The Reinforcement Sensi

CW00958520

One of the major neuropsychological models of personality, developed by world-renowned psychologist Professor Jeffrey Gray, is based upon individual differences in reactions to punishing and rewarding stimuli. This biological theory of personality – now widely known as 'Reinforcement Sensitivity Theory' (RST) – has had a major influence on motivation, emotion and psychopathology research. In 2000, RST was substantially revised by Jeffrey Gray, together with Neil McNaughton, and this revised theory proposed three principal motivation/emotion systems: the 'Fight-Flight-Freeze System' (FFFS), the 'Behavioural Approach System' (BAS) and the 'Behavioural Inhibition System' (BIS). This is the first book to summarize the Reinforcement Sensitivity Theory of personality and bring together leading researchers in the field. It summarizes all of the pre-2000 RST research findings, explains and elaborates the implications of the 2000 theory for personality psychology, and lays out the future research agenda for RST.

PHILIP J. CORR is Professor of Psychology at Swansea University. He has published over 60 scientific papers and is the author of the major textbook, *Understanding Biological Psychology* (2006).

Jeffrey Alan Gray (1934–2004)

The Reinforcement Sensitivity Theory of Personality

Edited by

Philip J. Corr

CAMBRIDGE UNIVERSITY PRESS
Cambridge, New York, Melbourne, Madrid, Cape Town, Singapore, São Paulo,
Delhi

Cambridge University Press
The Edinburgh Building, Cambridge CB2 8RU, UK

Published in the United States of America by Cambridge University Press,
New York

www.cambridge.org
Information on this title: www.cambridge.org/9780521851794

First published 2008

Printed in the United Kingdom at the University Press, Cambridge

A catalogue record for this publication is available from the British Library

Library of Congress Cataloguing in Publication Data

The reinforcement sensitivity theory of personality / [edited by]
Philip J. Corr.
   p. ; cm.
Includes bibliographical references and index.
ISBN 978-0-521-85179-4 (hardback : alk. paper) – ISBN 978-0-521-61736-9
(pbk. : alk. paper)
1. Reinforcement (Psychology) 2. Personality development. I. Corr,
Philip J.
   [DNLM: 1. Psychophysiology. 2. Reinforcement (Psychology)
3. Personality. 4. Psychological Theory. WL 103 R3675 2008]

   BF319.5.R4R45 2008
   155.2–dc22

                                                              2007051437

ISBN 978-0-521-85179-4 hardback
ISBN 978-0-521-61736-9 paperback

Contents

v

Abbreviations

ARAS	Ascending Reticular Activating System
BAS	Behavioural Approach System
BIS	Behavioural Inhibition System
CFA	common factor analysis or confirmatory factor analysis
CL	category learning
cns	conceptual nervous system
CNS	central nervous system
CR	conditioned response
CS	conditioned stimulus
DINN	dynamically interacting neural network
DMH	dorsomedial hypothalamus
ERP	event-related potential
FFFS	Fight-Flight-Freeze System
FFS	Fight-Flight System
fMRI	functional Magnetic Resonance Imaging
FNR	frustrative non-reward
GWPQ	Gray-Wilson Personality Questionnaire
IRT	Item Response Theory
JAMS	Jackson's Appetitive Motivation Scale
JSH	joint subsystems hypothesis
MDD	major depressive disorder
MMN	mismatch negativity
NA	negative affect
NAS	Non-specific Arousal System
OCD	obsessive-compulsive disorder
PA	positive affect
PAG	periaqueductal gray
PCA	Principal Components Analysis
PD	panic disorder
PEN	Psychoticism-Extraversion-Neuroticism
PET	Position Emission Tomography
PHOB	specific phobia

PTSD	post-traumatic stress disorder
QTL	quantative trait loci
RST	Reinforcement Sensitivity Theory
SHS	septo-hippocampal system
SPSRQ	Sensitivity to Punishment Sensitivity to Reward Questionnaire
S-R	stimulus-response
SSH	separable subsystems hypothesis
TMI	transmarginal inhibition
UCR	unconditioned response
UCS	unconditioned stimulus

Figures

Tables

Contributors

PROFESSOR CÉSAR ÁVILA, Department of Psychology, University of Jaume, Spain

DR XAVIER CASERAS, Department of Psychological Medicine, University of Barcelona, Spain

DR ANDREW COOPER, Department of Psychology, Goldsmiths College, University of London, United Kingdom

PROFESSOR PHILIP J. CORR, Department of Psychology, Swansea University, United Kingdom

PROFESSOR VILFREDO DE PASCALIS, Department of Psychology, University of Rome, Italy

PROFESSOR ADRIAN FURNHAM, Department of Psychology, University College, University of London, United Kingdom

PROFESSOR RAPSON GOMEZ, Department of Psychology, University of Tasmania, Australia

PROFESSOR CHRIS JACKSON, School of Business, University of New South Wales, Sydney, Australia

PROFESSOR LIISA KELTIKANGAS-JÄRVINEN, Department of Psychology, University of Helsinki, Finland

DR GENNADY KNYAZEV, State Research Institute of Physiology, Siberian Branch of the Russian Academy of Medical Sciences, Russia

PROFESSOR GERALD MATTHEWS, Department of Psychology, University of Cincinnati, USA

PROFESSOR NEIL MCNAUGHTON, Department of Psychology and Neuroscience Research Centre, University of Otago, New Zealand

JOSEPH P. NEWMAN, Department of Psychology, University of Wisconsin-Madison, USA

PROFESSOR ALAN PICKERING, Department of Psychology, Goldsmiths College, University of London, United Kingdom

PROFESSOR MARTIN REUTER, Department of Psychology, University of Bonn, Germany

PROFESSOR WILLIAM REVELLE, Department of Psychology, Northwestern University, USA

DR HELENA R. SLOBODSKAYA, State Research Institute of Physiology, Siberian Branch of the Russian Academy of Medical Sciences, Russia

DR LUKE D. SMILLIE, Department of Psychology, Goldsmiths College, University of London, United Kingdom

PROFESSOR JOHN F. WALLACE, Department of Psychology, University of Wisconsin-Madison, USA

PROFESSOR RAFAEL TORRUBIA, Department of Psychological Medicine, University of Barcelona, Spain

DR GLENN D. WILSON, Department of Psychology, Institute of Psychiatry, King's College London, University of London, United Kingdom

DR K. LIRA YOON, Department of Psychology, Northwestern University, USA

PROFESSOR RICHARD E. ZINBARG, Department of Psychology and the Family Institute, Northwestern University, USA

Preface

Jeffrey Alan Gray was known for his important contributions to many areas of psychology, latterly in his career, schizophrenia, stem-cell transplantation and a full-blown theory of the functions of consciousness. But his theory of anxiety and personality more generally – now known as Reinforcement Sensitivity Theory (RST) – is one of his greatest achievements and secures his place in the history books.

The high regard in which Jeffrey is held by colleagues world-wide was evident in the fact that all the authors I approached to contribute to this book readily agreed. I am grateful to them all for their scholarly chapters. I am especially grateful to William Revelle for agreeing to read all chapters before giving his reflections on the position of RST in the wider field of personality psychology. The contributors have given us much to consider, and in their work we may discern many of the landmarks that will surely characterize RST in the decades to follow.

This book testifies to the important developments that have taken place in Jeffrey's thinking over the years, as well as the thinking of others inspired by his ground-clearing work. As show-cased in this book, 'Gray's theory' is not a fossilized set of principles, assumptions and contentions; rather, it is a fecund scientific perspective that opens up new research possibilities. We witness this fecundity in the vitality and variety of theories and approaches that characterize RST research today, as well as in the variegated shoots of related reinforcement-based theories of motivation, emotion and personality. And we witness its true scientific credentials in its own refutation of some of the central elements of the original theory.

This book has one aim: to encourage the further development of RST. So in keeping with Jeffrey's scientific perspective, it is to the future that we must look, with all its challenges, rather than to the past with its seductive certitudes afforded by 20–20 hindsight. As the 2000 revision of Gray's 1982 *The Neuropsychology of Anxiety* marks a watershed in RST, this book serves to demarcate 'old' (pre-2000) RST from 'new' (post-2000) RST and, thereby, help to clarify new avenues of research.

This delineation should be of value to all students of personality, distinguished and novice alike.

I am very grateful to Cambridge University Press for agreeing to publish this work; especially to Sarah Caro, Commissioning Editor, for seeing the merit in the original proposal and for constant encouragement and advice; and then, after Sarah's departure, Andrew Peart, who saw the project through to its fruition.

PHILIP J. CORR

26 December 2006

1   Reinforcement Sensitivity Theory (RST): introduction

Philip J. Corr

The *Reinforcement Sensitivity Theory* (RST) of personality is a theoretical account of the neural and psychological processes underlying the major dimensions of personality. The first section of this introductory chapter traces the development of RST, from its official birth in 1970, through to Gray's highly influential 1982 *The Neuropsychology of Anxiety*, and on to its major revision in 2000 with the second edition of this book (co-authored with Neil McNaughton) – this section may be read as an overview tutorial of RST. The second section discusses some of the major issues facing future RST research. The third section turns attention to the question of the level of behavioural control exerted by 'biological' and 'cognitive' processes, and discusses the implications of findings from consciousness studies for conceptualizing the role of these processes in RST.

Past and present

At the time of writing (2006), most empirical studies continue to test the unrevised (pre-2000) version of RST. But, in many crucial respects, the revised (2000) theory is very different, leading to the formulation of new hypotheses, some of which stand in opposition to those generated from the unrevised theory. This reluctance, or slowness, to adopt the new model is, no doubt, motivated as much by unfamiliarity and research inertia as it is by a careful evaluation of the merits of both versions. But there may be a different reason for this state of affairs, and one that may continue to prevail in the RST research. Some personality researchers appreciate that RST encapsulates some of the core elements of emotion and motivation, as they relate to personality, especially the focus on approach and avoidance as the two fundamental dimensions of behaviour. But they also think that the specific details of Gray's work are not entirely appropriate at the human level of analysis. For example, Carver and Scheier (1998; see Carver 2004) has made changes to the emotions

1

associated with reward and punishment systems. Their view of these systems are reflected in the broad-band BIS-BAS scales of Carver and White (1994), which may be seen as reflecting general motivational tendencies of avoidance and approach rather than the specifics of the BIS and BAS as detailed in Gray's work. This shows that a 'family' of RST-related theories has developed, which serves, depending on one's opinion, either to enrich or confuse the literature, especially when the same term ('BIS') is used to measure theoretically different constructs. Because the revised theory is even more specific about neural functions, derived largely from typical animal learning paradigms, there is little reason to think that this attitude will change once the revised theory is fully assimilated into RST thinking. In order to help researchers make a choice of hypotheses, this section details and contrasts the two versions of the theory.

Foundations of RST

Jeffrey Gray's approach to understanding the biological basis of personality followed a particular pattern: (a) first identify the fundamental properties of brain-behavioural systems that might be involved in the important sources of variation observed in human behaviour; and (b) then relate variations in these systems to existing measures of personality. Of critical importance in this two-stage process was the assumption that the variation observed in the functioning of these brain-behavioural systems comprises what we term 'personality' – in other words, personality does not stand apart from basic brain-behaviour systems, but rather is defined by them. As we shall see below, relating *a* to *b* has proved the major, and still unresolved, problem for RST.

Gray's work was influenced by an appropriate respect for the implications of Darwinian evolution by natural selection. He took seriously the proposition that data obtained from (non-human) animals could be extrapolated to human animals (e.g., Gray 1987; see McNaughton and Corr, chapter 3). Gray's work may be seen in the larger scientific context foreshadowed by Darwin's (1859) prescient statement in the *Origin of Species*, 'In the distant future I see open fields for far more important researches. Psychology will be based on a new foundation, that of the necessary acquirement of each mental power and capability by gradation. Light will be thrown on the origin of man and his history.'

General theory of personality

Today, it may seem trite to link personality factors to emotion and motivational systems, but this neo-consensus did not prevail in the

1960s, when very few personality psychologists argued for the importance of basic systems of emotion underlying personality. It is a mark of achievement that Gray's (1970) hypothesis – novel as it was then in personality research – is today so widely endorsed. The emergence of a *neuroscience of personality* – an oxymoron not too long ago – was shaped in large measure by Gray's work. However, as we shall see below, the main elements of Gray's approach already existed in general psychology: like Hans Eysenck's (1957, 1967) theories, Gray's innovation was to put together the existing pieces of scientific jigsaw to provide the foundations of a general theory of personality. As with the construction of any complex structure, it is, indeed, prudent to have firm foundations – in the case of theory, verified concepts and processes from anywhere in the discipline (or from other disciplines) – upon which the further building blocks of theory may be placed. For this reason Gray, like Pavlov (1927) before him, advocated a twin-track approach: the conceptual nervous system (cns) and the *central nervous system* (CNS) (cf. Hebb 1955; see Gray 1972a); that is, the cns components of personality (e.g., learning theory; see Gray 1975) and the component brain systems underlying systematic variations in behaviour (*ex hypothesi*, personality). As noted by Gray (1972a), these two levels of explanation *must* be compatible, but given a state of imperfect knowledge it would be unwise to abandon one approach in favour of the other. Gray used the language of cybernetics, in the form of cns-CNS bridge, to show how the flow of information and control of outputs is achieved (e.g., the Gray-Smith 1969 Arousal-Decision model; see below). That RST focuses on a relatively small number of basic phenomena is in the nature of theory building; but this fact should not be interpreted, as it sometimes is, as implying that RST is restricted to explaining only these phenomena.

In contrast to Gray's general approach, Hans Eysenck adopted a very different 'top-down' one. His search for causal systems was determined by the structure of statistically-derived personality factors/dimensions. The possibility that the structure of these factors/dimensions may not correspond to the structure of causal influences was never seriously entertained. We shall have reason to question the premises underlying this particular assumption (see Corr and McNaughton, chapter 5). However, in one important respect, Eysenck's approach is viable: this was to understand the causal bases of *observed* personality structure, defined as a unitary whole (e.g., Extraversion and Neuroticism). For this very reason, it is perhaps not surprising that Eysenck's causal systems never developed beyond the postulation of a small number of very general brain processes, principally the Ascending Reticular Activating System (ARAS), underlying the dimension of introversion-extraversion and cortical arousal (for a summary, see Corr 2004). It should be noted that this was not a fault in Eysenck's work, because as argued elsewhere (Corr 2002a) there is considerable support for Eysenck's Extraversion-Arousal hypothesis and it does well to explain many forms of behaviours at the dimensional level of analysis. Taken together, Gray's and Eysenck's approaches are complementary, tackling important problems at different levels of analysis – we shall see below just how these levels of analysis can be integrated. Indeed, without Eysenck's work it is difficult to see how Gray's neuropsychological work would have led to a theory of *personality*. Also, Eysenck showed that a science of personality was possible and, in a wide variety of ways, of scientific importance (e.g., accounting for clinical neurosis).[1] (Fowles 2006 provides a superb summary of the development of Gray's work.)

The 'Hull-Eysenck' and 'Mowrer-Gray' perspectives   To understand the theoretical differences between the approaches adopted by Gray and Eysenck, it is necessary to delve into some of the scientific problems that dominated psychology during the middle of the twentieth century.

Eysenck's theory focused on a single factor underlying individual differences in arousal/arousability. This approach followed the well-trodden path of Hull (1952), whose learning theory concentrated on the single factor of drive reduction as underlying the effects of reinforcement. As noted by Gray (1975, p. 25), the 'Hullian concept of general drive, to the extent that it is viable, does not differ in any important respects from that of arousal'. To the extent that both Hull and Eysenck argued for one causal factor affecting learning, their position may be dubbed the 'Hull-Eysenck perspective' (Corr, Pickering and Gray 1995a).

In contrast to this perspective – and reflecting the changes in learning theory that were taking place in general psychology – Gray's alternative position argued for a two-process theory of learning based upon reward and punishment systems. This position, dubbed the 'Mowrer-Gray perspective' (Corr *et al.* 1995a), reflected the importance of Mowrer's (1960) influential work in which he argued that learning is composed of two processes: (a) associative (Pavlovian) conditioning and (b) instrumental learning. In addition, and of particular significance for RST, Mowrer also argued that the effects of reward and punishment had different behavioural effects as well as different underlying bases.

---

[1] On a personal level, Gray was influenced by the fact that he undertook clinical and doctoral training in Eysenck's own Department, who encouraged him to translate Russian works on personality (see Corr and Perkins 2006).

Emotion was introduced in this learning account by Mowrer's theory that such states (e.g., hope) played the role of the internal motivator of behaviour (also see Konorski 1967; Mackintosh 1983). This two-factor (punishment/reward) theory was supported by neurophysiological findings; e.g., the discovery of the 'pleasure centres' in the brain in the 1950s (e.g., Olds and Milner 1954). Thus, from Mowrer's theory came the claim that (a) reward and punishment are different processes and (b) states of emotion serve as internal motivators of behaviour. To link this theory to individual differences in the functioning of brain-behavioural systems – a theoretical claim that also came out of Hull's work – and, then, to well-known personality factors was a logical step; although as obvious as it may now appear it takes a scientist of exceptional insight to recognize and appreciate its potential.

Standard (1982) RST

Eysenck's arousal theory of Extraversion (Eysenck 1967) postulated that introverts and extraverts differ with respect to the sensitivity of their cortical arousal system in consequence of differences in response thresholds of their Ascending Reticular Activating System (ARAS). According to this theory, compared with extraverts, introverts have lower response thresholds and thus higher cortical arousal. In general, introverts are more cortically aroused and more arousable when faced with sensory stimulation. However, the relationship between arousal-induction and actual arousal is subject to the moderating influence of transmarginal inhibition (TMI: a protective mechanism that breaks the link between increasing stimuli intensity and behaviour at high intensity levels): under low stimulation (e.g., quiet or placebo), introverts should be more aroused/arousable than extraverts, but under high stimulation (e.g., noise or caffeine), they should experience over-arousal which, with the evocation of TMI, can lead to lower increments in arousal as compared with extraverts; conversely, extraverts under low stimulation should show low arousal/arousability, but under high stimulation, they should show higher increments in arousal. A second dimension, Neuroticism (N), was related to activation of the limbic system and emotional instability (see Eysenck and Eysenck 1985). It was against this backdrop that RST developed.

Gray (1970, 1972b, 1981) proposed his alternative theory to Eysenck's. This theory proposed changes: (a) to the position of Extraversion (E) and Neuroticism (N) in factor space; and (b) to the neuropsychological bases of E and N. Gray argued that E and N should be rotated by approximately 30° to form the more causally efficient axes

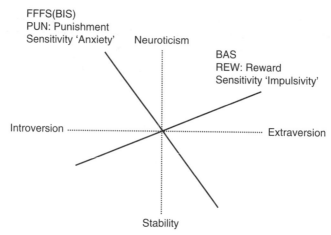

Figure 1.1 Position in factor space of the fundamental punishment sensitivity and reward sensitivity (unbroken lines) and the emergent surface expressions of these sensitivities, i.e., Extraversion (E) and Neuroticism (N) (broken lines). In the revised theory, a clear distinction exists between fear (FFFS) and anxiety (BIS), and separate personality factors may relate to these systems (see text); however, for the present exposition, these two systems are considered to reflect a common dimension of punishment sensitivity

of 'punishment sensitivity', reflecting Anxiety (Anx), and 'reward sensitivity', reflecting Impulsivity (Imp) (Figure 1.1; see Pickering, Corr and Gray 1999).[2]

In broad terms, the 1982 version of RST predicted that Imp+ individuals are most sensitive to *signals* of reward, relative to Imp− individuals; and Anx+ individuals are most sensitive to *signals* of punishment, relative to Anx− individuals. The orthogonality of the axes was interpreted to suggest: (a) that responses to reward should be the same at all levels of Anx; and (b) responses to punishment should be the same at all levels of Imp (this position has been named the 'separable subsystems hypothesis'; Corr 2001, 2002a). According to

---

[2] The relationship between Eysenck's and Gray's theories have not yet been fully clarified. For example, on the basis of empirical research, it seems likely that arousal is important in the initial conditioning of emotive stimuli which, then, serve as inputs into Gray's emotion systems; in turn, activation of these systems is expected to augment arousal and, thereby, influence conditioning processes quite independent of their role in generating emotion and motivational tendencies. If introversion-extraversion reflects the balance of reward and punishment sensitivities, then it may not be incompatible to argue that Eysenckian extraversion-arousal processes in conditioning continue to be relevant in Gray's RST.

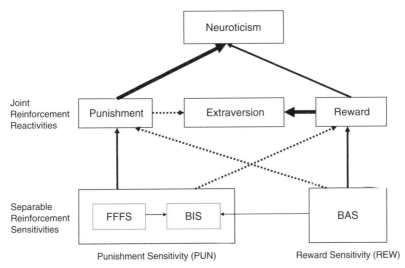

Figure 1.2 A schematic representation of the hypothesized relationship between (a) FFFS/BIS (punishment sensitivity; PUN) and BAS (reward sensitivity; REW); (b) their joint effects on reactions to punishment and reward; and (c) their relations to Extraversion (E) and Neuroticism (N). E is shown as the balance of punishment (PUN) and reward (REW) reactivities; N reflects their combined strengths. Inputs from the FFFS/BIS and BAS are excitatory (unbroken line) and inhibitory (broken line) – their respective influences are dependent on experimental factors (see text). The strength of inputs to E and N reflects the 30° rotation of PUN/REW and E/N: relatively strong (thick line) and weak (thin line) relations. The input from punishment reactivity to E is inhibitory (i.e., it reduces E), the input from reward reactivity is excitatory (i.e., it increases E). The BIS is activated by simultaneous activation of the FFFS and the BAS, and its activation increases punishment sensitivity. It is hypothesized that the joint effects of PUN and REW gives rise to the surface expression of E and N: PUN and REW represent the underlying biology; E and N represent their joint influences at the level of integrated behaviour

RST, Eysenck's E and N dimensions are derivative, secondary factors of these more fundamental punishment and reward sensitivities: E reflects the balance of punishment and reward sensitivities; N reflects their joint strengths (Gray 1981) (see Figure 1.2).

Gray's theory also explained Eysenck's arousal effects: *ex hypothesi*, on average, punishment is more arousing than reward, and introverts are more sensitive to punishment, therefore introverts experience more induction of arousal and tend to be more highly aroused. In contrast,

Eysenck maintained that, to the extent that reinforcement effects are mediated by personality, they are a consequence of arousal level and not sensitivity to reward and punishment per se.

Clinical neurosis

According to Eysenck's arousal theory, introverts are prone to suffer from anxiety disorders because they more easily develop classically conditioned (emotional) responses; this theory was expanded with the inclusion of 'incubation' in conditioning effects (Eysenck 1979) to account for the 'neurotic paradox' (i.e., the failure of extinction with continued non-reinforcement of the conditioned stimulus (CS)); coupled with emotional instability, reflected in N, this made the introverted neurotic (E–/N+) especially prone to the anxiety disorders.

However, from the inception of this arousal-based theory of personality, there were a number of problems. First, introverts show *weaker* classical conditioning under conditions conducive to high arousal (e.g., in eye-blink conditioning; Eysenck and Levey 1972); and a crossover pattern of E × arousal is easily confirmed (e.g., in procedural learning; Corr, Pickering and Gray 1995b), supporting Eysenck's *own* theory that introverts are transmarginally inhibited by high arousal (see above). Other problems attend Eysenck's arousal-conditioning claims. For example, Imp (inclined into the N plane), not sociability, is often associated with conditioning effects (Eysenck and Levey 1972); this places high arousability, and thus high conditionability, in the stable-introverted quadrant defined by E×N space, not in the neurotic-introvert quadrant required by the theory and clinical data. Thus, Eysenck's theory seems unable to explain the aetiology of anxiety in neurotic-introverts, which was one of the major aims of the theory from its early days. Time of day effects further undermine the central postulates of Eysenck's personality theory of clinical neurosis. Gray (1981) provides a masterly discussion of these problems, which according to him thrusts a dagger into the heart of Eysenckian theory.

Conditioning and emotion   Gray identified a more compelling reason for rejecting the classical conditioning theory of neurosis. In classical conditioning theory, as a result of the conditioned stimulus (CS) and unconditioned stimulus (UCS) being systematically paired, the CS comes to take on many of the eliciting properties of the UCS: when presented alone, the CS produces a response (i.e., the conditioned response (CR)) that resembles the unconditioned response (UCR) elicited by the UCS. Thus innate fear (UCS) may be elicited by a CS: hence the classic conditioning idea of neurosis. As so often the case, the devil is in the detail. The problem is that the CR does not substitute for the UCR – in several important respects, the CR does not even resemble the UCR. For example, a pain UCS will elicit a wide variety of reactions (e.g., vocalization and behavioural excitement) which are quite different to those elicited by a CS *signalling* pain: the latter produces anxiety and a different set of behaviours (e.g., quietness and behavioural inhibition). Thus, classical conditioning cannot explain the pathogenesis or phenomenology of neurosis, although it can explain how initially neutral stimuli (CSs) acquire the motivational power to elicit this state. Well, if the CR is not simply a version of the UCR then what generates the negative emotional state that characterizes neurosis? Gray's claim was an innate mechanism, namely the *Behavioural Inhibition System* (BIS) (Gray 1976, 1982).

Three systems of standard RST

RST gradually developed over the years to include three major systems of emotion:

(1) The Fight-Flight System (FFS) was hypothesized to be sensitive to *unconditioned* aversive stimuli (i.e., innately painful stimuli), mediating the emotions of rage and panic – this system was related to the state of negative affect (NA) (associated with pain) and Eysenck's trait of Psychoticism.

(2) The Behavioural Approach System (BAS) was hypothesized to be sensitive to *conditioned* appetitive stimuli, forming a positive feedback loop, activated by the presentation of stimuli associated with reward and the termination/omission of signals of punishment – this system was related to the state of positive affect (PA) and the trait of Imp.

(3) The Behavioural Inhibition System (BIS) was hypothesized to be sensitive to *conditioned* aversive stimuli (i.e., signals of both punishment and the omission/termination of reward) relating to Anx, but also to extreme novelty, high intensity stimuli, and innate fear stimuli (e.g., snakes, blood) which are more related to fear.

With respect to the CNS, Gray used data from a wide range of sources, principally (a) the effects of lesion of specific neural sites on behaviour and (b) the effects of drugs – initially the barbiturates and alcohol, and later anxiolytics – on specific classes of behaviour. Gray's 'philosopher's stone' was the detailed pattern of behavioural effects of classes of drugs known to affect emotion in human beings; in this way anxiety could be operationally defined as those behaviours changed by anxiolytic drugs. The obvious danger of circularity of argument was avoided by the postulation that anxiolytic drugs do not simply reduce anxiety (itself a vacuous tautology), but could be shown to have a number of behavioural effects in typical animal learning paradigms. It turned out that such drugs affected reactions to conditioned aversive stimuli, the omission of expected reward and conditioned frustration, all of which acted on a postulated Behavioural Inhibition System which was charged with the task of suppressing ongoing operant behaviour in the face of threat and enhancing information processing. Later, the Behavioural Approach System was added to account for behavioural reactions to rewarding stimuli, which was largely unaffected by anxiety-reducing drugs. The circularity of this argument was further broken by the behavioural profile of the newer classes of anxiolytics which, as it turned out, had the same behavioural effects, and acted on the same neural systems, as the older class of drugs, despite the fact that they had different psychopharmacological modes of action and side-effects (Gray and McNaughton 2000).

Revised (2000) RST

Chapters 2 and 5 provide a detailed account of the neuropsychology of the Gray and McNaughton (2000) revised theory. This section provides a brief overview of this new theory, which shows that there are a number of significant changes to the systems that hold important implications for conceptualization and measurement.

Revised RST postulates three systems.

(1) The Fight–Flight–Freeze System (FFFS) is responsible for mediating reactions to *all* aversive stimuli, conditioned and unconditioned. A hierarchical array of modules comprises the FFFS, responsible for avoidance and escape behaviours. Importantly, the FFFS mediates the 'get me out of this place' emotion of fear, not anxiety. The FFFS is an example of a negative feedback system, designed to reduce the discrepancy between the immediate threat and the desired state (i.e., safety). The associated personality factor comprises fear-proneness and avoidance, which clinically maps onto such disorders as phobia and panic. (In contrast, the original, 1982, theory assigned the FFFS to reactions to *unconditioned* aversive (pain) stimuli.)

(2) The Behavioural Approach System (BAS) mediates reactions to *all* appetitive stimuli, conditioned and unconditioned. This generates the appetitively hopeful emotion of 'anticipatory pleasure'. The associated personality comprises optimism, reward-orientation and impulsiveness, which clinically maps onto addictive behaviours (e.g., pathological

gambling) and various varieties of high-risk, impulsive behaviour, and possibly the appetitive component of mania. (The BAS is largely unchanged in the revised version of RST.) This is a positive feedback system, designed to move away from current appetitive goal-state towards the biological reinforcer.

It is important to distinguish the incentive motivation component and the consummatory component of the reactions to unconditioned appetitive stimuli. Gray believed that no single system mediates the consummatory component of such reactions (e.g., reactions to unconditioned stimuli): e.g., copulation and eating/drinking involve very different response systems (also see below for further work needed to the concept of the BAS). The BAS is responsible for reducing the temporo-spatial distance between current appetitive goal state and the final biological reinforcer.

(3) The Behavioural Inhibition System (BIS) is now responsible, not for mediating reactions to conditioned aversive stimuli and the special class of innate fear stimuli, but for the resolution of goal conflict in general (e.g., between BAS-approach and FFFS-avoidance, as in foraging situations, but it is also involved in BAS-BAS and FFFS-FFFS conflict). It is a negative feedback system aimed at countering the deviation from the reference state of no goal conflict. The BIS generates the 'watch out for danger' emotion of anxiety, which entails the inhibition of prepotent conflicting behaviours, the engagement of risk assessment processes, and the scanning of memory and the environment to help resolve concurrent goal conflict. The BIS resolves conflicts by increasing, by recursive loops, the negative valence of stimuli (these are adequate inputs into the FFFS), until behavioural resolution occurs in favour of approach or avoidance. Subjectively, this state is experienced as worry and rumination. The associated personality comprises worry-proneness and anxious rumination, leading to being constantly on the look-out for possible signs of danger, which clinically maps onto such conditions as generalized anxiety and obsessional-compulsive disorder (OCD) – both conditions reflect a lack of adequate goal conflict resolution appropriate to local environmental parameters. There is an optimal level of BIS activation: too little leads to risk-proneness (e.g., psychopathy) and too much to risk aversion (generalized anxiety), both with sub-optimal conflict resolution. It is intriguing to speculate that modern-day angst, and social malaise, is in part due to the conflict induced by reward-reward conflicts (e.g., which holiday to go on, which car to purchase and which career to pursue): choice per se has a negative component. The way in which the FFFS, BIS and BAS relate to Extraversion and Neuroticism is shown in Figure 1.2.

The revised Gray and McNaughton (2000) theory makes a number of new claims, some of which contradict those derived from unrevised RST theory.

(1) In contrast to the 1982 theory, the distinction between the BIS and FFFS is totally divorced from the conditioned or unconditioned nature of stimuli used to elicit emotion. In the 1982 version of the theory, the BIS was activated by conditioned aversive stimuli (as well as 'innate fear stimuli'), and the Fight-Flight System (as it was then called) by unconditioned aversive stimuli. This conditioned-unconditioned distinction is now not relevant to the revised theory: both types of stimuli can activate the FFFS and, provided there is conflict, the BIS. The importance of the conditioned-unconditioned distinction seems to have come from the strong correlation between, on the one hand, unconditioned and immediate threat, and, on the other hand, conditioned and potential threat. It also turned out that many, but not all, forms of conditioned stimuli are, in fact, conflict stimuli, and BIS effects were typically measured as the suppression of ongoing BAS-controlled behaviour (e.g., conditioned emotional suppression).

(2) There is now a sharp (ethological, behavioural and pharmacological) distinction between fear (FFFS) and anxiety (BIS). This distinction is still controversial. Consistent with the theory, Barlow (1988) associates anxiety with future danger and fear with imminent danger, but others challenge this distinction (see Fowles 2000). However, the theory shows how these two emotions are different. This difference is based on the concept of 'defensive direction': fear refers to the elicitation of a range of reactions that have the common function of facilitating the movement of the animal *away from* threat; anxiety refers to the elicitation of a range of reactions that have the common function of facilitating the movement of the animal *towards* threat (or more generally resolving conflict). The concept of defensive direction provides a single principle to define inputs to the BIS – the 1982 theory provided an essentially ad hoc list.

This conceptualization is based on the Blanchards' (e.g., Blanchard and Blanchard 1990) etho-experimental work which linked to a state of fear a set of behaviours elicited by a predator. These behaviours turn out to be sensitive to drugs that are panciolytic (i.e., panic reducing), but not to those drugs that are only anxiolytic (i.e., anxiety-reducing). Such behaviours include simple avoidance (fleeing), freezing and defensive attack.[3] In contrast, they link to a state of anxiety a quite different set of

---

[3] As noted by Eilam (2005), in fleeing, the prey physically removes itself from the vicinity of the predator; in freezing, the prey remains immobile in order to evade the attention of the predator; and in fighting (or defensive threat), the prey heads towards the predator in

behaviours (especially 'risk assessment'), elicited by the potential presence of a predator that turn out to be sensitive to anxiolytic drugs. Because of the detailed effects of anxiolytic drugs on behaviour (see Gray and McNaughton 2000), it is argued that the key factor distinguishing fear and anxiety is not that posited by the Blanchards, namely immediacy (or certainty) versus potentiality (or uncertainty) of threat but 'defensive direction': fear operates when *leaving* a dangerous situation (active avoidance), anxiety when *entering* it (e.g., cautious 'risk assessment' approach behaviour) or withholding entrance (passive avoidance).

(3) An important feature of the revised theory is it now explains the phenomenology of fear and anxiety in Darwinian adaptive terms; and at the specific neural module levels, specific reactions serve particular adaptive functions. Few theories of fear and anxiety attempt to explain *why* these emotions have their specific natures: *why* should anxiety should be related to rumination, worry, risk assessment, vigilance for potentially bad things?

(4) There are distinct systems in the brain that control specific functional classes of behaviour (e.g., fight, flight, freezing as separate classes). These systems can be viewed as the targets of particular perceptions/cognitions ('I am about to be eaten by the cat/lion' for rat/human respectively). They can also be viewed as the sources of particular emotional behaviours (e.g., panic) that, if excessive or inappropriate, represent particular types of clinical symptom (e.g., panic attack) or syndrome (e.g., panic disorder). These local systems are organized into clusters that control more global functional classes of behaviour (e.g., defence). Where several specific classes of behaviour (fight, flight, freeze) all have a high probability of being elicited in essentially the same global situation (predatory threat) their organization (through the course of evolution) into a more global system allows co-ordination and selection of just one of the primed classes of behaviour. Modulatory systems can affect specific global functional classes (e.g., threat sensitivity) or many together (e.g., arousal, attention).

(5) All of the above levels of neural organization can be assigned both state ('How active are they right now'; see chapter 2) and trait ('How reactive are they in general to a fixed stimulus'; see chapter 5). Macroscopic factors, affecting global classes of functional system (e.g., defence) or cutting across such systems (e.g., arousal), contribute to personality. Personality can be seen as reflecting global functional variations in these systems.

---

order to discourage its predatory behaviour – defensive fighting occurs when the prey has no possibility of freezing and fleeing and must face the predator.

(6) An important point for the personality theorist is the layer of complexity in the old (Gray and Smith 1969) and new theories – however, this is usually ignored in research – that focuses on the parametric interactions between approach and avoidance systems when each is concurrently activated. The key point is that when the BAS and FFFS are activated unequally (i.e., when there is little conflict between approach and avoidance), they nonetheless interact. This interaction is symmetrical. Activation of one system inhibits the other. This inter-action (in its purest form counterconditioning of one stimulus by a motivationally opposite stimulus) is insensitive to anxiolytic drugs and so practically as well as theoretically independent of the BIS. Thus, while the two systems are independent in that changes in the sensitivity of one will not affect the sensitivity of the other, they are not independent in that concurrent activation will cause interactions in their generation of behaviour output. The primary symmetrical inter-actions between the systems are also non-linear, accounting for such phenomena as behavioural contrast and peak shift (Gray and Smith 1969). Joint activation increases arousal while producing a subtractive effect on decision (Corr and McNaughton, chapter 5). This important matter is considered in detail below. Superimposed on these symmetrical interactions is the BIS. This is activated more as the difficulty of resolving the decision between the two (approach-avoid) increases (i.e., as the relative power of approach and avoidance become more equal). Its activation results in asymmetrical effects. It boosts arousal (over and above the additive effect of the existing conflicting motivations) while it amplifies activity in aversive system but not the appetitive one. Under conditions of conflict, then, it increases risk aversion.

(7) Abnormal levels of expressions of personality may result from three conditions: (a) as a normally adaptive reaction to their specific eliciting stimuli (e.g., mild anxiety before important examination); (b) at maladaptive intensity, as a result of excessive sensitivity to their specific eliciting stimuli (e.g., sight of harmless spider = fearful avoidance); and (c) at maladaptive intensity, as a result of excessive activation of a related structure by its specific eliciting stimuli but where the 'symptoms' are not excessive given the level of input (e.g., oncoming train = panic).

Defensive distance

Revised RST contends that defensive behaviour results from the superimposition on defensive direction (i.e., approach or avoid) of what is known as 'defensive distance'. According to this two-dimensional

Table 1.1 *Relationship between actual and perceived defensive distance in low, medium and high fearful individuals*

System state	Defensive distance	Real distance sufficient to elicit reaction
Low defensive individual:	Perceived distance > actual distance	Short
Normal defensive individual:	Percieved distance = actual distance	Medium
High defensive individual:	Perceived distance < actual distance	Long

model of McNaughton and Corr (2004), for a particular individual in a particular situation, defensive distance equates with real distance; but, in a more dangerous situation, the perceived defensive distance is shortened. In other words, defensive behaviour (e.g., active avoidance) will be elicited at a longer (objective) distance with a highly dangerous stimulus (corresponding to shortened perceived distance), as compared to the same behaviour with a less dangerous stimulus. According to the theory, neurotic individuals have a much shorter perceived defensive distance, and thus react more intensively to relatively innocuous (real distance) stimuli. For this reason, weak aversive stimuli are sufficient to trigger a neurotic reaction in highly defensive individuals; but for the braver individual, aversive stimuli would need to be much closer to elicit a comparable reaction. This set of relations is shown in Table 1.1 (taken from Corr and Perkins 2006).

Defensive distance operationalizes an internal cognitive construct of intensity of perceived threat. It is a dimension controlling the type of defensive behaviour observed. In the case of defensive avoidance, the smallest defensive distances result in explosive attack, intermediate defensive distances result in freezing and flight, and very great defensive distances result in normal non-defensive behaviour. The notion that there is a 'Distance-Dependent Defence Hierarchy' goes back a long way (e.g., Ranter 1977). Defensive distance maps to different levels of the FFFS (see chapter 2): as an animal cannot freeze and flee at the same moment, these behaviours must be controlled by different bio-behavioural mechanisms (Eilam 2005), and here we see the importance of a 'hierarchical' arrangement of defensive models, with higher-level modules inhibiting lower-level ones. The psychological state experienced at very short defensive distance would be labelled panic, which is often associated, at least at clinical extremes, with the cognition 'I'm going to die' – we may liken this cognition to whatever cognition runs through the rat's mind when nose-to-nose with a dangerous predator (e.g., hungry cat). The rat's cognition and emotion may be similar to the emotion we would feel if trapped in a car in the path of an oncoming high-speed train. At intermediate defensive distances, we would probably substitute panic for phobic avoidance (e.g., not driving over the train line if there is any chance of an oncoming train). With the opposite direction, defensive quiescence occurs; at intermediate distances, risk assessment is observed; and, at very long distances, defensive behaviour fades to be replaced by normal pre-threat behaviour. The first experimental test of this theory in human beings was made by Perkins and Corr (2006), who presented threat scenarios and correlated known measures of personality (including fear and anxiety scales) with the intensity and direction dimensions of chosen responses. The results broadly supported the differentiation of fear-related *avoidance* of threat and anxiety-related *cautious approach* to threat.

McNaughton and Corr (2004) view individual differences in defensive distance for a fixed real distance as a reflection of the personality dimension underlying 'punishment sensitivity', or 'threat perception' (or neurotic-introversion), which affects the FFFS directly, and the BIS indirectly (e.g., via FFFS-BAS goal conflict). Anxiolytic drugs alter (internally perceived) defensive distance relative to actual external threat. They *do not* affect defensive behaviour directly, but rather shift behaviour along the defensive axis, often leading to the output of a different behaviour (e.g., from freezing to flight; for discussion of a fundamental part of revised RST, see chapter 2). The modulation acts like a magnification factor. An important corollary of this claim is that comparison of individuals on a single measure of performance at only a single level of threat may produce confusing results (e.g., one person may be in a state of panic and so cease moving; another may actively avoid and so increase their movement). In other words, highly sensitive and insensitive individuals will show *different* behaviours *at the same level of threat* (defined in objective terms), as indeed will trait-identical individuals at different levels of threat. Thus, moving people along this axis of defensive distance (by drugs or by experimental means) will not simply affect the strength or probability of a given behaviour, but is expected to result in different behaviours. Thus, at the core of the revised theory are ethological considerations: specific behaviours relate to specific threats and environmental conditions.

A philosophical digress: utility theory

We have now covered the central tenets of the old and new versions of RST; the state and trait aspects of the theory are expanded in chapters 2 and 5, respectively. At this point, it might be appropriate to stand back from the details of the theory and consider RST in the broader domain of philosophy. Although not formally part of RST it is perhaps worth noting that the central tenets of RST, i.e., that behaviour is governed by two major affective dimensions of pleasure and pain, finds an echo in the view of the English philosopher, Jeremy Bentham (1748–1832), who formulated Utilitarian theory, which argues that society (and government public policy) should follow the principle of the 'greatest happiness to the greatest number'. Bentham's philosophy arose out of his views on the nature of individual behaviour; he wrote in *Introduction to the Principles of Morals and Legislation* (1781):

Nature has placed mankind under the governance of two sovereign masters, pain and pleasure. It is for them alone to point out what we ought to do as well as to determine what we shall do. On the other hand, the standard of right and wrong, on the other chain of causes and effects, are fastened to their throne. They govern us in all we do, in all we say, in all we think; every effort we can make to throw off our subjection, will serve but to demonstrate and confirm it. In words a man may pretend to abjure their empire: but in reality he will remain subject to it all the while.

Bentham introduced the principle of the individual's 'hedonic calculation', which maximizes the utility of the individual; in other words, individuals seek to maximize their 'happiness' (defined as the surplus of pleasure over pain), or minimize their pain (defined as the surplus of pain over pleasure). As a philosophy of individual behaviour, Bentham's view may be seen to border on the obvious and circular; but this circularity is broken once we have a scientific theory of the hedonic calculus – and this is what RST offers.

   This view of the governance of individual behaviour may be likened to the process of natural selection, that is, according to Darwin (1859/ 1968, p. 859) 'scrutinising, throughout the world, every variation, even the slightest; rejecting that which is bad ["pain"], preserving and adding up all that is good ["pleasure"]'. It is trite, but true, to say that most animals seek to minimize pain and maximize pleasure (although, in the case of the human animal, not necessarily in the crass, overt form that the word 'pleasure' usually implies).

   In his consideration of 'individual hedonic calculus', Bentham noted that the wealthier a person is, the greater their total happiness – all else being equal, it is better to be rich than to be poor! However, the wealth-happiness function is not linear; there is a 'marginal utility' function at work which states that the greater amount of utility a person *already* has (i.e., 'happiness'), the smaller will be the utility associated with an extra increment in wealth. (This principle of marginal utility is central to economic thinking today and is the rationale for, among other things, progressive rates of taxation.) Couched in the prosaic nomenclature of RST, this marginal utility function is likely to produce a non-linear relationship between an extra unit of reward (defined in some experimental manner) and experienced 'pleasure' (i.e., BAS-related emotion and behaviour). Perhaps it is for this reason that highly reward-sensitive gamblers need a large increment in reward to experience a perceptible increment in 'pleasure' – this general principle should hold also for highly BAS active individuals.

Bentham went on to state that the individual's hedonic calculus values pleasure or pain according to a number of parameters: (a) duration, (b) intensity, (c) certainty (or probability) and (d) propinquity vs. remoteness. It turns out that these are some of the very criteria that are important in operationalizing experimental variables in the RST laboratory. For example, certainty relates to defensive direction: a certain threat, of sufficient intensity and duration, should be avoided; propinquity vs. remoteness relates to defensive distance.

What this detour into political philosophy shows is that the types of constructs contained in RST do have a long tradition in intellectual thought and continue to underpin many public, and private, policies. Consideration of these domains lends support to the claim that RST, whilst perhaps not providing a complete account of emotion, behaviour and personality, focuses on some of their fundamental processes, as revealed by scientific findings as well as the wider realms of philosophical thought.

Future

We have now surveyed the main elements of RST, as encapsulated in their 1982 and 2000 versions. In this section we turn our attention to the future, asking which elements of RST require further development.[4]

The BAS and its parts

The Gray and McNaughton (2000) theory has little to say that is new about the BAS. But since the early 1990s, there has been debate in the

---

[4] The content of this section was influenced by discussions with two RST researchers, Mr Adam Perkins and Dr Andrew Cooper.

literature concerning its structure and psychometric properties. This section aims to show that the BAS is more complex than often thought, and that this complexity is not restricted only to its psychometric delineation.

Evolution of BAS complexity

There are several reasons for assuming that the BAS is much more complex than the FFFS (which motivates simple avoidance/escape), or indeed the BIS (which has a relatively simple process to resolve goal conflict). From an evolutionary perspective, this complexity may derive from the 'arms race' between predator and prey. The 'Life-Dinner Principle' (Dawkins and Krebs 1979) suggests that the evolutionary selective pressure on prey is much stronger than on predators: if a predator fails to kill its prey then is has lost its dinner, but if the prey fails to avoid/escape being the predator's dinner then it has lost its life. Although defensive behaviour, principally freezing, fleeing and defensive attack, are themselves relatively complex (Eilam 2005), it is nonetheless true that the behaviour of prey is intrinsically simpler than that of predator: all it has to do is avoid/escape – it really is life-or-death behaviour. In contrast, the predator has to develop counter-strategies to meet its BAS aims (to get its dinner, etc.), which entail a higher degree of cognitive and behavioural sophistication. This Life-Dinner Principle is related to the second reason for complexity, namely, heterogeneity of appetitive goals (e.g., securing food and finding/keeping a sexual mate), which demand a heterogeneity of BAS-related strategies. No one set of behaviours would be sufficient to achieve these very different BAS goals; therefore, it seems essential that the BAS entails a much more flexible repertoire of behaviours and planning processing than either the FFFS or the BIS.

BAS functions

The *primary* function of the BAS is to move the animal up the temporo-spatial gradient to the final biological reinforcer – it is for this reason that we should prefer the term 'approach' to the less precise 'activation'. This primary function is supported by a number of *secondary* processes. In its simplest form, the secondary process could comprise simple approach, perhaps with BIS activation exerting behavioural caution at critical points, designed to reduce the distance between current and desired appetitive state (e.g., as seen in foraging behaviour in a densely vegetated field); but in the case of human behaviour, this depiction of BAS-controlled approach behaviour is grossly oversimplified.

First, it is necessary to distinguish the *incentive* motivation component and the *consummatory* component of reactions to appetitive stimuli, as suggested by their distinct neuroanatomical substrates (Carver 2005). The neural machinery controlling reactions to unconditioned (innate) stimuli, and its associated emotion, must be different from that controlling the behaviour and emotion associated with *approach*, signalled by conditioned stimuli, to such stimuli. Even in the Gray and McNaughton (2000) revised theory, the BAS is still not sensitive to unconditioned stimuli.[5]

Second, moving to approach proper, we can discern a number of relatively separate, albeit overlapping, processes. At the simplest level, there seems an obvious difference between the 'interest' and 'drive' that characterizes the early stages of approach, and the behavioural and emotional excitement as the animal reaches the final biological reinforcer. Emotion in the former case may be termed 'anticipatory pleasure' (or 'hope'); in the latter case something akin to an 'excitement attack' – the resemblance with 'panic attack' is deliberate.[6]

There is, indeed, evidence, at the psychometric level of analysis, that the BAS behaviour/emotion is multidimensional. For example, the Carver and White (1994) BIS/BAS scales measure three aspects of BAS: reward responsiveness, drive and fun-seeking. As noted by Carver (2005, p. 9):

The three aspects of BAS sensitivity that are reflected in the three BAS scales derive from theoretical statements about the ways in which BAS functioning should be reflected experientially. That is, high BAS sensitivity should cause people to seek new incentives [reward responsiveness], to be persistent in pursuing incentives [drive], and to respond with positive feelings when incentives are attained [fun seeking].

In the conceptualization favoured here, Drive is concerned with actively pursing desired goals, and reward responsiveness is concerned with excitement at doing things well and winning, especially to rewarding

---

[5] However, in Gray and McNaughton (2000), Fig. 5.1 (p. 86) incorrectly shows adequate inputs to the BAS to include unconditioned reward (Gray, personal communication). To emphasize the important distinction between reactions to unconditioned and conditioned appetitive stimuli, Gray (personal communication) wryly commented: 'Try copulating with a ham sandwich!'

[6] 'Excitement attacks' may not only occur at the consummatory stage of approach – in a similar way panic attacks do not only occur when life is threatened – but may be triggered at the conclusion of fulfilment of important sub-goals in the cascade of approach behaviour. Indeed, such 'highs' would seem essential to maintain motivation directed to final-goal directed behaviour when approach entails a series of sub-goal procedures. (I am indebted to Margaret Wilson who, in sharing the experience of her own excitement attacks, first brought this felicitous term to my attention.)

stimuli associated with fulfilling sub-goal procedures: both processes seem to reflect the process of behavioural maintenance needed during complex approach behaviour involving multiple sub-goals. In contrast, fun-seeking may relate more to behaviours closer to the final biological reinforcer, which no longer entails planning and restraint of behaviour – fun-seeking is similar to impulsivity in this respect (see below). It is unlikely that *these* specific traits adequately capture the true nature of BAS behaviour, but they do usefully measure relatively separate (but overlapping) processes.

Sub-goal scaffolding

In order to move along the temporo-spatial gradient to the final primary biological reinforcer, it is necessary (at least in human beings) to engage in sub-goal scaffolding. This process consists of (a) identifying the biological reinforcer, (b) planning behaviour, and (c) executing the plan (i.e., 'problem solving') at each stage of the temporo-spatial gradient – this is in accordance with the type of cognitive operations first discussed by Miller, Gelenter and Pribram (1960), *Plans and the Structure of Behavior*.[7] Now, complex approach behaviour entails a series of behavioural processes, some of which oppose each other. For example, behaviour *restraint* and *planning* are often demanded to achieve BAS goals, but not at the final point of *capture* of the biological reinforcer, where non-planning and fast reactions (i.e., impulsivity) are more appropriate. Just being impulsive – that is, acting fast without thinking and not planning – would lead to being stranded on 'local highs' (in formal problems solving terms), moving the animal along the temporo-spatial gradient *away* from the final biological reinforcer. For this reason 'impulsivity' is perhaps not the most appropriate term for the personality factor corresponding to the full range of processes entailed by the BAS.

   Another way to look at restraint and impulsiveness in BAS approach is to think of closed and open feedback systems. A closed feedback system entails feedback which modifies behaviour. In the case of BAS this may entail some degree of restraint. But in an open feedback system there is no feedback to affect perception and behaviour: the output simply executes on the assumption that the consequence will be as intended (Carver and Scheier 1998). The latter form of feedback system is

---

[7] These authors argued that behaviour is guided by plans and goals and (self) regulated by discrepancy reducing feedback processes. They also noted that any general goal can be broken down into sub-goals; but this raises the problem of the control of sub-goals, which usually demands some form of hierarchical system of control of action plans.

appropriate to reflex-like responses, where there is little time for feedback to be processed. In the case of dysfunctional impulsivity (cf. Dickman 1990), it seems that the open feedback system is triggered long before environmental conditions warrant, with the result that behaviour comprises non-planning, lack of reflection and rigid behavioural repertoire (cf. Patterson and Newman 1993).

Sub-goal scaffolding, which is necessary for planning effective BAS approach to appetitive stimuli, will often entail the *inhibition* of impulsive behaviour, and for this reason we might suspect that BAS behaviours are hierarchically organized such that lower-level reactions (e.g., impulsiveness) are inhibited by high-level (control) modules, which involve the cognitive processing underlying sub-goal scaffolding.[8] In parallel with the example of FFFS-mediated panic attack, having an impulsivity-related behaviour when the biological reinforcer (i.e., unconditioned stimulus) is not proximal would be inappropriate. A panic attack is appropriate when suffocating; rash impulsivity is appropriate when cognitive planning can be replaced, at short temporo-spatial distance, by fast 'getting', or a physical grabbing, action (Carver 2005). Therefore, there is a need to take due consideration of two processes in BAS-controlled approach: (a) *behavioural restraint* is needed to plan and execute effective sub-goal scaffolding; and (b) *impulsive behaviour* is needed to get/capture the final biological reinforcer at near-zero temporo-spatial distance. However, this is not to imply that the emotional component of BAS behaviour would be attenuated at the early stages of approach behaviour; in fact, as noted above, the fulfilment of sub-goals is likely to entail periodic bursts of emotional excitement.

This restraint-impulsivity dimension, which is argued here to co-vary along a dimension of temporo-spatial distance to goal, may be illustrated by reference to the behaviour of careful financial planners and pathological gamblers. If the goal is to accumulate wealth, then gambling is an inappropriate strategy. In order to achieve this goal, restraint of impulsivity is needed, and short-term gains must be sacrificed for long-term success. As noted by Carver (2005, p. 312), 'unfettered impulse can interfere with the attainment of longer term goals'. This process may be labelled 'temporal bridging' to emphasize the need to maintain approach behaviour across time gaps during which approach behaviour

---

[8] It is to be expected that where goal conflict is present then the BIS will be engaged. This BIS influence on BAS functions provides another juncture at which systems interact. Such interaction may give rise to important effects on the BAS. For example, a hyperactive BIS would significantly disrupt functioning of the BAS by producing too much hesitation and risk assessment, thus impairing the adaptive approach behaviour.

is not being immediately reinforced. It would not make sense to define high BAS activity in terms of reckless impulsive behaviour that fails to achieve BAS ends: a longer timeframe is required to see fully how planning, involving scaffolding of sub-goals and temporal bridging, serves BAS ends.

Impulsivity   The concept of *sub-goal scaffolding* may shed new light on the role played by the trait of impulsivity in BAS behaviours. We have already seen that there is often the need for considerable planning in BAS behaviour, including reflection on likely outcome of alternative courses of action, for the BAS to achieve its goals. Let us now consider a typical measure of impulsivity (I_7; Eysenck, Pearson, Easting and Allsopp 1985), which is defined by aspects of fast reactions and non-planning:

(1) Do you often buy things on impulse?
(2) Do you often do things on the spur of the moment?
(3) Do you generally do and say things without stopping to think?
(4) Do you often get into a jam because you do things without thinking?

Such behaviours are insufficient to account for the full range of BAS-related processes and behaviours required to achieve BAS objectives. Differentiating functional and dysfunctional forms of impulsivity (Dickman 1990) does not help to resolve this debate. According to the position advanced here, 'dysfunctional' impulsivity is nothing more than the impulsive behaviour displayed at an inappropriate stage in the series of BAS processes involved in approach (e.g., as in the above example, pursuing the goal of being wealthy by engaging in impulsive gambling behaviour). There is a further conceptual confusion resulting from relating impulsivity to the BAS. This problem arises because impulsive behaviour may arise from either (a) an underactive BIS or (b) an overactive BAS (Ávila 2001) (see Ávila and Torrubia, chapter 7). As argued in chapter 5, impulsivity as a high-level personality construct may reflect the functioning of several underlying systems and not simply one (e.g., the BAS).

Item response theory

As discussed in chapters 5 and 6, there have been many attempts to develop psychometric measures of RST constructs: the aforementioned Carver and White BIS/BAS scales have been the most popular. The data pertaining to how these scales relate to the experimental manipulation of

RST variables has, however, proved problematic. The reason for this state of the literature may have much to do with inadequate psychometric definition of the central constructs of RST, as discussed above in the case of the BAS. However, there is a second factor that needs to be considered: the *precision* of measurement across the whole range of reinforcement sensitivities.

As argued by Gomez, Cooper and Gomez (2005), it is highly desirable to apply *Item Response Theory* (IRT) to ensure that RST scales contain sufficient items to measure reinforcement sensitivities along the entire length of the latent trait. Gomez *et al.* (2005) used IRT to examine the psychometric properties of the BIS/BAS scales and found that, although all items in all four scales (one BIS, three BAS) were reasonably effective in measuring their scales' designations, their precision of measurement was adequate only for low to moderately high trait level range: high sensitivities in particular are poorly measured, and it is in these extreme groups that RST has most interest. An item bank of FFFS, BAS and BIS items for all levels of the latent traits would prove a valuable addition to RST research. Such a bank of items, maybe using computerized adaptive testing to present the items relevant to the participant's latent trait, is needed to test with adequate precision in different populations experimental predictions based on RST constructs.

Basic and complex emotions

At its present stage of development, RST does not provide a complete account of emotion processing; rather it has focused on two fundamental negative emotions systems (underlying fear and anxiety),[9] and one positive emotion system (underlying appetitive drive and anticipatory pleasure). It has not addressed basic emotions (e.g., disgust and sadness). (Gray was working on the neural basis of disgust before his death, and had already published on this topic; e.g., Phillips *et al.* 2004.)

Gray (1985, 1994) suggested that emotional states are the blending of the more basic FFFS, BIS and BAS; for example, sadness may result from being confronted by punishment, which has to be approached, but

---

[9] As brought to my attention by Mr Adam Perkins, it is interesting to note that the emotion of 'anxiety' does not feature in Ekman's list of basic emotions, and nor does an 'approach' emotion, perhaps because of restricted and ambiguous facial expressions. According to Ekman (1994, p. 15), the 'use of the term basic is to emphasize the role that evolution has played in shaping both the unique and the common features that emotion display, as well as its current function', but it is questionable that emotions should be restricted to only those with prominent display (facial) features: 'display' should be expanded to include behavioural functions (e.g., risk assessment).

which is unavoidable (e.g., realizing you have a terminal illness). He likened this blending to that observed in colour perception: we perceive a vast number of colours from only three types of cones in the retina that are maximally sensitive to electro-magnetic energy of a given frequency; and the wonderful variety of colours seen on television is achieved with only three types of colour pixels. At this point, it should be noted that *how* the brain achieves this blending of basic emotional states to form complex ones is not known; far from being a limitation specific to RST, this problem represents one of the fundamental 'mysteries' in brain science.

However, some 'basic' emotions may not be as important as the name implies. For example, disgust is not likely to be a major emotional and motivational factor of general influence, as it is restricted to avoiding contaminated and rotting food – although by associative learning it can be linked to conditioned stimuli (e.g., one religion finding another religion's food preference as 'disgusting'; cf. Pinker 1997). In this respect, it is perhaps useful to distinguish between general systems of emotion and motivation (incentive and avoidance systems; FFFS and BAS) and those systems dealing with environmental demands in the form of response-specific processes (e.g., disgust and nausea).

There is also the real problem of essentially the same emotions being labelled with different terms, depending on the specifics of the situation. For example, McDonald and Leary (2005) make a strong case for considering the emotion associated with social exclusion as comparable to that associated with pain. Corr (2005) addresses this issue from the standpoint of RST and argues that, under some conditions (e.g., extreme psychological strain), differently labelled emotions (e.g., associated with distress and pain) may well be highly similar (if not identical), although this homology may break down under different conditions (e.g., mild psychological strain). An important challenge for future RST research will be to show just how far the blending theory of FFFS, BIS and BAS goes in understanding the multiple emotions that exist (see Table 1.2). Nonetheless, as pointed out by Matthews (chapter 17), there is a need to relate RST processes to specifically social brain processes (e.g., FFFS/BIS and attachment styles).

In the case of depression, a common example is the death of a loved one. The 'stimulus' – here the complex stimuli in memory and the environment relating to this person – cannot be avoided (i.e., forgotten) and thus is approached (via recurring thoughts, conversations with relatives, etc.). In this case, the stimulus (i.e., the person) elicits not the emotion of anxiety but an emotion that is usually called 'sadness'. As we shall see in chapter 2, therapeutic drugs effective for anxiety are also

Table 1.2 *Emotions/states and behaviours associated with: (a) the avoidance of (FFFS) and approach (BIS) to aversive stimuli, and (b) the approach to appetitive stimuli*

	Stimulus Conditions	Emotion/State	Behaviours
Aversive stimuli			
Avoid (FFFS):	Avoidable	Fear	Phobic avoidance, Escape, Flight
	Unavoidable	Panic	Fight (defensive aggression), Freeze
Approach (BIS):	Avoidable	Anxiety	Behavioural inhibition, Risk assessment
	Unavoidable	Depression	Behavioural suppression
Appetitive stimuli			
Approach (BAS)	Attainable	Hope, Anticipatory pleasure	Exploration, Sub-goal scaffolding
	Unattainable	Frustration, Anger	Fight (predatory aggression), Displacement activity

effective for depression, pointing to a close (but not homologous) association between these two states that seem prima facie unrelated. When this state entails thoughts about one's past behaviour, then sadness may be tinged with the emotion of regret.

This line of reasoning may help to throw light upon some very peculiar human states and beliefs. For example, in the above case of the death of a loved one, imagine the effect of this dead person, somehow, miraculously coming back to life: this would be an extreme form of 'relief of non-punishment', which is an input to the BAS. Given the power of the human brain to generate advanced states of fantasy, we may speculate that it is this very emotion that drives (i.e., provides the primary positive reinforcement in Skinnerian terminology) the hope that, one day, we shall all be reunited with dead loved ones – this is a very common belief, codified in many religions both primitive and advanced. Seen in the light of RST, we may start to understand why sadness is often accompanied by BAS-related 'hope' – for this reason, the emotions associated with bereavement tend to be complex. As this example shows, the blending of even only three major systems of emotion can give rise to many and complex emotional states, and by extension can be applied to explicating even fundamentally human beliefs.

As we can also see from Table 1.2, some appetitive stimuli that are being approached are unattainable – this fact might not be evident at the outset of the BAS sub-goal scaffolding process. This outcome would be related to a state of 'frustrative non-reward', which itself is an adequate input to the FFFS. Depending on its intensity it may produce fight/aggression and anger – the theoretical rationale for this process is given by Corr (2002b). Other authors have also argued that the BAS is related to anger (Carver 2004; Harmon–Jones 2003). Perhaps depending on personality factors outside the BAS (e.g., the *Violence Inhibition Mechanism*; see Blair, Jones, Clark and Smith 1995) we might also expect to see predatory aggression under conditions that signal reward unattainment, as well as various forms of displacement activity.

Cognition

One persistent criticism of RST is that it fails to consider adequately the importance of cognitive processes in emotion and personality (see Matthews, chapter 17). Revised RST has gone some way to remedying this situation. According to Gray and McNaughton (2000), the septo-hippocampal system is involved in cognitive and memorial processing, and this theory predicts that pathological anxiety is likely to result, at least in some cases, from abnormal cognitive processing. This brings revised RST much closer to recent cognitive theories of anxiety (e.g., Mathews 1993; Eysenck 1992). However, there are deeper criticisms of the form of the 'biological' approach adopted by RST, some of which may represent a misunderstanding, or a failure on behalf of RST researchers to be sufficiently clear in their theorizing. RST does not purport to offer a biological theory of personality that, in some way, supersedes or circumvents the need for the consideration of cognitive constructs; and nor does RST see cognitive processes as epiphenomenal froth – indeed, as argued below, it is possible to construct a theory that reveals the explicit role of higher-level cognitive constructs. For the moment, it may be noted that the influence of 'knowledge' is important – what, after all else, is a conditioned stimulus if not a form of knowledge about the relationship between stimuli? What RST does emphasize is that, whatever represents the eliciting stimuli for fear and anxiety – and these, of course, are influenced by primary and secondary appraisal and knowledge-level representations (see below) – the immediate behavioural reactions *must* be mediated by neural systems specifically evolved to control involuntary and fast-action processes. Irrespective of what we might consider the primary influence on anxiety – be it a specific threat stimulus, or the words on this page (that must require high-level cognitive processing and the engagement of knowledge structures) and which may be unique to the individual concerned (e.g., intense fear elicited by the sight of pink blancmange) – RST assumes that your *experience* of fear and anxiety is the same as everyone else's: these emotions are *not* themselves knowledge-level representations of symbolic interactions. According to this position, the type of constructs considered by RST, as well as the wider family of biological-level constructs in personality, are indispensable to a full account of emotion and personality: they are *necessary* processes. The extent to which RST possess *sufficient* processes to provide a full account of emotion and personality is a somewhat different issue.

We can see the problem more clearly in the following way. Any account that supposes that fear and anxiety result exclusively from information processing, unrelated to low-level neural systems in the brain, would have a difficult (impossible?) task of providing a cogent theoretical account, especially one that would explain the remarkable commonality observed in behaviour between non-human and human animals (e.g., effects of anxiolytics; see chapters 2 and 5). In contrast to some cognitive approaches, RST poses the question: why should we assert that, for example, the high fear induced in the rat when confronted suddenly and unexpectedly by a cat and the human being when attacked by a vicious predator – including the typical act of defecation (common in soldiers in combat) – is so qualitatively different so as to demand entirely different explanatory constructs, even when this emotion is affected by the same drugs? RST *does* need to invoke different explanatory constructs when talking about the factors *sufficient* to activate these primitive neural modules: the details of the knowledge structures and cognitive processes that activate *your* emotions do not, of necessity, need to be the same as those that activate *mine*, yet our emotional experience will be highly similar (in as far as we can ever make the general statement about inter-individual similarities, and between-species similarities, the former of which show commonality in verbal report, behaviour and reactions to drugs, as do the latter, save verbal report, although even non-human animals vocalize as part of the fear response repertoire).

None of the above is designed to detract from the important role played by cognitive factors (e.g., expectancy, primary and secondary appraisal, and 'knowledge' level factors): these play a central role in determining the adequate *inputs* to the FFFS, BAS and BIS; accordingly, they serve to regulate emotions and defensive behaviour: if inputs are changed *then* outputs of these systems are also changed.

Coping Coping is one area where the forging of RST and purely cognitive approaches could start. Hasking (2006) considered this question in the context of eating and drinking behaviours, noting that both reinforcement sensitivity and coping strategies have independently been related to these behaviours. Hasking hypothesized that if sensitivity to reward and punishment are biological predispositions that regulate behaviour, then it may be assumed that reinforcement sensitivity is a *distal* predictor of behaviour. On the other hand, coping strategies may be seen as the *proximal* predictor of behaviour. Hasking goes on to argue that these distal and proximal factors may be related in at least two ways. (a) High BIS sensitivity leads a person to adopt more avoidant coping strategies, such as denial, in order to avoid negative stimuli associated with the stressor, and the use of avoidant coping may in turn predict dysfunctional eating patterns or alcohol use. (b) Coping strategies may influence the relationship between reinforcement sensitivity and eating or drinking behaviour: there may be a positive relationship between BAS sensitivity and alcohol use, but only for people who engage in avoidant coping strategies, while a negative relationship may exist for those who use problem-focused strategies. In such a way, the coping strategies a person chooses may either mediate or moderate the relationship between predispositional reinforcement sensitivity and eating or drinking behaviour (and, by inference, many other forms of behaviour). The potential importance of a distinction between *distal* and *proximal* levels of explanation has been noted by other RST researchers (e.g., Jackson and Francis 2004).

Between-species and inter-individual differences

The question of the relevance of non-human animal data for human personality is often asked (see McNaughton and Corr, chapter 3); and the conclusion is sometimes drawn that any theory that relies so heavily upon animal data must have limitations when applied to complex human psychological processes. But RST assumes that neural systems of emotion and motivation are not species-specific; they are shared by a large variety of species. However, the specific demands of each species are quite different. RST assumes that the neural systems provide the general, background, evolutionary foundations to avoid (FFFS), approach (BAS) and be cautious (BIS), but the *specific stimuli* that we avoid, approach and are cautious of have important species-specific features.

The (relatively) strong BAS activation and (relatively weak) FFFS activation of a conference presenter should produce a cautious, risk assessment approach to preparation (e.g., checking for spelling mistakes in handout). A chimpanzee does not show these behaviours. He is not concerned with conference presentations; his concerns lie elsewhere (e.g., 'presenting' his genetic fitness to mates). But his concerns are no less reliant on basic emotional and motivational systems; and so too are ours. The fact that one species, in this case human beings, seem to have basic needs for competence, autonomy, social connection, even 'spiritual transcendence', is irrelevant to assessing the validity of RST, which does not purport to explain every 'basic need' of every species. Rather, it attempts to provide explanatory constructs that work at the general level, referring to general influences – irrespective of the specific content of the needs – related to avoidance, approach and cautious of, whatever set of stimuli dominate at the species level or individual level. Thus, the specific details of the life challenges facing a species, or individuals within a species, are not of primary importance. They, of course, need to be taken into account when trying to work out the types of stimuli which are sufficient to activate basic systems in a given species or individual.

Experimental assays

A number of putative experimental assays of the FFFS, BAS and BIS are shown in chapter 5 (Table 5.1). A challenge for RST is to develop 'pure' measures of these systems i.e., measures that allow the threshold and activation of the three systems to be measured without the influence of other systems. Only once such measures have been developed will it be possible to ask and answer questions about the interplay of these systems. In order to develop such paradigmatic assays, it will be necessary to undertake a detailed task analysis to define the parameters of the task and how these are likely to be affected by RST processes. In this respect, it would be useful to move beyond a verbal-qualitative description to a numerical-quantitative one using computational modelling procedures that capture the dynamics of behaviour and allow experimental predictions to be generated using different parameter values. (Examples of this approach are given in chapters 5 and 16.) Such computer simulations often produce results counter to verbal-qualitative description, and accordingly may help to explain the divergence of results reported in the RST literature (Corr 2004).

Much of previous RST research has not taken adequate account of the cognitive and behavioural demands of the task. In the 2000 revised theory, we can see that associated with each defensive distance is a specific set of cognitions/behaviours (e.g., flee vs. freeze). Even when there are significant RST-related individual differences on the task, the pattern of effects may confuse this relationship because of the match/ mismatch between task demands and specific RST cognitions/behaviours. A related problem concerns the range of effects: manipulation of reinforcement at only one point on the range (which is common in RST research) may be affecting performance on only one 'limb' of the performance curve. If this curve is inverted-U then sensitivity to reinforcement may be *either* positively related or negatively related to performance. This possibility may explain the diversity of results in the RST literature.

Levels of control

Discussion of the role of cognitive factors in RST processes raises a general problem of the appropriate level of control in emotion and motivation: 'biological' or 'cognitive'? Presenting the problem in this binary form is not helpful. Instead, what is needed is a model that clarifies the roles played by each level of control. The aim of this section is to embed RST in a wider literature which has already considered many of the issues of behavioural control. In so doing, the relevance – indeed, crucial importance – of considering consciousness in personality research will be highlighted.

Consciousness: what is controlling behaviour?

It is perhaps surprisingly that the nature of consciousness is all too rarely discussed alongside emotion and personality and, hitherto, never in relation to RST. However, this is not unique to personality research, as the problems of consciousness, especially those that seem so scientifically intractable, have, at least until the recent past, been largely ignored (or, more often, unrecognized).

We are, therefore, fortunate that Gray's (2004) last book, *Consciousness: Creeping up on the Hard Problem*, addressed the problems of consciousness for psychology in general, especially the problem of the relationship between systems controlling behaviour and conscious awareness. It is likely that, as with many other areas opened up by Gray's thinking, this hitherto delinquent area of psychology will come increasingly within the spotlight of personality psychology. (Space prevents a thorough discussion of this topic; for a more detailed description of Gray's model, see Corr 2006.) First, Gray does not offer an account of the 'Hard Problem' (Chalmers 1995), i.e., the *why* and *how* of conscious experience, especially how the brain *generates* conscious awareness. It instead addresses the *function* of consciousness: what it is for and how is it implemented?

    'Online' and 'Offline' processes   In addressing the function of consciousness, the distinction between different levels of behavioural control is important. Standard psychology textbooks continue to contrast 'learning theories' and 'cognitive theories'; and this approach follows the long-fought territorial battles between stimulus-response (S-R) theories (e.g., Skinner), who argued for automatic bonds between eliciting stimuli and responses, and cognitive theorists (e.g., Tolman), who argued that intervening variables between stimuli and responses, knowledge structures and processes are required (see MacPhail 1998). In reviews of the literature, Toates (1998, 2006) draws attention to the fact that both processes are observed in human and non-human animals, and that consideration of both processes may help us better to understand normal and abnormal behaviour in general, and consciousness in particular. This debate is also played out in the literatures concerned with implicit/procedural and explicit/declarative processes. In the context of personality research, some of the major dual-process theories of behavioural control are well rehearsed by Carver (2005).

    A similar distinction is seen in the field of visual perception. Milner and Goodale (1995) refer to two streams in visual processing: the 'online' and 'seeing' systems. The online system, is the 'action system' which can be indexed by various performance measures; it is automatic and reflex-like, occurring before the time needed to achieve conscious awareness of the action and the eliciting stimuli. This system seems to use the dorsal processing stream – Milner and Goodale propose that rather than being the 'where' stream, as suggested by Ungerleider and Mishkin (1982), it is the 'how' stream. The ventral stream, in contrast, is largely conscious: it is the 'what' stream, and is similar to the 'offline' processes discussed in this section.

    According to Toates' (1998) model (Figure 1.3), a stimulus (S) has a certain strength of tendency to produce a response (R; formerly called 'habit strength'); i.e., S has a response eliciting potential, which varies from zero to some maximum value (this strength depends upon innate factors and learning). 'Cognition' in this context refers to those processes that encode knowledge about the world in a form not tied to particular behaviours (Rs). Where there is uncertainly, novelty or a mismatch of actual against expected outcomes, behavioural control shifts from the S-R (online) processing, which is fast and coarse-grained in its analysis, to cognitive (offline) processing, that is slow and

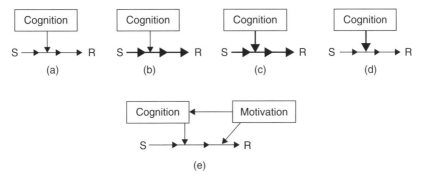

Figure 1.3 Representation of relationship between S–R and cognitive processes: (a) balanced weighting; (b) strong S–R and weak cognition; (c) strong S–R and strong cognition; (d) weak S–R and strong cognition; and (e) interaction with motivation

fine-grained in its analysis. The particular circumstance that gives rise to the different weightings is shown in Figure 1.3.

Toates' model helps us to understand the adaptive value of consciousness. This model contends that some actions that can be organized at a low (online) level can nonetheless be affected by conscious (offline) processes: higher-order, conscious processes can modulate the strength of connections controlling behaviour organized at a relatively low level of the control hierarchy. For example, a fear state that is processed consciously may sensitize the whole defensive system and thereby affect *subsequent* fast, automatic responses (such as the startle reflex). Thus, Toates emphasizes the weights attached to motor programs, and how cognitive, conscious (offline) processes can modify the weights (i.e., firing potential) of online responses. Online processes correspond to an open feedback system; whereas offline processes correspond to a closed feedback system (see above).

Gray's (2004) theory of the function of consciousness extends the line of argument pursued by Toates. Specifically, Gray takes seriously the implications of the findings of Libet (1985, 2003) which have shown a number of rather counterintuitive phenomena. Various forms of data point to the fact that it takes some 300–500 ms of brain activity for consciousness to occur: this is the 'lateness' of conscious experience.

The problem with such findings for any adaptive theory of consciousness is that long before 300–500 ms, motor actions have already been initiated (e.g., the removal of the hand from a hot stove occurs before awareness of the hand touching the stove). In this specific case, removal of the hand is involuntary and not controlled by conscious processes. However, events are not experienced as if they happened 300–500 ms ago: consciousness appears to refer to what is happening *now*. Libet suggests that the conscious experience of a stimulus is 'referred back in time' once neuronal adequacy has been achieved to make it *seem* as if there was no delay. This produces the illusion of voluntary control; arguably, it is an illusion that continues to dominate views on the role of cognition in personality.[10]

Now, there have been many criticisms of Libet's experiments as well as his interpretation of his data (e.g., Libet 2003; Zhu 2003; see Blackmore 2003), but the basic finding of the lateness of conscious awareness seems solid. As noted by Gray (2004, p. 23), 'The scandal of Libet's findings is that they show *the conscious awareness of volition to be illusory*' (emphasis added). However, from a physicalist point of view, all mind events (e.g., thinking and consciousness) must be *caused* by a physical process in the brain that *precedes* the conscious awareness of these events – how could it be otherwise? But, this leaves us with the problems of causation and behavioural control.

What does all of this mean for RST? Well, it implies that conscious awareness of emotion, volition, behaviour, etc. does not play any role in the emotion, volition and behaviour *to which it refers*. Now, we must be careful not to conflate 'cognitive processes' and 'conscious awareness'; but it remains the case that what we are consciously aware of does not have an *immediate* causal role to play – but we shall shortly see it does exert causal effects on *subsequent* behaviour. The main point is that the volition of behaviour is *always* non-conscious in terms of its *direct*, or primary, causal process. Thus, according to this position, RST relates to immediate causal processes, leaving higher-level cognitive processes (e.g., verbal mediation, but not exclusively so) to *indirect*, or secondary, causal effects on future (if only hundreds of milliseconds) behaviours.

Function of conscious awareness: late error detection   According to Gray (2004, p. 107):

Conscious experience serves three linked functions. (1) It contains a model of the relatively enduring features of the external world; and the model is experienced as though it *is* the external world; (2) within the framework afforded by this model, features that are particularly relevant to ongoing motor programs or which depart from expectation are monitored and emphasised; (3) within the

---

[10] Space prevents a full exposition of this matter. It is sufficient to say that 'cognition' does not relate solely to conscious processes, or necessarily only to slow, fine-grained analysis; but it is also germane to point out that fast-reflexive actions cannot entail much in the way of complex process *at the time* of execution of the response.

framework of the model, the controlled variables and set-points of the brain's unconscious servomechanisms can be juxtaposed, combined and modified; in this way, error can be corrected.

To understand these functions, imagine you are confronted by a dangerous snake and your fear system fires off an automatic (online) motor program: all this happens long before (i.e., hundreds of milliseconds) you are consciously aware of (i.e., 'see' and 'feel') the snake. It would now be highly adaptive to 'replay' the immediate past in order to analyse its contents, especially at those times when the online fear behaviour did not achieve its goal (in this instance, increasing defensive distance).

Central to this model of conscious awareness is the 'comparator',[11] which, in RST, serves to compare actual stimuli with expected stimuli (Gray and Smith 1969). Thus, the comparator compares the *expected* state of the world with the *actual* state of the world. When there is no discrepancy, and 'all is going to plan', the comparator is said to be in 'just checking mode'; however, when there is a mismatch between the expected and actual states of the world, then the comparator goes into 'control mode' (Gray 1981). According to Gray, in this control mode, the *contents* of consciousness are generated (e.g., attention to snake).

The relevance of online and offline systems can now be seen. According to this model, online (non-conscious) processes are modified by offline (conscious) processes; in Toates' terminology, the weights attached to response propensities in online processes are adjusted on the basis of the fine-grained offline processes. Gray (2004) uses the terminology of cybernetics with behavioural weights attached to specific stimuli (see Figure 1.4).[12]

Now, offline processes do have causal effects on *subsequent* online processes; in other words, our behaviour is modified by experience: we *learn*. Before our discussion slides blindly into a dualistic mode of thinking, it needs to be emphasized that both online and offline processes are products of the brain, but they have different functions. Specifically, they differ in (a) their temporal characteristics; (b) their level of analysis; and (c) their representation in conscious awareness. Online processes are

[11] Carver and Scheier (1998) put forward the intriguing idea that focusing attention on the self is often equivalent to engaging the comparator, which is centrally involved in self-regulating feedback control processes in general. In Gray's model, the comparator compares expected and actual reinforcing stimuli; in the case of personality, this leads to rumination, worry and anxiety; but in the case of consciousness, when behaviour is not going to plan (i.e., a feedback error signal is generated) offline processes are triggered (*ex hypothesi*, consciousness).

[12] Cybernetics is the science of communication and control, comprising end-goals and feedback processes containing control of values within the system that guide the organism towards its final goal (Wiener 1948).

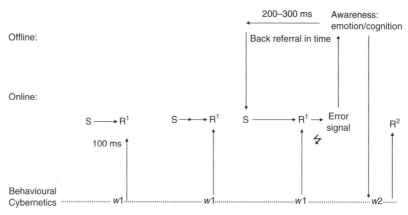

Figure 1.4 A schematic depiction of Gray's late error detection model of consciousness. Offline processes monitor the success of (automatic) online processes, and when 'everything is going to plan', online processes 'fire-off' and are not influenced by offline processes; but when an error signal (⚡) is detected, then the salient features of the error signal are transferred to offline processes which, among other things, is represented in the form of conscious perceptual experience (both perceptual in terms of imagery, etc. and affective, in terms of emotion). Although offline processes, of necessity, lag behind online processes, the process of 'back referral in term' provides the illusion that the experience is occurring at the same moment as the stimuli that it represents. Of importance, this offline process cannot affect responses to the stimuli it represents, but it can alter the behavioural weights of *subsequent* online processes (e.g., speed of response) and thus exerts a causal effect on future behaviour ('once bitten, twice shy')

very fast, involving coarse-grained analysis of salient features, and are not represented in conscious awareness; in contrast, offline processes are slow, taking hundreds of milliseconds to generate, entail (relatively) fine-grained analysis, and are represented in conscious awareness. This dual system serves evolutionary challenges well: a fast 'dirty' response system coupled with a slower 'cleaner' response system for post-action processing. (The distinction between 'fast-coarse', not involving conscious processing, and 'fine-detailed', involving conscious awareness, levels of processing has been noted before; LeDoux 1996, 2000.)

Thus, online behaviour, which *always* comes before the generation of conscious awareness, can be modified by offline processing that brings to the fore those salient features (e.g., novelty and mismatch) that require closer analysis. Although we may still want to talk about 'fast-and-dirty' primary cognitive analysis of data, we may also talk about 'cybernetic behavioural weights' that are central to RST – certainly, on this analysis, we cannot talk about conscious primary analysis, while secondary appraisal, that may be conscious, is not causally efficacious at all in relation to the stimuli it is appraising.

In relation to the BIS, one important consequence of modifying behavioural weights attached to online processes is to inhibit prepotent (online) responses. This mechanism solves one major evolutionary problem: how to ensure that online automatic responses are appropriate. It would be desirable to be able to inhibit the firing-off of these automatic behavioural routines in some circumstances (e.g., inhibiting avoidance behaviours when in foraging mode), even if this inhibition takes several hundreds of milliseconds (usually enough time to have important consequences). Gray notes that conscious control is exerted only at critical junctures, when a definite choice has to be made. But when in automatic mode, errors can occur. Thus, automatic routines are well suited to fixed tasks – crucially for RST, fixed action patterns associated with defensive distance and environmental parameters – but they are not so good for tasks requiring a departure from fixed routines (e.g., a novel task) or when automatic performance is not going to plan.

Extending the late detection model: what-if simulations

Consistent with the general form of Gray's (2004) model is the additional idea that consciousness allows 'what-if' simulations of future behaviour, produced offline in a virtual reality environment that contains the important features of the real physical environment (e.g., imagination). Indeed, this function seems highly important to human beings: much of our time is spent *imagining* the likely consequences of our behaviour and making plans for the future. Such behaviours require complex computational processes, specifically involving inferences concerning the likely behaviour of other people. It is obvious that personality does relate to such simulations, and, it may be speculated, that much of the 'energy' for neurotic disorders comes from these 'offline' cognitive processes. It is thus likely that variance in neuroticism will not be solely explained by standard RST processes, but by an elaboration of the theory to incorporate longer-term cognitive processes that decouple these processes from actual stimuli: thus, we can have 'free-floating' anxiety and 'worry about worry'. In reality it is highly probable that these higher-level effects are themselves shaped by basic RST processes in early development and are, in any event, refuelled by ongoing FFFS, BIS and BAS activation (or deactivation in the case of deficit syndromes, e.g., introvertive-anhedonia).

Let us now put to work our offline, what-if simulation modeller. Compare two phenotypes facing complex social problems: one phenotype simply computes errors in online programs; the second anticipates these errors by running realistic simulations, away from the (potentially punishing) stimuli in the real environment (informed by previous outcomes of online behaviours). Which phenotype would be more successful in terms of survival and reproduction? In many environments, it would be the latter. Now, if this same process could be used to solve complex social problems associated with approach motivation (e.g., securing and keeping a mate, influencing other conspecifics, achieving status and privileges in the social structure) then it is possible to conceive of the development of behaviour that is appropriate to complex natural and social environments that require a combination of fast, reflex-like processes, as well as more reflective analysis of the environment. Thus, the offline, late error detection mechanism seems to have acquired the capacity to be dissociated from immediately preceding online processes. This additional evolution of offline processing may well necessitate awareness (i.e., the experience of qualia, e.g., the 'redness' of a rose), especially when adequate sensory stimuli are not present in order to build an *apparently* real-time simulation model encompassing the central features of the external world.

It is tempting to associate FFFS, BIS and BAS with rapid 'online' behavioural procedures, and more 'frontal' systems, associated with restraint and deliberative, attentional control, with cognitive procedures of reflection and modification. If this approach has any merit then we might be able to understand how factors such as psychoticism[13] (in Eysenck's model) and constraint (in Tellegen's model) appear to be independent of neuroticism, anxiety and approach behaviour, yet seem able to modify these more basic reactions. However, it should be borne in mind that the above account of behavioural control provides only a very rough sketch; further elaboration and refinement of these processes is needed. In particular, it will be necessary to account for cognitive processes that operate automatically as it will be for those that operate at a more controlled level entailing slow deliberation and fine-grained analysis.

---

[13] Relating psychoticism to a higher level of cognitive control – that, as we have seen, according to Gray's theory is responsible for generating the contents of consciousness – is consistent with the association of psychoticism with the cognitive processes disrupted in schizophrenia (see Gray *et al.* 1991); of course, schizophrenia itself represents a disruption of conscious experience of self and the world. According to the theory promulgated here, the disruption seen in schizophrenia is, in part, a failure of this higher-level system to provide adequate constructions and inferences of the internal and external stimuli which are *re*presented, or displayed, in the form of conscious awareness.

Conclusion

RST will ultimately be tested against the criterion of *progressive science* (Lakatos 1970): will it only be interested in parochial theoretical issues, fortified by a restricted range of 'special case' data, or does it hold the potential to throw light on existing theoretical vistas as well as opening up new ones in personality psychology? Forging links with other theoretical perspectives will be especially crucial, as well as expanding the spheres of interest (e.g., occupational and financial behaviour). In the final analysis, it must be borne in mind that all scientific theories are, at best, approximations to the natural phenomena they attempt to explain; and if they are not to become conceptual fossils, they must change and grow.

References

Abler, B., Walter, H., Erk, S., Kammerer, H. and Spitzer, M. (2006), Prediction error as a linear function of reward probability is coded in human nucleus accumbens, *NeuroImage*, 31, 790–795

Ávila, C. (2001), Distinguishing BIS–mediated and BAS-mediated disinhibition mechanisms: a comparison of disinhibition models of Gray (1981, 1987) and of Patterson and Newman (1993), *Journal of Personality and Social Psychology*, 80, 311–324

Barlow, D.H. (1988), *Anxiety and its Disorders* (New York: Guilford Press)

Blanchard, R.J. and Blanchard, D.C. (1990), An ethoexperimental analysis of defense, fear and anxiety in N. McNaughton and G. Andrews (eds), *Anxiety* (Dunedin: Otago University Press), pp. 12–133

Blackmore, S. (2003), *Consciousness: An Introduction* (London: Hodder and Stoughton)

Blair, R.J.R., Jones, L., Clark, F. and Smith, M. (1995), Is the psychopath 'morally insane'?, *Personality and Individual Differences*, 19, 741–752

Carver, C.S. (2004), Negative affects deriving from the behavioral approach system, *Emotion*, 41, 3–22

  (2005), Impulse and constraint: perspectives from personality psychology, convergence with theory in other areas, and potential for integration, *Personality and Social Psychology Review*, 9, 312–333

Carver, C.S. and Scheier, M.F. (1998), *On the Self-Regulation of Behavior* (Cambridge: Cambridge University Press)

Carver, C.S. and White, T.L. (1994), Behavioral inhibition, behavioral activation, and affective responses to impending reward and punishment: the BIS/BAS scales, *Journal of Personality and Social Psychology*, 67, 319–333

Chalmers, D.J. (1995), Facing up to the problem of consciousness, *Journal of Consciousness Studies*, 2, 200–219

Cloninger, C.R. (1986), A unified biosocial theory of personality and its role in the development of anxiety states, *Psychiatric Developments*, 3, 167–226

Corr, P.J. (2001), Testing problems in J.A. Gray's personality theory: a commentary on Matthews and Gilliland (1999), *Personal Individual Differences*, 30, 333–352

Corr, P.J. (2002a), J.A. Gray's reinforcement sensitivity theory: tests of the joint subsystems hypothesis of anxiety and impulsivity, *Personality and Individual Differences*, 33, 511–532

(2002b), J.A. Gray's reinforcement sensitivity theory and frustrative nonreward: a theoretical note on expectancies in reactions to rewarding stimuli, *Personality and Individual Differences*, 32, 1247–1253

(2004), Reinforcement sensitivity theory and personality, *Neuroscience and Biobehavioral Reviews*, 28, 317–332

(2005), Social exclusion and the hierarchical defense system: comment on MacDonald and Leary (2005), *Psychological Bulletin*, 131, 231–236

(2006), *Understanding Biological Psychology* (Oxford: Blackwell)

Corr, P.J. and Perkins, A.M. (2006), The role of theory in the psychophysiology of personality: from Ivan Pavlov to Jeffrey Gray, *International Journal of Psychophysiology*, 62, 367–376

Corr, P.J., Pickering, A.D. and Gray, J.A. (1995a), Personality and reinforcement in associative and instrumental learning, *Personal Individual Differences*, 19, 47–71

(1995b), Sociability/impulsivity and caffeine-induced arousal effects: critical flicker/fusion frequency and procedural learning, *Personality and Individual Differences*, 18, 713–730

Darwin, C. (1859/1968), *On the Origin of Species by Means of Natural Selection, or the Preservation of Favoured Races in the Struggle for Life* (Princeton, NJ: Princeton University Press)

Dawkins, R. and Krebs, J.R. (1979), Arms races between and within species, *Proceeding of the Royal Society of London*, Series B, 205, 489–511

Dickman, S.J. (1990), Functional and dysfunctional impulsivity: personality and cognitive correlates, *Journal of Personality and Social Psychology*, 58, 95–102

Eilam, D. (2005), Die hard: a blend of freezing and fleeing as a dynamic defense: implications for the control of defensive behaviour, *Neuroscience and Biobehavioral Reviews*, 1181–1191

Ekman P. (1994), All emotions are basic in P. Ekman and R.J. Davidson (eds), *The Nature of Emotion: Fundamental Questions* (Oxford: Oxford University Press), pp. 15–19

Eysenck, H.J. (1957), *The Dynamics of Anxiety and Hysteria* (New York: Preger)

(1967), *The Biological Basis of Personality* (IL: Thomas Springfield)

(1979), The conditioning model of neurosis, *Behavioural and Brain Sciences*, 2, 155–199

Eysenck, H.J. and Eysenck, M.W. (1985), *Personality and Individual Differences: A Natural Science Approach* (New York: Plenum Press)

Eysenck, H.J. and Levey, A. (1972), Conditioning, introversion–extraversion and the strength of the nervous system in V.D. Nebylitsyn and J.A. Gray (eds), *Biological Bases of Individual Behaviour* (London: Academic Press), pp. 206–220

Eysenck, M.W. (1992), *Anxiety: the Cognitive Perspective* (Hillsdale, NJ: Erlbaum)

Eysenck, S.B.G., Pearson, P.R., Easting, G. and Allsopp, J.F. (1985), Age norms for impulsiveness, venturesomeness and empathy in adults, *Personality and Individual Differences*, 6, 613–619

Fowles, D.C. (2000), Electrodermal hypoactivity and antisocial behaviour: does anxiety mediate the relationship, *Journal of Affective Disorders*, 61, 177–189

Fowles, D.C. (2006), Jeffrey Gray's contributions to theories of anxiety, personality, and psychopathology in T. Canli (ed.), *Biology of Personality and Individual Differences* (New York: Guilford Press), pp. 7–34

Gray, J.A. (1970), The psychophysiological basis of introversion–extraversion, *Behaviour Research and Therapy*, 8, 249–266

(1972a), Learning theory, the conceptual nervous system and personality in V.D. Nebylitsyn and J.A. Gray (eds), *The Biological Bases of Individual Behaviour* (New York: Academic Press), pp. 372–399

(1972b), The psychophysiological nature of introversion-extraversion: a modification of Eysenck's theory in V.D. Nebylitsyn and J.A. Gray (eds), *The Biological Bases of Individual Behaviour* (New York: Academic Press), pp. 182–205

(1975), *Elements of a Two-Process Theory of Learning* (London: Academic Press)

(1976), The behavioural inhibition system: a possible substrate for anxiety in M.P. Feldman and A.M. Broadhurst (eds), *Theoretical and Experimental Bases of Behaviour Modification* (London: Wiley), pp. 3–41

(1981), A critique of Eysenck's theory of personality in H.J. Eysenck (ed.), *A Model for Personality* (Berlin: Springer), pp. 246–276

(1982), *The Neuropsychology of Anxiety: An Enquiry into the Functions of the Septo-Hippocampal System* (Oxford: Oxford University Press)

(1985), Anxiety and the brain: pigments aren't colour names, *Bulletin of the British Psychological Society*, 38, 299–300

(1987), *The Psychology of Fear and Stress* (Cambridge: Cambridge University Press)

(1994), Three fundamental emotion systems in P. Ekman and R.J. Davidson (eds), *The Nature of Emotion: Fundamental Questions* (Oxford: Oxford University Press)

(2004), *Consciousness: Creeping up on the Hard Problem* (Oxford: Oxford University Press)

Gray, J.A., Feldon, J., Rawlins, J.N.P., Hemsley, D.R. and Smith, A.D. (1991), The neuropsychology of schizophrenia, *Behavioral and Brain Sciences*, 14, 1–84

Gray, J.A. and McNaughton, N. (2000), *The Neuropsychology of Anxiety: An Enquiry into the Functions of the Septo-Hippocampal System* (Oxford: Oxford University Press)

Gray, J.A. and Smith, P.T. (1969), An arousal decision model for partial reinforcement and discrimination learning in R.M. Gilbert and N.S. Sutherland (eds), *Animal Discrimination Learning* (London: Academic Press), pp. 243–272

Gomez, R., Cooper, A. and Gomez, A. (2005), An item response theory analysis of the Carver and White (1994) BIS/BAS Scales, *Personality and Individual Differences*, 39, 1093–1103

Hasking, P.A. (2006), Reinforcement sensitivity, coping, disordered eating and drinking behaviour in adolescents, *Personality and Individual Differences*, 40, 677–688

Harmon-Jones, E. (2003), Anger and the behavioural approach system, *Personality and Individual Differences*, 35, 995–1005

Hebb, D.O. (1955), Drives and the CNS (conceptual nervous system), *Psychological Review*, 62, 243–254

Hull, C.L. (1952), *A Behavior System* (New Haven: Yale University Press)

Jackson, C.J. and Francis, L.J. (2004), Are interactions in Gray's reinforcement sensitivity theory proximal or distal in the prediction of religiosity: a test of the joint subsystems hypothesis, *Personality and Individual Differences*, 36, 1197–1209

Konorski, J. (1967), *Integrative Activity of the Brain* (Chicago: Chicago University Press)

Lakatos, I. (1970), Falsification and the methodology of scientific research programmes in I. Lakatos and A. Musgrave (eds), *Criticism and the Growth of Knowledge* (Cambridge: Cambridge University Press), pp. 91–196

LeDoux, J.E. (1996), *The Emotional Brain* (New York: Simon and Schuster)
    (2000), Emotion circuits in the brain, *Annual Review of Neuroscience*, 23, 155–184

Libet, B. (1985), Unconscious cerebral initiative and the role of conscious will in voluntary action, *Behavioral and Brain Sciences*, 8, 529–566
    (2003), Timing of conscious experience: reply to the 2002 commentaries on Libet's findings, *Consciousness and Cognition*, 12, 321–331

MacDonald, G. and Leary, M.R. (2005), Why does social exclusion hurt? The relationship between social and physical pain, *Psychological Bulletin*, 131, 202–223

Mackintosh, N.J. (1983), *Conditioning and Associative Learning* (Oxford: Clarendon Press)

MacPhail, E.M. (1998), *The Evolution of Consciousness* (Oxford: Oxford University Press)

Mathews, A. (1993), Biases in processing emotional information, *The Psychologist*, 6, 493–499

McNaughton, N. and Corr, P.J. (2004), A two-dimensional neuropsychology of defense: fear/anxiety and defensive distance, *Neuroscience and Biobehavioral Reviews*, 28, 285–305

Miller, G.A., Gelenter, E. and Pribram, K. (1960), *Plans and the Structure of Behavior* (New York: Holt, Rinehart and Winston)

Milner, A.D. and Goodale, M.A. (1995), *The Visual Brain in Action* (Oxford: Oxford University Press)

Mowrer, H.O. (1960), *Learning Theory and Behavior* (New York: Wiley)

Olds, J. and Milner, P. (1954), Positive reinforcement produced by electrical stimulation of septal area and other regions of rat brain, *Journal of Comparative and Physiological Psychology*, 47, 419–427

Patterson, C.M. and Newman, J.P. (1993), Reflectivity and learning from aversive events: towards a psychological mechanism for the syndromes of disinhibition, *Psychological Review*, 100, 716–736

Pavlov, I.P. (1927), *Reflexes: An Investigation of the Physiological Activity of the Cerebral Cortex* (Oxford: Oxford University Press, G.V. Anrep (trans. and ed.))

Perkins, A.M. and Corr, P.J. (2006), Reactions to threat and personality: psychometric differentiation of intensity and direction dimensions of human defensive behaviour, *Behavioural Brain Research*, 169, 21–28

Phillips, M.L., Williams, L.M., Heining, M., Herba, C.M., Russell, T., Andrew, C., Bullmore, E.T., Brammer, M.J., Williams, S.C.R. and Morgan, M.J. (2004), Differential neural responses to overt and covert presentations of facial expressions of fear and disgust, *Neuroimage*, 21, 1484–1496

Pickering, A.D., Corr, P.J., Gray, J.A. (1999), Interactions and reinforcement sensitivity theory: a theoretical analysis of Rusting and Larsen (1997), *Personality and Individual Differences*, 26, 357–365

Pinker, S. (1997), *How the Mind Works* (New York: Norton)

Ranter, S.C. (1977), Immobility in invertebrates: what can we learn? *Psychological Review*, 1, 1–14

Toates, F. (1998), The interaction of cognitive and stimulus-response processes in the control of behaviour, *Neuroscience and Biobehavioral Reviews*, 22, 59–83

(2006), A model of the hierarchy of behaviour, cognition, and consciousness, *Consciousness and Cognition*, 15, 75–118

Ungerleider, L.G. and Mishkin, M. (1982), Two cortical vision systems in D.J. Ingle, M.A. Goodale and R.J.W. Mansfield (eds), *Analysis of Visual Behaviour* (Cambridge, MA: MIT Press)

Weiner, N. (1948), *Cybernetics, or Control and Communication in the Animal and the Machine* (New York: John Wiley & Sons)

Zhu, J. (2003), Reclaiming volition: an alternative interpretation of Libet's experiment, *Journal of Consciousness Studies*, 10, 61–77

2 The neuropsychology of fear and anxiety: a foundation for Reinforcement Sensitivity Theory

Neil McNaughton and Philip J. Corr

Personality factors, as normally studied, are sources of variation that are stable over time and that derive from underlying properties of an individual more than current changes in their environment. They account for behavioural differences between individuals presented with identical environments that show consistent patterns within that individual across time. As such, an ultimate goal of personality research must be to identify the relatively static biological variables that determine the superficial factor structure evident in behaviour and other measures. This is not to deny the importance of the environment in controlling personality. But, to produce consistent long-term effects, environmental influences must be mediated by, and instantiated in, biological systems. Biology can also be viewed as more fundamental in that environmental events (such as an impact to the front of the head) have permanent effects on personality not in relation to the external parameters of the event (such as the force of impact) but rather in relation to the precise extent of change the event induces in the brain.

Those interested in individual variation in the tendency to neurotic disorders have been particularly inclined to theorize in terms of either the real or the conceptual nervous system. Pavlov saw variation in the response of his dogs to both traumatic and everyday events as arising from the 'Strength of the Nervous System' – a purely theoretical construct, albeit with a consistent behavioural structure (Gray 1964, 1967). H.J. Eysenck (1944, 1947) used factor analysis of a medical checklist of neurotic symptoms in a clinical population to identify and then develop, in the normal population, the constructs of Extraversion and Neuroticism. He then linked these constructs to conditionability of neural connections and so to the development of neurotic behaviour. The most extensive exegesis has been that of Gray. He (Gray 1970) first proposed an alternative theoretical account of the genesis of the *same* neurotic behaviour as Eysenck starting with a modest rotation of Eysenck's original factor axes. This allowed him to attribute neurotic disorder to a factor of punishment sensitivity, which he then linked (Gray 1976, 1982), via his theory of a 'Behavioural Inhibition System' (BIS), to a detailed neural architecture.

Gray's theory of the BIS is primarily an account of state changes. His personality theory, from which modern *Reinforcement Sensitivity Theory* (RST) derives, assumes that the entire BIS is subject to global modulation that accounts for trait/personality variation. As a result, the predictions of his personality theory are strongly related to the details of his account of state changes. This chapter[1] describes recent refinements of the state aspects of the BIS at both the conceptual and neural levels (Gray and McNaughton 2000; McNaughton and Corr 2004). Much of the revised theory is clarification and repackaging of the old theory. But some changes that are minor at the state level represent significant alterations to the foundations of RST. They demand the reformulation of experimental tests of RST in terms of the revised theory. For research purposes, this revised theory replaces the old theory. The specific implications of these alterations for theories of personality are dealt with in a separate chapter (see Corr and McNaughton, chapter 5). The key differences and similarities between Gray's (1982) neuropsychological theory and the updated theory are summarized in Table 2.1 The justification for, and main details of, the updated theory are presented below.

A 'state' level analysis of defence

To understand large-scale, long-term ('trait') modulation of neural systems it is first necessary to have at least an approximate idea of the functioning of those systems on shorter ('state') timescales. It is in these state variations that the structure and processes of neuropsychological systems are most evident. Neural level analysis also requires, as a precursor, some degree of coherent conceptualization of the structure of behaviour. We need to know what the theory is attempting to explain. This section, therefore, deals with some critical psychological constructs derived largely from Gray (1982) and Gray and McNaughton (2000).

Reward and punishment

Substantive affective events can be viewed as falling into just two distinct major classes: positive and negative (Gray 1975, 1982; Gray

---

[1] This chapter is based substantially on McNaughton and Corr (2004).

Table 2.1 *Comparison of original and updated theories of the neuropsychology of anxiety (bold items represent significant changes)*

Concept	Gray (1982)	Gray and McNaughton 2000 McNaughton and Corr 2004
Fear and anxiety		
Fear (FFFS)	Fight-Flight	Fight-Flight-**Freeze**
Anxiety (BIS)	behavioural inhibition increased arousal, attention, exploration	behavioural inhibition increased arousal, attention, **risk assessment**
Fear/Anxiety	unconditioned/ conditioned	**threat avoidance/threat approach**
The Behavioural Inhibition System		
BIS defined by	anxiolytic action	anxiolytic action
Inputs to BIS	stated ad hoc	**derived from conflict/threat approach**
Conflict	activates BIS, includes: approach-approach approach-avoidance avoidance-avoidance	activates BIS, includes: approach-approach approach-avoidance avoidance-avoidance
Neuropsychology		
Anxiolytic drugs	act via theta rhythm	act via theta rhythm, **and amygdala and other areas**
Anxiety (cognition)	via hippocampus	via hippocampus + **other areas**
Anxiety (arousal)	via hippocampus	**via amygdala**
Overall system	unitary	**distributed**
Personality/Disorders		
Neurotic disorders	unitary control	separate control
Neurotic personality	punishment sensitivity (anxiety)	punishment sensitivity (**fear** + anxiety)
Trait anxiety	= neurotic personality	#**neurotic personality** (see text)

and McNaughton 2000). Rewards and punishments are the obvious exemplars of positive and negative events, respectively. But, importantly for human experiments, the absence of an expected positive event is functionally the same as the presence of a negative event and vice versa (Gray 1975). Omission of expected reward is thus punishing. Similarly, the absence of an expected negative event is functionally the same as the presence of a positive event. Omission of punishment is rewarding.

This creates a significant problem for human testing. Given the right context, a 'non-event' is motivationally significant. If we wish to measure pure reward sensitivity, then we must do so in paradigms that do not involve omission of reward as a consequence of error. As will become clear below, we must particularly guard against equivalent levels of reward and punishment as these generate conflict, with additional consequences. Since conditional stimuli acquire secondary reinforcement value, we must take care also that 'neutral' stimuli are actually neutral for each person tested and do not have some previously acquired value.

Fear and anxiety: defensive direction

The revised theory treats fear and anxiety as not only quite distinct but also, in a sense, as opposites. A categorical separation of fear from anxiety as classes of defensive responses has been demonstrated by Robert and Caroline Blanchard (Blanchard and Blanchard 1988, 1989, 1990; Blanchard, Griebel, Henrie and Blanchard 1997).

The Blanchards used 'Etho-experimental analysis' of the innate reactions of rats to cats to determine the functions of specific classes of behaviour. One class of behaviours was elicited by the immediate presence of a predator. This class could clearly be attributed to a state of fear. The behaviours, grouped into the class on purely ethological grounds, were sensitive to panicolytic drugs but not to drugs that are anxiolytic but not panicolytic (Blanchard, Griebel, Henrie and Blanchard 1997). This is consistent with the insensitivity to anxiolytic drugs of active avoidance in a wide variety of species and of phobia in humans (Sartory, MacDonald and Gray 1990). A second, quite distinct, class of behaviours (including 'risk assessment') was elicited by the potential presence of a predator. This class of behaviours was sensitive to anxiolytic drugs. Both functionally and pharmacologically this class was distinct from the behaviours attributed to fear and could be attributed to a state of anxiety.

The Blanchards distinguished their classes of behaviour (and so their attribution of fear or anxiety) in terms of whether the behaviours were elicited by an actual or a potential predator. However, similar behaviours, and similar differential drug sensitivities, in more formal learning experiments (Gray 1977) show that fear is more the result of a requirement to avoid danger than of the immediacy (or certainty) of threat. (Of course, with strong dangers avoidance will be mandatory.) Likewise, anxiety is more the result of a requirement to approach danger than of the potentiality (or uncertainty) of it. Fear operates when leaving a dangerous situation (active avoidance), anxiety when entering it (e.g., cautious 'risk assessment' approach behaviour) or withholding entrance (passive avoidance). The critical factor distinguishing fear from anxiety can, then, be called 'defensive direction'.

While they are directionally opposed, there is, nonetheless, considerable functional overlap between the generation of fear and anxiety. In particular, anxiety involves modulation of pre-existing fear (or frustration). Also, in natural situations, there is a strong correlation between uncertainty of threat and the need to approach the source of potential threat. This correlation, we argue, has resulted in a greater elaboration of the neural control of fear relative to anxiety at lower levels of the neural hierarchy and a relatively greater elaboration of anxiety relative to fear at the higher levels.

On this view, there is a sharp (functional, behavioural and pharmacological) distinction between fear and anxiety. Fear has the function of moving the animal away from danger. It involves fight-flight-freezing, and is *insensitive* to anxiolytic drugs. When in an approach-avoidance conflict situation, anxiety has the function of moving the animal toward danger. It involves inhibition of prepotent behaviours, increased risk assessment and defensive quiescence. All these manifestations of the core state of anxiety are *sensitive* to anxiolytic drugs. Unlike Gray's 1982 theory (and many others) this distinction between fear and anxiety does not depend on the conditioned or unconditioned nature of stimuli used.

This is one crucial difference (Table 2.1) between Gray's original (1976, 1982) formulation and the revised theory (Gray and McNaughton 2000; McNaughton and Corr 2004). In the old theory, anxiety (activation of the BIS) resulted primarily from *conditioned* aversive stimuli. Strong unconditioned stimuli would lead to fear and so avoidance behaviour. But, almost by definition, anxiety would only be induced by potential threat (i.e., the conditioned signal, or warning, of threat). However, anxiety could also, according to Gray (1982), be induced by a rag-bag of 'innate fears' – confusingly included on an ad hoc basis. The new theory resolves this confusion and is explicit as to *exactly* what leads to fear and anxiety, respectively. With both innate and conditioned stimuli, it is defensive direction. In the old theory, fear played a pivotal role. It was necessary for aversive conditioning: it provided the central state to which neutral stimuli got associated. However, the personality theory, and so RST personality research, emphasized the BIS. The new theory suggests that fear is equally important in relation to personality and, in particular, the clinical consequences of extreme personality. In particular, the neurotic disorders are equally divided between what the theory defines as fears and what the theory defines as anxieties.

Conflict

We have just defined anxiety in terms of defensive approach. However, embedded in this idea is the more fundamental concept of conflict – because one only approaches a threat if there is some positive, conflicting, reason that makes avoidance inappropriate. Although this chapter focuses largely on defensive approach and defensive avoidance, it should be noted that the BIS is held to be engaged with any type of conflict, including approach-approach conflict (see Gray and McNaughton 2000, Appendix 1 and Appendix 8). Thus, defensive approach (approach to a threat) is paradigmatic in having clear appetitive and aversive components that are easily identified. But threats are not the only sources of aversion and avoidance that we experience. Indeed, in modern society omission of an expected reward (frustration) is a much more common source of aversion and stress than stimuli that produce pain or the threat of death. The theory holds that anxiety results from conflicts between competing available goals, whatever their source. The classic form of such conflict (Miller 1944; Kimble 1961; Gray 1987), and the most familiar for those studying anxiety, is approach-avoidance (McNaughton 2001). However, in principle, approach-approach and avoidance-avoidance conflicts would involve activation of the same system and have essentially the same effects as approach-avoidance. Approach-approach conflict (e.g., which of two competing job offers to take) is not likely normally to generate high levels of anxiety. The aversive component of the conflict resides in the frustration that could result from the relative loss incurred if the wrong choice is made and this will usually be small. However, it seems likely that the chronic stress that can, over a long period, precipitate anxiety disorders will, in developed societies, often reflect such conflicts more than classic approach-avoidance. According to this view, this process underlies the vague sense of dissatisfaction that is said to pervade advanced capitalist societies: we are spoiled for choice!

It is also important to realize that the presence or absence of conflict is something determined at least as much by the participant as by the experimenter. It is not necessary or sufficient that there be a nominal conflict in the formal description of a paradigm. Conflict can arise between an unexpected innate tendency and a conditioned response. Conversely, there may be no real conflict even in what is formally passive avoidance – which might be thought to be the quintessence of behavioural inhibition. For example (Okaichi and Okaichi 1994), rats with septo-hippocampal lesions showed no passive avoidance deficit in a running wheel *in which there was little spontaneous running* – unless they were first trained on a contrary active avoidance response. In refutation of radical behaviourism, it is the internal state of the animal that is as much to blame for conflict as the formal arrangement of environmental contingencies (see chapter 3).[2]

Defensive distance

A simple two-dimensional categorization of all defensive behaviour (and neurotic disorders) is provided by the superimposition on the categorical dimension of defensive direction (i.e., approach threat or avoid threat) of a graded dimension 'defensive distance', as defined by the Blanchards. For a particular individual in a particular situation, defensive distance equates with real distance. But, in a more dangerous situation, a greater real distance will be required to achieve the same defensive distance. Likewise, in the same situation, but with a braver individual, a smaller real distance will be required to achieve the same defensive distance. Defensive distance thus operationalizes an internal cognitive construct of intensity of perceived threat. It is a dimension controlling the type of defensive behaviour observed. We will later show that it is the conceptual basis of individual differences in sensitivity to aversive reinforcement.

In the case of defensive avoidance, the smallest defensive distances result in explosive attack, intermediate defensive distances result in freezing and flight, and very great defensive distances result in normal non-defensive behaviour (Figure 2.1A). In humans, the psychological state at very small defensive distance would be labelled panic. The commonly associated cognition in panic 'I'm going to die' would seem homologous to whatever cognitions can be attributed to a rat when it is nose-to-nose with a cat (one of the situations analysed by the Blanchards). Intermediate defensive distances can be equated with phobic avoidance.

With the opposite direction, defensive approach (Figure 2.1B), defensive quiescence occurs at the closest defensive distances (and, in rats, can be distinguished from freezing only by minor postural features and its sensitivity to anxiolytic drugs). At intermediate distances, risk assessment behaviour occurs and, at very great distances, defensive behaviour disappears and normal pre-threat behaviour reappears.[3]

---

[2] Diehard radical behaviourists would argue that these 'fictional' internal states are themselves the product of prior reinforcement history. For our analysis, this argument is irrelevant because the influence of such history must be instantiated in brain systems – and we know that variations in the neural functioning of these systems should influence both the sensitivity and reactivity to reinforcement and thus to their long-term influence.

[3] It might be thought that a highly active BIS would be associated with greater goal conflict resolution, thus BIS active individuals should be superior conflict resolvers. However, it

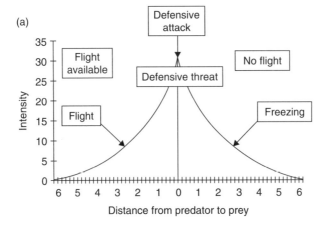

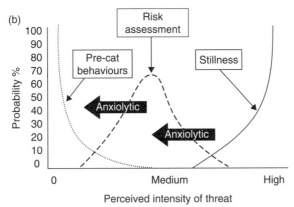

Figure 2.1 The relationship between defensive distance and behaviour. A. For defensive avoidance, from Blanchard and Blanchard (1990). B. For defensive approach. The grey arrows represent a fixed change in defensive distance produced by anxiolytic drugs both increasing and decreasing risk assessment behaviour depending on the initial defensive distance

should be borne in mind that there is an important adaptive balance between being too risk averse (BIS+) and too risk prone (BIS−). In other words, there is an optimal point of BIS activation: at high levels, the BIS is likely to resolve conflict in terms of FFFS-avoidance, which does not resolve the goal conflict in the longer term, although it may offer a temporary solution. In addition, a hyperactive BIS is likely to detect conflict at low level of objectively-defined conflict and thus engage in risk assessment cognitions/behaviours, which themselves generate more goal conflict (as perhaps seen in the pathological checking in OCD).

It is crucial to note here that anxiolytic drugs are not only specific to defensive approach as opposed to defensive avoidance but also affect defensive distance itself rather than specific defensive approach behaviours. If perceived intensity of threat is high (small defensive distance), an undrugged rat is likely to remain still. Under these conditions (lower grey arrow in Figure 2.1B), an anxiolytic drug will increase risk assessment (this will increase approach to the source of threat). But, if perceived threat is medium, an undrugged rat is likely to engage in risk assessment behaviour. Under these conditions (upper grey arrow in Figure 2.1B), an anxiolytic drug will decrease risk assessment (which again increases approach to the source of threat) and replace it with normal non-threat behaviours. Thus, the drug does not alter specific observable behaviours consistently but produces changes in behaviour that are consistent with an increase in the internal construct of defensive distance (Blanchard, Blanchard, Tom and Rodgers 1990; Blanchard and Blanchard 1990). This is a crucial point to understand about the new theory.

Conceptually, we see individual differences in defensive distance for a fixed real distance as a reflection of the personality dimension under-lying punishment sensitivity (Corr and McNaughton, chapter 5). Anxiolytic drugs alter (internally perceived) defensive distance relative to actual external threat. If endogenous anxiolytic compounds can produce similar effects they would lead to trait differences in conflict sensitivity – they would alter trait anxiety. As will become clear below, trait anxiety, in this sense, would not be identical to neuroticism (which would control sensitivity to threat both with avoidance and approach). But we argue that neuroticism operates in the same general way, modifying defensive distance rather than having a consistent effect on any individual measurable behaviour.

Trait anxiety, in this sense, would represent a specific risk factor for generalized anxiety disorder that would be quite independent of risks for panic disorder, obsessive compulsive disorder or depression. (Anxiolytic drugs, as a class, do not affect these.) In this very narrow sense of trait anxiety, we can liken the low trait anxious individual to the drugged rat. We can thus use the X axis of Figure 2.1B (but not 2.1A) to indicate the types of defensive approach behaviour elicited by different perceived intensities of aversive stimuli produced by (a) changes in actual inten-sity; (b) trait differences in conflict sensitivity; (c) anxiolytic drug effects; and (d) their interactions. At present there is little clear evidence for such an anxiety-specific personality factor.

Similarly, the X axis of Figure 2.1A can be used to indicate the types of defensive avoidance behaviour elicited by different perceived

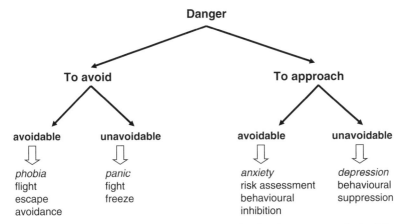

Figure 2.2 Categories of emotion and defensive response derived from defensive direction (avoid or approach the danger) and avoidability of the threat

intensities of aversive stimuli produced by (a) changes in the actual intensity of aversive stimuli; (b) trait differences in responses to aversive stimuli (different to trait differences in conflict sensitivity); (c) effects of drugs acting on threat sensitivity; and (d) their interactions. The bulk of the evidence for variation in proneness to DSM 'anxiety disorders', which include anxiolytic-insensitive symptomatologies such as panic and obsession, suggests that the key personality factor relates to a general punishment or threat sensitivity. We return to these issues in chapter 5.

So far, we have encompassed threats that should be avoided (defensive avoidance) but that produce different behaviours depending on whether the threat can be avoided or not (Figure 2.1A), as well as threats that should be approached but which in principle can be avoided. Indeed, the whole purpose of risk assessment behaviour (Figure 2.1B) is to allow approach to occur while avoiding the consequences of a perceived threat. There remains a further possibility (Figure 2.2). There can be threats that require approach (because of positive outcomes that could be obtained) but where the aversive consequence is perceived as unavoidable and where it is so great as to prevent the appetitive behaviour from occurring. This last possibility has not been subjected to the kind of analysis on which *The Neuropsychology of Anxiety* (1982) is based but has been tentatively identified with depression (McNaughton 1993).

Goals and goal conflict

A critical aspect of the recent formulations of the theory is that conflict is something that (from the point of view of the BIS) occurs between goals more than it does between stimuli or responses or action patterns. For those raised in a behaviourist environment it is natural to talk about conditioning of responses or the elicitation of innate responses. But behaviour is not simply controlled by some chain of stimulus-response connections (McNaughton 1989; Cahill, McGaugh and Weinberger 2001). Even well-conditioned behaviour is not invariant and what is important in determining the behaviour actually observed is the nature of the goal held in the animal's mind. Animals immediately produce completely novel response sequences to reach the unchanged goal location when their original response is blocked (Towe and Luschei 1981; Hinde 1966). Thus the conflict that activates the BIS is one between goals experienced by the subject rather than one inherent in a paradigm. In the case of human personality this realization has important implications: for example, it is not sufficient to manipulate reward and punishment without first assessing or manipulating expectations (Corr 2001).

Goal conflict, as a concept, has interesting implications. First, it should be clear that where there are equal tendencies to approach two incompatible goals the core problem to be resolved is independent of the motivational systems supporting the goals. This provides a simple account for the common effects of anxiolytic drugs on approach-approach, approach-avoidance, and avoidance-avoidance conflicts – while motivationally different, they have in common goal conflict. Second, it should be noted that goal conflict is only a significant problem when competing goals are approximately equally activated. In all other circumstances a simple winner-take-all mechanism will solve the problem. Thirdly, but less obviously, when the net worth of two goals is balanced we would expect evolution to favour risk aversion. Getting a larger reward is not advantageous in the long run if you are regularly running the risk of getting killed to obtain it rather than selecting a smaller, safe reward. Fourthly, and a corollary to the third point, conflict can best be resolved by gaining additional information to determine the true level of risk.

We have now entered the conceptual heart of the BIS: once conflict, in the sense of a close balance between competing goals, is detected, there is a selective potentiation of the power of affectively negative current perceptions and affectively negative remembered consequences. Affectively positive ones (although increased by simple drive summation) are not potentiated by conflict. In simple approach-avoidance, this will favour avoidance over approach. There are thus three distinct elements to consider in relation to anxiety (but not fear): approach, avoidance, and the conflict between the two. It will be important for our analysis below that, while fear and anxiety are fundamentally distinct, there will be many cases where anxiety (as indexed by anxiolytic action) involves an amplification of fear. There will also be cases where anxiety involves an amplification of frustration. Amplification of fear and of frustration occur through quite distinct neural circuits.

We see anxiety, then, as being most often generated by *concurrent* and equivalent activation of fear (or frustration) and approach systems, with the BIS acting to assess risk, and increase risk aversion in conflict situations. However, conflict is not restricted to approach-avoidance: approach-approach and avoidance-avoidance conflicts are also possible – and theoretically operate in the same way as approach-avoidance conflict.

Behavioural inhibition

A key aspect of conflict, from which the BIS derived its name, is that *prepotent* behaviour (both approach and avoidance) is inhibited. The result can be pure behavioural inhibition (behavioural quiescence) or exploratory and risk assessment behaviour or displacement activity. However, behavioural inhibition itself is so paradigmatic that it can appear more fundamental than the conflict that we have suggested gives rise to it.

Thus, in 'conditioned suppression', a stimulus classically conditioned with a shock suppresses responding despite there being no response-shock contingency. This is usually seen as a form of conditioned fear in which one might, therefore, 'not see any conflict, but only the impossibility of an escape response' (Frederico Graeff, personal communication). However, conditioned suppression appears to be insensitive to anxiolytic drugs unless the conditioning takes place in the same apparatus as the operant testing (i.e., it is 'on the baseline'). This, together with a range of other data (Gray and McNaughton 2000, Appendix 1 and Appendix 8), suggests that contextual conditioning is resulting in approach-avoidance conflict and, in particular, eliciting defensive quiescence that (unlike freezing proper) is sensitive to anxiolytic drugs (Melia, Ryabinin, Corodimas, Wilson and LeDoux 1996).

Behavioural elicitation

Although termed 'the behavioural inhibition system', the BIS is, and has always been, postulated to generate additional outputs related to exploration, attention and arousal. It is the *prepotent* conflicting behaviours that are inhibited and, while they can be replaced by simple quiescence, they are more usually replaced by special behaviours designed to resolve the conflict (or occasionally by displacement activities).

The elicitation of behaviour by conflict is particularly obvious in the work of the Blanchards (see above). They showed that behavioural quiescence at high levels of threat was replaced, at intermediate levels of defensive approach, with rearing and a range of related anxiolytic-sensitive behaviours. Defensive burying is another particularly characteristic threat-elicited, anxiolytic-sensitive behaviour that has been extensively studied by Treit and colleagues (Degroot, Kashluba and Treit 2001; Gray, Terlecki, Treit and Pinel 1981; Menard and Treit 1996a, 1996b, 1999; Treit and Fundytus 1988; Treit, Robinson, Rotzinger and Pesold 1993). In the 'shock-probe burying test' rats are shocked by an electrified probe, and the duration of time that they spend spraying bedding material towards the probe (i.e., burying) is the major index of 'anxiety'. Standard anxiolytic drugs suppress this burying behaviour, and abolish the elevations in plasma corticosterone and adrenaline induced by the probe-shock. The suppression of burying by the benzodiazepines does not appear to be secondary to behavioural sedation, associative learning deficits or analgesia. Critically, 'defensive burying is an interesting behaviour not least because it involves approach to the source of noxious stimulation, and because it is so reliably and strongly elicited by a single aversive experience ... [and] unconditioned burying of novel objects in the absence of shock has also been observed' (Blampied and Kirk 1983). Thus, burying fulfils our major criterion for an anxiety-related reaction in that it involves *approach* to a source of potential threat. Of course, when no conflict is present, the animal would simply leave the situation (FFFS-controlled behaviour).

Psychological structure of the theory

It should be clear from the above that the most recent versions of the BIS theory, derived from animal data, are explicitly two-dimensional (Gray and McNaughton 2000; McNaughton and Corr 2004).

The first dimension, defensive direction, is categorical. It rests on a functional distinction between behaviours that remove an animal from a source of danger (FFFS-mediated) and those that allow it to approach a source of danger (BIS-mediated). These functions are ethologically and pharmacologically distinct and, on each of these separate grounds, can be identified with fear and anxiety, respectively. An important point is that the focus on approach and avoidance is derived from detailed experimental analysis of animal behaviour which subsumes, but does not entirely match, the focus on certainty versus uncertainty of threat common to both clinical perspectives on fear and anxiety and the original ethological base of the current theory.

Shock-probe burying is probably the clearest, well-studied example of elicited behaviour that is sensitive to anxiolytics where the presence of the threat is absolutely certain and where the behaviour is elicited by approach to threat. In the conditioning literature, the most obvious example is in approach-avoidance conflict in the runway. Here, the rat is both certain of reward and equally certain of punishment. With low levels of shock the rat will suffer the shock to get the reward. At higher levels it will approach but not reach the goal and anxiolytic drugs increase this approach behaviour in both cases (changing defensive distance but not reward-related distance).

The second dimension, defensive distance, is graded. It rests on a functional hierarchy that determines appropriate behaviour in relation to defensive distance (i.e., perceived distance from threat – a cognitive dimension). This, second, hierarchical functional dimension applies equally to fear and anxiety but is instantiated separately in each (anxiolytic drugs change it in one case but not the other).

Neural systems of fear and anxiety

Although based on only two dimensions, this theory is comprehensive, combining previous theories of fear and anxiety within a single consistent rubric. In the process, it includes a large number of brain structures ranging from the prefrontal cortex, at the highest level, to the periaqueductal grey, at the lowest level, assigning to each structure (a) a specific place in the theory; (b) a specific fundamental class of function; and (c) a specific class of mental disorder. Thus, the most fundamental change to the old view of the BIS is that, in the new theory, it is *distributed* among a number of neural structures. At the state level, this detailed pigeon-holing shatters the unity that might be expected from the normal linkage of personality (and genetics) to individual neurotic disorders. But it will be seen that at the trait level we can 'put Humpty Dumpty back together again', delineating a small set of classes of disorder, via an analysis of modulatory systems. But the result is not identical to the unitary personality perspective taken by Gray originally (1976) and as recently as 1982. In this section we detail the neural architecture of these systems.

General architecture

The concepts of defensive direction and defensive distance provide a two-dimensional schema within which, in principle, all defensive behaviours can be categorized. The theory translates this two-dimensional psychological schema into a matching two-dimensional neurological one. The categorical distinction *between* defensive approach and defensive avoidance is translated into two distinct parallel streams of neural structures. The dimension of defensive distance is translated into the levels of a hierarchy of structures *within* each of the parallel streams.

The neural mapping of defensive distance into the two hierarchies is rendered simple by two architectural features. First, smaller defensive distances map to more caudal, subcortical neural structures while larger defensive distances map to more rostral, cortical neural structures with intermediate structures arranged in caudo-rostral order in between (see Figure 2.3). The result is a two-dimensional variant of the hierarchical organization originally proposed by Deakin and Graeff (1991). Second, this mapping occurs in a symmetrical fashion, with matching structures located within each of the parallel streams – often being different subdivisions or nuclei of the same named area.

Despite this symmetry, it should be noted that, given the functional distinction between fear (avoid threat) and anxiety (approach threat), fear is more likely than anxiety to be engaged with more immediate threats while anxiety is more likely to be engaged under conditions of distant or anticipated threat – with the balance varying as the intensity of the threat varies. Figure 2.3 therefore represents the relative extent of the neural systems controlling fear and anxiety as varying systematically. At the lower levels, fear has a greater neural representation and at the higher levels anxiety has a greater neural representation.

Finally, for simplicity, we have represented the levels of the system as each being reciprocally connected to adjacent levels. But, in practice, the prefrontal cortex, for example, can influence the periaqueductal gray directly (Floyd, Price, Ferry, Keay and Bandler 2000; Shipley, Ennis, Rizvi and Behbehani 1991; An, Bandler, Öngür and Price 1998), maintaining the topographic organization of more indirect connections. There will be similar by-passing of levels between all parts of the system. However, this has no significant consequences for the arguments about personality to be presented later.

Anxiolytic drugs as markers for the BIS

We have already appealed (but without detailed justification) to the effects of anxiolytic drugs as a basis for identifying behaviours associated with the BIS, and hence anxiety, and as a basis for distinguishing anxiety from fear. A post hoc justification for doing this is simply that it was successful. Defensive behaviours do fall into functional classes. The

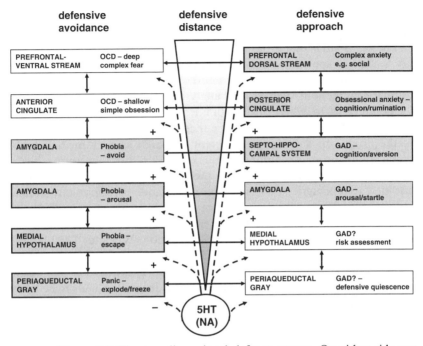

Figure 2.3 The two-dimensional defence system. On either side are defensive avoidance and defensive approach respectively (a categorical dimension). Each is divided, down the page, into a number of hierarchical levels. These are ordered from high to low (top to bottom) both with respect to neural level (and cytoarchitectonic complexity) and to functional level. Each level is associated with specific classes of behaviour and so symptom and syndrome. Syndromes are associated with hyper-reactivity of a structure and symptoms with high activity. Given the interconnections within the system (and effects of e.g., conditioning) symptoms will not be a good guide to syndromes

resultant classes are anxiolytic-insensitive and anxiolytic-sensitive respectively. But, equally important, is the fact that 'anxiolytic drugs' are effective in the clinic in treating disorders that clinicians recognize as having a common core, 'anxiety'.

This then permits an important strategic step. There is good agreement as to which drugs are anxiolytic and which not. Indeed, this agreement obtains even when there is radical disagreement as to the definition of anxiety. This allows the use of the drugs as markers for a class of behaviours and it was the experimental analysis of the effects of the drugs (as a class) that gave rise to the concept of the BIS (Gray 1976, 1982). Modern developments in the pharmacology of the drugs now also allow the identification of the critical brain systems mediating their actions – and so the neural location of the BIS.

The key point is that drugs must act on specific brain structures if they are to change specific emotions. They act like temporary lesions. Suitable alterations in those target structures should, then, produce sub-sets of the drugs' actions. Behavioural analysis of lesion effects can thus give us pointers as to where in the brain to look for functional changes underlying the drugs' actions. Once these are known, direct application of the drugs can determine the extent to which an area mediates systemic anxiolytic action. Prior to 1982, a problem with this approach was that all known anxiolytics acted via the neurotransmitter GABA and, in addition to anxiolytic action had various extents of euphoriant, addictive, muscle relaxant, anti-convulsant and other side-effects. With the advent of 'novel anxiolytics' that act through the serotonergic system we have drugs that have equivalent anxiolytic action (Wheatley 1982, 1990) but that have opposite side-effects. This allows us then to conclude that where any structure is affected, directly or indirectly, in the same manner by *both* classical and novel anxiolytic drugs, it is likely to be a key component of the BIS.

We will focus below on structures involved in the BIS and anxiety as it is in our treatment of these that the theory is most distinctive. The model we give below also deals with the FFFS and fear and our treatment of this is not covered in the same detail as it largely follows previous views (Deakin and Graeff 1991; Davis 1992b; LeDoux 1994; Graeff 1994; Gray and McNaughton 2000).

We will consider many neural structures, from the periaqueductal gray to the prefrontal cortex. For all of these structures it should be emphasized that we are dealing with only some parts of them. Particularly in the case of cingulate and frontal cortex, while we assign to parts of them specific defensive functions, this does not imply that any large part is devoted to defence as opposed to other affective systems. Nor do we imply that they are devoted to emotion as opposed to cognition. The amygdala is particularly noteworthy here. It can be viewed as more concerned with affect than cognition. But it is generally accepted to be important for all types of emotion not just fear and anxiety. Our allocation of both fear and anxiety to it is, then, consistent with its additional roles in various appetitive emotions.

Periaqueductal gray

The lowest neural level at which integrated defensive behaviour is controlled is the periaqueductal gray (PAG). As we will see, despite being associated with the smallest defensive distances, it plays at least some role in anxiolytic action and so the BIS, although its contribution to the FFFS is much greater. Its role, here, is represented at the bottom left of Figure 2.3, associated with *undirected* escape/panic (Deakin and Graeff 1991).

The PAG contains functionally discrete areas (Holstege 1989; Zhang and Barrett 1990; Shipley, Ennis, Rizvi and Behbehani 1991; Carrive, Leung, Harris and Paxinos 1997; Bandler and Shipley 1994) that are topographically organized with respect to specific outputs to areas that control, e.g., autonomic responses (Carrive and Bandler 1991) and with respect to higher-level inputs from areas such as the amygdala (Rizvi, Ennis, Behbehani and Shipley 1991), prefrontal cortex (Shipley, Ennis, Rizvi and Behbehani 1991; Floyd, Price, Ferry, Keay and Bandler 2000; Reinvang, Magnussen, Greenlee and Larsson 1998; An, Bandler, Öngür and Price 1998; Bandler, Keay, Floyd and Price 2000) and particularly medial hypothalamus (Canteras, Simerly and Swanson 1994; Veening, Buma, Ter Horst, Roeling, Luiten and Nieuwenhuys 1991) – all of which are considered separately below.

Anxiolytics act directly on the ventral PAG to affect conditioned hypoalgesia (Harris and Westbrook 1995; Fanselow 1991), a passive coping response. Other anxiolytic-sensitive, passive coping behaviours are controlled by the ventral PAG (Bandler, Price and Keay 2000; Bandler and Shipley 1994) including contextual fear (Aboufatima, Chait, Dalal and De Beaurepaire 1999; Carrive, Leung, Harris and Paxinos 1997; Fanselow 1991) and suppression of bar-pressing in a conflict task (Liebman, Mayer and Liebeskind 1970). More active, anxiolytic-sensitive coping behaviours are controlled by the dorsal PAG (De Souza, Schenberg and Carobrez 1998; Matheus and Guimaraes 1997; Matheus, Nogueira, Carobrez, Graeff and Guimaraes 1994), including + maze open arm entries (Audi, de Oliveira and Graeff 1991), social interaction (Kask, Rägo and Harro 1998) and fear-potentiated startle (Woo, Pucak, Kye, Matus and Lewis 1997).

The PAG also, and more clearly, mediates anxiolytic-insensitive defensive behaviours. The lateral portion of the PAG controls the immediate activity burst in response to a shock but not conditioned freezing – and so is doubly dissociated from the ventral PAG (Fanselow 1991). It is also generally involved in confrontational defensive reactions (Bandler, Price and Keay 2000), including flight and rage (Bandler 1982), and it is strongly activated by the presence of a predator (Canteras and Goto 1999). These lateral, fear-related portions of the PAG receive input from the anterior cingulate cortex, which we will suggest below is a higher level of the fear control system.

The functional and anatomical topographic organization of PAG suggests it contains two distinct, intertwined defence systems – one anxiolytic-sensitive, one anxiolytic-insensitive – that we can relate to fear and anxiety (Fanselow 1991). It also appears to support distinct systems related to escapable and inescapable threat (Bandler and Shipley 1994; Bandler, Price and Keay 2000; Bandler, Keay, Floyd and Price 2000; Keay and Bandler 2002). It may then be topographically organized not only with respect to functions related to fear and anxiety but also depression (McNaughton 1993).

We suggest, below, that monoamine input exerts a general control of the entire defence system. But an unexpected feature of serotonergic modulation is that the lowest level (panic) is suppressed by input that activates higher levels. This explains not only the differential effects of many drugs but also such apparently anomalous phenomena as relaxation-induced panic (Graeff 1994).

Consistent with this neural differentiation, the strong genetic homogeneity of most neurotic disorders is only partially shared by panic. Neurotic disorder and panic share only about half of their genetic control, each having a distinct other half (Scherrer, True, Xian et al. 2000). In the case of panic, then, genetic influences on anxiety, via polymorphisms of aminergic systems, could operate in parallel with panic susceptibility, via polymorphisms of cholecystokinin (CCK) systems (Wang, Valdes, Noyes, Zoega and Crowe 1998a; Wang, Valdes, Noyes, Zoega and Crowe 1998b). This strengthens the picture, derived from epidemiology, of panic as a distinct entity that can be both a cause and a symptom of anxiety and can also occur alone.

Hypothalamus

Above the periaqueductal gray, in the medial hypothalamus, we have *directed* escape/phobic escape (Deakin and Graeff 1991). The hypothalamus is topographically connected to the PAG (Veening, Buma, Ter Horst, Roeling, Luiten and Nieuwenhuys 1991) as well as to higher levels of the defence hierarchy such as the prefrontal cortex (Floyd, Price, Ferry, Keay and Bandler 2001) that are themselves topographically connected to PAG.

Anxiolytics act directly on the dorsomedial hypothalamus (DMH) to reduce the aversive reaction produced by DMH stimulation (Milani and Graeff 1987) and GABA blockade of the DMH has 'anxiolytic' effects in the + maze, increasing open arm entries. The hypothalamus also contains the supramammillary area which is the direct site of action of anxiolytics for a range of effects mediated by changes in hippocampal theta (see below) as well as being an area that controls defensive behaviour through its interactions with a range of areas including the PAG (Pan and McNaughton 2004). In particular, the supramammillary area controls a range of anxiolytic-sensitive behaviours including ambulation in the open field, contextual but not simple fear conditioning, consolidation of passive avoidance, punished responding in a conflict schedule, suppression in a fixed interval schedule and suppression in a differential reinforcement of low rates schedule (see Pan and McNaughton 2004, for review).

Amygdala

The amygdala controls active avoidance/phobic avoidance (Davis 1992b; LeDoux 1994). We have explicitly separated the components of the amygdala that deal with autonomic arousal and with active avoidance behaviour. Given the complexity of the amygdala (which includes areas with both cortical and subcortical architectonics) this is not unreasonable. However, our main reason for making this particular separation in our model, at its present stage of development, will be discussed in the next section. We also include the amygdala in both of the parallel hierarchies.

For many, the amygdala was a glaring omission from Gray's 1982 hippocampal theory of anxiety. However, at that time, this set of structures seemed involved in avoidance in general (mediated by what was, then, named the Fight-Flight System, FFS) rather than in the behavioural inhibition specifically affected by anxiolytic drugs. Even now, the parallels between anxiolytic action and hippocampal lesions are much closer (with respect to both effects and lacks of effect) than those between anxiolytic action and amygdala lesions (Gray and McNaughton 2000).

However, since 1982 it has become well accepted that the amygdala is involved in the control of both fear and anxiety (LeDoux 1994). In particular, anxiolytic drugs of all chemical classes act directly on the amygdala to reduce the arousal associated with anxiety (Davis 1992b), and this arousal is not mediated by the septo-hippocampal system (McNish, Gewirtz and Davis 1997). We are faced, then, with an amygdala that appears to mediate some but not all aspects of anxiolytic action, as well as a hippocampus that appears to mediate some but not all aspects of anxiolytic action. There is also significant overlap in the behaviours controlled by each – which is not surprising given their extensive interconnections (Gray and McNaughton 2000).

How can 'the amygdala' control both fear and anxiety? First we should note that it has equivalent involvement in many other types of motivation, positive and negative. It must be differentiated to deal with these and so fear and anxiety would be similarly separated. 'The amygdala' achieves these multiple separations, at least in part, because it is a complex set of highly differentiated cortical and subcortical structures. The boundaries of the amygdalar complex are not well defined and may include the 'extended amygdala' (Davis and Shi 1999). Conversely, the term 'amygdala', even without extension, is viewed by some as a set of distinct structures rather than being a unitary entity with multiple parts (Swanson and Petrovich 1998).

Whether fundamentally unitary or an arbitrary set of unrelated parts, it is clear that some parts of 'the amygdala' are functionally distinct from other parts in terms of mediating anxiolytic action. It appears that the anxiolytic-sensitive parts (with the highest density of benzodiazepine receptors) are the lateral and basal nuclei, with the central nucleus being insensitive (Davis 1992a).

Septo-hippocampal system

Above the amygdala, within the defensive approach system, we have the hippocampal formation. This constituted the core of Gray's 1982 neuropsychology of anxiety and is still the central structure in the currently proposed hierarchy. It also remains special within the theory in that it is at present the only complex area that is represented in only one of the two hierarchies.

To it we attribute cognitive aspects of conventional anxiety and generalized anxiety disorder (McNaughton 1997). However, as we noted above, the arousal associated with anxiety is controlled by the amygdala (Davis 1992b) not the septo-hippocampal system (McNish, Gewirtz and Davis 1997). So, within the defensive approach hierarchy we place a component of the amygdala below the septo-hippocampal system. By implication, therefore, there could be two forms of generalized anxiety disorder: one, more hippocampally centered, in which pathologically increased negative affective bias results in increased arousal; and a second, more amygdala centred, in which pathologically increased arousal results in increased negative cognitive bias. Both of these could, then, present clinically in a similar fashion.

An important point is that in both of these cases we have good evidence for direct effects of anxiolytic drugs producing distinct effects in these different neural targets (Gray and McNaughton 2000). Equally, active avoidance involves equivalent effects on cognition and arousal that are not sensitive to anxiolytic drugs. This is the basis for the three different boxes labelled 'amygdala' in Figure 2.3. Further work is required to precisely identify the different neural components of the amygdala corresponding to each.

The origin and core of Gray's theory was the extensive similarities between the behavioural effects of anxiolytic drugs and hippocampal lesions. When the theory was expanded (Gray and McNaughton 2000; McNaughton and Corr 2004) this core had been hugely strengthened by the extension of this similarity to novel anxiolytic drugs. As noted above, these drugs do not interact with the $GABA_A$ receptor and so do not share the side-effects of classical anxiolytics. The parallels between anxiolytic action and hippocampal dysfunction cannot now be, as they could have been in 1982, attributed to the anti-convulsant action, for example, of the classical anxiolytics. The novel anxiolytics are, if anything, pro-convulsant.

More importantly, both classical and novel anxiolytics are effective in tests thought to be specific to hippocampal-sensitive forms of memory (McNaughton and Morris 1992; McNaughton and Morris 1987; Tan, Kirk, Abraham and McNaughton 1990; Tan, Kirk, Abraham and McNaughton 1989; Money, Kirk and McNaughton 1992). This links anxiolytic action to changes in memory function of the sort typically attributed to the hippocampus.

Equally important for the 1982 theory was the fact that anxiolytic drugs produce characteristic changes in hippocampal electrical activity. By 2000 this was shown to be true of all classes of anxiolytic drug, including those (like anti-depressants) that have no overlapping side-effects with classical anxiolytics (Coop and McNaughton 1991; Coop, McNaughton, Warnock and Laverty 1990; Coop, McNaughton and Scott 1992; McNaughton and Coop 1991; Zhu and McNaughton 1991a, 1991b, 1994a, 1994b, 1994c, 1995a, 1995b).

A further link with memory is forged by the fact that all these drugs have immediate neural effects that change little with time and have immediate actions in tests of animal learning – while the truly anxiolytic (as opposed to euphoriant and muscle relaxant) clinical actions of even the classical anxiolytics take time to develop (Wheatley 1990). The drugs appear, then, to reduce the formation of new threatening memories leaving old ones intact. This is a parallel to the more anterograde than retrograde character of hippocampal amnesia.

While massive and consistent across many domains of evidence, the above linking of anxiolytic drugs and the hippocampus was correlational. Many of the parallels could be attributed to the fact that anxiolytics alter noradrenergic input to the hippocampus (McNaughton and Mason 1980) but some could not. Now, recent data have shown that intra-cranial anxiolytic injections that specifically reduce hippocampal theta frequency change both this and noradrenergic-insensitive behaviour as extensively as systemic injections (Woodnorth and McNaughton 2002). Importantly, when theta frequency is specifically changed by intra-cranial injections, formation of spatial memory is changed to an equivalent extent (Pan and McNaughton 1997). Thus 'hippocampal effects' of anxiolytic drugs can be attributed to these two distinct changes the drugs produce in the control of hippocampal theta as well as direct effects of the drugs on the hippocampus itself (Crestani, Lorez, Baer *et al.* 1999).

It is important to emphasize here that inclusion of any structure within the distributed network that is the BIS does not imply that its role in the BIS is that structure's sole raison d'être. In our theory the hippocampus resolves conflicts that are largely cognitively laden (as in delayed matching to sample) as much as it does those that are emotionally laden (as in the innate suppression of a rat's 'pre-cat' behaviours in response to the smell of a cat). The theory in its present form assigns cognitive conflict resolution more to the entorhinal cortex and response-oriented conflict resolution more to the subiculum. However, it is likely that future elaboration of the theory will extend this parcellation to the hippocampus proper – there being evidence that the septal pole of the hippocampus is more involved in cognitive and the temporal in emotional control (Bannerman, Rawlins, McHugh *et al.* 2004).

Cingulate cortex

As with the amgydala, the cingulate cortex has distinct parts, each with different roles within the new theory. We consider each in turn.

Anterior cingulate   Above the amygdala, in the stream of fear-related structures, we place the anterior cingulate cortex. It controls more complex active avoidance that will require a greater degree of anticipation and a less tight temporal linkage of warning stimuli with actual threat than the amygdala. Higher-level processing, here, does not imply less involvement in fundamental features of defence. Anterior cingulate is involved in the perception of pain (Koyama, Tanaka and Mikami 1998; Chang and Shyu 2001; Davis 2000; Coghill, Talbot, Evans *et al.* 1994; Davis, Wood, Crawley and Mikulis 1995), the production of anger (Dougherty, Shin, Alpert *et al.* 1999), Pavlovian fear conditioning (Knight, Smith, Stein and Helmstetter 1999) and avoidance learning (Kubota, Wolske, Poremba, Kang and Gabriel 1996).

Likewise, anterior cingulate lesions impair avoidance and lick suppression conditioned to an aversive stimulus (Bussey, Everitt and Robbins 1997).

Anterior cingulate thus deals with fundamental outputs of the FFFS – but involves stimulus inputs that may be as complex as guilt (Shin, Dougherty, Orr *et al.* 2000) with a focus on the affective rather than sensory aspects of pain (Rainville, Duncan, Price, Carrier and Bushnell 1997). In particular, we see the anterior cingulate as controlling active avoidance behaviours that include those that cannot be terminated by safety signals. There is a wide range of both innate and acquired rituals of this sort. Hand washing to avoid infection is an example. We, following others, thus assign their pathological form, obsessive compulsive disorder, to the anterior cingulate (Rapoport 1989; Ebert, Speck, Konig, Berger, Hennig and Hohagen 1997).

However, using the idea of defensive distance as the basis for speculation, we suggest that the anterior cingulate deals with relatively simple 'surface' expectations of nebulous threat (with prefrontal cortex dealing with deeper, more complex, expectations). Likewise, using the idea of defensive direction, we suggest that it deals only with obsessional active avoidance with posterior cingulate dealing with obsessional passive avoidance. Also, as with all of the other areas we include in Figure 2.3, the cingulate is held to deal with goal representations. More detailed motor control is elsewhere. In the case of the cingulate this control involves compulsions controlled largely by the basal ganglia (Rapoport 1989).

Our present allocation of anterior cingulate cortex to defensive avoidance is tentative. A possible role in defensive approach is suggested by involvement in the resolution of conflicts between approach and avoidance (MacDonald, Cohen, Stenger and Carter 2000; Riekkinen, Kuitunen and Riekkinen 1995) and in more general response conflicts 'in which a prepotent response tendency has to be overcome' (Barch, Braver, Akbudak, Conturo, Ollinger and Snyder 2001; Bussey, Muir, Everitt and Robbins 1996). Indeed, there is evidence that it is more involved in conflict monitoring than in selection for action (Botvinick, Nystrom, Fissell, Carter and Cohen 1999; Carter, Braver, Barch, Botvinick, Noll and Cohen 1998; Carter, Macdonald, Botvinick *et al.* 2000). These data would, nonetheless, be consistent with our assignment of anterior cingulate to the active defence system if the tasks used (e.g., Stroop test) are in fact eliciting *multiple responses* (Diehl, Dinner, Mohamed *et al.* 2000) that conflict in the attempt to achieve a *single goal*. The paradigm case here is mirror drawing. This involves a single clear goal but a high level of competition between prepotent and correct response tendencies and is not dependent on the BIS (Gray and McNaughton 2000). The inhibitory aspects of anterior cingulate function in avoidance may also relate more to the correct timing of responses held in working memory (Gabriel 1990) and the co-ordination of response sequences (Kermadi, Liu and Rouiller 2000; Ochsner, Kosslyn, Cosgrove et al. 2001; Procyk and Josephy 2001) than to conflict per se.

There is also evidence that anterior cingulate is involved in the generation of mania (Blumberg, Stern, Martinez et al. 2000) and in Pavlovian reward conditioning (Parkinson, Willoughby, Robbins and Everitt 2000). This suggests 'that the anterior cingulate cortex may be involved in learning about the significance of stimuli that predict both aversive and appetitive events, thus endowing these stimuli with both negative and positive affective value' (Bussey, Everitt and Robbins 1997). So, given its anatomical complexity, it is possible that it contains components of each of the BAS, FFFS and BIS. Certainly, pain and Stroop tasks activate different parts of anterior cingulate cortex (Derbyshire, Vogt and Jones 1998; Peterson, Skudlarski, Gatenby, Zhang, Anderson and Gore 1999) and different parts appear to be involved in more cognitive and more emotional processing respectively (Whalen, Bush, McNally et al. 1998; Kwan, Crawley, Mikulis and Davis 2000; Takenouchi, Nishijo, Uwano, Tamura, Takigawa and Ono 1999). Defensive approach and defensive avoidance may then be represented in both anterior and posterior cingulate systems (Gabriel 1990) rather than, as we suggest here, distributed between them.

Posterior cingulate   Posterior cingulate cortex is anatomically close to the hippocampal formation and like the hippocampus shows theta rhythm controlled from the medial septum (Feenstra and Holsheimer 1979; Borst, Leung and MacFabe 1987) – making its function as likely to be altered by anxiolytic drugs as is that of the hippocampus. The parallels are strengthened by the fact that, unlike the anterior cingulate cortex but like anxiolytic drugs and hippocampus, posterior cingulate is involved in water maze learning (e.g., Riekkinen, Kuitunen and Riekkinen 1995) and high interference working memory tasks (Murray et al. 1989) and seems specifically involved in behavioural inhibition (Berger, Weikart, Bassett and Orr 1986).

Consistent with our linking of posterior cingulate to hippocampal function, it appears to deal with longer-term encoding of information as compared to anterior cingulate which appears to deal with shorter term encoding (Gabriel 1990) and to contribute to dysfunction in dementia (Minoshima, Foster and Kuhl 1994; Ishii, Sasaki, Yamaji, Sakamoto, Kitagaki and Mori 1997; Joyce, Rio, Ruttimann et al. 1994; Maddock,

Garrett and Buonocore 2002; Minoshima, Giordani, Berent, Frey, Foster and Kuhl 1997). It is noteworthy here that spatial dysfunction resulting from posterior cingulate damage, like hippocampal amnesia, is anterograde but not retrograde (Katayama, Takahashi, Ogawara and Hattori 1999).

As noted in relation to anterior cingulate, an important point about the fundamental division between defensive approach and defensive avoidance, for which we are arguing, is that there should be both fear-related and anxiety-related forms of obsession. Hand washing is a paradigmatic form of the former – a simple avoidance response removes the organism from danger and allows it to proceed about its normal affairs. We would argue that, 'fear of the dark', given our behavioural analysis above, is one candidate for an anxiety that lacks safety signals. It should be seen as anxiety rather than fear since it involves entering a threatening dark area from a safe lit area.

Fear of the dark can also be viewed as assigning threat to a set of locations and posterior cingulate cortex appears to be involved in spatial analysis particularly in the dark (Harkin and Whishaw 2002; Sutherland, Whishaw and Kolb 1988; Hirono, Mori, Ishii et al. 1998; Cooper, Manka and Mizumori 2001; Riekkinen, Kuitunen and Riekkinen 1995; Cooper and Mizumori 1999) although its exact involvement and the contribution of fibres of passage remains to be determined (Neave, Lloyd, Sahgal and Aggleton 1994; Meunier and Destrade 1997; Neave, Nagle, Sahgal and Aggleton 1996; Warburton, Aggleton and Muir 1998).

A related form of anxiety is agoraphobia (which in the theory would be better classified as 'agoranxiety'). This and other equivalent possible higher-order anxieties are classified by a lack of any simple avoidance strategy for the danger (which requires a high level of the defence system for their processing) and the fact that what is required for normal function is the capacity to approach and deal with the source of threat (which engages the defensive approach, anxiety, system in addition to the pure fear system). A possibility, then, is that pathology of the posterior cingulate cortex could give rise to pure agoraphobia. (This is not inconsistent with the suggestion that agoraphobia is the result of conditioning to pathological panic – primarily controlled by the periaqueductal grey.) Space, here, may simply be a special case of stimulus complexity or involvement of contextual factors since verbally mediated threat can also be processed by posterior cingulate (Maddock and Buonocore 1997).

At least in the case of agoraphobia, the clinical condition appears only weakly sensitive to anxiolytic drugs. This leads us to the possibility that, having used the drugs to define anxiety in terms of approach to danger, the latter definition may take precedence. Posterior cingulate may be an area that we would want to see as part of the BIS even with behaviours that are not sensitive to anxiolytic drugs (the tool we have used so far in this section). In what could be argued are the most extreme cases of clinical anxiety, resistant to both psychological and pharmacological treatment, lesions of the cingulate have been used as treatment with some degree of success (Marks, Birley and Gelder 1966; Powell 1981; Rapoport 1989). However, it is not clear from the data on such cases as to whether it is fear or anxiety (in terms of the current theory) that is the critical problem.

Prefrontal cortex

Ventral stream   At the top left-hand side of Figure 2.3 we have the ventral stream of prefrontal cortex. This is, of course, a hierarchy of structures in itself not a single structure. It also includes (as we noted the cingulate might include) components of the BAS (Figure 2.4) with cells that are sensitive to the valence and value of reinforcement or related behaviours (O'Doherty, Kringelbach, Rolls, Hornak and Andrews 2001; Pratt and Mizumori 2001; Poucet 1997) including positive sensations (Francis, Rolls, Bowtell *et al.* 1999). But we have insufficient evidence at present to sub-divide it with respect to symptoms and syndromes. To it we assign those expectations of threat that involve the most complex assessment and the greatest distance in the future. Such assessments would involve processes as complex as gender stereotyping (Milne and Grafman 2001). This would suggest that there may be a form of 'deep' obsessive compulsive disorder that is to some extent neurally distinct from more 'surface' obsession – but still, nonetheless, involves simple avoidance of, rather than approach to, the source of danger. This suggestion is consistent with the fact that both cingulate and prefrontal damage can alleviate obsessionality (Powell 1981) and that abstract forms of punishment (e.g., monetary loss) appear to be represented in the ventral stream of frontal cortex (O'Doherty, Kringelbach, Rolls, Hornak and Andrews 2001). There are some indications that BIS output (possibly from the dorsal stream of the prefrontal cortex, see below) suppresses activity in the ventral stream (Simpson, Snyder, Gusnard and Raichle 2001; Simpson, Drevets, Snyder, Gusnard and Raichle 2001).

Dorsal stream   Like cingulate lesions, prefrontal lesions have been used with some success to treat otherwise intractable anxiety (Powell 1981; Marks, Birley and Gelder 1966) and we would assign the

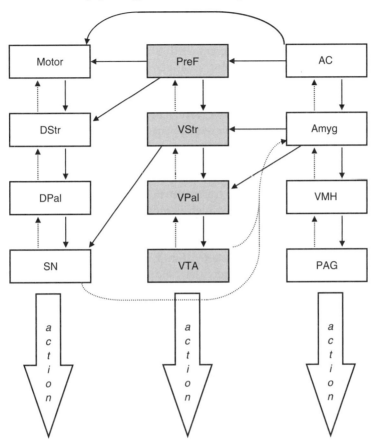

Figure 2.4 Structures included by Gray in the behavioural approach system (left two columns) with a suggested hierarchical organization similar to that of the defence systems. We argue in the text that the BAS is instantiated only within the column of shaded structures (operating on goal representations) rather than the unshaded ones (that operate on response rather than goal selection). Abbreviations: AC = anterior cingulate; Amyg = amygdala; DPal = dorsal pallium; DStr = dorsal striatum; PAG = periaqueductal gray; VMH = ventro-medial hypothalamus; VPal = ventral pallium; VStr = ventral striatum; VTA = ventral tegmental area

highest levels of control of anxiety to the dorsal stream of frontal cortex. Like the hippocampus, the dorsal stream appears to be involved in dealing with interference (MacDonald, Cohen, Stenger and Carter 2000) and given the involvement of the hippocampus in contextual tasks, it is noteworthy that cells in the dorsal (as opposed to the ventral) stream of prefrontal cortex are sensitive to the context of reinforcement (Watanabe, Hikosaka, Sakagami and Shirakawa 2002). The dorsal stream could, therefore, involve a variety of complex anxieties, in particular, social anxiety.[4]

Social behaviour is sufficiently complex that different aspects of it must be controlled at multiple levels of the defence system. Social situations also are likely to involve approach-avoidance conflict as they are at one and the same time a source of some of the most potent rewards and punishments faced by social organisms. Both imaging of those with social anxiety disorder compared to controls and imaging of changes induced by effective treatment indicate a fairly consistent pattern of changes in activation, which is most obvious in the dorsolateral prefrontal cortex (Argyropoulos, Bell and Nutt 2001; Furmark, Tillfors and Matteinsdottir 2002; Nutt, Bell and Malizia 1998; Van der Linden, Van Heerden and Warwick 2000). Similar results have been obtained with anxiety (and cortisol increases) induced by maternal separation both acutely in Rhesus monkeys (Rilling, Winslow, O'Brien, Gutman, Hoffman and Kilts 2001) and chronically in human infants. Given the complexity of prefrontal cortex there must be many other higher-level forms of anxiety to be described.

Behavioural approach system

We now have an outline of the FFFS and the matching components of the BIS. The revised BIS theory also has a central place for the *Behavioural Approach System* (BAS) – the BIS would often be activated with the simultaneous activation of the FFFS and the BAS (when there is approach-avoidance conflict). However, the BAS remains conceptually distinct from the FFFS and the BIS. All three systems can be viewed as hierarchically organized (Figure 2.4). Gray has previously (Gray and McNaughton 1996; Gray, Feldon, Rawlins, Hemsley and Smith 1991) described the BAS as having a 'caudate' component (left column in the figure) and an 'accumbens' component (shaded boxes in the figure). However, he also made clear that 'accumbens holds a list of subgoals making up a given motor program and is able to switch through the list in an appropriate order, but to retrieve the specific content of each step, it needs to call up the appropriate subroutine by way of its connections to the [caudate] system' (Gray and McNaughton 1996). Such caudate

---

[4] This suggestion and the literature we quote in the following paragraph were provided by Dr Caroline Bell.

motor command sub-routines are quite distinct from the affect-laden goals that are the subject of the FFFS, BAS and BIS (Gray and McNaughton 2000). We will, therefore, take here the BAS, proper, to be instantiated only in the structures represented in the figure by filled boxes.

As with the FFFS, the hierarchical organization of the BAS makes it difficult for any part of it to control overall BAS sensitivity. Where a personality factor is to alter such sensitivity generally, we must look for appropriate modulatory systems. The most likely neural candidate here is the mesolimbic system that employs the monoamine dopamine as its transmitter (mirroring the modulation by the monoamine serotonin of the FFFS and BIS). At the hormonal level, endogenous opioids are likely candidates.

The idea that the accumbens is a key node of the BAS is consistent with its involvement in appetitive arousal, facilitation of reward processes, and flexible response sequences including approach to safety signals (Ikemoto and Panksepp 1999).We cannot treat the dopamine system as homogenous, however. In the prefrontal cortex there is often a greater release of dopamine to aversive stimuli than is shown in the nucleus accumbens. It can also show increased dopamine release to both appetitive and aversive stimulation at times when the nucleus accumbens shows an increase to appetitive but a decrease to aversive stimuli (Di Chiara, Loddo and Tanda 1999). The BAS is further discussed by Pickering and Smillie in chapter 4.

From syndrome to sensitivity: putting Humpty Dumpty back together again

The key feature of our present view is that, independent of the precise correctness of the details suggested above, defensive distance and defensive direction map onto a series of distinct neural modules, to each of which can be attributed a particular class of function and so generation of a particular symptomatology, e.g., panic, phobia, obsession. These 'symptoms' may be generated in several different ways:

- as a normally adaptive reaction to their specific eliciting stimuli;
- at maladaptive intensity, as a result of excessive sensitivity to their specific eliciting stimuli;
- at maladaptive intensity, as a result of excessive activation of a related structure by its specific eliciting stimuli but where the 'symptoms' are not excessive given the level of input from the related structure.

For example, pathologically excessive anxiety could generate panic with the latter, in itself, being entirely appropriate to the level of apprehension experienced. Conversely pathological panic could, with repeated experience, condition anxiety with the level of the latter being appropriate to the panic experienced despite the anxiety being nominally pathological from the point of view of overall function.

This very modular view of the defence system, partitioned into distinct syndrome and symptom-specific components, was developed largely on the basis of animal experiments. But the linking of this view to terms such as panic, phobia and obsession is also justified by the clinical effects of drugs – taken class by class. As shown in Table 2.2, phobia, anxiety, panic, obsession and depression are dependent on distinct brain systems in that drugs that affect one need not affect another. For example, both benzodiazepines and buspirone are anxiolytic. But benzodiazepines (with a few exceptions such as alprazolam) do not affect depression and buspirone does not affect panic. Anxiety, depression and panic must each, then, depend on different parts of the brain. This separability of effects (comparing *classes* of drugs) is mapped by the theory to the distinct levels of the defence system. A multitude of specific behaviours, symptoms and syndromes can each, then, be pigeon-holed within a multitude of neural structures. While being a satisfactory explanation of the plethora of clinical phenomena this seems to shatter completely the idea, fundamental to the notion of a personality factor, that clusters and indeed swathes of such phenomena can have some fundamental unity, which is based on a personality.

Personality theory could be rescued, of course, by a simple appeal to the fact that, genetically speaking, there seems to be a common fundamental predisposition to the plethora of clinical neurotic phenomena even though that predisposition manifests differently in different individuals (Kendler, Prescott, Myers and Neale 2003; Andrews, Stewart, Morris-Yates, Holt and Henderson 1990). However, it can be rescued much more directly. The same pharmacology (Table 2.2) that allows us, through a comparison of classes of drug, to differentiate syndromes allows us, when we look at individual drugs, to arrive at a similar perspective to the genetic one. The action of many clinically effective drugs is best viewed as an interaction with more global modulatory systems. For example, 5HT neurones innervate virtually the entire defence system (Figure 2.3). Drugs such as imipramine or specific serotonin re-uptake inhibitors that have a general effect on 5HT synapses, therefore, have more general clinical actions. They can affect anxiety, depression and panic because they increase the levels of 5HT in the different parts of the system controlling each. Even so, their

Table 2.2 *Pharmacological dissection of disorders. Various classes of drugs effective in treating neurotic disorders and their relative effects on different neurotic syndromes and the extent to which they share classical anxiolytic side-effects (muscle relaxant; anti-convulsant, sedative, addictive). Exceptional effects of individual members of a class are ignored (e.g., the anti-depressant and panicolytic actions of specific benzodiazepines such as alprazolam). It should be noted that anti-depressant monoamine oxidase inhibitors, in particular phenelzine, are like novel anxiolytics such as buspirone and tricyclic drugs such as imipramine that have separate anxiolytic and anti-depressant action. They treat depression but also appear particularly effective in treating atypical depression (in which many symptoms overlap anxiety disorders but are resistant to anxiolytic drugs). They have not been reported to be effective in generalized anxiety. Key: class, classical anxiolytics such as benzodiazepines, barbiturates and meprobamate; CMI, Clomipramine; IMI, imipramine and closely related tricylic anti-depressants; MAOI, MonoAmine Oxidase Inhibitor; novel, novel, 5HT1A active, anxiolytics such as buspirone; SSRI, Specific Serotonin Reuptake Inhibitor; 0, no effect; – reduction; –, extensive reduction; +, increase; ( ), small or discrepant effects. From McNaughton (2002); Stein, Vythilingum and Seedat (2004)*

	class	novel	IMI	CMI	MAOI	SSRI
Simple phobia	0^a	?	0	?	(–)	(–)
Generalized anxiety	–	–	–	–	0?	–
Social phobia	–	(–)	0	(–)	–	–
Panic attacks	0^b	0	–	$–^c$	–	–
Obsessions/Compulsions	0	(–)	(–)	•–	(–)	–
Unipolar depression	0	–	–	–	–	–
Atypical depression	0	?	(–)	?	–	?

Notes:
[a] Sartory, MacDonald and Gray (1990).
[b] Excluding alprazolam, e.g., Sanderson, Wetzler and Asnis (1994).
[c] Gentil *et al.* (1993).

effects on, say, anxiety are not linked to, say, their concurrent effects on depression. These are each the result of independent effects of 5HT in different areas of the brain and of differentiation between 5HT systems (Deakin 1999).

It should be noted here that the genetic influences on the 5HT system that have been identified so far in humans, and that could easily underlie personality factors, operate to alter the system generally rather than impacting on specific receptors. Indeed, via actions on enzymes rather than receptors or uptake systems, genes could have even more widespread actions than tricyclic and related drugs.

So, comparison of drug classes can be used to dissect out different parts of the defence system. But this comparison must involve several different drugs within each class if specific conclusions are to be drawn about specific brain systems. Conversely, the systems as a joint whole, and each system individually, may be globally susceptible to modulation controlled by the biological substrates underlying personality. Humpty Dumpty in one sense remains broken but in another has been put back together again. In detail, then, the system underlying clinical drug action consists of two sets of parallel, interconnected modules dealing with defensive avoidance and defensive approach respectively. Superimposed on these specialized modules are general modulatory systems.

It would be expected, and seems on current evidence to be the case, that it is these latter modulatory systems that are crucial for personality. There is also a conceptual requirement for some such wholistic control. At least with the BIS, anxiolytics clearly alter defensive distance. They alter which point of the neural hierarchy is in control given progressive variations in the external situation – and they do so in a lawful manner. Assuming that the control of fear by the monoamines operates in a similar manner to the control of anxiety by anxiolytic drugs we would expect the personality factor of 'punishment sensitivity' would be one that simply alters the internal defensive distance in relation to any particular real distance. Put another way, a personality factor of fearfulness multiplies the level of fear experienced to a particular stimulus, producing many different levels with different stimuli. It does not consistently produce a particular class of fear-related behaviour – and it is only the latter that are linked to specific modules of the system outlined in Figure 2.3.

BAS, FFFS and BIS

With certain caveats, our argument has now come almost full circle. We start and finish with the idea that personality factors operate in a relatively simple fashion over large swathes of cognition, emotion and their related behavioural output.

Our caveats relate to the connection between factors and behavioural output and to the number and nature of the factors. There is a mass of defensive behaviour that can be pigeon-holed within a two dimensional matrix that is replicated at the functional/psychological and the neural levels. Global personality factors will interact with the different cells of the matrix to produce somewhat different patterns of output depending on the specific sensitivities of those cells. In factor analytic terms this should lead to substantial shared variance across a wide range of variables but to no particular variable having a much higher loading than any other on the factor. In our current analysis we will need to consider factors relating to global threat sensitivity (acting directly on the FFFS and indirectly on the BIS), to more specific conflict sensitivity (acting on the BIS) and, of course, global reward sensitivity (acting directly on the BAS and indirectly on the BIS). We can, and will below, consider these three systems in their global form, ignoring the differences in pattern of response between individuals discussed already. Clinicians would also need to concern themselves with a specific panic-related factor (which supplements threat sensitivity as a source of genetic variance in panic) but this seems unlikely to be significant for the experiments normally carried out by personality researchers.

The left-hand side of Figure 2.3 describes the neural machinery of the FFFS. It copes with an explicit danger that can be explicitly escaped or avoided. Obsession can be viewed as a special case where active avoidance is required but where it is in the nature of the danger (e.g., contagion) that there can be no explicit signal of safety. A single box in Figure 2.5 represents this entire system.

Figure 2.4 describes the neural machinery of the BAS and the right hand side of Figure 2.3 describes that of the BIS. Both are, like the FFFS, represented by a single box in Figure 2.5

The BIS is to some extent in parallel with the FFFS, but provides a range of functions when there is conflict. The most important of these functions with respect to the FFFS is that the BIS inhibits ongoing behaviour. Note, however, that the outputs of the BIS (Figure 2.5) include not only inhibition of avoidance (and approach) behaviour that would otherwise be produced but also increased arousal and attention.

Output from the BIS does not, however, entail immobility. An important active output, mediated by the septo-hippocampal system, is risk assessment behaviour, sometimes involving vigorous and extensive exploration. This behaviour can be seen as supporting the functions of the decision mechanism that would normally select approach or avoidance behaviour but which is incapable of doing so during conflict when (by definition) approach and avoidance are balanced. It gathers the information necessary to tip the balance in favour of approach (if the threat proves less than initially perceived) or avoidance (if the threat proves greater). While activation of the BIS inhibits avoidance behaviour (Figure 2.5), it does not decrease the motivational aspects of fear or frustration. Rather, the normal resolution of conflict by the BIS involves

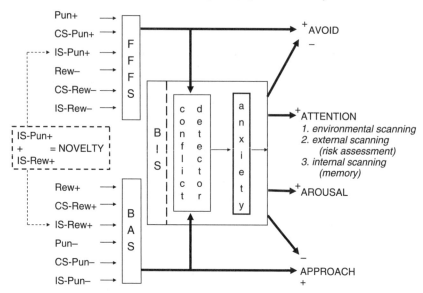

Figure 2.5 Relationship between stimuli, the Fight-Flight-Freeze System (FFFS), the Behavioural Approach System (BAS) and the Behavioural Inhibition System (BIS). Inputs consist of rewards (Rew) or punishers (Pun) that may be presented (+) or omitted when expected (−) and of innate stimuli (IS) or conditioned stimuli (CS) that predict these events. Note that the compound CS-Pun− can stand for either a CS that predicts Pun− or for the omission of a CS that predicts Pun+. The simplest means of activating the BIS is concurrent activation of the FFFS and the BAS, i.e., approach-avoidance conflict. However, approach-approach conflict and avoidance-avoidance conflict (as in two-way avoidance) will also activate the BIS

an increase in the effects of fear or frustration that favours avoidance over approach.

The decision to approach or to avoid is affected in a subtractive fashion by activation of the opposing motivational tendency. This subtraction operates both with respect to which decision (approach or avoid depending on whether the net sum is affectively positive or negative) and with respect to the vigour of goal-directed behaviour once the choice is made. Thus, even if a rat decides to run down a runway and collect the food at the end, prior experience of a mild shock will often reduce the speed with which it runs. It is important to note that the simple antagonism of reward value by associated punishment and of punishment by associated reward is symmetrical, is independent of

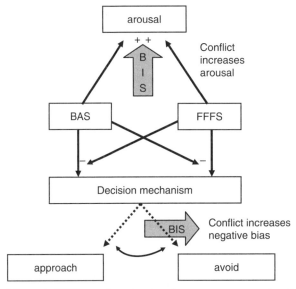

Figure 2.6 Effects of motivational systems on arousal and decision. The BAS and FFFS provide inputs that subtract to control decision and add to generate arousal. Arousal also operates on a much slower timescale than decision. The BIS increments arousal similarly to both the BAS and FFFS. It affects decision by increasing the effect of motivationally negative stimuli on decision

whether a response is required, and does not involve the BIS since it is not affected by anxiolytic drugs (McNaughton and Gray 1983).

In contrast to decision-making, the autonomic arousal accompanying approach or avoidance is affected in an additive fashion by activation of the opposing motivational tendency. This increased arousal also impacts on responses such as startle that are unrelated to the decision between the goals of the conflicting responses. Although 'fear potentiated startle' has received much analysis, it should be noted that 'hunger potentiated startle' also occurs (Drobes, Miller, Hillman, Bradley, Cuthbert and Lang 2001). The opposite interactions of the FFFS and BAS in decision-making and on arousal are shown in Figure 2.6 These different classes of computation must clearly be carried out by different parts of the brain.

Activation of the BIS by conflict (i.e., when approach and avoidance tendencies are not only each present but relatively closely matched in intensity of activation) also necessarily has different effects on choice than it does on arousal. As far as the decision mechanism that selects approach or avoidance is concerned, detection of conflict by the BIS has three distinct effects: it suppresses approach and avoidance;[5] it increases the tendency to avoid (lower BIS arrow in Figure 2.6); and it elicits risk analysis behaviour. By contrast, the arousal mechanism that summates the intensity of approach and avoidance motivation has its activity potentiated rather than suppressed by conflict via the 'increase arousal' output of the BIS (upper BIS arrow in Figure 2.6). Increased arousal might result (when approach and avoidance are closely balanced and both are inhibited) in the release of extraneous 'displacement' activities.

We need, therefore, to add to the picture of the amygdala painted in the 2000 theory. It is generally accepted that the amygdala not only receives information about both positive and negative events but also controls 'emotional' output for both positive and negative events. It is known, at least for negative events, to be the site at which an incoming signal of threat (e.g., a simple stimulus relayed from the thalamus) is registered and then generates a cascade including both motor and autonomic output. Intensity of amygdala activation can be equated here with arousal. The amygdala would be the logical site to locate the summing of the arousal inputs (see Figure 2.6).

It is not clear whether anxiolytic drugs affect this summing, in its most fundamental form. Nor, to our knowledge, has their effect on positive, e.g., hunger-potentiated, startle been tested. It may be that both positive and negative arousal feed into the amygdala and are anxiolytic-sensitive. However, it is also possible that positive and negative arousal are individually anxiolytic-insensitive but that the amygdala also contains additional circuitry that can detect when there is an even balance between arousal due to approach tendencies and arousal due to avoidance tendencies. When it detects such a balance, it implements the 'increase arousal' output of the BIS. Certainly, whether the circuitry is simple or complex, it is not contained in the septo-hippocampal system (lesion of which does not affect, for example, fear potentiated startle). Equally certainly, circuitry involved in this control of arousal is located in the amygdala since this is where the anxiolytics act directly to alter arousal.

The critical point not emphasized in the 2000 theory is that the effect of conflict is asymmetric (negative bias – increasing avoidance only) for the decision-making mechanism but symmetric (affecting components

[5] The suppression of conflicting behaviours is quite specific. Not only does conflict encourage risk analysis behaviour it also (mentioned only in passing in the 2000 theory) can unmask other 'displacement' behaviours. This can only occur if the behavioural inhibition is specific to the conflicting behaviours.

of both approach and avoidance) for arousal. This entails differential neural control. It should also be noted that the time course for decision-making will be very swift, of the order of tens of milliseconds, while that for arousal is necessarily slow with autonomic and hormonal actions having latencies of the order of seconds. The mutually antagonistic interactions between the FFFS and BAS, independent of the BIS, are also not emphasized in the 2000 theory. This antagonism can be presumed to occur at all relative levels of activation of the two systems. By contrast it is only when their activations are fairly evenly balanced that conflict results and the BIS is activated to resolve the problem faced by the decision mechanism.

Conclusion

Our theory makes a categorical distinction between two systems: one controlling defensive avoidance (fear) and one controlling defensive approach (anxiety). Why should one attempt to give precise behavioural/psychopharmacological definitions of fear and anxiety when these are used interchangeably by the general public and in clinical psychiatry? The fast answer, of course, is that we can. But, more importantly, there are many confusions for members of the public and psychiatrists that our distinction lays to rest. Why do 'anxiolytic drugs' only affect some defensive responses and not others? It is not tautological for us to reply that it is only anxious defence (i.e., approach to threat) that these drugs affect. How can relaxation induce panic – a sign of fear? Because fear and anxiety are not only distinct but anxiety (as defined by us) often inhibits fear (as defined by us). Further, as noted by Graeff, the nature of the responses elicited by the two states are often opposite in kind (fear producing speed and anxiety slowness) although the autonomic reactions are similar. So, not only can we distinguish fear and anxiety, especially in the clinic, we must do so if we are to have a clear picture of the world – and some chance of ultimately being able to categorize genuine syndromes of defensive reactions.

Our theory (Figure 2.3) also invokes a second dimension of hierarchical organization that is both functional (in terms of defensive distance) and neural (in terms of rostro-caudal level and cytoarchitectonic complexity). This does not have quite the fundamental impact of our first dimension. But again, both for the public and the psychiatrist, it can make clear both the potential diversity of reactions and hence syndromes and also a means of categorizing a multitude in terms of a simple, externally defined dimension. Importantly, it explains why many different drugs are needed to cope with individual pathologies of defence.

These two dimensions account for the differentiation between different defensive behaviours and between different syndromes and symptoms. Serotonergic and noradrenergic fibres that essentially mediate global threat sensitivity modulate all the structures controlling defence. The different levels of each system and the two systems as a whole are heavily interconnected to allow parallel control by both 'quick and dirty' and 'slow and sophisticated' systems (LeDoux 1994) and to allow rapid switching between defensive approach and defensive avoidance as conditions change. The monoamine systems can be thought of as operating on longer timescales, underpinning therapeutic drug actions and providing the basis for personality variables that determine risk of morbidity. Critically, they can be thought of as interacting with all levels of the systems, acting on defensive distance (which selects the neural level for current control) – and so having a more unitary function than the various parts we have delineated.

Omitted from the above account is the nature of the interactions between the levels of the system. That these will not be entirely simple is shown by the example of relaxation-induced panic – the result of an inhibitory interaction between the outputs of the anxiety and fear systems (Graeff 1994). Also absent is the highly detailed topographic mapping between the levels (Risold and Swanson 1996; Bandler, Keay, Floyd and Price 2000; Heidbreder and Groenewegen 2003). Each component of the model of Figure 2.3, then, is not a simple box but a patchwork of modules; each arrow represents a mass of parallel connections. But these do not really complicate the theory. They represent strands that allow the choice of particular responses once both defensive direction and defensive distance have determined the general nature of the required response. Finally, we should note that the detailed account presented here is only of the control of acute reactions. Control can pass from one system to another in an instant. The reactions to chronic threats are different and controlled by distinct systems (Deakin 1999) as may be entities such as anti-social personality disorder (Deakin 2003). We turn to the specifics of the theory for personality in the next chapter.

References

Aboufatima, R., Chait, A., Dalal, A. and De Beaurepaire, R. (1999), Calcitonin microinjection into the periaqueductal gray impairs contextual fear conditioning in the rat, *Neuroscience Letters*, 275, 101–104

An, X., Bandler, R., Öngür, D. and Price, J.L. (1998), Prefrontal cortical projections to longitudinal columns in the midbrain periaqueductal gray in macaque monkeys, *Journal of Comparative Neurology*, 401, 455–479

Andrews, G., Stewart, G., Morris-Yates, A., Holt, P. and Henderson, S. (1990), Evidence for a general neurotic syndrome, *British Journal of Psychiatry*, 157, 6–12

Argyropoulos, S.V., Bell, C.J. and Nutt, D. (2001), Brain function in social anxiety disorder, *Psychiatric Clinics of North America*, 24, 707–722

Audi, E.A., de Oliveira, R.M.W. and Graeff, F.G. (1991), Microinjection of propranolol into the dorsal periaqueductal gray causes an anxiolytic effect in the elevated plus-maze antagonized by ritanserin, *Psychopharmacology (Berl)*, 105, 553–557

Bandler, R. (1982), Induction of 'rage' following microinjections of glutamate into midbrain but not hypothalamus of cats, *Neuroscience Letters*, 30, 183–188

Bandler, R., Keay, K.A., Floyd, N. and Price, J. (2000), Central circuits mediating patterned autonomic activity during active vs. passive emotional coping, *Brain Research Bulletin*, 53, 95–104

Bandler, R., Price, J.L. and Keay, K.A. (2000), Brain mediation of active and passive emotional coping, *Progress in Brain Research*, 122, 331–347

Bandler, R. and Shipley, M.T. (1994), Columnar organization in the midbrain periaqueductal gray: modules for emotional expression?, *Trends in Neuroscience*, 17, 379–389

Bannerman, D.B., Rawlins, J.N.P., McHugh, S.B., Deacon, R.M.J., Yee, B.K., Bast, T., Zhang, W.-N., Pothuizen, H.H.J. and Feldon, J. (2004), Regional dissociation within the hippocampus: memory and anxiety, *Neuroscience and Biobehavioral Reviews*, 28, 273–283

Barch, D.M., Braver, T.S., Akbudak, E., Conturo, T., Ollinger, J. and Snyder, A. (2001), Anterior cingulate cortex and response conflict: effects of response modality and processing domain, *Cerebral Cortex*, 11, 837–848

Berger, T.W., Weikart, C.L., Bassett, J.L. and Orr, W.B. (1986), Lesions of the retrosplenial cortex produce deficits in reversal learning of the rabbit nictitating membrane response: implications for potential interactions between hippocampal and cerebellar brain systems, *Behavioral Neuroscience*, 100, 802–809

Blampied, N. and Kirk, R.C. (1983), Defensive burying: effects of diazepam and oxprenolol measured in extinction, *Life Sciences*, 33, 695–699

Blanchard, D.C. and Blanchard, R.J. (1988), Ethoexperimental approaches to the biology of emotion, *Annual Review of Psychology*, 39, 43–68

(1990), Effects of ethanol, benzodiazepines and serotonin compounds on ethopharmacological models of anxiety in N. McNaughton and G. Andrews (eds), *Anxiety* (Dunedin: Otago University Press), pp. 188–199

Blanchard, D.C., Blanchard, R.J., Tom, P. and Rodgers, R.J. (1990), Diazepam changes risk assessment in an anxiety/defense test battery, *Psychopharmacology (Berl)*, 101, 511–518

Blanchard, R.J. and Blanchard, D.C. (1989), Antipredator defensive behaviors in a visible burrow system, *Journal of Comparative Psychology*, 103(1), 70–82

(1990a), An ethoexperimental analysis of defense, fear and anxiety in N. McNaughton and G. Andrews (eds), *Anxiety* (Dunedin: Otago University Press), pp. 124–133

(1990b), Anti-predator defense as models of animal fear and anxiety in P.F. Brain, S. Parmigiani, R.J. Blanchard and D. Mainardi (eds), *Fear and Defence* (Church Harwood Academic Publishers), pp. 89–108

Blanchard, R.J., Griebel, G., Henrie, J.A. and Blanchard, D.C. (1997), Differentiation of anxiolytic and panicolytic drugs by effects on rat and mouse defense test batteries, *Neuroscience and Biobehavioral Reviews*, 21, 783–789

Blumberg, H.P., Stern, E., Martinez, D., Ricketts, S., De Asis, J., White, T., Epstein, J., McBride, P.A., Eidelberg, D., Kocsis, J.H. and Silbersweig, D.A. (2000), Increased anterior cingulate and caudate activity in bipolar mania, *Biological Psychiatry*, 48, 1045–1052

Borst, J.G.G., Leung, L.-W. S. and MacFabe, D.F. (1987), Electrical activity of the cingulate cortex. II, Cholinergic modulation, *Brain Research*, 407, 81–93

Botvinick, M., Nystrom, L.E., Fissell, K., Carter, C.S. and Cohen, J.D. (1999), Conflict monitoring versus selection-for-action in anterior cingulate cortex, *Nature*, 402, 179–181

Bussey, T.J., Everitt, B.J. and Robbins, T.W. (1997), Dissociable effects of cingulate and medial frontal cortex lesions on stimulus-reward learning using a novel Pavlovian autoshaping procedure for the rat: implications for the neurobiology of emotion, *Behavioral Neuroscience*, 111, 908–919

Bussey, T.J., Muir, J.L., Everitt, B.J. and Robbins, T.W. (1996), Dissociable effects of anterior and posterior cingulate cortex lesions on the acquisition of a conditional visual discrimination: facilitation of early learning vs. impairment of late learning, *Behavioural Brain Research*, 82, 45–56

Cahill, L., McGaugh, J.L. and Weinberger, N.M. (2001), The neurobiology of learning and memory: some reminders to remember, *Trends in Neurosciences*, 24, 578–581

Canteras, N.S. and Goto, M. (1999), Fos-like immunoreactivity in the periaqueductal gray of rats exposed to a natural predator, *Neuroreport*, 10, 413–418

Canteras, N.S., Simerly, R.B. and Swanson, L.W. (1994), Organization of projections from the ventromedial nucleus of the hypothalamus: a *Phaseolus vulgaris*-leucoagglutinin study in the rat, *Journal of Comparative Neurology*, 348, 41–79

Carrive, P. and Bandler, R. (1991), Viscerotopic organization of neurons subserving hypotensive reactions within the midbrain periaqueductal grey: a correlative functional and anatomical study, *Brain Research*, 541, 206–215

Carrive, P., Leung, P., Harris, J. and Paxinos, G. (1997), Conditioned fear to context is associated with increased fos expression in the caudal ventrolateral region of the midbrain periaqueductal gray, *Neuroscience*, 78, 165–177

Carter, C.S., Braver, T.S., Barch, D.M., Botvinick, M.M., Noll, D. and Cohen, J.D. (1998), Anterior cingulate cortex, error detection, and the online monitoring of performance, *Science*, 280, 747–749

Carter, C.S., Macdonald, A.M., Botvinick, M., Ross, L.L., Stenger, V.A., Noll, D. and Cohen, J.D. (2000), Parsing executive processes: strategic vs. evaluative functions of the anterior cingulate cortex, *Proceedings of the National Academy of Sciences of the United States of America*, 97, 1944–1948

Chang, C. and Shyu, B.C. (2001), A fMRI study of brain activations during non-noxious and noxious electrical stimulation of the sciatic nerve of rats, *Brain Research*, 897, 71–81

Coghill, R.C., Talbot, J.D., Evans, A.C., Meyer, E., Gjedde, A., Bushnell, M.C. and Duncan, G.H. (1994), Distributed processing of pain and vibration by the human brain, *Journal of Neuroscience*, 14, 4095–4108

Coop, C.F. and McNaughton, N. (1991), Buspirone affects hippocampal rhythmical slow activity through serotonin$_{1A}$ rather than dopamine D_2 receptors, *Neuroscience*, 40, 169–174

Coop, C.F., McNaughton, N. and Scott, D.J. (1992), Pindolol antagonizes the effects on hippocampal rhythmical slow activity of clonidine, baclofen and 8-OH-DPAT, but not chlordiazepoxide and sodium amylobarbitone, *Neuroscience*, 46, 83–90

Coop, C.F., McNaughton, N., Warnock, K. and Laverty, R. (1990), Effects of ethanol and Ro 15-4513 in an electrophysiological model of anxiolytic action, *Neuroscience*, 35, 669–674

Cooper, B.G., Manka, T.F. and Mizumori, S.J.Y. (2001), Finding your way in the dark: the retrosplenial cortex contributes to spatial memory and navigation without visual cues, *Behavioral Neuroscience*, 115, 1012–1028

Cooper, B.G. and Mizumori, S.J.Y. (1999), Retrosplenial cortex inactivation selectively impairs navigation in darkness, *Neuroreport*, 10, 625–630

Corr, P.J. (2001), Testing problems in J.A. Gray's personality theory: a commentary on Matthews and Gilliland (1999), *Personality and Individual Differences*, 30, 333–352

Crestani, F., Lorez, M., Baer, K., Essrich, C., Benke, D., Laurent, J.P., Belzung, C., Fritschy, J.-M., Lüscher, B. and Mohler, H. (1999), Decreased GABA$_A$-receptor clustering results in enhanced anxiety and a bias for threat cues, *Nature Neuroscience*, 2, 833–839

Davis, K.D. (2000), The neural circuitry of pain as explored with functional MRI, *Neurological Research*, 22, 313–317

Davis, K.D., Wood, M.L., Crawley, A.P. and Mikulis, D.J. (1995), fMRI of human somatosensory and cingulate cortex during painful electrical nerve stimulation, *Neuroreport*, 7, 321–325

Davis, M. (1992a), The role of the amygdala in conditioned fear in J.P. Aggleton (ed.), *The Amygdala: Neurobiological Aspects of Emotion, Memory, and Mental Function* (Wiley-Liss Inc.), pp. 255–305

(1992b), The role of the amygdala in fear and anxiety, *Annual Review of Neuroscience*, 15, 353–375

Davis, M. and Shi, C.J. (1999), The extended amygdala: are the central nucleus of the amygdala and the bed nucleus of the stria terminalis differentially involved in fear versus anxiety?, *Annals of the New York Academy of Sciences*, 877, 281–291

De Souza, M.M., Schenberg, L.C. and Carobrez, A.D.P. (1998), NMDA-coupled periaqueductal gray glycine receptors modulate anxioselective drug effects on plus-maze performance, *Behavioural Brain Research*, 90, 157–165

Deakin, J.F.W. (1999), Making sense of serotonin (5HT) and its role in common psychopathology in M. Tansella and G. Thornicroft (eds), *Common Mental Disorders in Primary Care: Essays in Honour of Professor Sir David Goldberg* (London and New York: Routledge), pp. 17–33

——— (2003), Depression and antisocial personality disorder: two contrasting disorders of 5HT function, *Journal of Neural Transmission*, 64, 79–93

Deakin, J.F.W. and Graeff, F.G. (1991), 5-HT and mechanisms of defence, *Journal of Psychopharmacology*, 5, 305–315

Degroot, A., Kashluba, S. and Treit, D. (2001), Septal GABAergic and hippocampal cholinergic systems modulate anxiety in the plus-maze and shock-probe tests, *Pharmacology, Biochemistry and Behavior*, 69, 391–399

Derbyshire, S.W.G., Vogt, B.A. and Jones, A.K.P (1998), Pain and Stroop interference tasks activate separate processing modules in anterior cingulate cortex, *Experimental Brain Research*, 118, 52–60

Di Chiara, G., Loddo, P. and Tanda, G. (1999), Reciprocal changes in prefrontal and limbic dopamine responsiveness to aversive and rewarding stimuli after chronic mild stress: implications for the psychobiology of depression, *Biological Psychiatry*, 46, 1624–1633

Diehl, B., Dinner, D.S., Mohamed, A., Najm, I., Klem, G., LaPresto, E., Bingaman, W. and Lüders, H.O. (2000), Evidence of cingulate motor representation in humans, *Neurology*, 55, 725–728

Dougherty, D.D., Shin, L.M., Alpert, N.M., Pitman, R.K., Orr, S.P., Lasko, M., Macklin, M.L., Fischman, A.J. and Rauch, S.L. (1999), Anger in healthy men: a PET study using script-driven imagery, *Biological Psychiatry*, 46, 466–472

Drobes, D.J., Miller, E.J., Hillman, C.H., Bradley, M.M., Cuthbert, B.N. and Lang, P.J. (2001), Food deprivation and emotional reactions to food cues: implications for eating disorders, *Biological Psychology*, 57, 153–177

Ebert, D., Speck, O., Konig, A., Berger, M., Hennig, J. and Hohagen, F. (1997), [1]H-magnetic resonance spectroscopy in obsessive-compulsive disorder: evidence for neuronal loss in the cingulate gyrus and the right striatum, *Psychiatry Research: Neuroimaging Section*, 74, 173–176

Eysenck, H.J. (1944), Type of personality: a factorial study of 700 neurotics, *Journal of Mental Sciences*, 90, 851–861

——— (1947), *Dimensions of Personality* (London: K. Paul Trench Trubner)

Fanselow, M. S. (1991), The midbrain periaqueductal gray as a coordinator of action in response to fear and anxiety in A. Depaulis and R. Bandler (eds), *The Midbrain Periaqueductal Gray Matter* (New York: Plenum Press), pp. 151–173

Feenstra, B.W.A. and Holsheimer, J. (1979), Dipole-like neuronal sources of theta rhythm in dorsal hippocampus, dentate gyrus and cingulate cortex of the urethane-anesthetized rat, *Electroencephalography and Clinical Neurophysiology*, 47, 532–538

Floyd, N.S., Price, J.L., Ferry, A.T., Keay, K.A. and Bandler, R. (2000), Orbitomedial prefrontal cortical projections to distinct longitudinal columns of the periaqueductal gray in the rat, *Journal of Comparative Neurology*, 422, 556–578

(2001), Orbitomedial prefrontal cortical projections to hypothalamus in the rat, *Journal of Comparative Neurology*, 432, 307–328

Francis, S., Rolls, E.T., Bowtell, R., McGlone, F., O'Doherty, J., Browning, A., Clare, S. and Smith, E. (1999), The representation of pleasant touch in the brain and its relationship with taste and olfactory areas, *Neuroreport*, 10, 453–459

Furmark, T., Tillfors, M. and Matteinsdottir, I. (2002), Common changes in cerebral blood flow in patients with social phobia treated with citalopram or cognitive behaviour therapy, *Archives of General Psychiatry*, 59, 425–433

Gabriel, M. (1990), Functions of anterior and posterior cingulate cortex during avoidance learning in rabbits, *Progress in Brain Research*, 85, 467–483

Gentil, V., Lotufo-Neto, F., Andrade, L., Cordás, T., Bernik, M., Ramos, R., Maciel, L., Miyakawa, E. and Gorenstein, C. (1993), Clomipramine, a better reference drug for panic/agoraphobia, I. Effectiveness comparison with imipramine, *Journal of Psychopharmacology*, 7, 316–324

Graeff, F.G. (1994), Neuroanatomy and neurotransmitter regulation of defensive behaviors and related emotions in mammals, *Brazilian Journal of Medical and Biological Research*, 27, 811–829

Gray, D.S., Terlecki, L.J., Treit, D. and Pinel, J.P.J. (1981), Effect of septal lesions on conditioned defensive burying, *Physiology and Behavior*, 27, 1051–1056

Gray, J.A. (1964), *Pavlov's Typology* (Oxford: Pergamon)

(1967), Disappointment and drugs in the rat, *Advancement of Science*, 23, 595–605

(1970), The Psychophysiological basis of introversion–extroversion, *Behaviour Research and Therapy*, 8, 249–266

(1975), *Elements of a Two-Process Theory of Learning* (London: Academic Press)

(1976), The behavioural inhibition system: a possible substrate for anxiety in M.P. Feldman and A.M. Broadhurst (eds), *Theoretical and Experimental Bases of Behaviour Modification* (London: Wiley), pp. 3–41

(1977), Drug effects on fear and frustration: possible limbic site of action of minor tranquilizers in L.L. Iversen, S.D. Iversen and S.H. Snyder (eds), *Handbook of Psychopharmacology*, vol. 8, *Drugs, Neurotransmitters and Behaviour* (New York: Plenum Press), pp. 433–529

(1982), *The Neuropsychology of Anxiety: an Enquiry into the Functions of the Septo-hippocampal System* (Oxford: Oxford University Press)

(1987), *The Psychology of Fear and Stress* (London: Cambridge University Press)

Gray, J.A., Feldon, J., Rawlins, J.N.P., Hemsley, D.R. and Smith, A.D. (1991), The Neuropsychology of Schizophrenia, *Behavioral and Brain Sciences*, 14, 1–20

Gray, J.A. and McNaughton, N. (1996), The neuropsychology of anxiety: reprise in D.A. Hope (ed.), *Perspectives on Anxiety, Panic and Fear* (Nebraska: University of Nebraska Press), pp. 61–134

(2000), *The Neuropsychology of Anxiety: an Enquiry into the Functions of the Septo-hippocampal System* (Oxford: Oxford University Press)

Harkin, A. and Whishaw, I.Q. (2002), Impaired spatial performance in rats with retrosplenial lesions: importance of the spatial problem and the rat strain in identifying lesion effects in a swimming pool, *Journal of Neuroscience*, 22, 1155–1164

Harris, J.A. and Westbrook, R.F. (1995), Effects of benzodiazepine microinjection into the amygdala or periaqueductal gray on the expression of conditioned fear and hypoalgesia in rats, *Behavioral Neuroscience*, 109, 295–304

Heidbreder, C.A. and Groenewegen, H.J. (2003), The medial prefrontal cortex in the rat: evidence for a dorso-ventral distinction based upon functional and anatomical characteristics, *Neuroscience and Biobehavioral Reviews*, 27, 555–579

Hinde, R.A. (1966), *Animal Behaviour* (New York: McGraw-Hill Book Company)

Hirono, N., Mori, E., Ishii, K., Ikejiri, Y., Imamura, T., Shimomura, T., Hashimoto, M., Yamashita, H. and Sasaki, M. (1998), Hypofunction in the posterior cingulate gyrus correlates with disorientation for time and place in Alzheimer's disease, *Journal of Neurology, Neurosurgery, and Psychiatry*, 64, 552–554

Holstege, G. (1989), Anatomical study of the final common pathway for vocalization in the cat, *Journal of Comparative Neurology*, 284, 242–252

Ikemoto, S. and Panksepp, J. (1999), The role of nucleus accumbens dopamine in motivated behavior: a unifying interpretation with special reference to reward-seeking, *Brain Research Reviews*, 31, 6–41

Ishii, K., Sasaki, M., Yamaji, S., Sakamoto, S., Kitagaki, H. and Mori, E. (1997), Demonstration of decreased posterior cingulate perfusion in mild Alzheimer's disease by means of $H_2^{15}O$ positron emission tomography, *European Journal of Nuclear Medicine*, 24, 670–673

Joyce, E.M., Rio, D.E., Ruttimann, U.E., Rohrbaugh, J.W., Martin, P.R., Rawlings, R.R. and Eckardt, M.J. (1994), Decreased cingulate and precuneate glucose utilization in alcoholic Korsakoff's syndrome, *Psychiatry Research*, 54, 225–239

Kask, A., Rägo, L. and Harro, J. (1998), NPY Y_1 receptors in the dorsal periaqueductal gray matter regulate anxiety in the social interaction test, *Neuroreport*, 9, 2713–2716

Katayama, K., Takahashi, N., Ogawara, K. and Hattori, T. (1999), Pure topographical disorientation due to right posterior cingulate lesion, *Cortex*, 35, 279–282

Keay, K.A. and Bandler, R. (2002), Parallel circuits mediating distinct emotional coping reactions to different types of stress, *Neuroscience and Biobehavioral Reviews*, 25, 669–678

Kendler, K.S., Prescott, C.A., Myers, J. and Neale, M.C. (2003), The structure of genetic and environmental risk factors for common psychiatric and substance use disorders in men and women, *Archives of General Psychiatry*, 60, 929–937

Kermadi, I., Liu, Y. and Rouiller, E.M. (2000), Do bimanual motor actions involve the dorsal premotor (PMd), cingulate (CMA) and posterior parietal

(PPC) cortices? Comparison with primary and supplementary motor cortical areas, *Somatosensory and Motor Research*, 17, 255–271

Kimble, G.A. (1961), *Hilgard and Marquis' Conditioning and Learning* (New York: Appleton-Century-Crofts)

Knight, D.C., Smith, C.N., Stein, E.A. and Helmstetter, F.J. (1999), Functional MRI of human Pavlovian fear conditioning: patterns of activation as a function of learning, *Neuroreport*, 10, 3665–3670

Koyama, T., Tanaka, Y.Z. and Mikami, A. (1998), Nociceptive neurons in the macaque anterior cingulate activate during anticipation of pain, *Neuroreport*, 9, 2663–2667

Kubota, Y., Wolske, M., Poremba, A., Kang, E. and Gabriel, M. (1996), Stimulus-related and movement-related single-unit activity in rabbit cingulate cortex and limbic thalamus during performance of discriminative avoidance behavior, *Brain Research*, 721, 22–38

Kwan, C.L., Crawley, A.P., Mikulis, D.J. and Davis, K.D. (2000), An fMRI study of the anterior cingulate cortex and surrounding medial wall activations evoked by noxious cutaneous heat and cold stimuli, *Pain*, 85, 359–374

LeDoux, J.E. (1994), Emotion, memory and the brain, *Scientific American*, 270, 50–59

Liebman, J.M., Mayer, D.J. and Liebeskind, J.C. (1970), Mesencephalic central gray lesions and fear-motivated behavior in rats, *Brain Research*, 23, 353–370

MacDonald, A.W. III, Cohen, J.D., Stenger, V.A. and Carter, C.S. (2000), Dissociating the role of the dorsolateral prefrontal and anterior cingulate cortex in cognitive control, *Science*, 288, 1835–1838

Maddock, R.J. and Buonocore, M.H. (1997), Activation of left posterior cingulate gyrus by the auditory presentation of threat-related words: an fMRI study, *Psychiatry Research: Neuroimaging Section*, 75, 1–14

Maddock, R.J., Garrett, A.S. and Buonocore, M.H. (2002), Remembering familiar people: the posterior cingulate cortex and autobiographical memory retrieval, *Neuroscience*, 104, 667–676

Marks, I.M., Birley, J.L.T. and Gelder, M.G. (1966), Modified leucotomy in severe agoraphobia: a controlled serial inquiry, *British Journal of Psychiatry*, 112, 757–769

Matheus, M.G. and Guimaraes, F.S. (1997), Antagonism of non-NMDA receptors in the dorsal periaqueductal grey induces anxiolytic effect in the elevated plus maze, *Psychopharmacology (Berl)*, 132, 14–18

Matheus, M.G., Nogueira, R.L., Carobrez, A.P., Graeff, F.G. and Guimaraes, F.S. (1994), Anxiolytic effect of glycine antagonists microinjected into the dorsal periaqueductal grey, *Psychopharmacology (Berl)*, 113, 565–569

McNaughton, N. (1989), *Biology and Emotion* (Cambridge: Cambridge University Press)

(1993), Stress and behavioural inhibition in S.C. Stanford and P. Salmon (eds), *Stress: an Integrated Approach* (Academic Press), pp. 191–206

(1997), Cognitive dysfunction resulting from hippocampal hyperactivity: a possible cause of anxiety disorder, *Pharmacology, Biochemistry and Behavior*, 56, 603–611

(2001), Approach-avoidance conflict in W.E. Craighead and C.B. Nemeroff (eds), *The Corsini Encyclopedia of Psychology and Behavioral Science* (New York: John Wiley and Sons), pp. 126–127

(2002), Aminergic transmitter systems in H. D'haenen, J.A. Den Boer, H. Westenberg and P. Willner (eds), *Textbook of Biological Psychiatry* (John Wiley and Sons), pp. 895–914

McNaughton, N. and Coop, C.F. (1991), Neurochemically dissimilar anxiolytic drugs have common effects on hippocampal rhythmic slow activity, *Neuropharmacology*, 30, 855–863

McNaughton, N. and Corr, P.J. (2004), A two-dimensional neuropsychology of defense: fear/anxiety and defensive distance, *Neuroscience and Biobehavioral Reviews*, 28, 285–305

McNaughton, N. and Gray, J.A. (1983), Pavlovian counterconditioning is unchanged by chlordiazepoxide or by septal lesions, *Quarterly Journal of Experimental Psychology*, 35B, 221–233

McNaughton, N. and Mason, S.T. (1980), The neuropsychology and neuropharmacology of the dorsal ascending noradrenergic bundle: a review, *Progress in Neurobiology*, 14, 157–219

McNaughton, N. and Morris, R.G.M. (1987), Chlordiazepoxide, an anxiolytic benzodiazepine, impairs place navigation in rats, *Behavioural Brain Research*, 24, 39–46

(1992), Buspirone produces a dose-related impairment in spatial navigation, *Pharmacology, Biochemistry and Behavior*, 43, 167–171

McNish, K.A., Gewirtz, J.C. and Davis, M. (1997), Evidence of contextual fear after lesions of the hippocampus: a disruption of freezing but not fear-potentiated startle, *Journal of Neuroscience*, 17, 9353–9360

Melia, K.R., Ryabinin, A.E., Corodimas, K.P., Wilson, M.C. and LeDoux, J.E. (1996), Hippocampal-dependent learning and experience-dependent activation of the hippocampus are preferentially disrupted by ethanol, *Neuroscience*, 74, 313–322

Menard, J. and Treit, D. (1996a), Does tolerance develop to the anxiolytic effects of septal lesions, *Physiology and Behavior*, 59, 311–318

(1996b), Lateral and medial septal lesions reduce anxiety in the plus-maze and probe-burying tests, *Physiology and Behavior*, 60, 845–853

(1999), Effects of centrally administered anxiolytic compounds in animal models of anxiety, *Neuroscience and Biobehavioral Reviews*, 23, 591–613

Meunier, M. and Destrade, C. (1997), Effects of radiofrequency versus neurotoxic cingulate lesions on spatial reversal learning in mice, *Hippocampus*, 7, 355–360

Milani, H. and Graeff, F.G. (1987), GABA-Benzodiazepine modulation of aversion in the medial hypothalamus of the rat, *Pharmacology, Biochemistry and Behavior*, 28, 21–27

Miller, N.E. (1944), Experimental studies of conflict in J.M. Hunt (ed.), *Personality and the Behavioural Disorders* (New York: Ronald), pp. 431–465.

Milne, E. and Grafman, J. (2001), Ventromedial prefrontal cortex lesions in humans eliminate implicit gender stereotyping, *Journal of Neuroscience*, 21, NIL1–NIL6

Minoshima, S., Foster, N.L. and Kuhl, D.E. (1994), Posterior cingulate cortex in Alzheimer's disease, *Lancet*, 344, 895–895

Minoshima, S., Giordani, B., Berent, S., Frey, K.A., Foster, N.L. and Kuhl, D.E. (1997), Metabolic reduction in the posterior cingulate cortex in very early Alzheimer's disease, *Annals of Neurology*, 42, 85–94

Money, E.A., Kirk, R.C. and McNaughton, N. (1992), Alzheimer's dementia produces a loss of discrimination but no increase in rate of memory decay in delayed matching to sample, *Neuropsychologia*, 30, 133–145

Murray, E.A., Davidson, M., Gaffan, D., Olton, D.S. and Suomi, S. (1989), Effects of fornix transection and cingulate cortical ablation on spatial memory in rhesus monkeys, *Experimental Brain Research*, 74, 173–186.

Neave, N., Lloyd, S., Sahgal, A. and Aggleton, J.P. (1994), Lack of effect of lesions in the anterior cingulate cortex and retrosplenial cortex on certain tests of spatial memory in the rat, *Behavioural Brain Research*, 65, 89–101

(1996), The effects of discrete cingulum bundle lesions in the rat on the acquisition and performance of two tests of spatial working memory, *Behavioural Brain Research*, 80, 75–85

Nutt, D., Bell, C.J. and Malizia, A.L. (1998), Brain mechanisms of social anxiety disorder, *Journal of Clinical Psychiatry*, 59, 4–9

O'Doherty, J., Kringelbach, M.L., Rolls, E.T., Hornak, J. and Andrews, C. (2001), Abstract reward and punishment representations in the human orbitofrontal cortex, *Nature Neuroscience*, 4, 95–102

Ochsner, K.N., Kosslyn, S.M., Cosgrove, G.R., Cassem, E.H., Price, B.H., Nierenberg, A.A. and Rauch, S.L. (2001), Deficits in visual cognition and attention following bilateral anterior cingulotomy, *Neuropsychologia*, 39, 219–230

Okaichi, Y. and Okaichi, H. (1994), Effects of fimbria-fornix lesions on avoidance tasks with temporal elements in rats, *Physiology and Behavior*, 56, 759–765

Pan, W.-X. and McNaughton, N. (1997), The medial supramammillary nucleus, spatial learning and the frequency of hippocampal theta activity, *Brain Research*, 764, 101–108

(2004), The supramammillary area: its organization, functions and relationship to the hippocampus, *Progress in Neurobiology*, 74, 127–166

Parkinson, J.A., Willoughby, P.J., Robbins, T.W. and Everitt, B.J. (2000), Disconnection of the anterior cingulate cortex and nucleus accumbens core impairs Pavlovian approach behavior: further evidence for limbic cortical-ventral striatopallidal systems, *Behavioral Neuroscience*, 114, 42–63

Peterson, B.S., Skudlarski, P., Gatenby, J.C., Zhang, H.P., Anderson, A.W. and Gore, J.C. (1999), An fMRI study of Stroop word-color interference: evidence for cingulate subregions subserving multiple distributed attentional systems, *Biological Psychiatry*, 45, 1237–1258

Poucet, B. (1997), Searching for spatial unit firing in the prelimbic area of the rat medial prefrontal cortex, *Behavioural Brain Research*, 84, 151–159

Powell, G.E. (1981), A survey of the effects of brain lesions upon personality in H.J. Eysenck (ed.), *A Model for Personality* (Springer-Verlag), pp. 65–87

Pratt, W.E. and Mizumori, S.J.Y. (2001), Neurons in rat medial prefrontal cortex show anticipatory rate changes to predictable differential rewards in a spatial memory task, *Behavioural Brain Research*, 123, 165–183

Procyk, E. and Josephy, J.P. (2001), Characterization of serial order encoding in the monkey anterior cingulate sulcus, *European Journal of Neuroscience*, 14, 1041–1046

Rainville, P., Duncan, G.H., Price, D.D., Carrier, B. and Bushnell, M.C. (1997), Pain affect encoded in human anterior cingulate but not somatosensory cortex, *Science*, 277, 968–971

Rapoport, J.L. (1989), The biology of obsessions and compulsions, *Scientific American*, 63–69

Reinvang, I., Magnussen, S., Greenlee, M.W. and Larsson, P.G. (1998), Electrophysiological localization of brain regions involved in perceptual memory, *Experimental Brain Research*, 123, 481–484

Riekkinen, P. Jr, Kuitunen, J. and Riekkinen, M. (1995), Effects of scopolamine infusions into the anterior and posterior cingulate on passive avoidance and water maze navigation, *Brain Research*, 685, 46–54

Rilling, J.K., Winslow, J.T., O'Brien, D., Gutman, D.A., Hoffman, J.M. and Kilts, C.D. (2001), Neural correlates of maternal separation in Rhesus monkeys, *Biological Psychiatry*, 49, 146–157

Risold, P.Y. and Swanson, L.W. (1996), Structural evidence for functional domains in the rat hippocampus, *Science*, 272, 1484–1486

Rizvi, T.A., Ennis, M., Behbehani, M.M. and Shipley, M.T. (1991), Connections between the central nucleus of the amygdala and the midbrain periaqueductal gray: topography and reciprocity, *Journal of Comparative Neurology*, 303, 121–131

Sanderson, W.C., Wetzler, S. and Asnis, G.M. (1994), Alprazolam blockade of CO_2-provoked panic in patients with panic disorder, *American Journal of Psychiatry*, 151, 1220–1222

Sartory, G., MacDonald, R. and Gray, J.A. (1990), Effects of diazepam on approach, self-reported fear and psychophysological responses in snake phobics, *Behaviour Research and Therapy*, 28, 273–282

Scherrer, J.F., True, W.R., Xian, H., Lyons, M.J., Eisen, S.A., Goldberg, J., Lin, N. and Tsuang, M.T. (2000), Evidence for genetic influences common and specific to symptoms of generalized anxiety and panic, *Journal of Affective Disorders*, 57, 25–35

Shin, L.M., Dougherty, D.D., Orr, S.P., Pitman, R.K., Lasko, M., Macklin, M.L., Alpert, N.M., Fischman, A.J. and Rauch, S.L. (2000), Activation of anterior paralimbic structures during guilt-related script-driven imagery, *Biological Psychiatry*, 48, 43–50

Shipley, M.T., Ennis, M., Rizvi, T.A. and Behbehani, M.M. (1991), Topographical specificity of forebrain inputs to the midbrain periaqueductal gray: evidence for discrete longitudinally organized input columns in A. Depaulis and R. Bandler (eds), *The Midbrain Periaqueductal Gray Matter* (New York: Plenum Press), pp. 417–448

Simpson, J.R. Jr, Drevets, W.C., Snyder, A.Z., Gusnard, D.A. and Raichle, M.E.(2001), Emotion-induced changes in human medial prefrontal cortex, II. During anticipatory anxiety, *Proceedings of the National Academy of Sciences of the United States of America*, 98, 688–693

Simpson, J.R. Jr, Snyder, A.Z., Gusnard, D.A. and Raichle, M.E. (2001), Emotion-induced changes in human medial prefrontal cortex, I. During cognitive task performance, *Proceedings of the National Academy of Sciences of the United States of America*, 98, 683–687

Stein, D.J., Vythilingum, B. and Seedat, S. (2004) Pharmacotherapy of phobias: a review, ch. 3, in M. Maj, H.S. Akiskal, J.J. López-Ibor and A. Okasha (eds), *Evidence and Experience in Psychiatry*, vol. 7 *Phobias*

Sutherland, R.J., Whishaw, I.Q. and Kolb, B. (1988), Contributions of cingulate cortex to two forms of spatial learning and memory, *Journal of Neuroscience*, 8(6), 1863–1872

Swanson, L.W. and Petrovich, G.D. (1998), What is the amygdala?, *Trends in Neurosciences*, 21, 323–331

Takenouchi, K., Nishijo, H., Uwano, T., Tamura, R., Takigawa, M. and Ono, T. (1999), Emotional and behavioral correlates of the anterior cingulate cortex during associative learning in rats, *Neuroscience*, 93, 1271–1287

Tan, S., Kirk, R.C., Abraham, W.C. and McNaughton, N. (1989), Effects of the NMDA antagonists, CPP and MK-801 on delayed conditional discrimination, *Psychopharmacology*, 98, 556–560

(1990), Chlordiazepoxide reduces discriminability but not rate of forgetting in delayed conditional discrimination, *Psychopharmacology*, 101, 550–554

Towe, A.L. and Luschei, E.S. (1981), Preface in A.L. Towe and E.S. Luschei (eds), *Motor Coordination* (New York: Plenum Press), pp. vii–viii

Treit, D. and Fundytus, M. (1988), A comparison of buspirone and chlordiazepoxide in the shock-probe/burying test for anxiolytics, *Pharmacology, Biochemistry and Behavior*, 30, 1071–1075

Treit, D., Robinson, A., Rotzinger, S. and Pesold, C. (1993), Anxiolytic effects of serotonergic interventions in the shock-probe burying test and the elevated plus mase, *Behavioural Brain Research*, 54, 23–34

Van der Linden, G., Van Heerden, B. and Warwick, J. (2000), Functional brain imaging and pharmacotherapy in social phobia: single photon emission computed tomography before and after treatment with the selective serotoninreuptake inhibitor citalopram, *Progress in Neuropsychopharmacology and Biological Psychiatry*, 24, 419–438

Veening, J., Buma, P., Ter Horst, G.J., Roeling, T.A.P., Luiten, P.G.M. and Nieuwenhuys, R. (1991), Hypothalamic projections to the PAG in the rat: topographical, immuno-electronmicroscopical and function aspects in A. Depaulis and R. Bandler (eds), *The Midbrain Periaqueductal Gray Matter* (New York: Plenum Press), pp. 387–415

Wang, Z., Valdes, J., Noyes, R., Zoega, T. and Crowe, R.R. (1998a), Possible association of a cholecystokinin promotor polymorphism (CCK_{-36CT}) with panic disorder, *American Journal of Medical Genetics*, 81, 228–234

(1998b), Possible association of a cholecystokinin promotor polymorphism (CCK_{-36CT}) with panic disorder, *American Journal of Medical Genetics*, 81, 228–234

Warburton, E.C., Aggleton, J.P. and Muir, J.L. (1998), Comparing the effects of selective cingulate cortex lesions and cingulum bundle lesions on water maze performance by rats, *European Journal of Neuroscience*, 10, 622–634

Watanabe, M., Hikosaka, K., Sakagami, M. and Shirakawa, S. (2002), Coding and monitoring of motivational context in the primate prefrontal cortex, *Journal of Neuroscience*, 22, 2391–2400

Whalen, P.J., Bush, G., McNally, R.J., Wilhelm, S., McInerney, S.C., Jenike, M.A. and Rauch, S.L. (1998), The emotional counting Stroop paradigm: a functional magnetic resonance imaging probe of the anterior cingulate affective division, *Biological Psychiatry*, 44, 1219–1228

Wheatley, D. (1982), Buspirone: multicenter efficacy study, *Journal of Clinical Psychiatry*, 43(12), 92–94

(1990), The new alternatives in D. Wheatley (ed.), *In the Anxiolytic Jungle: Where Next?* (Chichester: John Wiley), pp. 163–184

Woo, T.U., Pucak, M.L., Kye, C.H., Matus, C.V. and Lewis, D.A. (1997), Peripubertal refinement of the intrinsic and associational circuitry in monkey prefrontal cortex, *Neuroscience*, 80, 1149–1158

Woodnorth, M.-A. and McNaughton, N. (2002), Similar effects of medial supramammillary or systemic injections of chlordiazepoxide on both theta frequency and fixed-interval responding, *Cognitive, Affective, and Behavioral Neuroscience*, 2, 76–83

Zhang, L. and Barrett, J.E. (1990), Interactions of corticotropin-releasing factor with antidepressant and anxiolytic drugs: Behavioural studies with pigeons, *Biological Psychiatry*, 27(9), 953–967

Zhu, X.-O. and McNaughton, N. (1991a), Effects of long-term administration of anxiolytics on reticular-elicited hippocampal rhythmical slow activity, *Neuropharmacology*, 30, 1095–1099

(1991b), Effects of long-term administration of imipramine on reticular-elicited hippocampal rhythmical slow activity, *Psychopharmacology*, 105, 433–438

(1994a), A comparison of the acute effects of a tricyclic and a MAOI antidepressant on septal driving of hippocampal rhythmical slow activity, *Psychopharmacology (Berl)*, 114, 337–344

(1994b), Effects of long-term administration of antidepressants on septal driving of hippocampal RSA, *International Journal of Neuroscience*, 79, 91–98

(1994c), The interaction of serotonin depletion with anxiolytics and antidepressants on reticular-elicited hippocampal RSA, *Neuropharmacology*, 33, 1597–1605

(1995a), Minimal changes with long-term administration of anxiolytics on septal driving of hippocampal rhythmical slow activity, *Psychopharmacology (Berl)*, 118, 93–100

(1995b), Effects of long-term administration of phenelzine on reticular-elicited hippocampal rhythmical slow activity, *Neuroscience Research*, 21, 311–316

(1995c), Similar effects of buspirone and chlordiazepoxide on a fixed interval schedule with long-term, low-dose administration, *Journal of Psychopharmacology*, 9, 326–330

3 Animal cognition and human personality

Neil McNaughton and Philip J. Corr

Reinforcement Sensitivity Theory (RST) is based, both in terms of data and concepts, on the experimental analysis of (non-human) animal behaviour. Some workers in emotion and human personality research question its validity on this count alone. But, since Galileo and Copernicus, our world has clearly not been the centre of the wider universe. Likewise, since Darwin, biology has accepted the essential continuity between our own and other species (with chimpanzees, genetically speaking, being 98 per cent human), where the human form and characters have not been the goal of evolution. In this chapter we evaluate the claim that emotion and personality, nonetheless, remain distinct from the rest of biology; that with them it is still the case that 'the only proper study of mankind is man'. This will clarify the foundations on which RST rests.

Emotion and personality can be approached from more 'cognitive' (e.g., Matthews, chapter 17) or 'biological' (McNaughton and Corr, chapter 2) perspectives. But these are really different sides of the same coin. There are cases where cognitive or biological factors may seem relatively more important. But both kinds of case exist. This requires a true theoretical and empirical integration to take a combined 'biocognitive' perspective. Each approach fills the gaps left by the other. Their combination leads to a richer picture and a deeper understanding.

To many this is so obvious that to argue is to attack a straw man. But resistance to the idea of non-human cognition, or that human emotion and personality are just like those of other animals, while tacit is widespread. It is fuelled by a range of anthropocentric fallacies that diehard. But neural and behavioural homologies across species have illuminated much of human cognition, emotion and personality – perhaps nowhere more so than with RST.

A focus on language or surface aspects of cognition can blind us to this fact. But, after many years in the scientific wilderness, emotion (which in terms of everyday application is the most important aspect of psychology) is now receiving due attention and highlighting biological factors. But many assumptions and practices still remain that prevent integration of cognitive and biological constructs. RST provides a framework for such integration.

The question 'What is an emotion' (James 1884) is now tractable. Biological, and particularly evolutionary, analyses (McNaughton 1989) explain human emotions through the immense commonalities in internal and skeletal behaviours as well as through illuminating differences. Darwin (1872, reprinted 1965) devoted a whole book to the functional analysis of emotion and much more is known now.

We expose, below, fallacies that are a barrier to the wholesale transfer of the biological analysis of emotion and personality to the human species. For many these are so obvious that our treatment will seem otiose. But there are still others who view the role of 'pure cognition' as so central to human psychology as to make biology irrelevant, or at least a second-best level of analysis. But, even were cognition independent of emotion, it is not hardware-independent. Perceptual illusions result from processes such as lateral inhibition that can be exemplified in organisms as different from us as the horseshoe crab *Limmulus*. Human cognitive processes depend on neural mechanisms and are evident in behavioural data that are also general to non-human species. Pharmacology and imaging technologies (and on occasion more invasive techniques) confirm this generality directly (Gray and Braver 2002).

Neural mechanisms can be too low a level of analysis for some behaviours in any species. The psychology of non-human cognition can often provide a clearer picture of the psychological fundamentals of human cognition than analysis restricted to humans and particularly analysis restricted to the verbal channel. Indeed, Charles Darwin distrusted human verbal behaviour and preferred observation of non-human animals as being 'less likely to deceive us' (Darwin 1965).

'Behaviour analysis', or at least radical behaviourism, can also be blamed for a lack of interest in non-human animal cognition. Simplified artificial laboratory environments and limited ranges of measured behaviour made the rules underlying behaviour easier to discover. Even if we allow that animals could have cognitions, many of us were brought up with the idea that, 'according to behaviourism, the job of psychology is to specify the relationship between some physical event and the response, without reference to mental processes' (Dickinson 1980). But to insist that you should only use behaviour as *evidence* is not the religious aberration of radical behaviourism. Rather, this held that all you could *talk* about was behaviour – an obvious error to either a cognitive or a biological psychologist. But most theorists now believe that observing behavioural changes does not commit one to a strict behaviourist perspective, radical or otherwise. Mental processes can, and should, be inferred from behaviour (Dickinson 1980). Scientific psychology, except where it embraces neuroscience, must draw conclusions from behavioural observations, verbal and non-verbal. Where it does embrace neuroscience it is embracing even more the doctrine that we can use external observables to deduce 'what is going on inside the head'.

Conversely, an aversion to radical behaviourism can also blind one to the fact that the behaviour analysts' own data is often the best evidence for changes in internal cognitive structures (see Fallacy 8 below). More importantly, the very artificiality of the procedures used was specifically designed to eliminate species-specific behaviours and discover species general rules. So, despite the behaviourists' distaste for cognitive constructs, they were in fact analysing species-general cognitive processes. Such processes would be expected, given phylogenetic continuity, to form the basis of human cognition whatever species-specific additional processes might also be involved. 'Cognitivism', then, can ignore the importance both of behaviour (or neural activity) as fundamental evidence and comparative analysis as the key to unlocking function.

The focus of this chapter is on how far human cognition can be expected to conform to commonalities in non-human cognition. Given the assumption that the human species will have conserved functions that are generally conserved across other species, the details of such clear specific differences (e.g., colour vision), as can be found when selected pairs of species are compared, can be dealt with later as special cases.

Fallacies: biology or cognition

We suspect that the following fallacies underlie the separation of biological and cognitive constructs in psychology in general and personality psychology in particular. Each may seem a straw man but, inside them, we believe are the bones of strongly-held implicit positions that are seldom enunciated, but frequently distort reasoning – and so the type and direction of research carried out in the psychology of emotion and personality.

The root source of many of these fallacies is Cartesian dualism. This still reigns (albeit silently) in many areas of psychological science. Dualism allows a disregard for the central tenets of Darwinian biology and promotes an implicit anthropocentrism that supports major theoretical divides in psychology. The arguments advanced here adhere to two fundamental beliefs in biology: the continuity of species implied by Darwinian evolution; and the mapping of mind to brain as different levels of description of the same fundamental entity. Mind is not here identical to brain. It is a property of brain *processes*.

Fallacy 1: primary anthropocentrism

Although seldom nowadays stated in its raw form, anthropocentrism is often at the core of many of the other reasons given for treating human beings as categorically different in some specific way from 'the animals'. Explicable in terms of ingroup-outgroup bias or human egocentrism, it is no better a basis for modern psychological science than it was for astronomy in Galileo's time.

The human species is, of course, unique. But, for scientific purposes, all species are unique (at least in some important respects). The general argument against anthropocentrism is that there is no combination of characters that would truly set us apart from all 'the animals'. Specific more or less unique characters can, of course, be found individually on a species-by-species basis. But no character sets us apart from other animals in a way that other characters do not set each species apart from all others (Macphail and Bolhuis 2001).

The general argument for inclusivity is Darwinian. Genetically and ontogenetically, human beings are just one part of a massive radiation of species in time where unique characters are dwarfed by massive cross-species communalities in the majority of characters. Species-specific differences can be important – these are often much more marked along the phylogenetic scale (e.g., echo-location in the dolphin) – but such differences are best characterized *after* a proper scientific account of cross-species communalities. Such communalities are particularly strong for the systems controlling the fundamental emotions, and individual differences in these systems (*ex hypothesi*, personality). Cognition is just one (albeit important) component of these systems.

Love and hatred are common to the whole of sensitive creation, [and] their causes ... are of so simple a nature that they may easily be suppos'd to operate on mere animals. (David Hume (1739/1985), *A Treatise on Human Nature* (London: Penguin))

Truly unique characters (as opposed to character combinations) are also extremely rare and the number of nominally unique human characters much fewer than is commonly believed (McNaughton 1989; Macphail

1996; Cahill, McGaugh and Weinberger 2001). For example, tool use (Tebbich, Taborsky, Fessl and Blomqvist 2001); language capability (Macphail 1996); and even culture, a higher order externalization of our cognitions (Rendell and Whitehead 2001; Pepperberg and Lynn 2000; Whiten 2001) all appear to occur in other species. Chimpanzee cultures reveal 'patterns of variation far more extensive than have previously been documented for any animal species except human' (Whiten *et al.* 1999, p. 682); and, as a result, chimpanzee cultures cannot be cleanly separated from human cultures (Boesch and Tomasello 1998). In this respect, the orang-utan appears truly 'the old man of the forest' (Smuts 2004). Cross-species continuity seems to be the rule; it is not the exception.

Fallacy 2: cognitive anthropocentrism

We may accept that humans are 'just an improved form of ape' but feel that for emotion and personality the nominal 2 per cent difference between human and chimpanzee genomes is sufficient justification for a belief that we have cognition and they do not – or, at least, not a sufficiently developed cognitive system to be useful for understanding human data. To disavow anthropocentrism may seem, then, to reject a role for cognition in emotion and personality. To the contrary, cognition is seen as central to emotion and personality in all species. Arguably the role of cognition will be better understood (especially in terms of mechanism) when it is tied to biological, and particularly neuropsychological, constructs. A cognitive psychology without neurobiology lacks any connection to the rest of science – and little chance of making sense of underlying processes. But this is not to argue for a pure reductionism. A neurobiology without cognition would have little relevance to psychology – and indeed little way of making global sense of its detailed findings. What is required, then, is parallel, interlinked study at the cognitive and neural levels. For many phenomena, translation between them will require an additional sub-cognitive level (Smolensky 1988) of which 'neural network' models are the most obvious example. One of the strengths of RST is its explicit attempt to achieve this goal (see Pickering, chapter 16).

Of course, some specific human cognitions may be qualitatively different from those of *all* non-human species. But this is just the standard caveat for all generic biological research that each species differs somewhat from others. Human cognitions depend on the same fundamental neural machinery as those of other animals. There are massive similarities in organization, components, pharmacological responses and many other features of the brains of mammals as a class.

Certainly, there are constraints on cognition that derive directly from biology (you cannot comprehend the aesthetics of colour if you are born completely colour blind), but the influence of biology goes beyond mere constraints to the very structure and processes of cognition.

In a fundamental sense it can never be proved that different species have the same kinds of cognitions, however close their behaviour or neural machinery is shown to match. But to argue this is little short of a counsel of despair. Using this criterion, we can never prove that your cognition is the same as mine, or indeed that you have cognitions as such at all. On such a view there can be no 'cognitive science'. One might counter this by referring to the similarities in neural structure and behavioural phenomenology across individuals. But this argument for commonality holds equally well for the relations across species.

To take a biological perspective is not to imply that all aspects of cognition can be understood biologically. Some aspects of the cognitions of *any species* can only be understood in terms of their historical and social context. Many anthropologists would argue that different peoples have different cognitions by virtue of their different cultures. For example, the Yanomamo Indians, who live in Southern Venezuela and the adjacent portions of northern Brazil, like to be described as the 'fierce people' and are often at war with neighbouring tribes (Chagnon 1977). They have their own customs, marriage system, hierarchy, etc. and their lack of material culture is more than compensated by the richness and complexity of their theological concepts, myths and legends. Their ideas of the cosmos, origin myth, the soul and shamans are very unlike that of the high-rise Manhattan dweller. There is no merit in trying to explain these differences of cognition in biological terms.

However, such salient differences in superficial content mask deeper similarities that are taken for granted: they have a marriage system, they have hierarchies, they have an origin myth, and they have shamans. These in turn mask even greater underlying similarities in processes: in how cultural information is transmitted; how facts about the world are learned; and how facts and beliefs can be distorted. In the specific case of associative learning, the basic underlying processes of neural plasticity are likely to be identical across all species. In what *fundamental* ways are the Yanomamo-Manhattan cultural differences qualitatively distinct from the cultural differences (learned patterns of behaviour) observed in isolated populations of chimpanzees? Or, for that matter, do they differ in their means of transmission and implementation from the cultural differences observed in killer whales? (Whales teach their young the best method to ride the surf onto, and off, the beach; they teach them to attack prey, and to recognize the characteristic sound of engines of tuna-trawlers for an easy meal.) They *must* have the mental processes that we like to refer to as cognitions in human beings.

Of course, the particular stimulus (perhaps something you just read) that causes your emotion will not produce the same result in other animals. But that is equally true of human animals who speak a different language, or of any individual of any species that merely had different life experience, or indeed yourself on different occasions. Despite such variations in the effects of eliciting stimuli, however, brain activation is similar across individuals and occasions with different elicitations of the same basic perceptual or emotional state. Importantly, the brain activation associated with any particular state in human animals occurs in homologous parts of the brain in non-human ones.

Our concern should not, then, be with these superficial differences, which are often highly salient in the human animal, but are dependent on individual history. Our concern should be with the more general underlying cognitive processes that are common to cultures and that are tied to neurobiological processes. The stimulus that elicits your fear may be arbitrary but the processes required to make that stimulus fearful are quite general and the fear itself is a stereotyped compound of cognitive, affective and bodily tone. At this level of description, the marked similarities between non-human and human animals are obvious.

Fallacy 3: language is cognition

It is possible to accept that the neural organization of cognitive centres and so cognitive processes is the same across species but nonetheless argue that the content of those cognitions is categorically different because of some emergent property of human cognitive processing – in particular, language.

However, this view is a result of the fact that the *discussion* of cognition is necessarily verbal and that any inherently non-verbal aspects of cognition cannot easily be shared. Cognitions are also often thought to be most easily manipulated and assessed in humans using the verbal channel. (It should be noted, however, that delusions and phobic cognitions are more frequently altered by guided experience or drugs than by rational argument or persuasion.) Cognitions tend, therefore, to be perceived by those who analyse them as necessarily or at least substantially verbal – and nothing approaching our level of verbal ability appears to be present in the standard laboratory subject, the rat.

When linking panic disorder with the periaqueductal grey, one of us (McNaughton 2002) found it convenient to say that 'where [panic disorder] does present, the most dramatic associated cognition, "I am going to die" is what we would expect if a normal person were very close to a predator. This type of situation provides an animal analogue, e.g., a rat faced with a cat, that is sensitive to panicolytic drugs.'

For one neurobiologist of our acquaintance, at least, this labelling of the rat's cognition as 'I am going to die' looked like a joke or at least a poorly-chosen metaphor.

Certainly, a rat does not have the equipment to verbalize its cognition. But many would agree that the rat nose-to-nose with a cat would, in a sense *feel* very much like you or I would if we were nose-to-nose with a lion. The rat, like us, would experience an immense compulsion to leave the vicinity, coupled with palpitations, release of adrenaline, etc. But, equally importantly, if you have ever been in a truly threatening situation you should agree that, like the rat, you would not verbalize sub-vocally 'I'm going to die'; indeed verbalization of any sort would be blocked by the racing of your pure thoughts. 'I'm going to die' is merely how we interpret and describe the feeling, post-mortem as it were. The phrase is then, in our language, the closest we can get to what would be running through our heads at that precise moment. But, what was running through the animal's head would not be language, irrespective of whether the animal is human or non-human. *Talk* about emotion is not the same thing as the emotion itself.

Nor is emotion necessary to demonstrate the uncoupling of thought and language. We can certainly verbalize silently, and run verbal arguments through our head. But a moment's consideration will usually allow us to realize that the thoughts behind a normal argument run much faster than the words used to express it. Indeed, multiple strands of possible upcoming lines of argument can be run through our mind in the time it takes for one line to be verbalized. There is even imaging evidence that we make decisions hundreds of milliseconds before we are consciously aware of them (Gray 2004) and this conscious awareness must be more hundreds of milliseconds ahead of verbal translation of the associated cognition.

It is also worth noting that there are mental operations that cannot be verbalized, which we would label as 'cognitive'. Mental rotation is one example. One can describe the phenomenon to someone else: it involves deciding which of two mirror images matches a copy of one of them displayed rotated with respect to them. But *doing* mental rotation does not involve verbalization. The evidence is that it involves the actual rotation, in the brain, of the test image – a rotation that occurs at a fixed rate and is totally unconscious.

Modern cognitive psychology does not, of course, equate cognition with words. But we have dealt with this fallacy at length because so much manipulation of human cognition is based on word usage. For example, *cognitive*-behavioural therapy not only stresses the importance of thoughts, attributions, etc., but typically operates by trying to alter attributions via verbal routes (but not, be it noted, by logical argument). Arguments for the uniqueness of humans also very seldom focus on non-verbal examples.

Let us take more complex emotional phenomena, compulsions and obsessions, which when they are excessive in frequency or dysfunctional in type, allow diagnosis of Obsessive Compulsive Disorder (OCD). Many people would grant that a rat could have a compulsion (e.g., highly repetitive risk assessment behaviour in the absence of a predator); but could the rat have an obsession? Obsessions are 'a bridge too far', even for some strictly neurobiological psychologists. However, much of the rat's information processing could be 'obsessive' in the same sense that a human being's would be. The rat would attend selectively to possible sources of danger; other potentially important stimuli in the environment would be ignored; and usual motor plans would be disrupted. All of this could occur in the absence of overt behaviour. The parallel between rat and human seems fairly obvious with functional obsessions (such as the checking of the whereabouts of offspring). But even dysfunction is not specific to humans. Experimental neurosis can be produced in other species in much the same way as post-traumatic stress disorder in human beings. In a rat, this would disrupt cognitive processing producing a mental life that was 'obsessed' with threat. The fact that the rat cannot talk about being obsessed is irrelevant: if we are to restrict cognitive processes to verbalizations then we would have to eliminate, as we have seen above, many of the most complex human cognitions! Certainly, with OCD, the source of the obsession in the initial stages of the disease appears senseless, intrusive and non-verbalizable. It is only when we try and analyse the condition that words become involved. Even here, words are usually chosen as the cheapest means of assessment rather than the best.

Thus cognitions proper are internal and silent despite the need for verbalization *or some other behaviour* as evidence for their nature and existence. As evidence of internal states, verbal behaviour may be no better and no worse, in principle, than any other kind of behaviour. Internal verbalization may even work to deceive us about the true nature of our own cognitions, especially when those are pathological.

Cognitions are pre-verbal and indeed often, pre-conscious (Velmans 1991) and pre-volitional (Libet 1985).

Fallacy 4: cognitions are emotionally neutral

Even if one is not thinking in terms of verbalization, cognition (and particularly 'reason') can seem peculiarly human. Cognitions are seen as pure, valence-free, ideas. We would not expect rats to indulge in mental arithmetic. But, because we cannot use the verbal channel, non-human animals must be judged by their behaviour and this can be viewed as solely the result of emotion. This allows us to believe that humans are the only possessors of pure, emotion-free, cognition.

But perception and action are more mixed in the brain than this account allows. Ironically, it is the study of the perception and production of language that has produced some of the clearest evidence for perception and action being quite generally intertwined (MacKay 1987).

It also appears that language originated more as an efficient way of communicating emotions rather than pure ideas. Monitoring of conversations in a university cafeteria, peopled by university students and academic staff, has shown that the vast majority of language is used to determine who did what and with what and to whom and not to discuss emotionally neutral concepts (Dunbar 1992). The world still awaits a TV channel that screens only neutral information (all 'information' channels are contaminated by infotainment).

Verbalization, then, appears to have evolved as a specialization of emotional expression – essentially a form of grooming (Dunbar 1992) – that has only then been exapted to allow less emotionally laden communication. This idea is consistent with the fact that the brain areas devoted to the understanding and production of language in the dominant hemisphere are devoted to the understanding and production of emotional expression in the non-dominant hemisphere. The latter are also fully capable of supporting language if the dominant hemisphere is damaged early in development (Ogden 1988, 1989).

Now, this is not to deny the existence of pure thoughts ('$2 + 2 = 4$') that can be essentially motivation-free. But these are relatively rare and their proper manipulation requires considerable training. Indeed, as academics, we know all too well that formal education takes many years, often unsuccessfully, to attempt to develop such motivation-free thoughts. In both the uneducated and highly educated, thoughts are typically embedded in a motivational framework. In any case, the cognitions involved in emotion *are* embedded in a motivational framework. This said, even rats can have 'pure thoughts' (see Fallacy 8).

Fallacy 5: cognitions are unconstrained

We have so far dealt with what cognitions are not. We have not yet dealt with what we mean by 'cognition'. Many cognitive scientists believe that cognitions are knowledge-level mental representations that are not constrained (apart from in an obviously trivial sense) by the brain. When applied to emotion and personality, these scientists believe that personal meaning, values and other cognitions are the only important constructs as they are hardware-independent (see below). Most forms of cognitive therapy are predicated on the belief that disordered emotion results from 'irrational' thinking (irrationality implying less a lack of logic than the presence of self-defeating cognitions).

In its most general form, a true lack of constraint would imply that an intact brain can have an infinite number of different cognitions. But there are obvious storage and processing limitations: we cannot possibly remember the correct sequence of the 3 billion base pairs that comprise the human genome.

But what of flexible cognitive content (the human equivalent of the data stored in a digital computer)? What about qualitative rather than quantitative constraints? A few moments thought should show that cognitions must be constrained within a particular person or species. In the same way that perception of colour is impossible for the colour blind, cognitions of certain sorts are impossible for those with other neural birth defects or with focal brain dysfunction. Focal brain dysfunction is particularly interesting as it shows gaps in cognition and cognitive performance that can be remarkably selective. For example, a person may be incapable of naming only one particular class of object (e.g., living as opposed to non-living). Equally, schizophrenia (involving loose connection of thought streams), delusions (involving distorted conceptions of reality), mania (involving distorted decision-making) and paranoia (involving distorted attribution of motives) all show that so called 'normal' thinking depends on neural and chemical systems that can suffer from quite selective dysfunctions.

Why, then, is it not obvious that there are gaps in our cognitive armoury? Well, first, it should be noted that the gaps are often obvious, but only when they are in someone else's armoury. Agraphia, aphasia and various agnosias or even everyday misattribution are striking when we see them in others. 'But of course' we, the general community, do not suffer from these by definition.

But, we should note that the comparison can also be made in the reverse direction. Autistic savants can carry out mental operations that are starkly incomprehensible to the rest of us. They thus define mental operations of which a human brain could be capable but that seem available only at the expense of other faculties. Likewise, where differences can be determined in general between male and female functions and brain organization, there is evidence of trade-offs (Kimura 1992). Specific capacities brought to a high pitch appear to reduce or translocate other capacities within the brain and removal of the non-dominant half of the brain results in migration of dominant functions (Ogden 1988, 1989). Even in the intact adult brain, expansion of cortical representations of some entities are at the expense of the representations of adjacent ones (Nudo, Milliken, Jenkins and Merzenich 1996). Different people may have had their cognitions constrained in different ways but their very differences demonstrate that cognition is constrained.

It is also important to consider the constraints that are imposed on higher-order cognition by perception. A cognition, defined as the representation of some fact about the world within some symbology of which a mind is capable, is a deduction or inference. Any percept can be thought of as a cognition (although some may prefer to distinguish individual percepts from clusters of percepts or rules relating to them). Yet even the simplest percept is an inference from available evidence based on a coherent picture of the world. It melds bottom-up and top-down information. What we see is not the world. It is subject to illusions that result from the detailed physiology of your peripheral systems. It is also subject to illusions based on our expectations, including socially derived expectations. Thus, even 'veridical perception' is a distortion of the world that in turn will affect those cognitions that derive from that perception.

Fallacy 6: cognitions are hardware-free

There is a subtler variant of Fallacy 5 that deserves separate consideration. Some cognitive theorists hold the belief that cognitive processes cannot, in principle, be related to neural processes since they are different philosophical things (Matthews 2000; Matthews, Derryberry and Siegle 2000; Matthews 1997). Important in this regard is the hardware-software distinction which most cognitive psychologists would endorse as marking cognition apart from neural processes. As one prominent cognitive theorist in personality, Gerald Matthews, stated clearly:

There is a remaining difference regarding the hardware-software distinction, which I (along with most cognitive psychologists) do not see as a straw man. Philosophically, everything is doubtless the same brain/mind stuff, but development of coherent and empirically testable models requires choices to be made about which of the different descriptive languages of hardware and software (and intentionality) is appropriate for the research problem at hand. A conservative position is that these languages are not readily compatible with one another, and trying to describe software constructs in hardware terms is an arduous task (though connectionism may help). I have some sympathy with the more radical Pylyshyn-Newell position that there are some emergent software phenomena that cannot be reduced to neural constructs ... [There is also] the cognitive science argument that rule-bound computational systems ('software') are not readily reducible to physical processes ('hardware'). One wouldn't try to explain the operation of MS Word in terms of silicon, so is it really wise to apply hardware explanations to brain software? (Matthews, Personal Communication, 26 May 1999).

Note that this point of view does not require either limitless hardware, or even limitless possible encodings of information within the hardware. All it requires is that the flexibility of programming of the machine is sufficiently great that the output from it (while constrained to what may be a considerable extent) is much more determined by the software currently loaded than the hardware into which it has been loaded.

There is a risk in over-applying the silicon computer metaphor. Certainly, your mother tongue cannot be predicted from the structure of your brain. Nor is a neural analysis appropriate if we want to find out from you what you had for breakfast. In respect to the specific details of much current content, your mind is like the computer. But the computer is designed to be a truly general machine. The brain and mind, by contrast, co-evolved and both have been shaped by Darwinian processes – much of the 'programming' is therefore 'hardwired' and much more like a robot that has been designed to perform some specific set of tasks than a general-purpose computer. Genes operate on the developing brain (in interaction with the environment) to deliver mental characteristics that interact with the environment to generate behaviours that are then selected for. In some cases the selection of such genes has given rise to quite specific 'innate' reactions to equally specific classes of external stimuli. This has been particularly studied with a rat's fear of a cat or a duck's fear of a hawk. But the human species has similar innate selectivities. Separation anxiety, fear of the dark and fear of spiders are among a host of 'cognitively' unlikely emotional reactions. They attach selectively to particular objects (spiders even in countries where these are not venomous) and not others (guns). These selectivities are best explained by in-built neural tendencies rather than by current developmental history (although developmental triggers are often required for the behaviours to appear).

Returning to the computer analogy, there is one way that the brain is quite unlike a digital computer. You cannot suddenly reprogram the visual cortex for auditory processing, but you could easily load Micro-Soft PowerPoint© into memory locations that just a moment ago stored MicroSoft Word©. The software of the computer can run from any part of the memory segments of the hardware:[1] the brain and mind are very different in this important respect.[2] This difference is not trivial, because relatively hardwired emotion processes seem designed to respond to any adequate eliciting stimuli in a highly structured manner and the triggers for these emotion processes are specific classes of cognition – the identity of which must be similarly hardwired. The highest cognitive levels, found in the cortex, allow specific identification of arbitrary signals. But these are then assigned meanings that exercise control over lower brain stem and limbic structures. Cognitive-behavioural therapy works precisely because it operates on cognitions to alter the assignment of stimuli as inputs to the lower brain systems of emotion.

Emotion processes also drive cognitions. Neurotic people are hypervigilant to threat and assign more threatening meanings to motivationally ambiguous stimuli. These biases arise because of the specific neurochemistry of inputs to crucial structures involved in monitoring the environment. We can change these neurochemical processes and so the person's cognitions by appropriate drug treatment.

Fallacy 7: radical behaviourism

The aberration of radical behaviourism has led many behavioural scientists to throw out the baby with the bath water. This is because the radical behaviourist revolution in psychology has generated a common residual fallacy, peculiarly afflicting only scientists and not the general public. Many personality theorists feel that biopsychology, learning theory and other analyses of non-humans are solely concerned with stimulus-response relationships. As such, these disciplines are held to be irrelevant to analysis of the sophisticated products of human cognition.

Simple behavioural observations, quite devoid of the ghost of introspection, make clear that behaviour is controlled by cognition. The nature of a goal is held in the animal's mind: its behaviour is not simply controlled

---

[1] Note that the software is not indifferent to the hardware. An IBM program will not run (without recompilation) on a MAC and will not run, or often fit, in an older IBM machine. A program cannot run on a hard disk, it needs a CPU.

[2] The brain has a certain degree of plasticity, and reprogramming is possible on a longer timescale. For example, in those blind from birth the spatial processing units normally driven by vision may acquire auditory input; and, in animals like the blind mole rat, evolutionary rewiring of other inputs to what was visual cortex is complete (Catania 2002). But this is much more like rebuilding the machine than reprogramming it.

by some chain of stimulus-response connections (McNaughton 1989; Cahill, McGaugh and Weinberger 2001). Animals immediately produce completely novel response sequences to achieve their unchanged internal goal when their original response is blocked (Towe and Luschei 1981; Hinde 1966). Internal representations of the external world are not unique to the human species.

Cognition also plays a deeper role in the observed actions. Physiological evidence shows that the cognitive restructuring that is the primary 'response' to 'conditioning' is the generation of an appropriate novel mental structure and not simply the recurrence of an older mental structure. Conditioning can result in physiological reactions that are quite different from those elicited by the conditional or unconditional stimulus before conditioning (Brady 1975a, 1975b) but that are entirely appropriate to the *anticipation* of the arrival of the unconditional stimulus. Learning does not, then, always (or necessarily) involve stimulus substitution[3] (Pavlov 1927). The behavioural changes observed by learning theorists, consequently, are evidence for new cognitions.

Of course, given their relatively larger brain, we would expect human beings to experience more elaborate and richer cognitions than the rat. We also know that our visual world is richer, being in colour whereas the rat's is not. Conversely, the rat's olfactory world is much richer than ours. But this does not mean that rat vision (or rat cognition during panic, or rat olfaction) is fundamentally different from the human variety, except in the trivial sense that the rat's cognition will be different from the chimpanzee's – we use the word 'trivial' to emphasize the much more important cross-species continuities.

Fallacy 8: silent cognitions

A weaker form of the radical behaviourist fallacy derives from the fact that cognitions, per se, are behaviourally silent. We know that we have thoughts that do not lead to behaviour. While our only evidence for *another* person's cognitions is behaviour (including verbalization as behaviour), we infer silent cognitions in them from the combination of this behaviour and our own experience. But we resist making this inference with non-human animals. Indeed, strictly, we should not make it even with other people on the basis solely of our own experience. It is tempting, therefore, to see non-human animals as not having any mental

---

[3] Stimulus substitution: the acquisition by a previously neutral conditional stimulus of responses elicited by a motivationally significant unconditional stimulus.

processes that are behaviourally silent and hence as not having cognitions in the 'true human' form.

Simple behavioural observations, nonetheless, can show that the knowledge that ultimately guides the behaviour of a rat or pigeon can be behaviourally silent while it is being learned and become evident only later, as in demonstrations of latent learning (Kimble 1961; Mackintosh 1974) and 'sensory preconditioning' (Dickinson 1980). Sensory preconditioning[4] is something of a misnomer, with the term 'preconditioning' reflecting the radical behaviourist fallacy that conditioning (i.e., learning) can only have occurred when a response changes. 'Silent conditioning' would better describe the fact that a rat can learn that a tone follows a light as easily as the fact that a shock follows the light. All conditioning would clearly be the same if we did not require behavioural evidence for its occurrence. Likewise, the same behaviour results whether a particular cognition is elicited by a conditioned or by an innate stimulus.

Fallacy 9: the cortex is the seat of cognition

This is a fallacy linked to a particular view of neuroanatomy. The idea is that the neocortex is the primary engine of cognition, the seat of our self-awareness. Indeed, there are those who have argued that fish, for example, can have no perception of pain simply because they lack a neocortex (Rose 2002). Animals with relatively less neocortex, it is argued, cannot have our kind of cognitions. But, if we look at the cytoarchitecture of the cortex we find that the most recently evolved, most 'neo', neocortical cells are those closest to the peripheral inputs and outputs (Pandya and Barnes 1987). Each new level of the system has evolved by being interposed between the pure sensory periphery and a core of ancient essentially noncortical material (Nauta and Feirtag 1986).

---

[4] Sensory preconditioning is demonstrated with three experimental phases, the latter two allowing inferences to be drawn about processes occurring in the first:

Phase 1: Stimulus A (a light) is paired with stimulus B (a tone) in a series of classical (Pavlovian) conditioning-like trials. Neither A nor B produces any observable response, before or after the conditioning-like trials.

Phase 2: Stimulus B (the tone) is next paired with a food in a series of conditioning trials. Initially the subject salivates when the food is presented; after a number of trials, they salivate when B is presented.

Phase 3: Stimulus A is now presented to the subject without any previous pairing of A with food. In experiments of this type it is usually found that the subject will salivate when A is presented.

A has never been paired with food. Before Phase 2 it did not produce salivation. In Phase 3 it produces salivation showing that during Phase 1 the animal learned the relation between A and B. But, because neither was motivationally significant at the time of learning, it did not demonstrate this change in its cognitions by any change in behaviour.

The highest order processing (perhaps self or consciousness) therefore occurs in the oldest centres with the most archaic cytoarchitecture. This suggests that such 'top-end' processing exists, in however primitive a form, in the earliest creatures that can be said to have a telencephalon. Indeed, treating the end product as integration between modalities and combining perception and action into a unitary whole, it must have existed in a limited form primordially with increases in brain capacity only increasing the number and resolution of the sensory filters and motor mechanisms attached to it.

Before we turn to the specifics of emotion and personality research, we must stress that we are not arguing here that all relevant cognitive processes in human beings can be readily found and understood in non-human animals. The rat with its relatively small brain cannot have values, beliefs or expectations of the same order as you or I. But the nature of the rat's processes can inform us about human processes. In some cases, it should do so more readily because of the relative simplicity of the fundamental cognitions of an animal reared and tested in an impoverished environment. In other cases it may do so more readily because basic processes are not interacting with additional more complex ones. Our argument is, then, that both biological and cognitive constructs derived from work on non-human animals are relevant to an analysis of human emotion and personality. The human processes include and will often be largely like the non-human. That does not mean they all have to be exactly like.

Nor, even if all processes could be shown to be the same in all species, would we want to say that there could be nothing left to explain in a qualitative way in human beings. But the relevance of this uniqueness pales into insignificance once the considerable cross-species similarities are appreciated, especially in basic emotional processes.

Biology *and* cognition

Science has not yet reached a point where it can be shown that cognitive and biological explanations of emotion and personality *must* always be intertwined. But it would seem to us sensible to entertain this possibility seriously. This section turns to a positive path of identifying the integral links between biology and cognition, showing how personality research, and much of psychology in general, requires what we might term a *biocognitive* perspective.

Even at this early stage of scientific development, a common language would help to unite cognitive and biological levels of explanation. This does not imply that we may not have purely cognitive or neural theories within limited phenomenological domains. But it would seem wise to try to develop constructs that, in theoretical and operational terms, may be translated across the various levels of analysis. In the specific areas of emotion and personality, RST seems to go a long way to achieving this aim.

Brain-mind relations

It is a given in modern cognitive and behavioural neuroscience (although still contested in some areas of psychology) that if you change the activity of the brain, you change the mind. There are already neural prosthetics that deliver auditory input to the deaf, visual input to the blind and control of the world to the paralysed. Less exotically, drugs can produce global changes in perception, mood and cognition. Above all, genetics, development and physical trauma, such as closed head injury or brain-splitting operations, can produce changes in neural circuits sufficient to produce massive, and usually consistent, changes in specific mental capacity and predisposition.

More recently, imaging techniques have led to a wealth of studies that show that if you change the mind (via external perceptual input) you change the activity of the brain in consistent ways. This activity usually changes in those structures previously implicated by invasive brain manipulation in the control of the relevant mental processes. For example, visual input activates the striate cortex and lesions of the striate cortex produce functional blindness. Faces showing fear activate the amygdala (Morris, Frith, Perrett et al. 1996; Morris, Friston, Büchel et al. 1998; Breiter, Etcoff, Whalen et al. 1996) and amygdala lesions produce impaired recognition of fearful expressions (Broks, Young, Maratos et al. 1998; Adolphs, Tranel, Damasio and Damasio 1994, 1995). There is also a wealth of other data implicating the amygdala in the control of fear responses more generally (Aggleton 1993; Davis 1992; LeDoux 1994, 1998).

To treat the mind as a property of brain activity is not, however, to give physiological events causal primacy over psychological events. Certainly, any particular internal psychological change will be represented by a physiological change. For example, learning of a particular fact will be represented by altered strengths of particular synapses and blocking this alteration will prevent learning (LeDoux 1993, 1994; Gewirtz and Davis 1997; Lee and Kim 1998). But it is the *information* encoded in external events, not the physical nature of the neural changes, that is critical for the details of the underlying mental and physical changes. The same can be true even when there are traumatic physical changes in the brain. Post-traumatic Stress Disorder (PTSD) results in major physical changes in the brain, including loss of neurones in areas like the hippocampus (Bremner, Randall, Scott *et al.* 1995; Nadel and Jacobs 1996). Yet the disorder is in many cases the result of an *interpretation* of a pattern of light energy (visual images) where the light cannot itself damage the brain physically. Thus, what is best thought of as an internal mental event (a perception of threat) can produce physical damage in the brain (of course, 'mental' events are no less neural events). Nor need psychologically induced changes in brain morphology be pathological. Rats exposed to complex and interesting environments develop larger cortices.

The linking of these different types of observation is nicely exemplified in analysis of spatial memory. A spatial mapping task activates the hippocampus (Maguire, Frackowiak and Frith 1997); and lesions of the hippocampus impair spatial learning (Morris, Garrud, Rawlins and O'Keefe 1982). Most interestingly, sufficient use of the cognitive facility of spatial mapping, as shown in London taxi drivers, seems to have the physiological effect of increasing the size of the hippocampus (Maguire, Gadian, Johnsrude *et al.* 2000).

Emotion and personality

Many aspects of cognition, emotion and personality can be understood by studying homologous behavioural and neural phenomena in non-human animals. This position is epitomized in recent higher level applications of the concept of the BIS (Gray and McNaughton 2000, ch 11):

Inasmuch, then, as the septo-hippocampal system is involved in cognitive and memorial processing, a consequence of our theory is that pathological anxiety itself is likely to result, at least in some cases, from abnormal cognitive and mnemonic processing (McNaughton 1997). This brings the anxiety aspects of our theory quite close to more recent cognitive theories of generalised anxiety (Mathews 1993; Eysenck 1992). 'Cognitive dysfunction' suggests affective neutrality and a focusing of hippocampal processing on cortical information. But when emergency threatens, the messages received from older structures located in the brainstem take precedence and a fundamentally cognitive dysfunction can have, nonetheless, affective consequences ... It has recently been suggested that the critical pathology in this disorder lies in the functioning of cognitive, particularly working memory, *system* (Eysenck and Calvo 1992; Eysenck 1992) or the control of attentional resources (Mathews and MacLeod 1994). While the cognitive processes we invoke are different, our theory has much in common with these views, sharing in particular the idea that generalised anxiety is primarily a cognitive disorder.

Personality, in particular, can be viewed as largely independent of the specific cognition through which we assess its effect at any particular point in time. Personality acts as a general filter on all evaluation. As noted by Gray and McNaughton (2000, pp. 366–367):

> Neuroticism reflects principally a *perceptual* bias (that is to say, a *cognitive* bias ... [requiring] interpretation of what is perceived) towards the identification or magnification of threat of all kinds [both fear and anxiety] ... Anxiolytic drug treatment, in contrast, would alter the increased negative biasing associated with conflict, and so reduce anxiety only ... Neuroticism [should] amplify the operation of systems that detect threat generally, and thus the entirety of the networks that subserve defence ... Cognitive behavioural therapy works in the reverse manner, by dampening the operation of these same systems.

Thus RST, despite being predominantly based on data obtained from rats, emphasizes that cognitions, including high-level cognitions, are fundamental to threat processing in general (Neuroticism) and conflict between cognitive goals specifically (Anxiety).

With respect to clinical conditions, there is no question that the cognitions of a specific human individual in a particular situation will be different from those of a non-human animal. But they will also be quite different from those of other human individuals. Indeed it is the extent of certain individual differences that allow us to identify certain thoughts as pathological. However, cognitive biases, personality factors and most obviously the effects of drugs are factors that operate on *broad classes* of stimuli rather than on specific individual stimuli. Understanding of the resultant behaviour (which we need as scientific evidence) depends much more on categorizing such a class in terms of its affective value (e.g., immediate threat) than its cognitive complexity (possibly relating to a disadvantaged childhood and unloving mother). Once it is accepted that non-human animals are also driven by cognition, they can give us a clearer view of the factors driving our own behaviour than will study restricted to human beings.

Conclusion

This chapter starts from the position that emotion and personality researchers *are* divided into cognitive and behavioural (neural) camps (Corr 2001; Matthews 1997; Matthews and Gilliland 1999; Matthews, Derryberry and Siegle 2000). This is likely to be the result, in both cases, of a tacit rejection of a joint cognitive-neural perspective – an either-or type of thinking that portrays these two perspectives as somehow mutually exclusive. We see them, by contrast, as necessarily complementary – each level of analysis filling gaps left by the other.

Amalgamation is also necessary between academic and clinical perspectives. We agree with Luu, Tucker and Derryberry (1998) that 'anxiety may be a necessary component (motivator) of normal planning and regulation of behaviour' (p. 577). In the case of clinical anxiety, the most pronounced feature is the excessive motivational bias towards threat. It is not the specific behaviours or affect which are distinguishable from non-pathological anxiety but their excessive occurrence. Here we come full circle, because it is with extreme clinical conditions that neural analysis and non-human homologies are most apparent. This is true in particular of impaired executive functions (e.g., planning). Clinically, these demonstrate the involvement of the frontal lobes in cognitive processes and, in doing so, also link cognition to emotion. It is difficult to think of a frontal lobe related cognitive impairment that does not also entail an emotional component. The evolution of the neocortex may then not have acted to divorce cognition from emotion but to elaborate on a relationship between perception and action as two sides of the same coin.

This chapter has tried to bring the two sides together – or, at least, to have drained some of the conceptual swamp-land barring the start of this journey. In particular, it has listed a number of fallacies that we believe continue to pervade psychology in general, but especially emotion and personality psychology, which is still re-emerging from the dark days of neglect. As noted by Corr (2004, p. 318):

Personality has long been the Cinderella of psychology: its scientific potential thwarted by psychoanalysis, social constructivism and statistical indeterminism, and neglected by experimental (cognitive) psychology.

As the contributors to this volume have shown, this dismal state of affairs is fast passing. Taken together with the other chapters in this volume, this chapter suggests that RST provides a general framework for the integration of the biological and cognitive into a biocognitive perspective, but this will be achieved only by putting to rest a number of diehard fallacies concerning the relevance of non-human animal data and concepts for human emotion and personality

References

Adolphs, R., Tranel, D., Damasio, H. and Damasio, A.R. (1994), Impaired recognition of emotion in facial expressions following bilateral damage to the human amygdala, *Nature*, 372, 669–672
(1995), Fear and the human amygdala, *Journal of Neuroscience*, 15, 5879–5891
Aggleton, J.P. (1993), The contribution of the amygdala to normal and abnormal emotional states, *Trends in Neuroscience*, 16, 328–333
Boesch, C. and Tomasello, M. (1998), Chimpanzee and human cultures, *Current Anthropology*, 39, 591–604

Brady, J. V. (1975a), Toward a behavioural biology of emotion, in L. Levi (ed.), *Emotions: their Parameters and Measurement* (New York: Raven Press), pp. 17–46

(1975b), Conditioning and emotion in L. Levi (ed.), *Emotions: their Parameters and Measurement* (New York: Raven Press), pp. 309–340

Breiter, H.C., Etcoff, N.L., Whalen, P.J., Kennedy, W.A., Rauch, S.L., Buckner, R.L., Strauss, M.M., Hyman, S.E. and Rosen, B.R. (1996), Response and habituation of the human amygdala during visual processing of facial expression, *Neuron*, 17, 875–887

Bremner, J.D., Randall, P., Scott, T.M., Bronen, R.A., Seibyl, J.P., Southwick, S.M., Delaney, R.C., McCarthy, G., Charney, D.S. and Innis, R.B. (1995), MRI-based measurement of hippocampal volume in patients with combat-related posttraumatic stress disorder, *American Journal of Psychiatry*, 152, 973–981

Broks, P., Young, A.W., Maratos, E.J., Coffey, P.J., Calder, A.J., Isaac, C.L., Mayes, A.R., Hodges, J.R., Montaldi, D., Cezayirli, E., Roberts, N. and Hadley, D. (1998), Face processing impairments after encephalitis: amygdala damage and recognition of fear, *Neuropsychologia*, 36, 59–70

Cahill, L., McGaugh, J.L. and Weinberger, N.M. (2001), The neurobiology of learning and memory: some reminders to remember, *Trends in Neurosciences*, 24, 578–581

Catania, K.C. (2002), The nose takes a starring role, *Scientific American*, 287, 38–43

Chagnon, N.A. (1977), *Yanomamo: The Fierce People* (London: Holt, Rinehart and Winston)

Corr, P.J. (2001), Testing problems in J. A. Gray's personality theory: a commentary on Matthews and Gilliland (1999), *Personality and Individual Differences*, 30, 333–352

(2004), Reinforcement sensitivity theory and personality, *Neuroscience and Biobehavioral Reviews*, 28, 317–332

Darwin, C. (1872, reprinted in 1965), *The Expression of the Emotions in Man and Animals* (Chicago, Illinois: University of Chicago Press)

Davis, M. (1992), The role of the amygdala in fear and anxiety, *Annual Review of Neuroscience*, 15, 353–375

Dickinson, A. (1980), *Contemporary Animal Learning Theory* (Cambridge: Cambridge University Press)

Dunbar, R. (1992), Why gossip is good for you, *New Scientist*, 28–31

Co-evolution of neocortex size, group size and language in humans, *Behavioral and Brain Sciences*, 16, 681–735

Eysenck, M. W. (1992), The nature of anxiety in A. Gale and M.W. Eysenck (eds.), *Handbook of Individual Differences: Biological Perspectives* (John Wiley and Sons), pp. 157–178

Eysenck, M.W. and Calvo, M.G. (1992), Anxiety and performance: the processing efficiency theory, *Cognition and emotion*, 6, 409–434

Gewirtz, J.C. and Davis, M. (1997), Beyond attention: the role of amygdala NMDA receptors in fear conditioning, *Behavioral and Brain Sciences*, 20, 618

Gray, J.A. (2004), *Consciousness: Creeping Up on the Hard Problem* (Oxford: Oxford University Press)

Gray, J.A. and McNaughton, N. (2000), *The Neuropsychology of Anxiety: an Enquiry into the Functions of the Septo-hippocamoal System* (2nd edn, Oxford: Oxford University Press)

Gray, J.R. and Braver, T.S. (2002), Personality predicts working-memory-related activation in the caudal anterior cingulate cortex, *Cognitive, Affective, and Behavioral Neuroscience*, 2, 64–75

Hinde, R.A. (1966), *Animal Behaviour* (New York: McGraw-Hill Book Company)

James, W. (1884), What is an emotion?, *Mind*, 9, 188–205

Kimble, G.A. (1961), *Hilgard and Marquis' Conditioning and Learning* (New York: Appleton-Century-Crofts)

Kimura, D. (1992), Sex differences in the brain, *Scientific American*, 267, 118–125

LeDoux, J.E. (1993), Emotional memory: in search of systems and synapses, *Annals of the New York Academy of Sciences*, 702, 149–157

(1994), Emotion, memory and the brain, *Scientific American*, 270, 50–59

(1998), Fear and the brain: where have we been, and where are we going?, *Biological Psychiatry*, 44, 1229–1238

Lee, H. and Kim, J.J. (1998), Amygdalar NMDA receptors are critical for new fear learning in previously fear-conditioned rats, *Journal of Neuroscience*, 18, 8444–8454

Libet, B. (1985), Unconscious cerebral initiative and the role of conscious will in voluntary action, *Behavioral and Brain Sciences*, 8, 529–566

Luu, P., Tucker, D.M. and Derryberry, D. (1998), Anxiety and the motivational basis of working memory, *Cognitive Therapy and Research*, 22, 577–594

MacKay, D.G. (1987), *The Organization of Perception and Action: a Theory for Language and Other Cognitive Skills* (New York: Springer-Verlag)

Mackintosh, N.J. (1974), *The Psychology of Animal Learning* (New York: Academic Press)

Macphail, E.M. (1996), Cognitive function in mammals: the evolutionary perspective, *Cognitive Brain Research*, 3, 279–290

Macphail, E.M. and Bolhuis, J.J. (2001), The evolution of intelligence: adaptive specializations *versus* general process, *Biological Reviews*, 76, 341–364

Maguire, E.A., Frackowiak, R.S.J. and Frith, C.D. (1997), Recalling routes around London: activation of the right hippocampus in taxi drivers, *Journal of Neuroscience*, 17, 7103–7110

Maguire, E.A., Gadian, D.G., Johnsrude, I.S., Good, C.D., Ashburner, J., Frackowiak, R.S.J. and Frith, C.D. (2000), Navigation-related structural change in the hippocampi of taxi drivers, *Proceedings of the National Academy of Sciences of the United States of America*, 97, 4398–4403

Mathews, A. (1993), Biases in processing emotional information, *The Psychologist*, 6, 493–499

Mathews, A. and MacLeod, C. (1994), Cognitive approaches to emotion and emotional disorders, *Annual Review of Psychology*, 45, 25–50

Matthews, G. (1997), An introduction to the cognitive science of personality and emotion in G. Matthews (ed.), *Cognitive Science Perspectives on Personality and Emotion* (Amsterdam: Elsevier), pp. 3–30

(2000), A cognitive science critique of biological theories of personality traits, *History and Philosophy of Psychology*, 2, 1–17

Matthews, G., Derryberry, D. and Siegle, G. J. (2000), Personality and emotion: cognitive science perspectives in S.E. Hampson (ed.), *Advances in Personality Psychology* (London: Routledge), pp. 199–237

Matthews, G. and Gilliland, K. (1999), The personality theories of H. J. Eysenck and J. A. Gray: a comparative review, *Personality and Individual Differences*, 26, 583–626

McNaughton, N. (1989), *Biology and Emotion* (Cambridge: Cambridge University Press)

(1997), Cognitive dysfunction resulting from hippocampal hyperactivity: a possible cause of anxiety disorder, *Pharmacology, Biochemistry and Behavior*, 56, 603–611

(2002), Aminergic transmitter systems in H. D'haenen, J.A. Den Boer, H. Westenberg and P. Willner (eds.), *Textbook of Biological Psychiatry* (John Wiley and Sons), pp. 895–914

Morris, J.S., Friston, K.J., Büchel, C., Frith, C.D., Young, A.W., Calder, A.J. and Dolan, R.J. (1998), A neuromodulatory role for the human amygdala in processing emotional facial expressions, *Brain*, 121, 47–57

Morris, J.S., Frith, C.D., Perrett, D.I., Rowland, D., Young, A.W., Calder, A.J. and Dolan, R.J. (1996), A differential neural response in the human amygdala to fearful and happy facial expressions, *Nature*, 383, 812–815

Morris, R.G.M., Garrud, P., Rawlins, J.N.P. and O'Keefe, J. (1982), Place navigation impaired in rats with hippocampal lesions, *Nature*, 297, 681–683

Nadel, L. and Jacobs, W. J. (1996), The role of the hippocampus in PTSD, panic and phobia in N. Kato (ed.), *The Hippocampus: Functions and Clinical Relevance* (Elsevier Science B. V.), pp. 455–463

Nauta, W.J.H. and Feirtag, M. (1986), *Fundamental Neuroanatomy* (New York: W. H. Freeman and Co.)

Nudo, R.J., Milliken, G.W., Jenkins, W.M. and Merzenich, M.M. (1996), Use-dependent alterations of movement representations in primary motor cortex of adult squirrel monkeys, *Journal of Neuroscience*, 16, 785–807

Ogden, J. (1988), Language and memory functions after long recovery periods in left-hemispherectomised subjects, *Neuropsychologia*, 26, 645–659

(1989), Visuospatial and other 'right-hemispheric' functions after long recovery periods in left-hemispherectomised subjects, *Neuropsychologia*, 27, 765–776

Pandya, D. N. and Barnes, C. L. (1987), Architecture and connections of the frontal lobe in E. Perceman (ed.), *The Frontal Lobe Revisited* (New York: IRBN Press), pp. 41–72

Pavlov, I.P. (1927), *Conditioned Reflexes* (London: Oxford University Press, G. V. Anrep (trans.))

Pepperberg, I.M. and Lynn, S.K. (2000), Possible levels of animal consciousness with reference to grey parrots (*Psittacus erithacus*), *American Zoologist*, 40, 893–901

Rendell, L. and Whitehead, H. (2001), Culture in whales and dolphins, *Behavioral and Brain Sciences*, 24, 309–324

Rose, J.D. (2002), The neurobehavioral nature of fishes and the question of awareness and pain, *Reviews in Fisheries Science*, 10, 1–38

Smolensky, P. (1988), On the proper treatment of connectionism, *Behavioral and Brain Sciences*, 11, 1–41

Smuts, B. (2004), Orangutan technology, *Scientific American*, 291, 112–114

Tebbich, S., Taborsky, M., Fessl, B. and Blomqvist, D. (2001), Do woodpecker finches acquire tool-use by social learning?, *Proceedings of the Royal Society of London.B:Biological Sciences*, 268, 2189–2193

Towe, A. L. and Luschei, E. S. (1981), Preface in A.L. Towe and E.S. Luschei (eds.), *Motor Coordination* (New York: Plenum Press), pp. vii–viii

Velmans, M. (1991), Is human information processing conscious?, *Behavioral and Brain Sciences*, 14, 651–726

Whiten, A. (2001), Imitation and cultural transmission in apes and cetaceans, *Behavioral and Brain Sciences*, 24, 359–360

Whiten, A., Goodall, J., McGrew, W.C., Nishida, T., Reynolds, V., Sugiyama, Y., Tutin, C.E.G., Wrangham, R.W. and Boesch, C. (1999), Cultures in chimpanzees, *Nature*, 399, 682–685

4   The behavioural activation
        system: challenges and opportunities

Alan D. Pickering and Luke D. Smillie

The influence of *Reinforcement Sensitivity Theory* (RST) on personality psychology has been far greater than Jeffrey Gray would ever have conceived. This is especially the case for the *Behavioural Activation System* (or *Behavioural Approach System*) (BAS), which was introduced to his model on a somewhat arbitrary basis, only to be embraced by others as a major organizing framework for trait explanation. In the last few years, RST has been substantially revised in a number of aspects (as discussed in other chapters of this book), particularly centring on the role of the *Behavioural Inhibition System* (BIS) and *Fight-Flight-Freeze System* (FFFS). This might give the impression that the changes in thinking about the BAS have been relatively minor. We would argue that this impression is misleading and that an equally radical review of the BAS is called for (as we have been arguing in a series of articles: Pickering and Gray 1999, 2001; Pickering 2004; Smillie, Pickering and Jackson 2006). In this chapter we highlight the opportunities ahead at this time of theoretical flux, sketch some of the challenges to be met by future research, and suggest what we believe may be some promising initial steps in this process.

A time for rethinking the BAS within RST

Like Gray's other brain-behavioural systems, such as the BIS, the BAS was originally defined in ethological terms (see Gray 1987c). While the BIS was originally seen as a mediator of responses to conditioned punishment and frustrative non-reward (although not any more, see McNaughton and Corr, chapter 2), the BAS was proposed as a mediator of conditioned signals of reward and relieving non-punishment. These two specific inputs were seen to elicit two specific behavioural outputs from the BAS: approach and active avoidance. Approach concerns locomotion towards signals of a reward, while active avoidance concerns locomotion away from signals of punishment (or, more correctly, towards signals of relief or safety). In both cases, the function of the behaviour is to bring the animal in contact with positive reinforcement; like a heat-seeking missile, to use the metaphor chosen by Gray. A more generalized view of the BAS has since been proposed (see Gray and McNaughton 2000): it is now thought to be activated by all signals of reward along with actual (i.e., unconditioned) rewarding stimuli.

Two conceptually distinct processes describe BAS-mediated effects of reward on behaviour (see Pickering and Gray 2001; Smillie, Dalgleish and Jackson, in press). The first we shall call the *motivational* effect of BAS activation by reward. This refers to the redirection of behaviour toward sources of reward, and invigoration of ongoing behaviour when a reward contingency is introduced. Through this process, the BAS has the effect of increasing the intensity and shaping the direction of rewarded behavioural output. The second effect we shall call the effect of BAS activation relating to *learning* or *reinforcement*. This refers to the redirection of attention and arousal resources toward the rewarding stimuli, facilitating increased information processing and the learning of stimulus-stimulus and stimulus-response contingencies. As we have noted for BAS-mediated behavioural outputs themselves, these two processes underlying that behaviour serve the single function of bringing the animal into contact with rewarding stimuli and states.

The relevance of Gray's reward system to human personality rests upon the assumption that there are individual differences in the sensitivity or *reactivity* of the BAS. Individual differences in the activation of the BAS by reward, as indicated by variation in behavioural responses of the kind we have just discussed, translate to individual differences in the susceptibility to motivational and reinforcing effects of rewarding stimuli. Such differences are, in turn, thought to characterize some major dimension of personality; identifying *which* major dimension of personality this might be has become an unexpectedly complicated enterprise. Gray originally suggested impulsivity as a candidate for the personality correlate of the BAS; however, as we shall discuss later, this proposal was almost entirely arbitrary. Because of this, we will adopt the term used by Pickering and Gray (2001), and refer to 'the BAS-related trait' throughout this chapter. In its most general form, then, RST proposes that individuals with high levels of the BAS-related trait should respond most strongly (as seen in consequent motivational and/or reinforcing effects) to input stimuli which activate the BAS.

In addition to specific behaviours and certain (although almost certainly unknown) personality manifestations, the BAS has been secondarily linked to the regulation of emotion. While not detailed in the original version of RST (e.g., Gray 1973), it has since become a point of wide agreement that the BAS produces positive affect when activated by reward (Fowles 1993). Furthermore, it is typically found that putative measures of BAS-reactivity are strongly associated with trait positive affectivity (e.g., Smillie and Jackson 2005; see also Gomez and Cooper, chapter 9). However, a growing body of literature suggests that the BAS may also be implicated in negative emotions in response to aversive events (see Carver 2004). This compelling research is at odds with the original formulation of the BAS, but, as we shall see in the following section, can be incorporated within more modern delineations of Gray's reward system.

This first section has outlined the BAS conceptually, and in terms of its supposed effects upon behaviour, personality and emotion. Much more remains to be said on these topics, especially concerning the identification of the BAS-related trait. First, however, it is necessary to delineate the BAS in neurophysiological terms.

Challenges and opportunities created by neuroscience research

In a masterful and wide-ranging review, Schultz (1998) summarized the evidence relating to reward systems in the brain as follows:

One of the principal neuronal systems involved in processing reward information appears to be the dopamine system. Behavioural studies show that dopamine projections to the striatum and prefrontal cortex play a central role in mediating the effects of rewards on approach behaviour and learning. (p. 1)

In line with this widely-held view, Gray has suggested (e.g., Gray 1987b; Pickering and Gray 1999) that the BAS is located, in part, within frontal and striatal brain regions that are richly innervated by ascending dopaminergic projections; thus, the biological basis of the BAS-related trait is proposed to be at least partly dopaminergic. Other personality theorists have proposed fundamental personality traits based on the functioning of an explicitly BAS-like system (e.g., Cloninger *et al.* 1993; Depue and Collins 1999; Zuckerman 1991), and they have each stressed that the biological basis of such traits is likely to involve variations in dopaminergic neurotransmission.

Perhaps the most widely cited research concerning dopaminergic responses to reward involves single-cell recording experiments in monkeys. These studies have shown that dopaminergic cells (in both the ventral tegmental area, VTA, or substantia nigra pars compacta, SNc) fire phasically in response both to primary rewards (e.g., an unsignalled drop of fruit juice placed into the animal's mouth) and to conditioned visual or auditory stimuli that have become valid predictors of reward. After learning has established the conditioned stimulus as a reward predictor, the primary reward no longer elicits phasic firing in the dopaminergic cell (see Brown, Bullock and Grossberg 1999 and Schultz 1998 for references and details). The dopaminergic cells, from which such recordings are taken, project widely to many brain regions, including the striatum (to both dorsal striatal structures such as the caudate and ventral striatal regions such as the nucleus accumbens), prefrontal cortex, and the limbic system.

These findings make it seem very likely that the firing of the ascending dopaminergic projection cells will form a key part of BAS functioning. The fact that they respond to both primary and conditioned rewards (although at different stages of learning), implies that the BAS will respond both to primary rewards and stimuli associated with these rewards. As noted earlier, while the BAS was originally thought to be activated only by conditioned rewards, the revised version (Gray and McNaughton 2000) no longer distinguishes between conditioned and unconditioned rewards, and has therefore fallen into line with the above neuroscience literature.[1] In addition, the phasic bursts of firing of these dopaminergic cells are thought to represent a reinforcement signal which controls subsequent learning (see Schultz 1998 and Pickering and Gray 2001 for details). This view, and wealth of associated data, strongly implies that the BAS is involved not only in the responses to (conditioned) reward stimuli, but also in the *process* by which initially neutral stimuli become associated with reward. Thus, a person with a highly reactive BAS would be expected to develop reward conditioning more rapidly and more strongly than a person with a less reactive BAS. Initially, this was another grey area within RST (see Gray 1987a) but we have noted elsewhere that the existing personality data indicate an influence of potentially BAS-related personality traits on the conditioning process itself (see the discussion of the study by Corr, Pickering and Gray 1995, in Pickering *et al.* 1997). Zinbarg and Mohlman (1998) responded to the uncertainties over this point by distinguishing between the standard ('motivational') version of RST and an 'associative' version in which BAS-related personality traits are predicted to correlate with the strength of the association formed between a conditioned stimulus and a reward. Once again, the neuroscience contributes to the debate, specifically by supporting an associative version of RST.

---

[1] Of course, the BAS must interface with consummatory systems; these have more-or-less hardwired and specific responses that are directed towards only unconditioned rewards.

There is another, somewhat surprising, implication of these animal data concerning the dopaminergic substrate of the BAS. To appreciate this point one must be familiar with the view that a reinforcement signal is thought to act as part of a so-called 'three-factor' learning rule. This rule is so named because it proposes that three separate components are necessary for synaptic modification (the neural substrate of learning) to occur. Let us consider this learning rule specifically in relation to the synapses which form the junction between cortical input terminals and the dendritic spines of the striatal neurons receiving those inputs. This is a major site for learning that is under the control of the BAS's dopaminergic projection system. Synaptic strengthening is proposed to occur only when: (i) the *presynaptic* terminal from the cortical input is activated; (ii) the *postsynaptic* striatal neuron is strongly depolarized (i.e., beyond the threshold for this cell to fire); and (iii) an appropriately-timed *reinforcement* signal has arrived at the synapse. As already noted, it is widely suggested that the dopamine projections (in this case, those projecting to the striatum) carry the reinforcement signal. The dopaminergic projection fibres contain varicosities (sites from which dopamine is released) and it is known that these varicosities are usually found in very close proximity to the corticostriatal synapses referred to above, a physical arrangement ideal for the proposed reinforcement action (see Figure 4.1 and Schultz 1998 for details).

Wickens and Kotter (1995), in an excellent review, summarize much of the relevant information relating to three-factor learning: the evidence implicating mesolimbic/nigrostriatal dopamine neurons in reinforcement mechanisms; the theoretical development of the three-factor rule and its utility in explaining reinforcement processes; and the electrophysiological evidence concerning the role of dopamine in synaptic plasticity in the striatum. Furthermore, Wickens and Kotter propose a specific set of neurophysiological mechanisms by which the firing of dopamine cells may act as a reinforcement signal within the three-factor learning rule framework. The full details are beyond the scope of this chapter and so only a very brief summary is given here. A critical component is the binding of dopamine at a specific sub-type of post-synaptic dopamine receptor (the D-1 sub-type), located on the dendritic spines of striatal neurons. Binding at these receptors is driven by phasic bursts of firing in the ascending dopamine cells (and recall that just these phasic bursts of firing occur in response to rewards, or to conditioned stimuli associated with reward). These dopaminergic events (factor three of the three-factor rule) interact with processes occurring at other synapses located on the same dendritic spines of the striatal neurons (specifically the corticostriatal synapses at the junctions

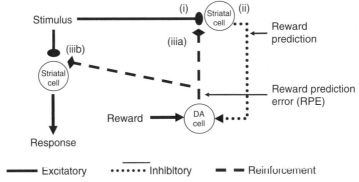

Figure 4.1 Schematic representation of three-factor learning and reward prediction error (RPE). Learning is thought to require: (i) activation of the presynaptic terminal by the stimulus; (ii) firing of the postsynaptic striatal neuron (which is involved in reward prediction); and (iii) the arrival of an appropriately-timed reinforcement signal at the synapse. This signal is provided by phasic dopamine cell firing and is thought to act as a reward prediction error (RPE). The RPE determines the learning of the reward prediction (iiia) and may participate in learning of stimulus-response connections at other striatal neurons (iiib)

between terminals of cortical input neurons and the striatal dendritic spines). Firing of the cortical neurons (factor one) releases glutamate at these corticostriatal synapses and this binds at post-synaptic N-methyl-D-aspartic acid (NMDA) receptors on the dendritic spines. This NMDA receptor activation leads to depolarization of the striatal cell (factor two) and an increase in calcium concentration within the dendritic spine. The interaction between these dopamine- and glutamate-activated processes is proposed to lead to a long-term strengthening (or 'potentiation') of the corticostriatal synapses.

Interestingly, there is evidence to suggest that if the glutamate-activated processes occur (factors one and two) but are not followed, at the appropriate time, by dopamine cell firing (and the associated changes at striatal dendritic spines, factor three), then the corticostriatal synapses may undergo long-term weakening (or 'depression'). Such synaptic depression will occur when an erroneous non-rewarded response has been made, resulting in 'unlearning' or 'extinction' of the active corticostriatal synapses; these synapses will be those which were just recruited during the execution of the response. Schultz's (1998) review of such data persuasively demonstrates that the phasic dopaminergic cell firing is more than simply a reinforcement signal occurring when an unconditioned or conditioned reward is encountered: it acts as a 'reward prediction error' (RPE) signal (see Figure 4.1). The first piece of evidence consistent with this interpretation is the observation that only unexpected unconditioned reward stimuli elicit dopamine cell firing: when the reward is well-predicted by a conditioned stimulus, the primary reward no longer elicits firing (see Schultz 1998, fig. 3). Moreover, in such situations, if the expected reward does not occur (or occurs at an unexpected time) then there is a depression of dopamine firing at the time when the reward would normally have occurred (see Schultz 1998, fig. 5).

The implication of these findings is that dopamine cell firing reflects the size of the actual reward minus the size of the predicted reward (thereby communicating the RPE). Thus, when an unexpected reward of size R occurs then the RPE is R minus 0 (0 = the predicted size of the reward, as it is unexpected), therefore, R. This positive quantity is reflected in a phasic increase in dopamine cell firing. When the actual reward is zero but a predicted reward of size R occurs the RPE is –R. This negative quantity is reflected in the phasic depression of dopamine cell firing observed in the experiments. Thus, within three-factor learning, the negative RPE (and associated depression of dopamine cell firing) is seen as responsible for the weakening of corticostriatal synapses, and this notion has been employed in a number of computational models of dopaminergic reinforcement-based learning (e.g., Brown, Bullock and Grossberg 1999).

In the terms of RST, one can consider the reinforcement scenarios in which a negative RPE signal occurs. This would be when one is expecting a reward, but it does not occur. This scenario was described in the classic RST literature as *frustrative non-reward* (FNR; see Gray 1975) and, within the original version of RST, was considered to elicit activation of the punishment system (originally the BIS, now the FFFS). In the revised version of RST, which stresses that the BIS is activated by conflict (e.g., between FFFS and BAS activations) then it seems possible that FNR might activate the BIS. When FNR occurs a number of times in a particular context, then there is potential for both activation of the BAS (associated with reward expectation) followed by activation of other systems (in relation to non-reward expectation). Such joint activation might plausibly constitute conflict.

The neuroscience reviewed in the preceding paragraphs suggests an alternative viewpoint. Both reward and FNR have effects upon firing of dopaminergic cells (phasic increases and decreases of firing respectively); these are occurring within the same neuronal system – a system we have argued is a central part of the neural substrate of the BAS. Interestingly, the neuroscientific evidence – and its controversial implication that FNR might relate to changes in BAS functioning – is now finding support in behavioural work. A recent paper by Carver (2004) explored the relationships between negative emotional states and BAS-related personality traits (as measured by the Carver and White 1994 BAS scales). In one experiment, Carver studied the effects of frustrative non-reward. This was induced in healthy student participants by leading them to expect that they would obtain reward (extra course participation credits) when performing an apparently simple experimental task (predicting the next item in a short sequence). Regardless of their responses, all participants received eight lots of identical feedback, during the task, which consistently indicated that they had received no rewards. Participants then completed items rating negative emotions for a second time (they had completed them prior to the start of the task). Ratings of frustration and sadness both increased significantly from the start to the end of the experiment. Scores on the Fun Seeking sub-scale (a sub-scale of the more general BAS scale) were associated with the increases in both frustration and sadness, while no significant associations were observed for a measure constructed to assess punishment system activation (the BIS scale). The relevance of FNR to the BAS is clearly supported by these findings, and suggests a radical but biologically plausible revision to current understanding of Gray's reward system.

In addition to informing our theoretical understanding of the BAS, the mainstream neuroscience literature can also provide some constraints on the experimental methods that should be used for testing RST and other theoretical perspectives on the BAS. In particular, one should ideally seek to employ tasks known to be sensitive to dopaminergic manipulations or to lesions to the striatum and/or prefrontal cortex. The development of neuroscience-driven paradigms is a promising means to address what we see as a major barrier to progress in the conceptualization and measurement of the BAS-related trait: the lack of any clear behavioural criteria for assessing reactions to reward. The usual approach taken when validating a putative measure of the BAS (or, similarly, using a supposedly valid psychometric measure of BAS to test some prediction of RST), is to introduce a reward contingency to any convenient behavioural task. Tasks which have been used range from go/no-go discrimination paradigms (Gomez and McClaren 1997; Smillie and Jackson 2006) to maze-learning tests (Pickering, Díaz and Gray 1995); from mood induction procedures (Carver and White 1994) to verbal operant conditioning (Gupta 1990). In each case, the degree to which the subjects' responses are influenced by the reward contingency is used as an index of BAS-reactivity.

With the benefit of hindsight it is possible to see this traditional approach as extremely arbitrary; it is almost certain that not all behavioural scenarios require forms of learning which are strongly dependent upon the motivational or reinforcing effects of reward. For instance, episodic memory-dependent learning primarily relies upon medial temporal lobe structures (Squire 1992), and is probably not greatly influenced by the dopaminergic processes thought to be central to BAS functioning. In the 'go/no-go' task often employed in RST research, participants have to memorize which stimuli (usually a small set of unrelated two-digit numbers) are associated with go responses, and which are associated with no-go responses (another small but arbitrary collection of two-digit numbers). There is no other basis on which to perform this task; as such, it seems likely to be heavily dependent upon the memory systems of the medial temporal lobes and relatively unlikely to be strongly influenced by reward-related processes. It seems likely, therefore, that we have not only been employing a range of trait measures which may or may not conceptually relate to the BAS, but we have often been attempting to use those measures to predict behavioural criteria which may or may not be much influenced by rewards. By being aware of contemporary cognitive neuroscience research, the RST researcher can better select the kinds of task that are likely to be influenced by the motivational-reinforcement processes with which he or she is directly concerned.

We have recently argued that certain kinds of category learning (CL) tasks may offer a paradigm for studying the BAS, due to compelling evidence that they rely strongly on the neural systems and structures which mediate reward-based learning. CL tasks vary considerably in appearance, but typically involve the assignment of stimuli that differ on one or more physical dimensions (length, colour, shape, etc.) into two or more (often arbitrary) categories. Most CL tasks can be described as either exemplar, rule-based or information-integration tasks. Exemplar tasks are learned by memory; there is typically a small number of stimuli per category that are each shown several times throughout the task. There is no system underlying category membership, hence the subject learns to recognize stimuli as belonging to category A or B (the go/no-go task cited earlier is an example of such a task). For rule-based tasks there is such a system; category membership is determined by an easily verbalizable rule. These can be unidimensional rules (e.g., 'if the stimulus is long it is from category A'), conjunctive rules (e.g., 'if the stimulus is long and on a 45° angle it is from category A'), or rules-with-exceptions (e.g., 'if the stimulus is long it is from category A, unless it is on a 45° angle'). Subjects learn these tasks by hypothesis testing, experimenting

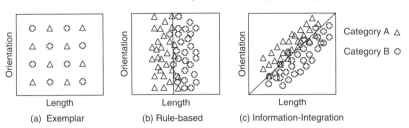

Figure 4.2 Illustration comparing: (a) exemplar; (b) rule-based; and (c) information-integration category-learning task structures. All stimuli consist of straight lines varying in length and orientation (angle). In the exemplar structure there are very few stimuli in each category, and no pattern of length or orientation determines category membership; the category to which each stimulus belongs must be learned by trial and error and then remembered. In the rule-based structure long lines belong in category B and short lines belong in category A, while orientation does not vary systematically with category membership. In the information-integration structure, a non-verbalizable combination of length and orientation determines category membership. Learning of these structures is procedural, and thought to be strongly dependent upon reinforcement. Note the between-category stimulus overlap for the rule-based and information-integration structures, indicating that category membership is probabilistic

with different possible rules until they identify the correct one. Like rule-based tasks, information integration tasks also have a system which determines category membership, but that system can be described only by a non-verbalizable combination of multiple dimensions. Whereas rule-based tasks are learned explicitly, information-integration tasks are learned implicitly (Ashby, Alfonso-Reese, Turken and Wladron 1998).

An extensive body of literature indicates that information integration tasks depend critically upon the dopaminergic (DA) pathways believed to form the substrate of the BAS (Ashby *et al.* 1998). Among this evidence is the finding that performance on such tasks is impaired for patients with Parkinsons' disease, a disorder characterized by degradation of ascending DA pathways (Brown and Marsden 1988; Knowlton, Mangels and Squire 1996). The importance of these pathways for learning seems to be specific to information integration tasks. Ashby, Maddox and Bohil (2002) compared the effect that different training methods have on learning for rule-based and for information integration tasks. Learning on rule-based tasks was not strongly influenced by training method, but learning on information integration tasks was significantly improved when reinforcing feedback was used (rather than observational training). From this it is reasonable to suggest that learning information integration tasks is strongly dependent upon reinforcement, and therefore, upon BAS reactivity.

There have been very few published studies of CL paradigms to test predictions from RST. Ball and Zuckerman (1990) were, to our knowledge, the first to report such a study, whose potential importance we have highlighted elsewhere (e.g., Pickering 2004; Pickering and Gray 2001). In their task, participants had to learn an explicit rule for classifying novel stimuli (patterns consisting of a letter within a shape, surrounded by a border) as targets or distractors. The task was completed under four reinforcement conditions (verbal reward, verbal punishment, monetary reward and monetary punishment), and it was predicted that Sensation-Seeking (a construct based strongly upon Gray's notion of BAS; Zuckerman 1979) would be positively associated with learning in the reward conditions only. However, sensation-seeking positively predicted learning in *all four* conditions. In light of the recent CL literature this is not a surprising finding, and we would argue that an information integration task would have been more likely to yield the predicted results. Indeed, rule-based CL tasks like the one used by Ball and Zuckerman do not depend strongly upon reinforcement during learning (Ashby, Maddox and Bohil 2002). This further suggests that the sensation-seeking trait effects observed by Ball and Zuckerman are probably not related to the reinforcing properties of the training regimes used.

In the last few years we have explored the usefulness of CL tasks as a paradigm for reactivity of the BAS. Most of these findings we have summarized in recent review articles (Pickering 2004; Smillie, Pickering and Jackson 2006) while further work is in progress at the time of writing. These studies have tended to converge with the CL literature in suggesting that reward manipulations are more effective, and more reliably accounted for, by potential psychometric measures of the BAS, when information integration tasks are used as opposed to other CL task structures. For example, Smillie, Dalgleish and Jackson (in press) used the BAS measure from Carver and White's 1994 BIS/BAS scales to predict motivational effects of reward while completing an information integration task. Employing an identical design, Smillie and Jackson (2006) report a second experiment using a go/no-go discrimination learning task (putatively exemplar-based) rather than an information integration task. For this latter experiment the relationship between the Carver and White BAS scale and reward-based motivational effects was considerably weaker – less than half the observed effect size reported by Smillie *et al.* for an information integration task. The discrepancy between these findings is directly predicted by the recent research concerning the neuropsychological bases of category learning which we have cited, and reinforces the view that in not all behavioural paradigms will learning be strongly dependent upon brain structures which mediate the effects of reward.

Beyond category learning, there is also now a rapidly growing number of neuroscientific publications, with human participants, that are of direct relevance to RST. Such research has examined individual differences in relation to neuro-imaging measures, or used modern neuroscience methods to study the neurophysiological and/or functional properties of the brain regions thought to be central to one of Gray's systems (e.g., the nigrostriatal and mesocorticolimbic dopamine projection systems underpinning the BAS). However, the researchers, although aware of Gray's pre-eminence in this area, may not frame their research in exact alignment with the central issues of RST. RST researchers who want to develop a coherent neurobiological model of personality need to be aware of the burgeoning research in this area and, we believe, employ these methods to address some of the core issues for RST. In the following paragraphs we review a couple of interesting recent studies and argue that RST researchers should be aware of such studies and adapt the methods concerned for their own purposes.

A recent experiment by Martin and Potts (2004) analysed Event Related Potential (ERP) responses to reward and related signals, adopting the general 'reward prediction error' (RPE) framework noted above in relation to the functioning of the mesocorticolimbic dopamine system. Although not addressing RST specifically, this work provided some support for RST's basic personality predictions, and offers a method for testing these predictions more comprehensively. In addition to the single-unit recording studies from the animal literature noted earlier in this chapter, Martin and Potts (2004) cite fMRI studies from the human literature, which also suggest a role for DA projections from the ventral tegmental area (VTA) to the orbitofrontal cortex (OFC) in reward prediction. They then suggest that ERPs assessed at P300 or Anterior P2 (P2a) components, which have been suggested to index motivational aspects of stimulus processing, might also index similar dopaminergically mediated aspects of reward prediction. If correct, such ERP markers should prove invaluable for personality researchers investigating the BAS.

Martin and Potts recorded continuous EEG from a 128-channel electrode array while twenty-eight subjects completed a task in which sequential pairs of stimuli (presented 1,000ms apart on computer screen) were imperfectly predictive of small financial reward and non-reward events. A pair of cherries or a pair of gold bars was predictive of reward, while a lemon followed by either a cherry or a second lemon was predictive of non-reward. A cherry which was not followed by a second cherry, or a gold bar which was not followed by another, was a non-predicted non-reward. Finally, a lemon which was followed by a gold bar was a non-predicted reward. The EEG was segmented into 1,000 ms epochs, time-locked to the onset of the second stimulus event; the moment when a prediction was either confirmed or violated.

According to the single-unit and fMRI research cited by the authors, and the wider literature concerning the role of DA neurons (Schultz 1998), the reward-processing system should show phasic activation to non-predicted reward (in response to a positive RPE) and phasic depression to non-predicted non-reward (which causes a negative RPE). According to RST, a BAS-related personality trait would be expected to moderate this effect, such that high scorers show the strongest response to non-predicted reward and, as we argued earlier, to non-predicted non-reward. While Martin and Potts did not focus explicitly on RST or the BAS, they did assess impulsivity using the Barratt Impulsiveness Scale (Patton, Stanford and Barratt 1995; we shall avoid the convention of abbreviating this measures as 'BIS-11' for obvious reasons!). They divided their healthy student sample about the median into 'high' and 'low' impulsives. On separate theoretical grounds, they predicted impulsivity to relate to reward reactivity in the same way we would predict for the BAS-related trait.

The key findings reported by Martin and Potts are as follows: ERPs for both P2a (averaged from twelve inferior frontal electrodes) and P300 (averaged from twenty centroparietal electrodes) were larger for rewarding than non-rewarding outcomes. Further, the pattern of results for P2a indicated that ERPs were largest after non-predicted reward and smallest after non-predicted non-reward. Source analysis indicated that the P2a arose in the medial OFC, supporting the authors' hypothesis that such activity might reflect reward-elicited DA projections from the VTA to the OFC. We find this very encouraging, in that it suggests a tool for examining reactivity of the BAS in an ERP paradigm. Effects relating to impulsivity were also interesting: in the high-impulsive group, P2a to non-predicted non-reward was significantly lower compared with (in order of increasing magnitude) predicted non-reward predicted reward and non-predicted reward. Differences were non-significant in the low-impulsive group. Thus, it seems that high impulsive individuals showed a more reactive DA reward system than low impulsive individuals. The reactivity of the reward system was shown, in this study, by a positive P2a after unexpected reward, and a large negative P2a after unexpected non-reward (consistent with the neuroscience literature reviewed earlier).

We believe the Martin and Potts study is a clear example of research outside of the mainstream RST and BAS literature which is strongly deserving of the attention of RST and BAS researchers. Admittedly, as an investigation into the BAS there are some limitations worth mentioning. For instance, as we do not know what personality scales offer the most pure or reliable index of BAS (see below), it is unclear what we can conclude about the BAS from the effects relating to the Barratt Impulsiveness Scale. Furthermore, the statistical comparisons reported omit those which would be of particular interest to the RST view. A clear test to determine if the Barratt Impulsiveness Scale reflected reactivity of the BAS would compare neural responses to non-predicted reward in the high-impulsive group to that of the low-impulsive group (rather than comparing responses to non-predicted reward with responses to non-predicted non-reward *within* the high- and low-impulsive groups). The same comparison would be of interest for responses to non-predicted non-reward. But these limitations only arise because the RST researcher would have slightly different aims to Martin and Potts. The value of this experiment for those interested in the BAS, such as ourselves, is a promising paradigm for assessing neural reactivity to reward. The paper offers, for example, a clear means to compare the validity of various candidate BAS-traits.

The next example of highly relevant neuroscience research is a recent paper linking fMRI, a dopamine-related genotype and extraversion (Cohen, Young, Baek, Kessler and Ranganath 2005). In this small-scale fMRI study, two experiments (N = 17 and N = 16) were conducted with healthy student volunteers. In both experiments participants chose between two gambles (one: low payout, high probability of reward vs. another: higher payout, lower probability of reward) while in the scanner. Despite the difference in risk the gambles were of equal expected value. The researchers quantified the brain areas in which there was the strongest fMRI response to rewarded versus unrewarded trials. The reward activated regions were in brain areas widely implicated in reward processing (orbitofrontal cortex, amygdala and nucleus accumbens). In most of these regions, in both experiments 1 and 2, the Big Five Personality Inventory measure of extraversion (John, Donahue and Kentle 1991) was significantly positively correlated with the strength of the reward activation. Moreover, in experiment 2, the researchers had DNA from participants which they genotyped for the presence of the A1 allele of the so-called Taq1A polymorphism of the dopamine D2 receptor (DRD2) gene. This polymorphism was targeted as it has been repeatedly linked to reward-related processes, and is believed to be associated with numbers of dopamine D2 receptors (see Cohen *et al.* 2005 for references).

In the brain regions showing fMRI reward activation, presence of the A1 allele was associated with significantly reduced reward activation. Although the absence of the A1 allele and increasing extraversion scores had a similar effect on reward association, these two predictor variables did not show a significant association between themselves (although power to detect this was very low). In experiment 2, the researchers were able to separate out a neural response of anticipation of reward (a state of waiting to learn whether reward will be received or not), from that associated with the experience of reward itself. This anticipation neural response was not associated with either extraversion or the DRD2 Taq1A polymorphism, and occurred in different regions (dorsal caudate, ventral prefrontal cortex and parietal cortex) from those which responded to the experience of reward relative to the experience of non-reward. Interestingly, neither the polymorphism, nor the extraversion scores, were associated with behavioural response measures taken during the task (e.g., proportion of higher-risk gambles chosen, proportion of higher-risk gambles chosen after a high-risk win, or the probability of adopting a win-stay lose-shift strategy). This suggests that the neuroimaging measures are more strongly associated with the personality trait and polymorphism than are the relevant behavioural measures, although the interpretation of null results in this study is severely limited by the restricted power available with such small samples.

We predict that genetic studies, such as the above work by Cohen *et al.*, will become an increasingly common method to investigate RST. Some years ago we (Pickering and Gray 1999) reported one of our first unpublished attempts to carry out work in this area (investigating a possible association between the dopamine D4 receptor gene and hypothetically BAS-related behaviours). Cohen *et al.*'s findings, showing that the DRD2 gene may be linked with the BAS-related personality trait, gain some qualified support from work by Reuter, Schmitz, Corr and Hennig (2005). They also showed that the Taq 1A polymorphism of the DRD2 gene (the same one investigated by Cohen *et al.* 2005) may be linked with the BAS-related trait. However, they found the association when the personality measure was the BAS scale (Carver and White 1994) and the relationship emerged only in interaction with a polymorphism of another dopamine-related gene (the so-called COMT gene, which affects the functioning of a major catabolic enzyme that degrades cortical dopamine).

A major question left unanswered by these early genetic and neuro-imaging studies concerns exactly which personality measure shows the strongest and most reliable correlations with the neural measures. It is conceivable that different types of trait measure may be associated with different components of the underlying neural systems, but much more data needs to be gathered before such a possibility can be assessed.

We have seen, in this section, that RST research can profit from integrating the latest neuroscience into our quest for, and understanding of, the biological substrates of systems such as the BAS, and how they might relate to personality. However, we feel that, for those RST researchers who are less intrigued by neurobiological questions than we are, there is plenty of RST-relevant research, outside the neuroscience domain, which also has not been fully considered. In the following section we illustrate this by reviewing some recent, purely psychological, findings which speak directly and powerfully to RST.

A need for psychological and conceptual reframing?

As already intimated above, the influence of Gray's model of brain-behaviour relationships, and the associated RST of personality, has become very widespread within psychology. It is very common to see RST cited in general support of a related position in other, less biological areas of psychological discourse (e.g., BAS-related traits as predictors of workplace performance when incentives are used; Jackson 2001; Stewart 1996). For those working with the detailed predictions of RST these other areas of research often seem to contribute little, as they are typically painted with very broad brush-strokes. However, we would argue that RST should try to use what has been learned in these other areas to inform the revisions that it is currently undergoing. This is possible as there is now some empirical work, generated by these other accounts, which speaks directly to the predictions of RST.

One example is the 'regulatory focus' framework advocated by Higgins (1987, 1997). This account makes broad reference to RST by distinguishing between approach and avoidance stimuli. Individuals may have two distinct kinds of regulatory focus: promotion and prevention. Under a promotion focus, individuals are sensitive to the presence or absence of approach stimuli. Alternatively, they may have a prevention focus, in which they are sensitive to the presence or absence of avoidance stimuli. Regulatory focus can be a state variable (induced experimentally) and this has been shown to influence cognitive processing and decision-making (e.g., in a difficult task individuals are more persistent when in a situationally-induced promotion focus condition than when in a prevention focus condition; Crowe and Higgins 1997). The model also proposes individuals may have a preferred regulatory focus (i.e., a trait variable), and furthermore argues that people prefer a fit between their trait regulatory focus and the focus being presented by the environment (e.g., Higgins 2000). The links between this framework and RST are clear (e.g., an individual who has a preference for a promotion focus would be a high BAS individual under RST), but they have not been considered in detail.

A recent study by Markman, Baldwin and Maddox (2005), drawing upon the concept of regulatory focus, poses some very interesting questions for RST. As a result we will review this study in some detail. The authors used a simple probabilistic category learning (CL) task in which participants viewed stimuli comprising single small dots. The stimuli varied only in their position on the screen (e.g., to the left or right of the screen centre). Participants had to learn, via trial and error plus feedback, that stimuli to one side of the screen tended to be in category A and those to the other side of the screen tended to be in category B, although the probabilistic nature of the task meant that it was difficult and many stimuli violated this simple rule. In essence the task consists of gradually learning where to place a simple decision criterion to optimize task success. To maximize accuracy, individuals should place their criterion midway between the means of the distributions of each category. Thus if dots in category A have a mean position of 275 pixels from the left of the screen, and dots in category B have a mean position of 375 pixels from the left of the screen,[2] then optimal accuracy can be gained by placing a decision criterion at 325 pixels from the left of the screen and responding to all stimuli to the left of the criterion with a 'category A' response, with the rest of the stimuli receiving 'category B' responses.

Markman *et al.* tested participants under each of three conditions; each condition employed a different biased payoff matrix.[3] Such biased matrices (described below) mean that an optimum accuracy decision criterion, as described above, will not yield maximal winnings. The framing of the task and the feedback presentation encouraged participants to maximize winnings (or minimize losses) rather than maximizing task accuracy. In two of the matrix conditions ('gain' and 'mixed') the payoff (i.e., points won) for making a correct category A response was higher (gain: 400 points; mixed: 200 points) than the payoff for making

---

[2] The dots varied in position about the mean with a standard deviation of 100 pixels for each category.

[3] A payoff matrix simply describes the gains and losses that follow correct responses and errors, for each possible type of response.

a correct category B response (gain: 200 points; mixed: 0 points). The consequence of an erroneous A and B response were equivalent to each other in either matrix condition (gain: 100 points for each; mixed: 100 points loss for each). In the mixed condition, the fact that error responses attracted losses of points meant that both positive and negative incentives were used in this condition, hence its name. In the gain condition there were no losses of points at all, as a small number of points were won even when making erroneous responses to either category A or B (the same for each category). From the point of view of RST, then, the gains condition seems likely to be the purest BAS-activating condition, as this delivers only rewards.

In the third matrix condition ('loss'), points were lost for all responses, but the points lost for correct category A responses (-111 points) were smaller than those lost for correct category B responses (-311 points). The losses for errors were the same for A and B items (-411 points).

Using such biased payoff matrices, one can estimate the optimal decision criterion for maximizing reward (or minimizing losses). In each of the three matrices used by Markman *et al.* the optimal reward decision criterion should be shifted away from the centre of the high payoff category by the same amount. In the example above, for each of the matrices that they used, the optimal criterion for maximizing reward (or minimizing losses) should be placed at 434.5 pixels from the left of the screen; that is, shifted well beyond the optimal accuracy criterion (325 pixels) in the direction away from the centre of the high payoff category. Consider the gains matrix condition. To understand why this decision criterion placement optimizes winnings, one must note that it ensures that one misses very few A items (and so gains a very high number of the large rewards for all the correct A responses). This more than compensates for the increased number of B items that are erroneously called A items; as B is the low payoff category, one can afford to sacrifice getting these items correct (and losing potential points) in order to make sure of getting most of the high-paying A items correct.

When one considers this task from the perspective of RST, one would predict that the degree of shift to an optimal reward criterion (away from an optimal accuracy criterion) would be greatest in high BAS-trait individuals, under task conditions which primarily activated the BAS (such effects were predicted and found by Smillie and Jackson 2006, and Smillie *et al.*, in press, using somewhat similar experimental manipulations). This follows because the criterion shift is a reward-maximizing strategy, of exactly the kind that the BAS was intended to describe in animals. As already argued, the gain matrix condition seems likely to be a relatively pure BAS-activating condition. Although

Markman *et al.* did not examine individual differences, their manipulation of regulatory focus yielded some interesting results. A promotion focus was elicited for half of the subjects by telling them that they could win tickets for a US $50 raffle if their points total exceeded a specific score at the end of the task. The remaining subjects were given a prevention focus by giving them the raffle tickets at the start and telling them that they could keep the tickets only if their score at the end was above the criterion. Markman *et al.* found that, on average, the subjects in the promotion focus condition with the gains matrix showed a tendency to place their decision criterion near to the optimal criterion for maximizing reward; however, subjects in the prevention focus with the gains matrix did not show this tendency (their mean decision criterion was quite close to that required for optimum accuracy). This suggests that BAS-related processes were strongly engaged in the gains condition with a promotion focus manipulation, but were much less strongly engaged in the gains condition with a prevention focus manipulation.

The above result is surprising for RST, which would predict that the BAS should have been strongly engaged under *either* regulatory focus manipulation in the gains matrix condition. With either focus the responses in the gains condition received only rewards (in the form of points) which could be exchanged for a potentially financially valuable prize at the end of the experiment. Those rewards, delivered during the task, should therefore activate the BAS and allow it to control responding. It appears instead that the prevention focus manipulation in some way reduced BAS activation and control of behaviour during the gains condition. We believe it is very informative and important for developing clear accounts of the BAS within RST to understand how regulatory focus operates in situations like this.

The result above also tells us that the BAS is not always activated by the occurrence of rewards per se. The context in which those rewards are delivered seems critical. This insight is not particularly new: for example, when Gray and Smith (1969) first formalized the operations of reward and punishment-based systems, they argued that a reward which was smaller than expected would not activate the reward system (a point developed further by Zinbarg and Revelle 1989, and revisited later by Corr 2002). This is another example of context affecting the ability of reward stimuli to activate the BAS. What must now be explained is how the prevention focus context suppresses BAS activation. One possibility might be that the prevention focus induced a mildly fearful or anxious state (based on the prospect of losing the valued reward that had already been given at the start of the task). As such, this could correspond to the activation of a punishment-based or anxiety system (the FFFS, or

BIS, respectively, in the Gray and McNaughton revised model). If this system is being engaged, it should impair the engagement of the system which otherwise would take control and so shift behaviour to a reward-maximizing strategy (i.e., the BAS). This interpretation is consistent with Markman et al.'s observation from the mixed condition: under either a prevention or promotion focus the participants behaved very similarly; in both cases participants, on average, placed their criterion close to the maximum accuracy criterion. Once again, joint activation of both systems (e.g., by the mixed incentives available in the task) could be impairing the ability of the subjects to shift behaviour to the most adaptive reward-maximizing/loss-minimizing strategy. This suggestion would also fit with the growing interest in system interactions (see chapter 16). Finally, it would also encourage the search for tasks in which joint system activation would be adaptive for the individual.

An alternative interpretation suggests that the BAS is not activated in the gains condition with a prevention focus because the highest level goal of behaviour (to win the lottery tickets) is already achieved at the start of the task (in prevention focus condition the tickets are given at the start of the task; they have to be gained in promotion and are awarded only at the end). This idea supposes that there is a system which monitors how far an individual is from their ultimate goal and allows BAS activation only when the goal has not been reached. We might think of this as a 'BAS gate' which is open only when we are at a distance from our goal. Whether, and to what extent, the BAS is actually activated would depend upon the number and intensity of reward stimuli encountered while the BAS gate is open (and the reactivity of the individual's BAS, of course). Also, for this idea to work in the context of the gain condition of the Markman task, the goal operating the BAS gate must be the final desired outcome (getting the lottery tickets). There are other 'goals' presented in the task; in particular, raising one's point score from zero to exceed the criterion (33,700 points), which determines winning the lottery tickets. This goal is presented on the screen throughout the task and a participant's progress towards that goal is physically displayed (by a thermometer bar which gradually moves towards the criterion point). This very obvious and available goal, and distance from it, is present identically in both the promotion and prevention focus conditions to an equivalent extent. It cannot therefore be controlling the 'BAS gate' as suggested above. In order to explain the data, the higher-level abstract goal (achievement of which is assessed via the question: 'have I got the lottery tickets yet') must be critical in opening/closing the BAS gate.

This view is distinct from the ideas presented by Gray. However, it chimes closely with ideas espoused by Carver and colleagues (see Carver 2004 for a review). Carver stresses two sets of feedback processes. First, there are feedback signals which relate to approach and avoidance, as suggested by the majority of biobehavioural models of emotion-motivation (of which RST was probably the first). However, Carver argues that the subjective experience of affect is critically controlled by other feedback loops: specifically, ones that monitor the effectiveness of movement towards positive incentives or away from threats. The rate of progress of these second feedback processes, against some kind of reference value, is seen as an 'error signal' which creates subjective affect. If the rate of progress is too low then negative affect arises; whereas if the rate is acceptable, or exceeds the criterion, then positive affective states will ensue. This model enables Carver to explain his findings (e.g., Carver 2004) in which personality traits related to the approach system can predict both positive and negative affective changes.

Our idea of a 'BAS gate' could relate directly to Carver's feedback processes. Clearly, some form of feedback is required in order to determine whether a desired goal has been reached. It is not clear, however, whether this fits more with the first set of processes Carver has posited (ones which determine which type of motive is in play) or the second (those that determine rate of progress towards that goal). Perhaps it is distinct from, or supplementary to, both. Further experimental work on these kinds of ideas is needed and would seem likely to cast light on the operation of the BAS. In addition, it is tempting to relate Carver's second set of feedback processes to the RPE signal we discussed in the neuroscience section. Thus, the same neural system (the dopaminergically-mediated BAS) can show increases or decreases of dopamine cell firing depending on how well the environmental feedback signals concerning rewards match the predictions made by the individual. Consequently, the same neural system can produce either type of affective state (happiness or frustration) depending on the direction of change of dopamine cell firing. Schultz (1998) shows how the RPE account extends to chains of initially neutral stimuli which are encountered en route to an ultimate goal/reward (e.g., see Schultz 1998, fig. 10). This makes the analogy drawn here more compelling still. When the conceptual developments mesh with the neuroscience, both are placed on firmer ground: we are sure that these are the kinds of developments to his theory that Gray himself would have found most persuasive.

Psychometric issues: which trait relates to variation in BAS functioning?

In an integrative review of personality processes in the *Annual Review of Psychology*, William Revelle (1995) observes that:

the cluster of approach traits of extraversion (Eysenck 1990), impulsivity (Barratt 1994, Gray 1994, Zinbarg and Revelle 1989), novelty seeking (Cloninger 1987), and positive affectivity (Depue and Iacano 1989), as well as the states resulting from approach of reward, energetic arousal (Thayer 1989) and positive affect (Watson *et al.* 1994) have all been discussed in terms of the BAS. (p. 312)

One could infer from this description that either the BAS has a powerful and dominating influence on a wide range of personality variables, or, almost the opposite: that identification of the BAS-related trait has proved a difficult task and is a subject of much disagreement. To be sure, the concept of the BAS has had a profound influence on personality research, inspiring theoretical accounts of many and varied traits (see Elliot and Thrash 2002). On the other hand, it is a striking fact that, thirty years after the BAS was proposed as a cause of personality, an empirically supported consensus has not been reached as to where in the spaces of personality we might observe its principal effects. Conceptualization and measurement of the trait which corresponds to the BAS is indeed one of the greatest theoretical and practical challenges to RST as a model for personality; it is to this issue we turn in the final section of this chapter.

The confusion surrounding the BAS as a cause of a personality is not surprising given the ad hoc manner in which this system was introduced to RST. As noted by Gray, Owen, Davis and Tsaltas (1983), RST was:

first proposed (Gray, 1970) as a theory of Anxiety ... It was natural to suggest that, if Anxiety reflects sensitivity to signals of punishment and nonreward, [an orthogonal rotation of this dimension] might correspond to sensitivity to signals of reward and non-punishment [and] might underlie the trait of high impulsivity. (pp. 184–185)

Clearly, the trait description Gray suggested for the BAS was entirely arbitrary. The taxonomic personality landscape within which Gray had originally situated RST was provided by Eysenck's (1967) spaces of Extraversion and Neuroticism. At this time, Impulsivity was conceived of as lying approximately at right angles to Anxiety; the trait for which Gray was seeking an orthogonal rotation. The end result was the now well-known representation of Gray's (1970, 1981) model of Anxiety-Impulsivity as a 30° rotation to Eysenck's (1967) model of Extraversion-Neuroticism.

An initial difficulty with making a bottom-up link from the BAS to trait impulsivity concerns the fact that impulsivity is a complex *cluster* of traits, associated with more varied and numerous psychometric measures, trait definitions and theoretical explanations than any other dimension in personality psychology (for reviews, see Evenden 1999, and Parker and Bagby 1997).[4] Within Eysenck's taxonomy, Impulsivity began as a facet of Extraversion and migrated to Psychoticism (Revelle 1997). In the Five Factor scheme it has been an even faster-moving target, wandering from Neuroticism to Extraversion to Conscientiousness (not just over time, but also depending on which version of this taxonomy one adopts; Block 1995). In addition, the many taxonomies concerned exclusively with impulsivity also tend to provide multiple conceptualizations of this trait (e.g., Barratt 1985; Dickman 1990; Eysenck, Pearson, Easting and Allsop 1985). Perspectives on the theoretical bases of impulsivity are also many and varied, with putative causal mechanisms ranging from serotonin (Coscina 1997) to attention regulation (Dickman 2000) to cortical arousal (Revelle, Humphreys, Simon and Gilliland 1980) – often depending upon which 'kind' of impulsivity one is talking about. The dilemma which quickly confronted the RST researcher is, then, to which kind of impulsivity did Gray refer?

In response to this problem, and (initially) to provide consistency in the operationalization of RST traits in personality research, numerous purpose-built measures have been published over the last twenty years. The Gray-Wilson Personality Questionnaire (GWPQ; Wilson, Barrett and Gray 1989) included two measures of BAS reactivity modelled on human analogues of *approach* and *active avoidance* behaviour seen in the animal learning research upon which RST is based. This was quickly followed by the Generalized Reward and Punishment Expectancy Scales (GRAPES; Ball and Zuckerman 1990), which offered a measure of BAS variation in terms of optimistic expectations regarding future rewarding events. Next in line were the BIS/BAS scales (Carver and White 1994), which included three interpretations of the BAS-related trait: Fun-Seeking, Reward-Responsiveness and Drive. The Sensitivity to Reward and Sensitivity to Punishment Questionnaire (SPSRQ; Torrubia, Ávila, Caseras and Moltó 2001) followed shortly afterward along with the Appetitive Motivation Scale (Jackson and Smillie 2004). This list

---

[4] To our knowledge, the link between the BIS and anxiety has not proved so difficult. This is probably owing to the fact that the BIS was proposed from the outset as a theory of anxiety, combined with the fact that different measures of anxiety are not nearly as heterogeneous as different measures of impulsivity.

becomes even longer if we include measures based indirectly upon the BAS or proposed as alternative conceptualizations of the BAS (e.g., Novelty Seeking, Cloninger, Svrakic and Przybeck 1993; Sensation-Seeking, Zuckerman 1979).

In addition to impulsivity and purpose-built BAS measures, a common (and relatively successful) operationalization of the BAS-related trait has been achieved using measures of Extraversion (e.g., Bartussek, Diedrich, Naumann and Collet 1993; Boddy, Carver and Rowley 1986; Gupta 1990; Senuath 1975). The use of Extraversion as a proxy for the BAS might be questioned in light of Gray's explicit proposal that the BAS-related axis lies at a 30° angle to Extraversion. Nevertheless, it is important to emphasize the hypothetical nature of Gray's critique of, and proposed rotation to, Eysenck's personality factors. Specifically, Gray was not arguing against the number or even the nature of Eysenck's factors – at least not in the same way that, for instance, Goldberg (e.g., 1982) criticized Cattell's (1950) sixteen factor taxonomy. Rather, he was arguing that Eysenck's top-down approach to personality – first identifying descriptive factors and then searching for their biological correlates – risks overlooking the most central biological causes of variation in behaviour. Put simply, if one cannot be certain that their model represents the 'true' descriptive dimensions of personality – as is *always* the case when that model is derived from factor analysis (Block 1995; Gray 1981) – then biological correlates of those dimensions may not represent the 'true' underlying causes of personality. As it turns out, Gray's bottom-up alternative to Eysenck's theory postulated the existence of a major descriptive trait being located somewhere near Extraversion; hence it seems perfectly reasonable from the outset to include this trait among those which may potentially reflect BAS functioning.

The psychometric net which has been cast in the search for the BAS-related trait is clearly very wide. Nevertheless, to our knowledge, there is no comprehensive review of the evidence favouring generic impulsivity measures, purpose-built BAS measures, or the various incarnations of Extraversion, as valid reflections of Gray's reward system. Furthermore, as different measures tend to be favoured by different researchers using different paradigms, we believe that the data presently do not exist to permit such an appraisal. There is, however, a wealth of recent data to make a strong case for the validity of one of these BAS candidates in particular – Extraversion – and we shall briefly consider this evidence here.

As we have found to be the case for other issues relating to the BAS, the neuroscience literature has made a particularly valuable contribution here. In a detailed review which provides a cornerstone of modern understanding of the BAS, Depue and Collins (1999) provide convincing evidence that dopaminergic processes which form the substrate of the BAS have their strongest and most reliable correlation with certain measures of Extraversion. Depue and colleagues refer to this reward-sensitive component of Extraversion as *agency*, separate from a second component, *affiliation*, which they do not relate to the BAS. DA D_2 receptor effects are strongly and significantly correlated with agentic Extraversion, but only modestly with measures such as trait impulsivity. (Recent pharmacologic and psychophysiological data in direct support of these findings are reported by Wacker, Chavanon and Stemmler 2006.) According to the neuroscience literature reviewed earlier, which underlines the central importance of the dopamine system to the BAS, these are important findings.

Our own experiments in category learning, mentioned earlier, appear to support the view espoused by Depue and Collins. For example, Pickering (2004) describes a category learning study in which participants served under either a paired-associate or a reward-contingent training condition. In paired-associate training, each trial consisted of a stimulus presentation together with the category to which it belonged. Participants could therefore associate stimuli with categories without exposure to any explicit rewarding stimuli likely to engage the BAS (e.g., positive feedback). Conversely, in reward-contingent training, participants learned by trial-and-error, with rewards (positive feedback and 10 UK pence) being given for each correct categorization. Learning was then assessed by a test phase, in which the stimuli were presented a second time and all participants were required to assign to the correct category without assistance. Results showed that, for subjects who served in the paired-associate training condition, EPQ-Psychoticism (being a key correlate of most impulsivity measures) was significantly associated with learning, $r = 0.30$, $p = 0.02$, but EPQ-Extraversion was not, $r = 0.13$, $p = 0.21$. By contrast, for subjects who served in the reward-contingent training condition, EPQ-Psychoticism was not associated with learning, $r = -0.001$, *ns*, but EPQ-Extraversion was, $r = 0.34$, $p = 0.015$.

Complementary evidence has been obtained more recently by Smillie and colleagues, who compared purpose-built BAS measures with generic trait impulsivity scales in the prediction of reward-based learning and motivational effects (Smillie 2005; Smillie *et al.* in press; Smillie and Jackson 2006). For example, two experiments using an information intergration category learning paradigm showed that a purpose-built measure of BAS correlating primarily with Extraversion predicted learning and motivation criteria, but measures of impulsivity which were strongly associated with Psychoticism did not. In the first experiment, Carver and White's (1994) BAS-total scale (being the sum of the three sub-scales, Fun-Seeking, Reward-Responsiveness and Drive) predicted a shift in response bias indicating a preference for a rewarded response, but a general measure of Impulsivity (the Impulsiveness sub-scale of Psychoticism from the Eysenck Personality Profiler; Eysenck, Barrett, Wilson and Jackson 1992) did not. In the second experiment, the Carver and White BAS-total scale predicted learning (in terms of increases in response-sensitivity) when rewarding rather than punishing feedback was given, while a trait-Impulsivity scale (I^7 Impulsiveness; Eysenck et al. 1985) did not.

Recent psychometric research also appears to support the view that the BAS is more clearly related to Extraversion than to Impulsivity. For example, Zelenski and Larsen (1999) factor analysed psychometric measures relating to the theories of Gray, Eysenck and Cloninger, and obtained three independent factors. The first comprised Neuroticism along with a number of measures relating to the BIS or anxiety. The second was composed of Extraversion along with a number of measures developed to assess the BAS (from both Cloninger's and Gray's theories). The third was composed of Psychoticism along with various measures associated with Impulsivity. Very similar results to these have since been obtained using factor analysis, structural equation modelling and multivariate regression (Caseras, Ávila and Torrubia 2003; Knyazev, Slobodskaya and Wilson 2004; Quilty and Oakman 2004; Smillie, Jackson and Dalgleish 2006).

While we believe it is presently strongly supported, the BAS = Extraversion view is not free from uncertainty. As already noted, it is widely agreed that typical measures of Extraversion reflect multiple distinct concepts, only one of which may relate to the BAS (e.g., Depue and Morrone-Strupinsky 2005; Revelle 1997). We have recently had the opportunity to analyse a large dataset (collected by Lessiter 1999) in which healthy participants completed eight scales that potentially reflect the reward system (EPQ-Extraversion and Psychoticism; Cloninger's Novelty Seeking and Reward Dependence scales; Carver and White's BAS scale; Mason et al.'s (1995) Introvertive Anhedonia and Impulsive Nonconformity Scales;[5] and the Venables, Wilkins, Mitchell, Raine and

---

[5] The introvertive anhedonia scale contains some extraversion items (reverse scored) plus items concerning failure to experience physical or social pleasures. The extraversion items were removed and the remaining anhedonia items were reverse scored so as to make the direction of the scale score consistent with the other putative reward traits used. The

Bailes (1990) Anhedonia scales).[6] If we excluded Extraversion, these putative reward traits were found to form two orthogonal factors. Factor 1 was loaded on by Psychoticism, Novelty Seeking, Impulsive Nonconformity and the BAS scale. Factor 2 was loaded on by Reward Dependence and the two Anhedonia scales. Extraversion had robust positive correlations with both factors ($r > 0.4$, $p < 0.001$ in each case), and lay approximately midway between the axes formed by the other two factors. We (Pickering 2004) have suggested that the first of the above axes (which we have referred to as Impulsive Antisocial Sensation Seeking) may not relate to BAS functioning directly, but rather to episodic memory functioning. This does not rule out a partly dopaminergic basis for such traits, although such a basis would have to lie in components of the brain's dopaminergic projection systems that are not directly concerned with rewards. The second axis may correspond more closely to the functioning of the BAS, however, further research is clearly needed to affirm this.

Our impression of the data in this area, at this point in time, provides two possible conceptualizations of the BAS-related trait, echoing the two possible interpretations we offered of Revelle's (1995) observation quoted at the beginning of this section. The first possibility is that the BAS manifests as a single, specific personality dimension, probably lying somewhere between Extraversion and Psychoticism. Extraversion would then correspond to some measures of reward reactivity due to a partial overlap with the BAS-related trait. Some varieties of impulsivity would also be expected to overlap with the BAS-related trait, such as we (Smillie and Jackson 2006) have suggested for Dickman's (1990) concept of 'Functional Impulsivity'. The alternative to this view is that the BAS underlies a broader cluster of traits, which may vary in their strength of association with BAS-related criteria depending on a range of mitigating factors. This is the view offered by Carver and White (1994) in relation to their three-facet psychometric tool for assessing the BAS, who suggest that the sub-scales may reflect different aspects of the BAS which manifest in difference situations (for example, seeking out rewards versus experiencing pleasure when rewards are given). This

impulsive non-conformity scale contains several EPQ-Psychoticism and lie scale items and these were removed.

[6] This scale contains similar anhedonia items to the Mason *et al.* scale and was also reverse scored for consistency with the other scales. In the category learning experiment noted above, the association between learning under positive reinforcement conditions was found for Extraversion but also for the introvertive anhedonia measure, suggesting it may also have an important relationship with reactions to reward.

view conceptualizes the BAS as a framework for personality rather than a causal basis of one particular trait.

In sum, despite promising advances, the uncertainty of the BAS-related trait continues to dominate. That different researchers use different proxy measures of the BAS, and sometimes claim replication of findings despite a change in scale choice, is possibly as much a cause of this uncertainty as it is an effect. A key agenda for RST is to determine which of the available BAS candidates are associated with which biological and/or behavioural markers of BAS functioning. In pursuing this goal, we would urge researchers to employ more than just their own favourite psychometric tools; a wide range of measures should be reported until clear patterns of associations with biobehavioural markers are established.

Conclusion

In this chapter we have tried to illustrate the reasons for our belief that the time is ripe for reframing ideas concerning the BAS within RST. At a time when RST is emphasizing the greater integration between the component systems, and changes in functioning are being proposed for the BIS and FFFS, it seems likely that previous views of BAS functioning may require updating. Recent tests of Gray's model (e.g., Carver 2004) confirm that our older views are at best incomplete, while other more general frameworks, relevant to RST (e.g., Higgins' notion of regulatory focus), also provide data which needs to be incorporated within a remodelled RST, and may throw light on our understanding of the BAS. Accounts of the role of dopaminergic neuronal systems have now become well-established (see Schultz 1998) and are beginning to lead to data in the individual differences literature which are highly relevant and informative for RST (e.g., Martin and Potts 2004). Other techniques in neuroscience (fMRI and genomics) are now very widely used, and we have noted that publications are now emerging which employ these techniques, and they show great promise for enriching our understanding of the neural basis of the BAS. Finally, there is wide consensus that the family of trait measures used in RST research into the BAS is factorially complex, and questions about which trait measures are associated with which BAS-mediated effects need to be answered. Presently, we are persuaded by the view championed by Depue and colleagues, that Extraversion provides the most promising trait representation of the BAS, however, more research is needed.

In conclusion, we feel that research into the BAS is at an exciting crossroads with many possibilities ahead. We are certain that Jeffrey

Gray would have been enthused by these possibilities, and can imagine both the challenging questions he would have posed and the numerous ideas he would have conceived for pursuing them experimentally. Our excitement is thus tinged with sadness that he can no longer contribute to the development of the work that he began.*

References

Ashby, F.G., Alfonso-Reese, L.A., Tuken, A.U. and Wladron, E.M. (1998), A neuropsychological theory of multiple systems in category learning, *Psychological Review*, 105, 442–481

Ashby, F.G., Maddox, W.T. and Bohil, C.J. (2002), Observational versus feedback training in rule-based and information-integration category learning, *Memory and Cognition*, 30, 666–677

Ball, S.A. and Zuckerman, M. (1990), Sensation seeking, Eysenck's personality dimensions and reinforcement sensitivity in concept formation, *Personality and Individual Differences*, 11, 343–353

Barratt, E.S. (1985), Impulsiveness subtraits: arousal and information processing in J.T. Spence and C.E. Izard (eds), *Motivation, Emotion, and Personality* (New York: Elsevier Science Publishers), pp. 137–146

(1994), Impulsiveness and aggression in J. Monohan and H.J. Steadman (eds), *Violence and Mental Disorder* (Chicago: University of Chicago Press), pp. 61–79

Bartussek, D., Diedrich, O., Naumann, E. and Collet, W. (1993), Introversion-extraversion and event-related potentials (ERP): a test of J.A. Gray's theory, *Personality and Individual Differences*, 14, 565–574

Block, J. (1995), A contrarian view of the five-factor approach to personality description, *Psychological Bulletin*, 117, 187–215

Boddy, J., Carver, A. and Rowley, K. (1986), Effects of positive and negative verbal reinforcement on performance as a function of extraversion-introversion: some tests of Gray's theory, *Personality and Individual Differences*, 7, 81–88

Brown, J., Bullock, D. and Grossberg, S. (1999), How the basal ganglia use parallel excitatory and inhibitory learning pathways to selectively respond to unexpected rewarding cues, *Journal of Neuroscience*, 19, 10502–10511

Brown, R.G. and Marsden, C.D. (1988), Internal versus external cues and the control of attention in Parkinson's disease, *Brain*, 111, 323–345

Carver, C.S. (2004), Negative affects deriving from the behavioural approach system, *Emotion*, 4, 3–22

Carver, C.S. and White, T.L. (1994), Behavioural inhibition, behavioural activation, and affective responses to impending reward and punishment: the BIS/BAS scales, *Journal of Personality and Social Psychology*, 67, 319–333

*Preparation of this chapter was facilitated by an Economic and Social Research Council grant (PTA-026-27-0708) awarded to Luke D. Smillie.

Caseras, X., Ávila, C. and Torrubia, R. (2003), The measurement of individual differences in behavioural inhibition and behavioural activation systems: a comparison of personality scales, *Personality and Individual Differences*, 34, 999–1013

Cattell, R.B. (1950), *Personality: a Systematic Theoretical and Factual Study*, (New York, NY: McGraw-Hill)

Chico, E., Tous, J.M., Lorenzo-Seva, U. and Vigil-Colet, A. (2003), Spanish adaptation of Dickman's impulsivity inventory: its relationship to Eysenck's personality questionnaire, *Personality and Individual Differences*, 35, 1883–1892

Cloninger, C.R. (1987), A systematic method for clinical description and classification of personality variants, *Archives of General Psychiatry*, 44, 573–588

Cloninger, C.R., Svrakic, D.M. and Przybeck, T.R. (1993), A psychobiological model of temperament and character, *Archives of General Psychiatry*, 50, 975–990

Cohen, M.X., Young, J., Baek, J.M., Kessler, C. and Ranganath, C. (2005), Individual differences in extraversion and dopamine genetics reflect reactivity of neural reward circuitry, *Cognitive Brain Research*, 25, 851–861

Corr, P.J. (2002), J.A. Gray's reinforcement sensitivity theory and frustrative nonreward: a theoretical note on expectancies in reactions to rewarding stimuli, *Personality and Individual Differences*, 32, 1247–1253

Corr, P.J., Pickering, A.D. and Gray, J.A. (1995), Personality and reinforcement in associative and instrumental learning, *Personality and Individual Differences*, 19, 47–71

Coscina, D.V. (1997), The biopsychology of impulsivity: focus on brain serotonin in C.D. Webster and M.A. Jackson (eds), *Impulsivity: Theory, Assessment and Treatment* (London: Guilford Press), pp. 95–115

Crowe, E. and Higgins, E.T. (1997), Regulatory focus and strategic inclinations: promotion and prevention in decision-making, *Organizational Behavior and Human Decision Processes*, 69(2), 117–132

Dawe, S., Gullo, M. and Loxton, N.J. (2004), Reward drive and rash impulsiveness as dimensions of impulsivity: implications for substance misuse, *Addictive Behaviours*, 29, 1389–1406

Dawe, S. and Loxton, N.J. (2004), The role of impulsivity in the development of substance use and eating disorders, *Neuroscience and Biobehavioural Reviews*, 28, 343–351

Depue, R.A. and Collins, P.F. (1999), Neurobiology of the structure of personality: dopamine, facilitation of incentive motivation, and extraversion, *Behavioural and Brain Sciences*, 22, 491–569

Depue, R. and Iacono, W. (1989), Neurobehavioral aspects of affective disorders, *Annual Review of Psychology*, 40, 457–492

Depue, R.A. and Morrone-Strupinsky, J.V. (2005), A neurobehavioral model of affiliative bonding: implications for conceptualizing a human trait of affiliation, *Behavioral and Brain Sciences*, 28, 313–395

Derryberry, D. and Tucker, D.M. (1991), The adaptive base of the neural hierarchy: elementary motivational controls on network function in

R. Dienstbier (ed.), *Nebraska Symposium on Motivation*, vol. 38, *Perspectives on Motivation* (Lincoln: University of Nebraska Press), pp. 289–342

Dickman, S.J. (1990), Functional and dysfunctional impulsivity: personality and cognitive correlates, *Journal of Personality and Social Psychology*, 58, 95–102

(2000), Impulsivity, arousal and attention, *Personality and Individual Differences*, 28, 563–581

Elliot, A.J. and Thrash, T.M. (2002), Approach-avoidance motivation in personality: approach avoidance temperaments and goals, *Journal of Personality and Social Psychology*, 82, 804–818

Evenden, J.L. (1999), Varieties of impulsivity, *Psychopharmacology*, 146, 348–361

Eysenck, H.J. (1967), *The Biological Basis of Personality* (Springfield, IL: Charles C. Thomas)

Eysenck, H.J., Barrett, P., Wilson, G.D. and Jackson, C.J. (1992), Primary trait measurement of the 21 components of the P-E-N System, *European Journal of Psychological Assessment*, 8, 109–117

Eysenck, S.B.G., Pearson, P.R., Easting, G. and Allsopp, J.F. (1985), Age norms for impulsiveness, venturesomeness and empathy in adults, *Personality and Individual Differences*, 6, 613–619

Fowles, D.C. (1993), Biological variables in psychopathology: a psychobiological perspective in P.B. Sutker and H.E. Adams (eds), *Comprehensive Handbook of Psychopathology* (2nd edn, New York: Plenum Press), p. 5782

Goldberg, L.R. (1982), From ace to zombie: some explorations in the language of personality in C.D. Spielberger and J.N. Butcher (eds), *Advances in Personality Assessment* (Hillsdale, NJ: Erlbaum), vol. 1, pp. 203–234

Gomez, R. and McLaren, S. (1997), The effects of reward and punishment on response disinhibition, moods, heart rate and skin conductance level during instrumental learning, *Personality and Individual Differences*, 23, 305–316

Gray, J.A. (1970), The psychophysiological basis of introversion-extraversion, *Behaviour Research and Therapy*, 8, 249–266

(1973), Causal models of personality and how to test them in J.R. Royce (ed.), *Multivariate Analysis and Psychological Theory* (London: Academic Press), pp. 409–463

(1975), *Elements of a Two-Process Theory of Learning* (London: Academic Press)

(1981), A critique of Eysenck's theory of personality in H.J. Eysenck (ed.), *A Model for Personality* (Berlin: Springer), pp. 246–276

(1987a), Perspectives on anxiety and impulsivity: a commentary, *Journal of Research in Personality*, 21, 493–509

(1987b), The neuropsychology of emotion and personality in S.M. Stahl, S.D. Iversen and E.G. Goodman (eds), *Cognitive Neurochemistry* (Oxford: Oxford University Press), pp. 171–190

(1987c), *The Psychology of Fear and Stress* (Cambridge: Cambridge University Press)

(1994), Framework for a taxonomy of psychiatric disorder in S.H.M. Van Goozen, N.E. Van de Poll and J.A. Sergeant (eds), *Essays on Emotion Theory* (Hove: Lawrence Erlbaum), pp. 29–59

Gray, J.A. and McNaughton, N. (2000), *The Neuropsychology of Anxiety* (Oxford: Oxford University Press)

Gray, J.A., Owen, S., Davis, N. and Tsaltas, E. (1983), Psychological and physiological relations between anxiety and impulsivity in M. Zuckerman (ed.), *The Biological Bases of Sensation Seeking, Impulsivity, and Anxiety* (Hillsdale: Earlbaum), pp. 189–217

Gray, J.A. and Smith, P.T. (1969), An arousal-decision model for partial reinforcement and discrimination learning in R.M. Gilbert and N.S. Sutherland (eds), *Animal Discrimination Learning* (London: Academic Press), pp. 243–272

Gray, N.S., Pickering, A.D. and Gray, J.A. (1994), Psychoticism and dopamine D2 binding in the basal ganglia using single photon emission tomography, *Personality and Individual Differences*, 17, 431–434

Gupta, S. (1990), Impulsivity sociability and reinforcement in verbal operant conditioning: a replication, *Personality and Individual Differences*, 11, 585–589

Higgins, E.T. (1987), Self-discrepancy: a theory relating self and affect, *Psychological Review*, 94, 319–340

(1997), Beyond pleasure and pain, *American Psychologist*, 52, 1280–1300

(2000), Making a good decision: value from fit, *American Psychologist*, 55(11), 1217–1230

Jackson, C.J. (2001), Comparison between Eysenck and Gray's models of personality in the prediction of motivational work criteria, *Personality and Individual Differences*, 31, 129–144

Jackson, C.J. and Smillie, L.D. (2004), Appetitive motivation predicts the majority of personality and an ability measure: a comparison of BAS measures and a re-evaluation of the importance of RST, *Personality and Individual Differences*, 36, 1627–1636

John, O.P., Donahue, E.M. and Kentle, R.L. (1991), *The Big Five Inventory: Version 4a and 5* (Technical report, Berkeley, CA: Institute of Personality and Social Research, University of California)

Knyazev, G.G., Slobodskaya, H.R. and Wilson, G.D. (2004), Comparison of the construct validity of the Gray-Wilson personality questionnaire and the BIS/BAS scales, *Personality and Individual Differences*, 37, 1565–1582

Knowlton, B.J., Mangels, J.A. and Squire, L.R. (1996), A neostriatal habit learning system in humans, *Science*, 273, 1399–1402

Kruschke, J.K. (2005), Category learning in K. Lamberts and R.L. Goldstone (eds), *The Handbook of Cognition* (London: Sage), pp. 183–201

Lessiter, J. (1999), *A Dopaminergic Model of Reward Motivation: A Test of Implications for Personality and Schizophrenia* (Doctoral thesis, London: University of London)

Markman, A.B., Baldwin, G.C. and Maddox, W.T. (2005), The interaction of payoff structure and regulatory focus in classification, *Psychological Science*, 16, 852–855

Martin, L.E. and Potts, G.F. (2004), Reward sensitivity in impulsivity, *Cognitive Neuroscience and Neuropsychology*, 15, 1519–1522

Mason, O., Claridge, G., and Jackson, M. (1995), New scales for the assessment of schizotypy, *Personality and Individual Differences*, 18, 7–13

Parker, J.D.A. and Bagby, R.M. (1997), Impulsivity in adults: a critical review of measurement approaches in C.D. Webster and M.A. Jackson (eds), *Impulsivity: Theory, Assessment and Treatment* (London: Guilford Press), pp. 142–157

Patton, J.H., Stanford, M.S. and Barratt, E.S. (1995), Factor structure of the Barratt impulsiveness scale, *Journal of Clinical Psychology*, 51, 768–774

Pickering, A.D. (1999), Personality correlates of the dopaminergic facilitation of incentive motivation: impulsive sensation seeking rather than extraversion?, *Behavioural and Brain Sciences*, 22, 534–535

(2004), The neuropsychology of Impulsive antisocial sensation seeking personality traits: from dopamine to hippocampal function? in R.M. Stelmack (ed.), *On the Psychobiology of Personality: Essays in Honour of Marvin Zuckerman* (Oxford: Elsevier Ltd), pp. 453–476

Pickering, A.D., Corr, P.J., Powell, J.H., Kumari, V., Thornton, J.C. and Gray, J.A. (1997), Individual differences in reactions to reinforcing stimuli are neither black nor white: to what extent are they Gray? in H. Nyborg (ed.), *The Scientific Study of Human Nature: Tribute to Hans J. Eysenck at Eighty* (London: Elsevier Sciences), pp. 36–67

Pickering, A.D., Díaz, A. and Gray, J.A. (1995), Personality and reinforcement: an exploration using a maze-learning task, *Personality and Individual Differences*, 18, 541–558

Pickering, A.D. and Gray, J.A. (1999), The neuroscience of personality in L. Pervin and O. John (eds), *Handbook of Personality* (2nd edn, New York: Guilford Press), pp. 277–299

(2001), Dopamine, appetitive reinforcement, and the neuropsychology of human learning: an individual differences approach in A. Eliasz and A. Angleitner (eds), *Advances in Individual Differences Research* (Lengerich, Germany: PABST Science Publishers), pp. 113–149

Quilty, L.C. and Oakman, J.M. (2004), The assessment of behavioural activation: the relationship between impulsivity and behaviour activation, *Personality and Individual Differences*, 37, 429–442

Reuter, M., Schmitz, A., Corr, P. and Hennig, J. (2005), Molecular genetics support Gray's personality theory: the interaction of COMT and DRD2 polymorphisms predicts the behavioural approach system, *International Journal of Neuropsychopharmacology*, 1, 1–12

Revelle, W. (1995), Personality processes, *Annual Review of Psychology*, 6, 295–328

(1997), Extraversion and impulsivity: the last dimension in H. Nyborg (ed.), *The Scientific Study of Human Nature: Tribute to Hans J. Eysenck at Eighty* (Elsevier Science Press), pp. 189–212

Revelle, W., Humphreys, M.S., Simon, L. and Gilliland, K. (1980), The interactive effect of personality, time of day, and caffeine: a test of the arousal model, *Journal of Experimental Psychology: General*, 109, 1–31

Schultz, W. (1998), Predictive reward signal of dopamine neurons, *Journal of Neurophysiology*, 80, 1–27

Senuath, O.M. (1975), Personality, reinforcement and learning, *Percept Motor Skills*, 41, 459–463

Smillie, L.D. (2005), *Trait Representation of J.A. Gray's Behavioural Activation System: Distinguishing between Reward-Reactivity and Impulsivity* (Doctoral Thesis, University of Queensland)

Smillie, L.D., Dalgleish, L.I. and Jackson, C.J. (2007), Distinguishing between learning and motivation in behavioural tests of the reinforcement sensitivity theory of personality, *Personality and Social Psychology Bulletin*, 33, 476–489

Smillie, L.D. and Jackson, C.J. (2005), The appetitive motivation scale and other BAS measures in the prediction of approach and active avoidance, *Personality and Individual Differences*, 38, 981–994

(2006), Functional impulsivity and reinforcement sensitivity theory, *Journal of Personality*, 74, 47–83

Smillie, L.D., Jackson, C.J. and Dalgleish, L.I. (2006), Conceptual distinctions among Carver and White's (1994), BAS scales: a reward-reactivity versus trait impulsivity perspective, *Personality and Individual Differences*, 40, 1039–1050

Smillie, L.D., Pickering, A.D. and Jackson, C.J. (2006), The new reinforcement sensitivity theory: implications for personality measurement, *Personality and Social Psychology Review*, 10, 320–335

Squire, L.R. (1992), Memory and the hippocampus: a synthesis from findings with rats, monkeys, and humans, *Psychological Review*, 99, 195–231

Stewart, G.L. (1996), Reward structure as a moderator of the relationship between extraversion and sales performance, *Journal of Applied Psychology*, 81, 619–627

Thayer, R.E. (1989), *The Biopsychology of Mood and Arousal* (New York: Oxford University Press)

Torrubia, R., Ávila, C., Caseras, X. and Moltó, J. (2001), The sensitivity to punishment and sensitivity to reward questionnaire (SPSRQ) as a measure of Gray's anxiety and impulsivity dimensions, *Personality and Individual Differences*, 31, 837–862

Venables, P.H., Wilkins, S., Mitchell, D.A., Raine, A. and Bailes, K. (1990), A scale for the measurement of schizotypy, *Personality and Individual Differences*, 11, 481–495

Wacker, J., Chavanon, M. and Stemmler, G. (2006), Investigating the dopaminergic basis of extraversion in humans: a multilevel approach, *Journal of Personality and Social Psychology*, 91, 171–187

Watson, D. and Clark, L.A. (eds) (1994), Personality and Psychopathology, *Journal of Abnormal Psychology*, 103 [Special Issue].

Wickens, J. and Kotter, R. (1995), Cellular models of reinforcement in J.C. Houk, J.L. Davis, D.G. Beiser (eds), *Models of Information Processing in the Basal Ganglia* (London: MIT Press), pp. 189–214

Wilson, G.D., Barrett, P.T. and Gray, J.A. (1989), Human reactions to reward and punishment: a questionnaire examination of Gray's personality theory, *British Journal of Psychology*, 80, 509–515

Wilson, G.D., Gray, J.A. and Barrett, P.T. (1990), A factor analysis of the Gray-Wilson personality questionnaire, *Personality and Individual Differences*, 11, 1037–1045

Zelenski, J.M. and Larsen, R.J. (1999), Susceptibility to affect: a comparison of three personality taxonomies, *Journal of Personality*, 67, 761–791

Zinbarg, R. and Mohlman, J. (1998), Individual differences in the acquisition of affectively valenced associations, *Journal of Personality and Social Psychology*, 74, 1024–1040

Zinbarg, R. and Revelle, W. (1989), Personality and conditioning: a test of four models, *Journal of Personality and Social Psychology*, 57, 301–314

Zuckerman, M. (1979), *Sensation Seeking: Beyond the Optimal Level of Arousal* (Hillsdale, NJ: Erlbaum)

(1991), *Psychobiology of Personality* (Cambridge: Cambridge University Press)

5 Reinforcement Sensitivity Theory and personality

Philip J. Corr and Neil McNaughton

Reinforcement Sensitivity Theory (RST) is composed of two main components: (a) a *state* description of neural systems and associated, relatively short-term, emotions and behaviours; and (b) a *trait* description of longer-term dispositions to such emotions and behaviours. McNaughton and Corr (chapter 2) outlined the state level of description; this chapter explores the trait level of description and takes a more general view of the problems posed by the revised Gray and McNaughton (2000) theory.

'Top-down' and 'bottom-up' approaches to personality

The standard biological approach to personality adopts the well-established procedure from biology: first describe (taxonomy) and then explain (theorize about form of taxonomy; e.g., evolution). As noted by Gray (1972a, p. 372), 'The study of personality is the attempt (a) to discover consistent patterns of individual differences and (b) to account for the form taken by these patterns.' This 'top-down' approach has considerable merit and many empirical successes to its name. But it cannot be applied in a simple one-step fashion. Even within species and genera, taxonomy ((*a*) above) is not independent of causal theories ((*b*) above) – findings in molecular biology can alter taxonomy based on superficial description. With the study of personality it is a moot point whether the underlying variation in sensitivity of causal brain systems – which *must* control the psychological phenomena we classify under 'personality' – correspond in any obvious fashion to the manifest aspects of personality (i.e., factors, traits, facets, etc.). This chapter draws out some of the implications for personality research of understanding the relationship between (a) causal systems and (b) behavioural expressions, in an attempt to clarify the problems that future RST research will need to tackle.

Defining the problem?

The problem of relating causal and descriptive systems of personality is best illustrated by the seminal work of Hans Eysenck. Starting in 1944 with a statistical classification of individual variation in medical checklist items of 700 'war neurotics', which led to the postulation of the factors of Extraversion (E) and Neuroticism (N), Eysenck went on to propose causal theories to account for the brain-behavioural bases of these differences (inhibition-excitation theory in 1957, and arousal theory in 1967). This approach was adopted by Gray (1970, 1972b), who accepted that factor analysis can identify the minimum number, and thus the necessary (albeit not necessarily sufficient) factor space of personality, but not the rotation of axes (and hence causal systems) within that factor space.

However, close attention to the details of biological systems suggest that the factor analytic approach provides a description of personality that, whilst valid at the level of behavioural expression, fails adequately and sufficiently to reflect separable causal influences: thus, it may not be possible to use existing structural models of personality as a useful guide to discovering underlying causal systems. The conclusion from the analysis developed in this chapter is that if the phenotypic description of personality is not anchored to known brain systems then it will provide factors that are ill-matched to the underlying (genotypic and ontogenetic) causal processes. Accordingly, the growth in understanding the biology of personality will be stunted.

It needs to be borne in mind that the current uncertainty as to the best way to relate fundamental systems of emotion and motivation to personality factors is not a flaw in RST, but part of its ongoing development process, the nature of which has been described by Smillie, Pickering and Jackson (2006). They note that although RST is most often seen as a theory of anxiety and impulsivity, it is 'more accurately identified as a neuropsychology of emotion, motivation and learning. In fact, RST was born of basic animal learning research, initially not at all concerned with personality' (p. 320); they go on to remark, 'RST did not develop as a theory *of* specific traits, but as a theory of specific biological systems which were later suggested to relate, inter alia, to personality' (p. 321). There is another reason why basic emotion and motivational systems do not map neatly onto personality factors: basic emotion and motivation theory has extended beyond the point at which Gray suggested that the BIS and BAS relate to anxiety and impulsivity, respectively; and RST researchers have developed scales to measure the BIS and BAS that were influenced by Gray's original thinking and which do not reflect more recent developments in the basic theory. Thus, RST research represents two distinct bodies of knowledge, the first concerned with neural processes, the second with personality measurement. The Janus-face of RST is a strength, making it a dynamically evolving theory, but it also poses obvious problems for, at any given time, specifying a consensual model agreed by researchers. In particular, 'as if it were frozen in time, Gray's "personality model" is a relatively discrete slice of an otherwise continuous and ongoing field of knowledge' (Smillie *et al.* 2006, p. 321).

A biological approach to factor analysis

The class of statistical reduction methods that fall under the rubric of 'factor analysis' have played a fundamental role in personality research. The number, but not nature, of the sources of variance can be estimated by Principal Components Analysis (PCA) or one of the various forms of common factor analysis (CFA). These statistical techniques have been criticized for allowing arbitrary decisions to be made concerning the number of factors to be extracted and the location of the factors within the factor space. A biological perspective shows that such apparently arbitrary choices concerning the relation of variables (including items in a questionnaire) are not the correct means of settling the matter of the structure of personality, either in terms of the location of the axes within the space or, indeed, of whether factor axes should be orthogonal (for a discussion of the limitations of factor analysis, especially of complex biological systems, see Lykken 1971).

A purely mathematical choice of which scales to use, based on some criterion such as the nominal factorial purity of a pair of scales, has nothing to do with where a real underlying causal factor is controlling variance within the data space. The choice of scales is, however, important if we wish them each to be pure measures of a real causal factor. It is merely a convenient initial simplification to use orthogonal axes and rotate these so that the first factor captures the maximum shared variance among all the measured variables. As we get more knowledge of underlying causal systems, then *this* knowledge should influence the description of personality. Nor does the identification of a single real factor (e.g., Extraversion) commit one to dependence of this factor on a single cause. Thus, genetic influences, developmental changes, infection, long-term social factors and some single event in the previous week may all be important in causing personality expression. Of course, there is no necessary conflict between factor analytically-derived personality factors and those suggested by biological theory.

Extraversion and Neuroticism may make a good job of accounting for systematic individual differences at the highest level of description; but they may be a poor starting point if we wish to understand the complex of underlying causal systems – but often a 'poor' starting point is better than none at all. What is needed is a dynamic descriptive model, showing all levels of the structural hierarchy and how each level relates to each other – but we need to understand the functioning of the underlying causal systems first.

It might seem that we have manoeuvred ourselves into a somewhat awkward position: we have argued that factor analysis, upon which most of the established models of personality are based, may not provide a reliable guide to the biological basis of personality, yet that is where RST started and continues to thrive: i.e., on factor analytically-derived Extraversion and Neuroticism and other psychometric models of reward and punishment sensitivities. But experimental analysis cannot proceed until at least some kind of descriptive framework is in place for personality characters to be explained. Personality psychology must, therefore, start with factors discoverable by factor analysis. But crucially it must also move beyond this technique in developing and refining its description of personality, undertaking a continual process of anchoring descriptive axes and extending the dimensions of the factor space already discovered.

We must, therefore, conclude that factor analysis provides only a preliminary guide to the biological processes underlying the most common sources of variation in a population. This conclusion is demanded by the fact that factor analysis will not be able to differentiate, for example, separate causes that are conflated in development, and nor is it able to identify primary causes. It works on measures of the phenotype that may be (and often are) the end product of a long chain of causal, and interacting, influences. Causal and phenotypic factors may be so similar as to allow a one-to-one correspondence, but this would be the outcome of serendipity not of the logic of factor analysis. Therefore, 'discovering' a nominally single factor of personality and then *assuming* that there is a single causal basis of that factor is, to our way of thinking, a flawed strategy in the neuroscience of personality. It is an open empirical question whether there exists a single causal factor for the recovered personality factor.

Extraversion/neuroticism and reward/punishment sensitivity

Let us now take a closer look at the personality factors in the context of RST. Gray and Eysenck both accept that factor analysis recovers, at least, two personality dimensions: Extraversion and Neuroticism. The critical issues in relation to the factors within such a two-dimensional space is whether they are independent of each other (orthogonal) or not, and where in the space they should be placed. But the item loadings on Eysenck's (1944, 1947) factor analysis of neurotic symptoms/behaviours show that a large number of decisions had to be made concerning the nature of the normal personality dimensions corresponding to the (four original) factors of the factor analysis.[1] The later choice of items for the measurement of Extraversion and Neuroticism scales was not based on consideration of causal factors; it was based on preconceptions (i.e., a theory) about the most appropriate scales to *describe* the phenotypic nature of personality seen in the light of then current psychiatric nosology and other theoretical accounts of personality (e.g., Jung's Introversion-Extraversion). Eysenck's model was a 'best-guess'; indeed, it should be acknowledged as 'excellent-guess' given the ubiquity of these factors in virtually every other structural model of personality. But, as we have already seen, a valid structural model of factors at the most general level of description (i.e., dimensions) does not necessarily inform investigation of the associated causally-efficacious underlying systems.

Psychometric refinement

Eysenck's structural model has seen a number of changes over the years, and this psychometric refinement cannot be quoted in strong support of the original model (Gray 1981). Corr and McNaughton (submitted) discuss this matter at some length. Here it is sufficient to note that Eysenck's (e.g., Eysenck and Eysenck 1975) attempt to create factorial purity represents, in essence, an arbitrary choice of axis rotation: he could have added a large number of other items to his scales and then, provided the item population had retained dimensional purity, he could have created orthogonal scales of reward sensitivity and punishment sensitivity. RST researchers have done exactly this in their creation of scales of reward and punishment sensitivity. Psychometric tinkering can take us only so far in understanding the causal bases of personality – it leaves whole areas barren of either description or explanation. The substantive issue for RST is how far our current knowledge of the brain

---

[1] When the four factors of Eysenck's (1944) matrix are rotated in accordance with conventional techniques, then these factors could, equally as well, be interpreted as reward and punishment sensitivity (Perkins, Revelle and Corr, unpublished); it is important to note that E and N were hypothesized from unrotated factors in 1944.

can identify the location of real factor (causal) axes. It is only when this matter is decided that the issue of the best measurement scale need be addressed. McNaughton and Corr (chapter 2) shows much progress has been made in identifying putative brain systems underlying personality; i.e., the *Fight-Flight-Freeze System* (FFFS), the *Behavioural Inhibition System* (BIS) and the *Behavioural Approach System* (BAS).

Nature of the extracted factors

The rotation of Extraversion and Neuroticism by 30° suggested by Gray (1970, 1972b), is sufficiently small that, to a first approximation, 'Neuroticism' could be seen as composed largely of 'Sensitivity to Punishment' (perhaps comprising both fear and anxiety). Independent of whether we choose to rotate the axes, there is a separate question of the psychological nature of the factors being measured. There are thus two problems to solve:

(1) the location of the axes: Eysenck may have appeared to resolve this issue for his theory by fiat – refining the Extraversion scale to become independent to Neuroticism – but, as we have seen, either an alternative conception of his 1944 factor matrix or subsequent refinement of scales would have produced scales reflecting alternative rotations;

(2) underlying systems: the specific functional nature of the underlying factor giving rise to each dimension; in practice, solving this issue should also solve issue 1, but until this solution is definitely achieved both need to be assessed.

Neural systems and personality factors

The main issue to be faced is to what extent variation in the sensitivity of neural or hormonal modulatory systems does or could result in personality factors. Tightly linked to this is the question of how the neural systems (BAS, FFFS, BIS) are modulated. There are a number of quite distinct (but not mutually exclusive) possibilities.

(1) The simplest possibility is that a specific modulatory system could act solely on one single functional system and could act uniformly on all the elements of that system. With three separate modulatory systems, this would generate a separate personality factor for each of the BIS, FFFS and BAS. According to this view, a single personality factor would predict all behaviour mediated by the FFFS, irrespective of the specific

neural circuits mediating specific behaviours (e.g., phobia = hypothamalus + amgydala), and likewise for the BAS and BIS.

(2) Next in complexity is the possibility that a specific modulatory system could act on two systems and would act uniformly on all the elements of both systems. There could, for example, be a single personality factor representing the sensitivity of both the FFFS and BIS concurrently (perhaps identifiable with 'threat sensitivity') or of both the BAS and FFFS (perhaps identifiable with 'reinforcer sensitivity'). At the personality level, we would need to take into account the distinct nature of the single modulatory system and of the two functional systems modulated. Critically we would expect co-variation, at the personality level, between measures that, at the state level, were selective for each of the systems.

(3) Most general and complex is the possibility that a specific modulatory system could act on selected parts of one or more functional systems. At the personality level, we would need to take into account both the nature of the modulatory system and the detailed nature of its selective action on the functional systems affected.

When we look more closely at the detailed neurology of the Gray and McNaughton (2000) theory, the situation becomes clearer. Both the FFFS and the BIS are represented by very large numbers of interlinked brain structures. But this multiplicity reflects a hierarchical organization that selects particular behaviours to match particular 'defensive distances' (or threat perception; see McNaughton and Corr, chapter 2). Threat perception itself represents the dimension of defensive distance (i.e., actual or perceived distance from threat) that selects, from all of the levels of the system, the currently appropriate one.

For the operation of any general factor underlying sensitivity to threat there must, then, be some neural or hormonal system that can modulate all levels of the BIS and/or FFFS concurrently. There are a number of potential candidates for this role in the theory: noradrenergic input, serotonergic input (BIS and FFFS), the endogenous hormonal ligand of the benzodiazepine receptor (the latter is restricted to the BIS only) and the various hormones in the hypothalamus-pituitary-adrenal (HPA) axis stress cascade (BIS and FFFS). Each of these has the capacity to affect many structures, in the same way, in parallel. Both noradrenergic and serotonergic systems can do this because they have multiple divergent collaterals targeting many structures. An endogenous benzodiazepine ligand and the various stress hormones could do this because of the widespread distribution of the relevant receptors across the critical structures and the delivery of the critical compounds to those structures via the blood stream.

Finally, cutting across the BAS, FFFS and BIS, is physiological arousal. Concurrent activation of different motivational systems within each of the BAS and FFFS is held (Gray and Smith 1969) to sum in the production of arousal. Activation of the BIS also increases arousal directly via the amygdala in a way that by-passes the septo-hippocampal control of behavioural inhibition. This common summation of input from all the systems provides an obvious potential source for a very general factor of 'arousability' that reflects changes in the responsiveness of the autonomic nervous system that are significant for all three of the BAS, FFFS and BIS.

We have, then, a range of physical substrates in which long-term changes in sensitivity could give rise to personality factors.

(1) An effect general within the BIS but relatively specific to it could be produced by changes in benzodiazepine-like hormones or their receptors. Determination as to whether any particular trait measure (or factor score) reflected activity in this system would be straightforward: such a trait measure should be reduced by repeated administration of a benzodiazepine agonist over a period of at least two weeks. As an additional check, buspirone could be repeatedly administered: this drug has the same action on the BIS as a benzodiazepine but essentially opposite side-effects and the latter, again, diminish with repeated administration. Any scale or measure intended to relate to the BIS should have, as a primary criterion, that it be similarly affected by long-term administration of these two chemically distinct types of anxiolytic. Given such a relation, its specificity would then have to be determined.

(2) Effects restricted to parts of the BIS could be produced by changes in noradrenaline or serotonin. To determine whether any particular trait measure (or factor score) reflected activity in the monoamine systems one would use chronic administration of either serotonin or noradrenaline re-uptake inhibitors, or a combination of the two. Changes in both together can also be produced by monoamine oxidase inhibitors. Any scale or measure affected by such monoaminergic manipulations but not by both benzodiazepines and buspirone would not be assessing BIS activity.

(3) General effects could be produced by changes in autonomic reactivity or by changes in circulating hormones, such as adrenaline.

(4) There are insufficient data to be sure whether the FFFS could be specifically modulated. While there are drugs that are panicolytic these tend to also be anxiolytic. Genetic or long-term environmental effects on the serotonin system are likely to be general to the FFFS and BIS rather than specific to the FFFS. Given the special focus of BIS output on the

FFFS (as a means of increasing negative bias), it may not be reasonable to expect there to be any system that modulates the FFFS without also having separate direct effects on the BIS – however, the functional hierarchies of the FFFS and BIS are clearly different, and the existence of specific psychometric measures of fear and anxiety, which can be shown to be relatively uncorrelated, points to the existence of separate causal influences.

(5) Effects selective to the BAS can probably be produced by chronic alterations in dopaminergic and/or opiodergic systems.

Monoamine systems and personality

The monoamine systems have been implicated in anxiety and the clustering of anxiety disorders is the basis for Gray's suggestion that Eysenck's factors should be rotated. An immediate point to note is that serotonin and noradrenaline are affected in similar ways by stress. They also have effects that combine synergistically. It follows that many genetic sources controlling serotonin and noradrenaline, and especially those that control monoamine oxidase (which has parallel effects on serotonin and noradrenaline), could underlie a single recoverable personality dimension. This point is of particular relevance to the only animal model we have for a relevant personality dimension.

There is evidence that 'emotionality' in rats is a homologue of neurotic introversion, or perhaps 'trait anxiety' (Broadhurst 1960). It has a major genetic component (Hall 1951; Gray 1987). Selective breeding for high and low emotional defecation ('emotionality') has resulted in the Maudsley Reactive and Maudsley Non-reactive strains of rat, respectively. Such defecation in anticipation of an aversive event occurs in many species (Candland and Nagy 1969), including our own (Stouffer et al. 1969; cited by Broadhurst 1960). It appears to be an indicator of very high levels of fear or anxiety (Hunt and Otis 1953).

Despite being selected for a single, rather basic, character, the two Maudsley strains differ on a huge range of items (Broadhurst 1975; Blizard 1981; Gray 1987). Overall, these items suggest that Maudsley Reactive rats have a greater response to threats in general rather than to anxiety-provoking stimuli in particular. The two strains also differ in an animal model of depression (Abel, Altman and Commissaris 1992; Viglinskaya et al. 1995) and this effect shows a strong linkage between changes in scores on an anxiety test with those on the depression test (Commissaris et al. 1996). Just like human neurotic introversion, the genetic differences between Reactive and Non-reactive rats appear to influence susceptibility to the full spectrum of neurotic reactions.

Long-term changes in the monoamine systems appear, then, to have general effects on defensive distance (i.e., actual or perceived distance from threat) that are independent of defensive direction (i.e., to avoid or approach the threat). Both with the direct alteration of serotonergic function (Deakin and Graeff 1991) and with the indirect genetic alteration of both noradrenergic and serotonergic function in the Maudsley strains, there are changes in both defensive approach and defensive avoidance. As noted above, the breadth of monoamine effects is consistent with the very broad morbidity (ranging from obsessive compulsive disorder through neurotic depression) associated with genetic and environmental alterations in neurotic introversion and 'punishment sensitivity' in general.

However, although these effects clearly range across the FFFS and BIS, they do not appear to be a change in threat sensitivity, pure and simple. It has been emphasized by Deakin and Graeff (Graeff 1994; Deakin and Graeff 1991) that the serotonergic system has opposite effects on panic to other aspects of defence. The separation between components of threat extends further. Serotonergic dysfunction appears to impair fear-related behaviour that requires a specific decision, such as passive avoidance and conditioned suppression, but appears to increase fear responses related to arousal, such as fear potentiated startle and immediate responses to aversive stimulation (Gray and McNaughton 2000, table 5.2). Although the available evidence is slim, it suggests that neurotic-introversion, or what Gray (1970) labelled 'trait anxiety', personality results from genetic or environmental changes in the long-term tone of the serotonin and noradrenaline systems – probably interacting synergistically. It also suggests that such changes will involve a general increase in many fear-(FFFS) and anxiety-(BIS) related behaviours but, at least in the general population, could involve a modest decrease in the tendency to panic.

Benzodiazepine receptors, BIS and personality

There could also be a personality factor more specifically restricted to the sensitivity of the BIS. The BIS itself is defined in terms of sites of action of anxiolytic drugs. In the case of the novel anxiolytic drugs, acting at 5HT1A receptors, we are probably looking at a serendipitous selectivity for serotonergic terminals located in the BIS. When serotonin itself binds to 5HT1A receptors, it would also be binding to many other receptors, served by collaterals in other parts of the defence system. However, the most commonly used classical anxiolytics, the benzodiazepines, operate by modulating the sensitivity of the GABA-A receptor without binding to it themselves. This would be an ideal site at which a circulating 'anxiety-specific' hormone could act. There is evidence for endogenous compounds that bind to benzodiazepine receptors and which could have such a hormonal action (George *et al.* 1994; Lamacz *et al.* 1996; Sudakov *et al.* 2001; Aufdembrinke 1998; Ozawa *et al.* 1994). We might expect, then, that longer-term changes in the reactivity of such a system could lead to a personality factor that would influence specific morbidity for generalized anxiety disorder and would not affect morbidity for obsessive compulsive disorder, panic disorder or depression.

General modulation

That personality factors should operate at a more global level also makes evolutionary sense. Specific responses (risk assessment, panic) are appropriate to particular levels of threat. But there is a delicate balance in normal ecological situations between general risk-proneness (which could cause you to be killed by a predator before you reproduce) and risk aversion (which could cause you or your offspring to starve to death while avoiding a predator and so, again, fail to reproduce). Specific learning tied to local stimuli will deal with specific special risks, but we would expect that, in addition, there would be longer-term feedback mechanisms that adjust non-specific risk-proneness both within an individual and within a genetic pool. Critically, such long-term adjustments cannot be specific to a particular defensive distance (and hence symptomatology). They must modulate the overarching factor of defensive distance itself.

In principle, there might be a wide range of negative affective events combining to create a general avoidance tendency reflecting activation of a single FFFS. Conversely, positive affective events would activate the BAS. Activation of inputs to FFFS and inputs to BAS will sum to produce general arousal (Gray and Smith 1969) and subtract to produce behavioural output. The more similarly the FFFS and BAS are activated, the more conflict will result and activate the BIS. This will increase arousal further and bias decisions towards avoidance (Gray and McNaughton 2000).

Gray and McNaughton (2000) and McNaughton and Corr (2004) deliberately held back from specifying the relationship of the components of the revised theory and personality factors; we now incline to the view that the old 'Anxiety' axis (i.e., neurotic-introversion) should be relabelled as 'Punishment Sensitivity', or 'Threat Perception', or simply 'Defensive Distance', with lower order factors of this orthogonal 'dimension' breaking down into specific, lower-order, oblique FFFS-fear and BIS-anxiety factors. It should be noted here that we encounter another asymmetry: fear can be generated without a significant degree of anxiety (i.e., in the absence of goal-conflict), but BIS activation always leads to FFFS activation via the increase in negative valence. For this reason FFFS and BIS will often be co-activated.

Two important issues spring from these conclusions: (a) the (inter) dependence of the Punishment Sensitivity (fear + anxiety) and the BAS; and (b) the relationship between fear and anxiety measures on behavioural and psychophysiological measures in the laboratory (in this latter case, it is important to remember the distinction between (i) the *subtractive* nature of reward and punishment on the 'decision' mechanism, *direction*; and (ii) the *additive* effect of reward and punishment on the arousal component, *intensity*).

FFFS/BIS and BAS interactions

An important point for RST is that the theory focuses on *state* changes and considers three basic scenarios: approach, avoid and conflict. But there is a layer of complexity that is old (Gray and Smith 1969) that focuses on the parametric interactions between approach and avoidance systems when each is concurrently activated. The key point is that when the BAS and FFFS are activated unequally (that is, when there is little conflict between approach and avoidance), they nonetheless interact: this interaction is symmetrical. Activation of one system inhibits the other with respect to decision-making. This inhibitory interaction (in its purest form counterconditioning of one stimulus by a motivationally opposite stimulus) is insensitive to anxiolytic drugs and so is in practice as well as theoretically independent of the BIS (McNaughton and Gray 1983). Thus, while the two systems are independent in that changes in the sensitivity of one will not affect the sensitivity of the other, they are not independent in that *concurrent* activation will cause interactions in their generation of *behavioural output*. The primary symmetrical interactions between the systems are also non-linear (see below), accounting for such phenomena as behavioural contrast and peak shift (Gray and Smith 1969). Joint activation increases arousal while producing a subtractive effect on the decision process of the model.

Superimposed on these symmetrical interactions is the BIS. This is activated more as the difficulty of resolving the decision between the two (approach-avoid) increases, i.e., as the relative power of approach and avoidance become more equal. Its activation results in asymmetrical effects. It boosts arousal (over and above the additive effect of the existing conflicting motivations) while it amplifies activity in the aversive system but not the appetitive one. Under conditions of conflict, then, it increases risk aversion.

Corr (2001, 2002a) argued that much of the human experimental data designed to test the BIS and BAS are consistent with the *joint subsystems hypothesis* of BIS/BAS effects (for a review of this limited literature, see Corr 2004). Interactions are often found between psychometric measures of the BIS/BAS in predicting behavioural effects. The state account of the theory presented above, however, essentially retains the *separable subsystems hypothesis* (i.e., BIS/BAS effects are functionally independent) of the 1982 version of the theory. While the systems are *neurally* independent, and can be assessed for separate trait sensitivities, their *outputs* will interact when they are *concurrently activated*. We argue that such concurrent activation is usual, but not necessary, under typical human laboratory conditions (e.g., mixed reward/punishment stimuli, weak stimuli) on tasks sensitive to motivational influences.[2]

Separability and dominance of systems

There are two distinct issues here. The first is the issue of intrinsic separability of the systems, and the second is the idea of dominance. Under normal ecological circumstances, the 2000 theory assumes (as did the 1982 theory) that an approach or an avoidance tendency will often capture response mechanisms. But, where approach and avoidance are too evenly matched for straightforward capture, activation of the BIS will enhance the avoidance tendency and so usually lead to avoidance. This might seem to imply that either the BAS or FFFS will be dominant at all times (with the FFFS needing help from the BIS on occasion). However, there are two scenarios where this dominance will be less than absolute. First, is when activation of the BIS changes a weak net approach tendency into an only marginal avoidance tendency.

---

[2] They are other ways in which the systems may interact to produce complex forms of behaviour. Corr (2002b) noted that frustative non-reward should be generated first in those individuals sensitive to reward (i.e., those who are highly BAS-sensitive), and that the detection of 'non-reward' (i.e., a lower frequency or magnitude of reward than expected) should serve as an input to the BIS (which generates the aversive state; this position is consistent with the Arousal-Decision model presented by Gray and Smith 1969). The experimental prediction is that such a state should be highest in BAS+/ BIS + individuals and lowest in BAS −/BIS − individuals. Despite some initial work (e.g., Carver 2004), this prediction has yet to be adequately investigated. Clarity on this matter, as well as others, may, however, need to wait for adequate psychometric measures of the revised FFFS and BIS.

Under these circumstances the observed behaviour will be dominated by risk assessment and exploration (of the external world or of memory) with prepotent approach and avoidance tendencies both suppressed. Second, is when we view behaviour on a longer timescale. In a straight alley, in which both food and shock have been experienced in the goal box, a rat will initially run towards the goal since approach gradients are shallower than avoidance gradients (Miller 1944). This approach to the goal (since it involves passive avoidance) will engage the BIS and so slow approach even more than would the subtraction of the avoidance tendency from the approach tendency. If the memory of the shock is sufficiently aversive, the rat will stop at some distance from the goal box, turn and move away. From this point, the rat is engaged in active avoidance, the BIS is no longer engaged, and so the memory of the shock is perceived as relatively less aversive than when approaching. The rat therefore reverses its direction. This relatively fast switching between states, coupled with the assumption of behavioural momentum, explains the dithering observed in rats during approach-avoidance conflict in runways and that is experienced cognitively, and not always behaviourally silently, in ourselves when faced with difficult choices.

This analysis would deliver the results predicted by the joint subsystems hypothesis provided that, in the vast majority of human experiments, there is simultaneous weak activation of appetitive and aversive systems. Given the presence of goal gradients, there is little reason to assume that, across the whole task, one system dominates the other. Rather, the FFFS, BIS and BAS may be simultaneously activated and the control of behaviour pass from one to the other as a result of the weakness of activating stimuli, variations in memories currently being recalled or, as is often the case, changing task demands.

Different forms of interaction

To say that the systems are fundamentally independent does not mean that their effects on behaviour will be independent. This, in turn, means that assessment of underlying personality factors will involve variables that are likely not to be factorially pure. When tested at the state level, appetitive and aversive systems will frequently be co-activated – albeit unintentionally. Omission of reward is punishing and so it can be difficult to arrange a truly pure reward schedule. With concurrent activation of the systems (one weaker and the other stronger) the more there is heightened activity in one system the more there will be a general suppression of the other (Gray and Smith 1969). This joint subsystems view is, at a fundamental neural level, wholly consistent with Gray's original view of the two critical personality factors as reflecting independent *sensitivities* to punishment and reward. Sensitivity of one system can be assessed by a carefully purified test, in the absence of contamination from the other, and the personality factor loadings extracted from such pure tests will be independent. The interaction between the systems when they are co-activated even modestly can, however, be complicated.

Pure activation of the BAS or FFFS involves cognitions that, if they lead to action, will result in pure approach (BAS) or pure avoidance (FFFS) of some situation without any tendency to produce cognitions of the opposite affective valence. In such situations, trait differences in the reactivity of the inactivated system will not affect responses to the activated system.

Unequal activation of the BAS and FFFS involves strong activation of one system with weak activation of the system inducing the opposite tendency. Here trait increases in the reactivity of the less activated system will result in decreased cognitive and hence behavioural output from the more activated system and a contrasting increase in arousal. Trait decreases would have the opposite effects. This interaction in the output of the co-activated systems is symmetrical – it does not matter which is the weak and which the strong system. In human experiments this interaction could appear as an attentional bias. The cognitions of the more weakly activated system would be made even weaker and so less able to capture attention. If one is waiting for the executioner's bullet (FFFS activation) then news of a US$100 wage bonus is unlikely to lead to much (BAS-mediated) pleasure!

Similar activation of the BAS and FFFS produces conflict that has effects over and above the interactions produced with unequal activation. The more equal is the activation of the opposing tendencies, the more we have conflict. At low levels, conflict results (via mild BIS activation) in an amplification of the effects of the FFFS on behavioural output while the BAS is controlling behaviour (but not vice versa). Conflict changes the behavioural output qualitatively when the approach and avoidance tendencies (behaviourally silent or not) are sufficiently balanced to make a decision between approach and avoidance difficult to make on the basis of choosing that one which is clearly the more activated. At this point, both approach and avoidance behaviours (as opposed to the positive and negative cognitions represented by activity in the BAS and FFFS) are blocked and exploration and risk analysis are initiated to gather information, positive or negative, that will resolve the conflict. Exploration and risk analysis are most easily detected as behaviour but it is a crucial feature of the theory that they involve behaviourally silent scanning of memory as well as of the environment. Here, trait changes in any of the systems will alter cognitive and so, often, behavioural output. They will also, as a result of changes in cognition, change memory and so future behaviour. Changes in the BAS will alter the external stimulus values at which a BAS/FFFS balance results in conflict. Changes in the FFFS will alter both this balance and, probably, the effect of output from the BIS since, as the theory stands at present, BIS output will often amplify FFFS activity. Increased sensitivity of the BIS will alter the balance by triggering increased FFFS activity at lower levels of conflict. Indeed, the theory attributes some cases of generalized anxiety disorder to excessive output from the BIS that results in negative cognitive bias, i.e. excessive activity in the FFFS for a given input during approach to a (perhaps very mildly) threatening situation.

Testing the systems

As we have seen, the 2000 theory argues for independence of the systems in the sense that all three systems have their own unique, non-overlapping biological control: (a) anxiolytic drugs affect BIS but not BAS nor FFFS;[3] (b) panicolytic drugs affect FFFS but (probably) not BIS; and (c) addictive drugs affect BAS but not BIS or FFFS. The critical point here is that you can change trait features of one system without affecting the outputs from the other systems and detect these changes selectively *provided* you have pure tests of the other systems.

Testing BAS sensitivity without FFFS or BIS is theoretically simple. All that is needed is a task that determines pure sensitivity to reward with no slightest hint of aversive consequences. In practice, some care must be taken as many net positive stimuli have both appetitive and aversive aspects and (a core aspect of the theory) any omission of an expected appetitive stimulus will result in aversion. Error-free learning paradigms (equivalent to the rat finding food in a straight alley) are probably necessary to achieve this. Testing FFFS sensitivity is the same but with the affective signs reversed.

Testing uncontaminated BIS sensitivity is more difficult because the most usual way of generating conflict pits punishment against reward. As a result, changes in sensitivity of either the BAS or FFFS will shift the balance of the conflict and so alter the apparent output of the BIS in that situation. The same is true with variations in the stimuli used in a task.

---

[3] This description is of the classes of drugs rather than of individual drugs. Some anxiolytic drugs are panicolytic and addictive but that is as a result of side-effects and is not a necessary feature of anxiolysis since other equally anxiolytic drugs are neither panicolytic nor addictive.

Solution of what is *formally* a passive avoidance task does not require the BIS, provided the nominally competing tendency is weak enough not to generate significant conflict (Okaichi and Okaichi 1994). The simplest task without this problem is two-way active avoidance. This involves an avoidance-avoidance conflict rather than an approach-avoidance conflict. Changes in the sensitivity of the FFFS will therefore affect avoidance, as such, equally for the two locations, and changes in passive avoidance *relative to* active avoidance must be due to changes in sensitivity of the BIS.

The procedure to assess the BIS would be as follows: (a) Test groups of individuals in both a one-way and a two-way active avoidance task at varying levels of shock. Determine the normal variation (if any) in one-way active avoidance learning (or perhaps performance) with shock level – this must be due to variation in activation of FFFS without any change in the 'sensitivity' of the BIS. (b) Then look at the additional differences between individuals in two-way avoidance. The drug data say that low BIS sensitivity will result in 'improved' two-way avoidance learning relative to one-way, since anxiolytic drugs improve the former and do not change the latter. Thus, the drugs allow active avoidance, in the two-way situation, to occur without interference from the normally competing passive avoidance tendency. Elsewhere, we have presented other state challenge tests to assess the reactivity of FFFS and BIS modules (McNaughton and Corr 2004).

A computational model

In an attempt to put a bit more flesh on the bare bones of the concepts outlined above, we have constructed a simple computational model. The parameters of the model derive from the interrelations between the FFFS, BIS and BAS that we have outlined above. These interrelations were always implicit in the original (1982) BIS theory. But the revised theory stresses that simultaneous activation of the FFFS and the BAS activates the BIS. This, and the largely ignored symmetrical interactions of the BAS and FFFS, have significant implications for the interdependencies in functional outputs of these systems.

Model specifications The model (see Figure 5.1) is based primarily on the symmetric BAS-FFFS interactions of the Gray and Smith arousal-decision model. To their basic model we have added the asymmetric effects on these systems of the BIS. (The model is not intended to be quantitative.) Input units and response output units are expressed as percentages of some nominal standard. Sensitivities are

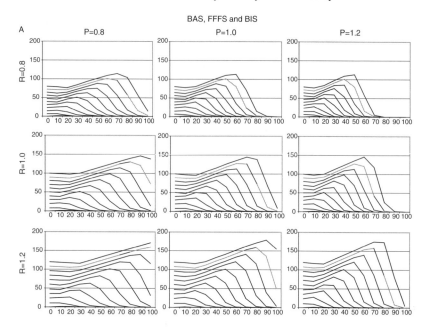

Figure 5.1 Output from the modified Gray and Smith model of Figure 2.6 (see chapter 2). R, P represent changes in personality factors of reward sensitivity and punishment sensitivity, respectively. The Y axis represents the output of reward-related behaviour. The different lines plotted result from different reward input values (0–100 %). The X axis represents different punishment input values (0–100 %) on the same nominal scale as reward values. A: BAS, FFFS and BIS: output of the full model (see D for block diagram). B: BAS and FFFS (no BIS): output of the model when the BIS component (see D) is eliminated. C: Effect of loss of BIS: difference between the two models in A and B. This represents the type of effect to be expected with people treated with anxiolytics or with very low scores on a factor relating to BIS sensitivity. By contrast, variation due to 'trait anxiety' would be expected to follow the changes in P. D: Modified Gray and Smith model: a block diagram of the model is shown at D. R_i, P_i are inputs to the BAS and FFFS, respectively. These are multiplied by a sensitivity value (R = 0.8, 1.0, 1.2; P = 0.8, 1.0, 1.2 in the graphs) to deliver internal representations R'_i, P'_i. These sum to produce arousal (a). Their difference is input to a decision mechanism that assumes a normal distribution of their inputs with a particular standard deviation (s). Conflict detection in the BIS is modelled as a function that increases with increasing activation of the more activated of the two systems (FFFS or BAS) and decreases as the unsigned difference between the two systems increases

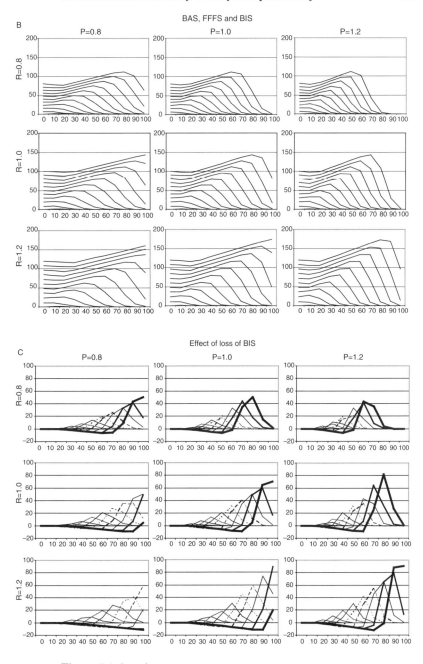

Figure 5.1 (*cont.*)

D   Modified Gray and Smith model

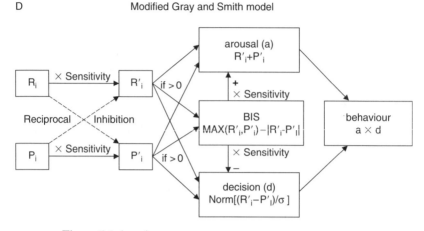

Figure 5.1 (*cont.*)

expressed as proportions of some nominal mean or median of a normal population and are used as multipliers. Thus with reward sensitivity (impulsivity) at the mean for the population (R=1.0) changes in reward input between 0–100 per cent produce changes in output between 0–100 per cent, respectively, provided there is no punishment input. With R=1.2 (representing reward sensitivity 20 per cent above the norm), input between 0–100 per cent produces changes in output between 0–120 per cent, respectively.

Computationally, reward and punishment sensitivities are implemented as multipliers between the external input (R_i, P_i) and its internal representation (R'_i, P'_i). We depart slightly from the Gray and Smith model in that the mutual inhibition of the reward and punishment systems is represented as being fed-forward from the external inputs to the internal representations rather than involving recursive connections. This provides computational simplicity (requiring no recursion) and is likely to be closer to neural reality. The internal representations of reward and punishment (R'_i, P'_i) are then separately summed (to calculate *arousal*) or subtracted (to calculate *decision*). We have made a second minor modification to the Gray and Smith model, here, preventing R'_i or P'_i from taking negative values. This was done to match the fact that neurons cannot be inhibited below a zero firing rate. An important feature, retained from the original model, is that the decision mechanism operates on the assumption of a normal distribution of the strength of its inputs. The arousal and decision components are then multiplied to generate the overall behavioural output observed. This latter step allows generation of such phenomena as behavioural contrast and peak shift when a free operant measure is being used. The separate arousal and decision outputs can be used if, say, autonomic output or, say, choice in a two choice paradigm is to be modelled, respectively.

While the architecture of the model is quite specific, its outputs are not tightly constrained, except in general form. Not only are the input and output values expressed in arbitrary units but the model contains a large number of free parameters. Figure 5.1 shows the effects of explicitly varying reward and punishment sensitivity by 20 per cent up and down from the nominal norm. Other parameters that could be varied are: the extent of reciprocal inhibition between R'_i and P'_j; the sensitivity of the BIS to detect conflict; the extent to which output from the BIS affects arousal and decision, respectively; and the way that arousal and decision combine to deliver predicted output. What the model does therefore is illustrate only the general overall form of the kind of interactions that can be expected between the systems in their generation of output. Any attempt to produce a neurally faithful model should start with separate estimations of individual components (such as reward sensitivity) and only later combine these (now parametrically rigid) components into a full model.

Two features are of particular interest. First, is the non-linear behaviour of the basic model (even without the BIS contribution). This is the result, transferred from the original Gray and Smith model, of including the assumption of a normal distribution of inputs to the decision mechanism. Second, is the prediction that changes in the BIS can produce (at least small) opposite effects at certain parameter values to those that would normally be expected. Such effects have very occasionally been observed by one of us (Monahan 1989) with anxiolytic drugs in animals.

The output of the model represented in Figure 5.1 is focused on a single free operant behaviour generated by the reward system. Activation of the BAS, uncontaminated by activation of the FFFS, is represented by the outputs graphed when input to the punishment system is zero (i.e., the left-most point of each curve). This is represented as being a simple linear relationship between input and output. In practice this would be expected to be at least a sigmoid function. Any attempt at a quantitative version of the model should, therefore, start with a purely appetitive task and systematically vary reward value in a substantial number of steps that cover the entire normal range of the input.

Output corresponding to a single behaviour generated by the punishment system would be identical in form to that represented for reward, in the absence of a BIS – but with the axes reversed. The effect of the BIS would, of course, be the opposite of that shown in Figure 5.1. Again, any attempt at a quantitative version of the model should start with a purely aversive task and systematically vary punishment value in a substantial number of steps that cover the entire normal range of the input.

The estimation of the free parameters in the model and of the linearity or otherwise of the BIS-arousal and BIS-decision interactions could proceed in a similar fashion once the basic reward and punishment functions had been determined. So while there are a large number of free parameters, each can be independently constrained by data.

Hidden complexity

Consideration of the interdependence of the FFFS and BAS – or the BIS and BAS in the 1982 version of RST – reveals the complexity of prediction. Corr (2004) noted that RST has received mixed support from laboratory studies, which stems in part from a failure to translate theoretical constructs into operational variables amenable to a fair test in the human laboratory. This issue is especially important when we ask the question: what empirical findings would disconfirm modified RST? (See Matthews, chapter 17.) At first sight it may seem that there have been (too) many personality-reinforcement associations that are prohibited by RST, whether conceived in terms of the separable subsystems hypothesis or the joint subsystems hypothesis. But sometimes this apparent predictive failure reflects the finer details of the theory being neglected. For example, RST allows the situation in which the presentation of punishment leads to enhanced BAS-related behaviour (and, indeed, was based on animal data that demonstrated this phenomenon, such as behavioural contrast and peak shift). For example, in a study of sexual response, Barr and McConaghy (1974) found that anxiety enhanced appetitive electrodermal conditioning. This experimental outcome is permitted within RST because the presentation of punishment during the performance of a BAS-controlled behaviour has two effects: (a) arousal-induced enhancement of any ongoing response, and (b) inhibition of behaviour. It is a matter of experimental detail which of these effects is witnessed: with relatively weak punishment, the arousal enhancing effect may more than compensate for behavioural inhibition (which, in any event, may not be so apparent in some psychophysiological measures, e.g., eye-blink conditioning). These possible effects are evident from the original Gray and Smith (1969) model.

It is often possible in RST terms to provide a post hoc account, even for seemingly contradictory findings; but this is an unsatisfactory way to test theory. Much better is (a) rigorous specification of parameters of any given task; (b) consideration of mutually inhibitory effects of the FFFS and BAS; (c) operational specification of prevailing reinforcement; and (d) consideration of level and effects of non-specific arousal induction. With this information in hand, it is then possible to *predict* (rather than postdict) the outputs of the FFFS, BIS and BAS in any given experimental situation. Even so-called simple learning tasks (e.g., eye-blink conditioning) hold hidden complexities. A priori hypothesis formation and rigorous testing are required to avoid the possibility that 'the new RST may perhaps afford excessive "wriggle room" for explaining unexpected effects' (Matthews, chapter 17).

Existing RST personality measures

The small amount of evidence available suggests that genetic and long-term environmentally-induced changes in a combination of noradrenergic and serotonergic systems could underlie a personality factor that is normally measured as 'neurotic-introversion' (*ex hypothesi*, 'Punishment Sensitivity': a shift along the dimension of defensive distance for any fixed level of external threat) – reflecting principally the activity of the FFFS (but, due to the close relationship between the FFFS and BIS, also sharing variance with BIS-related anxiety). At the neural level, this factor would represent significant co-variation of noradrenergic and serotonergic function. Co-variance could result for two reasons that are not mutually exclusive:

(a) if the primary agent were monoamine oxidase or stress this would act jointly on the two monoamines;
(b) synergistic changes in both systems may be required to alter behaviour appropriately.

Conceptualization of the factor as punishment-related rather than as 'trait anxiety' is driven by two facts. First, at the neural level, the factor is related to risk not only for generalized anxiety but for many other pharmacologically separate conditions (see McNaughton and Corr, chapter 2), including depression. An increased sensitivity to higher levels of punishment (spanning both the fear and anxiety systems), then, has much in common with the older concept of neurotic disorders. Secondly, at the personality level, 'trait anxiety' would seem to suggest permanent anxiousness. In fact, it is only a risk factor for the later development of anxiety-related disorder. Here it is worth noting that Taylor himself did not see 'manifest anxiety' (which we can identify with punishment sensitivity/neurotic introversion) as related in any direct way to clinical anxiety and thought 'the test might better have been given a more non-committal label' (Taylor 1956). One issue to be dealt with in relation to 'anxiety' measures, such as the Spielberger Trait Anxiety scale is that items span a range of FFFS and BIS situations, and do not reflect anxiety as conceptualized here. A second is that they share only about 50 per cent of variance with Eysenck's Neuroticism.

What of the scales developed in recent years to measure the FFFS, BIS and BAS? These have been developed to replace more general ones of anxiety and impulsivity that provided convenient names for Gray's rotation of Extraversion and Neuroticism. Some are related to the systems' functioning (e.g., the BIS/BAS scales; Carver and White 1994); others to general expectancies of reward and punishment (e.g., the Generalised Reward and Punishment Sensitivity scales; Ball and Zuckerman 1991); and still others to the characteristic (animal-analogue) behavioural outputs of these systems (e.g., the Gray-Wilson Personality scales; Wilson, Barrett and Gray 1989).

To demonstrate how far the revised theory has gone in clarifying the distinction between the FFFS (fear) and BIS (anxiety), consider the BIS items from the highly popular Carver and White BIS/BAS scales (hypothesized FFFS/BIS designations shown in brackets):

(1) Even if something bad is about to happen to me, I rarely experience fear or nervousness. (FFFS)
(2) Criticism or scolding hurts me a lot. (FFFS/BIS)
(3) I feel pretty worried or upset when I think or know somebody is angry at me. (FFFS/BIS)
(4) If I think something unpleasant is going to happen I usually get pretty 'worked up'. (BIS)
(5) I feel worried when I think I have done poorly at something. (BIS)
(6) I have few fears compared to my friends. (FFFS)
(7) I worry about making mistakes. (BIS)

This 'catch-all' scale has proved highly popular in experimental studies, perhaps because it does mix FFFS and BIS items, and thus measures the more general construct of 'Punishment Sensitivity'. However, the need to distinguish between fear and anxiety is important in the new theory, because, in some situations, FFFS-fear and BIS-anxiety control opposite motivational tendencies (i.e., avoidance vs. cautious approach). Therefore, we are likely to need separate scales that are sensitive (a) to perceptual sensitivity (input variables), comprising defensive distance and general punishment sensitivity (also general appetitive motivations, so corresponding to perceptual distance to reward); and (b) processes (outputs) of the FFFS (e.g., avoidance), BIS (e.g., risk assessment) and BAS (e.g., exploration).

Implications of revised RST for testing

Revised RST holds a number of important implications for the laboratory testing of personality hypotheses (Corr and Perkins 2006; McNaughtion and Corr 2004). For example, consider a standard question in the psychophysiology of emotion: what are the psychophysiological correlates of fear and anxiety? The conventional psychophysiological approach to personality is to take a psychophysiological measure (e.g., EMG startle) and relate this measure to psychometric traits (e.g., trait anxiety). At best, approximate relations may be found, for example, between arousal and the BIS. The problem with this approach is the *atheoretical* nature of the relationship between personality and psychophysiological parameters. As shown by the discussion of 'defensive distance' (see McNaughton and Corr, chapter 2), a threat stimulus of a fixed intensity leads to different behavioural reactions depending on the individual's *perceived* defensive distance; and with each distinct defensive behaviour (e.g., avoidance vs. freezing) different psychophysiological processes are engaged. With psychophysiological measures that may measure whole defensive system functioning (e.g., skin conductance), this may not be too much of a problem. But it is altogether a different matter when we want to measure activation of specific neural modules, or even to distinguish between fear and anxiety. The widely reported 'fractionation' (Lacey 1967) of psychophysiological measures may be a result of the activation of different neural modules at different defensive intensities.

We should also expect, though, that the introduction of reinforcement during the performance of a cognitive task would have definite consequences, but the precise pattern of effects observed would depend on the nature of the reinforcement and cognitive parameters of the task. As already discussed, specific modules have specific reactions, and we would need to know in advance the precise cognitive demands before predicting outcomes. The observation that cognitive parameters interact with personality traits does not strengthen or weaken RST.

An important conclusion of RST is that it should be possible to separate different syndromes of defensive disorder by using theoretically-based challenge tests and so by-pass the problem that (given the interconnectedness of structures) different syndromes can present with much the same symptoms. Indeed, a key feature of the tests we propose is that they should seldom be directed towards the most obvious symptoms and should be administered when state anxiety and hence symptoms are minimal. The same would, of course, be true of any challenges used to activate the brain for imaging (McNaughton and Corr 2004). The central idea behind the suggestion for differential diagnosis is that the specific nodes of the defence system should be selectively challenged to determine whether they are functioning normally. Such challenges should be designed to produce *minimal* reactions from the rest of the defence system. Otherwise, anxiety (or fear or panic) will automatically spill over into activation of much of the remainder of the system, so making it impossible to determine at which point excessive reactions begin. An important corollary of this recursiveness (and an idea gradually creeping into conventional diagnosis) is that co-morbidity is likely to be extensive. For there is little reason to suppose that just one node of the overall defence system should often be the only one overreactive in any one individual at any one time.

Testing specific neural modules in the defensive hierarchy

Considering the FFFS first, starting at the bottom of the defence system with the periaqueductal gray, what we require is a stimulus maximally activating this region accompanied by minimal activation of other parts of the defence system. With such a challenge we could then test patients for the extent to which the periaqueductal gray itself is overreactive, as opposed to being secondarily triggered by excessive activity elsewhere in the defence system. The periaqueductal gray controls 'fight-flight reactions to impending danger, pain, or asphyxia' (see McNaughton and Corr, chapter 2). 'Danger' in any general sense could clearly produce widespread activation of the defence system before activating the periaqueductal gray. To detect not only clinical panic disorder (which some define as involving anxiety), but also those who show panic without anxiety, one could determine the *threshold* level of CO_2 required to elicit an attack. More subtle assessment could be necessary; and, indeed, it seems that panic disorder may be detectable from irregularities in respiratory rhythm and perhaps the response to respiratory challenge. As soon as panic is elicited, other parts of the defence system could contribute to the attack. So, challenge with fixed levels of CO_2 is not only theoretically unattractive but does not discriminate panic well from, e.g., specific phobias. Threshold measurements, on the other hand, should detect supersensitivity in the periaqueductal gray independent of other abnormalities in the defence system. There may also be relatively input-specific abnormalities of the periaqueductal gray whose detection would require testing with, say, painful stimuli or adrenaline challenge as well as asphyxia.

We have linked amygdalar dysfunction with the arousal component of anxiety. The most obvious relevant challenge would be fear-potentiated

Table 5.1 *A sample of experimental assays to measure the activity in the Fight-Flight-Freeze System (FFFS), Behavioural Approach System (BAS) and Behavioural Inhibition System (BIS)*

Motivational system	Experimental assays
FFFS:	One-way avoidance Anticipatory arousal (e.g., electrodermal activity) Conditioned freezing (no conflict) – electromyographic Cold pressor test Hyponeophagia (inhibition of eating in novel environment) Serotonin challenge
BAS:	Simple approach (e.g., CARROT task)[a] Reaction time to appetitive cue (vs. neutral cue) Attentional bias to appetitive stimuli (e.g., dot probe) Reactions to omission/termination of punishment (e.g., psychomotor activity) Error-free learning Dopamine challenge
BIS:	Approach-avoidance conflict (classic test; e.g., interpersonal interaction, 'performance anxiety') Avoidance-avoidance conflict (pure test; e.g., flight vs. freezing) Approach-approach conflict (frustration test) Counter-conditioning Two-way avoidance (low anxiety = better performance) Q-task (behavioural inhibition)[b] 'Fear' (anxiety)-related startle (arousal potentiation) Geller-Seifter test (frequency of conditioned response with aversive stimulus) Vogel conflict (frequency of conditioned consumption with aversive stimulus) Extinction Reversal learning Benzodiazepine agonist challenge

Note: [a] The CARROT task was developed by Powell, Al-Adawi, Morgan and Greenwood (1996).
[b] The Q-task was developed by Newman, Wallace, Schmitt and Arnett (1997). References and descriptions of the other essays may be found in Flint (2002, 2004) and Pickering, Corr, Powell, Kumari, Thornton and Gray (1997).

Table 5.2 *Summary of 1982 and 2000 versions of Reinforcement Sensitivity Theory (RST) and suggested personality scales and neural systems[a]*

		1982 theory	2000/2004 theory
FFS/FFFS:	**Adequate input**	UCS-Pun+, UCS-Rew−	Punishment of all kinds: UCS-Pun+, CS-Pun+, UCS-Rew−, CS-Rew−,
	Output	Avoidance, defensive attack	Avoidance, freezing, defensive attack
	Emotion	Panic and rage	Panic, phobia, rage, fearfulness
	Trait	Psychoticism	Fear ('neurotic-introversion')
BAS:	**Adequate input**	CS-Rew+, CS-Pun−	Reward of all kinds:[b] *CS-Rew+, UCS-Pun−, CS-Pun−*
	Output	Approach, active avoidance	Approach, active avoidance
	Emotion	Anticipatory pleasure, 'hope'	Anticipatory pleasure, 'hope'
	Trait	Impulsivity (purpose-built BAS scales; see text)	'Impulsivity' (purpose-built BAS scales; see chapter 1)
BIS:	**Adequate input**	CS-PUN+, IS-Pun+, CS-Rew−, IS-Rew− Novelty (IS-Rew+/IS-Pun+compound)	Conflict stimuli of any kind (e.g., CS-Rew+/ UCS-Pun+)
	Output	Passive avoidance, extinction enhanced information processing, arousal	Passive avoidance, risk assessment, enhanced information processing and arousal
	Emotion	Anxious rumination of impending danger	Anxious rumination of impending danger
	Trait	Anxiety ('neurotic-introversion')	Anxiety (but not 'neurotic-introversion' per se)

Note: [a] FFF = Fight-Flight System; FFFS = Fight-Flight-Freeze System; BAS = Behavioural Approach System; BIS = Behavioural Inhibition System. UCS-Pun+ = unconditioned (innate) fear stimulus; UCS-Rew − = unconditioned omission/termination of expected reward; CS-Rew+ = conditioned appetitive stimulus; UCS-Pun − = unconditioned 'relief of non-punishment'; CS-Pun − = conditioned 'relief of non-punishment' stimulus; CS-Pun+ = conditioned fear stimuli; IS = Pun+ = innate anxiety stimulus (e.g., cat odour); CS-Rew − = conditioned frustrative stimuli; IS-Rew − = innate frustrative stimuli.
[b] The BAS is not formally involved in controlling reactions to unconditioned appetitive stimuli (i.e., UCS-Rew+).

startle, since this is not only sensitive to anxiolytic drugs (including when injected into the amygdala),[4] but is also insensitive to hippocampal lesions.

Next we come to the septo-hippocampal system. What is required is a test sensitive to septo-hippocampal system damage and anti-anxiety drugs, but *not* to amygdalar or periaqueductal gray lesions. The most obvious tasks, here, are spatial navigation, delayed matching to sample and behaviour on a fixed interval schedule of reward. Of these, delayed matching to sample can be most clearly set up in an anxiety-free form and so would probably be preferable, but it might be too specific in the aspects of septo-hippocampal function which it engages.

Global activity of FFFS, BAS and BIS

A number of promising laboratory tasks and naturalistic procedures have either already been designed or are suggested by careful consideration of the details of the theory to provide empirical tests of RST. These tests are important in verifying predictions of the theory but, equally important, they are required to provide opportunities for disconfirmation which is necessary for the theory to develop – this is important in RST which can be seen to be in a state of continuous development. Table 5.1 shows some of the existing test and possible tests that may be used to index the sensitivity of the three systems.

Out of the woods: putting it all together Description of the neuropsychology of the FFFS, BAS and BIS is complicated. In an attempt to provide some degree of clarity, Table 5.2 show the differences between the old and new RST versions, as suggested by the above analysis.

Conclusion

Assuming that RST has correctly specified the neuroanatomical bases of defensive and approach systems, it has yet to specify how these systems relate to overt behaviour and individual differences in overt behaviour, namely personality. What was called 'Anxiety' (i.e., running from E – /N+ to E+/N –) can no longer be so labelled. This axis may either be (a) FFFS-fear, or (b) Punishment Sensitivity or Defensive Distance or Threat Perception (incorporating FFFS and BIS). However, given the independence

---

[4] One of Gray's PhD students, Jasper Thornton (1998), reported that, in healthy volunteer subjects, 'fear-potentiated' startle was selectively reduced by the anxiolytic drug, diazepam (15 mg oral) – this effect was not, however, observed with 5mg (also see Patrick, Berthot and Moore, 1996).

of the FFFS and BIS, we should expect significant and important individual differences in BIS sensitivity and functioning that are independent of FFFS sensitivity and functioning. In addition to the obvious links between FFFS and fear/phobia, and BIS and generalized anxiety, we could imagine other varieties of individuals, for example, an individual with a weak FFFS and BAS who had a hypersensitive BIS, who would ruminate in a non-emotional way about almost anything; or a hyperactive FFFS individual, highly prone to fear, but where conflict does not activate the hypoactive BIS, leading to pure non-ruminative fear; or a BIS-insensitive, BAS-sensitive individual with a weak FFFS who may be especially prone to psychopathic-type behaviour. Arguably, the distinction between FFFS-fear and BIS-anxiety renders the variety of clinical conditions more amenable to theoretical analysis and explanation.

References

Abel, E.L., Altman, H.J. and Commissaris, R.L. (1992), Maudsley reactive and nonreactive rats in the forced swim test: comparison in fresh water and soiled water, *Physiology and Behavior*, 52, 1117–1119

Aufdembrinke, B. (1998), Abecarnil, a new beta-carboline, in the treatment of anxiety disorders, *British Journal of Psychiatry*, 173, 55–63

Ball, S.A. and Zuckerman, M. (1991), Sensation seeking, Eysenck's personality dimensions and reinforcement sensitivity in concept formation, *Personality and Individual Differences*, 11, 343–353

Barr, R.F. and McConaghy, N. (1974), Anxiety in relation to conditioning, *Behaviour Theraphy*, 5, 193–202

Blizard, D.A. (1981), The Maudsley reactive and nonreactive strains: a North American perspective, *Behavior Genetics*, 11, 469–489

Broadhurst, P.L. (1960), Applications of biometrical genetics to the inheritance of behaviour in H.J. Eysenck (ed.), *Experiments in Personality*, vol. 1, *Psychogenetics and Psychopharmacology* (London: Routledge Kegan Paul), pp. 1–102

(1975), The Maudsley reactive and nonreactive strains of rats: a survey, *Behavior Genetics*, 5, 299–319

Candland, D.K. and Nagy, Z.M. (1969), The open field: some comparative data, *Proceedings of the National Academy of Sciences*, 159, 831–851

Carver, C.S. (2004), Negative affects deriving from the Behavioral Approach System, *Emotion*, 41, 3–22

Carver, C.S. and White, T.L. (1994), Behavioral inhibition, behavioral activation, and affective responses to impending reward and punishment: the BIS/BAS scales, *Journal of Personality and Social Psychology*, 67, 319–333

Commissaris, R.L., Verbanac, J.S., Markovska, V.L., Altman, H.J. and Hill, T.J. (1996), Anxiety-like and depression-like behavior in Maudsley reactive (MR) and non-reactive (MNRA) rats, *Progress in Neuropsychopharmacology and Biological Psychiatry*, 20, 491–501

Corr, P.J. (2001), Testing problems in J.A. Gray's personality theory: a commentary on Matthews and Gilliland (1999), *Personal Individual Differences*, 30, 333–352

(2002a), J.A. Gray's reinforcement sensitivity theory: tests of the joint subsystem hypothesis of anxiety and impulsivity, *Personality and Individual Differences*, 33, 511–532

(2002b), J.A. Gray's reinforcement sensitivity theory and frustrative nonreward: a theoretical note on expectancies in reactions to rewarding stimuli, *Personality and Individual Differences*, 32, 1247–1253

(2004), Reinforcement sensitivity theory and personality, *Neuroscience and Biobehavioral Reviews*, 28, 317–332

Corr, P.J. and McNaughton, N. (submitted), J.A. Gray's behavioural inhibition system and the anchoring problem in the neuroscience of personality

Corr, P.J. and Perkins, A.M. (2006), The role of theory in the psychophysiology of personality: from Ivan Pavlov to Jeffrey Gray, *International Journal of Psychophysiology*, 62, 367–376

Deakin, J.F.W. and Graeff, F.G. (1991), 5-HT and mechanisms of defence, *Journal of Psychopharmacology*, 5, 305–315

Eysenck, H.J. (1944), Types of personality: a factorial study of seven hundred neurotics, *Journal of Mental Science*, 90, 851–861

(1947), *Dimensions of Personality* (London: Kegan Paul)

(1957), *The Dynamics of Anxiety and Hysteria* (New York: Preger)

Eysenck, H.J. (1967), *The Biological Basis of Personality* (IL: Thomas, Springfield)

Eysenck, H.J. and Eysenck, S.B.G. (1975), *Manual of the Eysenck Personality Questionnaire (Adults)* (London: Hodder and Stoughton)

Flint, J. (2002), Animal models of personality in R.P. Ebstein, R.H. Belmaker and J. Benjamin, *The Molecular Genetics of the Human Personality* (Washington DC: APA), pp. 63–90

(2004), The genetics of neuroticism, *Neurosciencce and Biobehavioral Reviews*, 28, 307–316

George, M.S., Guidotti, A., Rubinow, D., Pan, B., Mikalauskas, K. and Post, R.M. (1994), CSF neuroactive steroids in affective disorders: pregnenolone, progesterone, and DBI, *Biological Psychiatry*, 35, 775–780

Gray, J.A. (1970), The psychophysiological basis of introversion-extraversion, *Behaiour Research and Therapy*, 8, 249–266

(1972a), Learning theory, the conceptual nervous system and personality in V.D. Nebylitsyn and J.A. Gray (eds), *The Biological Bases of Individual Behaviour* (New York: Academic Press), pp. 372–399

(1972b), The psychophysiological nature of introversion-extraversion: a modification of Eysenck's theory in V.D. Nebylitsyn and J.A. Gray (eds), *The Biological Bases of Individual Behaviour* (New York: Academic Press), pp. 182–205

(1981), A critique of Eysenck's theory of personality in H.J. Eysenck (ed.), *A Model for Personality* (Berlin: Springer), pp. 246–276

(1982), *The Neuropsychology of Anxiety: An Enquiry into the Functions of the Septo-Hippocampal System* (Oxford: Oxford University Press)

(1987), *The Psychology of Fear and Stress* (Cambridge: Cambridge University Press)

Gray, J.A. and McNaughton, N. (2000), *The Neuropsychology of Anxiety: An Enquiry into the Functions of the Septo-Hippocampal System* (2nd edn, Oxford: Oxford University Press)

Gray, J.A. and Smith, P.T. (1969), An arousal decision model for partial reinforcement and discrimination learning in R.M. Gilbert and N.S. Sutherland (eds), *Animal Discrimination Learning* (London: Academic Press), pp. 243–272

Graeff, F.G. (1994), Neuroanatomy and neurotransmitter regulation of defensive behaviors and related emotions in mammals, *Brazilian Journal of Medical and Biological Research*, 27, 811–829

Flint, J. (2002), Animal models of personality in J. Benjamin, R.P. Ebstein and R.H. Belmaker (eds), *Molecular Genetics and the Human Personality* (London: American Psychiatric Publishing), pp. 63–90

(2004), The genetics of neuroticism, *Neuroscience and Biobehavioral Reviews*, 28, 307–316

Hall, C.S. (1951), The genetics of behavior in S.S. Stevens (ed.), *Handbook of Experimental Psychology* (New York: Wiley), pp. 304–329

Hunt, H.F. and Otis, L.S. (1953), Conditioned and unconditioned emotional defecation in the rat, *Journal of Comparative and Physiological Psychology*, 46, 378–382

Lacey, J.I. (1967), Somatic response patterning and stress: some revisions of activation theory in M.H. Appley and R. Trumbull (eds), *Psychological Stress* (New York: Appleton Century Crofts), pp. 14–43

Lamacz, M., Tonon, M.C., Smih-Rouet, F., Patte, C., Gasque, P., Fontaine, M. and Vaudry, H. (1996), The endogenous benzodiazepine receptor ligand ODN increases cytosolic calcium in cultured rat astrocytes, *Molecular Brain Research*, 37, 290–296

Lykken, D.T. (1971), Multiple factor analysis and personality research, *Journal of Experimental Research in Personality*, 5, 161–170

McNaughton, N. and Corr, P.J. (2004), A two-dimensional neuropsychology of defense: fear/anxiety and defensive distance, *Neuroscience and Biobehavioral Reviews*, 28, 285–305

McNaughton, N. and Gray, J.A. (1983), Pavlovian counterconditioning is unchanged by chlordiazepoxide or by septal lesions, *Quarterly Journal of Experimental Psychology*, 35, 221–233

Miller, N.E. (1944), Experimental studies of conflict in J.M. Hunt (ed.), *Personality and the Behavioural Disorders* (New York: Ronald), pp. 431–465

Monahan, A.M. (1989), The involvement of endogenous opiate systems in the anxiolytic actions of the benzodiazepines and melatonin (unpublished MSc thesis, University of Otago, Dunedin, New Zealand)

Newman, J.P., Wallace, J.F., Schmitt, W.A. and Arnett, P.A. (1997), Behavioral inhibition system functioning in anxious, impulsive and psychopathic individuals, *Personality and Individual Differences*, 23, 583–592

Okaichi, Y. and Okaichi, H. (1994), Effects of fimbria-fornix lesions on avoidance tasks with temporal elements in rats, *Physiology and Behavior*, 56, 759–765

Ozawa, M., Nakada, Y., Sugimachi, K., Yabuuchi, F., Akai, T., Mizuta, E., Kuno, S. and Yamaguchi, M. (1994), Pharmacological characterization of the novel anxiolytic carboline abecarnil in rodents and primates, *Japanese Journal of Pharmacology*, 64, 179–187

Patrick, C.J., Berthot, B.D. and Moore, J.D. (1996), Diazepam blocks fear-potentiated startle in humans, *Journal of Abnormal Psychology*, 105, 89–96

Perkins, A.M., Revelle, W. and Corr, P.J. (Unpublished), A reanalysis of H.J. Eysenck's (1994) medical checklist data

Pickering, A.D., Corr, P.J., Powell, J.H., Kumari, V., Thornton, J.C. and Gray, J.A. (1997), Individual differences in reactions to reinforcing stimuli are neither black nor white: to what extent are they Gray? in H. Nyborg (ed.), *The Scientific Study of Human Nature: Tribute to Hans J. Eysenck at Eighty* (London: Elsevier), pp. 36–67

Powell, J.H., Al-Adawi, S., Morgan, J. and Greenwood, R.J. (1996), Motivational deficits after brain injury: effects of bromocriptine in 11 patients, *Journal of Neurology, Neurosurgery, and Psychiatry*, 60, 416–421

Smillie, L.D., Pickering, A.D. and Jackson, C.J. (2006), The new reinforcement sensitivity theory: implications for personality measurement, *Personality and Social Psychology Review*, 10, 320–335

Stouffer, S.A., Lumsdaine, A.A., Lumsdaine, M.H., Williams, R.M., Smith, M.B. and Janis, I.L. (1949), Studies in social psychology in world war II: vol 2. The american soldier: combat and its aftermath. Princeton, cited by Broadhurst (1960), p. 37

Sudakov, S.K., Medvedeva, O.F., Rusakova, I.V., Terebilina, N.N. and Goldberg, S.R. (2001), Differences in genetic predisposition to high anxiety in two inbred rat strains: role of substance P, diazepam binding inhibitor fragment and neuropeptide Y, *Psychopharmacology*, 154, 327–335

Taylor, J. (1956), Drive theory and manifest anxiety, *Psychological Bulletin*, 53, 303–320

Thornton, J.C. (1998), *The Behavioural Inhibition System and Anxiety in Human Subjects* (unpublished Doctoral Thesis, Institute of Psychiatry, University of London)

Viglinskaya, I.V., Overstreet, D.H., Kashevskaya, O.P., Badishtov, B.A., Kampov-Polevoy, A.B., Seredenin, S.B. *et al.* (1995), To drink or not to drink: tests of anxiety and immobility in alcohol-preferring and alcohol-nonpreferring rat strains, *Physiology and Behavior*, 57, 987–991

Wilson, G.D., Barrett, P.T. and Gray, J.A. (1989), Human reactions to reward and punishment: a questionnaire examination of Gray's personality theory, *British Journal of Psychology*, 80, 509–515

6   Reinforcement sensitivity scales

Rafael Torrubia, César Ávila and Xavier Caseras

Gray's (1970, 1981, 1982) personality theory, currently referred to as the *Reinforcement Sensitivity Theory* (RST) (Pickering, Díaz and Gray 1995) has defined the existence of three conceptual nervous systems that underlie three orthogonal personality dimensions. These systems reflect brain structures that influence sensitivity to reinforcing events and control the experience of emotion. The best known is the Behavioural Inhibition System (BIS); this system normally functions as a comparator, taking control of behaviour in response to signals of punishment, frustrative non-reward and novel stimuli. In terms of individual differences in personality, the BIS is related to the trait-anxiety dimension. As regards its relationship with Eysenckian dimensions, the BIS runs from the neurotic introvert quadrant (maximum BIS activity) to the stable extravert quadrant (minimum BIS activity). The second system is called the Behavioural Approach System (BAS) and is considered independent of the BIS; this system is responsible for approach behaviour in response to incentives (signals of reward or non-punishment). Individual differences in the functioning of the BAS are related to the impulsivity dimension of personality. This dimension is orthogonal to anxiety, and runs from stable introvert (minimum BAS activity) to neurotic extravert (maximum BAS activity) quadrants. The third system, the Fight-Flight System (FFS) is the most recently proposed of the three (Gray 1987a) and is the least clearly defined. It is activated by the presence of unconditioned aversive stimuli promoting fight or escape behaviour.

The theory initially put forward by Gray (1970) was intended as a modification of Eysenck's descriptive model (Eysenck 1967), the development of which had principally been based on the application of factor analysis techniques. Its main aim was to locate the descriptive axes in such a manner that they could most likely reflect the activities of brain systems that control emotional behaviour. According to Gray (1981), factor analysis techniques are useful to establish how many independent dimensions there are in a given personality space, but not

188

where they should be located. If any location of these axes reflects systematic individual differences in the functioning of a separable sub-system of the brain, this cannot be established by factor analysis techniques alone, but must be justified by other empirical or theoretical considerations.

The modification proposed by Gray (1970, 1981, 1982) was prompted partly by knowledge built up from animal research into the effects of ansiolitic drugs on behaviour, and partly by the findings that in studies with humans (1) introverts do not have better conditioning than extraverts in all situations, but only when the conditioning is aversive; (2) extraverts have better appetitive conditioning; and (3) neuroticism strengthens the effects of the interaction between the type of conditioning and extraversion. The anxiety and impulsivity dimensions were initially proposed as a 45° rotation of the neuroticism and extraversion dimensions as the best way of reflecting these learning effects. However, based on the relative loadings of Extraversion (E) and Neuroticism (N) on anxiety questionnaires, Gray (1988) proposed that the angle between anxiety and N was likely to be closer to 30° than 45°. Preserving the orthogonality between anxiety and impulsivity, the angle between impulsivity and E must also be 30° (Pickering, Corr and Gray 1999). In accordance with the model, Eysenck's extraversion and neuroticism dimensions would be derivative factors of the more fundamental punishment and reward sensitivities: extraversion would reflect the balance between punishment and reward sensitivities, whereas neuroticism would reflect their joint strengths (see Wallace and Newman 1990). Gray (1988) completed his descriptive model by placing impulsivity and anxiety within the Eysenckian three-dimensional space, and proposed that impulsivity inclined into psychoticism, and anxiety away from psychoticism.

During the last three decades, a great deal of human experimental or psychometric research with normal and clinical populations has been carried out, taking as a point of departure Gray's RST (see, for instance, Corr 2004). Furthermore, interest in the model has grown steadily in recent years. Though results have been divergent, they clearly illustrate the vitality of the model. RST-derived hypotheses have usually been tested in humans by examining the behavioural, psychophysiological, clinical or psychometric correlates of a number of self-report measures which were used to assess the habitual level of functioning of the BIS and the BAS dimensions. However, the different nature of the various measurement strategies employed makes it difficult to compare results from a lot of studies. Moreover, when different measures of BIS or BAS have been used in the same study, the results do not always coincide with regard to the relationship between these measures and behaviour (see, for instance, Pickering, Corr, Powell, Kumari, Thornton and Gray 1997).

One of the main problems in RST is the lack of a standard measure of the constructs. This is an important difference between RST and other well known personality models, such as Cloninger's or Eysenck's, in which one of the priorities was to elaborate psychometric measures of the proposed personality dimensions, and much of the work was devoted to the development of questionnaires and the study of their behavioural, psychophysiological and social behaviour correlates. Experience over the years now tells us that the lack of an 'official' widely accepted psychometric measure of the BIS, the BAS and FFS has encouraged researchers to develop their own way to measure RST dimensions, which has led to greater heterogeneity in the measures used and the results obtained.

In the present chapter we will do the following: briefly revise strategies used for the measurement of BIS and BAS dimensions by using scales not directly derived from RST; describe BIS and BAS scales developed on the basis of RST assumptions; analyse the psychometric properties of the RST-based BIS and BAS scales and discuss some controversial issues related to BIS and BAS measurement; revise laboratory and social behaviour correlates of BIS and BAS purpose-built scales; present some conclusions about the validity of RST purpose-built measures; discuss to what extent scales based on RST assumptions and other anxiety and impulsivity scales are interchangeable; and present some concluding remarks.

Strategies for the measurement of BIS and BAS dimensions by using scales not directly derived from RST

Three basically different strategies have been used in the measurement of BIS and BAS dimensions, using scales not directly derived from RST: (1) a combination of the Eysenckian dimensions of personality; (2) measures related to traits of anxiety and impulsivity, but not specifically designed to tap the dimensions depicted by RST; and (3) scales based on other personality models sharing common theoretical grounds. These procedures have been used mainly prior to the more recent publication and dissemination of purpose-built BIS and BAS measures.

*Measures based on a combination of the Eysenckian
dimensions of personality*

Based on Gray's (1981) hypothesis that extraversion and neuroticism as
formulated by Eysenck (1967) are derivative factors resulting from
combinations of the BIS and the BAS, some researchers have used the
N, E and P scales from the Eysenck Personality Questionnaire (EPQ)
(Eysenck and Eysenck 1975). In some cases, Gray's conditioning
hypotheses have been successfully tested using the E scale (see chapter 7).
In other cases, classification of subjects was based on the four quadrants
derived from their scores on E and N scales (see, for instance, Patterson,
Kosson and Newman 1987). A third related procedure is the one
recently proposed by Corr (2001) based on deriving BIS and BAS
dimensions from the combinations of E, N and P. As the impulsivity
dimension derives from a 30° rotation of extraversion, anxiety from a
30° rotation of neuroticism, impulsivity inclined into psychoticism,
and anxiety away from psychoticism, EPQ derived impulsivity would
be: Impulsivity $= ((E \times 2) + N + P)$, and EPQ derived anxiety would
be: Anxiety $= ((n$ of items $E - E) + (N \times 2) - P)$ (see, for instance,
Kambouropoulos and Staiger 2004).

*Measures related to traits of anxiety and impulsivity, but not
specifically designed to tap the dimensions depicted by RST*

The Trait-Anxiety scale from the State-Trait Anxiety Inventory (STAI-
T) (Spielberger, Gorsuch and Lushene 1970) and the Anxiety scale
from the Eysenck Personality Profiler (EPP) (Eysenck, Barrett, Wilson
and Jackson 1992) have been used as measures of BIS (see, for
instance, Caseras, Ávila and Torrubia 2003; Jackson and Smillie
2004). A number of scales such as the Impulsiveness (I_7) scale from
the Impulsiveness, Venturesomeness and Empathy Questionnaire
(Eysenck, Pearson, Easting and Allsop 1985), the Impulsivity sub-scale
from the Eysenck Personality Inventory (EPI) (Eysenck and Eysenck
1964) and the Impulsivity scale from the EPP (Eysenck *et al.* 1992)
have been proposed as effective measures of the BAS (see, for instance,
Caseras, Ávila and Torrubia 2003; Gomez and Gomez 2005; Jackson
and Smillie 2004; Pickering *et al.* 1997; Quilty and Oakman 2004;
Zinbarg and Mohlman 1998). However, as anxiety and impulsivity
are more complex structures than those described in Gray's model,
not just any scale designed to measure anxiety or impulsivity can
necessarily be considered an appropriate measure of the RST BIS and
BAS dimensions, respectively. Gray, Owen, Davis and Tsaltas (1983),

for example, defined four different types of impulsive behaviours, only one of them being related to BAS.

Scales based on other personality models sharing common theoretical ground

Cloninger's model can be considered to be an example of this approach. Gray (1987b) highlighted the resemblance of two dimensions proposed by Cloninger (named harm avoidance and novelty seeking) with his dimensions of anxiety and impulsivity, respectively. However, it proved more difficult to fit reward dependence in his model. Harm avoidance is related to behavioural inhibition in response to aversive stimuli; the similarities between this dimension and anxiety as defined in RST are obvious. Novelty seeking would be responsible for behavioural responses to novel stimuli or cues for potential rewards or potential relief of punishment. A number of studies have used the above-mentioned scales as measures of BIS and BAS respectively (see, for instance, Corr, Wilson, Fotiadou, Kumari, Gray, Checkley and Gray 1995; Pickering *et al.* 1997).

BIS and BAS scales developed on the basis of RST assumptions

Taking RST as a theoretical framework, a number of authors have developed several scales aimed at measuring individual differences in the functioning of the BIS and the BAS respectively. In general, scales constructed using this procedure usually provide good face and content validities. However, the approaches used in their development and the results obtained are not homogeneous. Following a chronological order, these are as follows.

Susceptibility to punishment scale

As far as we know, the first attempt to develop a scale for the measurement of RST dimensions was carried out by Torrubia and Tobeña (1984). They published a thirty-six-item scale named Susceptibility to Punishment, aimed at measuring individual differences in BIS activity. Item content was related to habitual behaviours in response to cues of punishment, frustrative non-reward and novel stimuli. Preliminary psychometric results showed adequate internal consistency and a good convergent and discriminant validity in accordance with Gray's (1981) model.

Gray-Wilson personality questionnaire

The second attempt was made by Wilson, Barrett and Gray (1989) and Wilson, Gray and Barrett (1990), who developed the Gray-Wilson Personality Questionnaire (GWPQ) based on six different scales of twenty items each, with a 'Yes, ?, No' format. It was designed to measure individual differences in the activity of the three RST systems. The aim of the authors was to link animal laboratory paradigms to clinical phenomena and they tried to develop a personality questionnaire derived explicitly from animal research. The main hypothesis was that scales designed to measure human equivalents of the six laboratory phenomena relevant for the RST would link up into pairs corresponding with Gray's three major proposed neuropsychological systems. Ten items were devised to tap each of the six laboratory-established types of behaviour (approach, active avoidance, passive avoidance, extinction, fight and flight) and each of the ten items was then matched with an approximate logical reversal of itself to reduce the likelihood that agreement response bias would influence scale scores. Two scales were constructed to assess individual differences in the BAS: Approach (reward seeking) and Active Avoidance (taking positive steps to avoid punishment); two scales, to assess individual differences in the BIS: Passive Avoidance (avoiding punishment by inactivity and submission) and Extinction (abandoning behaviours that do not bring reward); and two scales to assess individual differences in the FFS: Fight ('defensive' as distinguished from predatory, aggression toward aversive stimulus) and Flight (rapid escape from aversive stimulus). Although the six scales showed satisfactory internal consistencies, they failed to link up into the three major systems suggested by the theory. The validity data were not completely successful in finding the expected relationships between scales, because some results did not fit well in the RST model. The strongest associations were between Fight and Approach and between Flight and Passive Avoidance; some of the relationships observed with E, N and P did not confirm theoretical predictions. Factor analysis of the items provided only limited confirmation of the a priori structure of the GWPQ; impartial criteria did suggest a six-factor solution as optimal, but the six factors did not correspond exactly to those initially built into the questionnaire (see also Wilson, Barrett and Iwawaki 1995 for a later replication).

   Recently, taking as a point of departure a shortened version of the GWPQ translated into Russian, a short form (twenty-eight items) of the GWPQ (the GWPQ-S) was developed by Slobodskaya, Knyazev, Safronova and Wilson (2003). The authors reduced the original questionnaire to two major scales, the Behavioural Activation System and the Behavioural Inhibition System. The reduction was based on factor loadings from a sample of Russian adolescents and correlations with previously validated criteria. Internal consistency was satisfactory. Items included in each one of the new scales belonged to several original GWPQ scales. Balanced direction of scoring prevented agreement response bias.

Since then, a further attempt by the same group to develop a new version of the GWPQ (New GWPQ) aimed at measuring the RST constructs has been published (Knyazev, Slobodskaya and Wilson 2004). Using exploratory factor analysis, a three-factor solution was chosen and three new scales of twelve items each were created. The first comprised four passive avoidance items, four flight items, two extinction items and two fight items and was identified as the BIS (GWPQ-BIS). The second scale, which was identified as Fight, included seven fight items, one approach item and four active avoidance items of the original GWPQ. The third scale, named Approach, comprised six approach items, two active avoidance items, one extinction item, two fight items and one flight item of the original GWPQ. A Confirmatory Factor Analysis showed that the Fight and Approach scales should be treated as sub-scales of a common BAS factor. Consequently, the authors recommended that these scales should be regarded as facets of the BAS rather than independent factors.

General reward and punishment expectancy scales

Ball and Zuckerman (1990), following a cognitive interpretation of Gray's model, developed a questionnaire named General Reward and Punishment Expectancy Scales (GRAPES) by factor analysing items reflecting expectations regarding outcomes for various life events in the future. Their assumption was that subjects with high BAS reactivity will anticipate positive consequences from their behaviours (high reward expectancies) resulting in a high activity. In contrast, high BIS subjects will expect negative consequences from their behaviours (high punishment expectancies) resulting in inhibition. Items were constructed using a 'True-False' format. Two scales were developed: Reward Expectancy and Punishment Expectancy. The validity study only partially confirmed the hypotheses, as little support was found for the Reward Expectancy scale. Another problem found was that both scales correlated negatively, violating RST assumptions of orthogonality. The results obtained suggested that the Reward Expectancy scale could be considered an inverse measure of the anxiety dimension rather than a direct measure of the BAS construct.

BIS scale

Following an empirical procedure, MacAndrew and Steele (1991) developed an MMPI-derived scale to measure BIS sensitivity: the BIS scale (MS-BIS). Selected items of the scale were included because (1) they were able to differentiate between three different samples of females: psychiatric outpatients with distimic disorder, putative normal subjects and incarcerated prostitutes (supposed to have an underactive BIS); and (2) they correlated positively with the N scale and negatively with the E scale of the EPQ. The final scale comprised thirty items, some of them with a content that did not reflect directly the functioning of the BIS.

BIS/BAS scales

Carver and White (1994) developed the most widely-used scales in the field: the BIS/BAS scales. They include a seven-item scale (five positively scored) to measure BIS functioning (CW-BIS) and three scales related to BAS functioning (CW-BAS), called Drive (five items positively scored), Fun Seeking (four items positively scored) and Reward Responsiveness (four items positively scored) respectively. The answer format to items follows a Likert-type scale with four possibilities ordered from 'absolute agreement' to 'absolute disagreement'. Good reliability was obtained for each scale and some data about validity were also reported. The authors justified the sub-division of the BAS dimension in three facets after the results of factor analysis with oblique rotation. They reported that a four-factor structure was obtained and also that the three BAS scales loaded on a second-order factor which should be considered a BAS factor. However, no clear theoretical justification was given in the original publication for the sub-division of the BAS dimension. The CW-BIS scale includes items referencing reactions to the anticipation of punishment; the Drive scale is composed of items related to the persistent pursuit of desired goals; the Fun Seeking scale includes items reflecting a desire for new rewards and a willingness to approach a potentially rewarding event on the spur of the moment; the Reward Responsiveness scale is composed of items that focus on positive responses to the occurrence or anticipation of reward. In recent years a number of studies have used the BAS Total score, which is the sum of the scores in the three scales (Gomez and Gomez 2002; Quilty and Oakman 2004). Recently, a short version of the questionnaire (Carver, Meyer and Antoni 2000), a parent report version for the assessment of children (Blair 2003; Blair, Peters and Granger 2004), and a self-report version for children (Colder and O'Connor 2004) have been developed.

Sensitivity to punishment and sensitivity to reward questionnaire

The Sensitivity to Punishment and Sensitivity to Reward Questionnaire (SPSRQ) was recently developed by Torrubia, Ávila, Moltó and Caseras (2001). It is composed of two scales: Sensitivity to Punishment and Sensitivity to Reward. The Sensitivity to Punishment scale is a revision of the previously published Susceptibility to Punishment scale (Torrubia and Tobeña 1984); it is intended to measure BIS activity and includes twenty-four positively scored items. The Sensitivity to Reward scale is aimed at measuring BAS activity and is also composed of twenty-four positively scored items. Items have a 'Yes-No' format. The published SPSRQ was derived from an experimental version previously used in a number of studies (see, for instance, Valdés and De Flores 1986). Principal component analysis showed that the two scales are orthogonal. The two scales were correlated with other personality variables in accordance with theoretical predictions. As in the 1984 version, items of the Sensitivity to Punishment scale were designed to measure individual differences in some functions dependent on the BIS in checking and control modes: (1) behavioural inhibition (passive avoidance) in general situations involving the possibility of aversive consequences or novelty; and (2) worry or cognitive processes produced by the threat of punishment or failure. Sensitivity to Reward items deal with specific rewards such as money, sex partners, social events, power, sensation seeking and so on, always trying to describe situations in which people could adopt approach behaviours to obtain them. A junior unpublished version of the SPSRQ has also been developed by the same group (Torrubia, Garcia-Carrillo, Ávila, Caseras and Grande, in preparation).

Appetitive motivation scale

The most recent attempt to construct a measure of RST dimensions has been carried out by Jackson and Smillie (2004). They developed a twenty positively scored item scale called Appetitive Motivation which assesses individual differences in BAS from the perspective of impulsively approaching appetitive stimuli with the goal of obtaining a rewarding experience. Items have a 'True-False' format and their content reflects a motivation to approach ideas and physical stimuli, as well as reflecting the appraisal of obtaining rewards. Data on internal consistency were acceptable and preliminary evidence of construct validity of the scale was promising.

Comparison of questionnaires: approaches to scale development and number of traits assessed

Despite the fact that all the purpose-built BIS and BAS questionnaires are based on the same theoretical model, they differ on how they were developed and how many traits they assess. With regard to the first aspect, the GWPQ was constructed on the basis of developing items related in human beings to learning theory defined as typical animal defensive and approach behaviours; GRAPES items were based on expectations regarding outcomes (reward or punishment) for various life events in the future; items of the MS-BIS were selected using an empirical approach, and content was not necessarily related to the functioning of the BIS; items of the BIS/BAS scales were developed in order to assess sensitivities but not typical experience in general and non-specific situations and in accordance with the authors assertion that 'assessment of BIS and BAS sensitivities would seem to benefit from assessing response to appropriate classes of situations rather than assessing general affective tone' (Carver and White 1994, p. 321); SPSRQ items were constructed to detect individual differences in behavioural inhibition or approach behaviours in response to diverse specific stimuli or situations involving the possibility of aversive or rewarding consequences respectively; and Appetitive Motivation scale items were intended to measure individual differences in approaching appetitive stimuli with the aim of obtaining a rewarding experience.

A basic difference between BIS/BAS scales and the other scales is that the item content of BIS/BAS scales does not include situations with rewards or specific punishments, as do all the other scales, but is based instead on a generic concept of reward and punishment. This means that the items in the other scales describe situations with specific reinforcers (sex, money, social recognition, etc.), to which subjects might show different preferences (quality of reinforcement), while the BIS/BAS scales measure individual differences in intensity of seeking and reaction to a non-specific reinforcement.

As regards the second source of differences, some of the question- naires measure a single trait (MS-BIS and Appetitive Motivation), while the others measure BIS and BAS traits (New GWPQ, GRAPES, BIS/ BAS scales and SPSRQ). Furthermore, the BIS/BAS scales include three scales for the measurement of the BAS and New GWPQ includes two scales for the same purpose; the remaining questionnaires only include one scale per dimension. In summary, the approaches used to develop BIS and BAS scales are diverse, and neither the number of dimensions measured by each questionnaire nor the number of scales per dimension are homogeneous.

Psychometric properties of the BIS and BAS purpose-built scales

The existence of several measures for the assessment of BIS and BAS dimensions leaves some important questions to be answered; for instance, the extent to which these scales assess the same constructs, and if they do not, what the main differences between them are. In the following sections, an analysis is made of (1) reliabilities, score distributions and gender differences; and (2) validity on the basis of either correlational data or factor analysis studies.

Reliability, score distributions and gender differences

In this section, a brief review of these aspects is made based on information available in the seminal publications of the scales (Table 6.1). The data are itemized by gender where this information was provided in these publications. When the original validation studies did not provide the necessary information, data from later studies were used. As a whole, it can be observed that the scales presented satisfactory internal consistency as indicated by Cronbach's alpha coefficients, although the values for the two GRAPES scales were below par. Only test-retest reliability data for the BIS/BAS scales and the SPSRQ were available; the interval between administrations was eight weeks in the case of the former, and three months in the latter. In both cases, the correlations were acceptable, though the results pointed to greater consistency over time for the SPSRQ scales.

The observation of means and standard deviations in Table 6.1 lead us to deduce that for most of the scales the range of possible scores oscillated approximately between -2 SD and $+2$ SD from the mean. The only exception to this rule were the CW-BAS scales, the reported means of which were located at the upper part of the scale range, probably indicating that the response range was extremely limited within the response format of 1–4. This asymmetric distribution would tend to limit the dispersion of the scores at the upper range of the distribution, and indicates that many individuals select the maximum score in many of the items. Thus, for example, if there is a need to select extreme subjects with scores higher than a standard deviation above the mean on

Table 6.1 *Psychometric characteristics of purpose-built RST scales and correlation coefficients of each scale with Eysenck's E, N and P (data published in seminal studies)*

	No. items	Alpha reliab.	Test-retest (r)	Mean	SD	Gender differences	Correlations E	N	P
BIS scales									
GWPQ-BIS									
Knyazev, Slobodskaya and Wilson 2004	12	.79		11.64	5.70	F > M	$-.20^a$	$.47^a$	$-.19^a$
Punishment expectancy	15								
Ball and Zuckerman 1990		.60					$-.27^a$	$.36^a$	$-.20$
Zuckerman *et al.* 1999 (females)				8.34	2.89	F > M			
(males)				7.35	2.79				
MS-BIS	30								
MacAndrew and Steele 1991 (females)[b]		.85		12.66	6.13	F > M	$-.45^a$	$.74^a$	$.22^a$
(males)		.82		10.83	5.60		$-.41^a$	$.69^a$	$.14^a$
CW-BIS	7								
Carver and White 1994[c]		.74	.66	19.99	3.79	F > M	$-.14$	$.64^a$	$-.31^a$
Jorm *et al.* 1999							$-.19^a$		

Table 6.1 (*cont.*)

	No. items	Alpha reliab.	Test–retest (r)	Mean	SD	Gender differences	Correlations		
							E	N	P
Sensitivity to punishment	24								
Torrubia *et al.* 2001									
(females)		.82		11.98	5.06	n.s.	−.48[a]	.53[a]	−.07
(males)		.83	.89	11.65	5.27		−.53[a]	.62[a]	−.04
BAS scales									
Fight	12								
Knyazev, Slobodskaya and Wilson 2004		.71		13.95	5.12	M > F	.20[a]	.13	.40[a]
Approach	12								
Knyazev, Slobodskaya and Wilson 2004		.67		6.18	4.47	F > M	.04	.30[a]	.35[a]
Reward expectancy	15								
Ball and Zuckerman 1990									
Zuckerman *et al.* 1999									
(females)		.63		7.35	2.73		.50[a]	−.26[a]	−.01
(males)				8.13	2.72	M > F			
Drive	4								
Carver and White 1994[c]		.76	.66	12.05	2.36	n.s.	.41[a]	.01	.20[a]
Jorm *et al.* 1999							.32[a]		
Reward responsiveness	5								
Carver and White 1994[c]		.73	.59	17.59	2.14	F > M	.39[a]	.21[a]	−.02
Jorm *et al.* 1999							.28[a]		

Scale	Items	α	α[b]	Mean	SD	Sex diff	GWPQ-BIS	CW-BIS	MS-BIS
Fun seeking	4								
Carver and White 1994[c]		.66	.69	12.43	2.26	n.s	.59[a]	.02	.23[a]
Jorm et al. 1999							.46[a]		
Sensitivity to reward	24								
Torrubia et al. 2001		.75	.87						
(females)				10.11	4.05		.37[a]	.25[a]	.19[a]
(males)				12.18	4.48	M > F	.41[a]	.33[a]	.24[a]
Appetitive motivation	20								
Jackson and Smillie 2004		.78	.74						
(females)				14.09	3.42				
(males)				15.25	2.42	M > F	.38[a]	−.18	.34[a]

Notes: GWPQ-BIS: BIS scale from the New GWPQ (Knyazev, Slobodskaya and Wilson 2004); MS-BIS: BIS scale from MacAndrew and Steele (1991); CW-BIS: BIS scale from BIS/BAS scales (Carver and White 1994).
F: females; M: males.
[a] $p < 0.01$ (2-tailed).
[b] Data from student's cross-validation samples.
[c] A short version of E (10 items) was used in this study.

the Reward Responsiveness scale, only those obtaining the maximum score of 20 can be selected.

With regard to gender differences for BIS scales, the data in Table 6.1 shows that GWPQ-BIS, Punishment Expectancy, MS-BIS and CW-BIS presented significantly higher scores in women than in men, while the Sensitivity to Punishment did not show significant differences between genders. In relation to BAS scales, males scored higher than females in Fight, Reward Expectancy, Sensitivity to Reward and Appetitive Motivation, whereas females scored higher than males in Approach and Reward Responsiveness.

Validity: correlational data

Concurrent validity As noted above, Gray (1970, 1982) hypothesized that BAS-related measures should be positively related to extraversion and neuroticism and that BIS-related measures should be positively related to neuroticism and negatively to extraversion. Later on, he proposed that psychoticism should be negatively related to BIS measures and positively to BAS measures (Gray 1988). However, this relationship is hard to interpret, since Gray also proposed that P was related to the activity of the FFS system, which should be independent from the BIS and the BAS. Concurrent validity of the purpose-built RST scales is analysed below by observing their relationships with E, N and P in seminal publications.

Table 6.1 also shows correlation coefficients published in the original validation studies of each BIS and BAS scales and E, N and P. As no correlations were presented for N and P in the original publication of the BIS/BAS scales, results from a study with a large sample were taken for this analysis (Jorm, Christensen, Henderson, Jacomb, Korten and Rodgers 1999). In the case of BIS scales, all were negatively related to E and positively to N. Correlations with N were high for all the scales, although correlations with E tended to be low for GWPQ-BIS, Punishment Expectancy and CW-BIS, and high for Sensitivity to Punishment and MS-BIS. Correlations of BIS scales with P were either negative (GWPQ-BIS, Punishment Expectancy and CW-BIS), near zero (Sensitivity to Punishment) or positive (MS-BIS). A differential aspect is noticeable in this general pattern of results: the Sensitivity to Punishment and the MS-BIS scales clearly showed a higher correlation with E than the other scales, being located at almost 45° from E and N.

As for the relationship between BAS scales and E, N and P scales, correlation coefficients with E were all positive with the exception of

Approach, which was close to zero. With regard to correlations with N, it is necessary to consider three different patterns of results: (1) a near zero or a low positive correlation for CW-BAS scales; (2) a positive (low or moderate) correlation for both New GWPQ scales and Sensitivity to Reward; and (3) a negative correlation for Reward Expectancy and Appetitive Motivation. The relationship with P tended to be positive in most of the scales with the exception of Reward Responsiveness and Reward Expectancy, which were near zero. These results will be commented on below.

Convergent and discriminant validity   With respect to correlational data, the conditions that BIS and BAS measures should meet in order to demonstrate their convergent and discriminant validity would be: (1) positive and significant correlations among BIS measures; (2) positive and significant correlations among BAS measures; and (3) orthogonality of BIS and BAS scales both within and between questionnaires. An analysis will be presented of these issues, using results published in a number of papers that include correlational data on at least two of the BIS and/or BAS questionnaires developed on the basis of RST assumptions.

Inspection of data from Table 6.2 provides some support for convergent validity of BIS scales: intercorrelations were all positive and significant and ranged between .23 (MS-BIS with Punishment Expectancy) and .75 (MS-BIS with Sensitivity to Punishment), with Punishment Expectancy being the least related to other scales. With regard to convergent validity for BAS scales (Table 6.3), correlations across scales were all low or moderate. Several specific results were noticeable: (1) Approach and Fight scales were neither related to Drive nor Reward Responsiveness scales and only moderately to Fun Seeking scale; (2) Reward Expectancy scale was only moderately related to CW-BAS scales and Sensitivity to Reward scale; (3) the three CW-BAS scales were only moderately related to Sensitivity to Reward and Appetitive Motivation scales, however, when a total score of the three CW-BAS scales was considered, correlations with Sensitivity to Reward clearly improved; (4) intercorrelations among CW-BAS scales were positive and in general higher than between each one of these scales and any of the other questionnaires' BAS scales. To sum up the results, the magnitude of intercorrelations was lower than the one obtained for BIS measures and the limited data available (only one study) did not give support for the convergent validity of both Approach and Fight scales as compared with Drive and Reward Responsiveness scales.

Table 6.2 *Intercorrelations between BIS purpose-built scales obtained from studies that include data on at least two of the BIS scales*

	MS-BIS	CW-BIS	Sensitivity to punishment
GWPQ-BIS			
Knyazev, Slobodskaya and Wilson 2004		.53[a]	
Punishment expectancy			
Caseras, Ávila and Torrubia 2003	.23[a]	.37[a]	.31[a]
Gomez and Gomez 2005[b]		.59[a]	
MS-BIS			
Carver and White 1994		.59[a]	
Caseras, Ávila and Torrubia 2003		.53[a]	.75[a]
CW-BIS			
Carver and White 1994[c]			.39[a]
Caseras, Ávila and Torrubia 2003			.53[a]
O'Connor, Colder and Hawk 2004			.54[a]
Smillie and Jackson 2005			.56[a]
Franken and Muris 2006			.52[a]

Note: [a] $p < 0.01$ (2-tailed).
[b] In this study correlations between latent scores were calculated.
[c] Correlation with Susceptibility to Punishment scale (Torrubia and Tobeña 1984).
GWPQ-BIS: BIS scale from the New GWPQ (Knyazev, Slobodskaya and Wilson 2004); MS-BIS: BIS scale from MacAndrew and Steele (1991); CW-BIS: BIS scale from BIS/BAS Scales (Carver and White 1994).

In relation to discriminant validity and taking into account the same sources of information consulted in the convergent validity analyses, most worthy of mention is the orthogonality between the majority of BIS and BAS scales; this orthogonality was both intra- and inter-questionnaire. However, two exceptions should be made to this general rule: (1) the Reward Expectancy scale was negatively related to Punishment Expectancy, MS-BIS, CW-BIS and Sensitivity to Punishment (Caseras, Ávila and Torrubia 2003); and (2) the Reward Responsiveness scale tended to show a positive relationship with CW-BIS (Carver and White 1994; Franken and Muris 2006; Johnson, Turner and Iwata 2003; O'Connor, Colder and Hawk 2004; Smillie and Jackson 2005).

Validity: factor analyses studies

A number of studies using exploratory factor analysis and confirmatory factor analysis have been carried out in order to investigate the relationship

Table 6.3 *Intercorrelations between BAS purpose-built scales obtained from studies that include data on at least two of the BAS scales*

	Approach	Drive	Reward responsiveness	Fun seeking	Sensitivity to reward	Appetitive motivation
Fight						
Knyazev, Slobodskaya and Wilson 2004	$.20^a$		.01	$-.03$	$.32^a$	
Approach						
Knyazev, Slobodskaya and Wilson 2004		$-.03$	.01	$.28^a$		
Reward expectancy						
Caseras, Ávila and Torrubia 2003		$.33^a$	$.23^a$	$.21^a$	$.29^a$	
Drive						
Caseras, Ávila and Torrubia 2003			$.36^a$	$.36^a$	$.41^a$	
Knyazev, Slobodskaya and Wilson 2004			$.29^a$	.03		
Jackson and Smillie 2004			$.49^a$	$.47^a$		.31
O'Connor, Colder and Hawk 2004			$.38^a$	$.49^a$	$.32^a$	
Smillie and Jackson 2005			$.34^a$	$.36^a$	$.29^a$	$.32^a$
Franken and Muris 2006			$.45^a$	$.43^a$	.28	
Reward responsiveness						
Caseras, Ávila and Torrubia 2003				$.34^a$	$.33^a$	
Knyazev, Slobodskaya and Wilson 2004				.14		
Jackson and Smillie 2004				$.52^a$		.04
O'Connor, Colder and Hawk 2004				$.53^a$	.17	
Smillie and Jackson 2005				$.50^a$	$.30^a$	$.32^a$
Franken and Muris 2006				.22	$.29^a$	
Fun Seeking						
Caseras, Ávila and Torrubia 2003					$.41^a$	
Jackson and Smillie 2004						$.37^a$
O'Connor, Colder & Hawk 2004					$.22^a$	
Smillie and Jackson 2005					$.28^a$	$.50^a$
Franken and Muris 2006					$.35^a$	
CW-BAS						
Quilty and Oakman (2004)					$.46^a$	
Sensitivity to Reward						
Smillie and Jackson 2005						$.35^a$

Note: CW-BAS: Sum of the scores in the three BAS scales from BIS/BAS scales.
[a] $p < 0.01$ (2-tailed).

between some of the scales aimed at measuring individual differences in BIS and BAS. The results also provide valuable information in order to know the convergent, discriminant and concurrent validity of the different questionnaires.

Caseras, Ávila and Torrubia (2003) carried out a study including five questionnaires aimed at measuring individual differences in BIS and BAS, the EPQ, the TPQ (Cloninger 1987), the I_7 and the STAI-T. A principal component analysis with Varimax rotation was performed, which yielded four-factors with eigenvalues > 1. The first was a BIS factor with positive loadings from all the BIS scales, STAI-T and N, and negative from Reward Expectancy and E; the second was positively loaded by Novelty Seeking, I_7, P, Fun Seeking, E and Sensitivity to Reward; the third was mainly loaded by Drive, Sensitivity to Reward, Reward Responsiveness and Fun Seeking; and the fourth by Reward Dependence, E, and P (in negative). The results were very similar when an oblique rotation was performed: factors approached orthogonality, the BIS factor showed low correlations with the other three factors and the highest correlation was found between the 'impulsivity-thrill seeking' (second) and 'reward interest' (third) factors (.23; p < .001). Thus, the results show a single factor for BIS scales and a two factor structure for BAS-related scales (the fourth factor was not considered as a BAS-related factor by the authors). However, when a two-factor solution with oblique rotation was forced, an orthogonal solution was found (r = − .06; ns); a BIS factor was obtained which was loaded positively by N and negatively by E, and also positively by all anxiety, neuroticism and BIS scales; the second was a BAS factor which was positively loaded by E, N and P and all the BAS/impulsivity scales. Results also showed that Cloninger's Reward Dependence scale did not show relevant loadings on either BIS or BAS factors.

Useful data for the analysis of convergent validity of some BIS and BAS scales have also been published by Knyazev, Slobodskaya and Wilson (2004). These authors performed an exploratory factor analysis including the three scales of the New GWPQ, the BIS/BAS scales, E, N, P, two impulsivity and two anxiety scales. As in the Caseras, Ávila and Torrubia (2003) study, BAS/impulsivity measures loaded on two different factors: Approach, Fight, Fun Seeking, P and I_7 loaded on a 'P' factor, whereas Drive, Reward Responsiveness and E loaded on an 'E' factor. A third factor named 'N' was positively loaded by BIS, anxiety and N scales and negatively by E. Similar results have been published by Franken and Muris (2006), Smillie and Jackson (2006), Zelenski and Larsen (1999) and Zuckerman, Joireman, Kraft and Kuhlman (1999). A noteworthy aspect of the above-mentioned studies is that the Fun

Seeking scale usually loads on 'P'/impulsivity factors, the Drive and Reward Responsiveness scales usually load on 'E'/Appoach motivation factors and Sensitivity to Reward loads on the two factors. Using confirmatory factor analysis, Quilty and Oakman's (2004) conclusions about the structure of BAS rating scales were similar to those reached in studies which used exploratory factor analysis. Their results showed that (1) a good fit was obtained for a model based on a single factor with all the BAS/impulsivity scales; (2) impulsivity measures decreased the overall fit of the model and were somewhat less strong indicators of the BAS than purpose-built BAS scales; (3) when a two-factor model was formed, including the measures of BAS as indicators of the latent variable of BAS and the measures of impulsivity as indicators of the latent variable of impulsivity, a better fit was obtained; and (4) the correlation between these two constructs was found to be statistically different from unity. Summing up, the results of both exploratory and confirmatory factor analysis have corroborated convergent validity for all the BIS scales developed on the basis of RST assumptions. As regards convergent validity for BAS scales, the two BAS/impulsivity-related factors observed in many of the studies seem to be indicating that not all BAS/impulsivity scales are measuring the same construct, but that impulsivity-thrill seeking and approach motivation seem to be related, though not identical, facets of an impulsivity and action-oriented superfactor. In addition, the differences between the BAS scales in the New GWPQ and those in the BIS/BAS scales observed by Knyazev, Slobodskaya and Wilson (2004) using exploratory factor analysis, would indicate again that the BAS scales in the two questionnaires measure clearly different traits.

Exploratory factor analysis results confirmed discriminant validity for almost all of the scales: in all studies but one (Reward Expectancy in Caseras, Ávila and Torrubia 2003), BIS and BAS scales loaded on different factors.

As regards concurrent validity based on exploratory factor analysis results, a BIS-related factor was loaded by N (positively) and E (negatively) in two of the studies (Caseras, Ávila and Torrubia 2003; Knyazev, Slobodskaya and Wilson 2004) but not in the other two (Zelenski and Larsen 1999; Zuckerman et al. 1999), where only N loadings were observed. These results are probably related to the fact that some BIS scales do not meet the requirement of being negatively related to E. Results for BAS scales showed that in three of four studies (Knyazev, Slobodskaya and Wilson 2004; Zelenski and Larsen 1999; Zuckerman et al. 1999) E loaded on a approach motivation factor (also including scales such as Drive, Reward Responsiveness, Sensitivity to Reward and Reward Expectancy) and in all four studies, P loaded on an impulsivity-thrill seeking factor (including Fun Seeking in all the studies and both Approach and Fight in one case). This would indicate that the impulsivity-thrill seeking factor could be a facet which is more related to P, and that the approach motivation factor would be more related to E. Though much less related to BAS than the other two Eysenckian dimensions, N would be more associated with impulsivity-thrill seeking than approach motivation. The negligible loadings from N in BAS/impulsivity-related factors would be a reflection of the low correlation which many of the scales show with this personality dimension.

BIS and BAS purpose-built scales and controversial issues related to the measurement of the RST dimensions

How important to the validity of the scales are the correlations with E, N and P predicted in the RST?

The results from psychometric analyses carried out in the previous section raise two important issues: (1) BIS scales differ in the strength of correlations with E, N and P; and (2) serious divergence is detected between BAS scales and important deviations in some of them with regard to the relation which might be expected with Eysenckian variables. To take the first point, the RST indicates that both the E and N dimensions should contribute to a greater sensitivity to punishment (Gray 1970, 1981). Some of the scales (see Table 6.1), however, have shown low correlations with E. This might suggest a problem of validity, as there are many behavioural studies which show a strong relationship between introversion and greater sensitivity to punishment (see, for example, Newman 1987; Pickering, Díaz and Gray 1995; and chapter 7), while there are no behavioural data only relating neuroticism to greater learning in situations of punishment. The correlation with extraversion seems therefore to be, a priori, an important requirement for scales which evaluate the BIS. Scales which fail to meet this requirement should demonstrate their capacity to predict passive avoidance learning in the laboratory.

As regards the second point, it must be pointed out that Gray's work was focused more on the description of the BIS, and various aspects of the description of the BAS emerge through its parallelism with the BIS. A consequence of this is that in a number of important issues, either no clear theoretical formulation exists about the BAS in some aspects, or there is a lack of consensus among researchers in others. Several theoretical formulations have stressed that sensitivity to reward is related to extraversion (Depue and Collins 1999; chapter 7), though there are data to indicate that neurotic extraverts display better appetitive learning than stable introverts (see Ávila, Moltó, Segarra and Torrubia 1995; Gupta and Shukla 1989; Nichols and Newman 1986; Patterson, Kosson and Newman 1987). Wallace and Newman ((1990); see also Patterson and Newman 1993) have even argued that the role of neuroticism is to increase arousal and focus attention on reward, which heightens sensitivity to reward and makes it more difficult to modify appetitive response patterns. Behavioural studies therefore show that neuroticism seems to play an important part in sensitivity to reward, suggesting that BAS scales should correlate positively with this dimension.

In the case of BAS measures, it is very hard to decide which of the scales best reflects the construct, only using psychometric criteria. One possible explanation for the low correlations between N and BAS measures may come from the moderate negative correlation between E and N (approximately $-.15$ to $-.20$), given that some items in the N scale have a negative content. In this sense, N might not reflect sensitivity to all kinds of reinforcers. For this reason, BAS scales must be validated with laboratory and neuro-imaging studies (see above).

Is BAS better assessed from a multidimensional approach than a unidimensional one?

There is no a priori approach in the RST to the question of whether the structure of the BAS should be uni- or multi-dimensional. The fact that there is no clear definition in the RST about the way that the BAS should be manifested at trait level has generated different forms of approaching the measurement of the construct (Díaz and Pickering 1993). In the development of the BIS/BAS scales, Carver and White (1994) proposed a three-factor structure for the measurement of the BAS, while Knyazev, Slobodskaya and Wilson (2004) suggested considering their Approach and Fight scales as two facets of a broad BAS factor when developing the New GWPQ. In both cases, the choice of a multiple factor structure for BAS measurement was mainly based on empirical results of exploratory and confirmatory factor analyses respectively, rather than on any theoretical model. However, other authors have chosen a unidimensional structure in the development of their BAS scales (Ball and Zuckerman 1990; Jackson and Smillie 2004; Torrubia et al. 2001).

As regards BIS/BAS scales, each one of the scales focuses on different relevant aspects of the approach processes. The factor structure of the BIS/BAS scales has been replicated on several occasions using confirmatory factor analysis (Heubeck, Wilkinson and Cologon 1998; Leone, Perugini, Bagozzi, Pierro and Mannetti 2001), and in some studies the authors even highlighted the importance of treating BAS sub-scales as independent constructs (Ross, Millis, Bonebright and Bailley 2002). To date, however, no suggestion has been made about the theoretical significance of these three constructs in relation to the BAS.

Since their original publication, the three BAS scales of Carver and White's scales presented certain divergences between them with regard to their relationship with other variables. Thus, for example, the Reward Responsiveness scale proved to be positively related to CW-BIS and Cloninger's Reward Dependence scale, while the other two tended towards orthogonality; in contrast, Drive and Fun Seeking were negatively related to Cloninger's Harm Avoidance, while Reward Responsiveness failed to produce this correlation. In the seminal study, it was also observed that in a situation in which subjects anticipated a reward, subjects with high scores in Drive and Reward Responsiveness were happier than low scorers, controlling for initial happiness; however, this result was not found for Fun Seeking (Carver and White 1994). In a recent study, each of the scales was related to different kinds of negative affect: Fun Seeking to frustration and sadness after frustrative non-reward; Reward Responsiveness to anger in response to scenarios; and Drive to anger after the terrorist attacks of September 11, 2001 (Carver 2004).

The results mentioned above obtained in various studies using exploratory factor analysis and including the BIS/BAS and different BAS activity-related scales could provide a suitable framework for answering our question. Caseras, Ávila and Torrubia (2003), Knyazev, Slobodskaya and Wilson (2004) and Zelenski and Larsen (1999) coincide in finding that scales related to BAS activity clustered in two different factors which we could call approach motivation and impulsivity-thrill seeking. This would seem to indicate that the scales which have been used so far to assess the BAS would be measuring two different constructs. In the three studies, the Fun Seeking scale shows greater loadings on the second factor, while the other two load more heavily on the first. Also, in a study carried out to examine the component structure of impulsivity, by performing a principal components analysis with Varimax rotation of 10 sub-scales from four different BAS/impulsivity-related measures, Miller, Joseph and Tudway (2004) found a three-component structure, with the third factor being loaded by Reward Responsiveness and by Drive. The other two factors were labelled Non-Planning Dysfunctional and Functional Venturesomeness respectively. It is also noticeable that Fun Seeking showed similar loadings on all the three factors, Drive also loaded on the Functional Venturesomeness factor and that Reward Responsiveness loaded exclusively on the third factor. As well as revealing that Reward Responsiveness is not related to three well known impulsivity questionnaires, the results once again confirm the differences between Fun Seeking and the other two BAS scales of the BIS/BAS scales. All these data lead us to a clear conclusion: both the Drive and the Reward Responsiveness scales assess aspects which are related to the approach motivation construct, while the Fun Seeking scale would instead measure aspects related to impulsivity and sensation-seeking.

There is currently a wealth of empirical evidence to show that the three scales often differ in their relation to other behavioural or psychometric variables. Also, the availability of scales related to different aspects of a particular construct may contribute to a better understanding of the phenomenon being studied. However, the main drawback in the case of Carver and White's scales is that the lack of theoretical foundation to support the assessment of these facets makes it difficult to interpret the information obtained.

With regard to the New GWPQ scales, it would be premature to draw conclusions about the usefulness of the two factors, as so far there have been no studies to replicate this structure and reveal the behavioural and psychometric correlates of these scales. As happens with the BIS/BAS scales, however, justification of them has been made a posteriori, without being based on a theoretical model.

The answer to the question asked at the beginning of this section should be based on (1) analysis of the predictive capacity of the scales when considered separately, compared to when they are computed as the sum of scores; (2) comparison between the predictive capacity of multifactor and single factor scales; and (3) analysis of the factor structure of the different BAS scales, which have so far only been used from a unidimensional perspective to find out the extent to which the structures mentioned above could be replicated with other sets of items.

Laboratory and social behaviour correlates of BIS and BAS scales

Analysis of the psychometric characteristics of instruments based on correlational and factorial studies with other scales is only one of the steps necessary for the proper assessment of their validity. The RST is a neuropsychological model which permits a great variety of predictions about behaviour and physiological responses in controlled laboratory situations or in particular social contexts. The most important test for analysing the validity of BIS and BAS scales is demonstrating that high and low scorers on each one of them show behaviours anticipated in the theory.

A great deal of RST-related laboratory results have been obtained using the EPQ scales, anxiety scales like the STAI, impulsivity scales like the EPI-Impulsivity, or Cloninger's scales as instruments to evaluate the BIS and BAS. The results sometimes confirm the model, while at other times they do not (Corr 2004). Very little work has been done in this sense, however, with some purpose-built scales of reward and punishment sensitivity, and this perhaps is the area which future research must address. Although with some differences, only the BIS/BAS scales and the SPSRQ have been submitted to a sufficient number of non-psychometric studies to test different aspects of their validity.

Going by the recent review by Corr (2004), it can clearly be seen that the BIS/BAS scales are those which can boast a greater number of behavioural, psychophysiological and neuro-imaging studies to support them. Many of the behavioural studies have been conducted by Carver himself (Carver 2004; Carver, Meyer and Antoni 2000; Carver and White 1994), though other authors have also obtained results which lend validity to the scales (Gomez and Gomez 2002; Heponiemi, Keltikangas-Järvinen, Puttonen and Ravaja 2003; Kambouropoulos and Staiger 2001; Zinbarg and Mohlman 1998). Usually, however, the measures used as a dependent variable which have produced significant results have been of the self-reporting variety. The capacity of the questionnaire to predict laboratory behaviours based on execution (i.e., using dependent variables such as reaction time (RT) and learning) which comply to the model is thus still to be proven; specifically, (1) the capacity of the CW-BIS scale to predict greater sensitivity to punishment in aversive learnings; and (2) the capacity of the CW-BAS scales to predict greater sensitivity to reward. The results published so far have been inconsistent (Pickering 1997) or negative (Smillie and Jackson 2005; Zinbarg and Mohlman 1998).

To date, published psychophysiological, psychopharmacological or functional neuro-imaging studies have only given partial support to the RST and hence to the validity of the questionnaire. Thus, for example, the BIS/BAS scales have been shown to predict asymmetries in resting levels of cortical arousal (Harmon-Jones and Allen 1997; Sutton and Davidson 1997); affective modulation and pre-pulse inhibition of startle reflex (Hawk and Kowmas 2003); and heart rate reactivity and parasympathetic withdrawal during laboratory tasks (Heponiemi, Keltikangas-Järvinen, Kettunen, Puttonen and Ravaja 2004). However, other authors have not found any relation between these scales and physiological measures of BIS and BAS reactivity (Brenner, Beauchaine and Sylvers 2005), or between CW-BAS scores and dopaminergic activity (Stuettgen, Hennig, Reuter and Netter 2005), as might be expected according to the model. Functional neuro-imaging studies have found that CW-BIS scores are associated with a greater responsivity (right amygdala or hippocampus) to fearful faces (Cools, Clark, Owen and Robbins 2002), to aversive pictures (Mathews, Yiend and Lawrence 2004) and also to fear, disgust and erotic visual stimuli (Reuter, Stark, Hennig, Walter, Kirsch, Schiene and Vaitl 2004); in this last study, however, few associations were detected between CW-BAS and brain activity in response to disgust and erotic stimuli. Many studies have shown the BIS/BAS scales to be related to social behaviours in natural environments. To quote some examples, BIS and BAS assessed by BIS/BAS scales have been shown to be related to reactions to negative and positive events in everyday life (Gable, Reis and Elliot 2000), and in a study carried out by Kasch, Rottenberg, Arnow and Gotlib (2002), it was found that depressed participants reported lower BAS levels and higher BIS levels than non-depressed controls and that in the depressed group, lower CW-BAS scales scores were associated with greater concurrent depression severity and predicted eight-month outcome. A similar result, albeit only for CW-BIS, was found by Johnson, Turner and Iwata (2003) in an epidemiological study carried out in a large non-clinical sample. CW-BAS scales scores have been related to manic symptoms in non-clinical populations (Meyer, Johnson and Carver 1999); and to stronger desires and intentions to drink alcohol and negative reinforcement craving during exposure to alcohol-related cues (Franken 2002).

The SPSRQ displays the opposite pattern to BIS/BAS scales, in that different behavioural studies using laboratory tasks test Gray's model (see Corr 2004; and chapter 7), though few psychophysiological studies (Brunelle, Assaad, Barrett, Ávila, Conrod, Tremblay and Pihl 2004; Caseras, Fullana, Riba, Barbanoj, Aluja and Torrubia 2006; De Pascalis, Arwari, Matteucci and Mazzocco 2003; Fullana, Caseras, Riba, Barbanoj and Torrubia 2006) have been carried out with this questionnaire. No functional neuro-imaging studies have been published which use the SPSRQ and only two voxel-based morphometry studies have investigated the relationship between gray matter concentration in the brain and SP and SR respectively. The first showed a positive correlation between SP and gray matter volume in the amygdala, the septo-hippocampal system, the cingulate and the hypothalamus (Barrós-Loscertales, Meseguer, Sanjuán, Belloch, Parcet, Torrubia and

Ávila 2006a), and the second a negative correlation between SR scores and gray matter volume in right striatum (including caudate, putamen, globus pallidus and nucleus accumbens; Barrós-Loscertales, Meseguer, Sanjuán, Belloch, Parcet, Torrubia and Ávila 2006b).

The results of behavioural studies have been an evident source of support for the RST, as they demonstrate that individuals who are highly sensitive to punishment have better passive avoidance learning (Ávila 2001; Ávila, Parcet, Ibáñez and Ortet 1999; Ávila and Torrubia, in press; Torrubia, Ávila, Moltó and Grande 1995), and extinction learning (Ávila 1994; Ávila and Parcet 2001), in addition to a greater tendency to focus their attention on threatening stimuli (Ávila and Parcet 2002a). Sensitivity to Reward, meanwhile, is associated behaviourally with a better appetitive and active avoidance learning, as well as a greater difficulty in modifying appetitive response patterns (Ávila 2001; Ávila and Parcet 2001, 2002b; Kambouropuolos and Staiger 2004; Smillie and Jackson 2005). Studies with cognitive paradigms have also shown how the Sensitivity to Reward scale is associated with a greater conscious focalization of attention on stimuli associated with reward (Ávila and Parcet 2002b; Poy, Eixarch and Ávila 2004) and a greater facility for disengagement from non-relevant stimuli (Ávila and Parcet 1997; Ávila, Barrós, Ortet, Parcet and Ibáñez 2003).

With regard to social behaviour correlates in natural settings, the Sensitivity to Punishment and Sensitivity to Reward scales have been shown to be related to the infringement of road traffic rules (Castellà and Pérez 2004), response strategies in multiple-choice question examinations in university students (Ávila and Torrubia 2004) and sexual experiences, excitability and satisfaction levels in females (Aluja 2004). In the clinical field, low scores on the Sensitivity to Reward scale have been shown to be associated with the diagnosis of major depression in both patients with current major depression and recovered patients (Pinto-Meza, Caseras, Soler, Puigdemont, Pérez and Torrubia 2006), and high scores on this scale have been related to problematic drinking patterns in students (O'Connor and Colder 2005). High Sensitivity to Punishment scores made it possible to differentiate patients with cluster C personality disorders from patients with other personality disorders or without personality disorder (Caseras, Torrubia and Farré 2001); scores were also found to be high in obsessive compulsive disorder patients (Fullana, Mataix-Cols, Trujillo, Caseras, Serrano, Alonso, Menchón, Vallejo and Torrubia 2004) or associated with some of the symptom dimensions of this disorder (Fullana, Mataix-Cols, Caseras, Alonso, Menchón, Vallejo and Torrubia 2004).

Summary of psychometric properties and predictive capacity in the laboratory of purpose-built RST measures

In Table 6.4, a summary is provided of psychometric properties and available data on predictive capacity in the laboratory of purpose-built RST measures. Adopting exclusively psychometric criteria, data may be found which give support to the reliability and, to a certain extent, the validity of all the scales analysed. This being said, although the BIS scales generally display good convergent validity, our impression is that, in relation to the BAS scales, each of them offers different nuances as regards the actual nature of this construct. Three examples of this are the low convergent validity between the CW-BAS scales and the BAS scales in the New GWPQ, the merely moderate correlations between the CW-BAS and Sensitivity to Reward scales, and the very slight convergent validity between the Reward Expectancy scale and the other BAS scales.

Also, psychometric studies do not suffice as confirmation of the validity of measurement instruments, as pointed out earlier. We have stressed the need for scales developed to measure individual differences in the activity of different systems to be tested in learning situations in the laboratory. Applying this criterion, only two of them have been sufficiently studied to confidently confirm their predictive capability: BIS/BAS scales and SPSRQ. The former are, without doubt, the scales most commonly used to measure BIS and BAS activity and the current yardstick for evaluating RST dimensions, although further laboratory studies using learning tasks are required to demonstrate their validity. The latter was published more recently and the number of researchers who have used it in RST-related studies is logically smaller.

To what extent are scales based on RST assumptions and other anxiety and impulsivity scales interchangeable?

Gray introduced the labels 'anxiety' and 'impulsivity' to identify individual differences in BIS and BAS activation, respectively. These labels have frequently led many authors to use anxiety and impulsivity scales to measure the activity of the BIS and the BAS. To what extent, however, is this option the right one? Both anxiety and impulsivity seem to be more complex concepts which go beyond the BIS and BAS constructs in the RST. This fact is more complicated if we consider that, in the development of many BIS and BAS scales, anxiety and impulsivity scales have been used as a criterion for studying convergent validity.

Table 6.4 Summary of psychometric properties and predictive capacity in the laboratory of purpose-built RST measures

BIS scales	Psychometric properties					Prediction of behaviour in laboratory	
	Alpha reliab.	Test-retest reliab.	Convergent validity	Discriminant validity	Relationship with E and N	Learning and performance	Self-reported affect
GWPQ-BIS (1)	Good	Not reported	Good: 4 No data: 2; 3; 5	Good: 6; 7; 9; 10; 11 No data: 8; 12; 13	Good	Insufficient data	Insufficient data
Punishment expectancy (2)	Moderate	Not reported	Good: 3; 4; 5 No data: 1	Good: 9; 10; 11; 12 Poor: 8 No data: 6; 7; 13	Good	Insufficient data	Insufficient data
MS-BIS (3)	Very good	Not reported	Good: 2; 4; 5 No data: 1	Good: 9; 10; 11; 12 Poor: 8 No data: 6; 7; 13	Good	Insufficient data	Insufficient data
CW-BIS (4)	Good	Good	Good: 1; 2; 3; 5	Good: 6; 7; 9; 10; 11; 12; 13 Poor: 8	Low corr with E	Insufficient data	Very good
Sensitivity to punishment (5)	Very good	Very good	Good: 2; 3; 4 No data: 1	Good: 9; 10; 11; 12; 13 Poor: 8 No data: 6; 7	Good	Very good	Insufficient data

BAS

Fight (6)	Good	Not reported	Good: 7; 11 Poor: 9; 10 No data: 8; 12; 13	Good: 1; 4 No data: 2; 3; 5	Low corr with N	Insufficient data	Insufficient data
Approach (7)	Moderate	Not reported	Good: 6; 11 Poor: 9; 10 No data: 8; 12; 13	Good: 1; 4 No data: 2; 3; 5	Low corr with E	Insufficient data	Insufficient data
Reward Expectancy (8)	Moderate	Not reported	Good: 9; 10; 11; 12 No data: 6; 7; 13	Poor: 2; 3; 4; 5 No data: 1	Neg. corr with N	Insufficient data	Insufficient data
Drive (9)	Good	Good	Good: 8; 10; 11; 12; 13 Poor: 6; 7	Good: 1; 2; 3; 4; 5	Low corr with N	Insufficient data	Very good
Reward Responsiv. (10)	Good	Good	Good: 8; 9; 11; 12; 13 Poor: 6; 7	Good: 1; 2; 3; 4; 5	Good	Insufficient data	Very good
Fun Seeking (11)	Moderate	Good	Good: 6; 7; 8; 9; 10; 12; 13	Good: 1; 2; 3; 4; 5	Low corr with N	Insufficient data	Very good
Sensitivity to Reward (12)	Good	Very Good	Good: 8; 9; 10; 11; 13 No data: 6; 7	Good: 2; 3; 4; 5 No data: 1	Good	Very good	Insufficient data
Appetitive Motivation (13)	Good	Not reported	Good: 9; 10; 11; 12 No data: 6; 7; 8	Good: 4; 5 No data: 1; 2; 3	Neg. corr with N	Insufficient data	Insufficient data

Note: The numbers in the Convergent validity and Discriminant validity columns correspond to the scales numbered in the first column. Scales 1, 6 and 7 (New GWPQ); Scales 2 and 8 (GRAPES); Scale 3 (BIS scale from MacAndrew and Steele 1991); Scales 4, 9, 10 and 11 (BIS/BAS scales); Scales 5 and 12 (SPSRQ); Scale 12 (BAS scale from Jackson and Smillie 2004).

The results of exploratory and confirmatory factor analysis studies mentioned above also provide support for the convergent validity of a number of anxiety scales not developed within the framework of RST (for instance, STAI-T, Harm Avoidance and Anxiety from de EPP), as these scales usually loaded on the same factor as the BIS scales in all of these studies. Moreover, the strength of correlations between these scales and purpose-built BIS scales was no weaker than that observed among the latter (Caseras, Ávila and Torrubia 2003).

The results obtained with impulsivity measures not developed within the framework of RST show a somewhat different picture: When included in exploratory factor analyses, these measures usually loaded on a different factor than some purpose-built BAS scales related to approach motivation, although, when a single factor for all BAS/impulsivity measures was forced, a homogeneous BAS factor was obtained. Data from Quilty and Oakman (2004) using confirmatory factor analyses corroborated these results, showing that though a good fit was obtained for one-factor solutions including BAS and impulsivity scales, a better fit was observed when two different factors were considered. This difference between these two types of BAS/impulsivity measures seems to be confirmed at a neurobiological level by a number of recent studies (Dawe, Gullo and Loxton 2004; Stuettgen et al. 2005).

In our opinion, it would be premature to claim that the purpose-built BIS and BAS scales are more recommendable than anxiety and impulsivity scales for use in RST research. There have so far been insufficient laboratory studies which simultaneously use both types of scales to decide which of them present better predictive capacity (see, however, Gomez and Gomez 2002; Pickering et al. 1997; Zinbarg and Mohlman 1998).

In summary, it may be affirmed that anxiety and BIS scales assess roughly the same construct, though impulsivity-thrill seeking scales and some BAS scales developed on the basis of RST assumptions assess related, but not identical, constructs. Among the purpose-built BAS scales, only Sensitivity to Reward seems to encompass the two constructs.

Conclusion

Gray's model was perhaps one of the first proposals to highlight the independence of appetitive and aversive motivation. This principle is currently championed by several authors (Caccioppo and Bernston 1994; Davidson 1998; Lang 1995) who, rather than personality models as such, refer to ones of emotion. Aversive motivation is defined in terms of sensitivity and reactivity to punishment cues, whereas appetitive motivation is defined in terms of sensitivity and reactivity to reward cues. As well as demonstrating the independence of the two types of motivation, Gray's model shows that the relevant personality dimensions (which he called anxiety and impulsivity) are associated with the differential functioning of these systems. Taking Eysenck's model as a reference point, the specific proposal is that introvert neurotic subjects display greater aversive motivation than extravert stable subjects, while extravert neurotic subjects display greater appetitive motivation than introvert stable subjects. This suggestion stems from the observation, which has since received general support in the literature, that introverts display greater aversive learning, while extroverts display greater appetitive learning, and that neuroticism enhances these effects.

One of the problems found in the model is the lack of a valid psychometric instrument derived by the author himself. This has led other authors to construct measures following the BIS and BAS formulation, but taking different approaches to their development and requiring rather different degrees of validity and validity criteria. Despite having, to a greater or lesser extent, a particular level of convergent and discriminant validity, it cannot be said that these measures are evaluating the same constructs or that they may be used indiscriminately. We believe that any assessment of the validity of instruments must be based not only on the apparent validity of items, but also on their capacity to satisfy the predictions of the RST. These predictions are very specific: (1) BIS measures should correlate negatively with E and positively with N; (2) BAS measures should correlate positively with E and N; (3) BIS measures should be positively related to aversive learning; (4) BAS measures should do likewise with appetitive learning; (5) BIS measures should be associated with a differential functioning of the septohippocampal system; (6) BAS measures should be associated with a differential functioning of cerebral reward systems. At present, none of the scales meet all of these criteria, although two of them (BIS/BAS scales and SPSRQ) are supported by a wealth of data to confirm their validity.

From a psychometric viewpoint, BIS evaluation seems much clearer than in that of the BAS. With regard to the latter, on the basis of the scales analysed, two constructs emerge which, though related, are distinct: Impulsivity-sensation seeking and approach motivation. Among the purpose-built BAS scales examined in this chapter, SR is the only one that clearly shows loadings on the two constructs. Future studies, especially those of the psychophysiological and neuro-imaging types, will have to set out the common elements and the differences between these different approaches to BAS measurement.

The BIS and the BAS are not constructs which match the traits of anxiety and impulsivity respectively, as these last two are much broader concepts than the first two. It would seem appropriate to have specific instruments for evaluating these constructs. Despite this, there is insufficient empirical evidence to show that scales developed specifically to evaluate the BIS and BAS have greater predictive capability than some anxiety and impulsivity scales.

In order to ascertain which set of measures provide the best predictions of reward and punishment sensitivities in laboratory studies, the simultaneous use of BIS/BAS purpose-built scales together with anxiety, impulsivity, E and N scales would be valuable in the future.

In this chapter we have assumed the association between sensitivity to punishment and BIS functioning, as was originally defined in light of the model depicted by Gray (1982). However, if we take into account the redefinition of the model made by Gray and McNaughton (2000) and lately by McNaughton and Corr (2004), it must be pointed out that there are no instruments specifically designed to evaluate the new version of the BIS and Fight-Flight-Freeze System (FFFS) constructs, and we still do not know how useful the instruments reviewed in the present chapter are in this task. In the framework of the new model, sensitivity to punishment as measured by the present BIS scales could be considered either an index of the BIS, an index of the FFFS or an index of the combined BIS/FFFS functioning. Future research will have to address this issue, and also that of whether it is possible to use questionnaires to measure these constructs independently. Present knowledge would seem to indicate, however, that it is too early to abandon Gray's (1982) RST model without first having a more solid formulation of what such systems represent in the domain of personality traits or the right instruments for evaluating them. As regards the BAS, we believe that the new formulation of the model has no substantial effect on the measurement of this construct, and that currently available instruments could be a good starting point for going about future research.*

References

Aluja, A. (2004), Sensitivity to punishment, sensitivity to reward and sexuality in females, *Personality and Individual Differences*, 36, 5–10
Ávila, C. (1994), Sensitivity to punishment and resistance to extinction: a test of Gray's behavioural inhibition system, *Personality and Individual Differences*, 17, 845–847

*Preparation of this chapter was supported by a grant (BSO2001-2556) from the Dirección General de Investigación, Ministerio de Ciencia y Tecnología of Spain.

(2001), Distinguishing BIS-mediated and BAS-mediated disinhibition mechanisms: a comparison of disinhibition models of Gray and Patterson and Newman, *Journal of Personality and Social Psychology*, 80, 311–324

Ávila, C., Barrós, A., Ortet, G., Parcet, M.A. and Ibáñez, M.I. (2003), Set-shifting and sensitivity to reward: a dopamine mechanism for explaining disinhibitory disorders, *Cognition and Emotion*, 17, 951–959

Ávila, C., Moltó, J., Segarra, P. and Torrubia, R. (1995), Sensitivity to primary or secondary reinforcers, what is the mechanism underlying passive avoidance: deficits in extraverts?, *Journal of Research in Personality*, 29, 373–394

Ávila, C. and Parcet, M.A. (1997), Impulsivity and anxiety differences in cognitive inhibition, *Personality and Individual Differences*, 23, 1055–1064

(2001), Personality and inhibitory deficits in the stop-signal task: the mediating role of Gray's anxiety and impulsivity, *Personality and Individual Differences*, 29, 975–986

(2002a), The role of attentional anterior network on threat-related attentional biases in anxiety, *Personality and Individual Differences*, 32, 715–728

(2002b), Individual differences in reward sensitivity and attentional focus, *Personality and Individual Differences*, 33, 979–996

Ávila, C., Parcet, M.A., Ibañez, M.I. and Ortet, G. (1999), The role of the behavioral inhibition system in the ability to associate aversive stimuli with future rewards, *Personality and Individual Differences*, 27, 1209–1219

Ávila, C. and Torrubia, R. (2004), Personality, expectations and response to multiple choice question examinations in university students: a test of Gray's hypotheses, *European Journal of Personality*, 18, 45–59

(2006), Personality differences in suppression of behavior as a function of the probability of punishment, *Personality and Individual Differences*, 41, 249–260

Ball, S. and Zuckerman, M. (1990), Sensation seeking, Eysenck's personality dimensions and reinforcement sensitivity in concept formation, *Personality and Individual Differences*, 11, 343–345

Barrós-Loscertales, A., Meseguer, V., Sanjuán, A., Belloch, V., Parcet, M.A., Torrubia, R. and Ávila, C. (2006a), Behavioral inhibition system activity is associated with increased amygdala and septo-hippocampal gray matter volume: a voxel-based morphometry study, *Neuro Image*, 33, 1011–1015

(2006b), Striatum gray matter reduction in males with an overactive behavioral activation system (BAS), *European Journal of Neuroscience*, 24, 2071–2074

Blair, C. (2003), Behavioral inhibition and behavioural activation in young children: relations with self-regulation and adaptation to preschool in children attending head start, *Deviant Psychobiology*, 42, 301–311

Blair, C., Peters, R. and Granger, D. (2004), Physiological and neuropsychological correlates of approach/withdrawal tendencies in preschool: further examination of the behavioral inhibition system/behavioral activation system scales for young children, *Deviant Psychobiology*, 45, 113–124

Brenner, S.L., Beauchaine, T.P. and Sylvers, P.D. (2005), A comparison of psychophysiological and self-report measures of BAS and BIS activation, *Psychophysiology*, 42, 108–115

Brunelle, C., Assaad, J.M., Barrett, S.P., Ávila, C., Conrod, P.J., Tremblay, R.E. and Pihl, R.O. (2004), Heightened heart rate response to alcohol intoxication is associated with a reward–seeking personality profile, *Alcoholism, Clinical and Experimental Research*, 28, 394–401

Caccioppo, J.T. and Bernston, G.G. (1994), Relationship between attitudes and evaluative space: a critical review, with emphasis on the separability of positive and negative substrates, *Psychological Bulletin*, 115, 401–423

Carver, C.S. (2004), Negative affects derived from the behavioral approach system, *Emotion*, 4, 3–22

Carver, C.S., Meyer, B. and Antoni, M.H. (2000), Responsiveness to threats and incentives, expectancy of recurrence, and distress and disengagement: moderator effects in women with early stage breast cancer, *Journal of Consulting and Clinical Psychology*, 68, 965–975

Carver, C.S. and White, T.L. (1994), Behavioral inhibition, behavioral activation, and affective responses to impending reward and punishment: the BIS/BAS scales, *Journal of Personality and Social Psychology*, 67, 319–333

Caseras, X., Ávila, C. and Torrubia, R. (2003), The measurement of individual differences in behavioural inhibition and behavioural activation systems: a comparison of personality scales, *Personality and Individual Differences*, 34, 999–1013

Caseras, X., Fullana, M.A., Riba, J., Barbanoj, M.J., Aluja, A. and Torrubia, R. (2006), Influence of individual differences in the behavioral inhibition system and stimulus content (fear vs. blood/disgust) on affective startle reflex modulation, *Biological Psychology*, 72, 251–256

Caseras, X., Torrubia, R. and Farré, J.M. (2001), Is the behavioural inhibition system the core vulnerability for cluster C personality disorders?, *Personality and Individual Differences*, 31, 349–359

Castellà, J. and Pérez, J. (2004), Sensitivity to punishment and sensitivity to reward and traffic violations, *Accident Analysis and Prevention*, 36, 947–952

Cloninger, C.R. (1987), A systematic method for clinical description and classification of personality variants, *Archives of General Psychiatry*, 44, 573–588

Colder, C.R. and O'Connor, R.M. (2004), Gray's reinforcement sensitivity model and child psychopathology: laboratory and questionnaire assessment of the BAS and BIS, *Journal of Abnormal Child Psychology*, 32, 435–451

Cools, R., Clark, L., Owen, A.M. and Robbins, T. (2002), Defining the neural mechanisms of probabilistic reversal learning using event-related functional magnetic resonance imaging, *Journal of Neuroscience*, 22, 4563–4567

Corr, P.J. (2001), Testing problems in J.A. Gray's personality theory: a commentary on Matthews and Gilliland (1999), *Personality and Individual Differences*, 30, 333–352

(2004), Reinforcement sensitivity theory and personality, *Neuroscience and Biobehavioral Reviews*, 28, 317–332

Corr, P.J., Wilson, G.D., Fotiadou, M., Kumari, V., Gray, N.S., Checkley, S. and Gray, J.A. (1995), Personality and affective modulation of the startle reflex, *Personality and Individual Differences*, 19, 543–553

Davidson, R.J. (1998), Affective style and affective disorders: perspectives from affective neuroscience, *Cognition and Emotion*, 12, 307–320

Dawe, S., Gullo, M.J. and Loxton, N.J. (2004), Reward drive and rash impulsiveness as dimensions of impulsivity: implications for substance misuse, *Addictive Behaviors*, 29, 1389–1405

De Pascalis, V., Arwari, B., Matteucci, M. and Mazzocco, A. (2005), Effects of emotional visual stimuli on an auditory information processing: a test of J.A. Gray's reinforcement sensitivity theory, *Personality and Individual Differences*, 38, 163–176

Depue, R.A. and Collins, P.F. (1999), Neurobiology of the structure of personality: dopamine, facilitation of incentive motivation, and extraversion, *Behavioral and Brain Sciences*, 22, 491–569

Díaz, A. and Pickering, A.D. (1993), The relationship between Gray's and Eysenk's personality spaces, *Personality and Individual Differences*, 15, 297–305

Eysenck, H.J. (1967), *The Biological Basis of Personality* (Springfield, IL: Charles C. Thomas)

Eysenck, H.J., Barrett, P.T., Wilson, G.D. and Jackson, C.J. (1992), Primary trait measurement of the P-E-N system, *European Journal of Psychological Assessment*, 8, 109–117

Eysenck, H.J. and Eysenck, S.B.G. (1964), *The Manual of the Eysenck Personality Inventory* (London: University of London Press)
(1975), *Manual of the Eysenck Personality Questionnaire (Junior and Adult)*, (London: Hodder and Stoughton)

Eysenck, S.B.G., Pearson, P.R., Easting, G. and Allsop, J.F. (1985), Age norms for impulsiveness, venturesomeness and empathy in adults, *Personality and Individual Differences*, 6, 613–619

Franken, I.H.A. (2002), Behavioural approach system (BAS) sensitivity predicts alcohol craving, *Personality and Individual Differences*, 32, 349–355

Franken, I.H.A. and Muris, P. (2006), Gray's impulsivity dimension: a distinction between reward sensitivity versus rash impulsiveness, *Personality and Individual Differences*, 40, 1337–1347

Fullana, M.A., Caseras, X., Riba, J., Barbanoj, M. and Torrubia, R. (2006), Influence of individual differences in behavioral inhibition system on the magnitude and time course of the fear-potentiated startle, *International Journal of Psychophysiology*, 60, 323–329

Fullana, M.A., Mataix-Cols, D., Caseras, X., Alonso, P., Menchón, J.M., Vallejo, J. and Torrubia, R. (2004), High sensitivity to punishment and low impulsivity in obsessive-compulsive patients with hoarding symptoms, *Psychiatry Research*, 129, 21–27

Fullana, M.A., Mataix–Cols, D., Trujillo, J.L., Caseras, X., Serrano, F., Alonso, P., Menchón, J.M., Vallejo, J. and Torrubia, R. (2004), Personality characteristics in obsessive-compulsive disorder and individuals with sub-clinical obsessive-compulsive problems, *British Journal of Clinical Psychology*, 43, 387–398

Gable, S.L., Reis, H.T. and Elliot, A.J. (2000), Behavioral activation and inhibition in everyday life, *Journal of Personality and Social Psychology*, 78, 1135–1149

Gomez, A. and Gomez, R. (2002), Personality traits of the behavioural approach and inhibition systems: associations with processing of emotional stimuli, *Personality and Individual Differences*, 32, 1299–1316

(2005), Convergent, discriminant and concurrent validities of measures of the behavioural approach and behavioural inhibition systems: confirmatory factor analytic approach, *Personality and Individual Differences*, 38, 87–102

Gray, J.A. (1970), The psychophysiological basis of introversion–extraversion, *Behavior Research and Therapy*, 8, 249–266

(1981), A critique of Eysenck's theory of personality. In H.J. Eysenck (ed.), *A Model of Personality* (New York: Springer), pp. 246–276

(1982), *The Neuropsychology of Anxiety* (New York: Oxford University Press)

(1987a), *The Psychology of Fear and Stress* (2nd edn, New York: Cambridge University Press)

(1987b), Discussion arising from: Cloninger C.R. A unified theory of personality and its role in the development of anxiety states, *Psychiatric Developments*, 4, 337–394

(1988), The neuropsychological basis of anxiety in C.G. Last and M. Hersen (eds.), *Handbook of Anxiety Disorders* (Oxford: Pergamon Press), pp. 10–37

Gray, J.A. and McNaughton, N.J. (2000), *The Neuropsychology of Anxiety* (2nd edn, Oxford: Oxford Medical Publications)

Gray, J.A., Owen, S., Davis, N. and Tsaltas, E. (1983), Psychological and physiological relations between anxiety and impulsivity, in M. Zuckerman (ed.), *The Biological Bases of Sensation Seeking, Impulsivity and Anxiety* (Hillsdale, NJ: Erlbaum), pp. 189–217

Gupta, S. and Shukla, A.P. (1989), Verbal operant conditioning as a function of extraversion and reinforcement, *British Journal of Psychology*, 80, 39–44

Harmon-Jones, E. and Allen, J.J.B. (1997), Behavioral activation sensitivity and resting frontal EEG asymmetry: covariation of putative indicators related to risk for mood disorders, *Journal of Abnormal Psychology*, 106, 159–163

Hawk, L.W. Jr and Kowmas, A.D. (2003), Affective modulation and prepulse inhibition of startle among undergraduates high and low in behavioural inhibition and approach, *Psychophysiology*, 40, 131–138

Heponiemi, T., Keltikangas-Järvinen, L., Kettunen, J., Puttonen, S. and Ravaja, N. (2004), BIS-BAS sensitivity and cardiac autonomic stress profiles, *Psychophysiology*, 41, 37–45

Heponiemi, T., Keltikangas-Järvinen, L., Puttonen, S. and Ravaja, N. (2003), BIS/BAS sensitivity and self-rated affects during experimentally induced stress, *Personality and Individual Differences*, 34, 943–957

Heubeck, B.G., Wilkinson, R.B. and Cologon, J. (1998), A second look at Carver and White's (1994) BIS/BAS scales, *Personality and Individual Differences*, 25, 785–800

Jackson, C.J. and Smillie, L.D. (2004), Appetitive motivation predicts the majority of personality and an ability measure: a comparison of BAS measures and a re-evaluation of the importance of RST, *Personality and Individual Differences*, 36, 1627–1636

Johnson, S.L., Turner, R.J. and Iwata, N. (2003), BIS/BAS levels and psychiatric disorder: an epidemiological study, *Journal of Psychophysiology and Behavioral Assessment*, 25, 25–36

Jorm, A.F., Christensen, H., Henderson, A.S., Jacomb, P.A., Korten, A.E. and Rodgers, B. (1999), Using the BIS/BAS scales to measure behavioural inhibition and behavioural activation: factor structure, validity and norms in a large community sample, *Personality and Individual Differences*, 26, 49–58

Kambouropoulos, N. and Staiger, P.K. (2001), The influence of sensitivity to reward on reactivity to alcohol-related cues, *Addicton*, 96, 1175–1185

(2004), Personality and responses to appetitive and aversive stimuli: the joint influence of behavioural approach and inhibition systems, *Personality and Individual Differences*, 37, 1153–1165

Kasch, K.L., Rottenberg, J., Arnow, B.A. and Gotlib, I.H. (2002), Behavioral activation and inhibition systems and the severity and course of depression, *Journal of Abnormal Psychology*, 111, 589–597

Knyazev, G.G., Slobodskaya, H.R. and Wilson, G.D. (2004), Comparison of the construct validity of the Gray-Wilson personality questionnaire and the BIS/BAS scales, *Personality and Individual Differences*, 37, 1565–1582

Lang, P.J. (1995), The emotion probe: studies of motivation and attention, *American Psychologist*, 50, 372–85

Leone, L., Perugini, M., Bagozzi, R.P., Pierro, A. and Mannetti, L. (2001), Construct validity and generalizability of the Carver-White behavioural inhibition system/behavioural activation system scales, *European Journal of Personality*, 15, 373–390

MacAndrew, C. and Steele, T. (1991), Gray's behavioural inhibition system: a psychometric examination, *Personality and Individual Differences*, 12, 157–171

Mathews, A., Yiend, J. and Lawrence, A.D. (2004), Individual differences in the modulation of fear-related brain activation by attentional control, *Journal of Cognitive Neuroscience*, 16, 1683–1694

McNaughton, N. and Corr, P.J. (2004), A two-dimensional neuropsychology of defense: fear/anxiety and defensive distance, *Neuroscience and Behavioral Reviews*, 28, 285–305

Meyer, B., Johnson, S.L. and Carver, C.S. (1999), Exploring behavioral activation and behavioral inhibition sensitivities among college students at risk for bipolar spectrum symptomatology, *Journal of Psychopathology and Behavioral Assessment*, 21, 275–292

Miller, E., Joseph, S. and Tudway, J. (2004), Assessing the component structure of four self–report measures of impulsivity, *Personality and Individual Differences*, 37, 349–358

Newman, J.P. (1987), Reaction to punishment in extraverts and psychopaths: implications for the impulsive behavior of disinhibited individuals, *Journal of Research in Personality*, 21, 464–480

Nichols, S. and Newman, J.P. (1986), Effects of punishment on response latency in extraverts, *Journal of Personality and Social Psychology*, 50, 624–630

O'Connor, R.M. and Colder, C.R. (2005), Predicting alcohol patterns in first-year college students through motivational system and reasons for drinking, *Psychology of Addictive Behaviors*, 19, 10–20

O'Connor, R.M., Colder, C.R. and Hawk, L.W. Jr (2004), Confirmatory factor analysis of the sensitivity to punishment and sensitivity to reward questionnaire, *Personality and Individual Differences*, 37, 985–1002

Patterson, C.M., Kosson, D.S. and Newman, J.P. (1987), Reaction to punishment, reflectivity, and passive avoidance learning in extraverts, *Journal of Personality and Social Psychology*, 52, 565–575

Patterson, C.M. and Newman, J.P. (1993), Reflectivity and learning from aversive events: toward a psychological mechanism for syndromes of disinhibition, *Psychological Review*, 100, 716–736

Pickering, A.D. (1997), The conceptual nervous system and personality: from Pavlov to neural networks, *European Psychologist*, 2, 139–163

Pickering, A.D., Corr, P.J. and Gray, J.A. (1999), Interactions and reinforcement sensitivity theory: a theoretical analysis of Rusting and Larsen (1997), *Personality and Individual Differences*, 26, 357–365

Pickering, A.D., Corr, P.J., Powell, J.H., Kumari, V., Thornton, J.C. and Gray, J.A. (1997), Individual differences in reactions to reinforcing stimuli are neither black nor white: to what extent are they Gray? in A.H. Nyborg (ed.), *The Scientific Study of Human Nature: Tribute to Hans J. Eysenck at Eighty* (Oxford: Pergamon), pp. 36–67

Pickering, A.D., Diaz, A. and Gray, J.A. (1995), Personality and reinforcement: an exploration using a maze-learning task, *Personality and Individual Differences*, 18, 541–558

Pinto-Meza, A., Caseras, X., Soler, J., Puigdemont, D., Pérez, V. and Torrubia, R. (2006), Behavioural inhibition and behavioural activation systems in current and recovered major depression patients, *Personality and Individual Differences*, 40, 215–226

Poy, R., Eixarch, M.C. and Ávila, A. (2004), On the relationship between attention and personality: covert visual orienting of attention in anxiety and impulsivity, *Personality and Individual Differences*, 36, 1471–1481

Quilty, L.C. and Oakman, J.M. (2004), The assessment of behavioural activation: the relationship between impulsivity and behavioural activation, *Personality and Individual Differences*, 37, 429–442

Reuter, M., Stark, R., Hennig, J., Walter, B., Kirsch, P., Schienle, A. and Vaitl, D. (2004), Personality and emotion: test of Gray's personality theory by means of an fMRI study, *Behavioral Neuroscience*, 118, 462–469

Ross, S.R., Millis, S.R., Bonebright, T.L. and Bailley, S.E. (2002), Confirmatory factor analysis of the behavioural inhibition and activation scales, *Personality and Individual Differences*, 33, 861–865

Slobodskaya, H.R., Knyazev, G., Safronova, V. and Wilson, G.D. (2003), Development of a short form of the Gray-Wilson personality questionnaire: its use in measuring personality and adjustment among Russian adolescents, *Personality and Individual Differences*, 35, 1049–1059

Smillie, L.D. and Jackson, C.J. (2005), The appetitive motivation scale and other BAS measures in the prediction of approach and active avoidance, *Personality and Individual Differences*, 38, 981–999

(2006), Functional impulsivity and reinforcement sensitivity theory, *Journal of Personality*, 74, 1–37

Spielberger, C.D., Gorsuch, R.L. and Lushene, R. (1970), *Manual for the State Trait Anxiety Inventory* (Palo Alto: Consulting Psychologist Press)

Stuettgen, M.C., Hennig, J., Reuter, M. and Netter, P. (2005), Novelty seeking but not BAS is associated with high dopamine as indicated by a neurotransmitter challenge test using mazindol as a challenge substance, *Personality and Individual Differences*, 38, 1597–1608

Sutton, S.K. and Davidson, R.J. (1997), Prefrontal brain asymmetry: a biological substrate of the behavioral approach and inhibition systems, *Psychological Science*, 8, 204–210

Torrubia, R., Ávila, C., Moltó, J. and Caseras, X. (2001), The sensitivity to punishment and sensitivity reward questionnaire (SPSRQ) as a measure of Gray's anxiety and impulsivity dimensions, *Personality and Individual Differences*, 31, 837–862

Torrubia, R., Ávila, C., Moltó, J. and Grande, I. (1995), Testing for stress and happiness: the rôle of the behavioral inhibition system, in C.D. Spielberger, I.G. Sarason, J. Brebner, E. Greenglass, P. Langani and A.M. O'Roark (eds.), *Stress and Emotion: Anxiety, Anger, and Curiosity* (Washington, DC: Taylor and Francis), vol. 15, pp. 189–211

Torrubia, R., Garcia-Carrillo, M., Ávila, C., Caseras, X. and Grande, I. (in preparation), A junior questionnaire for the measurement of sensitivity to punishment and sensitivity to reward

Torrubia, R. and Tobeña, A. (1984), A scale for the assessment of susceptibility to punishment as a measure of anxiety: preliminary results, *Personality and Individual Differences*, 5, 371–375

Valdés, M. and De Flores, T. (1986), Behaviour pattern A: reward, fight or punishment?, *Personality and Individual Differences*, 7, 319–326

Wallace, J.F. and Newman, J.P. (1990), Differential effects of reward and punishment cues on response speed in anxious and impulsive individuals, *Personality and Individual Differences*, 11, 999–1009

Wilson, G.D., Barrett, P.T. and Gray, J.A. (1989), Human reactions to reward and punishment: a questionnaire examination of Gray's personality theory, *British Journal of Psychology*, 80, 509–515

Wilson, G.D., Barrett, P.T. and Iwawaki, S. (1995), Japanese reactions to reward and punishment: a cross-cultural personality study, *Personality and Individual Differences*, 19, 109–112

Wilson, G.D., Gray, J.A. and Barrett, P.T. (1990), A factor analysis of the Gray-Wilson personality questionnaire, *Personality and Individual Differences*, 11, 1037–1045

Zelenski, J.M. and Larsen, R.J. (1999), Susceptibility to affect: a comparison of three personality taxonomies, *Journal of Personality*, 67, 761–791

Zinbarg, R.E. and Mohlman, J. (1998), Individual differences in the acquisition of affectively valenced associations, *Journal of Personality and Social Psychology*, 74, 1024–1040

Zuckerman, M., Joireman, J., Kraft, M. and Kuhlman, D.M. (1999), Where do motivational and emotional traits fit within three factor models of personality, *Personality and Individual Differences*, 26, 487–504

7 Performance and conditioning studies

César Ávila and Rafael Torrubia

Since 1970, J.A. Gray (1970, 1981, 1982, 1987a) has outlined several aspects of a personality model called *Reinforcement Sensitivity Theory* (RST). This model has generated a great amount of experimental research and has been applied to adult psychopathology (Fowles 1988), psychophysiology (Fowles 1980), child psychopathology (Quay 1988; Nigg 2000, 2001) and disinhibited behaviour (Patterson and Newman 1993). The impression one has thirty years on, however, is that the model still has some grey areas since it was first proposed, which are lacking in detail and in some ways limit its development (see Pickering, Corr, Powell, Kumari, Thornton and Gray 1997).

Theoretical contributions and controversial issues of RST

Considering basically performance and conditioning studies, the aim of the present chapter is to raise some of the model's problematic aspects and to put forward some hypotheses and practical issues in regard to its application to humans. The chapter begins by setting out Gray's model in its initial formulation, and further theoretical contributions (Corr 2002, 2004; Patterson and Newman 1993; Wallace and Newman 1990). We shall then deal with aspects which we consider essential with regard to application to humans, and compile the results of the research work in this field from a new point of view. Owing to the fact that measures of BIS and BAS are based on Gray's classical model (Gray 1982), and that it remains to be seen how the new model by Gray and McNaughton (2000) fits in, the basis of this review will be the classical RST model.

Gray's reinforcement sensitivity theory

One of the most important aims of Gray's work since the late 1960s has been to describe the neuropsychological bases of emotion, focusing especially on the limbic system and its connections (Gray 1982; Gray and McNaughton 2000). His studies have mainly been based on animal research, though his theoretical contributions have been directly applied to the areas of emotion and human personality.

Gray's RST model postulates the existence of three independent systems which interact in the control of emotional behaviour. These three systems differ with regard to the stimuli which are capable of activating them, the emotions they generate and the learning they mediate (Gray 1987b). The first is the Behavioural Inhibition System (BIS), which is activated in the presence of stimuli which indicate the possibility of receiving aversive or non-reward stimuli, and new stimuli. According to Gray's description (1982), the BIS has two different functioning modes: a checking mode and a control mode. In the first case, the BIS acts as a comparing device, monitoring all environmental information in order to detect relevant information which might activate it (specifically, aversive stimuli and stimuli which do not match expectations). BIS activation implies a switch to the control mode, thus creating a state of anxiety which has its behavioural manifestations in the inhibition of the appetitive motor programme currently in operation, and an increase in activation and attention to the environment. BIS activation in control mode generates feelings of fear (in the case of aversive and new stimuli) or frustration (in the case of non-reward stimuli), which facilitates the learning of passive avoidance and extinction, respectively.

A second system is the Behavioural Approach or Activation System (BAS). This system is activated in the presence of conditioned reward stimuli or safety cues, promoting approach to the stimulus in order to achieve the positive features associated with it. This system generates feelings of hope (in the case of cues associated with reward) and relief (for safety cues), intervening in the learning of reward and active avoidance, respectively. The least developed system in Gray's model is undoubtedly the Fight-Flight System, which is activated in the presence of unconditioned aversive stimuli, promoting reactions of fight or flight. This system produces feelings of anger and terror.

According to Gray's model in its theoretical application to humans, the stable individual differences in the level of activation and response of each of these emotional systems give rise to three basic orthogonal personality dimensions. The neuropsychological description of these three emotional control systems led Gray to propose that basic human personality traits must depend on their differential functioning. Thus, individual differences in BIS, BAS and Fight-Flight System functioning are related to the basic personality dimensions of Anxiety, Impulsiveness and Psychoticism, respectively (Gray 1981, 1987b). Although the ascription of the third dimension to Eysenck's Psychoticism is for the time being merely tentative, the Anxiety and Impulsiveness dimensions have served to develop a great deal of research on performance correlates differences of the BIS and the BAS. However, some caution should be taken in using anxiety scales as measures of the BIS and, especially, impulsivity scales as measures of the BAS (see chapter 6).

Different predictions have been derived from RST relating, in humans, to personality and performance on different tasks. The three most accepted and that have been the main focus of research were that: (a) individuals with a hyperactive BIS (BIS+) would have better aversive learning (i.e., passive avoidance and extinction) than those with a hypoactive BIS (BIS−); (b) individuals with a hyperactive BAS (BAS+) would have better appetitive learning (i.e., reward and active avoidance learning) than those with a hypoactive BAS (BAS−); (c) activation of the BIS and the BAS was independent (Gray 1981). Although the predictions are clear, results from the various studies do not appear to have given them total verification.

In spite of the very wide acceptance that Gray's model has generally enjoyed, it should not be forgotten that its neuropsychological bases have been developed from animal research, and that its application in humans, therefore, requires a more complex framework. One of the schematic forms currently most used to apply Gray's model is shown in Figure 7.1. This Conceptual Nervous System was developed by Gray and Smith (1969) to explain situations of attraction-avoidance conflict. As revealed in the scheme, the BIS and BAS are sensitive to aversive and appetitive conditioned stimuli respectively, producing the responses described above. Moreover, the two systems mutually inhibit each other once activated. A third relevant component is the Non-specific Arousal System (NAS), which receives inputs from the BIS and the BAS when the systems are activated. As can be seen, its function is to intensify the vigour of the effects of the BIS and the BAS. In a situation of conflict, the relative activity of the three systems will determine the predominance of either appetitive (response) or aversive motivation (response inhibition).

Newman's model

Newman has conducted several studies in humans, taking as a starting point a disinhibition model which entailed a different reading from that made by Gray himself of the animal literature on septal injuries (Gorenstein and Newman 1980). His initial idea was that disinhibition observed in psychopathological disorders like psychopathy, addictions or child hyperactivity resembled that observed in animals with septal injuries. Such disinhibition should not be understood as an inhibitory deficit due to BIS hypoactivty but is defined as a difficulty in inhibiting

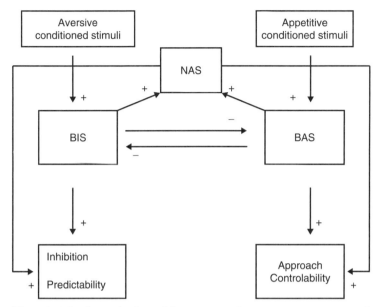

Figure 7.1 A schematic view of the conceptual nervous system proposed by Gray

appetitive dominant responses because of the presence of punishment, or other contingencies which indicate the need to suppress this response (a mechanism more related to BAS hyperactivity).

After several experiments, Patterson and Newman (1993) proposed a four-phase mechanism which accounted for the deficit in the prediction of aversive events characteristic of BAS+ in approach-avoidance conflicts:

(1) The learning of an appetitive dominant response pattern leading to reward: everybody is capable of learning this response pattern, although, following Gray's model, BAS+ would be quicker to learn this relationship, would be activated with greater intensity in the presence of the discriminatory stimulus which marks this response option, and would be more prepared to execute it. In short, an appetitive relationship is learnt in this first phase, which then generates in BAS+ a focalization of attentional resources on the relevant stimuli, as well as a greater tendency towards the emission of responses.

(2) An aversive or unexpected event occurs after the emission of the appetitive response: the unexpected introduction of an aversive stimulus after the appetitive stimulus produces two reactions in all subjects: an automatic increase in the processing of information and an increase in activation because a positive expectation has not been

fulfilled. Of the two, the key element is the NAS-mediated increase in activation, which is higher in BAS+, and leads to greater vigour in responses made later on (Gray 1987a). In the case of BAS+, these responses consist more of reward-seeking defence reactions than an increase in the processing of information characteristic of the BIS.

(3) Response modulation deficit: response modulation is related with reflection (an increase in information processing) produced after an unexpected or aversive event. Generally, response modulation consists of a passive coping reaction by which the causes of the aversive stimulus are analysed, and which aims to increase the likelihood of predicting in future when the aversive stimulus will reappear. BAS+, when compared with BAS−, will display response modulation deficits, owing to the fact that the greater tendency to seek reward will lead them to persevere in the appetitive response pattern. These deficits are due to the fact that the increase in the likelihood of responding impulsively after unexpected events reduces the possibility of reflecting and predicting the aversive event in future.

(4) The nature of learning deficits: the lower *retrospective* reflection which follows aversive stimuli described in the previous phase produces a deficit in the learning of the causal mechanism which produces them. The result is that BAS+ retain in the memory a smaller number of aversive associations in situations of responding to obtain reward. This smaller number of aversive associations will generate lower *prospective* prediction when the subject must process aversive event cues, thus producing a deficit in the prediction of these events, and facilitating impulsive, persevering and reward-seeking behaviour.

To sum up, the model explains the mechanism which produces inhibition deficits in appetitively motivated responses in BAS+. From our point of view, Newman's group have made some of the most relevant contributions to Gray's model, based on careful research work which has produced very important results. One of the key points in Newman's research is to highlight the importance of the interaction between the BIS and the BAS.

Joint subsystems hypothesis

Although the reader may find more detailed information elsewhere, these mutual inhibitory BIS-BAS processes described by Newman have been more explicitly highlighted by Corr (2004). He distinguished the separable subsystems hypothesis (SSH, which predicts the independent functioning of the BIS and BAS) from the joint subsystems hypothesis (JSH, which highlights the influence of the inhibitory pathways between both systems). His proposal is that the subsystems will work separately (a) when strong appetitive/aversive stimuli are used; (b) when individuals with extreme scores on dimensions are used; (c) in experimental situations that do not contain mixed appetitive and aversive stimuli; and (d) when there is not a need for rapid attentional and behavioural shifts between aversive and appetitive stimuli. In opposing situations to those described, however, results compatible with the JSH will be obtained. The practical consequence of this difference lies in the relevant systems for predicting behaviour: in the case of the SSH, these will be the BIS or BAS, whereas it will be the interaction between the BIS and BAS in the case of the JSH.

Controversial issues in Gray's model

In general, the approaches taken to Gray's model have been highly faithful to its initial formulation, without considering that it needs adapting prior to application to humans. Our basic idea is to take a functional approach to the model, based on previously established aims which we consider vital to such an application. Four different issues should be considered before summarizing performance studies.

(1) *Human research is different from animal research: the role of expectations and the motivational context.* One of the chief supports on which Gray's model is based is animal experimentation. In animal experimentation on punishment and reward, motivationally-significant stimuli are assumed to act with the same efficiency in different subjects, i.e., an electric discharge will be an aversive stimulus in all cases, and food will always be an appetitive stimulus for hungry animals. In other words, animal experiments only served to test the *separable* subsystems hypothesis. This sort of claim is often not directly applicable in human research, where there is enormous variability in the motivational significance of the stimuli used and the context where these stimuli are used (Gray 1987c). Therefore, Gray's model should allow for variability not only in responsiveness to motivational stimuli, but also in reactivity/sensitivity to appetitive and aversive motivational stimuli.

Importantly, the concepts of expectations and goals are relevant in performance studies in humans (Ball and Zuckerman 1992; Depue and Collins 1999; Zinbarg and Mohlman 1998). The level of control that research has in humans is often lower than in animals, a fact which generates the problem of which factor is the relevant one. In the animal procedures used by Gray, motivational context coincides in most cases with the type of stimulus used: discharges produce aversive motivational contexts, while food generates appetitive contexts in the case of hungry animals. In humans, this parallelism between type of stimulus and motivational context is not so clear. If, for instance, an individual stammers when speaking in public, the effect on performance will be different in the case of the first-timer (aversive context) than in that of the experienced university lecturer (appetitive context). In the application of Gray's model to humans, we therefore believe it necessary to take into account motivational context (in addition to the type of learning task) to be able to predict execution. Once review has been made of the different studies carried out, we shall define appetitive and aversive motivational contexts with greater precision.

(2) *Cognitive biases to detect motivational stimuli.* A different capacity for detecting motivational stimuli should emerge not only through a different cognitive system in the presence of motivationally-significant stimuli, but also in their absence. In the case of the anxiety dimension, for example, various authors have described an information processing system termed hypervigilant, which serves to detect aversive stimuli more rapidly and efficiently (Beck and Clark 1997, Eysenck 1992). Similarly, in the case of the BAS, we have suggested the existence of a system for processing which facilitates the detection of appetitive stimuli (see Ávila and Parcet 2002a; Avila, Barros, Ibañez, Parcet and Ortet 2003). A complete approach to Gray's model should, therefore, take a step backwards and explain how differences in the detection and evaluation of motivational stimuli are generated.

(3) *Are the appetitive and aversive systems symmetric?* Gray's work has focused more on the description of the BIS, and various aspects of the description of the BAS emerge through this parallelism with the BIS. In fact, in animal experimentation in which stimulation is controlled and its motivational relevance is assured, this parallelism may be more easily inferred. However, we believe that with regard to humans, this parallelism is not totally complete, as appetitive and aversive motivation differ in certain relevant aspects (Caccioppo and Bernston 1994). The BIS is activated in the face of threatening stimuli which provoke fear and behavioural inhibition. Whether contact with the aversive stimulus is avoided or not, in future it is highly likely that passive avoidance strategies will be employed to avoid coming into contact with these (and similar) aversive stimuli again. For this reason, the aversive effects of these stimuli have a low probability of being extinguished (Gray 1987a). The BAS, on the other hand, is involved in starting up and maintaining locomotor activity, incentive motivation processes, exploratory behaviour and, in general, goal-directed behaviour (Depue and Collins 1999). The BAS promotes the expression of motivational excitement and anticipatory eagerness, which leads to the start of goal-directed behaviour (Panksepp 1986), though it does not guarantee

goal-achievement. Also, this appetitive motivation can sometimes lead to the reception of aversive stimuli (Fowles 1987). As a result of the action of the BAS, therefore, appetitive motivational effects can increase, be maintained or decrease. In short, the activity of the BIS tends to perpetuate the motivational effects of the aversive stimuli, and so to diminish inter-individual variability in aversive stimuli. The activity of the BAS, on the other hand, shows a tendency to modulate, increasing, maintaining or suppressing the appetitive effects of the appetitive stimuli.

This asymmetry generates differences in the way motivation is manifested. In any motivational process, there would be two relevant aspects: one bottom-up, by which a stimulus triggers motivation and the action of the BIS and the BAS, and another, top-down, by which previous experience modulates the action in response to this stimulus. The previous analysis leads us to hypothesize that the action of the BIS would be guided more by bottom-up systems in which the stimulus leads to behavioural inhibition, whereas in the action of the BAS, the more relevant is the top-down process which modulates inhibitory control over the diverse options of approach to the stimulus (Nigg 2000, 2001). For instance, the sight of a nearby wasp could rapidly and intensely generate fear and behavioural inhibition. The sight of a plasma TV in a shop window, on the other hand, could generate the urge to buy it, though in this case inhibitory control (i.e., I haven't got any money) would act to suppress approach behaviour. Approach tendencies are continuously reviewed, whereas inhibitory tendencies are prone to be maintained.

This view explains the differences in the slope of the motivation gradient as we approach the appetitive or aversive stimulus. The appetitive gradient grows slowly as the reward stimulus is approached, whereas the aversive gradient grows rapidly (Fowles 1987). On most occasions, the BAS would be activated more often, and weakly, and only rarely with intensity. The BIS, however, would be less likely to be activated, but more intensely when it was. These differences in activation would lead to the appetitive experiences in each individual being numerous, less intense and more dependent on experience, whereas aversive experiences would be less frequent, more intense and more clearly remembered. The general effect produced would be that of greater inter-individual variability (heterogeneity) for appetitive motivations, which would be more easily modulated by experience, whereas stimuli capable of activating the BIS would be similar for most individuals.

(4) *Necessity of a functional approach.* A personality model like the one aimed at here cannot be based on the explanation of reactivity in the face of specific events, but should predict habitual behaviour, and do so in a functional way, that is, specifying three different issues: (1) how the

BIS and BAS work in the absence of motivationally significant stimuli; (2) taking into account each system's function, in other words, that the BIS is a system aimed to determine which stimuli *predict* the appearance of aversive stimuli, while the BAS is a system aimed to select the responses which lead to obtaining a reward; and (3) the differential adaptive mechanisms of individuals located at both ends of a dimension. Regarding the third point, we believe therefore, that both extremes of a dimension (for example, a hypo- or hyperactive BIS) suppose equally valid forms of adaptation to the environment which must be described. However, a shallow appraisal of Gray's model gives the idea, for example, that BIS+ have a better aversive learning and a greater capacity for detecting aversive stimuli than BIS−. What happens then in the case of the latter? How do they cope with aversive situations? From a functional point of view, the RST model should explain how these individuals adapt to such situations.

BIS, BAS and performance on laboratory tasks

In this section, we shall review the various studies which have been designed to test Gray's model, taking into consideration the importance of the aforementioned aspects. This is not a simple task, as there is tremendous variability in both experimental situations and the measures of BIS and BAS activity used. The aim of this review is to try and clarify for future researchers the conditions in which Gray's model should be tested, whilst attempting to identify what we believe to have been the ideal experimental situations for testing the model. The outline is divided into three sections. In the first, we briefly review the results derived from the Extraversion dimension (E), as we believe the literature here is both extensive and useful for Gray's model. In the second, we review studies on BIS and BAS functioning in checking mode, that is to say, differences in the detection of motivationally significant stimuli. Finally, and after developing a new framework to better understand data on these studies based on giving relevance to new variables such as motivational context and task learning type, we review data on individual differences in reactions to stimuli with motivational significance, in other words, control mode.

Extraversion and performance

The appraisal of cognitive functioning in the BIS and BAS may be made based on the huge amount of existing literature on E. According to Gray, however, E does not reflect BIS or BAS activity, but rather the differential activity of both systems. Regardless of the controversial role which arousal might play in E (see Matthews 1992), several studies exist that describe the differences between extroverts (E+) and introverts (E−) in different cognitive tasks. Matthew's excellent review (1992) concluded:

(1) At the level of perception and attention, E+ perform worse than E− in vigilance tasks with visual stimuli than in perceptive discrimination tasks with rapid cues.
(2) E+ perform better in short-term memory tasks than E−, but possibly worse (at least in associated pairs tasks) in long-term memory tasks.
(3) E+ perform difficult tasks better than E−. It has also been observed, however, that E− perfom better than E+ at difficult problem-solving tasks (Kumar and Kapila 1987).
(4) E+ have a slacker response criterion than E−.

Although these differences are general, they largely coincide with Brebner's model (Brebner and Cooper 1985), which, in short, indicates that E− base their approach to tasks on the processing of stimuli and caution in their responses, while E+ display a system of tackling tasks based on the organization of response and appraisal of its effects, with a lesser degree of stimulus processing. This approach coincides with the view that BIS− and BAS+ facilitate the emission of responses, while BIS+ and BAS− facilitate response inhibition (and the resulting greater processing of stimulus) (see Fowles 1987).

At the motivational level, different studies have been devised to test Gray's (1981) hypothesis that E+ show better execution when the correct response is rewarded, while E− do the same when the incorrect response is punished. This result has been found in various studies in different situations, such as persecution rotor learning (Seunath 1975), complex learnings (Boddy, Carver and Rowley 1986), operant verbal conditioning (Gupta and Nagpal 1978; Gupta and Shukla 1989), in-class arithmetic learning (McCord and Wakefield 1981) and Posner's orientation paradigm (Derryberry 1987).

Cognitive functioning: checking mode

As mentioned above, a functional approach to the BIS and BAS relies on the orientation of cognitive functioning to the detection of aversive and appetitive stimuli, respectively. Let us now consider the existing evidence for this, taken from the various studies made.

Cognitive functioning of the BIS   Although these studies did not directly aim to study the BIS, the set of studies on cognitive biases in anxiety conducted using the STAI scale may serve to illustrate how it works (Eysenck 1992; Mathews and MacLeod 1994; Williams, Watts, MacLeod and Mathews 1998). The paradigms most frequently used to test these biases are the emotional Stroop task and the spatial attention task (Mathews and MacLeod 1994). The emotional Stroop task required subjects to name the colours of two lists of words as quickly as possible, one list containing neutral words, and the other threatening words. While with non-anxious subjects naming performance was similar for the two lists, anxious subjects typically obtained slower naming times for the threat-related than for the neutral words. The spatial attention task presented vertically two different words for 500 ms: one had a neutral significance and the other had a threatening significance. The subjects' task was to read aloud the top word and ignore the bottom word. Distribution of attention is measured by a secondary task involving detection of a dot which could appear in the spatial location of either upper or lower word after display is terminated. Results showed that anxious subjects were faster in detecting probes when they occurred in the area where a threat word had just occurred. Non-anxious subjects showed the opposite pattern, suggesting that they orient away from the location at which threat had occurred. Both the emotional Stroop and the spatial attention tasks have shown that anxious subjects have a processing bias toward supraliminal threat-related stimuli (Mathews and MacLeod 1994).

Pre-attentive selection of threat-related material has also been studied in anxious and non-anxious subjects. A hypervigilant (Eysenck 1992) or an orienting (Beck and Clark 1997) mode that permits an early detection of threatening stimuli has been described in anxious subjects. Their attentional system seems to have evolved for the search and early detection of aversive, personally relevant and threat-related stimuli. Although this functioning will have evolutionary value, the problem in anxiety comes from an excessive detection and further elaboration of this negative material (Beck and Clark 1997). This functioning has been supported through different important findings. If compared with non-anxious subjects, anxious subjects: (a) process subliminal threat-related stimuli more deeply (Fox 1996; Mogg, Bradley, Williams and Mathews 1993); (b) give threat-related significance to homophones with an alternative neutral significance (Mathews, Richards and Eysenck 1989; Richards and French 1992); and (c) are more distracted by neutral and aversive peripheral stimuli (Broadbent, Broadbent and Jones 1986; Fox 1994; Mathews, May, Mogg and Eysenck 1990). However, a critical point is to explain why this processing bias does not normally facilitate a better recall of negative material (Mathews and MacLeod 1994).

Such a wealth of research would be compatible with the idea that the cognitive functioning of the BIS is geared to detecting aversive stimuli (see Ávila and Parcet 2002b; Derryberry and Reed 1994; Poy, Eixarch and Ávila 2004). These studies not only show that BIS+ have a greater capacity for detecting aversive stimuli, but also that BIS− are more able to disengage from aversive stimuli once they are detected.

Cognitive functioning of the BAS   Available data on the cognitive functioning of the BAS are much less abundant. However, the association between sensitivity to reward and dopamine facilitates the development of a more global cognitive theory of BAS functioning. Thus, the BAS may play a more general role in processing relevant stimuli, and in preparing and programming goal-directed behaviour (Robbins and Everitt 1995; Pickering and Gray 2001). Our research group has conducted different studies to illustrate this relationship, which may be summarized in two points:

(1) BAS+ over-focus on locations where rewarding stimuli are present (Ávila 1995; Derryberry and Reed 1994) and on reward-associated stimuli (Ávila and Parcet 2002a). This process is not automatic, but is consciously produced.
(2) Different paradigms such as negative priming (Ávila and Parcet 1997), latent inhibition (Pickering and Gray 2001), set-shifting (Ávila *et al.* 2003) and the endogenous orientation paradigm (Poy, Eixarch and Ávila 2004) suggest that BAS+, when compared with BAS−, disengage faster from semantic information automatically derived from previous stimuli once disappeared, and this allows them to reconfigure conditions of relevancy (i.e., goals) easily, in order to cope with new stimuli (see Dickman 1993, 2000, for a similar proposal). In other words, an overactive BAS seems to be more associated with responding on the basis of present than past stimuli. This view of the role of dopamine is consistent with that of Redgrave, Prescott and Gurney (1999). The presence of a relevant stimulus would cause a short latency, short duration burst of firing in dopaminergic neurones that serves to disengage attention from previous stimuli and to reallocate it in new, unexpected stimuli. This response of dopaminergic cells would suppress the influence of past stimuli when coping with new stimuli.

To sum up, the BAS is associated with an attentional mechanism directed at seeking and effectively detecting relevant environmental stimuli, by means of the conscious focalization of attention on zones or stimuli associated with reward, and rapid semantic disengagement from previously analysed stimuli. An example of the utility of this capacity for disengagement in detecting rewards can be seen in the recent study by Smillie and Jackson (2005).

Coping with motivational stimuli: control mode

Studying the functioning of the BIS and the BAS in control mode means basically the study of performance in the presence of motivationally significant stimuli. In accordance with Gray's model, the BIS participates in aversive instrumental learnings (passive avoidance and extinction processes), while the BAS does so in appetitive learnings (reward and active avoidance processes). From our point of view, rather than learning systems, the BIS and BAS are systems which facilitate or deteriorate motivational learning as a secondary consequence of response style. Thus, BIS activation leads to behavioural inhibition and a heightening of attention and arousal, which allow greater reflection and analysis of the source of the stimulus and how to deal with it. Similarly, BAS outputs allow appetitive associations to be learnt better, since approach behaviours increase the likelihood of obtaining reward and predicting it in the future.

The direct application of Gray's model appears to demonstrate that BIS+ or BAS+ learn better than BIS− or BAS−, and therefore that these individuals have simply an inferior learning, and a lower capacity for predicting and coping with stimuli of a motivational meaning. Such a conclusion would not only be hasty, but would obviously clash with the functional approach defended here. It is for this reason that the positive consequences of having a hypoactive BIS or BAS must be described to highlight that the corresponding personalities may also be environment-adaptive. Specifically, our proposal is that a hypoactive BIS facilitates appetitive learning, since the non-detection of aversive stimuli, or the evaluation of them as being less aversive, increases the likelihood of disengagement from them, thus fostering the emission of BAS-mediated responses which favour appetitive learnings (the BAS is not hypoactivated). In the same way, BAS− would have a greater capacity for aversive learning in situations of reward, as a strategy for coping with problems that the search for reward might bring about (see Patterson and Newman 1993). The obtainment of reward is based on the execution of motor programmes (i.e., dominant responses) which had led to reward in the past. The modification of these programmes or self-regulation requires reflection on the associated contingencies of any given moment, and their subsequent modification. According to Patterson and Newman's model, this capacity for learning adverse contingencies is greater in BAS−.

This proposal makes the learning-related predictions deriving from Gray's model much more complex. The activation of one system by the presence of a relevant stimulus implies the inhibition of the other, and it could therefore be said that both the BIS and BAS systems can mediate individual differences in appetitive and aversive learning processes (see Corr 2004). Thus, aversive learning may arise through different channels of activation: directly through the BIS (see Figure 7.1), or indirectly through the BAS (see in Figure 7.1 inhibitory influences on the BIS from the BAS). Does this mean that aversive and appetitive motivations are not independent? Not at all: they are mutually exclusive, that is, the activation of one system implies the inhibition of the other.

Some additional considerations are necessary before developing our proposal. First, laboratory tasks used to investigate performance differences associated with the BIS or the BAS, when not based in RT measures, should be sufficiently difficult to yield differences between personality groups. That is, learning tasks based on performance should include latent contingencies that would be differently learnt by participants. Secondly, tasks normally include performance of approach responses and inhibition of approach responses, so both the BIS and the BAS are activated during a task. The ideal task to test the RST model is that which activates predominantly one system. Diverse characteristics of the task will determine which one: intensity of aversive and appetitve stimuli, percentage of aversive and appetitve stimuli, instructions, etc. What then are the variables which determine the system more involved in each type of instrumental learning and the way to proceed? The most important is *motivational context*, but *the type of learning task* should also be considered.

Motivational context and differential BIS and BAS activation Motivational context will determine the entry channel of the stimulus, and then the system which takes control of behaviour, and is determined by the expectation of reward or punishment. Our proposal is that motivational context will not only depend on actual stimulus (as proposed by Gray 1981) but is dynamically related to expectations (formed from previous reinforcements during the task, previous experiences, difficulty of the task, instructions, etc.). Using three examples with experimental tasks used by our group, we aim to illustrate the importance of motivational context in Gray's model. Using the same paradigm or situation, a different motivational context leading to the BIS or the BAS will determine individual differences in performance. These studies will help us describe how appetitive and aversive motivational contexts are generated.

The 'go-no go' discrimination task   This task was used by Newman, Widom and Nathan (1985) to study the conditions in which passive avoidance deficits are produced in extraverts and psychopaths. This task required the trial and error learning of when to respond, and when to suppress responses. The task was based on ten two-figure numbers which were repeated eight times. There were two learning conditions, based on motivational context. In that of Reward and Punishment, participants had to learn to respond to half of these numbers to get a reward (earning money) and to suppress the response in reaction to the other half, to avoid immediate punishment (withdrawal of money). No feedback was given if the subject did not respond, which served the purpose of establishing an appetitive motivational context in which it is compulsory to respond in order to seek reward, despite the probability of obtaining reward being the same as that of receiving punishment. In the second condition of Punishment Only, participants received an initial amount of money, and could only lose money. In the case of half of the numbers, the way to avoid losing some of it was to respond, while for the other half, it was necessary to suppress the response in order not to lose money (either way, feedback was produced). The results showed that neurotic extraverts and psychopaths displayed passive avoidance deficits in the Reward and Punishment condition, but not in that of Punishment Only; in other words, passive avoidance deficits only appeared when it was necessary to suppress reward-seeking responses (Newman and Kosson 1986; Patterson, Kosson and Newman 1987).

Ávila, Moltó, Segarra and Torrubia (1995) studied this task in individuals classified by the EPQ. The results revealed that the relevant system in the Punishment Only condition was the BIS, as BIS+ tended to try not to receive punishment by suppressing the response, whereas BIS− showed a greater tendency to respond. In the Reward and Punishment condition, however, they confirmed that the relevant system was the BAS. In summary, aversive contexts produce learning differences depending on the BIS, and appetitive contexts on the BAS.

Extinction task   Extinction theoretically depends on the BIS (Gray 1982). Ávila (1994) designed the two-phase selection task to be completed without interruption. In the first phase, subjects were required to adopt a behaviour of selecting between two reinforcement programmes which, though different, were equivalent with regard to the size of reward obtained: one response was associated with a smaller and more contingent reward, while the other was associated with a larger and less contingent reward. In the second phase (no information given to subjects beforehand or interruption in the task), one of the two responses was chosen at random in a way that it was no longer rewarded, while the other continued to be rewarded in identical fashion to the first phase. The number of times the never-rewarded response was made in the second phase was used as the measure of resistance to extinction. The analyses showed that BIS+ had a lower resistance to extinction than BIS− (Ávila 1994). In our second study, Ávila and Parcet (2000) replicated the results of the first, but also demonstrated the importance of motivational context. Individuals were divided into two groups on the basis of selection in the first phase: those who had established a dominant response by choosing one response option more than the other, and those whose responses were equally split between the two options. The former had established a dominant response for reward which would strongly activate the BAS, and would therefore be harder to extinguish. The results confirmed that BAS+ had more difficulty extinguishing a dominant response for reward than BAS−. Once again, therefore, motivational context determined which system, the BIS or the BAS, took control of behaviour.

A real situation: multiple-choice exams. One last study that has enabled us to demonstrate the relevance of motivational context is a real situation in the shape of the multiple-choice exams often used to test knowledge in universities (Ávila and Torrubia 2004). The approach taken was that each question in a multiple-choice exam when correction for guessing is applied poses an approach-avoidance conflict which offers the possibility of reward (getting a mark) or punishment (losing a mark) after responding, while no marks are awarded for failing to respond. For this reason, we believe that the BIS and BAS might affect responses in such exams, once each student's knowledge in the subject matter has been allowed for. We hypothesized that BIS+ and BAS− would be more likely to make errors of omission (i.e., leaving items unanswered), whereas BIS− and BAS+ would be more likely to make mistakes by choosing the wrong answers. This being said, the relevance of the role of each system would depend on the motivational context. The results showed that BIS+, in exams with a lower average mark, made more omssion errors and fewer incorrect responses than BIS−. In contrast, in exams perceived as being easier (those with a higher percentage of responses), BAS− made more omission errors and fewer incorrect responses than BAS+. To sum up, in an identical situation (multiple-choice exams), the BIS was the relevant system in an aversive motivational context, while the BAS was when the motivational context was more appetitive.

Definition of motivational context. The different studies outlined above indicate that motivational context (appetitive or aversive) is more relevant than the type of learning (aversive or appetitive) to determining which system will mediate learning and/or performance. The overall principle would therefore be that, in appetitive motivational contexts, BAS activation would mediate performance differences in all types of appetitive and aversive instrumental learning, whereas in aversive contexts, the BIS would mediate the differences in all types of instrumental learning. With the experience gained in this field, and bearing in mind the absence of parallelism between appetitive and aversive motivation, it may be argued that it is much easier to generate an aversive context than an appetitive one in the laboratory. How are they defined? It must first be considered that motivational contexts vary in the degree of aversiveness or appeal, and can show intra-task and between-subject variability. When an attempt is made to test the RST, the aim is to create laboratory conditions which are more likely to produce homogeneous motivational contexts (always aversive or appetitive) that are perceived in the same way by a high percentage of individuals, and that activate a single system (i.e., the BIS or the BAS). Two aspects should be considered here: (1) it is easier for an appetitive context to become an aversive one (the aversive gradient is generated quickly and intensely), while the transformation from aversive into appetitive is more complicated (the appetitive gradient is generated more slowly) (see Fowles 1987; Caccioppo and Bernston 1994); and (2) contexts may be dynamic: as an experimental situation unfolds and one gradually learns the contingencies involved in the task, context tends to become gradually and slowly more appetitive and less aversive.

With these premises as a starting point, we may address the concept. In general, aversive motivational contexts are those in which the expectation that behaviour can be punished or extinguished is maintained throughout the task. This expectation comes from the reception of punishments. These situations rapidly generate a dominant inhibition response to cope with the situation (Gray 1987a). As the inhibitory learning progresses, punishments will be less frequent, and the inhibition will become more circumscribed to the presence of the conditioned stimulus (CS). However, if punishments are received throughout the task, expectations will be maintained. Thus, aversive contexts are those that initially establish a strong dominant inhibition response set based on frequent punishments, which is maintained across the task by the appearance of more sporadic punishments. These situations firmly maintain expectation of punishment throughout the task.

The difficulty of finding appropriate appetitive stimuli makes the task of generating appetitive contexts much more complicated. On the face of it, they would be defined as situations in which the expectation that behaviour may be rewarded is maintained. Some researchers have pointed to the need to create at the outset a dominant reward response, which must then be modified by the appearance later on of an aversive contingency (Ávila 2001; Patterson, Kosson and Newman 1987). In order to generate appetitive contexts, situations are required in which the percentage of reward is very high. Another way of doing this is to establish the need to respond in order to tackle the task in all of the participants (no feedback is given for no response) (see Newman, Widom and Nathan 1985). This dominant response set for reward would resemble the genetically determined inhibition response observed in aversive contexts. However, the combination of the facts that it is not genetically determined and that a single aversive stimulus can transform appetitive contexts into aversive ones, means that caution should be exercised in the application of aversive (or non-reward) stimuli, because frequent or intense stimuli may transform the context. Unlike aversive contexts, the appetitive variety require a very low percentage of aversive (or unrewarded) stimuli, which would depend on diverse factors such as the dominance of the appetitive response and the intensity of aversive and appetitive stimuli. An as yet little studied factor which could be relevant is the performance of pre-tasks with a high aversive component. The establishment of appetitive contexts is so vulnerable that the execution of pre-tasks in aversive motivational contexts could prevent them from being generated (see Ávila et al. 1995; Segarra, Moltó and Torrubia 2000).

In other situations with mid-range percentages of rewards and punishments, there is a risk that the context is interpreted differently, depending on personality. Motivationally mixed situations may be interpreted as aversive for BIS+ and appetitive for BIS−, thus making it difficult to interpret results, as the effect of a single system is not being studied.

In short, appetitive motivational context is not determined simply by the possibility of obtaining reward in the absence of punishment, but rather by the fact that these rewards are frequent, easy to obtain and/or of varying sizes, and are not mixed with or preceded by frequent aversive situations (or even neutral ones, lacking both reward and punishment). This is why such situations have very seldom been used in studies designed to study the BAS.

Task type: the point scoring reaction time task   The type of learning task is also a relevant aspect in determining whether BIS or BAS will be the relevant system (see Patterson and Newman 1993). By definition, the BIS is related to aversive instrumental learnings, that is, to passive avoidance and extinction behaviour. When studying individual differences in BIS functioning in humans with these tasks, the fundamental learning on most occasions is that which permits the detection and subsequent future prediction of aversive signals. The aim in activating the BIS is, therefore, to control the environment by predicting future aversive situations. Hyperactivation of the BIS will make it possible to know the stimuli which signal aversive stimuli, while its hypoactivation will produce a faster disengagement from averisve stimulus which will slow down or prevent aversive learning, but will allow the emission or learning of new appetitive response patterns, which on occasion serve to put an end to the aversive stimulus. For example, when first speaking in public (aversive context), BIS− would be less sensitive to aversive conditioned stimuli than BIS+ (e.g., diction errors, bored looks from the audience, etc.) and would be better able to develop their presentation.

BAS-mediated learning, however, involves the detection of signals which predict appetitive stimuli, as well as the acquisition of behavioural patterns of approach which lead to reward. The aim of such learning will therefore be to control the environment through the acquisition of response patterns suited to the obtainment of reward. The hyperactive BAS facilitates the starting-up of motor programmes which were dominant in the past for obtaining reward, while the lower appetitive motivation of BAS− will make it possible to carry out aversive learnings which lead to the modification of response patterns as circumstances dictate. For example, driving a little over the speed limit is an appetitively-motivated behaviour. If we are shocked after miscalculating the sharpness of a bend, BAS− are more likely to reduce speed and adopt greater caution (sensitivity to punishment), while BAS+ will carry on driving fast (see Castellà and Perez 2004 for a study on personality and the infringements of the road traffic rules).

Ávila (2001) conducted a series of experiments based on a Point Scoring Reaction Time Task (PSRT), with the aim of demonstrating two types of disinhibition, one associated with the BAS, and the other with the BIS. In the same motivational context, this study showed how stimulus-detection based learning depended on the BIS, and response-based learning on the BAS. The main task involved discriminating between two-digit odd and even numbers. The task had to be performed in three different conditions, depending on the meaning of a circle which changed colour from trial to trial: Pre-punishment, Punishment and Post-punishment. In the Pre-punishment and Post-punishment conditions, the colour of the circle was of no relevance. In the Punishment phase, the sporadic appearance of a particular colour was associated with the punishment of losing half of the points accumulated up to that moment, if a response was made in the discrimination task. It was therefore necessary to inhibit the response so as not lose them. Without fail before the start of the Post-punishment condition, individuals were informed that the colour of the circle associated with punishment no longer had this effect. In experiment 1, instructions were given on the colour of the circle and the need to suppress the response before starting the Punishment phase. The results, which confirmed previous results obtained in other studies by our group (Torrubia *et al.* 1995) proved the existence of two types of disinhibition. Individual differences in BAS activation correlated negatively with the general reaction time in the punishment phase; in other words, BAS− displayed an inhibition of dominant appetitive response for money in a situation in which there was a sporadic threat of punishment. Individual differences in BIS activation, however, were observed if they were only taken into account in the magnitude of inhibition response once the aversive stimulus was no longer associated with aversive consequences. The results showed that the greater the activity of the BIS, the greater was TR to aversive CS in the Post-punishment phase, independently of appetitive behaviour and caution.

Experiments 2 and 3 provided further information about the mechanisms underlying the BIS and BAS. These experiments revealed how the lower cautiousness of response in BAS+ leads to the poorer learning of aversive contingency; in other words, in accordance with our proposal, high appetitive motivation leads to quicker responding, despite the threat of punishment, which produces a deficit in aversive conditioning. With regard to the mechanism associated with the BIS, experiment 3 demonstrated that BIS+ show a greater aversive generalization, that is to say, the presence of a neutral stimulus physically similar to an aversive CS generates a response inhibition (BIS activation) which increases with BIS activity. This study proved, therefore, that the disinhibition mechanisms associated with BIS were related to the capacity for extinguishing the aversive motivational effects of the CS, while those of the BAS were associated with the capacity of the threat of punishment for suppressing appetitive responses.

This example illustrates how the type of task interacts with the BIS and the BAS within a mixed motivational context. After generating an appetitve motivational context, the introduction of an aversive CS transformed it to a situation of approach-avoidance conflict. Results showed that the BAS was relevant when we studied dominant response suppression by the introduction of punishment, whereas the BIS was relevant when we studied aversive learning (i.e., the strength of association between CS and the aversive stimulus). In sum, BIS+ should have better aversive learning than BIS− in mixed motivational contexts when tasks require to learn which CS predicts the appearence of the aversive stimulus. By contrast, BAS+ should persevere more than BAS− in dominant responses for reward in the same contexts.

Performance studies dependent on the BIS

BIS and aversive learning   Many studies show that BIS+ develop aversive learning more quickly than BIS−. Indeed, probably this is the aspect which has most data to support it. In several studies, comparison between BIS+ and BIS− has revealed that the former have greater resistance to the extinction of a previously reinforced behaviour (Ávila 1994; Ávila and Parcet 2000), maintain aversive learning for longer (Ávila 2001, Experiment 1; Kambouropoulos and Staiger 2004; Newman, Wallace Schmitt and Arnett 1997; and Pickering *et al.* 1997), display better procedural learning (Corr, Pickering and Gray 1997), have better verbal operant conditioning in aversive conditions (Gupta 1990), have greater aversive generalization (Ávila 2001, Experiment 3), show greater behavioural inhibition (Ávila *et al.* 1995; Avila and Torrubia 2004; Hagopian and Ollendick 1994), are better at learning a latent aversive contingency in Lykken's mental maze (Torrubia 1983) and display greater conditioned suppression or conditioned fear (Ávila 2001, Experiment 4). All these studies were based on aversive contexts and the task was based on the learning of which (conditioned) stimulus predicts the appearance of the aversive stimulus, or the extinction of an aversive association (i.e., prediction of when an aversive conditioned stimulus failed to predict the appearance of the aversive stimulus). All these data are consistent with the idea that a hyperactive BIS is related to a greater propensity for detecting and learning the aversive stimulus relationships proposed by Gray (1987a). It is worth noting that in few of these studies does the BAS play a relevant role in execution.

BIS and appetitive learning   A second idea deriving directly from our model is that in aversive motivational contexts, a hypoactive BIS predisposes to a greater likelihood of appetitive learning. The data mentioned earlier show how a hypoactive BIS predisposes to action more than inhibition in response to aversive stimuli (Ávila *et al.* 1995; Torrubia *et al.* 1995), while a hyperactive BIS does the opposite. In aversive contexts, once punishment has been perceived, this active coping response could be attributed to a faster disengagement from aversive stimuli which 'disinhibits' the BAS. Then, the individual acts by responding, and this increases the likelihood of learning new appetitive relationships.

In our laboratory, we devised a counterconditioning task to test this hypothesis (Ávila, Parcet, Ibañez and Ortet 1999). We designed a procedure in which it was necessary to choose between two possible responses: A responses always produced small rewards (7.5 points average), while B responses always led to punishments of a much bigger size (20 points average). B responses, however, were also associated with a subsequent larger reward (115 points average) for the first A response after two trials, meaning that the best strategy for gaining points was to choose response B (inflicting self-punishment) in order to receive a greater reward later on. The results showed that BIS− were quicker to learn this contingency than BIS+. Moreover, this learning was not related to BAS activity.

Several reviews made by Gray's research group (Pickering et al. 1997; Pickering 1997), have highlighted studies in which BIS− showed lower behavioural inhibition than BIS+, which enabled better appetitive learning or reactivity in response to appetitive stimuli. Specifically, Pickering (1997) cites three experiments in which BIS− show a greater response to reward than BIS+ using different tasks: (1) instrumental conditioning in which appetitive, aversive and neutral trials were equally mixed (Corr, Pickering and Gray 1995); (2) in a maze-learning task (Pickering, Diaz and Gray 1995); and (3) speed of classification of cards (cited in Pickering et al. 1997). In all these cases, and according to our definition, an appetitive motivational context could not be considered to exist, as dominant responses were not established and aversive and appetitive stimuli were equally frequent. Instead, these tasks represent aversive motivational contexts in which, from our standpoint, BIS− have a greater capacity for disengaging from aversive stimuli and learning appetitive relationships than BIS+. Significantly, BAS does not seem to play an important role in these studies.

Cognitive-behavioural mechanisms How do these differences come about? The concepts of inhibition and passive avoidance associated by Gray with BIS functioning are key to explaining them. In aversive contexts, humans rapidly establish a dominant inhibition response to avoid punishment in presence of aversive CS. When the CS is not specifically known, inhibition is more generalized than when the CS is known. Because of their higher fear response to aversive stimuli, BIS+ establish stronger and more generalized inhibition responses than BIS−, being more likely to resort to passive coping which makes it possible to analyse and predict in the future which conditioned stimuli predict the appearance of aversive stimuli (passive avoidance learning). As BIS− have a low fear response to aversive stimuli, they may disengage physically and cognitively from the aversive properties of the stimuli, and are more able to modify this dominant inhibition response when contingencies impel them to do so. The modification of inhibition response allows the BAS to act without the inhibitory influences of the BIS.

Ávila and Torrubia (2006) have recently demonstrated that BIS differences (but not BAS) arise in situations with a mixed motivational context. Following an adaptation of procedure by Siegel (1978), participants had to complete eight series of forty trials which were followed by monetary rewards and punishments. Each series had a different probability of punishment of between 20 and 90 per cent, and the task of the participants was to decide after each response if they should make another, or quit the series. There were no BAS determined differences but BIS+ made fewer responses than BIS− in all of the series between 40 and 80 per cent of punishment (no differences were found for the 20, 30 and 90 per cent series). In other words, the BIS, but not the BAS, mediates performance in situations of mixed reward and punishment. Two conclusions are relevant: (1) situations with 40 per cent of punishment are aversive contexts; and (2) perception of aversiveness is lower in BIS−.

One finding of this and other studies has been a differential reaction to aversive stimuli, which would reinforce the mechanism proposed here: BIS+ reflect for longer after punishment than BIS− (see also Derryberry 1987; Nichols and Newman 1986). As BIS+ has greater *retrospective* reflection which follows aversive stimuli, they retain in the memory a greater number of aversive associations, which allows a greater *prospective* prediction in the presence of aversive CS. BIS−, on the contrary, would show lower reflection after punishment, which facilitates disengaging from it.

There are also data on the generation of aversive expectations after negative experiences or the emotional interpretation of situations. In general, the various studies show that BIS+ have a greater tendency to develop negative expectations (Ávila and Torrubia 2004; Chan and Lovibond 1996; Eysenck and Derakshan 1997; Pearce-McCall and Newman 1986; Zinbarg and Mohlman 1998), have a greater tendency to experience or self-report negative mood (Carver and White 1994), report lesser happiness and positive affect and more negative affect (Fullana, Caseras and Torrubia 2003), and show more punishment expectancies and less reward expectancies (Caseras, Ávila and Torrubia 2003).

In sum, the appearance of aversive stimuli generates in BIS+ a greater tendency to behavioural inhibition, the retrospective processing of aversive cues, the storing in memory of aversive relationships, and the better prospective prediction of when they will re-appear, which will mean a greater likelihood of developing negative expectations. BIS− display the opposite pattern and, in consequence, are more prone to disengaging from aversive stimuli and to developing BAS-mediated positive expectations after the appearance of aversive stimuli.

Performance studies dependent on the BAS

BAS and appetitive learning   As we have already pointed out, it is difficult to establish appetitive motivational contexts. It is an even harder task, however, to study individual differences in appetitive learning in appetitive contexts, since the excess of non-reward (or aversive) situations would rapidly transform the context into an aversive one. One exception to this is the study by Gupta (1990), which shows that, in reward conditions, extravert neurotics condition better than introvert stables, without BIS-based differences or differences associated with BAS in the punishment condition. It should be highlighted that the methodology used in the verbal operant conditioning procedure measures execution once the dominant response has been established. Other relevant studies are those which address approach-approach conflicts, in which it has been observed that BAS+ prefer contingent rewards of a smaller size (Ávila and Parcet 2000) or transfer their attention more rapidly to bigger rewards (Smillie and Jackson 2005). A different attempt is the CARROT task devised by Powell, Al-Adawi, Morgan and Greenwood (1996). This seeks to compare the speed of classification of cards between a neutral situation and one in which the speed of response is rewarded. Although the participants improved their execution, the results were consistent with what was expected in one study (Kambouropoulos and Staiger 2004) but not in another (Pickering *et al.* 1997).

BAS and aversive learning   In relation to the BAS, this has been the most well studied aspect, and one which has generated the most consistent data. Various studies show that once a dominant response pattern has been established leading to reward, BAS− have a greater capacity for learning aversive relationships which in some way involve a modification of this dominant response (see Ávila 2001; Ávila and Parcet 2001; Newman, Widom and Nathan 1985; Patterson, Kosson and Newman 1987).

Mechanisms.   Patterson and Newman's model (1993), described earlier, explains in detail the conditions of this process: to establish a dominant response set, with a negative or unexpected consequence appearing after the response. Nichols and Newman (1986) demonstrated that BAS+ spend less time reflecting after punishment than BAS−, which would generate a tendency to persevere with the dominant response, while the hypoactive BAS increases the probability of reflecting on the signal which predicts the aversive or unexpected stimulus, and modifies the dominant response (Newman 1987). In some way, this mechanism could be interpreted as a contrary counter-conditioning to the previous one; in other words, a hypoactive BAS would facilitate the transformation of appetitive into aversive learning.

At the emotional level, several theoretical contributions seem to relate the BAS to positive emotions (Caccioppo, Gardner and Berntson 1999; Davidson 1998; Lang, Bradley and Cuthbert 1990). This has been seen in situations such as happiness about coping with a challenging task (Carver and White 1994). Recent studies, however, indicate that BAS+ show greater frustration and anger with negative feedback than BAS− (Carver 2004) and a greater tendency to anger (Harmon-Jones 2003). This second aspect could explain why BAS+ persevere in appetitive response patterns. BAS+ also show high reward expectancies.

General discussion

The approach of making a systematic review of performance studies on the premises of Gray's model is no easy task, owing to the variability of the previous research in (a) the experimental procedures selected to validate the model; (b) the measures used to study the different activity of the BIS and BAS; and (c) the results obtained. We guess that this variability might be a little discouraging for future researchers and suggest the need to elaborate an RST model with predictions which are both more specific and directly verifiable. In the light of all this, we have opted for a review of those studies which allows readers to: (a) weigh up specific proposals about how to set up studies to verify the model; and (b) form more specific hypotheses to test.

The key premises to be considered are as follows:

(1) The application of the RST model to humans must consider the importance of cognitive variables such as motivational context and expectations, and also establish that experimental procedures are methodologically dynamic.

(2) Appetitive and aversive motivation are not symmetrical: appetitive gradients are generated slowly and are low in intensity, whereas aversive gradients are generated more quickly and intensely. This makes appetitive contexts more difficult to generate than aversive ones.

(3) A functional approach is required to the personality dimensions proposed in the RST which explains how each pole of the personality dimensions adapts to the environment.

(4) The model will have to explain not only the nature of differences in reaction to motivational stimuli, but also which cognitive biases exist in the processing of information, which lead to a different probability of detecting motivational stimuli.

Adhering to these points, we have put together a proposal about how the BIS and BAS work. The two systems would be activated at different times, would have different functions and their functioning would be relatively independent (see Table 7.1). The BIS would be a system with

Table 7.1 *A summary of the model proposed in this chapter*

Motivational context	Personality	BIS activation	BAS activation	Predictability aversive associations	Learning approach responses	Extinction of aversive associations	Extinction of appetitive responses
Aversive	BIS+	High	Low	Good	Poor	Poor	Good
Aversive	BIS−	Low	Normal	Poor	Good	Good	Poor
Appetitive	BAS+	Low	High	Poor	Good	Good	Poor
Appetitive	BAS−	Normal	Low	Good	Poor	Poor	Good

the function of predicting the appearance of aversive stimuli, and reacting to them in conditions in which they are expected. The best conditions for studying how it works are aversive motivational contexts in which it is highly likely that aversive stimuli will be received (without creating a sensation of helplessness). In such circumstances, BIS+ would have more capacity for detecting threat, and would attempt to study, by means of analysis and behavioural inhibition, which specific stimuli predict the arrival of the aversive stimulus (i.e., better passive avoidance learning). BIS−, meanwhile, would disengage more rapidly from threat, would have less capacity for learning inhibitory associations, but would have better appetitive learning.

As we have pointed out, studying the BAS would be a more complicated task owing to the difficulty of establishing lasting appetitive contexts and the greater individual variability in rewards. The BAS-associated cognitive system is based on the ability to disengage from previously processed stimuli which have disappeared, so as to be able to focus on new appetitive stimuli. This system makes it easier to detect such stimuli quickly, and to establish dominant responses to achieve rewards or aims. At the performance level, the action of the BAS is determinant in appetitive contexts, or in other words, in situations in which a dominant response for reward is established, and aversive contingencies are infrequent. In these conditions, BAS+ would be more able to establish the dominant response, experience greater frustration at not achieving their aim, and have less capacity for modifying the response (i.e., perseverance). BAS−, on the other hand, would be slower to make appetitive associations but would be more able to detect later an aversive contingency, analyse the change of situation and modify their pre-established dominant response.

What would happen in mixed motivational contexts with appetitive and aversive components? There would be a greater likelihood that they would not be uniformly perceived by all individuals (although they are always more likely to be perceived as aversive) and the two mechanisms could co-exist. Thus, some participants would activate the BIS and others the BAS, meaning the task would be of little use for studying a single system. From our point of view, these situations arise in the numerous studies which support the JSH (see Corr 2004). Also these situations would in some way produce similar results to those obtained when E− and E+ are compared for motivation: E− (and BIS+) would activate the BIS and E+ (BAS+) would activate the BAS to perform the same task.

Conclusion

To sum up, studying the independent activity of the BIS and the BAS at the level of learning and performance requires conditions which have not always been properly formulated. The study of differential BIS activity preferably requires (1) aversive motivational contexts, in other words, situations in which a frequent threat of receiving aversive stimuli is maintained; and (2) aversive learnings in which the most relevant factor is to determine which conditioned stimulus more reliably predicts the appearance of the aversive stimulus or that of non-reward. As for studying differential BAS activity, this may only be carried out in appetitive situations, the most effective of which require (1) the setting up of powerful motivational contexts through the establishment of dominant responses for reward; (2) the introduction of latent aversive contingencies which make it necessary to modify appetitive behaviour; and (3) the study of differences in modification speed (i.e., modulation) versus perseverance in dominant response patterns.

Finally, and despite the fact our proposal is designed to fit in Gray's 1982 model, we do not believe it is difficult to make it compatible with recently appeared modifications (Gray and McNaughton 2000). Based on the premise that the aversive system (now associated with the Fight-Flight-Freeze System) and the appetitive system (i.e., BAS) are maintained, the present review should lead us to reflect on the need to establish a different brain structure to settle conflicts, or if, as we have suggested, the aversive and appetitive systems will suffice to explain motivated behaviour. We feel that the standpoint of greater FFS-BIS closeness which controls behaviour in aversive contexts in the presence of conditioned and unconditioned aversive stimuli (see Corr 2004), and a BAS system which controls behaviour while dominant reward responses are made, will be enough.

References

Ávila, C. (1994), Sensitivity to punishment and resistance to extinction: a test of Gray's behavioral inhibition system, *Personality and Individual Differences*, 17, 845–847

(1995), Facilitation and inhibition of visual orienting as a function of personality, *Personality and Individual Differences*, 18, 503–509

(2001), Distinguishing BIS–mediated and BAS-mediated disinhibition mechanisms: a comparison of disinhibition models of Gray and Patterson and Newman, *Journal of Personality and Social Psychology*, 80, 311–324

Ávila, C., Barrós, A., Ibáñez, M.I., Ortet, G. and Parcet, M.A. (2003), Set-shifting and sensitivity to reward: a dopamine mechanism for explaining disinhibitory disorders, *Cognition and Emotion*, 17, 951–959

Ávila, C., Moltó, J., Segarra, P. and Torrubia, R. (1995), Sensitivity to primary or secondary reinforcers: what is the mechanism underlying passive avoidance deficits in extraverts?, *Journal of Research in Personality*, 29, 373–394

Ávila, C. and Parcet, M.A. (1997), Impulsivity and anxiety differences in cognitive inhibition, *Personality and Individual Differences*, 23, 1055–1064

(2000), The rôle of Gray's impulsivity in anxiety-mediated differences in resistance to extinction, *European Journal of Personality*, 14, 185–198

(2001), Personality and inhibitory deficits in the stop-signal task: the mediating role of Gray's anxiety and impulsivity, *Personality and Individual Differences*, 29, 975–986

(2002a), Individual differences in reward sensitivity and attentional focus, *Personality and Individual Differences*, 33, 979–996

(2002b), The role of attentional anterior network on threat-related attentional biases in anxiety, *Personality and Individual Differences*, 32, 715–728

Ávila, C., Parcet, M.A., Ibañez, M.I. and Ortet, G. (1999), The role of the behavioral inhibition system in the ability to associate aversive stimuli with future rewards, *Personality and Individual Differences*, 27, 1209–1219

Ávila, C. and Torrubia, R. (2004), Personality, expectations and response to multiple choice question examinations in university students: of Gray's hypotheses, *European Journal of Personality*, 18, 45–59

(2006), Personality differences in suppression of behavior as a function of the probability of punishment, *Personality and Individual Differences*, 41, 249–260

Ball, S.A. and Zuckerman, M. (1992), Sensation seeking and selective attention: focused and divided attention on a dichotic listening task, *Journal of Personality and Social Psychology*, 63, 825–831

Beck, A.T. and Clark, D.A. (1997), An information processing model of anxiety: automatic and strategic processes, *Behavior Research and Therapy*, 35, 49–58

Boddy, J., Carver, A. and Rowley, K. (1986), Effect of positive and negative-reinforcement on performance as a function of introversion–extraversion: some tests of Gray's theory, *Personality and Individual Differences*, 7, 81–88

Brebner, J. and Cooper C. (1985), A proposed unified model of extraversion in J.T. Spence and C.E. Izard (eds.), *Motivation, Emotion and Personality* (Amsterdam: North-Holland), pp. 219–227

Broadbent, D.E., Broadbent, M.H. and Jones, J.L. (1986), Performance correlates of self-reported cognitive failure and of obsessionality, *British Journal of Clinical Psychology*, 25, 285–299

Caccioppo, J.T. and Bernston, G.G. (1994), Relationship between attitudes and evaluative space: a critical review, with emphasis on the separability of positive and negative substrates, *Psychological Bulletin*, 115, 401–423

Caccioppo, J.T., Gardner, W.L. and Bernston, G.G. (1999), The affect system has parallel and integrative processing components: form follows function, *Journal of Personality and Social Psychology*, 76, 839–855

Carver, C.S. (2004), Negative affects derived from the behavioral approach system, *Emotion*, 4, 3–22

Carver, C.S. and White, T.L. (1994), Behavioral inhibition, behavioral activation, and affective responses to impending reward and punishment: the BIS/BAS scales, *Journal of Personality and Social Psychology*, 67, 319–333

Caseras, X., Ávila, C. and Torrubia, R. (2003), The measurement of individual differences in behavioural inhibition and behavioural activation systems: a comparison of personality scales, *Personality and Individual Differences*, 34, 999–1013

Castellà, J. and Pérez, J. (2004), Sensitivity to punishment and sensitivity to reward and traffic violations, *Accident Analysis and Prevention*, 36, 947–952

Chan, C. and Lovibond, P.F. (1996), Expectancy bias in trait anxiety, *Journal of Abnormal Psychology*, 105, 637–647

Corr, P.J. (2001), Testing problems in J.A. Gray's personality theory: commentary on Matthews and Gilliland (1999), *Personality and Individual Differences*, 30, 333–352

(2002), J.A. Gray's reinforcement sensitivity theory: tests of the joint subsystems hypothesis of anxiety and impulsivity, *Personality and Individual Differences*, 33, 511–532

(2004), Reinforcement sensitivity theory and personality, *Neuroscience and Biobehavioural Reviews*, 28, 317–332

Corr, P.J., Pickering, A.D. and Gray, J.A. (1995), Personality and reinforcement in associative and instrumental learning, *Personality and Individual Differences*, 19, 47–71

(1997), Personality, punishment, and procedural learning: a test of J.A. Gray's anxiety theory, *Journal of Personality and Social Psychology*, 73, 337–344

Corr, P.J., Wilson, G.D., Fotiadou, M., Kumari, V., Gray, N.S., Checkley, S. and Gray, J.A. (1995), Personality and affective modulation of the startle reflex, *Personality and Individual Differences*, 19, 543–553

Davidson, R.J. (1998), Affective style and affective disorders: perspectives from affective neuroscience, *Cognition and Emotion*, 12, 307–330

Depue, R.A. and Collins, P.F. (1999), Neurobiology of the structure of personality: dopamine, facilitation of incentive motivation, and extraversion, *Behavioral and Brain Sciences*, 22, 491–569

Derryberry, D. (1987), Incentive and feedback effects on target detection: a chronometric analysis of Gray's model of temperament, *Personality and Individual Differences*, 8, 855–865

Derryberry, D. and Reed, M.A. (1994), Temperament and attention: orienting toward and away from positive and negative signals, *Journal of Personality and Social Psychology*, 66, 1128–1139

Dickman, S.J. (1993), Impulsivity and information processing in W.G. McCown, J.L. Johnson and M.B. Shure (eds.), *The Impulsive Client: Theory, Research, and Treatment* (Washington, DC: American Psychological Association), pp. 151–184

(2000), Impulsivity, arousal and attention, *Personality and Individual Differences*, 28, 563–581

Eysenck, M.W. (1992), *Anxiety: The Cognitive Perspective* (Hillsdale, NJ: Lawrence Erlbaum Associates)

Eysenck, M.W. and Derakshan, N. (1997), Cognitive biases for future negative events as a function of trait anxiety and social desirability, *Personality and Individual Differences*, 22, 597–606

Fowles, D.C. (1980), The three arousal model: implications of Gray's two-factor learning theory for heart rate, electrodermal activity, and psychopathy, *Psychophysiology*, 17, 87–104

(1987), Application of a behavioral theory of motivation to the concepts of anxiety and impulsivity, *Journal of Research in Personality*, 21, 417–435

(1988), Psychophysiology and psychopathology: a motivational approach, *Psychophysiology*, 25, 373–391

Fox, E. (1994), Attentional bias in anxiety: a defective inhibition hypothesis, *Cognition and Emotion*, 8, 165–195

(1996), Selective processing of threatening words in anxiety: the role of awareness, *Cognition and Emotion*, 10, 449–480

Fullana, M.A., Caseras, X. and Torrubia, R. (2003), Psychometric properties of the personal state questionnaire in a Catalan sample, *Personality and Individual Differences*, 34, 605–611

Gorenstein, E.E. and Newman, J.P. (1980), Disinhibitory psychopathology: a new perspective and a model of research, *Psychological Review*, 87, 301–315

Gray, J.A. (1970), The psychophysiological basis of introversion–extraversion, *Behavior Research and Therapy*, 8, 249–266

(1981), A critique of Eysenck's theory of personality in H.J. Eysenck (ed.), *A Model of Personality* (New York: Springer), pp. 246–276

(1982), *The Neuropsychology of Anxiety* (New York: Oxford University Press)

(1987a), *The Psychology of Fear and Stress* (2nd edn, New York: Cambridge University Press)

(1987b), The neuropsychology of personality and emotion in S.M. Stahl, S.D. Iversen and E.C. Goodman (eds.), *Cognitive Neurochemistry* (Oxford: Oxford University Press), pp. 171–190

(1987c), Perspectives on anxiety and impulsivity: a commentary, *Journal of Research in Personality*, 21, 493–509

(1991), Neural systems, emotion and personality in J. Madden IV (ed.), *Neurobiology of Learning, Emotion and Affect* (New York: Raven Press), pp. 273–306

(1994), Framework for a taxonomy of psychiatric disorder in S.H.M. Van Goozen, N.E. Van de Poll and J.A. Sergeant (eds.), *The Emotions: Essays on Emotion Theory* (Hillsdale, NJ: Lawrence Erlbaum Associates), pp. 29–59

Gray, J.A. and McNaughton, N.J. (2000), *The Neuropsychology of Anxiety* (Oxford: Oxford Medical Publications)

Gray, J.A. and Smith, P.T. (1969), An arousal-decision model for partial reinforcement and discrimination learning in R. Gilbert and N.S. Sutherland (eds.), *Animal Discrimination Learning* (New York: Academic Press), pp. 243–272

Gupta, B.S. and Nagpal, M. (1978), Impulsivity/sociability and reinforcement in verbal operant conditioning, *British Journal of Psychology*, 68, 203–206

Gupta, S. (1990), Personality and reinforcement in verbal operant conditioning: a test of Gray's theory, *Psychological Studies*, 35, 157–162

Gupta, S. and Shukla, A.P. (1989), Verbal operant conditioning as a function of extraversion and reinforcement, *British Journal of Psychology*, 80, 39–44

Hagopian, L.P. and Ollendick, T.H. (1994), Behavioral inhibition and test anxiety: an empirical investigation of Gray's theory, *Personality and Individual Differences*, 16, 597–604

Harmon-Jones, E. (2003), Anger and the behavioural approach system, *Personality and Individual Differences*, 35, 995–1005

Kambouropoulos, N. and Staiger, P.K. (2004), Personality and responses to appetitive and aversive stimuli: the joint influence of behavioural approach and inhibition systems, *Personality and Individual Differences*, 37, 1153–1165

Kumar, D. and Kapila, A. (1987), Problem solving as a function of extraversion and masculinity, *Personality and Individual Differences*, 8, 129–132

Lang, P.J., Bradley, M.M. and Cuthbert, B.N. (1990), Emotion, attention, and the startle reflex, *Psychological Review*, 97, 377–395

Mathews, A. and MacLeod, C. (1994), Cognitive approaches to emotion and emotional disorders, *Annual Review Psychology*, 45, 25–50

Mathews, A., May, J., Mogg, K. and Eysenck, M.W. (1990), Attentional bias in anxiety: selective search or defective filtering?, *Journal of Abnormal Psychology*, 99, 166–173

Mathews, A. and Milroy, R. (1994), Processing of emotional meaning in anxiety, *Cognition and Emotion*, 8, 535–553

Mathews, A., Richards, A. and Eysenck, M. (1989), Interpretation of homophones related to threat in anxiety states, *Journal of Abnormal Psychology*, 98, 31–34

Matthews, G. (1992), Extraversion in A. Smith and D. Jones (eds.), *Handbook of Human Performance*, vol. 3, *State and Trait* (London: Academic Press), pp. 95–126

McCord, R.R. and Wakefield, J.A. (1981), Arithmetic achievement as a function of introversion–extraversion and teacher-presented reward and punishment, *Personality and Individual Differences*, 2, 145–152

Mogg, K., Bradley, B.P., Williams, R. and Mathews, A. (1993), Subliminal processing of emotional information in anxiety and depression, *Journal of Abnormal Psychology*, 102, 304–311

Newman, J.P. (1987), Reaction to punishment in extraverts and psychopaths: implications for the impulsive behavior of disinhibited individuals, *Journal of Research in Personality*, 21, 464–480

Newman, J.P. and Kosson, D.S. (1986), Passive avoidance learning in psychopathic and nonpsychopathic offenders, *Journal of Abnormal Psychology*, 95, 252–256

Newman, J.P., Wallace, J.F., Schmitt, W.A. and Arnett, P.A. (1997), Behavioral inhibition system functioning in anxious, impulsive and psychopathic individuals, *Personality and Individual Differences*, 23, 583–592

Newman, J.P., Widom, C.S. and Nathan, S. (1985), Passive avoidance in syndromes of disinhibition: psychopathy and extraversion, *Journal of Personality and Social Psychology*, 48, 1316–1327

Nichols, S. and Newman, J.P. (1986), Effects of punishment on response latency in extraverts, *Journal of Personality and Social Psychology*, 50, 624–630

Nigg, J.T. (2000), On inhibition/disinhibition in developmental psychopathology: views from cognitive and personality psychology and a working inhibition taxonomy, *Psychological Bulletin*, 126, 220–246

—— (2001), Is ADHD a disinhibitory behavior?, *Psychological Bulletin*, 127, 571–598

Panksepp, J. (1986), The anatomy of emotions in E. Plutchik and H. Kellerman (eds.), *Emotion: Theory Research and Experience,* vol. 3, *Biological Foundations* (New York: Academic Press), pp. 91–124

Patterson, C.M., Kosson, D.S. and Newman, J.P. (1987), Reaction to punishment, reflectivity, and passive avoidance learning in extraverts, *Journal of Personality and Social Psychology*, 52, 565–575

Patterson, C.M. and Newman, J.P. (1993), Reflectivity and learning from aversive events: toward a psychological mechanism for syndromes of disinhibition, *Psychological Review*, 100, 716–736

Pearce-McCall, D.P. and Newman, J.P. (1986), Expectation of success following non-contingent punishment in introverts and extraverts, *Journal of Personality and Social Psychology*, 50, 439–466

Pickering, A.D. (1997), The conceptual nervous system and personality: from Pavlov to neural networks, *European Psychologist*, 2, 139–163

Pickering, A.D., Corr, P.J., Powell, J.H., Kumari, V., Thornton, J.C. and Gray, J.A. (1997), Individual differences in reactions to reinforcing stimuli are neither black nor white: to what extent are they Gray? in H. Nyborg (ed.), *The Scientific Study of Personality: Tribute to Hans J. Eysenck at Eighty* (London: Elsevier Sciences), pp. 36–67

Pickering, A.D., Diaz, A. and Gray, J.A. (1995), Personality and reinforcement: an exploration using a maze-learning task, *Personality and Individual Differences*, 18, 541–558

Pickering, A.D. and Gray, J.A. (2001), Dopamine, appetitive reinforcement, and the neuropsychology of human learning: an individual differences approach in A. Eliasz and A. Angleitner (eds.), *Advances in Individual Differences Research* (Lengerich, Germany: PABST Science Publishers), pp. 113–149

Powell, J.H., Al-Adawi, S., Morgan, J. and Greenwood, R.J. (1996), Motivational deficits after brain injury: effects of bromocriptine in 11 patients, *Journal of Neurology, Neurosurgery, and Psychiatry*, 60, 416–421

Poy, R., Eixarch, M.C. and Ávila, A. (2004), On the relationship between attention and personality: covert visual orienting of attention in anxiety and impulsivity, *Personality and Individual Differences*, 36, 1471–1481

Quay, H.C. (1988), The behavioral reward and inhibition system in childhood behavior disorder in L.M. Bloomingdale (ed.), *Attention Deficit Disorder*, vol. 3, *New Research in Attention, Treatment, and Psychopharmacology* (Elmsford: Pergamon Press), pp 176–186

Redgrave, P., Prescott, T.J. and Gurney, K. (1999), Is short-latency dopamine response too short to signal reward error?, *Trends in Neuroscience*, 22, 146–151

Richards, A. and French, C.C. (1992), An anxiety-related bias in semantic activation when processing threat/neutral homographs, *Quarterly Journal of Experimental Psychology*, 45A, 503–525

Robbins, T.W. and Everitt, B.J. (1995), Arousal systems and attention in M.S. Gazzaniga, *The Cognitive Neurosciences* (Cambridge: MIT Press), pp. 703–720

Segarra, P., Moltó, J. and Torrubia, R. (2000), Passive avoidance learning in extraverted females, *Personality and Individual Differences*, 29, 239–254

Seunath, O.M. (1975), Personality, reinforcement and learning, *Perceptual and Motor Skills*, 41, 459–463

Siegel, R.A. (1978), Probability of punishment and suppression of behavior in psychopathic and non-psychopathic offenders, *Journal of Abnormal Psychology*, 87, 330–350

Smillie, L.D. and Jackson, C. (2005), The appetitive motivation scale and other BAS measures in the prediction of approach and active avoidance, *Personality and Individual Differences*, 38, 981–994

Torrubia, R. (1983), *Personalitat, ansietat i susceptibilitat al càstig: aplicació de la teoria de Gray als humans* (unpublished Master thesis, Universitat Autònoma de Barcelona)

Torrubia, R., Ávila C., Moltó, J. and Grande I. (1995), Testing for stress and happiness: the rôle of the behavioral inhibition system in C.D. Spielberger, I.G. Sarason, J. Brebner, E. Greenglass, P. Langani and A.M. O'Roark (eds.), *Stress and Emotion: Anxiety, Anger, and Curiosity* (Washington, DC: Taylor and Francis), vol. 15, pp. 189–211

Wallace, J.F. and Newman, J.P. (1990), Differential effects of reward and punishment cues on response speed in anxious and impulsive individuals, *Personality and Individual Differences*, 11, 999–1009

Williams, J.M.G., Watts, F.N., MacLeod, C. and Mathews, A. (1998), *Cognitive Psychology and Emotional Disorders* (Chichester: Wiley)

Zinbarg, R.E. and Mohlman, J. (1998), Individual differences in the acquisition of affectively valenced associations, *Journal of Personality and Social Psychology*, 74, 1024–1040

8 Psychophysiological studies

Vilfredo De Pascalis

The original version of *Reinforcement Sensitivity Theory* (RST) (Gray 1982, 1987, 1991) postulated three basic emotion systems, identifiable in animal species, with relevance to human personality. The three systems are defined as the Behavioural Approach System (BAS), the Behavioural Inhibition System (BIS) and the Fight-Flight System (FFS). The BAS is thought to be a simple positive feedback system which is sensitive to stimuli associated with reward (approach) or with omission (active avoidance) or termination of punishment (escape). This system is responsible for positive affect. The BAS is involved in moving the organism up to the temporo-spatial gradient through the location of the reward.

The BIS is defined by inhibition of ongoing behavior programs in response to conditioned stimuli associated with punishment or non-reward (frustration), or novel stimuli. The BIS mechanism is thought as a comparator that continuously scans the environment by checking predicted against actual events (checking mode) and being able to stop programmed motor activity by other systems (control mode) if they do not match. The system also modulates the control of exploratory behavior by diverting attention toward the threatening or novel stimulus. When a mismatch between predicted and actual events occurs, the motor program is stopped and outputs of the BIS seek to take more information by enhancing attention and arousal. This system is responsible for negative affect.

Gray's third system, the FFS, was originally described to be sensitive to unconditioned aversive stimuli (i.e., innate painful stimuli) and unconditioned defense aggression or escape behavior reflecting emotions of rage and panic. The FFS has been originally described as having a very tentative relationship with the other systems of the model and there has been little research on the human information processing activities of the FFS, although it has been postulated that this system controls the behavioral expressions of anger and panic.

More recently, there has been a number of important revisions to the operation of the BAS, BIS and FFS (see Gray and McNaughton 2000). McNaughton and Corr (2004) have outlined that in the revised theory, the BAS is sensitive to both conditioned and 'unconditioned' appetitive stimuli and there is a sharp distinction between the incentive motivation component and the consummatory component of responses to unconditioned appetitive stimuli. The BAS is involved in moving the animal to reduce the spatio-temporal distance between the current and the likely location of the primary reinforcement. The BAS would not mediate the final act of consummatory behavior.

The original formulation of the FFS has been reconceptualized by incorporating, in this system, the function of 'freezing' and renamed as the Fight-Flight-Freeze System (FFFS). The freezing behavior occurs in the cases in which the actual threat stimuli are unavoidable while the avoidable ones induce anger-related fight or fear-related flight. The FFFS mediates all aversive stimulations, that is, the innate, unconditioned and 'conditioned' stimuli.

The revised RST theory suggests that the BIS becomes activated only when both the FFFS and the BAS are currently activated, that is, when the animal is faced with an approach/avoidance conflict. The state of anxiety is elicited by the approach/avoidance conflict.

Gray's original theory of personality (Gray 1970, 1976, 1982, 1987) suggests the rotation of Eysenck's major dimensions of personality to fit with the functions of the conceptualized underlying neurobiological structures (Figure 8.1).

The activity of the BIS supports punishment sensitivity and it is proposed as the causal basis of Anxiety (Anx). In terms of Eysenck's personality space Anx is rotated by $30°$ from N and it is ranging from high Anx (Anx $+ \rightarrow E - N + P -$) to low Anx (Anx $- \rightarrow E + N - P +$, or psychopathy). The FFS is the second emotional system which is thought to be aligned with Eysenck's psychoticism (P). Finally, the BAS supports reward sensitivity and it is proposed as the causal basis of Impulsivity (Imp). In terms of Eysenck's personality space Imp is rotated by $30°$ from E and ranges from the pole of high Imp (Imp $+ \rightarrow E + N + P +$, or neurotic extraversion) to the pole of low Imp (Imp $- \rightarrow E - N - P -$, or stable introversion). Considering that Anx lies at $30°$ angle from N, Imp at $30°$ from E, and Imp inclines into P, Pickering, Corr and Gray (1999) derived Anx and Imp from PEN measures with the following algebraic expression: Anx $= (2 \times N - E - P)$ and Imp $= (2 \times E + N + P)$. However, Anx and Imp factors derived from Eysenck Personality Questionnaire (EPQ; Eysenck and Eysenck 1975) dimensions do not seem to moderate behavior in the same way as more direct measures of Anx and Imp.

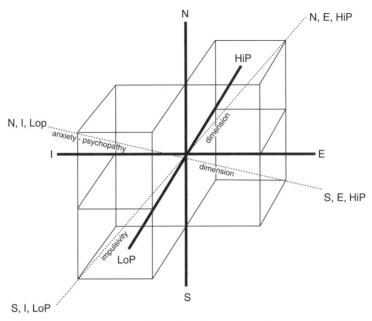

Figure 8.1 Gray's three-dimensional conceptualization of anxiety-psychopathy and impulsivity dimensions (dashed lines) within co-ordinates of Eysenck's three dimensions (thick solid lines) of extraversion (E)-intraversion (I), neuroticism (N)-stability (S) and psychoticism (P)

Corr (2001), in his commentary to Matthews and Gilliland's (1999) comparative review of H. J. Eysenck's arousal and J. A. Gray's rein-forcement theories, pointed out the weakness of the psychometric measurements of BIS/BAS functions.

Electroencephalogram and RST

The EEG is one of the most direct sources of data for monitoring CNS activity during a variety of conditions including perceptual and cognitive activities. Fourier spectrum analysis is one of the most used methods to decompose EEG waveform into various range activities such as delta (<4Hz), theta (4–8Hz), alpha (8–13Hz), beta (13–35Hz), gamma (>35Hz). Usually, the alpha activity has been assumed to reflect states of low arousal and relaxation, while the beta and gamma ranges are associated, respectively, with wakefulness and focused arousal. In spite of their poor spatial resolution and the impossibility of making definitive conclusions about the sources that give rise to the scalp voltage distributions, EEG measures have the virtues of fast time resolution and are good tools for studying physiological processes underlying arousal, attention, memory, vigilance, emotion and cognitive activities (Davidson, Jackson and Larson 2000). The desynchronization of the EEG, i.e., the transition from high amplitude, low frequency alpha activity to low amplitude, high frequency beta activity, was associated to the increased activity of the ascending reticular activating system (ARAS) when attention is directed to incoming stimulation or to response generation (Moruzzi and Magoun 1949; Magoun 1963).

In his theory of personality, Eysenck proposed that individual differences in E and N are determined by differences in cortical arousal as indexed by EEG measures (Eysenck 1967; Eysenck and Eysenck 1976, 1985). However, because of methodological difficulties in obtaining response-specific measures in the ongoing EEG, the enthusiasm for exploring individual differences in EEG-arousal and psychological processes has received a decreasing interest in personality research (Gale 1983; Stelmack 1990; Stelmack and Geen 1992; De Pascalis 2004).

Very few studies have been addressed to evaluate the relation between individual differences in BIS/BAS sensitivity and ongoing EEG activity. This is probably because Gray's theory does not devote a critical role to the arousal system in differentiating individual differences in Anx and Imp.

In an EEG study by Stenberg (1992), two dimensions of Anx and Imp were derived from factor analysis of the N, E and other known personality sub-scales. Signs of lower EEG arousal were found in Imp + subjects as compared to Imp − ones. Anx + subjects showed greater frontal theta activity in the right hemisphere suggesting higher emotionality. Anx + subjects also displayed higher beta rhythm activation to negative emotions, but, in contrast with expectations, Imp + subjects did not display a higher beta activation to positive emotions. These findings have the limit that the sample size (N = 40) used for factor analysis was insufficient to derive Anx and Imp dimensions. However, both these findings are consistent with the assumption that it is easier to induce a negative emotional feeling than a positive emotional one (Pickering et al. 1997; Zinbarg and Mohlman 1998; Corr 2004) and that Anx predicts the potentiation of the startle response to unpleasant stimuli (Cook, Hawk, Davis and Stevenson 1991; Corr et al. 1995c; 1997).

Barratt (1971), using EEG recordings during a classical differential eyelid conditioning, observed that Imp − / Anx + subjects emitted the highest number of conditioned responses, while Imp + / Anx − were less aroused with the onset of the stimulus and emitted fewer conditioned responses. The hypothesis that Imp + subjects would condition better to a positively valenced stimulus than to negatively valenced one was confirmed. These findings can be clearly explained with RST assuming that BIS and BAS have two functions, one facilitatory and the other antagonistic (Corr 2001). In the case of BIS behaviors, Anx + facilitates and Imp + antagonizes. In the case of BAS behaviors, Imp + facilitates and Anx − antagonizes.

In the EEG literature two hypotheses have been formulated on the relationship between cortical trait activity and BIS/BAS functioning (e.g., Gray and McNaughton 2000). The first hypothesis is suggested by Sutton and Davidson (1997) and proposes that greater relative left frontal cortical activity is related to higher BAS scores and greater relative right frontal cortical activity is related to higher BIS scores (Sutton and Davidson 1997; Wacker, Heldmann and Stemmler 2003). A number of findings are in support to the suggested link between the activation of left anterior cortical activity and BAS (Coan and Allen 2003; Harmon-Jones and Allen 1997; Sutton and Davidson 1997) and may indicate a positive association between the BAS and approach motivation. The second hypothesis was formulated by Harmon-Jones and Allen (1997) and implied that greater bilateral frontal cortical activity may be related to higher BAS activity. The bilateral BAS model proposed that not only the approach system but also the withdrawal system is related to the behavioral activation system (BAS), i.e., that BAS is related to behavioral activation irrespective of motivational direction (see Harmon-Jones and Allen 1997; Coan and Allen 2003; Wacker, Heldmann and Stemmler 2003). According to Harmon-Jones and colleagues it is vital to differentiate between affective valence and motivational direction (see Harmon-Jones et al. 2002; Harmon-Jones and Allen 1998; Harmon-Jones and Sigelman 2001; Harmon-Jones et al. 2003). In particular, Harmon-Jones and Allen (1998), measuring resting EEG and trait anger with the Aggression Questionnaire by Buss and Perry (1992), debated that anger can be regarded as an emotion with an approach tendency (which is thought to be related to left anterior cortical activity), and a negative valence (which is thought to be related to right anterior cortical activity). Thus, anger discloses a contradiction between the constructs of motivational direction (approach/withdrawal) and affective valence (positive/negative) with respect to their relation to anterior cortical asymmetry. The study displayed a positive relation between left middle frontal cortical activity and trait anger and did not find significant relations for positive and negative emotions. Recently, Hewig et al. (2006) reported that subjects with greater bilateral frontal cortical activity had higher BAS scores as obtained with BIS/BAS scales of Carver and White (1994). These findings were seen by the authors as more in line with an approach/withdrawal model of anterior asymmetry (e.g., Harmon-Jones and Allen 1998) rather than a BIS/BAS model of anterior asymmetry, which corroborates the position that the BAS may be related to approach and withdrawal motivation.

BIS/BAS and event-related potentials

Event-related potentials (ERPs), or evoked potentials, are event-related voltage responses derived from the ongoing EEG activity that are time-locked to sensory, cognitive and motor events. The ERPs are usually obtained by summation of the time-locked electrocortical responses that occur on each repetition of the event (averaging procedure). This procedure assumes that the ERP and the background EEG summate independently. As averaging proceeds, the ERP waveform summates, while the random background EEG (noise) decreases in amplitude (for details, see Fabiani, Gratton and Coles 2000). It is assumed that ERPs represent the synchronized activity of multiple units whose fields are so aligned that they summate to produce recordable potentials. A distinction is made between 'exogenous' and 'endogenous' components (for details, see Hillyard and Picton 1987; Rugg and Coles 1995).

One of the useful applications of ERP measurements is to demarcate the timing and classification of specific stages of information processing. The majority of ERP studies investigated responses that occur in the first 100–1000 ms following a stimulus. Early components (N100, P200) relate to sensory properties of stimuli and to selective attention. Later ERP waves are used to index endogenous cognitive activity.

The positive going ERP component at about 300 ms (P300) is related to processes that involve classifying or updating memory representations of stimuli. The amplitude of the P300 increases as the demand for cognitive resources increases and as the significance of the event and its relevance to the subject increases. The latency of the P300 measure appears to be independent of the time needed for response-related processes. It is a good index of the time needed to categorize and evaluate the stimulus and appears to be independent of the time needed for response-related processes.

Another important ERP activity is the mismatch negativity (MMN) (Näätänen 1982). The MMN is typically elicited by low probability deviant tones delivered in a series of repetitive stimulations. One of the main characteristics of the MMN is that it can be obtained independently of the direction of attention of the subject, thus allowing the evaluation of auditory discrimination and passive attention in subjects unable or unwilling to co-operate. The MMN generally peaks 100–200 ms from the beginning of the change, it is the electrocortical expression of the neural traces through which the auditory cortex fixates the repetitive aspects of a sound (Näätänen et al. 1993). The MMN can be obtained through a classic oddball paradigm by presenting deviant, non-frequent, tones in a sequence of repetitive (standard) tones.

A number of ERP studies have addressed the relationship between P300 peak amplitude and Eysenck's E dimension, while few of them have attempted differential tests of Eysenck's and Gray's theories (for a review, see Matthews and Gilliland 1999). Eysenck (1994), on the basis of the fact that activities associated with P300, as orienting responses, habituation, and stimulus classification are tightly related to the concept of cortical activation, has suggested the measure of the P300 component to test the hypothesized link between arousal and E. Here it will be mainly concerned with experimental studies which afford direct tests of the original and reviewed forms of Gray's theory.

As an example, I will review ERP findings in some studies in which published data are usable for testing both the original and joint subsystems view of Gray's theory. Reward and punishment were exerted by winning and losing different amounts of money in a gambling task. Auditory ERPs were recorded to signals indicating winnings or losses and to the visual presentation of the amount to win or lose. The authors expected larger ERP peaks after signals of reward than after signals of punishment in extroverts; the opposite trend for reward and punishment signals was expected for the amplitudes of these ERP components in introverts. Subjects were selected by means of their extreme E and N scores in the Eysenck Personality Inventory (EPI). Four groups were formed with high or low scores in the E and N dimensions (E + N +, E − N −, E + N −, E − N +). Peak amplitudes of P2 and N2 components of the ERPs demonstrated the predicted interaction between extraversion and winning/losing, but no significant main or interaction effects including N were observed for these ERP components. The authors concluded that these findings were in line with Gray's theory predictions. This conclusion needs to be reconsidered since individual differences in the BAS and BIS sensitivities should be explained in terms of the contribution of both E and N (and not only E). More specifically, it is known that if we assume that the two-factor model involves combinations of N and E with unequal weightings (e.g., 30° rotation), the BAS and BIS sensitivities (or respectively the personality dimensions of Imp and Anx) can be expressed with the following formula: BAS $\propto$ (2E + N);

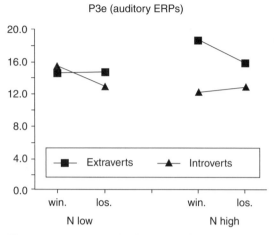

Figure 8.2 P3e amplitudes (μV) of extraverts and introverts scoring high (N high) and low (N low) in neuroticism to the tones indicating winning (win.) and losing (los.)

BIS ∝ (2N − E) (where ∝ represents proportionality, see Pickering, Corr and Gray 1999 for more details). The first equation implies that the auditory tones indicating winning of money should elicit higher ERP peak amplitudes in E + N + (Imp +) subjects as compared to E − N − (Imp −) ones. The second equation implies that tones signaling losing of money should elicit higher ERP peak amplitudes in E −N + (Anx +) subjects as compared to E +N − (Anx −). Since in the report P2, N2 and slow ERP measures are not available for the above-mentioned four experimental groups, it is not possible to derive more specific post-hoc conclusions in terms of Gray's theory. However, in this study, a significant E×N× Winning/Losing interaction was found for a P3e amplitude of the ERPs (known to reflect subjective stimulus meaning). A graph of this inter-action, available in the original paper, is here reported in Figure 8.2.

According to the original RST theory, P3e peak amplitude to tones indicating losing should be more pronounced in E −N + (Anx +) sub-jects compared to E +N − (Anx −) ones. On the other side, tones indicating winning should produce higher P3e peaks in E + N + (Imp +) subjects as compared to E − N − (Imp −) subjects. In Figure 8.2, there does not appear to be a difference between E −N + and E +N − groups on P3e peak amplitude. When P3e data to losing signals are averaged across E +N − and E −N + groups, there does not appear to be a difference of the

Corr (2002)

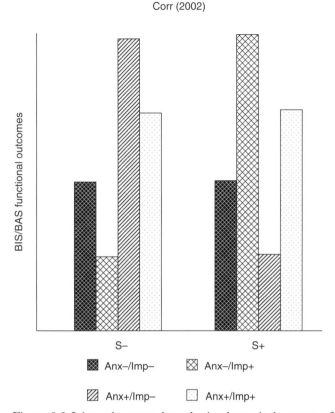

Figure 8.3 Joint subsystems hypothesis: theoretical pattern of effects between low (−) and high (+) Anxiety (Anx) and Impulsivity (Imp) groups in strength of reaction to aversive (S −) and appetitive (S +) conditioned stimuli

means between groups, while winning signals produced the highest P3e peaks in $E + N +$ subjects.

Finally, using P3e data reported in Figure 8.2, it may be interesting to test the validity of the 'joint subsystems hypothesis' of RST (see Figure 8.3; Corr 2002, p. 516). The trend of the means for P3e amplitude across high and low Anx and Imp groups for winning tones stimuli is: $(E + N − / E + N +) > (E − \quad N + / E + N +) \geq (E + N − / E − N −) \geq (E − N + / E − N −)$; for losing tones is: $(E + N − / E + N +) > (E − N + / E + N +) > (E + N − / E − N +) \simeq (E − N + / E − N −)$; where $E + N − \rightarrow Anx −$, $E − N + \rightarrow Anx +$, $E − N − \rightarrow Imp − E + N + \rightarrow Imp +$.

The P3e data pattern, obtained for appetitive stimuli, appears in line with prediction derived from the joint subsystems view, while data pattern obtained for aversive stimuli does not fit with predicted pattern derived from this view. The P3e finding that Imp + is related to individual differences in appetitive reactions is relatively rare in the literature (Matthews and Gilliland 1999; Pickering *et al.* 1997; Zinbarg and Mohlman 1998). Therein quite often Anx− is found to moderate appetitive reactions, whether assessed by induced positive emotion (Larsen and Katelaar 1991), instrumental approach behavior (Corr, Pickering and Gray 1995a), modulation of the eye-blink startle response (e.g., Corr *et al.* 1995c), or appetitive classical conditioning (e.g., Paisey and Mangan 1988). On the other hand, a common report in the literature is that Anx + is related to individual differences in aversive reactions, a finding which is consistent with the view that it is easier to experience or to induce a negative emotion than a positive one.

Later, Bartussek *et al.* (1996) examined the effect of positive, negative and neutral adjectives on the ERP of extraverts and introverts in two conditions, one where attention was drawn to the emotional words by asking subjects to rate the strength of valence and a different condition where subjects were distracted from the valence of the word by simply asking them to decide how long the word was. The authors reported a number of interactions between extraversion, the type of task and electrode site. They observed that none of these findings were consistent with RST, though at the frontal cortex they did find that, in line with RST, introverts had larger P300 amplitude to negative and neutral stimuli compared to positive stimuli. In a second experiment of this study the relationship between ERPs and affective modulation of a startle probe was evaluated. Again, ERP findings suggest that RST could not be supported since extraverts tend to have higher frontal cortex P2 peak amplitudes for both positive and negative stimuli.

De Pascalis and collaborators have also carried out a number of studies examining ERP in relation to RST. In particular, De Pascalis, Fiore and Sparita (1996) elicited ERPs by feedback words 'losing' or 'winning' of amount of money in sixty-two subjects. The GWPQ, EPQ and I₇ Questionnaires were used to measure BAS and BIS functions. In line with the original and revised RST theory are the following ERP findings: (1) high Approach (APPR) subjects exhibited larger P600 peaks to signals of winning and low APPR subjects larger P600 peaks to signals indicating losing of money; (2) high N subjects produced higher N800 peak amplitudes to stimuli indicating losing as compared to stimuli indicating winning of money, while low N subjects did not display differences between feedback stimuli; (3) high Passive Avoidance

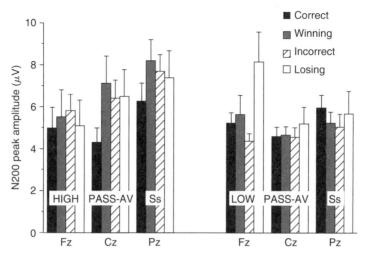

Figure 8.4 N200 amplitude of high passive avoidance and low passive avoidance subjects to words indicating winning, losing, correct and incorrect responses at three mid line electrode sites

(PASS-AV) subjects had greater N200 peaks to winning signals. The finding in (2) was seen to be in line with both Eysenck's and Gray's theory predictions. Eysenck's theory (Eysenck 1981; Eysenck and Eysenck 1985) suggests that high N values (but not low E), are associated with frequent experiences of negative emotions. This finding is also in line with Gray's original theory since it is known that the contribution of N to the BIS functioning is stronger than that of E, which, on the other hand, contributes to enhancing the activity of the BAS.

The finding in (3) (see Figure 8.4) was interpreted by the authors as indicating a higher sensitivity to signals of reward in high PASS-AV subjects, a result which appears in contrast with the Gray's original theory that predicts passive avoidance behavior as a reflection of the activity of the BIS. However, if we reconsider N2 peak amplitude data in the light of the recent revision of Gray's theory (Gray and McNaughton 2000; McNaughton and Corr 2004), it can be easily derived that over Cz, and even more over Pz scalp sites, high PASS-AV subjects had higher N2 peaks than low PASS-AV subjects during both 'winning' and 'losing' conditions. Given that the N200 component of the ERP has been associated with brain events of transient arousal and orienting responses (Näätänen 1992; Näätänen and Gaillard 1983), this finding may be seen as indicating that high PASS-AV subjects were simply more arousable than low PASS-AV subjects.

More recently, De Pascalis *et al.* (2004) recorded ERPs to emotionally positive and negative adjectives during four emotional-word recognition tasks using a visual oddball paradigm. Confirmatory factor analysis of popular personality and temperamental scales yielded a clear two-factor orthogonal solution of Anx (first factor) and Imp (second factor) which were congruently defined. Consistent with RST, frontal and temporal P300 peak amplitude was larger in Anx + individuals for unpleasant words; but Imp + showed smaller P300 peaks for negative targets over parietal and occipital cortical areas and longer P300 latencies across frontal, temporal, parietal and occipital recording sites. The expected amplification of the response to positive emotion in the Imp + group was not confirmed. These findings, however, appear in agreement with the joint subsystems hypothesis that predicts, for the Imp + subjects, as compared to Imp− ones, at all levels of anxiety a lower level of sensitivity to signals of punishment.

A new line of evidence is suggesting that Anx and Imp, or other BIS/BAS scales from alternative biological models of personality, modulate the MMN of the ERPs. This relationship is suggested by several findings demonstrating that a dysfunction of the BIS is responsible for the reduced frontal MMN found in patients with schizophrenia (Alain, Woods and Knight 1998; Alho *et al.* 1994; Javitt *et al.* 1995; Catts *et al.* 1995) and for the enhanced N200 peak amplitude of the ERPs in anxiety disorders, a sign of increased automatic processing (Towey *et al.* 1993).

In a study by Wang *et al.* (2001), frontal MMN amplitude was found to be positively correlated with Neuroticism-Anxiety (N-Anx), measured by Zuckerman-Kulman's Personality Questionnaire (ZKPQ) (Zuckerman *et al.* 1993), but negatively with Experience Seeking (ES), measured by Zuckerman's Sensation Seeking Scale (SSS) (Zuckerman 1979). These findings support RST predictions if we assume that N-Anx is related to the BIS activity and ES to the activity of the BAS. Later, Hansenne *et al.* (2003) investigated the relationship between the MMN and personality dimensions as measured by Tridimensional Personality Questionnaire (Cloninger 1986). Harm avoidance (HA) dimension, which is thought to reflect the activity of the BIS, was found significantly correlated with MMN amplitudes, indicating that higher MMN amplitude is associated with higher score on HA. This association was found to be more pronounced among women than men. This study suggests that individuals who exhibit higher MMN amplitude are characterized by increased inhibitory processes.

De Pascalis *et al.* (2004) tested separable and joint subsystems hypothesis using affective modulation (positive, neutral and negative

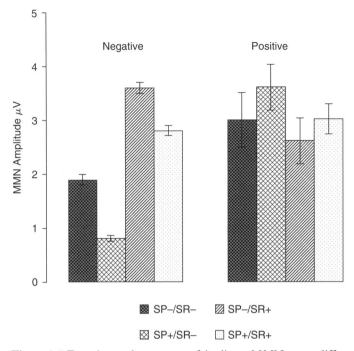

Figure 8.5 Experimental outcomes of Auditory MMN mean difference at midline scalp sites during positive and negative slide viewing conditions in high and low sensitivity to punishment(SP +, SP −) and sensitivity to reward (SR +, SR −) subjects

color pictures) of MMN derived from auditory ERPs. Participants were considered 'low' or 'high' in Sensitivity to Punishment (SP − or SP +) and in Sensitivity to Reward (SR − or SR +) as measured by the Sensitivity to Punishment and Sensitivity to Reward Questionnaire (SPSRQ) (Torrubia *et al.* 2001). The MMN findings, obtained for unpleasant pictures, were seen by the authors as in line with the joint subsystems hypothesis. These findings are summarized in Figure 8.5. The SP + subjects displayed higher MMN peak amplitudes over frontal and central scalp sites in the presence of unpleasant pictures as compared to positive and neutral pictures. This effect was found to be stronger in SP +SR − participants as compared to SP +SR + ones. The SP −SR + subjects had a smaller MMN amplitude than SP −SR − ones (see Figure 8.5). These differences do not fit with a separable subsystems view of Gray's theory, since we would expect the SP + subjects would have a similar response level to negative pictures, regardless of their SR scores. Although the MMN patterns for positive pictures resembled the theoretical predictions, it failed to reach any significant level of differences between groups and, therefore, the authors concluded that this outcome did not match the joint subsystems predictions. This result may be dependent on the nature/intensity of the experienced stimuli. It is known that we usually perceive negative emotion stimuli as more powerful than positive ones. Moreover, Pickering *et al.* (1997) suggested that, for evaluation of pure effects, the context of an experiment must be exclusively rewarding or exclusively punishing. When the order of presentation of positive and negative valenced stimuli change, as was the case in this study, the results are less predictable.

In conclusion, although some reports support Gray's original theory, some others do not fit and are better accounted for by a joint subsystems hypothesis (Corr 2001, 2002). The diversity of findings reported indicates that more theoretical and experimental research efforts must be made in the attempt to understand personality/emotion/cognition dynamics.

Autonomic activity and BIS/BAS

Among activities of the autonomic nervous system, measures of electrodermal activity (EDA) such as palmar skin conductance (SC) seem to be directly related to arousability and general cortical arousal and measures of cardiovascular activity such as heart rate (HR) seem to be directly related to somatic complying, incentive and arousal.

The base level of skin conductance (SCL) is considered as an index of tonic arousal. It reflects slow changes in conductance of the skin to an electrical current in prolonged response to a situation or internal level of activation. Electrodermal responses (EDRs), or skin conductance responses (SCRs), to a specific stimulus consist of two phases, a slow rise and a recovery to SCL baseline, which can be slow or fast. Measures of SCR include amplitude, frequency of response, onset latency and recovery time. These measures are usually thought of as a component of orienting response. Peak amplitude of the SCR is directly linked to stimulus intensity, and stronger to the first stimulation, but response reactions are usually habituated after some repetitions of the stimulus. Spontaneous skin conductance responses or non-specific SCRs (NSSCRs) may appear as fluctuations in the SCL when there are no apparent changes in the external environment, as when during common baseline recordings. Dawson *et al.* (1990) has outlined that electrodermal measures provide a direct representation of sympathetic activity which is relatively not affected by other somatic influences such as respiration and heart activity.

Measures of cardiovascular activity have also been used to explore arousal differences in personality and temperament. Although the cardiovascular system is influenced by respiratory activity, HR change in response to stimuli has been used as a dependent measure in many personality and psychopathology studies (e.g., Fowles 1987; De Pascalis, Strelau and Zawadzki 1999; Kaiser, Beauvale and Bener 1997). Lacey and Lacey (1970, 1974), using a fixed foreperiod (RT) paradigm, observed a phasic HR deceleration starting prior to an anticipated event in cases in which the 'intake' of sensory information conveyed by the signal was required. A body of empirical work has now firmly established that HR slowing indexes selective and even more global inhibition and that each successive heartbeat is slowed in anticipation of a specific action if the timing of performance demand can be expected with good accuracy (for a review, see e.g., Van der Molen et al. 1991; Van der Molen, Somsen and Jennings 2000; Jennings and Van der Molen 2002).

In contrast to HR slowing, the HR increases when brain modulation of cardiovascular activity is to support motivated action, mostly in support of anticipated action. A clearly understood cardiac response is HR increase and switching of blood to muscles from other districts of the body after a threat stimulus is perceived (i.e., the classic fight-flight reaction). According to Jennings et al. (1993), the autonomic nervous system acts on a central command to change the vascular distribution of the blood prior to the progression of a metabolic need. Experimental findings indicate that when individuals respond actively to impending aversive cues, there is an increase in HR, while passive acceptance of impending aversive cues produces no change in HR (Obrist 1976).

There is experimental evidence that HR increases in response to rewards (for a review, see Fowles 1980). Based on these findings as well as cardiac-somatic complying hypothesis, Fowles (1980) has advanced that HR is more strongly associated with BAS activity than BIS activity. This view is indirectly supported by findings indicating higher HR in high impulsive individuals as compared to low impulsive ones (for a review, see e.g., Hare 1978). Fowles (1980) has also suggested that changes in EDA reflect emotional reactions to anticipation of punishment, and thus provide a good index of BIS activity. The evidence for electrodermal hypo-reactivity in the anticipation of aversive stimuli in high impulsive individuals (e.g., psychopaths), compared with low impulsive ones (seen as reflecting a weak BIS), supports this view (Fowles 1980, 2000). Despite the number of studies using Fowles' (1980) adaptation of Gray's theory to explain syndromes of inhibition such as anxiety disorders (e.g., Geen 1987; Hagopian and Ollendick 1994), or syndromes of disinhibition such as psychopathy (e.g., Newman and Wallace 1993; Arnett 1997; Fowles 2000), there has been little research testing the general validity of Fowles' autonomic hypotheses.

Only a few studies have recorded both HR and EDA for testing Gray-Fowles hypotheses. Gomez and McLaren (1997) measured changes in HR, SCL and mood responses in two separate groups of participants, one group completing a reward only go/no-go task (Patterson, Kosson and Newman 1987) and the other completing a punishment only go/no-go task. In agreement with Gray/Fowles' predictions, subjects, in the reward condition, as compared with subjects in the punishment condition, made more commission errors, reported significantly higher happy mood scores and significantly lower nervous mood scores and displayed lower SCL activity. These findings were seen by the authors as in agreement with Gray's theory predictions. However, HR findings did not support predictions that HR would increase more in the reward condition than in the punishment condition. HR was not found to be associated with happy mood ratings, with any dimension of Eysenck's Impulsiveness Scale (Eysenck and Eysenck 1977), or with any of Carver and White's (1994) BAS scales. In addition, SCL did not correlate with Spielberger's STAI-trait anxiety (Spielberger et al. 1983) or Carver and White's (1994) BIS scale.

Arnett and Newman (2000) raised a number of possible reasons to account for the finding of the lack of the predicted HR/reward association in Gomez and McLaren's (1997) study. First, these authors suggested that the two go/no-go tasks may not have wholly elicited BIS and BAS activation since the punishment only condition also involved active avoidance which is putatively mediated by the BAS and may have masked any HR differences between the groups. Secondly, it may be that in the reward condition the failure to obtain monetary reward may result in some BIS activation that reduced any ongoing BAS activation since it is known that the BIS is activated by both punishment stimuli and frustrative non-reward (Gray 1987). Accordingly, both tasks may have involved BIS and BAS activation, although the problem of the elicitation of 'pure' BIS or BAS activation is not uniquely associated to the go/no-go task. Thirdly, to enhance the relationship between HR and BAS, a more demanding motor response may be needed. The last, but not least, possible reason may simply lie in the fact that HR may not be an accurate marker of BAS activity – a statement in contrast with Fowles' (1980) hypothesis. A relevant criticism may have been that, among EDA measures, the SCL measure used in Gomez and McLaren's (1997) study may have not been sensitive enough to reflect BIS activity. A fluctuating

NSSCR or a phasic SCR to a specific punishment stimulus have been suggested as more reliable markers of anxiety or BIS activity (Fowles 1980) and, thus, were chosen in Arnett and Newman's (2000) study. These authors attempted to improve Gomez and McLaren's (1997) study by developing a task involving much more demanding motor activity and thought to reduce the effects of frustrative non-reward on BAS activation. HR and response time to active avoidance signals were measured in addition to reward signals as elicitors of the BAS. Two experiments were carried out by engaging two different groups of participants: (a) a reward experiment (experiment 1), and (2) an active avoidance experiment (experiment 2). HR did not significantly correlate with trait impulsivity in either study, while they did indeed find that HR increased in reward and active avoidance situations. In terms of EDA measures their results were somewhat mixed, with SCL amplitude increasing in response to punishment in both studies, and SCRs increasing in experiment 1. Consistent with predictions for the BIS, participants showed significant increases in number of SCRs from a reward-only to a mixed incentive phase in experiment 1 and a significant increase in the amplitude of SCRs to punishment signals in both experiments. Contrary to expectations, no significant increase in number of SCRs occurred from the active-avoidance to mixed-incentive phases in experiment 2 and the change in number of SCRs from the reward-only to mixed-incentive phases was not significantly correlated with the amplitude of SCR to punishment signals in experiment 1. The most unexpected finding was that the anxiety measure was not correlated with either SCR measure in either experiment. Moreover, consistent with predictions of Gray/Fowles' model, that signals activating the BIS should reduce ongoing BAS activation, were the significant decreases in HR and response time found from the reward-only (experiment 1) or active-avoidance (experiment 2) phases to the mixed-incentive phases. In sum, response time and HR decreases to BIS signals appear to be more reliable indices of BIS activity than SCRs. It is surprising that BIS influenced HR and response time and both were correlated with self-reported anxiety in experiment 1, but none of the EDA indices of the BIS correlated with anxiety in either experiment. Participants showed significant increases in amplitude of SCR to punishment signals, a finding which is common to other studies (Fowles 1980, 1987). The lacking relationship between anxiety and SCR measures in Arnett and Newman's (2000) study contrasts with previous findings on criminal offenders by the same research group (Arnett *et al.* 1993) where a greater number of SCRs following punishment in high-anxiety, compared to low-anxiety, offenders was obtained. One of the main limitations of the Arnett and Newman study lies in the fact that no Anx and Imp measures were used. These dimensional traits are components of RST and individual differences in Anx and Imp can help in better understanding their relationship with behavioral and physiological measures of BIS/BAS functioning. In any event, this study appears an interesting investigation more generally oriented at supporting the validity of Gray/Fowles' model rather than to verify RST predictions in terms of the underlying temperamental components of this theory.

In another study, Sosnowski, Nurzynska and Polec (1991) recorded both HR and EDR during performance on a monetary reward or no reward task and a passive and active coping task. Electrodermal activity and HR, while subjects solved problems from Raven's progressive matrices, were evaluated. These authors found a significant interaction in relation to the active versus passive coping task, such that BIS mediated passive coping. Consistent with Gray/Fowles' predictions, subjects who actively solved the problems displayed higher HR and lower electrodermal activity than passive subjects whose bonus was dependent on their partner's performance. The results for HR in both tasks did not support RST, and Fowle's (1980) predictions were partially supported.

In an attempt to predict autonomic reactivity to public speaking, Schwerdtfeger (2004) recorded HR and the number of NSSCRs during a baseline and speech delivery period. HR reactivity was found significantly associated with subject's involvement in the task, a measure that is linked to BAS activation. NSSCR reactivity was significantly related to other-rated nervousness/unstableness, a measure that is clearly linked to BIS activation. Interestingly, the author noted that objectively assessed task engagement was not significantly correlated with NSSCRs and other-rated nervousness was not correlated with HR. Thus, these findings not only support Gray/Fowles' predictions that HR increase is an autonomic index of BAS functioning and NSSCR an index of BIS functioning, but also that these systems are automatically independent during a speaking task.

In a study by Keltikangas-Järvinen et al. (1999), the relationships between strength of excitation (SE) and strength of inhibition (SI), as measured by Strelau Temperament Inventory – Revised (Strelau, Angleitner and Ruch 1989), and autonomic stress reactivity were evaluated in middle-aged men. The SE and SI measures were seen by the authors as temperament dimensions serving as markers respectively of the BAS and BIS functioning. The number of NSSCRs and the amplitude of respiratory sinus arrhythmia (RSA) and HR reactivity, derived from interbeat interval, were measured during administration of the Rorschach's test. SE was found significantly correlated with task-induced change of RSA. SI was significantly related to low NSSCRs and increased HR reactivity, whereas SE was not associated with overall HR reactivity. In this study, SI was also significantly related to calmness and lack of it to anticipatory tension, a result which appears contrary to RST predictions, suggesting that behavioral inhibition would be related to increased level of Anx. These findings are clearly in contrast with Fowles' interpretation of Gray's theory of temperament, but support Kagan, Reznik and Snidman's (1987) findings that temperamental inhibition is primarily related to high cardiac reactivity. However, due to the types of task and temperamental measures used in this study, it is difficult to generalize findings in terms of Gray's BIS/BAS theory. First, as pointed out by the same authors, it is difficult to bring back the SE and SI dimensions in terms of Gray's Anx and Imp factors. Secondly, the task and nature of stimulus used in the Rorscharch test might be viewed as a passive coping task rather than an active coping one. Further, picture-viewing protocols similar to Rorschach testing induce sensory intake (Obrist 1981) and passive coping which produces parasympathetic activation modulated by primary appraisal (Tomaka et al. 1993).

Clements and Turpin (1995) enrolled six groups of undergraduate subjects into an easy or difficult sentence-verification task. In a first phase of the experiment, different groups received either performance-related monetary penalties, monetary incentives or no feedback on performance. During a second phase of the experiment, this feedback was unexpectedly terminated. According to Gray/Fowles' model it was expected that penalties would lead to elevated levels of SCL, while incentives would lead to increased HR. When the feedback signal was terminated, these effects were expected to reverse. Findings showed that SCL and HR measures did not behave as predicted on feedback trials. SCL measure revealed small and gradual effects of feedback signal, while HR revealed an interaction between feedback and task difficulty. Two groups showed higher HR levels on positive feedback for a difficult task and on a negative feedback for a easy task. One possible explanation of these findings lay in the weak assumption that positive and negative feedbacks are opposite in nature, but equivalent in activating the BIS or BAS systems. This may not be the case since the antagonizing effects of appetitive motivation on aversive motivation are relatively weak, while, in contrast to appetitive motivation, aversive motivation is easy to establish and difficult to extinguish (see Corr 2001).

Heponiemi et al. (2004) examined BIS and BAS sensitivity in relation to HR changes during baseline and task performance. HR measures were not found related to BIS sensitivity. In agreement with Fowles' (1980) predictions, these authors found that BAS sensitivity was related to increased HR reactivity across three stress-inducing tasks. They also found that BAS sensitivity was related to increased HR in a mental arithmetic task. This finding contrasts with Knyazev, Slobodskaya and Wilson's (2002) finding who reported, in the same task, that BAS sensitivity was related to decreased HR. However, Knyazev *et al.*'s (2002) task did not include incentives and plausibly induced BIS activity. Moreover, the two studies did use different questionnaire measures of the BAS, the BIS/BAS scales of Carver and White (1994) and the Gray-Wilson Personality Questionnaire (GWPQ) (Wilson, Barrett and Gray 1989). The results from both studies can be interpreted in support of Fowles' (1980) predictions. Ravaja (2004), using the spectral analysis of HR, obtained similar findings to those reported by Heponiemi *et al.* (2004) and outlined that the BAS may be mediated by the parasympathetic nervous system.

In a study already discussed above, De Pascalis, Destro Fiore and Sparita (1996) recorded ERPs and HR deceleration responses to feedback words indicating winning and losing of amounts of money. The following findings were obtained in terms of HR activity and personality. First, HR deceleration response to both punishment and reward feedback signals was significantly more pronounced in high N individuals as compared to low N ones. Secondly, extraverts disclosed greater HR decelerations for reward compared with punishment signals. The first finding was seen as supporting Gray's original prediction that differences in N are dependent on both BAS and BIS systems. The second finding was seen as indicating that a single arousal system may not account for the observed HR differences between introverts and extraverts and that two distinct neuronal systems could be necessary to mediate punishment and reward responses. Although HR findings may appear in agreement with RST predictions, this conclusion must be taken with reserve since Anx and Imp were not directly measured in this study.

De Pascalis and Speranza (2000), using a spatially word cued recognition task, reported that extraverted-sensation seekers, thought to have putative high BAS activity, had higher feeling ratings for pleasant words. Anx + individuals had larger HR accelerations for unpleasant cued target words and slower RTs in detecting both pleasant and unpleasant cued target words. Low P-SS subjects, compared to high P-SS ones, had greater HR accelerations and greater P300 peaks to neutral- and pleasant-cued words. Results obtained for E-SS and Anx factors appear in agreement with RST predictions. However, the physiological findings obtained for P-SS dimension cannot be easily explained in terms of RST since this factor is not clearly defined in terms of BIS/BAS or FFFS functioning.

In a study of our own, already reported above (De Pascalis *et al.* 2004), ERPs and HR were recorded to emotionally positive and negative adjectives during four emotional-word recognition tasks using a visual oddball paradigm. Consistent with RST, more pronounced HR decelerations and higher emotional feeling ratings to unpleasant words were obtained in Anx + subjects as compared to Anx − ones. No significant effects on emotional ratings and HR deceleration responses were obtained for an Imp factor.

Startle reflex and BIS/BAS

There is a growing literature on the eye-blink component of the startle reflex measured by the electromyogram (EMG) recorded from the orbiculari oculi muscle. It is known that conditioned fear increases the magnitude of startle reflex in animals (Davis 1986, 1989) and it is of clear survival significance. In humans, the most reliable and easy to measure component of the startle reflex is the magnitude of the eye-blink response to acoustic probe. This measure has been widely used after the finding that it can be influenced by a dominant emotion (for an overview, see Lang, Bradley and Cuthbert 1992). Fearful or unpleasant emotional states increase magnitude of startle reflex, while pleasant hedonic states attenuate startle response (Vrana, Spence and Lang 1988; Hamm *et al.* 1993). The measure of eye-blink startle response is a promising tool for studying emotional activity in the brain since it provides independent measures of reactivity to pleasant and unpleasant foreground events which is modality-free and reflects the activity of central motivation states. Startle reflex paradigm has proved to be a valid paradigm for studying individual differences in emotionality and, thus, particularly useful for testing Gray's theory. If we assume that Anx + individuals are highly sensitive to punishment signals, then we might expect them to exhibit an amplification of startle response to aversive stimulations. Impulsive individuals, on the other hand, being more sensitive to reward signals, should display more pronounced startle responses to pleasant stimuli. Corr, Pickering and Gray (1995b) found that Harm Avoidance (HA), a putative measure of trait anxiety derived from Cloninger's (1986) model of personality, significantly moderated fear potentiation since only high HA individuals showed startle modulation to unpleasant stimuli. These findings were replicated by Corr *et al.* (1997), giving support to the hypothesis that individual differences in trait anxiety are important in affective modulation of startle reflex and that Cloninger's HA personality dimension is a good tool for startle modulation experiments. Furthermore, Anx − is sometimes found to moderate appetitive responses, as happened in Corr, Pickering and Gray's (1995b) study in which there was evidence of an antagonism of anxiety and pleasure attenuation. Results from another startle reflex study (Kumari *et al.* 1996) failed to find an influence of Eysenck's and Cloninger's dimensions on affective modulation of startle reflex in subjects viewing emotionally toned pleasant, unpleasant and neutral film-clips.

On the basis of neuro-imaging findings (Phillips *et al.* 1997, 1998) that showed an anatomical dissociation of reactions to disgust and fear-inducing stimuli, Wilson *et al.* (2000) reanalyzed their previous film-clips data (Kumari *et al.* 1996) and found that individuals scoring high on Eysenck's N scale showed reduced startle reflexes to disgust-inducing film-clips, while they exhibited potentiated startle reflexes to fear-inducing film-clips. These findings outline the importance of clearly differentiating stimuli in terms of different emotional states.

More recently, Corr (2002) reported two experiments devoted to test predictions from the joint subsystems hypothesis on RST. The first experiment used the affective modulation of the acoustic startle reflex to measure the emotional state. Results from this study showed that Anx + individuals had the strongest affective reactions in the presence of unpleasant slides, compared with neutral slides, but this effect of 'fear potentiation' was found stronger in Anx + Imp − participants. This effect was not statistically significant in the Anx + Imp + group of participants. These findings were seen as indicating that Imp + antagonizes BIS-mediated reactions. In this experiment, however, there were no effects for reactions to appetitive stimuli. In the second experiment, Anx − Imp + individuals had the highest number of commission errors under monetary punishment on a rapid visual information processing task. This indicates that individuals who, putatively, have a weak BIS and strong BAS have a disinhibited pattern of reaction. However, given that this effect was observed only under caffeine-induced arousal, these findings also suggested that high levels of arousal may be necessary for strengthening inhibitory behavior.

Conclusion

In this chapter some psychophysiological accounts of RST are reviewed mainly in terms of personality traits. Findings from many of these studies outline the importance of RST in physiological understanding of personality, including how individual differences in personality are reflected in behavior and cognition. However, there is little consensus over the optimal set of psychometric measures and there is no reason to choose between alternative scales, although questionnaires providing more direct measures of BIS/BAS sensitivities appear to be more promising. During the last thirty years, the RST has been revised a number of times and the complexity of individual differences in personality in terms of reinforcement sensitivity has been recently outlined (Corr 2004; McNaughton and Corr 2004). Recent psychophysiological findings highlight the importance of cognitive factors for an explanation of electrocortical and autonomic responses in terms of RST. However, the diversity of findings obtained suggests that, in spite of recent progress, research has still a long way to go for the development of a neuroscience of personality. It is too early to say whether the recent reformulation of Gray's theory, including the joint subsystems hypothesis, will improve the capacity to predict psychophysiological responses to punishment and reward signals.

References

Alain, C., Woods, D.L. and Knight, R.T. (1998), A distributed cortical network for auditory sensory memory, *Brain Research*, 812, 23–37

Alho, K., Woods, D.L., Algasi, A., Knight, R.T. and Näätänen, R. (1994), Lesions of frontal cortex diminish the auditory mismatch negativity, *Electroencephalography and Clinical Neurophysiology*, 91, 353–362

Arnett, P.A. (1997), Autonomic responsivity in psychopaths: a critical review and theoretical proposal, *Clinical Psychology Review*, 17, 903–936

Arnett, P.A., Howland, E.W., Smith, S.S. and Newman, J.P. (1993), Autonomic responsivity during passive avoidance in incarcerated psychopaths, *Personality and Individual Differences*, 14, 173–184

Arnett, P.A. and Newman, J.P. (2000), Gray's three-arousal model: an empirical investigation, *Personality and Individual Differences*, 28, 1171–1189

Barratt, E.S. (1971), Psychophysiological correlates of classical differential eyelid conditioning among normal subjects selected on the basis of impulsiveness and anxiety, *Biological Psychiatry*, 3, 339–346

Bartussek, D., Becker, G., Diedrich, O., Naumann, E. and Maier, S. (1996), Extraversion, neuroticism and event-related potentials in response to emotional stimuli, *Personality and Individual Differences*, 20, 301–312

Bartussek, D., Diedrich, O., Naumann, E. and Collet, W. (1993), Introversion-extraversion and event related potential (ERP): a test of J.A. Gray's theory, *Personality and Individual Differences*, 14, 565–574

Buss, A.H. and Perry, M. (1992), The aggression questionnaire, *Journal of Personality and Social Psychology*, 63, 452–459

Carver, C.S. and White, T.L. (1994), Behavioral inhibition, behavioral activation, and affective responses to impending reward and punishment: the BIS/BAS scales, *Journal of Personality and Social Psychology*, 67, 319–333

Catts, S.V., Shelley, A.M., Ward, P.B., Liebert, B., McConaghy, N., Andrews, S. and Michie, P.T. (1995), Brain potential evidence for a sensory memory deficit in schizophrenia, *American Journal of Psychiatry*, 152, 213–219

Clements, K. and Turpin, G. (1995), Effects of feedback and task difficulty on electrodermal activity and heart rate: an examination of Fowles' three arousal model, *Journal of Psychophysiology*, 9, 231–242

Cloninger, C.R. (1986), A unified biosocial theory of personality and its role in the development of anxiety states, *Psychiatric Developments*, 3, 167–226

Coan, J.A. and Allen, J.J. B. (2003), Frontal EEG asymmetry and the behavioral activation and inhibition systems, *Psychophysiology*, 40, 106–114

Cook, E.W., Hawk, L.W., Davis, T.L. and Stevenson, V.E. (1991), Affective individual differences and startle reflex modulation, *Journal of Abnormal Psychology*, 100, 5–13

Corr, P.J. (2001), Testing problems in A.J. Gray's personality theory: a commentary on Matthews and Gilliland (1999), *Personality and Individual Differences*, 30, 333–352

(2002), J.A. Gray's reinforcement sensitivity theory: tests of the joint subsystems hypothesis of anxiety and impulsivity, *Personality and Individual Differences*, 33, 511–532

(2004), Reinforcement sensitivity theory and personality, *Neuroscience and Biobehavioral Reviews*, 28, 317–332

Corr, P.J. and Kumari, V. (1997), Sociability/impulsivity and haloperidol-induced de-arousal: critical flicker/fusion frequency and procedural learning, *Personality and Individual Differences*, 22, 805–815

Corr, P.J., Kumari, V., Wilson, G.D., Checkley, S. and Gray, J.A. (1997), Harm avoidance and affective modulation of the startle reflex: a replication, *Personality and Individual Differences*, 22, 591–593

Corr, P.J., Pickering, A.D. and Gray, J.A. (1995a), Personality and reinforcement in associative and instrumental learning, *Personality and Individual Differences*, 19, 47–71

(1995b), Sociability/impulsivity and caffeine-induced arousal: critical flicker fusion frequency and procedural learning, *Personality and Individual Differences*, 18, 713–730

Corr, P.J., Wilson, G.D., Fotiadou, M., Kumari, V., Gray, N.S., Checkley, S. and Gray, J.A. (1995c), Personality and affective modulation of the startle reflex, *Personality and Individual Differences*, 19, 543–553

Davidson, R.J., Jackson, D.C. and Larson, C.L. (2000), Human electroencephalography in J.T. Caccioppo and L.G. Tassinary (eds.), *Handbook of Psychophysiology* (2nd edn, New York: Cambridge University Press), pp. 27–52

Davis, M. (1986), Pharmachological and anatomical analysis of fear conditioning using the fear-potentiated startle paradigm, *Behavioural Neuroscience*, 100, 814–824

(1989), Sensitization of the acoustic startle reflex by footshock, *Behavioural Neuroscience*, 103, 495–503

Dawson, M.E., Schell, A.M. and Filion, D.L. (1990), The electrodermal system in J.T. Caccioppo and L.G. Tassinary (eds.), *Principles of psychophysiology: Physical, Social and Inferential Elements* (Cambridge: Cambridge University Press)

De Pascalis, V. (2004), On the psychophysiology of extraversion in R.M. Stelmack (ed.), *On the Psychobiology of Personality* (Oxford: Elsevier Ltd), pp. 295–327

De Pascalis, V., Destro Fiore, A. and Sparita, A. (1996), Personality, event-related potential (ERP) and heart rate (HR): an investigation of Gray's theory, *Personality and Individual Differences*, 20, 733–746

De Pascalis, V. and Speranza, O. (2000), Personality effects on attentional shifts to emotional charged cues: ERP, behavioural and HR data, *Personal and Individual Differences*, 29, 217–238

De Pascalis, V., Strelau, J. and Zawadzki, B. (1999), The effect of temperamental traits on event-related potentials, heart rate and reaction time, *Personality and Individual Differences*, 26, 411–465

De Pascalis, V., Strippoli, E., Riccardi, P. and Vergari, F. (2004), Personality, event-related potential (ERP) and heart rate (HR) in emotional word processing, *Personality and Individual Differences*, 36, 873–891

Eysenck, H.J. (1967), *The Biological Basis of Personality* (Springfield: Thomas)
(1981), General features of the model in H.J. Eysenck (ed.), *A Model for Personality* (Berlin: Springer-Verlag), pp. 1–37
(1994), Personality: biological foundations in P.A. Vernon (ed.), *The Neuropsychology of Individual Differences* (London: Academic Press)

Eysenck, H.J. and Eysenck, M.W. (1985), *Personality and Individual Differences* (New York: Plenum)

Eysenck, H.J. and Eysenck, S.B.G. (1975), *Manual of the Eysenck Personality Questionnaire (Adults)* (London: Hodder and Stoughton)
(1976), *Psychoticism as a Dimension of Personality* (London: Hodder and Stoughton)

Eysenck, S. and Eysenck, H. (1977), The place of impulsiveness in a dimensional system of personality description, *British Journal of Psychology*, 16, 57–68

Fabiani, M., Gratton, G. and Coles, M.G.H. (2000), Event-related brain potentials: methods, theory, and application in J.T. Caccioppo, L.G. Tassinary and G.G. Berntson (eds.), *Handbook of Psychophysiology* (2nd edn, Cambridge: Cambridge University Press), pp. 53–84

Fowles, D. (1980), The three arousal models: implications of Gray's two factor learning theory for heart-rate, electrodermal activity, and psychopathology, *Psychophysiology*, 17, 87–104
(1987), Psychophysiology and psychopathology: a motivational approach, *Psychophysiology*, 25, 373–391
(2000), Electrodermal hyporeactivity and antisocial behavior: does anxiety mediate the relationship?, *Journal of Affective Disorders*, 61, 177–189

Gale, A. (1983), Electroencephalographic studies of extraversion-introversion: a case study in the psychophysiology of individual differences, *Personality and Individual Differences*, 4, 371–380

Geen, R.G. (1987), Anxiety and behavioral avoidance, *Journal of Research in Personality*, 21, 481–488

Gomez, R. and McLaren, S. (1997), The effects of reward and punishment on response disinhibition, moods, heart rate, and skin conductance level during instrumental learning, *Personality and Individual Differences*, 23, 305–316

Gray, J.A. (1970), The psychophysiological basis of introversion-extraversion, *Behaviour Research and Therapy*, 8, 249–266

(1976), The behavioural inhibition system: a possible substrate for anxiety in M.P. Feldman and A.M. Broadhurst, *Theoretical and Experimental Bases of Behaviour Modification* (London: Wiley), pp. 3–41

(1982), *The Neuropsychology of Anxiety: an Enquiry into the Functions of the Septo-hippocampal System* (Oxford: Oxford University Press)

(1987), *The Psychology of Fear and Stress* (Cambridge: Cambridge University Press)

(1991), Neural systems, emotion and personality in J.I. V. Madden (eds.), *Neurobiology of Learning, Emotion and Affect* (New York: Raven Press), pp. 273–306

Gray, J.A. and McNaughton, N. (2000), *The Neuropsychology of Anxiety: an Enquiry into the Functions of the Septo-hippocampal System* (2nd edn, Oxford: Oxford University Press)

Hagopian, L.P. and Ollendick, T.H. (1994), Behavioral inhibition and test anxiety: an empirical investigation of Gray's theory, *Personality and Individual Differences*, 16, 597–604

Hamm, A.O., Greenwald, M.K., Bradley, M.M. and Lang, P.J. (1993), Emotional learning, hedonic change, and the startle probe, *Journal of Abnormal Psychology*, 102, 453–465

Hansenne, M., Pinto, E., Scantamburlo, G., Renard, B., Reggers, J., Fuchs, S., Pitchot, W. and Ansseau, M. (2003), Harm avoidance is related to mismatch negativity (MMN) amplitude in healthy subjects, *Personality and Individual Differences*, 34, 1039–1048

Hare, R.D. (1978), Electrodermal and cardiovascular correlates of psychopathy in R.D. Hare, and D. Schalling (eds.), *Psychopathic Behavior: Approaches to Research* (New York: Wiley), pp. 107–144

Harmon-Jones, E., Abramson, L.Y., Sigelman, J., Bohlig, A., Hogan, M.E. and Harmon-Jones, C. (2002), Proneness to hypomania/mania symptoms or depression symptoms and asymmetrical frontal cortical responses to an anger-evoking event, *Journal of Personality and Social Psychology*, 82(4), 610–618

Harmon-Jones, E. and Allen, J.J. B. (1997), Behavioral activation sensitivity and resting frontal EEG asymmetry: covariation of putative indicators related to risk of mood disorders, *Journal of Abnormal Psychology*, 106, 159–163

(1998), Anger and frontal brain asymmetry: EEG asymmetry consistent with approach motivation despite negative affective valence, *Journal of Personality and Social Psychology*, 74, 1310–1316

Harmon-Jones, E. and Sigelman, J. (2001), State anger and prefrontal brain activity: evidence that insult-related relative left-prefrontal activation is associated with experienced anger and aggression, *Journal of Personality and Social Psychology*, 80, 797–803

Harmon-Jones, E., Sigelman, J.D., Bohlig, A. and Harmon-Jones, C. (2003), Anger, coping, and frontal cortical activity: the effect of coping potential on anger-induced left frontal activity, *Cognition and Emotion*, 17, 1–24

Heponiemi, T., Keltikangas-Järvinen, L., Kettunen, J., Puttonen, S. and Ravaja, N. (2004), BIS-BAS sensitivity and cardiac autonomic stress profiles, *Psychophysiology*, 41, 37–45

Hewig, J., Hagemann, D., Seifert, J., Naumann, E. and Bartussek, D. (2006), The relation of cortical activity and BIS/BAS on the trait level, *Biological Psychology*, 71, 42–53

Hillyard, S.A. and Picton, T.W. (1987), Electrophysiology of cognition in V.B. Mountcastle, F. Plum and S.R. Geiger (eds), *Handbook of Physiology*, Section 1 *The Nervous System* (Bethesda, MD: American Physiological Society), pp. 519–571

Javitt, D.C., Doneshka, P., Grochowski, S. and Ritter, W. (1995), Impaired mismatch negativity generation reflects widespread dysfunction of working memory in schizophrenia, *Archives of General Psychiatry*, 52, 550–558

Jennings, J.R. and van der Molen, M.W. (2002), Cardiac timing and the central regulation of action, *Psychological Research*, 66, 337–349

Jennings, J.R., van der Molen, M.W., Brock, K. and Somsen, R.J. (1993), How are tonic and phasic cardiovascular changes related to central motor command?, *Biological Psychology*, 35, 237–254

Kagan, J., Reznik, J.S. and Snidman, N. (1987), The physiology and psychology of behavioral inhibition in children, *Child Development*, 58, 1459–1473

Kaiser, J., Beauvale, A. and Bener, J. (1997), The evoked cardiac response as a function of cognitive load differs between subjects separated on the main personality dimensions, *Personality and Individual Differences*, 22, 241–248

Keltikangas-Järvinen, L., Kettunen, J., Ravaja, N. and Näätänen, P. (1999), Inhibited and disinhibited temperament and autonomic stress reactivity, *International Journal of Psychophysiology*, 33, 185–196

Knyazev, G.G., Slobodskaya, H.R. and Wilson, G.D. (2002), Psycho-physiological correlates of behavioural inhibition and activation, *Personality and Individual Differences*, 33, 647–660

Kumari, V., Corr, P.J., Wilson, G.D., Kaviani, H., Thornton, J.C., Checkley, S.A. and Gray, J.A. (1996), Personality and modulation of the startle reflex by emotionally-toned filmclips, *Personality and Individual Differences*, 21, 1029–1041

Lacey, B.C. and Lacey, J.I. (1974), Studies of heart rate and other bodily processes in sensorimotor behavior in P.A. Obrist, A.H. Black, J. Brener and L.V. DiCara (eds.), *Cardiovascular psychophysiology* (Chicago: Aldine), pp. 538–564

Lacey, J.I. and Lacey, B.C. (1970), Some autonomic-central nervous system inter–relationships in P. Black (ed.), *Physiological Correlates of Emotion* (New York: Academic Press)

Lang, P.J., Bradley, M.M. and Cuthbert, B.N. (1992), A motivational analysis of emotion: reflex-cortex connections, *Psychophysiological Science*, 3, 44–49

Larsen, R.J. and Katelaar, T. (1991), Personality and susceptibility to positive and negative emotional states, *Journal of Personality and Social Psychology*, 61, 132–140

Magoun, H.W. (1963), *The Waking Brain* (2nd edn, Springfield, IL: Thomas)

Matthews, G. and Gilliland, K. (1999), The personality theories of H.J. Eysenck and J.A. Gray: a comparative review, *Personality and Individual Differences*, 26, 583–626

McNaughton, N. and Corr, P.J. (2004), A two-dimensional neuropsychology of defense: fear/anxiety and defensive distance, *Neuroscience and Behavioral Review*, 28, 285–305

Moruzzi, G. and Magoun, H.W. (1949), Brain stem reticular formation and activation of the EEG, *EEG Clinical Neurophysiology*, 1, 455–473

Näätänen, R. (1982), Processing negativity: an evoked potential reflection on selective attention, *Psychological Bulletin*, 92, 605–640

(1992), *Attention and Brain Function* (Hillsdale, NJ: Erlbaum)

Näätänen, R. and Gaillard, A.W. K. (1983), The orienting reflex and the N2 deflection of the event–related potential (ERP) in A.W. K. Gaillard and W. Ritter (eds), *Tutorials in Event-related Potential Research: Endogenous Components* (Amsterdam: Elsevier), pp. 119–141

Näätänen, R., Jiang, D., Lavikainen, J., Reinikainen, K. and Paavilainen, P. (1993), Event-related potentials reveal a memory trace for temporal features, *Neuroreport*, 13, 310–312

Newman, J.P. and Wallace, J.F. (1993), Diverse pathways to deficient self-regulation: implications for disinhibitory psychopathology in children, *Clinical Psychology Review*, 13, 690–720

Obrist, P.A. (1976), The cardiovascular–behavioral interaction: as it appears today, *Psychophysiology*, 13, 95–107

(1981), *Cardiovascular Psychophysiology: a Perspective* (New York: Plenum Press)

Paisey, T.H. J. and Mangan, G.L. (1988), Personality and conditioning with appetitive and aversive stimuli, *Personality and Individual Differences*, 9, 69–78

Patterson, C.M., Kosson, D.S. and Newman, J.P. (1987), Reaction to punishment, reflectivity, and passive avoidance learning in extraverts, *Journal of Personality and Social Psychology*, 52, 565–575

Phillips, M.L., Young, A.W., Scott, S.K., Calder, A.J., Andrew, C., Giampietro, V., Williams, S.C. R., Bullmore, E.T., Brammer, M. and Gray, J.A. (1998), Neural responses to facial and vocal expressions of fear and disgust, *Proceedings of the Royal Society of London Series B: Biological Sciences*, 265, 1809–1817

Phillips, M.L., Young, A.W., Senior, C., Brammer, M., Andrew, C., Calder, A. J., Bullmore, E.T., Perrett, D.I., Rowland, D., Williams, S.C. R., Gray, J.A. and David, A.S. (1997), A specific neural substrate of perceiving facial expressions of disgust, *Nature*, 389, 495–498

Pickering, A.D., Corr, P.J. and Gray, J.A. (1999), Interactions and reinforcement sensitivity theory: a theoretical analysis of Rusting and Larsen (1997), *Personality and Individual Differences*, 26, 357–365

Pickering, A.D., Corr, P.J., Powell, H.J., Kumari, V., Thornton, J.C. and Gray, J.A. (1997), Individual differences in reactions to reinforcing stimuli are neither black nor white: to what extent are they gray? in H. Nyborg (ed.), *The Scientific Study of Human Nature: Tribute to Hans J.Eysenck at Eighty* (London: Elsevier Sciences), pp. 36–67

Ravaja, N. (2004), Effects of a small talking facial image on autonomic activity: the moderating influence of dispositional BIS and BAS sensitivities and emotions, *Biological Psychology*, 65, 163–183

Rugg, M.D. and Coles, M.G. H. (1995), The ERP and cognitive psychology: conceptual issues in M.D. Rugg and M.G. H. Coles (eds), *Electrophysiology of Mind: Event-related Brain Potentials and Cognition* (Oxford: Oxford University Press), pp. 27–39

Schwerdtfeger, A. (2004), Predicting autonomic reactivity to public speaking: don't get fixed on self-report data!, *International Journal of Psychophysiology*, 52, 217–224

Sosnowski, T., Nurzynska, M. and Polec, M. (1991), Active-passive coping and skin conductance and heart rate changes, *Psychophysiology*, 28, 665–672

Spielberger, C.D., Gorsuch, R., Lushene, R., Vagg, P.R. and Jacobs, G.A. (1983), *Manual for the Stait-Trait Anxiety Inventory: STAI (Form Y)* (Palo Alto, CA: Consulting Psychologists Press)

Stelmack, R.M. (1990), Biological bases of extraversion: psychophysiological evidence, *Journal of Personality*, 58, 293–311

Stelmack, R.M. and Geen, R.G. (1992), The psychophysiology of extraversion in A. Gale and M.W. Eysenck (eds), *Handbook of Individual Differences: Biological Perspectives* (New York: Wiley), pp. 227–254

Stenberg, G. (1992), Personality and the EEG: arousal and emotional arousability, *Personality and Individual Differences*, 13, 1097–1113

Strelau, J., Angleitner, A. and Ruch, W. (1989), Strelau Temperament Inventory (STI): general review and studies on German samples in C.D. Spielberger and J.N. Butcher (eds), *Advances in Personality Assessment* (Hillsdale, NJ: Erlbaum), vol.8, pp. 187–241

Sutton, S.K. and Davidson, R.J. (1997), Prefrontal brain asymmetry: a biological substrate of the behavioral approach and inhibition systems, *Psychological Science*, 8, 204–210

Tomaka, J., Bascovich, J., Kelsey, R.M. and Leitten, C.L. (1993), Subjective, physiological, and behavioral effects of threat and challenge appraisal, *Journal of Personality and Social Psychology*, 65, 248–260

Torrubia, M., Avila, C., Molto, J. and Caseras, X. (2001), The sensitivity to punishment and sensitivity to reward questionnaire (SPSRQ) as a measure of Gray's anxiety and impulsivity dimensions, *Personality and Individual Differences*, 31, 837–862

Towey, J., Bruder, G., Tenke, C., Leite, P., DeCaria, C., Friedman, D. and Hollander, E. (1993), Event-related potential and clinical correlates of neurodysfunction in obsessive-compulsive disorder, *Psychiatry Research*, 49, 167–181

Van der Molen, M.W., Bashore, T.R., Halliday, R. and Callaway, E. (1991), Chronopsycho-physiology: mental chronometry augmented by psycho-physiological time markers in J.R. Jennings and M.G.H. Coles (eds.), *Handbook of Cognitive Psychophysiology: Central and Autonomic Nervous System Approaches* (Chichester: Wiley), pp. 9–179

Van der Molen, M.W., Somsen, R.J., and Jennings, J.R. (2000), Developmental change in auditory selective attention as reflected by phasic heart rate changes, *Psychophysiology*, 37, 626–633

Vrana, S.R., Spence, E.L. and Lang, P.J. (1988), The startle probe response: a new measure of emotion?, *Journal of Abnormal Psychology*, 97, 487–491

Wacker, J., Heldmann, M. and Stemmler, G. (2003), Separating emotion and motivational direction in fear and anger: effects on frontal asymmetry, *Emotion*, 3, 167–193

Wang, W., Zhu, S.Z., Pan, L.C. and Wang, Y.H. (2001), Mismatch negativity and personality traits in chronic primary insomniacs, *Functional Neurology*, 16, 3–10

Wilson, G.D., Barrett, P.T. and Gray, J.A. (1989), Human reactions to reward and punishment: a questionnaire measure of Gray's personality space, *British Journal of Psychology*, 80, 509–515

Wilson, G.D., Kumari, V., Gray, J.A. and Corr, P.J. (2000), The role of neuroticism in reflex reactions to fearful and disgusting stimuli, *Personality and Individual Differences*, 29, 1077–1082

Zinbarg, R.R. and Mohlman, J. (1998), Individual differences in acquisition of affectively valenced associations, *Journal of Personality and Social Psychology*, 74, 1024–1040

Zuckerman, M. (1979), *Sensation Seeking: Beyond the Optimal Level of Arousal* (Hillsdale, NJ: Lawrence Erlbaum)

Zuckerman, M., Kuhlman, D.M., Joireman, J., Teta, P. and Kraft, M. (1993), A comparison of three structural models for personality: the Big Three, the Big Five and the Alternative Five, *Journal of Personality and Social Psychology*, 65, 757–768

9 Reinforcement Sensitivity Theory and mood induction studies

Rapson Gomez and Andrew Cooper

In relation to affect, Gray's (1970) original version of the *Reinforcement Sensitivity Theory* (RST) suggests that positive emotion and negative emotion reflect independent activities of the Behavioural Approach System (BAS) and the Behavioural Inhibition System (BIS), respectively (Gray 1990). A recent revision of the RST (Corr 2001, 2004; Gray and McNaughton 2000) implies that the BAS will facilitate positive emotion and antagonize negative emotion, while the BIS will facilitate negative emotion and antagonize positive emotion. This chapter reviews the extent to which mood induction studies support the original and revised RST. Also covered are the limitations of these studies, and the implications of existing data for psychopathology. Suggestions for future research in this area are proposed.

Reinforcement sensitivity theory and mood states

In the initial RST (Gray 1970; see Corr, chapter 1), the BIS is hypothesized to be sensitive to signals of conditioned punishment, frustrative non-reward and novelty. It is involved in regulating aversive motivation, in that its activation will cause individuals to inhibit further responses to such cues. The BAS, by contrast, is sensitive to signals of conditioned reward and non-punishment. It is involved in regulating appetitive motivation as its activation increases goal directed responses. A third system, the Flight-Fight System, is hypothesized to regulate responses to unconditioned punishment and non-reward cues.

In the revised RST (Gray and McNaughton 2000), the BAS is linked to conditioned and unconditioned appetitive stimuli. Aversive stimuli that do not involve approach responses are mediated by a Fight-Flight-Freeze System. The BIS is hypothesized to be activated in conflict situations, involving both approach and avoidance goals. It interrupts and evaluates current behaviour, and it also serves to increase the negative salience of one of the competing goals. These activities facilitate the resolution of the approach-avoidance conflict. According to Corr (2001, 2002b, 2004), the revised RST implies that the BAS will facilitate responses to appetitive stimuli and antagonize responses to aversive stimuli, while the BIS will facilitate responses to aversive stimuli and antagonize responses to appetitive stimuli. Corr has referred to this as the joint subsystems hypothesis (JSH). This conceptualization differs from the initial RST, which links the BAS and the BIS with appetitive and aversive stimuli, respectively, which Corr refers to as the separable subsystems hypothesis (SSH).

In terms of the SSH perspective, the BIS is linked to negative affect, while the BAS is linked to positive affect (Gray 1990). Although the RST does not specify the nature of the positive and negative affect, it has been suggested that they are activated pleasant (AP) affect and activated unpleasant (AUP) affect, as conceptualized in the circumplex model of affect (Larsen and Diener 1992; Russell 1980; Tellegen 1985; Watson, Wiese, Vaidya and Tellegen 1999). If this view is accepted, then from a JSH perspective, the expectation is that AP affect will be induced positively and negatively by the BAS and the BIS, respectively, while AUP affect will be induced negatively and positively by the BAS and the BIS, respectively. Alternatively, AP and AUP affect states could result from BAS x BIS interaction.

Gray (1970) has proposed that impulsivity and anxiety are the personality traits of the BAS and BIS, respectively. Thus, the activities of the BAS and BIS on mood can be inferred by impulsivity and anxiety, or comparable trait measures that have since been proposed for the BAS and BIS. It is also possible to examine the activities of these systems using Eysenck's (1967) extraversion and neuroticism traits because in Eysenck's personality space, BAS impulsivity runs from the neurotic-extravert quadrant to the stable-introvert quadrant, while BIS anxiety runs from the neurotic-introvert quadrant to the stable-extravert quadrant. Thus, from a SSH perspective, BAS activity and AP affect will be positively predicted by both extraversion and neuroticism, while BIS activity and AUP affect will be predicted positively and negatively by neuroticism and extraversion, respectively. This conceptualization of how extraversion and neuroticism are related to the different affect states differs from the view proposed by others, i.e., positive affect is predicted by extraversion alone, and negative affect is predicted by neuroticism alone (Caccioppo, Gardner and Bernston 1999; Costa and McCrae 1980; Larsen and Diener 1992; Tellegen 1985; Watson *et al.* 1999).

Reinforcement sensitivity theory and mood induced studies

Table 9.1 provides a summary of RST relevant mood induction studies. It shows that a number of different mood induction approaches have been used, and that mood responses have been assessed through self-report, psychophysiological indices and neuro-imaging.

Table 9.1 shows that of the mood self-report studies that have used BAS and BIS trait measures, all but two studies (Carver 2004; Gomez and McLaren 1997) found results consistent with predictions from the SSH and not the JSH (Carver and White 1994; Gomez, Cooper and Gomez 2000; Heponiemi, Keltikangas-Jarvinen, Puttonen and Ravaja 2003; Leen-Feldner, Zvolensky, Feldner and Lejuez 2004; Zelenski and Larsen 1999). These findings are especially relevant to AP and AUP mood states (Heponiemi *et al.* 2003). Somewhat inconsistent with these findings, Carver (2004) found that sadness, frustration and anger correlated positively with the BAS trait, and not the BIS trait. In this respect, the finding for anger has been reported by others (e.g., Harmon-Jones 2003; Harmon-Jones and Sigelman 2001; Smits and Kuppens 2005).

Carver (2004) has suggested a 'velocity' hypothesis to explain his results. This hypothesis proposes feedback loops for monitoring the effectiveness of movement toward incentives, and away from threats. According to this hypothesis, one's current movement is compared against one's own reference movement rate. Acceptable rate and unacceptable rate will result in positive and negative affect, respectively, with a balanced rate leading to neutral affect. In this respect, Corr (2002a) has pointed out that as high BAS individuals have high expectation for positive stimuli, the absence or withdrawal of rewards would cause relatively higher frustration and anger. Harmon-Jones (2003) has suggested that the BAS may be involved in negative affect responses when these responses are associated with behavioural approach. In any case, the findings in the Carver study remain unclear and deserve further investigation.

With the exception of one study (Larsen and Ketelaar 1991), which found support for the SSH for negative affect, none of the studies shown in Table 9.1 that have used neuroticism and extraversion supported predictions from the SSH. While a handful of studies showed no relations for extraversion and neuroticism with mood (Carver and White 1994; Helmers, Young and Pihl 1997), most studies supported predictions from Eysenck's theory, i.e., an association between extraversion and AP mood state, and neuroticism and AUP mood state (Gomez,

Table 9.1 *Summary of mood induced studies relevant to the Reinforcement Sensitivity Theory*

Study	RST measures (mood measures)	Mood induction procedure	Findings	Interpretation
Induced mood studies based on BAS and BIS traits and self-reported affect				
Carver and White 1994	S3, S4 – BIS/BAS, MAS (S3 – nervous, S4 – happy)	S3. False performance feedback for impending punishment (NMI). S4. False performance feedback for reward (PMI)	In S3, only BIS was a significant (positive) predictor of nervous. In S4, D and RR were significant (positive) predictors of happy	Supports SSH
Gomez and McLaren 1997	EIS, STAI, BIS/BAS (Happy, nervous)	Reward only (PMI) and punishment only (NMI) for go/no-go task performance	None of the personality traits associated with either emotion during performance	No support for RST
Zelenski and Larsen 1999	S3. Reward, Punishment, Impulsivity (positive, negative)	Pleasant (PMI), unpleasant (NMI) and neutral (NUEMI) slides	Reward and punishment correlated positively with positive and negative emotion, respectively, during PMI and NMI, respectively. Impulsivity correlated positively with negative emotion during PMI	Supports SSH
Gomez, Cooper and Gomez 2000	STAI, BIS-11 (PANAS)	Reward only (PMI) and punishment only (NMI) for go/no-go task performance	For PMI, impulsivity predicted performance AP. For NMI, anxiety predicted performance AUP	Supports SSH

Heponiemi et al. 2003	BIS/BAS (All octants of the affect circumplex model)	Startle sound (So; NMI), rewarded mental arithmetic task (MA; PMI), choice-deadline reaction time task + loud noise (RT; more NMI)	BAS associated more with PA in MA than RT. BIS associated more with NA in So and RT than MA. For all affect octants, there was no BAS×BIS effect	Supports SSH. No support for JSH
Leen-Feldner et al. 2004	BIS/BAS (SAM)	Paced auditory serial addition task (NMI)	BIS correlated positively with negative mood	Supports SSH
Carver 2004	BIS/BAS (S1 used sad, frustration. S2 used angry, nervous)	For S1, after subjects were told that they could get reward, false performance feedback given indicating no gain of reward (frustration MI). For S2, guided imagery of anger-provoking events (anger MI)	In S1, sad and frustration correlated positively with FS. In S2, anger correlated positively with RR and BIS (RR > BIS), nervous correlated positively with RR & BIS, and negatively with DR and FS, BIS strongest predictor	No support for SSH or JSH
Induced mood studies based on extraversion and neuroticism and self-reported affect				
Larsen and Ketelaar 1989	EPI (4 opposite emotion pairs)	False feedback of good (PMI) and poor (NMI) performance	For PMI, E correlated positively with more positive mood. For NMI, N correlated positively with less positive mood	Supports EYS, not SSH or JSH
Larsen and Ketelaar 1991	EPQ (PA, NA)	Guided imagery of pleasant (PMI), unpleasant (NMI) and neutral (NEUMI) events	For PMI, PA correlated positively with E and negatively with N (2E, −1N). For NMI, NA correlated positively with N and negatively with E (i.e., 2N, −1E)	NA supports SSH, PA supports JSH

Table 9.1 (*cont.*)

Study	RST measures (mood measures)	Mood induction procedure	Findings	Interpretation
Carver and White 1994	S4: E-Short (Happy)	False performance feedback for reward (PMI)	E not related to performance happy when initial happy was controlled	No support for any model
Helmers, Young and Pihl 1997	EPQ (positive, negative and neutral mood)	Speech on one's recent personal happy/proud event (PMI), personal faults (NMI) and reading/ imagining neutral statements (NEUMI)	No change in any emotion from baseline to MI conditions for high and low E, and high and low N	No support for any model
Rusting and Larsen 1997	EPQ (PANAS)	Reading/imagining pleasant/rewarding events (PMI) and unpleasant/ painful events (NMI)	E (but not N or N×E) positively predicted performance AP for PMI. For NMI, N (but not E or N×E) predicted performance AUP positively	Supports E and N predictions (not SSH or JSH)
Rusting 1999	Study 2; EPQ (PANAS)	Guided imagery of pleasant event/pleasant music (PMI) and guided imagery unpleasant events/ unpleasant music (NMI)	For PMI, E did not predict post-induction AP. For NMI, post-induction AUP was not predicted by N	No support for any model
Gomez, Cooper and Gomez 2000	EPI (PANAS)	Reward only (PMI) and punishment only (NMI) for go/no-go task performance	For PMI, E (but not N) predicted performance AP. For NMI, N (but not E) predicted performance AUP	Supports E and N predictions (not SSH or JSH)

Morrone *et al.* 2000	MPQ E Agency, affiliation (AP)	Films inducing motivation-positive activation	AP correlated positively with agency and affiliation, with the correlation for agency much stronger	Supports E prediction
Morrone-Strupinsky and Depue 2004	MPQ E Agency, affiliation (AP and warmth-affection)	Films to induce motivation-positive activation (as opposed to amusement and pleasantness) and films to induce warmth and affection	AP correlated positively with only agency, while warmth-affection correlated positively with only affiliation	Supports E prediction
Lucas and Baird 2004	IPIP E (AP, pleasant)	S1 – guided imagery of pleasant (PMI) and neutral (NEUMI) events. S2, S3, S4 – films of comedy (PMI) and gardening (NEUMI). S5 films of comedy (PMI), gardening (moderate PMI) and stock report (NEUMI). S6 – reading/rating jokes (PMI)	In S1, S5 and S6, high E more closely associated with AP for PMI. This not found in other studies or pleasant in any study	Supports E prediction
Induced mood studies based on BAS and BIS related traits and neurological and physiological responses				
Gray and Braver 2002	BIS/BAS (fMRI of brain activity)	Exposure to pleasant (PMI), unpleasant (NMI) and neutral (NEUMI) pictures	For brain activities in different regions, BAS associated with unpleasant over neutral pictures and BIS associated with pleasant over neutral pictures	Inconsistent with RST models

Table 9.1 (cont.)

Study	RST measures (mood measures)	Mood induction procedure	Findings	Interpretation
Canli et al. 2001	NEO-FFI (fMRI of brain activity)	Exposure to pleasant (PMI) and unpleasant (NMI) pictures	For brain activities in different regions, E associated with pleasant (over unpleasant) pictures. N associated with unpleasant (over pleasant) pictures	Supports E and N predictions
Canli, Amin and Haas 2004	NEO-FFI (fMRI of brain activity)	Stroop task involving pleasant (PMI), unpleasant (NMI) and neutral (NEUMI) words	For brain activities in different regions, E associated with pleasant (over neutral) words. Negative mood associated with unpleasant (over neutral words)	Supports E and N prediction
Amin, Constable and Canli 2004	NEO-FFI (fMRI of brain activity)	Dot-probe attentional task involving pleasant (PMI), unpleasant (NMI) and neutral (NEUMI) pictures	E associated with faster reaction time when probe placed behind neutral than negative. For brain activities in certain regions, E associated with probe located behind negative stimuli for negative/neutral pair	No support for any model
Reuter, Stark and Hennig 2004	BIS/BAS (fMRI of brain activity)	Exposure to fear and disgust (NMI), erotic (PMI) and neutral (NEUMI) pictures	Disgust and erotic associated with mainly BIS	Partial support for SSH

Induced mood studies based on BAS and BIS related traits and emotional processing, stress reactivity, rumination and satisfaction

Study	Measure	Task	Results	Conclusion
De Pascalis et al. 2005	SPSRQ mismatch negativity	Viewing emotionally negative (NMI), positive (PMI) and neutral (NEUMI) slides	Unpleasant slides associated more with +SP than −SP. Pleasant slides associated more with +SR than −SR	More supportive of JSH
Ravaja and Kallinen 2004	BIS/BAS facial electromyography (EMD) and respiratory sinus arrhythmia (RSA)	Music with and without startling effect during reading news reports. Startling effect more pleasure for high BAS	For startling condition: EMD and RSA associated positively with BAS	Support for RST
Roger and Revelle 1998	EPI (modified MSQ)	S3. Pleasant (PMI), unpleasant (NMI) and neutral (NEUMI) films	Personality and mood unrelated to emotional processing. E×N predicted pleasant and unpleasant processing. High E associated with more pleasant processing and high N associated with more unpleasant processing	E×N predicts pleasant and unpleasant EP
Rusting 1999	Study 2; EPQ (PANAS)	Guided imagery of pleasant event/pleasant music (PMI) and guided imagery unpleasant events/unpleasant music (NMI)	E predicted pleasant emotional processing. N and N×AUP predicted unpleasant processing	E, N predicts EP and N×AUP predicts unpleasant EP
Leen-Feldner et al. 2004	BIS/BAS (SAM)	Paced auditory serial addition task (NMI)	BIS correlated positively with stress reactivity and rumination	SSH predicts stress reactivity and rumination.

Table 9.1 (cont.)

Study	RST measures (mood measures)	Mood induction procedure	Findings	Interpretation
Updegraaff, Gable and Taylor 2004	BIS/BAS (AP/pleasant, AUP/unpleasant)	False performance feedback for impending punishment (NMI) and impending reward (PMI) and unpleasant (NMI) and pleasant (PMI) films	AP and BAS×AP predicted end of study satisfaction, with high AP increasing the association between BAS and satisfaction	BAS moderates impact of AP on satisfaction

AP = activated pleasant, AUP = activated unpleasant, BAS = Behavioural Activation System scale (Carver and White 1994), BIS = Behaviour Inhibition System scale (Carver and White 1994), BIS-11 = Barratt Impulsiveness Scale (Patton, Stanford and Barratt 1995), BIS/BAS = Behavioural Inhibition System/Behavioural Activation System scales (Carver and White 1994), E = extraversion, D = drive, EIS = Eysenck Impulsiveness Scale (Eysenck and Eysenck 1977), EP = emotional processing, EPI = Eysenck Personality Inventory (Eysenck and Eysenck 1964), EPQ = Eysenck Personality Questionnaire (Eysenck and Eysenck 1975), E-Short = Extraversion-Short Form (Eysenck *et al.* 1985), EYS = Eysenck's theory, fMRI = functional magnetic resonance imaging, FS = fun seeking, JSH = joint subsystems hypothesis, IPIP = International Personality Item Pool (Goldberg 1999); MAS = Manifest Anxiety Scale (Taylor 1953, as revised by Bendig 1956), MI = mood induction, MPQ = Multidimensional Personality Questionnaire (Tellegen and Waller, in press), MQS = Motivation State Questionnaire-revised (Revelle and Anderson 1994; has emotions of all octants of the affect circumplex), N = neuroticism, NA = negative affect, NEO-FFI = NEO Five Factor Inventory (Costa and McCrae 1992); NEUMI = neutral mood induction, NMI = negative mood induction, PA = positive affect, PANAS = Positive Affect and Negative Affect Schedule (Watson, Clark and Tellegen 1988), PMI = positive mood induction, RR = reward responsiveness, RST = Reinforcement Sensitivity Theory, S = Study, SAM = Self-Assessment Manikin (Lang 1980, which provides pictures of human faces reflecting different levels of valence and arousal), SP = sensitivity to punishment, SR = sensitivity to reward, SPSRQ = Sensitivity to Punishment and Sensitivity to Reward Questionnaire (SPSRQ; Torrubia *et al.* 2001), SSH = separable subsystems hypothesis, STAI = State-Trait Anxiety Inventory (Spielberger *et al.* 1983).

Cooper and Gomez 2000; Gross, Sutton and Ketelaar 1998; Larsen and Ketelaar 1989; Lucus and Baird 2004; Morrone, Depue, Scherer and White 2000; Morrone-Strupinsky and Depue 2004; Rusting and Larsen 1997). Although Lucas and Baird (2004) found an association between extraversion and AP mood state for positive mood induction, they also found that extraversion was positively associated with pleasant mood across positive, negative and neutral mood induction conditions, thereby also supporting the affect-level model – a finding also supported by Gross et al. (1998).

Given that virtually all existing studies show that both BAS trait measures and extraversion predict AP mood, and that both BIS trait measures and neuroticism predict AUP mood, it would appear that extraversion and the trait for the BAS, and neuroticism and the trait for the BIS are isomorphic, as proposed by others (Eysenck and Eysenck 1985; Larsen and Ketelaar 1991; Rusting and Larsen 1997; Tellegen 1985; Watson et al. 1999). In support of this argument, a recent confirmatory factor analysis study found that several BAS measures correlated with extraversion at levels comparable to those between them, and, similarly, that several BIS measures correlated with neuroticism at levels comparable to those between them (Gomez and Gomez 2005). If this argument is accepted, then the findings from the mood induction studies involving extraversion and neuroticism can be reinterpreted to be supportive of the SSH.

It is, however, possible that the relation of extraversion and neuroticism with mood states may involve lower order factors in these traits. Indeed, at least two studies have shown that the agency component (comparable to behaviours characterized by the BAS) rather than the affiliation component (reflecting social relations and activities) of extraversion correlated positively with AP mood (Morrone et al. 2000; Morrone-Strupinsky and Depue 2004; see Table 9.1). For neuroticism, it is conceivable that its anxiety and depression components are the critical components relating to AUP mood. Future studies may wish to examine this possibility, and also the differences in the predictions of AP from extraversion and BAS specific traits, and also of AUP from neuroticism and the BIS specific traits (Gomez and Francis 2003).

As shown in Table 9.1, with some exceptions (Amin, Constable and Canli 2004; Gray and Braver 2002), most of the data from the other functional magnetic resonance imaging studies have all supported the SSH. Although Reuter, Stark and Hennig (2004) found brain activity linking erotic stimuli (believed to be positive) with the BIS, they have proposed that erotic pictures may be salient to high BIS individuals, in that they may be embarrassed by their content. Table 9.1 shows that the

Ravaja and Kallinen (2004) study, which used psychophysiological measures of emotion responses, supported the SSH. De Pascalis, Arwari, Matteucci and Mazzocco (2005) examined the RST using the amplitude of the mismatch-negativity (MMN) components of the evoked response potentials, which are known to be significantly attenuated when low arousal pictures of positive valence are viewed as compared to pictures of negative or neutral valence (Surakka, Tenhunen-Eskelinen, Hietanen, Jari and Sams 1998). The results were consistent with the RST, in particular the JSH.

Overall, the results of past mood induction studies mostly provide support for the SSH. Past studies have supported the affect-level model, i.e., the BAS and the BIS are related to pleasant and unpleasant mood states, respectively, independent of the valence of the situations. Taken together, this means that individuals with high BAS and BIS traits generally experience higher levels of basal positive and negative affect, respectively. However the activations of basal levels of the BAS and BIS would generally induce AP and AUP, respectively, with each system acting independently. It may be worth pointing out that this finding parallels that reported in experience-sampling studies of reactions to everyday real-life events (Costa and McCrae 1980, 1992; Gable, Reis and Elliot 2000; Lucas and Fujita 2000; Suls, Green and Hillis 1998; Updegraff, Gable and Taylor 2004).

The conclusion made here supporting the SSH needs to be viewed with a number of points in mind. First, the correlations between the RST traits and mood reactivity have generally been modest (Lucas and Baird 2004). In this respect, it would be useful if future studies were to examine the direct, mediating and moderating effects of a range of factors in mood reactivity (Gross, Sutton and Ketelaar 1998). Secondly, as already noted, Carver (2004) found results inconsistent with the conclusions made here as he found anger, frustration and sadness (all negative emotions) to be positively associated with the BAS. It may be that while the BAS is generally related to pleasant affect and AP mood reactivity states, this does not necessarily imply that only positive emotions are linked to the BAS (Wacker, Heldmann and Stemmler 2003). If so, the RST may need to be revised to accommodate why and how certain negative emotions are linked to the BAS.

Another point that needs to be considered is that the findings in support for the SSH can be explained from a cognitive perspective. A number of studies have shown that under natural mood condition, the BIS traits and neuroticism are associated positively with unpleasant emotional information processing and attention, while the BAS traits and extraversion are associated positively with pleasant emotional information processing and attention (Amin, Constable and Canli 2004; Canli, Amin and Haas 2004; Derryberry and Reed 1994; Gomez and Gomez 2002; Gomez, Gomez and Cooper 2002; Gomez, Cooper, McOrmond and Tatlow 2004; Rogers and Revelle 1998; Rusting 1999, 2001; Rusting and Larsen 1998; Tamir, Robinson and Clore 2002). Given that some researchers believe that mood induction procedures interact with cognitive processes (e.g., Martin 1990; Teasdale and Fogarty 1979), these findings raise the possibility that biases in cognitive emotional processing may have either mediated the relationship between BAS and BIS relations with mood reactivity, and/or that mood reactivity is involved in a vicious cycle with biased attention and cognitions, such as that proposed in some cognitive models of the affective and mood disorders (Beck 1976; Beck, Emery and Greenberg 1985).

Cognitive processes involved in emotion and mood regulation may also be of relevance here. These are strategies aimed at attempts to eliminate, maintain or change mood or emotion states (Lischetzke and Eid 2006; Morris and Reilly 1987; Rusting and Nolen-Hoeksema 1998; Rusting and DeHart 2000). As there is evidence that mood regulation may be related to neuroticism and self-esteem, a construct closely related to extraversion (Bradley, Mogg, Galbraith and Perrett 1993; Smith and Petty 1995), it is possible that the BAS and the BIS may also be directly related to individual differences in mood regulation. To date, the relevance of the BAS and the BIS in mood regulation has not been explored. Such studies would be useful.

A further issue that is worthy of note is the possibility that past studies may be unsuitable for testing the JSH. According to Corr (2002b), the SSH is applicable when there are strong appetitive or aversive stimuli, or when either reward or punishment is present, and when hyperactive BIS and BAS individuals are tested. The JSH is applicable when there are weak appetitive or aversive stimuli, or when both reward and punishment cues are present together, or when normal-active BIS and BAS individuals are tested. In addition, Gomez et al. (2004) have suggested that the SSH is also likely to apply to stimuli that require substantive and deliberate processing of their emotional content, while the JSH would apply when this is not the case. For virtually all RST mood induction studies, the procedures involved either strong pleasant (rewarding) or strong unpleasant (punishing) stimuli that required substantive and deliberate processing. Thus, it can be argued that existing RST mood induction studies are only suitable for evaluating the SSH, and not the JSH. Clearly, carefully designed mood induction studies are needed to test more directly the applicability of the JSH in mood reactivity.

Implications of existing RST mood induction data for psychopathology

Some researchers have noted that negative mood induction procedures are capable of providing emotional states that are comparable to clinical disorders (Clark 1983; Goodwin and Williams 1982; Martin 1990). Indeed, as found in past negative mood induction studies (Leen-Feldner *et al.* 2004; Rogers and Revelle 1998; Rusting 1999, 2001), there are now ample data linking the affective and mood disorders to biases in attending to and processing unpleasant cues, more reactivity to stress and use of rumination to cope and regulate emotion (American Psychiatric Association 1994; Cox, Enns and Taylor 2001; Harmon-Jones and Allen 1997; Tamir, Robinson and Solberg 2006). Thus, given existing data, it can be argued that the BIS is relevant in understanding the biased emotion and cognitive responses that characterize several psychological disorders, especially those related to anxiety and depression.

A major theory of psychopathology that has linked psychopathology with emotion and cognition is that proposed by Beck (1976). In brief, Beck's model proposes that external events will induce 'automatic thoughts', which are immediate, unpremeditated interpretations of events. These thoughts are believed to be influenced by underlying beliefs, assumptions and schemas. They also induce the appropriate emotional and behavioural responses. The induced emotion will bias recall and perceptions of past events in mood-congruent ways. For example, a depressed mood will induce recall of past sad events (for a recent review of mood-congruent effect, see Rusting 1998). As such biases can elicit more of the same mood, they tend to perpetuate the mood state.

Given the conclusion here that past mood induction studies link the BIS to AUP, and that the BIS is linked to biases in cognitive processing of unpleasant emotional cues, it would appear logical that Beck's model can be extended to include an overreactive BIS. Figure 9.1 depicts an extension of Beck's (1976) model to include the BIS. We refer to this model as the RST cognitive model of psychopathology. The shaded boxes in this figure are components of Beck's original cognitive model of psychopathology. Based on past mood induction studies, in our RST cognitive model of psychopathology, intense negative events and stimuli are hypothesized to induce overreactivity of the BIS. The resulting reactivity of the BIS is hypothesized to activate trait congruent schemas (which includes one's beliefs and assumptions). This is conceivable as one's schemas (and self-concepts) are closely intertwined with one's

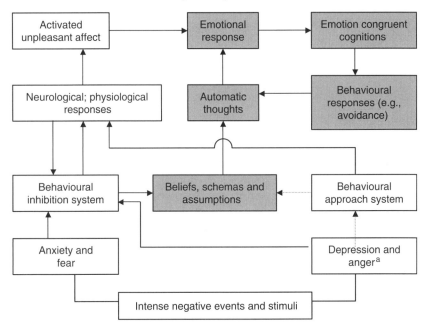

Figure 9.1 The RST cognitive model of psychopathology
Note: [a]Depression is related to decreased BAS activity and anger is related to increased BAS activity

personality (Robinson, Robinson and Syty 2002, as cited in Tamir, Robinson and Clore 2002), and as the BIS underlies one of the two dimensions (the other being the BAS) of personality. The over-activation of the BIS is also hypothesized to induce high AUP mood, with this relation being mediated by reactivity in specific sites of the brain and physiological responses (see chapters 8 and 10). The high AUP mood state also induces arousal and activation of specific emotional states, which, as proposed in Beck's model, is hypothesized to be induced by one's automatic thoughts, with their roots being in one's schemas. In terms of the network theory of affect (Bower 1981; see also Rusting 1998), it is probable that the energized emotional state induces activation of the relevant emotion nodes (i.e., network of cognitions associated with the emotion) that leads to emotion-congruent processing.

It will be noticed that our model is consistent with the SSH, which concurs with Corr's (2002b) argument that the SSH (and not the JSH) is applicable for individuals with hyperactive BIS and BAS. Also, our model linking high BIS reactivity to negative events and stimuli is consistent with some theories of anxiety and depression disorders (Gray 1994; Gomez and Francis 2003; Johnson, Turner and Iwata 2003; Meyer, Johnson and Winters 2001; see also chapters 11 and 12). However, as there is some support and theories linking some negative emotions and psychopathologies, such as those associated with depression and anger, to the BAS (underactive BAS for depression and overactive BAS for anger) rather than the BIS (Carver 2004; Depue, Krauss and Spoont 1987; Harmon-Jones and Sigelman 2001; Henriques, Glowacki and Davidson 1994; see also chapters 11 and 12) our RST cognitive model of psychopathology also includes a possible path involving the BAS (shown as dotted lines). Overall, the RST cognitive model of psychopathology proposed here broadens the scope of Beck's model of psychopathology by identifying the BIS (and possibly the BAS) as distal factor(s) associated with negative schemas, and contributing to negative emotional and behavioural responses associated with the mood and affective psychopathologies.

Limitations in mood induction studies and future studies

A number of limitations and omissions in existing data, and suggestions for future research were presented earlier. This section examines further limitations and provides additional suggestions for future research.

According to Morrone-Strupinsky and Depue (2004), most of the RST mood induction studies have used procedures that induce changes in general hedonic states of pleasantness or unpleasantness. Given that the BAS and BIS induce reactivity for AP and AUP mood states (rather than general pleasantness and unpleasantness), it is conceivable that mood induction procedures that induce AP and AUP mood states are needed for a better understanding of the impact of the BAS and BIS on mood responses. In this respect, Morrone-Strupinsky and Depue (2004) have provided guidelines and have developed films that specifically induce AP mood. These guidelines can also be adapted for the development of emotion specific mood induction procedures.

Another area overlooked in previous mood induction studies is that they have not considered the intensity of mood produced by the induction procedures. As the intensity of the emotional stimuli can be expected to impact on mood levels (Brenner 2000; Rusting 2001), it will be useful for future studies to also consider this variable in their studies, and examine how this variable interacts with the RST traits in the predictions of affect states. Morrone-Strupinsky and Depue (2004) have recently developed scales that allow measurement of PA and warm/affection mood states and their intensities. Also relevant here is the standardization of the emotional stimuli used for inducing mood and the mood response measures used so as to allow better comparability of the results across studies. The materials developed by Bradley and Lang (1999a, 1999b; Center for the Study of Emotion and Attention 1999) would be valuable for this purpose. Their emotion-inducing stimuli include photographs, digitized sounds and verbal stimuli, with each stimulus having norms for pleasantness, arousal and dominance. The pleasantness, arousal and dominance of each stimulus are assessed through the Self-Assessment Manikin (Lang 1980), in which each variable is measured on a continuum, depicted by appropriate graphic pictures of human faces.

Some problems with mood induction procedures in general have been identified (Brenner 2000; Martin 1990). Of particular importance is the demand characteristic effect, i.e., the cues in the mood induction procedure convey to participants expectations of particular mood (Gerrards-Hesse and Spies 1994; Larsen and Sinnett 1991; Westermann, Spies, Stahl and Hesse 1996). This effect is believed to be problematic when participants are asked to provide self-reports of their mood states. Given this, it is recommended that RST mood induction research studies evaluate this effect in their studies.

The demand characteristic effect can be avoided to a large degree by using psychophysiological measures of emotion (such as facial electromyography, heart rate, respiratory sinus arrhythmia, electrodermal activity, startle reflex, affective modulation of the mismatch-negativity components of cortical event-related potential) and brain-imaging techniques involving different blood flow patterns (such as positron emission tomography and functional magnetic resonance imaging) (see Table 9.1, and Bradley and Lang 2000; De Pascalis et al. 2005; Lane et al. 1997; see also chapters 8 and 10). Although psychophysiology and neuro-imaging techniques can be seen as invaluable in RST mood induction studies, these measures also have limitations. They are susceptible to the confounding effects produced by attention and cognitive biases arising from different reactivity levels of the BAS and BIS. In addition, they provide indications of only general valence, and not necessarily reactivity of the AP and AUP mood states or other specific emotions (Canli, Amin and Haas 2004; Ravaja 2004). Thus it will be useful if future studies also include self-reports of affect and emotions when psychophysiology and neuro-imaging techniques and measures are used (Bradley and Lang 2000).

Since mood induction procedures are believed to be capable of producing emotional states that are analogues to the corresponding clinical disorders (Fox, Knight and Zelinski 1998; Martin 1990), it would appear useful to conduct more mood induction studies to further understand the relevance of the BAS and BIS for a wide range of psychopathologies. Indeed, given the highly controlled environment of the laboratory setting, mood induction studies may allow examination of substantive clinical issues that may be difficult to examine in the actual disorders (Fox, Knight and Zelinski 1998). In this respect, it is notable that virtually all past RST mood induction relevant studies have examined university students or individuals without psychopathology. Future studies may wish to examine samples with specific clinical disorders, using emotion-specific induction procedures, as they will be critical for a comprehensive understanding of the relationships of the BAS, BIS and emotion states in psychopathology. Such studies would be worthwhile, given that there is now growing evidence that the BAS and BIS are relevant to a wide range of psychopathologies in both adults and children (Depue, Krauss and Spoont 1987; Gray 1994; Gomez 2003; Gomez and Francis 2003; Henriques, Glowacki and Davidson 1994; Johnson, Turner and Iwata 2003; Meyer, Johnson and Winters 2001; Newman et al. 1997; see also chapters 11 and 12).

Previous studies are also limited in terms of statistical treatment of the data. Although past studies have all assumed a linear relation between the RST traits and mood reactivity, it is conceivable that this relation may be more complex. Perhaps future studies can group participants into low, medium and high BAS and BIS groups, and not just high and low. Also, as past studies have used observed scores (that include error variance), the findings may have been confounded (Diener, Smith and Fujita 1995). Future studies may wish to use structural equation modelling procedures. For instance, the BAS and BIS latent traits can be modelled with various BAS and BIS measures, and the AP and AUP latent mood states can be modelled with their appropriate emotions. Following mood induction, the predictive relations of the BAS and BIS latent traits and the initial AP and AUP latent mood states with AP and AUP mood during or at the end of the mood induction can be examined using structural equation modelling methods.

Conclusion

Although there are some inconsistencies, existing mood induction studies are generally supportive of the SSH, i.e., BIS and BAS activities are associated with AP mood and AUP mood reactivity, respectively. Mood induction studies also appear to support the SSH in the prediction of emotional processing and responses, with induced negative mood by the BIS being associated with biases for processing unpleasant stimuli, more susceptibility to stress and use of coping strategies involving rumination. The findings involving negative mood induction were interpreted to suggest that the BIS is likely to be involved in affective and mood disorders. The findings involving positive mood induction can be interpreted to suggest that the BAS is likely to be involved in subjective well-being. It was, however, also noted that the support for the SSH has been modest, and that the lack of support for the JSH may actually reflect inadequacies of past studies to provide suitable tests of this hypothesis.

A number of limitations and omissions in existing data have been identified in this chapter, and numerous suggestions for future studies proposed. It is suggested that future studies examine (1) the relevance of the JSH in momentary mood; (2) the differences between extraversion and BAS traits, and neuroticism and BIS traits in predictions of affect states; (3) the role of lower order factors within these traits in affect reactivity; (4) the relevance of the BAS in certain negative mood states, such as anger; (5) the relation between the RST traits and cognitive factors in induced mood; (6) non-linear relations of the RST traits and mood states; (7) the relevance of the RST traits for specific emotional states, especially those corresponding to the affective and mood disorders; and (8) a wider cross-section of participants, including those with clinical disorders. It was pointed out that it will be useful for future studies to use a wide range of affect measures, test for demand characteristic effects, consider the intensity of the induced mood, and use structural models to analyse data. It was also proposed that research in this area could benefit from using standardized mood measurement and mood induction procedures. In concluding, it is hoped that this chapter has provided sufficient information for researchers to conduct the types of research studies that we perceive to be needed for extending further our understanding of the relevance of RST in mood reactivity and psychological disorders.

References

American Psychiatric Association (1994), *Diagnostic and Statistical Manual of Mental Disorders IV* (Washington, DC: APA)

Amin, Z., Constable, T.R. and Canli, T. (2004), Attentional bias for valenced stimuli as a function of personality in the dot–probe task, *Journal of Research in Personality*, 38, 15–23

Beck, A.T. (1976), *Cognitive Therapy and the Emotional Disorders* (Madison, CT: International Universities Press)

Beck, A.T., Emery, G. and Greenberg, R.C. (1985), *Anxiety Disorders and Phobias: A Cognitive Perspective* (New York: Guilford Press)

Bendig, A.W. (1956), The development of a short form of the manifest anxiety scale, *Journal of Consulting Psychology*, 20, 384

Bower, G.H. (1981), Mood and memory, *American Psychologist*, 36, 129–148

Bradley, B., Mogg, K., Galbraith, M. and Perrett, A. (1993), Negative recall bias and neuroticism: state vs trait effects, *Behaviour Research and Therapy*, 31, 125–127

Bradley, M.M. and Lang, P.J. (1999a), *Affective Norms for English Words (ANEW): Technical Manual and Affective Ratings* (Gainsville, FL: Center for Research in Psychophysiology, University of Florida)

(1999b), *International Affective Digitized Sounds: Technical Manual and Affective Ratings* (Gainsville, FL: Center for Research in Psychophysiology, University of Florida)

(2000), Measuring emotion: behaviour, feeling and physiology in R.D. Lane and L. Nadel (eds), *Cognitive Neuroscience of Emotion* (New York: Oxford University Press), pp. 242–276

Brenner, E. (2000), Mood induction in children: methodological issues and clinical implications, *Review of General Psychology*, 4, 264–283

Caccioppo, J.T., Gardner, W.L. and Berntson, G.G. (1999), The affect system has parallel and integrative processing components: form follows function, *Journal of Personality and Social Psychology*, 76, 839–855

Canli, T., Amin, Z. and Haas, B. (2004), A double dissociation between mood states and personality traits in the anterior cingulate, *Behavioral Neuroscience*, 118, 897–904

Canli, T., Zhao, Z., Desmond, J.E., Kang, E., Gross, J. and Gabrieli, J.D.E. (2001), An fMRI study of personality influences on brain reactivity to emotional stimuli, *Behavioral Neuroscience*, 115, 33–42

Carver, C.S. (2004), Negative affects deriving from the behavioral approach system, *Emotion*, 4, 3–22

Carver, C.S. and White, T.L. (1994), Behavioral inhibition, behavioral activation, and affective responses to impending reward and punishment: the BIS/BAS scales, *Journal of Personality and Social Psychology*, 67, 319–333

Center for the Study of Emotion and Attention (1999), *The International Affective Picture System* (Gainsville, FL: University of Florida)

Clark, D.M. (1983), On the induction of depressed mood in the laboratory: evaluation and comparison of the Velten and musical procedures, *Advances in Behaviour Research and Therapy*, 5, 27–49

Corr, P.J. (2001), Testing problems in J.A. Gray's personality theory: a commentary on Matthews and Gilliland (1999), *Personality and Individual Differences*, 30, 333–352

(2002a), J.A. Gray's reinforcement sensitivity theory and frustrative nonreward: a theoretical note on expectancies in reactions to rewarding stimuli, *Personality and Individual Differences*, 32, 1247–1253

(2002b), J.A. Gray's reinforcement sensitivity theory: tests of the joint subsystems hypothesis of anxiety and impulsivity, *Personality and Individual Differences*, 33, 511–532

(2004), Reinforcement sensitivity theory and personality, *Neuroscience and Biobehavioural Review*, 28, 317–333

Costa, P.T. and McCrae, R.R. (1980), Influence of extraversion and neuroticism on subjective well-being: happy and unhappy people, *Journal of Personality and Social Psychology*, 38, 668–678

(1992), *Revised NEO Personality Inventory (NEO PI–R) and NEO Five–Factor Inventory (NEO–FFI): Professional Manual* (Odessa, FL: Psychological Assessment Resources)

Cox, B.J., Enns, M.W. and Taylor, S. (2001), The effect of rumination as a mediator of elevated anxiety sensitivity in major depression, *Cognitive Therapy and Research*, 25, 525–535

De Pascalis, V., Arwari, B., Matteucci, M. and Mazzocco, A. (2005), Effects of emotional visual stimuli on auditory information processing: a test of J.A. Gray's reinforcement sensitivity theory, *Personality and Individual Differences*, 38, 163–176

Depue, R.A., Krauss, S.P. and Spoont, M.R. (1987), A two-dimensional threshold model of seasonal bipolar affective disorder in D. Magnusson and A. Ohman (eds.), *Psychopathology: An Interactional Perspective* (San Diego, CA: Academic Press Inc.), pp. 95–123

Derryberry, D. and Reed, M.A. (1994), Temperament and attention: orienting toward and away from positive and negative signals, *Journal of Personality and Social Psychology*, 66, 1128–1139

Diener, E., Smith, H. and Fujita, F. (1995), The personality structure of affect, *Journal of Personality and Social Psychology*, 69, 130–141

Diener, E., Suh, E.M., Lucas, R.E. and Smith, H.L. (1999), Subjective well-being: three decades of research, *Psychological Bulletin*, 125, 276–302

Eysenck, H.J. (1967), *The Biological Basis of Personality* (Springfield, IL: Charles C. Thomas)

Eysenck, H.J. and Eysenck, M.W. (1985), *Personality and Individual Differences: A Natural Science Approach* (New York: Plenum Press)

Eysenck, H.J. and Eysenck, S.B.G. (1964), *Manual of the Eysenck Personality Inventory* (London: University of London Press)

(1975), *Manual of the Eysenck Personality Questionnaire* (London: Hodder and Stoughton)

Eysenck, S.B.G. and Eysenck, H.J. (1977), The place of impulsiveness in a dimensional system of personality description, *British Journal of Social and Clinical Psychology*, 16, 57–68

Eysenck, S.B.G., Pearson, P.R., Easting, G. and Allsop, J.F. (1985), Age norms for impulsiveness, venturesomeness and empathy in adults, *Personality and Individual Differences*, 6, 613–619

Fox, L.S., Knight, B.G. and Zelinski, E.M. (1998), Mood induction with older adults: a tool for investigating effects of depressed mood, *Psychology and Aging*, 13, 519–523

Gable, S.L., Reis, H.T. and Elliot, A.J. (2000), Behavioural activation and inhibition in everyday life, *Journal of Personality and Social Psychology*, 78, 1135–1149

Gerrards-Hesse, A. and Spies, K. (1994), Experimental inductions of emotional states and their effectiveness: a review, *British Journal of Psychology*, 85, 55–79

Goldberg, L.R. (1999), A broad-bandwidth, public domain, personality inventory measuring the lower-level facets of several five–factor models in I. Mervielde, I. Deary, F. De Fruyt and F.Ostendorf (eds), *Personality Psychology in Europe* (Tilburg: Tilburg University Press), vol. 7, pp. 7–28

Gomez, R. (2003), Underlying processes in the poor response inhibition of children with attention-deficit/hyperactivity disorder, *Journal of Attention Disorders*, 6, 111–122

Gomez, R., Cooper, A. and Gomez, A. (2000), Susceptibility to positive and negative mood states: test of Eysenck's, Gray's and Newman's models, *Personality and Individual Differences*, 29, 351–365

Gomez, R., Cooper, A., McOrmond, R. and Tatlow, S. (2004), Gray's reinforcement sensitivity theory: comparing the separable and joint subsystems hypotheses in the predictions of pleasant and unpleasant emotional information processing, *Personality and Individual Differences*, 37, 289–305

Gomez, R. and Francis, L. (2003), Generalised anxiety disorder: relationships with Eysenck's, Gray's and Newman's theories, *Personality and Individual Differences*, 34, 3–17

Gomez, R. and Gomez, A. (2002), Personality traits of the behavioural approach and inhibition systems: associations with processing of emotional stimuli, *Personality and Individual Differences*, 32, 1299–1316

(2005), Convergent, discriminant and concurrent validities of measures of the behavioural approach and behavioural inhibition systems: exploratory and confirmatory factor analytic approaches, *Personality and Individual Differences*, 38, 87–102

Gomez, R., Gomez, A. and Cooper, A. (2002), Neuroticism and extraversion as predictors of negative and positive emotional information processing: comparing Eysenck's, Gray's and Newman's theories, *European Journal of Personality*, 16, 333–350

Gomez, R. and McLaren, S. (1997), The effects of reward and punishment on response disinhibition, moods, heart rate and skin conductance levels during instrumental learning, *Journal of Personality and Individual Differences*, 23, 305–316

Goodwin, A.M. and Williams, M.J. (1982), Mood–induction research: its implications for clinical depression, *Behaviour Research and Therapy*, 20, 373–382

Gray, J.A. (1970), The psychophysiological basis of intraversion–extraversion, *Behavior Research and Therapy*, 8, 249–266

(1990), Brain systems that mediate both emotion and cognition, *Cognition and Emotion*, 4, 269–288

(1994), Framework for a taxonomy of psychiatric disorder in S.H.M. Van Goozen, N.E. Van de Poll and J.A. Sergeant (eds), *Emotions: Essays on Emotion Theory* (New Jersey: Lawrence Erlbaum), pp. 29–59

Gray, J.A. and McNaughton, N. (2000), *The Neuropsychology of Anxiety* (2nd edn, Oxford: Oxford University Press)

Gray, J.R. and Braver, T.S. (2002), Personality predicts working–memory–related activation in the caudal anterior cingulate cortex, *Cognitive, Affective and Behavioral Neuroscience*, 2, 64–75

Gross, J.J., Sutton, S.K. and Ketelaar, T. (1998), Relations between affect and personality: support for the affect–level and affective reactivity views, *Personality and Social Psychology Bulletin*, 24, 279–288

Harmon-Jones, E. (2003), Anger and the behavioral approach system, *Personality and Individual Differences*, 35, 995–1005

Harmon-Jones, E. and Allen, J.J.B. (1997), Behavioral activation sensitivity and resting frontal EEG asymmetry: covariation of putative indicators related to risk for mood disorders, *Journal of Abnormal Psychology*, 106, 159–163

Harmon-Jones, E. and Sigelman, J. (2001), State anger and prefrontal brain activity: evidence that insult–related relative left–prefrontal activation is associated with experienced anger and aggression, *Journal of Personality and Social Psychology*, 80, 797–803

Helmers, K.F., Young, S.N. and Pihl, R.O. (1997), Extraversion and behavioral impulsivity, *Personality and Individual Differences*, 23, 441–452

Henriques, J.B., Glowacki, J.M. and Davidson, R.J. (1994), Reward fails to alter response bias in depression, *Journal of Abnormal Psychology*, 103, 460–466

Heponiemi, T., Keltikangas-Järvinen, L., Puttonen, S. and Ravaja, N. (2003), BIS/BAS sensitivity and self–rated affects during experimentally induced stress, *Personality and Individual Differences*, 34, 943–957

Johnson, S.L., Turner, J.R. and Iwata, N. (2003), BIS/BAS levels and psychiatric disorder: an epidemiological study, *Journal of Psychopathology and Behavioral Assessment*, 25, 25–36

Lane, R.D., Reiman, E.M., Bradley, M.M., Lang, P.J., Ahern, G.L., Davidson, R.J. and Schwartz, G.E. (1997), Neuroanatomical correlates of pleasant and unpleasant emotion, *Neuropsychologica*, 35, 1437–1444

Lang, P.J. (1980), Behavioural treatment and bio-behavioural assessment: computer applications in J.B. Sidowski, J.H. Johnson and T.A. Williams (eds), *Technology in Mental Health Care Delivery Systems* (Norwood, NJ: Ablex Publishing), pp. 119–137

Larsen, R.J. and Diener, E. (1992), Promises and problems with the circumplex model of emotion in M.S. Clark, *Emotion* (Thousand Oaks, CA: Sage Publications), pp. 25–59

Larsen, R.J. and Ketelaar, T. (1989), Extraversion, neuroticism, and susceptibility to positive and negative mood induction procedures, *Personality and Individual Differences*, 10, 1221–1228

(1991), Personality and susceptibility to positive and negative emotional states, *Journal of Personality and Social Psychology*, 61, 132–140

Larsen, R.J. and Sinnett, L.M. (1991), Meta-analysis of experimental manipulations: some factors affecting the Velten mood induction procedure, *Personality and Social Psychology Bulletin*, 17, 323–334

Leen-Feldner, E.W., Zvolensky, M.J., Feldner, M.T. and Lejuez, C.W. (2004), Behavioral inhibition: relation to negative emotion regulation and reactivity, *Personality and Individual Differences*, 36, 1235–1247

Lischetzke, T. and Eid, M. (2006), Why extraverts are happier than introverts: the role of mood regulation, *Journal of Personality*, 74, 1127–1161

Lucas, R.E. and Baird, B.M. (2004), Extraversion and emotional reactivity, *Journal of Personality and Social Psychology*, 86, 473–485

Lucas, R.E. and Fujita, F. (2000), Factors influencing the relation between extraversion and pleasant affect, *Journal of Personality and Social Psychology*, 79, 1039–1056

Martin, M. (1990), On the induction of mood, *Clinical Psychology Review*, 10, 669–697

Meyer, B., Johnson, S.L. and Winters, R. (2001), Responsiveness to threat and incentive in bipolar disorder: relations of the BIS/BAS scales with symptoms, *Journal of Psychopathology and Behavioral Assessment*, 23, 133–143

Morris, W.M. and Reilly, N.P. (1987), Toward the self regulation of mood: theory and research, *Motivation and Emotion*, 11, 215–249

Morrone-Strupinsky, J.V. and Depue, R.A. (2004), Differential relation of two distinct, film–induced positive emotional states to affiliative and agentic extraversion, *Personality and Individual Differences*, 36, 1109–1126

Morrone, J.V., Depue, R.A., Scherer, A.J. and White, T.L. (2000), Film–induced incentive motivation and positive activation in relation to agentic and affiliative components of extraversion, *Personality and Individual Differences*, 29, 199–216

Newman, J.P., Wallace, J.F., Schmitt, W.A. and Arnett, P.A. (1997), Behavioral inhibition system functioning in anxious, impulsive and psychopathic individuals, *Personality and Individual Differences*, 23, 583–592

Patton, J.H., Stanford, M.S. and Barratt, E.S. (1995), Factor structure of the Barratt impulsiveness scale, *Journal of Clinical Psychology*, 51, 768–775

Ravaja, N. (2004), Effects of a small talking facial image on autonomic activity: the moderating influence of dispositional BIS and BAS sensitivities and emotions, *Biological Psychology*, 65, 163–183

Ravaja, N. and Kallinen, K. (2004), Emotional effects of startling background music during reading news reports: the moderating influence of dispositional BIS and BAS sensitivities, *Scandinavian Journal of Psychology*, 45, 231–239

Reuter, M., Stark, R. and Hennig, J. (2004), Personality and emotion: test of Gray's personality theory by means of an fMRI study, *Behavioral Neuroscience*, 118, 462–469

Revelle, W. and Anderson, K.J. (1994), *Personality, Motivation and Cognition* (Paper presented at the Conference on Human Cognitive Abilities, University of Virginia, Charlottesville)

Rogers, G.M. and Revelle, W. (1998), Personality, mood, and the evaluation of affective and neutral word pairs, *Journal of Personality and Social Psychology*, 74, 1592–1605

Russell, J.A. (1980), A circumplex model of affect, *Journal of Personality and Social Psychology*, 39, 1161–1178

Rusting, C.L. (1998), Personality, mood and cognitive processing of emotional information: three conceptual frameworks, *Psychological Bulletin*, 124, 165–196

(1999), Interactive effects of personality and mood on emotion–congruent memory and judgment, *Journal of Personality and Social Psychology*, 77, 1073–1086

(2001), Personality as a moderator of affective influences on cognition in J.P. Forgas (ed.), *Handbook of Affect and Social Cognition* (New Jersey: Lawrence Erlbaum), pp. 371–391

Rusting, C.L. and DeHart, T. (2000), Retrieving positive memories to regulate negative mood: consequences for mood–congruent memory, *Journal of Personality and Social Psychology*, 78, 737–752

Rusting, C.L. and Larsen, R.J. (1997), Extraversion, neuroticism, and susceptibility to positive and negative affect: a test of two theoretical models, *Personality and Individual Differences*, 22, 607–612

(1998), Personality and cognitive processing of affective information, *Personality and Social Psychology Bulletin*, 24, 200–213

Rusting, C.L. and Nolen-Hoeksema, S. (1998), Regulating responses to anger: effects of rumination and distraction on angry mood, *Journal of Personality and Social Psychology*, 74, 790–803

Smith, S.M. and Petty, R.E. (1995), Personality moderators of mood congruency effects on cognition: the role of self-esteem and negative mood regulation, *Journal of Personality and Social Psychology*, 68, 1092–1107

Smits, D.J.M. and Kuppens, P. (2005), The relations between anger, coping with anger, and aggression, and the BIS/BAS system, *Personality and Individual Differences*, 39, 783–793

Spielberger, C.D., Gorsuch, R., Lushene, R., Vagg, P.R. and Jacobs, G.A. (1983), *Manual for the State–Trait Anxiety Inventory (Form Y)* (Palo Alto, CA: Consulting Psychologists Press)

Suls, J., Green, P. and Hillis, S. (1998), Emotional reactivity to everyday problems, affective inertia, and neuroticism, *Personality and Social Psychology Bulletin*, 24, 127–136

Surakka, V., Tenhunen-Eskelinen, M., Hietanen, J.K., Jari, K. and Sams, M. (1998), Modulation of human auditory information processing by emotional visual stimuli, *Cognitive Brain Research*, 7, 159–163

Tamir, M., Robinson, M.D. and Clore, G.L. (2002), The epistemic benefits of trait–consistent mood states: an analysis of extraversion and mood, *Journal of Personality and Social Psychology*, 83, 663–677

Tamir, M., Robinson, M.D. and Solberg, E.C. (2006), You may worry, but can you recognize threats when you see them? Neuroticism, threat identifications and negative affect, *Journal of Personality*, 74, 1481–1506

Teasdale, J.D. and Fogarty, S.J. (1979), Differential effects of induced mood on retrieval of pleasant and unpleasant events from episodic memory, *Journal of Abnormal Psychology*, 88, 248–257

Tellegen, A. (1985), Structures of mood and personality and their relevance to assessing anxiety with an emphasis on self–report in A.H. Tuma and J.D. Maser (eds), *Anxiety and the Anxiety Disorders* (Hillsdale, NJ: Erlbaum), pp. 681–706

Tellegen, A. and Waller, N.G. (in press), *Exploring Personality through Test Construction: Development of the Multidimensional Personality Questionnaire* (Minneapolis: University of Minnesota Press)

Torrubia, R., Ávila, C., Moltó, J. and Caseras, X. (2001), The sensitivity to punishment and sensitivity to reward questionnaire (SPSRQ) as a measure of Gray's anxiety and impulsivity dimensions, *Personality and Individual Differences*, 31, 837–862

Updegraaf, J.A., Gable, S.L. and Taylor, S.E. (2004), What makes experiences satisfying? The interaction of approach–avoidance motivations and emotions in well-being, *Journal of Personality and Social Psychology*, 86, 496–504

Wacker, J., Heldmann, M. and Stemmler, G. (2003), Separating emotion and motivational direction in fear and anger: effects on frontal asymmetry, *Emotion*, 3, 167–193

Watson, D., Clark, L.A. and Tellegen, A. (1988), Development and validation of brief measures of positive and negative affect: the PANAS scales, *Journal of Personality and Social Psychology*, 54, 1063–1070

Watson, D., Wiese, D., Vaidya, J. and Tellegen, A. (1999), The two general activation systems of affect: structural findings, evolutionary considerations, and psychobiological evidence, *Journal of Personality and Social Psychology*, 76, 820–838

Westermann, R., Spies, K., Stahl, G. and Hesse, F.W. (1996), Relative effectiveness and validity of mood induction procedures: a meta-analysis, *European Journal of Social Psychology*, 26, 557–581

Zelenski, J.M. and Larsen, R.J. (1999), Susceptibility to affect: a comparison of three personality taxonomies, *Journal of Personality*, 67, 761–791

10   Neuro-imaging and genetics

Martin Reuter

Jeffrey Gray's *Reinforcement Sensitivity Theory* (RST) (Gray 1970, 1982) is undoubtedly one of the most influential biological oriented personality theories available. Although the theory originated from animal research it could be extrapolated on humans and allows predictions on individual differences in behaviour. Moreover, RST can be applied to understand the mechanisms underlying the continuum between normal behaviour in healthy subjects and psychopathological syndromes like depression, anxiety, impulse control disorders and drug addiction.

In his initial 1982 theory Gray postulated that the three dimensions of his RST, the Behavioural Approach System (BAS), the Behavioural Inhibition System (BIS), and the Fight-Flight System (FFS) were mainly under the control of distinct neuroanatomical structures (Gray 1982). The BAS, which is activated by conditioned signals of reward or non-punishment, was assumed to be located in limbic brain structures and to be mainly under the control of the dopaminergic (DA) system. The neuroanatomical correlate of the BIS which is activated by conditioned signals of punishment should be the subiculum and septo-hippocampal structures. The FFS was hypothesized to be sensitive to unconditioned aversive stimuli (i.e., innately painful stimuli), mediating the emotions of rage and panic – this system was thought to be related to the state of negative affect (associated with pain). The neuroanatomical basis of the FFS systems are the basolateral and centromedial nuclei of the amygdala, the ventromedial nucleus of the hypothalamus, the central gray region of the midbrain, and the somatic and motor effector nuclei of the lower brain stem.

In 2000, Gray and McNaughton modified the 1982 theory (Gray and McNaughton 2000; see also McNaughton and Corr, chapter 2). However, the proposed adjustments and additions – the distinction between fear and anxiety, the refinement of the neural structures of the BIS and providing a specific account of the role of the hippocampus in human amnesia and the implications for psychopathology – do not contradict the major statements of the initial theory (for a review, see McNaughton and Corr 2004). Due to the fact that the number of genetic and imaging studies directly addressing RST is rare, this chapter will not concentrate on the differences between the 1982 and the 2000 theory but will outline future validation perspectives provided by these new technologies at the end of the chapter.

Until now, the RST could be confirmed by many studies from different fields of psychology including psychophysioloy, psychopharmacology and traditional experimental psychology (for a review, see Corr 2004). However, the fast moving field of biological psychology has brought up new fascinating techniques and methods allowing either a more direct approach, i.e., testing the neuroanatomical correlates of the RST dimensions, or a more fundamental approach, i.e., investigating the genetic underpinnings of RST. Therefore, the present chapter intends (a) to give a short introduction into the methods of neuro-imaging and molecular genetics, (b) to report the first results of those pioneer studies related to RST using neuro-imaging techniques and molecular genetic approaches, and (c) to give an outlook on future perspectives by using combinations of biological and experimental methods in gaining a deeper understanding of RST.

Molecular genetics and RST

Studies from behavioural genetics have demonstrated the high heritability (up to 60 per cent) of personality traits (e.g., Bouchard *et al.* 1990; Bouchard 1994; Lander and Schork 1994). By means of twin and adoption studies, researchers working in the field of behavioural genetics estimate the percentage of variance in a given phenotype (e.g., personality) that can be accounted for by genes. In twin study designs one method to estimate heritability is to compare correlation coefficients between mono- and dizygotic twins. Due to the fact that monozygotic twins share 100 per cent of the same genome, while dizygotic twins only have 50 per cent of the genetic material in common, a simple formula to estimate heritability of a given phenotype is twice the difference of the intra-pair correlation coefficients of mono- and dizygotic twins ($h^2 = 2$ ($r_{MZ} - r_{DZ}$)). Adoption studies compare the resemblance between adopted children and their biological parents/siblings with the resemblance between adopted children and their step-parents/step-siblings. The total variance in a given phenotype is then separated into genetic influences and influences of shared and non-shared environments, plus a measurement error representing a lack of reliability of the method by which the phenotype is assessed.

Once the heritability of a phenotype is demonstrated the hunt for candidate genes begins, because the mere fact that personality is highly heritable does not satisfy biological oriented researchers. The question to be answered is which genes underlie a personality trait. Since genes code for proteins involved in brain metabolism, the detection of an association between a gene and a personality trait would directly give information about the biochemical basis of this trait. Especially genes coding for enzymes, transporters or receptors of neurotransmitter systems are the focus of interest (for a review, see Reif and Lesch 2003) because several personality theories postulate a biochemical basis for their major traits (e.g., Cloninger 1987).

However, most of the studies from molecular genetics which are concerned with personality focus on single gene loci without considering gene interactions, although epistasis (i.e., gene-gene interactions) is thought to be important in behavioural phenotypes (Benjamin, Ebstein and Belmaker 2002). The limitation of association studies investigating the effect of a single gene on personality is primarily caused by economic reasons. The simultaneous investigation of many gene loci, especially if interactions of higher order are considered, causes high financial costs which are the consequence of the high demands on the sample size that is necessary to yield enough power for the statistical tests. However, the identification of single candidate genes for personality traits showing robust effects is the first step in the endeavour of identifying so called quantitative trait loci (QTLs) for personality. The term QTL refers to the fact that certain genes code for the expression of phenotypes which are normally distributed in the population. In contrast, monogenetically determined diseases like Huntington's Disease are not quantitative but categorical (ill/healthy).

Since RST makes clear assumptions on the biochemical substrates of its dimensions (e.g., the BAS should be related to the DA-system) Gray's theory is verifiable also by an approach from molecular genetics (see below).

Methods in molecular genetics: the polymerase chain reaction

The polymerase chain reaction (PCR) is a powerful tool which has revolutionized the field of molecular genetics. Kary Mullis invented this technique in 1983 which allows the amplification of a specific DNA sequence millions to billions of times in just one to two hours. In short, PCR is amplification without cloning. The PCR method mimics DNA replication occurring in a living cell. In the living cell DNA duplicates are gained by a series of enzyme-mediated reactions. First the DNA double helix has to be unwound into single strands. Then an RNA polymerase synthesizes a short stretch of RNA complementary to one of the DNA strands at the start site of replication. This DNA/RNA heteroduplex acts as a priming site for the coupling of the DNA polymerase which then synthesizes the complementary DNA strand.

During a PCR run the process of DNA replication consists of three different steps which are repeated between twenty-five and sixty times to get millions to billions of DNA copies of a specific DNA sequence. The three steps are hybridization, annealing and elongation and are conducted by different programs run by a PCR machine. The crucial difference between the three programs is the temperature they demand to obtain optimal results. During hybridization, DNA which had been extracted and purified from cells (blood cells, buccal cells or cells from tissue) by commercial test kits are heated up to 96°C for one to two minutes to unwind the DNA strands.

During the annealing phase the temperature is held between 50–65°C. This temperature is optimal to allow the primers to anneal to the DNA single strands. Primers are oligonucleotides of a length of fifteen to twenty base pairs which are complementary to the DNA strand. Two different primers are designed in a way that they mark the DNA sequence to be amplified. One of the most important aims of PCR is to detect polymorphic DNA regions and to genotype them.

Therefore the primers have to mark a DNA sequence which contains the polymorphic region between them. The primers left and right of the polymorphism are the starting points for DNA amplification which takes place in the next PCR step, the elongation. A polymerase which is added with additional nucleotides to the reaction tube starts elongation of the single DNA strands, beginning at the primers. Elongation only takes place in $5'$ to $3'$ direction at about 72°C. At the end of the three DNA phases of the first PCR cycle two double strands are synthesized. Now the second PCR cycle starts, beginning with hybridization, followed by annealing and ending with elongation, resulting in four double strands of DNA. The number of DNA copies of the target DNA sequence is 2^n with n specifying the number of PCR cycles. The principle of the PCR is illustrated in Figure 10.1.

As described above, the PCR is a method to amplify a specific DNA sequence. But what is it good for? The true aim is to have a technique allowing to genotype polymorphic gene loci because only polymorphic gene loci can account for individual differences in behaviour. However, PCR sets the stage for this because genotyping demands a strong signal

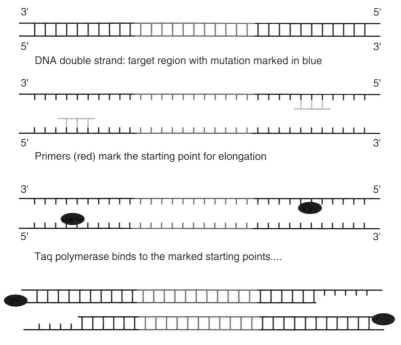

3'   5'

DNA double strand: target region with mutation marked in blue

3'   5'

5'   3'
Primers (red) mark the starting point for elongation

3'   5'

5'   3'
Taq polymerase binds to the marked starting points....

... and completes the DNA single strands

Figure 10.1 Principle of polymerase chain reaction (PCR)

which is given only after amplifying the polymorphic region billions of times. After the PCR product is gained, genotyping is done either by running a gel electrophoresis which makes different numbers of repeats in repeat polymorphisms visible or by sequencing the polymorphic region to make point mutations visible. Recently, newer PCR techniques have been invented which allow amplification and genotyping of point mutations in one single run. The so-called Real Time PCR marks the polymorphic regions by the use of so-called hybridization probes which are oligonucleotides containing fluorescence molecules. The fluorescence signal of the hybridization probes increases with the amount of replicated DNA and can be traced online on a computer screen. After amplification, point mutations can be detected by a melting-curve analysis. Hereby the temperature at which the hybridization probes are melted off the DNA strand is an indicator for the presence or absence of a mutation.

Evidence for the validity of Gray's RST from molecular genetics

During the last decade the number of publications reporting association studies between personality dimensions and certain gene polymorphisms is increasing. However, the majority of these papers deal more with personality disorders or psychopathological syndromes related to personality traits than with individual differences in character and temperament dimensions in healthy subjects. Moreover, we are confronted with the problem that most of the genetic association studies in healthy subjects only yield indirect evidence for the validity of Gray's theory because they use measures of personality which do not exactly match the RST dimensions. For example, association studies relating Extraversion (E) to a certain gene locus strictly speaking do not support a linkage with the BAS because Gray (1970) argues that the axes of E and Neuroticism (N) should be rotated by approximately 30° to form the more efficient BIS and BAS axes. According to Gray, the BAS represents Reward Sensitivity or Impulsivity (Imp) and is a combination of high E and high N (E+/N+) in Eysenck's terminology of personality, whereas the BIS represents Punishment Sensitivity or Anxiety (Anx) and is reflected by a combination of E−/N+ (a more detailed description of scales measuring the reinforcement sensitivity to reward and punishment is given by Torrubia, Ávila and Caseras in chapter 6).

Several studies have tried to relate the personality dimensions of Eysenck and Gray to positive affect (PA) and negative affect (NA). Eysenck himself proposed that E was related to PA and N to NA (Eysenck and Eysenck 1985), although his biological conceptualization of E and N was based on differences in arousal and made no assumptions on emotional reactivity. Gomez and colleagues (Gomez, Cooper and Gomez 2000) could indeed corroborate this hypothesis of relationships to PA and NA. With respect to RST, Larsen and Katellaar (1991) reported that NA was highest in E−/N+ (high Anx) and that PA was highest in E+/N− (low Anx) and not as expected according to RST in E+/N+ (high Imp) subjects. However, a common feature of all important personality theories is the concept of personality traits reflecting PA and NA. In order to become an impression of the conceptual proximity of these dimensions' reflecting PA and NA, data of the Giessen Gene Brain Behavior Project (GGBBP) on approximately 500 subjects are presented in Table 10.1, for whom besides genetic data an excessive personality assessment is available. In addition to the BAS of the Carver and White (1994) BIS/BAS scales, Novelty Seeking (NS) of the TCI (Cloninger 1987), Extraversion

Table 10.1 Intercorrelation matrix of traits measuring PA and NA: data taken from the Giessen Gene Brain Behavior Project (GGBBP)

		BAS	NS	EXT_NEO	EPQ_E	SEEK	PLAY	BIS	HA	NEU_NEO	EPQ_N	FEAR	SAD-NESS
BAS	r		.230**	.390**	.392**	.383**	.256**	.270**	-.269**	-.087	-.206*	-.119*	-.096
	p		.000	.000	.000	.000	.000	.000	.000	.117	.039	.034	.089
NS	r	.230**		.361**	.552**	.331**	.330**	-.061	-.379**	-.232**	-.315**	-.308**	-.133*
	p	.000		.000	.000	.000	.000	.270	.000	.000	.002	.000	.030
EXT_NEO	r	.390**	.361**		.699**	.409**	.707**	-.016	-.600**	-.459**	-.571**	-.436**	-.366**
	p	.000	.000		.000	.000	.000	.779	.000	.000	.000	.000	.000
EPQ_E	r	.392**	.552**	.699**		.424**	.633**	-.172	-.741**	-.610**	-.473**	-.596**	-.543**
	p	.000	.000	.000		.000	.000	.086	.000	.000	.000	.000	.000
SEEK	r	.383**	.331**	.409**	.424**		.354**	-.050	-.459**	-.337**	-.311**	-.232**	-.213**
	p	.000	.000	.000	.000		.000	.380	.000	.000	.000	.000	.000
PLAY	r	.256**	.330**	.707**	.633**	.354**		-.120*	-.498**	-.452**	-.604**	-.356**	-.286**
	p	.000	.000	.000	.000	.000		.032	.000	.000	.000	.000	.000
BIS	r	.270**	-.061	-.016	-.172	-.050	-.120*		.241**	.345**	.289**	.307**	.338**
	p	.000	.270	.779	.086	.380	.032		.000	.000	.003	.000	.000
HA	r	-.269**	-.379**	-.600	-.741**	-.459**	-.498**	-.241**		.785**	.698**	.777**	.629**
	p	.000	.000	.000	.000	.000	.000	.000		.000	.000	.000	.000

Table 10.1 (cont.)

		BAS	NS	EXT_NEO	EPQ_E	SEEK	PLAY	BIS	HA	NEU_NEO	EPQ_N	FEAR	SAD-NESS
NEU_NEO	R	-.087	-.232**	-.459**	-.610**	-.337**	-.452**	.345**	.785**		.799**	.829**	.781**
	p	.117	.000	.000	.000	.000	.000	.000	.000		.000	.000	.000
EPQ_N	r	-.206*	-.315**	-.571**	-.473**	-.31**	-.604**	.289**	.698**	.799**		.793**	.748**
	p	.039	.002	.000	.000	.004	.000	.003	.000	.000		.000	.000
FEAR	r	-.119*	-.308**	-.436**	-.596**	-.232**	-.356**	.307**	.777**	.829**	.793**		.701**
	p	.034	.000	.000	.000	.000	.000	.000	.000	.000	.000		.000
SADNESS	r	-.096	-.133	-.366**	-.543**	-.213**	-.286**	.338**	.629**	.781**	.748**	.701**	
	p	.089	.030	.000	.000	.000	.000	.000	.000	.000	.000	.000	

Note: * p < .05.
** p < .01.

of the NEO-FFI (Costa and McCrae 1989) and EPQ-R (Eysenck and Eysenck 1991) and SEEK of Panksepp's Affective Neroscience Personality Scales (ANPS) (Davis, Panksepp and Normansell 2003) were analysed as indicator scales for PA, and besides the BIS (Carver and White 1994), Harm Avoidance (HA) of the TCI, Neuroticism of the NEO-FFI and EPQ-R, and Sadness and Fear of the ANPS as indicators for NA were analysed. A principal component analysis (PCA) yielded two components with Eigenvalues > 1, reflecting PA and NA and explaining together 52.5 per cent of the total variance. Inspection of the correlation matrix presented in Table 10.1 reveals that BAS correlates significantly with the other scales representing PA and that the BIS correlates significantly with the other scales representing NA. However, all other PA and NA scales had higher intercorrelations with the scales of the respective component than BAS and BIS. Moreover, BAS and BIS were positively correlated with each other (.27) indicating that the two dimensions of the Carver and White scales were not orthogonal.

Despite the psychometric problems in measuring the RST dimensions, some of the contributions from molecular genetics that are of relevance for RST will be reviewed here.

Genetic association studies relevant to the BIS

In 1996, Lesch et al. detected an association between the short allele of the serotonin transporter gene (5-HTTLPR = 5-hydroxytryptamine-transporter-gene-linked polymorphic region) and neuroticism, a personality trait related to the BIS, anxiety, hostility and depression. The results could be replicated in independent samples (e.g., Greenberg et al. 2000) but there are also several studies with negative findings (e.g., Lang et al. 2004). The effect sizes of the studies with positive results show that the 5-HTTLPR polymorphism accounts for 3–4 per cent of the phenotypic variance. Based on previous studies indicating that a dysfunctional 5-HT system marks affective disorders and maladaptive behaviours like depression, aggression, and impulsivity (e.g., Asberg and Traskman 1981; Brown and Linnoila 1990) genes of the 5-HT system have been the most popular candidate genes to detect associations with traits related to NA. Of the fourteen 5-HT receptor sub-types known, in particular genes coding for the 5-HT1a, 5-HT1b, 5-HT2a, and 5-HT2c receptor have been successfully related to personality dimensions. Initially, studies on knockout mice have demonstrated the behavioural effects of the 5-HT receptor genes. For example, 5-HT1b knockout mice show increased aggressive but also increased exploratory behaviour (Ramboz et al. 1995; Malleret, Hen, Guillou, Segu and Buhot 1999) and mice with an inactivated 5-HT1a receptor show increased anxiety (Heisler *et al.* 1998). In humans, the 5-HT1a gene could also be demonstrated to be related to anxiety and depression related personality traits (Strobel *et al.* 2003). The 5-HT1b receptor was reported to be associated with suicide (New *et al.* 2001) and anti-social behaviour (Soyka, Preuss, Koller, Zill and Bondy 2004). An association between the 5-HT2a receptor gene and schizophrenia has been reported by several authors, a result which could not be replicated by others but a recent meta-analysis demonstrated an association of the C-allele of the T102C polymorphism of the 5-HT2a gene with schizophrenia (Abdolmaleky, Faraone, Glatt and Tsuang 2004). There is evidence that impulsive aggression in personality disorder correlates with platelet 5-HT2A receptor binding (Coccaro, Kavoussi, Sheline, Berman and Csernansky 1997). However, positive associations with personality traits are still rare. Ham *et al.* (2004) reported an association between the 5-HT2a A-1428G SNP and Spirituality, a temperament dimension of Cloninger's TCI, in a Korean population. Other authors did not find any associations between the TCI dimensions or the Karolinska Scales of Personality (KSP) inventory and several SNPs on the 5-HT2a gene (Kusumi *et al.* 2002; Jonsson *et al.* 2001). In knockout mice the 5-HT2c gene could be related to an increased vulnerability to seizures and overweight, supporting the role of 5-HT in the regulation of food intake and satiety. With respect to personality the reports are scarce. Schmidt *et al.* (Schmidt, Fox, Rubin, Hu and Hamer 2002) did not find an association between the 5-HT2c gene and aggression-related behaviours in pre-school children. In a study on subjects with a history of deliberate self-harm (DSH) Evans *et al.* (2000) reported that males with the serine variant of the 5-HT2c (cys-ser) polymorphism were more impulsive than those with the cysteine variant. Kuhn *et al.* (1999) could replicate the initial finding by Ebstein *et al.* (1997) reporting a significant interaction effect of the DRD4-exon-III and 5HT2c receptor polymorphisms on reward dependence, a temperament dimension of Cloninger's TCI. Besides receptor and transporter genes of the 5-HT system also genes coding for enzymes involved in the 5-HT metabolism are candidate genes for personality traits reflecting NA. One of these candidate genes refers to polymorphisms of the tryptophan hydroxylase (TPH) gene. THP1 is a rate limiting biosynthetic enzyme in the serotonin pathway and regulates levels of 5-HT by converting tryptophan into 5-hydroxytryptophan which is the direct precursor of 5-HT. Besides nicotine addiction (Sullivan *et al.* 2001; Lerman *et al.* 2001; Reuter and Hennig 2005a) the TPH1-gene located on chromosome 11p15.3-p14 has been found to be related to impulsive-aggressive personality traits (Rujescu *et al.* 2002;

Hennig *et al.* 2005; Reuter and Hennig 2005a) and behaviours including suicide which reflects an extreme type of auto-aggression (Nielsen *et al.* 1994; Mann *et al.* 1997; Abbar *et al.* 2001; Souery *et al.* 2001). Since the most prominent SNPs of the TPH1 gene which have been successfully related to behavioural phenotypes, the A779C and the A218C polymorphisms are located on an intron, it is assumed that these SNPs must be in linkage disequilibrium with another functional gene. Recently, Walther *et al.* (2003) have identified a second TPH isoform – referred to as TPH2 – in mice which is predominatly expressed in the brain stem, while the classical TPH gene – now called TPH1 – is expressed in the gut, pineal gland, spleen and thymus. The authors also identified a TPH2 homolog on chromosome 12 (GenBank: AY098914). Historical evidence for two TPH isoforms, predicted characteristics of TPH2 and clinical implications are discussed by Walther and Bader (2003). First polymorphisms on TPH2 are detected now which could be successfully related to affective disorders (Harvey *et al.* 2004; Zill *et al.* 2004). In two independent samples an association between the -703 G/T polymorphism located in the promoter region of the TPH2 gene and harm avoidance could be detected (Reuter, Küpper and Hennig 2007; Gutknecht *et al.* 2007).

Besides the anabolic enzyme TPH also the catabolic monoamine oxidase A (MAO-A) is an interesting candidate gene for personality traits. A long time before molecular genetic techniques had been available or had been used in personality research, results from biochemical studies have shown a negative correlation between the trait of Sensation Seeking (SS) and MAO-A levels (for a review, see Zuckerman 1993). However, an association between MAO-A and a trait does not answer the question which neurotransmitter is predominately involved because MAO-A metabolizes not only 5-HT but also catecholamines. Until now, associations between the MAO-A gene and personality in healthy humans are missing, but have been demonstrated in studies on alcoholism and personality. The X-chromosomal localized regulatory MAO-A gene promoter polymorphism can discriminate between antisocial and anxious-depressive alcoholics dependent on gender (Schmidt *et al.* 2000). In males the low-activity 3-repeat allele was significantly more prevalent in anti-social than in anxious-depressive alcoholics, whereas female anxious-depressive alcoholics showed a trend towards a low frequency of genotypes with the 3 repeat allele compared to female alcoholics without these symptoms. The usefulness of the MAO-A gene for discriminating sub-types of alcoholism was corroborated by others (Parsian, Cloninger, Sinha and Zhang 2003).

Genetic association studies relevant to the BAS

Studies which aimed to identify the molecular genetic basis of PA-related personality traits mainly focused on genes of the DA system. The concentration on DA-related genes resulted from the influential hypothesis of a final common pathway of reward postulating that the DA system mediates all positive emotions and reward related behaviours (for a critical review, see Spanagel and Weiss 1999). Therefore, DA-related genes are also candidate genes for addictive behaviours. As demonstrated for the 5-HT system and NA, also receptor-, transporter- and enzyme-polymorphisms – but this time of the DA system – are of interest for personality traits related to PA. Due to the fact that addictive behaviours and personality traits have often been shown to have the same candidate genes it is suggested that these genes have pleiotropic effects, i.e., these genes have more than one distinguishable effect in influencing two different phenotypes, addiction and personality (e.g., Reuter and Hennig 2005a). It still has to be clarified to which extent the influence of pleiotropic genes on addiction is mediated by personality. A strong mediator effect would support the existence of a drug prone personality.

The DRD2 gene is one of the most prominent candidate genes with respect to addiction that has also been linked to novelty seeking, persistence and extraversion (Noble 2000) in healthy subjects. Interestingly, in two independent samples we could demonstrate that the minor A1+ allele, which is characterized by a lower density of central D2 receptors (Pohjalainen *et al.* 1998), is also associated with lower neuroticism/anxiety in male but not in female subjects (Wacker, Reuter, Hennig and Stemmler 2005). These findings indicate that the A1+ allele of DRD2 is related to high PA and the absence of high NA, thus questioning the orthogonality of PA and NA.

Novelty Seeking (NS) is the trait which has attracted most attention with respect to a polymorphic 48-bp repeat in exon 3 of the DRD4 gene. The 7-repeat allele was related to higher NS scores in many studies although also negative results have been reported (for a review, see Reif and Lesch 2003). However, in Scandinavian samples the presence of the 2- or 5-repeat seems to be a marker for high NS indicating ethnic differences (for a review, see Elovainio *et al.* 2005). With respect to the DRD4 polymorphism also positive associations with alcoholism and attention deficit hyperactive disorder (ADHD) have been reported, indicating a risk factor in carriers of the 7-repeat allele (for a review, see DiMaio, Grizenko and Joober 2003; Vandenbergh *et al.* 2000).

Only two papers published so far related gene markers to the BIS/BAS scales. In a large population study the interaction of the DRD3 and the catechol-O-methyltransferase (COMT) gene with stressful life events and personality was investigated. While there was a positive association between the DRD3 gene and the BIS and EPQ-N in subjects who experienced a critical life event, this effect was not present in the total sample, indicating a gene-environment interaction (Henderson *et al.* 2000). With respect to the BAS, there was a weak association between the DRD3 gene and the BAS sub-scale DRIVE but again only in the sub-sample of subjects with a stressful life event. In one of our own studies we investigated the BIS/BAS scales with respect to two DA gene loci, the DRD2- and the COMT gene (Reuter *et al.* 2006). Results revealed no main effect but an epistasis effect DRD2 x VAL-allele of COMT. This interaction suggests that more than one genetic indicator of the DA system is necessary to account for DA activity related to the BAS. In a sub-sample of forty-eight subjects, we could demonstrate that those patterns of alleles of DRD2 and COMT which were associated with the BAS (A1+/VAL+ or A1−/VAL−) are characterized by low prolactin (PRL) levels (Reuter *et al.* 2006). Low PRL levels are a marker for high DA activity because DA is the inhibiting factor of PRL. These results indicate that the BAS is marked by high DA levels.

The COMT polymorphism has been the focus of interest in numerous genetic association studies investigating associations with psychopathology, personality and behaviour because the COMT VAL158MET SNP results in a severe variation in enzyme activity. The MET/MET genotype shows a fourfold reduction in COMT enzyme activity in comparison to the VAL/VAL genotype with intermediate enzyme activity in the heterozygous VAL/MET genotype (Lachman *et al.* 1996). As outlined for the MAO gene, the effects of the COMT gene are difficult to interpret, because COMT degrades all catecholamines and not only DA. In a female Chinese sample, COMT was related to NS and RD (Tsai, Hong, Yu and Chen 2004). Moreover, there is plenty of evidence that the COMT gene is a genetic marker of aggressive behaviours. The homozygous genotypes of COMT seem to differentiate between outwardly (MET/MET) and inwardly directed anger (VAL/VAL) (Rujescu, Giegling, Gietl, Hartmann and Moller 2003). In one of our own studies we could demonstrate an association between the VAL/VAL genotype of COMT and the CARE-scale of the ANPS (Netter, Reuter and Hennig 2005). The CARE dimension is psychometrically and neurobiologically almost identical with Depue's concept of affiliation (Depue and Collins 1999; Depue and Morrone-Strupinsky 2005) because it also refers to social closeness, nurturance and affiliative bonding and explains CARE behaviour to be associated with dopamine besides estrogen, prolactin, oxytocin, vasopressin and opioids. Recently, we found an association between the VAL/VAL genotype of the COMT VAL158MET polymorphism and the personality traits extraversion (as measured by the NEO-FFI) and the novelty seeking sub-scale exploratory excitability (Reuter and Hennig 2005b). Given the fact that the interaction of DRD2 and COMT predicts the BAS and COMT alone predicts extraversion and NS1, we can conclude that different facets of PA are related to different marker genes of the DA system.

Neuro-imaging and RST

Besides molecular genetics, neuro-imaging techniques have revolutionized the advances in biological-oriented personality research, because they allow monitoring brain activity in distinct cortical and subcortical brain circuits while behavioural tasks are executed, or they provide information on receptor occupancy and receptor density. Biological-oriented personality theories, like RST, define specific assumptions on the neuronal basis of personality. Especially the revised RST (Gray and McNaughton 2000) postulates different brain regions to be involved in fear and anxiety or in states that are dependent on the nature of threat, defensive avoidance or defensive approach behaviour is elicited accompanied by different activity patterns in distinct brain regions.

While in animal studies lesion techniques can be used, experiments in humans require non-invasive methods. Therefore, neuro-imaging techniques are the method of choice to investigate the neuroanatomical underpinnings of behaviour.

Methods in neuro-imaging studies: fMRI and PET

Although many more imaging techniques are available, the present review will focus on the two techniques that have been used in personality research until now, functional Magnetic Resonance Imaging (fMRI) and Positron Emission Tomography (PET).

fMRI is a technique that measures changes in blood circulation in different brain regions, that are caused by the energy demand of active nerve cells. The basis of fMRI is the blood-oxygen level dependent (BOLD) effect which uses differences in the magnetic characteristics of oxygenated and desoxygenated blood for signal detection, or in other words the difference between oxyhaemoglobin and desoxyhaemoglobin. Oxyhaemoglobin is diamagnetic and has no influence on the magnetic properties of the surrounding tissue, while desoxyhaemoglobin is paramagnetic and leads to measurable changes in the magnetic field. By means of fMRI nerve cell activity can be localized with a precision of less than a millimetre within a timeframe of a few seconds. Therefore, fMRI gives insights into the topography of cognitive and emotional processes under experimental conditions.

PET is a technique that uses radioactive labelled tracers to quantify regional blood circulation or receptor density in neuropsychobiological research. The PET signal is obtained by measuring the energy emission occurring during the decay of positrons. Positrons are positively loaded elementary particles stemming from the atomic nucleus of isotopes. If a radioactive isotope with a short half-life period accumulates in specific brain regions or is binding to certain receptors as a ligand then it is possible to relate physiological and biochemical processes to brain metabolism.

Evidence for the validity of Gray's RST from neuro-imaging studies

The situation for neuro-imaging studies and RST is the same as for molecular genetic studies and RST. There are only very few studies directly addressing RST. Therefore, imaging studies will be reviewed which are of relevance for RST.

fMRI studies

The most common strategy to 'map personality onto the brain' is to use emotional pictures as stimulus material to investigate the moderating influence of personality on brain reactivity to emotional stimuli by fMRI. In their influential pioneer work, Canli *et al.* (2001) reported that in a sample of healthy women, extraversion was correlated with brain reactivity to positive stimuli whereas neuroticism was correlated with brain reactivity to negative stimuli. Canli *et al.* identified brain regions which showed distinct significant correlations either with extraversion or with neuroticism: higher brain activity in response to positive relative to negative stimuli were significantly correlated with extraversion in the temporal lobe of the right hemisphere, with activation of the cingulate, the caudate nucleus and the amygdala and higher brain activation in response to negative relative to positive stimuli were significantly correlated with neuroticism in the temporal lobe of the left hemisphere. Moreover, results showed that activation in the frontal cortex, in the left middle gyrus, was significantly correlated with extraversion as well as with neuroticism, but that extraversion correlated with the response to positive pictures and neuroticism with the response to negative pictures in this brain area.

In a further fMRI study, Canli and colleagues (Canli, Sivers, Whitfield, Gotlib and Gabrieli 2002) reported a positive correlation between extraversion scores and the reactivity to happy facial expressions. This finding corroborates the high reactivity of extraverts towards positive stimuli. Since this study specifically focused on amygdala activation to emotional stimuli, it could not be excluded that the amygdala activation was caused by modulatory influences from other brain regions. The missing link was provided by three further fMRI studies. The first one used a matching task where participants had to select a matching face stimulus or word label from alternative choices (Hariri, Bookheimer and Mazziotta 2000). The face pictures portrayed different emotional expressions. Results showed significant amygdala activation in response to angry and fearful faces, but was reduced when subjects were engaged in the linguistic matching task. The decrease in amygdala activation was correlated with an increase in activation in the right prefrontal cortex indicating that higher cortical areas can inhibit amygdala reactivity to stimuli that would otherwise increase it. Hariri and colleagues (Hariri, Mattay, Tessitore, Fera and Weinberger 2003) could replicate these results in a paradigm presenting pictures of the International Affective Picture System (IAPS) (Lang, Bradley and Cuthbert 1995).

In line with these findings Ochsner and colleagues (Ochsner, Bunge, Gross and Gabrieli 2002) reported that the reappraisal of negative images was associated with increased activation in prefrontal regions and decreased activity in the amygdala indicating that the processing of negative emotions in the amygdala is modulated by cortical areas. In one of our own fMRI studies we directly tested RST by investigating differences in brain haemodynamic responses after exposure to positive, disgustive, fearful and neutral pictures of the IAPS dependent on scores on the Carver and White BIS/BAS scales (Reuter et al. 2004). It turned out that BIS was associated with the activity in numerous brain areas in response to fear (anterior cingulate, thalamus, posterior cingulate), disgust (anterior cingulate, amygdala, thalamus) and erotic visual stimuli (anterior cingulate, thalamus, amygdala, insula, basal ganglia, brain stem, posterior cingulate), whereas few associations could be detected between the BAS and brain activity in response to disgust, fear and erotic stimuli. It was striking that the anterior and posterior cingulate and the thalamus were involved in the processing of all three emotional categories suggesting some common aspects (see Figure 10.2). This is in line with previous findings: for the caudal anterior cingulate cortex (ACC) it has been reported that it is involved in the processing of stimuli which induce emotional recall or imagery independent of their content (Teasdale et al. 1999). Surprisingly, there was a significant positive

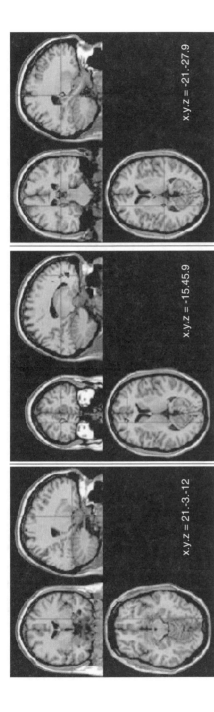

Figure 10.2 Results (selected examples) of the ROI analyses and scatter plots of correlations between BIS scores and brain activity in response to emotional stimuli. Triangles represent male subjects and circles represent female subjects left panel: amygdala (R), disgust greater neutral middle panel: anterior cingulate (L), disgust greater neutral lower panel: thalamus (L), disgust greater neutral middle panel: anterior cingulate (L), disgust greater neutral lower panel: thalamus (L), disgust greater neutral

x.y.z = 21.-3.-12   x.y.z = -15.45.9   x.y.z = -21.-27.9

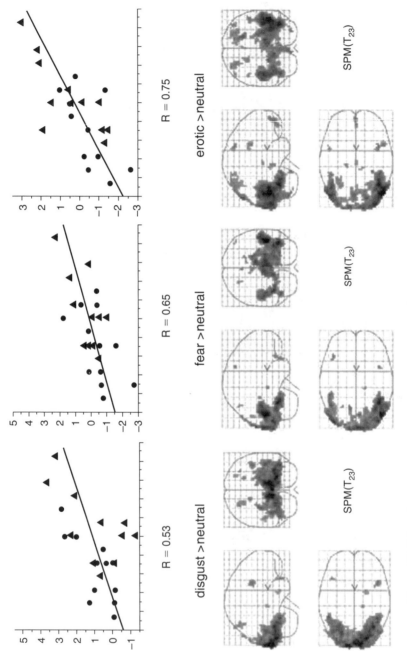

Figure 10.2 (cont.)

correlation between the BAS and brain activity during viewing erotic pictures in the hippocampus/parahippocampus area, a region that according to RST should be related to the BIS.

More and more well-established experimental paradigms are integrated in fMRI studies to detect the neuroanatomical correlates of personality. Horn and colleagues used a go/no-go task to relate brain activity to impulsivity (Horn, Dolan, Elliott, Deakin and Woodruff 2003). Results showed a strong association between posterior orbital activation and impulsivity. Furthermore, subjects scoring higher on impulsivity scales made more errors and had greater activation of paralimbic areas during response inhibition, while less impulsive individuals and those producing least errors activated higher order association areas.

In another fMRI study, the emotional Stroop test was used to detect individual differences in brain activity during emotional processing (Canli 2004). Activation to positive relative to negative stimuli in the anterior cingulate was positively correlated with extraversion. Gray and Braver (2002) tested whether Gray's BIS/BAS dimensions assessed by the Carver and White scales could predict differences in working memory-related activation in the caudal ACC after pre-exposure to emotional films of positive or negative valence. The ACC was considered as a region of interest (ROI) in this study because the caudal and posterior-rostral ACC had been reported to be involved in cognitive functioning and the rostral and subgenual ACC in affective processing. Results revealed individual differences in brain activity during the working memory (WM) task. Subjects scoring high on the BAS scale had significantly lower and subjects scoring high on the BIS scale significantly higher brain activity as compared to subjects with low BAS or low BIS scores respectively and this irrespective of the valence of the emotional pre-exposure. Moreover, for the caudal ACC, personality scores explained variance in the task-related activity that was not explained by activity in the neutral condition. Interestingly, this effect was only observable for BAS in the unpleasant condition and for BIS in the pleasant condition, a finding that was not in line with Gray's theory.

PET studies

As mentioned above, PET is an imaging technique which can give insights into the biochemical make up of neurotransmitter systems, e.g., by quantifying receptor density and binding affinity. For example, PET studies yielded evidence for a 30–40 per cent lower receptor density in carriers of the A1+ allele as compared to carriers of the A1− allele of the

DRD2 TAQ IA polymorphism (Thompson *et al.* 1997). In 1997 Farde and colleagues reported a negative correlation between the personality traits of detachment and irritability with D2 receptor density (Farde, Gustavsson and Jonsson 1997). Recent PET studies with dopaminergic tracers have demonstrated strong and specific negative relationships between D2 receptor density, striatal DA synthesis capacity and Neuroticism-Anxiety but not for other personality dimensions (Laakso *et al.* 2003; Kestler, Malhotra, Finch, Adler and Breier 2000).

In line with these findings Yasuno *et al.* (2001) found a relation among dopamine D2 receptor binding in the amygdala and the personality trait of Harm Avoidance in normal human subjects. In sum, there is considerable evidence that low D2 receptor density is related to NA.

Combination studies of molecular genetics and neuro-imaging

Although studies from behavioural genetics have demonstrated the high heritability of personality traits (e.g., Bouchard *et al.* 1990; Bouchard 1994; Lander and Schork 1994) the effect of a single gene on personality is estimated to be very modest. Therefore, the best strategy according to current opinions is to relate specific genes to endophenotypes of personality (Hamer 2002; Strobel *et al.* 2004). This approach was used by Hariri *et al.* (2002) who investigated if the amygdala response to fear-inducing stimuli is associated with the 5-HT-transporter gene, a gene that has been shown to be related to neuroticsm and anxiety-related traits (e.g., Lesch *et al.* 1996; see above). Indeed carriers of the short-allele had greater fMRI amygdala activation in response to fear-related stimuli. In a follow up study, Hariri *et al.* (2003) could replicate their findings and showed that this amygdala response in subjects with at least one copy of the s-form of 5-HTTLPR is associated with fearful temperament.

Future perspectives

The low number of studies combining imaging studies with molecular genetic approaches indicates that this is a new but nonetheless promising field of research. Only the combination of different psychobiological methods can help to understand the neurobiological basis of RST. It will be the aim of the future to explain the long way from genes to behaviour. Promising techniques like fMRI, PET and PCR are available now, but the problem to define RST dimensions properly is still unsolved. It may be asked if it is adequate to question results from biological-oriented studies if the criterion – a questionnaire measure – is not met. For example, most studies from molecular genetics define candidate genes for a personality trait by their capacity to be significantly associated with a questionnaire measure of which the reliability and especially validity is sometimes far from convincing. Therefore, endo-phenotypes of personality like behaviours in experimental paradigms (e.g., Stroop tasks, reactivity to emotional stimuli, startle responses or behaviours related to punishment or reward, etc.) observed by simul-taneous monitoring of brain activity in genotyped subjects will be a more straightforward approach. With respect to the exploration of the biochemical basis of personality, a combination of genotyping, phar-macological challenge-test, behavioural paradigms and brain-imaging techniques can be considered as the *via regia*. Especially the selection of subjects according to genotypes prior to testing is an efficient approach to avoid lack of power in statistical testing caused by low cell frequencies due to rare genotype or allele configurations (Reuter *et al.* 2005). Moreover, the hypothesis of a common dimension underlying person-ality as well as psychopathology is testable by the new techniques. For example, a common candidate gene for aggressive normal subjects and patients with psychopathological aggression supports this hypothesis (Rujescu *et al.* 2002).

Conclusion

In sum, molecular genetics and brain-imaging studies are highly promising tools to investigate the neurobiological basis of RST. None-theless, it is still a difficult endeavour, for the new techniques have their own problems (high costs, stratification problems, complexity of epistatsis effects, defining the functionality of certain genes or low sample sizes, correction biases, relating blood oxygenation in vessels to neighbouring tissue, etc.).

References

Abbar, M., Courtet, P., Bellivier, F., Leboyer, M., Boulenger, J. P., Castelhau, D., Ferreira, M., Lambercy, C., Mouthon, D., Paoloni-Giacobino, A., Vessaz, M., Malafosse, A. and Buresi, C. (2001), Suicide attempts and the tryptophan hydroxylase gene, *Molecular Psychiatry*, 6, 268–73

Abdolmaleky, H. M., Faraone, S. V., Glatt, S. J. and Tsuang, M. T. (2004), Meta-analysis of association between the T102C polymorphism of the 5HT2a receptor gene and schizophrenia, *Schizophrenia Research*, 67, 53–62

Asberg, M. and Traskman, L. (1981), Studies of CSF 5-HIAA in depression and suicidal behaviour, *Advances in Experimental Medicine and Biology*, 133, 739–752

Benjamin, J., Ebstein, R. P. and Belmaker, R. H. (2002), Genes for human personality traits in J. Benjamin, R. P. Ebstein and R. H. Belmaker (eds), *Molecular Genetics and the Human Personality* (Washington DC: American Psychiatric Publishing), pp. 355–380

Bouchard, T. J. Jr (1994), Genes, environment, and personality, *Science*, 264, 1700–1701

Bouchard, T. J. Jr, Lykken, D. T., McGue, M., Segal, N. L. and Tellegen, A. (1990), Sources of human psychological differences: the Minnesota study of twins reared apart, *Science*, 250, 223–228

Brown, G. L. and Linnoila, M. I. (1990), CSF serotonin metabolite (5-HIAA) studies in depression, impulsivity, and violence, *Journal of Clinical Psychiatry*, 51 Suppl, 31–41

Canli, T. (2004), Functional brain mapping of extraversion and neuroticism: learning from individual differences in emotion processing, *Journal of Personality*, 72, 1105–1132

Canli, T., Sivers, H., Whitfield, S. L., Gotlib, I. H. and Gabrieli, J. D. (2002), Amygdala response to happy faces as a function of extraversion, *Science*, 296, 2191

Canli, T., Zhao, Z., Desmond, J. E., Kang, E., Gross, J. and Gabrieli, J. D. E. (2001), An fMRI study of personality influences on brain reactivity to emotional stimuli, *Behavioral Neuroscience*, 115, 33–42

Carver, C. S. and White, T. L. (1994), Behavioral inhibition, behavioral activation, and affective responses to impending reward and punishment: the BIS/BAS Scales, *Journal of Personality and Social Psychology*, 67, 319–333

Cloninger, C. R. (1987), A systematic method for clinical description and classification of personality variants: a proposal, *Archives of General Psychiatry*, 44, 573–588

Coccaro, E. F., Kavoussi, R. J., Sheline, Y. I., Berman, M. E. and Csernansky, J. G. (1997), Impulsive aggression in personality disorder correlates with platelet 5-HT2A receptor binding, *Neuropsychopharmacology*, 16, 211–216

Corr, P. J. (2004), Reinforcement sensitivity theory and personality, *Neuroscience and Biobehavioral Reviews*, 28, 317–332

Costa, P. T. and McCrae, R. R. (1989), *The NEO PI/FFI Manual Supplement* (Odessa, FL: Psychological Assessment Resources)

Davis, K. L., Panksepp, J. and Normansell, L. (2003), The affective neuroscience personality scales: normative data and implications, *Neuro-Psychoanalysis*, 5, 57–69

Depue, R. A. and Collins, P. F. (1999), Neurobiology of the structure of personality: dopamine, facilitation of incentive motivation, and extraversion, *Behavioral and Brain Sciences*, 22, 491–569

Depue, R. A. and Morrone-Strupinsky, J. V. (2005), A neurobehavioral model of affiliative bonding: implications for conceptualizing a human trait of affiliation, *Behavioral and Brain Sciences*, 28, 313–350

DiMaio, S., Grizenko, N. and Joober, R. (2003), Dopamine genes and attention-deficit hyperactivity disorder: a review, *Journal of Psychiatry and Neuroscience*, 28, 27–38

Ebstein, R. P., Segman, R., Benjamin, J., Osher, Y., Nemanov, L. and Belmaker, R. H. (1997), 5-HT2C (HTR2C) serotonin receptor gene polymorphism associated with the human personality trait of reward dependence: interaction with dopamine D4 receptor (D4DR) and dopamine D3 receptor (D3DR) polymorphisms, *American Journal of Medical Genetics*, 74, 65–72

Elovainio, M., Puttonen, S., Heponiemi, T., Reuter, M., Kivimaki, M., Viikari, J. and Keltikangas-Järvinen, L. (2005), Relationship between DRD4 polymorphism and lipid metabolism: what is the role of novelty seeking?, *Neuropsychobiology*, 51, 53–58

Evans, J., Reeves, B., Platt, H., Leibenau, A., Goldman, D., Jefferson, K. *et al.* (2000), Impulsiveness, serotonin genes and repetition of deliberate self-harm (DSH), *Psychological Medicine*, 30, 1327–1334

Eysenck, H. J. and Eysenck, M. W. (1985), *Personal and Individual Differences: a Natural Science Approach* (New York: Plenum Press)

Eysenck, H. J. and Eysenck, S. B. G. (1991), *Manual of the Eysenck Personality Scales* (London: Hodder & Stoughton)

Farde, L., Gustavsson, J. P. and Jonsson, E. (1997), D2 dopamine receptors and personality traits, *Nature*, 385, 590

Gomez, R., Cooper, A. and Gomez, A. (2000), Susceptibility to positive and negative mood states: test of Eysenck's, Gray's and Newman's theories, *Personality and Individual Differences*, 29, 351–365

Gray, J. A. (1970), The psychophysiological basis of introversion-extraversion, *Behaviour Research and Therapy*, 8, 249–266
(1982), *The Neuropsychology of Anxiety: an Inquiry into the Functions of the Septo-hippocampal System* (1st edn, Oxford: Oxford University Press)

Gray, J. A. and McNaughton, N. (2000), *The Neuropsychology of Anxiety: an Inquiry into the Functions of the Septo-hippocampal System* (2nd edn, Oxford: Oxford University Press)

Gray, J. R. and Braver, T. S. (2002), Personality predicts working-memory-related activation in the caudal anterior cingulate cortex, *Cognitive, Affective and Behavioral Neuroscience*, 2, 64–75

Greenberg, B. D., Li, Q., Lucas, F. R., Hu, S., Sirota, L. A., Benjamin, J., Lesch, K. P., Hamer, D. and Murphy, D. L. (2000), Association between the serotonin transporter promoter polymorphism and personality traits in a primarily female population sample, *American Journal of Medical Genetics*, 96, 202–216

Gutknecht, G., Jacob, C., Strobel, A., Müller, J., Zeng, Y., Markert, C., Escher, A., Wendland, J., Reif, A., Mössner, R., Gross, C., Brocke, B. and Lesch, K. P. (2007), Tryptophan hydroxylase-2 gene variation influences personality traits and disorders related to emotional dysregulation, *International Journal of Neuropsychopharmacology*, 10, 309–320

Ham, B. J., Kim, Y. H., Choi, M. J., Cha, J. H., Choi, Y. K. and Lee, M. S. (2004), Serotonergic genes and personality traits in the Korean population, *Neuroscience Letters*, 354, 2–5

Hamer, D. (2002), Rethinking behavior genetics, *Science*, 298, 71–72

Hariri, A. R., Bookheimer, S. Y. and Mazziotta, J. C. (2000), Modulating emotional responses: effects of a neocortical network on the limbic system, *Neuroreport*, 11, 43–48

Hariri, A. R., Mattay, V. S., Tessitore, A., Fera, F. and Weinberger, D. R. (2003), Neocortical modulation of the amygdala response to fearful stimuli, *Biological Psychiatry*, 53, 494–501

Hariri, A. R., Mattay, V. S., Tessitore, A., Kolachana, B., Fera, F., Goldman, D. *et al.* (2002), Serotonin transporter genetic variation and the response of the human amygdala, *Science*, 297, 400–403

Hariri, A. R., Munoz, K. E., Kolachana, B., Goldsmith, D. R., Mattay, V. S. and Goldber, T. (2003), Genetically driven variation in serotonergic neurotransmission alters amygdala reactivity associated with fearful temperament, *Society for Neuroscience Abstracts*, 662

Harvey, M., Shink, E., Tremblay, M., Gagne, B., Raymond, C., Labbe, M. *et al.* (2004), Investigation of the tryptophan hydroxylase 2 (TPH2) gene in bipolar affective disorders, *American Journal of Medical Genetics, Part B Neuropsychiatric Genetics*, 130B, 151–152

Heisler, L. K., Chu, H. M., Brennan, T. J., Danao, J. A., Bajwa, P., Parsons, L. H. and Tecott, L. H. (1998), Elevated anxiety and antidepressant-like responses in serotonin 5-HT1A receptor mutant mice, *Proceedings of the National Academy of Sciences of the United States of America*, 95, 15049–15054

Henderson, A. S., Korten, A. E., Jorm, A. F., Jacomb, P. A., Christensen, H., Rodgers, B. *et al.* (2000), COMT and DRD3 polymorphisms, environmental exposures, and personality traits related to common mental disorders, *American Journal of Medical Genetics*, 96, 102–107

Hennig, J., Reuter, M., Netter, P., Burk, C. and Landt, O. (2005), Two types of aggression are differentially related to serotonergic acitvity and the A779C TPH polymorphism, *Behavioral Neuroscience*, 119, 16–25

Horn, N. R., Dolan, M., Elliott, R., Deakin, J. F. W. and Woodruff, P. W. R. (2003), Response inhibition and impulsivity: an fMRI study, *Neuropsychologia*, 41, 1959–1966

Jonsson, E. G., Nothen, M. M., Gustavsson, J. P., Berggard, C., Bunzel, R., Forslund, K. *et al.* (2001), No association between serotonin 2A receptor gene variants and personality traits, *Psychiatric Genetics*, 11, 11–17

Kestler, L. P., Malhotra, A. K., Finch, C., Adler, C. and Breier, A. (2000), The relation between dopamine D2 receptor density and personality: preliminary evidence from the NEO personality inventory-revised, *Neuropsychiatry, Neuropsychology, and Behavioral Neurology*, 13, 48–52

Kuhn, K. U., Meyer, K., Nothen, M. M., Gansicke, M., Papassotiropoulos, A. and Maier, W. (1999), Allelic variants of dopamine receptor D4 (DRD4) and serotonin receptor 5HT2c (HTR2c) and temperament factors: replication tests, *American Journal of Medical Genetics*, 88, 168–172

Kusumi, I., Suzuki, K., Sasaki, Y., Kameda, K., Sasaki, T. and Koyama, T. (2002), Serotonin 5-HT(2A) receptor gene polymorphism, 5-HT(2A) receptor function and personality traits in healthy subjects: a negative study, *Journal of Affective Disorders*, 68, 235–241

Laakso, A., Wallius, E., Kajander, J., Bergman, J., Eskola, O., Solin, O., Ilonen, T., Salokangas, R. K. R., Syvalahti, E. and Hietala, J. (2003), Personality traits and striatal dopamine synthesis capacity in healthy subjects, *American Journal of Psychiatry*, 160, 904–910

Lachman, H. M., Papolos, D. F., Saito, T., Yu, Y. M., Szumlanski, C. L. and Weinshilboum, R. M. (1996), Human catechol-O-methyltransferase pharmacogenetics: description of a functional polymorphism and its potential application to neuropsychiatric disorders, *Pharmacogenetics*, 6, 243–250

Lander, E. S. and Schork, N. J. (1994), Genetic dissection of complex traits, *Science*, 265, 2037–2048

Lang, P. J., Bradley, M. M. and Cuthbert, B. (1995), *International Affective Picture System* (Gainsville, FL: Center for Research in Psychophysiology, University of Florida)

Lang, U. E., Bajbouj, M., Wernicke, C., Rommelspacher, H., Danker-Hopfe, H. and Gallinat, J. (2004), No association of a functional polymorphism in the serotonin transporter gene promoter and anxiety-related personality traits, *Neuropsychobiology*, 49, 182–184

Larsen, R. J. and Katelaar, T. (1991), Personality and susceptibility to positive and negative mood states, *Journal of Personality and Social Psychology*, 61, 132–140

Lerman, C., Caporaso, N. E., Bush, A., Zheng, Y. L., Audrain, J., Main, D., Shields, P. G. (2001), Tryptophan hydroxylase gene variant and smoking behavior, *American Journal of Medical Genetics*, B105, 518–520

Lesch, K. P., Bengel, D., Heils, A., Sabol, S. Z., Greenberg, B. D., Petri, S., Benjamin, J., Muller, C. R., Hamer, D. H. and Murphy, D. L. (1996), Association of anxiety-related traits with a polymorphism in the serotonin transporter gene regulatory region, *Science*, 274, 1527–1531

Malleret, G., Hen, R., Guillou, J. L., Segu, L. and Buhot, M. C. (1999), 5-HT1B receptor knock-out mice exhibit increased exploratory activity and enhanced spatial memory performance in the Morris water maze, *Journal of Neuroscience*, 19, 6157–6168

Mann, J. J., Malone, K. M., Nielsen, D. A., Goldman, D., Erdos, J. and Gelernter, J. (1997), Possible association of a polymorphism of the tryptophan hydroxylase gene with suicidal behavior in depressed patients, *American Journal of Psychiatry*, 154, 1451–1453

Mattay, V. S., Goldberg, T. E., Fera, F., Hariri, A. R., Tessitore, A., Egan, M. F. *et al.* (2003), Catechol O-methyltransferase val(158)-met genotype and individual variation in the brain response to amphetamine, *Proceedings of the National Academy of Sciences of the United States of America*, 100, 6186–6191

McNaughton, N. and Corr, P. J. (2004), A two-dimensional neuropsychology of defense: fear/anxiety and defensive distance, *Neuroscience and Biobehavioral Review*, 28, 285–305

Netter, P., Reuter, M. and Hennig, J. (2005), Specificity of affiliation supported by neurotransmitter challenge tests and molecular genetics, *Behavioral and Brain Sciences*, 3, 359–360

New, A. S., Gelernter, J., Goodman, M., Mitropoulou, V., Koenigsberg, H., Silverman, J. and Siever, L. J. (2001), Suicide, impulsive aggression, and HTR1B genotype, *Biological Psychiatry*, 50, 62–65

Nielsen, D. A., Goldman, D., Virkkunen, M., Tokola, R., Rawlings, R. and Linnoila, M. (1994), Suicidality and 5-hydroxyindoleacetic acid concentration associated with a tryptophan hydroxylase polymorphism, *Archives of General Psychiatry*, 51, 34–38

Noble, E. P. (2000), Addiction and its reward process through polymorphisms of the D-2 dopamine receptor gene: a review, *European Psychiatry*, 15, 79–89

Ochsner, K. N., Bunge, S. A., Gross, J. J. and Gabrieli, J. D. (2002), Rethinking feelings: an FMRI study of the cognitive regulation of emotion, *Journal of Cognitive Neuroscience*, 14, 1215–1229

Parsian, A., Cloninger, C. R., Sinha, R. and Zhang, Z. H. (2003), Functional variation in promoter region of monoamine oxidase A and subtypes of alcoholism: haplotype analysis, *American Journal of Medical Genetics, Part B Neuropsychiatric Genetics*, 117B, 46–50

Pohjalainen, T., Rinne, J. O., Nagren, K., Lehikoinen, P., Anttila, K., Syvalahti, E. K. and Hietala, J. (1998), The A1 allele of the human D2 dopamine receptor gene predicts low D2 receptor availability in healthy volunteers, *Molecular Psychiatry*, 3, 256–260

Ramboz, S., Saudou, F., Amara, D. A., Belzung, C., Segu, L., Misslin, R. *et al.* (1995), 5-HT1B receptor knock out, behavioral consequences, *Behavioural Brain Research*, 73, 305–312

Reif, A. and Lesch, K. P. (2003), Toward a molecular architecture of personality, *Behavioral Brain Research*, 139, 1–20

Reuter, M. and Hennig, J. (2005a), Pleiotropic effect of the TPH A779C polymorphism on nicotine dependence and personality, *American Journal of Medical Genetics, Part B Neuropsychiatric Genetics*, 134B, 20–24

Reuter, M. and Hennig, J. (2005b), Association of the functional COMT VAL158MET polymorphism with the personality trait of extraversion, *NeuroReport*, 16, 1135–1138

Reuter, M., Küpper, Y. and Hennig, J. (2007), Association between a polymorphism in the promoter region of the TPH2 gene and the personality trait of harm avoidance, *International Journal of Neuropsychopharmacology*, 10, 401–404

Reuter, M., Peters, K., Schroeter, K., Koebke, W., Lenardon, D., Bloch, B. and Hennig, J. (2005), The influence of the dopaminergic system on cognitive functioning: a molecular genetic approach, *Behavioural Brain Research*, 164, 93–99

Reuter, M., Schmitz, A., Corr, P. and Hennig, J. (2006), Molecular genetics support for Gray's personality theory: the interaction of COMT and DRD2 polymorphisms predict BIS/BAS scales, *International Journal of Neuropsychopharmacolgy*, 9, 155–166

Reuter, M., Stark, R., Hennig, J., Walter, B., Kirsch, P., Schienle, A. *et al.* (2004), Personality and emotion: test of Gray's personality theory by means of an fMRI study, *Behavioral Neuroscience*, 118, 462–469

Rujescu, D., Giegling, I., Bondy, B., Gietl, A., Zill, P. and Moller, H. J. (2002), Association of anger-related traits with SNPs in the TPH gene, *Molecular Psychiatry*, 7, 1023–1029

Rujescu, D., Giegling, I., Gietl, A., Hartmann, A. M. and Moller, H. J. (2003), A functional single nucleotide polymorphism (V158M) in the COMT gene is associated with aggressive personality traits, *Biological Psychiatry*, 54, 34–39

Schmidt, L. A., Fox, N. A., Rubin, K. H., Hu, S. and Hamer, D. H. (2002), Molecular genetics of shyness and aggression in preschoolers, *Personality and Individual Differences*, 33, 227–238

Schmidt, L. G., Sander, T., Kuhn, S., Smolka, M., Rommelspacher, H., Samochowiec, J. et al. (2000), Different allele distribution of a regulatory MAOA gene promoter polymorphism in antisocial and anxious-depressive alcoholics, Journal of Neural Transmission, 107, 681–689

Souery, D., Van Gestel, S., Massat, I., Blairy, S., Adolfsson, R., Blackwood, D., Del-Favero, J., Dikeos, D., Jakovljevic, M., Kaneva, R., Lattuada, E., Lerer, B., Lilli, R., Milanova, V., Muir, W., Nothen, M., Oruc, L., Papadimitriou, G., Propping, P., Schulze, T., Serretti, A., Shapira, B., Smeraldi, E., Stefanis, C., Thomson, M., Van Broeckhoven, C. and Mendlewicz, J. (2001), Tryptophan hydroxylase polymorphism and suicidality in unipolar and bipolar affective disorders: a multicenter association study, Biological Psychiatry, 49, 405–409

Soyka, M., Preuss, U. W., Koller, G., Zill, P. and Bondy, B. (2004), Association of 5-HT1B receptor gene and antisocial behavior in alcoholism, Journal of Neural Transmission, 111, 101–109

Spanagel, R. and Weiss, F. (1999), The dopamine hypothesis of reward: past and current status, Trends in Neurosciences, 22, 521–527

Strobel, A., Debener, S., Anacker, K., Muller, J., Lesch, K. P. and Brocke, B. (2004), Dopamine D4 receptor exon III genotype influence on the auditory evoked novelty P3, Neuroreport, 15, 2411–2415

Strobel, A., Gutknecht, L., Rothe, C., Reif, A., Mossner, R., Zeng, Y., Brocke, B. and Lesch, K. P. (2003), Allelic variation in 5-HT1A receptor expression is associated with anxiety- and depression-related personality traits, Journal of Neural Transmission, 110, 1445–1453

Sullivan, P. F., Jiang, Y., Neale, M. C., Kendler, K. S. and Straub, R. E. (2001), Association of the tryptophan hydroxylase gene with smoking initiation but not progression to nicotine dependence, American Journal of Medical Genetics, B105, 479–484

Teasdale, J. D., Howard, R. J., Cox, S. G., Ha, Y., Brammer, M. J., Williams, S. C. R. and Checkley, S. A. (1999), Functional MRI study of the cognitive generation of affect, American Journal of Psychiatry, 156, 209–215

Thompson, J., Thomas, N., Singleton, A., Piggot, M., Lloyd, S., Perry, E. K., Morris, C. M., Perry, R. H., Ferrier, I. N. and Court, J. A. (1997), D_2 dopamine receptor gene (DRD2) TaqI A polymorphism: reduced dopamine D_2 receptor binding in the human striatum associated with the A1 allele, Pharmacogenetics, 7, 479–484

Tsai, S. J., Hong, C. J., Yu, Y. W. Y. and Chen, T. J. (2004), Association study of catechol-O-methyltransferase gene and dopamine D-4 receptor gene polymorphisms and personality traits in healthy young Chinese females, Neuropsychobiology, 50, 153–156

Vandenbergh, D. J., Rodriguez, L. A., Hivert, E., Schiller, J. H., Villareal, G., Pugh, E. W. et al. (2000), Long forms of the dopamine receptor (DRD4) gene VNTR are more prevalent in substance abusers: no interaction with functional alleles of the catechol-o-methyltransferase (COMT) gene, American Journal of Medical Genetics, 96, 678–683

Wacker, J., Reuter, M., Hennig, J. and Stemmler, G. (2005), Sexually dimorphic link between dopamine D2 receptor gene and neuroticism-anxiety, *NeuroReport*, 16, 611–614

Walther, D. J. and Bader, M. (2003), A unique central tryptophan hydroxylase isoform, *Biochemical Pharmacology*, 66, 1673–1680

Walther, D. J., Peter, J. U., Bashammakh, S., Hortnagl, H., Voits, M., Fink, H. *et al.* (2003), Synthesis of serotonin by a second tryptophan hydroxylase isoform, *Science*, 299, 76

Yasuno, F., Suhara, T., Sudo, Y., Yamamoto, M., Inoue, M., Okubo, Y. and Suzuki, K. (2001), Relation among dopamine D-2 receptor binding, obesity and personality in normal human subjects, *Neuroscience Letters*, 300, 59–61

Zill, P., Baghai, T. C., Zwanzger, P., Schule, C., Eser, D., Rupprecht, R., Moller, H. J., Bondy, B. and Ackenheil, M. (2004), SNP and haplotype analysis of a novel tryptophan hydroxylase isoform (TPH2) gene provide evidence for association with major depression, *Molecular Psychiatry*, 9, 1030–1036

Zuckerman, M. (1993), P-impulsive sensation seeking and its behavioral, psychophysiological and biochemical correlates, *Neuropsychobiology*, 28, 30–36

11 Reinforcement Sensitivity Theory and psychosomatic medicine

Liisa Keltikangas-Järvinen

Since the 1950s the importance of behavioural factors in the pathogenesis of somatic diseases has been decidedly accepted. The pioneers of this field were the psychiatrists Alexander and Dunbar, who in the 1940s suggested that emotions that cannot be expressed are likely to turn into somatic diseases. They identified the 'Holy Seven', that is, the list of seven somatic diseases that had psychological origins and were therefore called 'the psychosomatic diseases' (Dunbar 1947). The scientific evidence behind their claim was, however, indecisive. They used retrospective designs and biased, primarily psychiatric samples. Most of their claims lacked empirical evidence and their findings cannot be replicated. Therefore, their theory was not widely accepted.

Previous psychosomatic medicine

In the 1950s, the cardiologists Friedman and Rosenman discovered an association between behavioural factors and the risk of coronary heart disease, and created the concept of Type A behaviour, a composition of behavioural style and negative emotions (for a review, see Siegman and Smith 1994). This finding was of utmost significance and launched systematic and evidence-based research in psychosomatic medicine. It was no longer asked whether psychological or behavioural factors are of importance in the development of somatic diseases, but rather how they operate.

Since then, empirical evidence has consistently associated negative emotions like anger, anxiety, depression and hostility with negative health outcomes in general, not only with cardiovascular disease. Negative emotions or negative affects have been identified as a possible mediator of the association between psychosocial variables and health outcomes, more specifically, as a mediator between psychological variables and physiological stress reactions. Stress, in turn, is a key factor in the development of cardiovascular disease as well as many other diseases.

Stress is generally experienced as discomfort, tension or negative affect. It has even been found that stressors that do not evoke negative affects do not produce a physiological reaction. That means that a stressor has to include an emotional upset to produce a basic general stress response (e.g., Baum, Davidson, Singer and Street 1987).

Negative affectivity has been shown to be associated especially with high sympathetic arousal and low parasympathetic tone (e.g., Denollet 2000). These parameters are also of great importance in psychosomatic medicine. The tendency to show heightened HR responses to mental stress has been hypothesized to be a risk factor for the development of atherosclerosis, coronary heart disease (CHD) and hypertension (e.g., Krantz and Manuck 1984). Furthermore, high HR reactivity has been shown to be associated with stress-related plasma cortisol concentrations, natural killer cell cytotoxicity and immune responses to stress (Lovallo, Pincomb, Brackett and Wilson 1990; Manuck, Cohen, Rabin, Muldoon and Bachen 1991).

It appears that persons are differently disposed to respond with specific emotions when given everyday situations. People differ in the extent to which they are prone to experience negative or positive affects. Those with a disposition to high positive affectivity are shown to actively approach life with enthusiasm, cheerfulness and confidence. By contrast, regardless of the situation, people with high negative affectivity experience negative emotions more frequently and intensely than people with low negative affectivity (Watson, Clark and Harkness 1994).

Individual differences in proneness to experience affects might even be innate. Dispositions to experience negative or positive affects are suggested to be temperamental factors and, as such, genetically determined at least to some extent. An assertion of innate individual differences in the readiness to experience emotions raises the question of innate stress vulnerability. If an individual has a disposition to experience negative emotions, regardless of the situation, he or she can be assumed to be prone to generally experience more stress.

Gray's Reinforcement Sensitivity Theory (RST)

A suggestion that dispositions to positive and negative affects are temperamental factors has evoked the question whether temperament might explain the whole stress process, that is, individual differences in emotional distress, and the relationship between environmental stimulus, stress experience and somatic endpoint.

One of the first and most profound temperament models that associates an environmental stimulus, behaviour and emotional and physiological reactions was proposed by Gray (1982, 1990). Gray's RST assumes the existence of three fundamental systems with independent neurobiological mechanisms in the mammalian central nervous system (CNS). The systems are the Behavioural Inhibition System (BIS), the Behavioural Approach System (BAS) and the Fight-Flight System (FFS). Gray proposed that the individual differences in the functioning of these systems and their interaction underlie human temperament.

The BIS is activated primarily by aversive stimuli (punishment, non-reward) causing behavioural inhibition and an increase of arousal and attention levels. Activation of the BIS is seen to be responsible for the experience of negative affects, such feelings as fear, anxiety, frustration, sadness and depression (Gray 1990). In addition, the BIS is the proposed causal basis of trait anxiety. Gray proposed that the BIS comprises the septo-hippocampal system, its monoaminergic afferents from the brainstem, and its neurocortical projection in the frontal lobe. Later studies have shown that BIS might be associated with an increased sympathetic arousal (Fowles 1980).

The BAS is activated primarily by appetitive stimuli (reward, termination of punishment) causing approach behaviour or activation. Activation of the BAS is seen to be responsible for the experience of positive feelings such as hope, elation and happiness (Gray 1990). In addition, the BAS is the proposed causal basis of trait impulsivity. Gray proposed that the neural basis of the BAS is activity in the mesolimbic dopamine system focused on the nucleus accumbens. Later on, it was suggested that the activation of the BAS is associated with increased HR (Fowles 1980).

Given these factors, a person's emotional reactions to stimuli reflect his or her sensitivity of functioning of three neurobiologically independent systems, and as such, emotional reactions are at least partly innate. Individuals with a sensitive BAS would be highly engaged in reacting to incentives, and the BAS would be responsible for the disposition to experience positive feelings as a rule. Activity of the BIS would be, instead, responsible for the experience of negative feelings, and individuals with a sensitive BIS would, by nature, be fixed on possible threats and dangers.

Gray's original theory has been slightly modified by Gray and McNaughton in 2000, the most important adjustment focusing on the functional, behavioural and pharmacological distinction between fear and anxiety (for a review, see McNaughton and Corr 2004). From the point of view of psychosomatic medicine, this remodelling is of high importance since anxiety has been shown to play a role in the pathogenesis of many diseases, while this is not true with fear.

RST and disease prone emotionality

Recent empirical evidence supports Gray's theory on temperament-related proneness to experience positive or negative affects. Anxiety and depression have been shown to be characterized by low BAS and high BIS activity (Fowles 1988). In everyday life, persons with BIS sensitivity have been shown to report more negative affects, and persons with BAS sensitivity more positive affects, when measured using diaries (Gable, Reis and Elliot 2000) or questionnaires that ask how participants generally felt (Jorm et al. 1999).

BIS has also been shown to have a moderator effect. Gable, Reis and Elliot (2000) have found that persons with BIS sensitivity experienced more negative affects after negative life events than persons with a less sensitive BIS. BAS sensitivity, however, was not associated with an increased frequency of positive affects after positive life events.

In laboratory settings, the BIS scale has been found to predict negative emotions, whereas the BAS scale predicted positive emotions when participants viewed emotional public service announcements (Dillard and Peck 2001). Studies on the impact of BIS and BAS sensitivity on emotions are, however, very few in number, and only some have used appropriate BIS/BAS scales.

The most systematic study, perhaps, is a series of laboratory experiments by Heponiemi et al. (Heponiemi, Keltikangas-Järvinen, Puttonen and Ravaja 2003). That focused on the relationship between BIS/BAS sensitivity and experimentally induced physiological and emotional stress. They studied inter-individual differences in affects between persons with BIS or BAS sensitivity during different stressors (experimental tasks with varying reinforcements), and intra-individual differences in affects among persons with BIS or BAS sensitivity evoked by different stressors, that is, a stress-specificity related to BIS or BAS sensitivity (Heponiemi et al. 2003; Heponiemi, Keltikangas-Järvinen, Kettunen, Puttonen and Ravaja 2004). They used Carver and White's (1994) BIS/BAS scales, which were specially designed to measure BIS and BAS sensitivities. Circumplex model (Larsen and Diener 1992) was used in assessing emotions. According to this model, emotions are structured in a two-dimensional space, valence (positive-negative, i.e., pleasant and unpleasant affects) and intensity (activated and unactivated affects) being the co-ordinates of this space.

Heponiemi et al. (2003) found that in general, that is, independently of the nature of the stressor, BIS sensitivity was associated with unpleasant affects in all levels of emotional activation, whereas BAS sensitivity was unrelated to unpleasant affects (see Figure 11.1). That

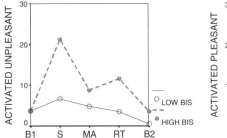 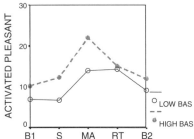

Figure 11.1 Emotional reactivity of persons with BIS or BAS sensitivity during public speech (S), mathematics (MA) and reaction time (RT)

means that during the experimental stress, the BIS sensitive people felt tired, sad, disappointed, anxious, uneasy and/or tense. From the point of view of psychosomatics, it was noteworthy that BIS sensitive people especially expressed a great increase of anxiety (activated unpleasant affect) during stress, anxiety being an important risk factor of CHD (see for a review, Siegman and Smith 1994). In contrast, BAS sensitivity was generally associated with pleasant affects in all levels of emotional activation, whereas BIS sensitivity was unrelated to pleasant affects. That means that during the experimental stress, the BAS sensitive people felt vigorous, lively, delighted, satisfied and calm.

The findings by Heponiemi *et al.* (2003) also showed that a difference in emotional experiences between BIS sensitive and BAS sensitive people refers to stress-induced emotional distress. That means that the difference was apparent during stress while no differences were true during the baselines, that is, before and after the tasks.

RST and disease prone physiological reactivity

Gray's theory is based on physiological evidence derived mainly from animal studies and lesion research. The theory has been supported by, for instance, procedural learning studies (Corr, Pickering and Gray 1997), performance studies (Gomez and McLaren 1997; Hagopian and Ollendick 1994) and EEG studies (De Pascalis, Fiore and Sparita 1996), although conflicting findings also exist (for a review, see Matthews and Gilliland 1999).

Gray's constructs can be applied to a wide range of traits, affective disorders and psychopathology. To date, only a few studies exist on the relationship between cardiac autonomic activity and direct measures of BIS and BAS sensitivity.

Beauchaine (2001) has suggested that both the BIS and the BAS would be mediated peripherally by the sympathetic nervous system. A significant increase in heart rate has indeed been found when the BAS has been activated by reward or active avoidance cues (Arnett and Newman 2000), although some studies have resulted in conflicting findings (e.g., Gomez and McLaren 1997).

Some studies have, instead, associated BIS-BAS sensitivity primarily with the parasympathetic nervous system. Knyazev, Slobodskaya and Wilson (2002) have found that BAS sensitivity scores were associated with a lower baseline RSA and, unexpectedly, lower HR reactivity during mental arithmetic. In addition, a socially relevant stimulus (a speaking facial image) has been found to elicit greater RSA withdrawal among high BAS individuals than among low BAS individuals (Ravaja 2004).

The findings of Heponiemi *et al.* (2004) showed that BAS sensitivity was associated with increased HR reactivity and greater RSA withdrawal during the tasks, but it was unrelated to PEP reactivity and baseline measures of HR, RSA and PEP. In addition, they did not find a relationship between BIS sensitivity and cardiac autonomic activity (see Figure 11.2).

Their finding was consistent with Fowles' (1980) suggestion that BAS activity is strongly associated with HR activity. It was, however, inconsistent with Knyazev, Slobodskaya and Wilson *et al.* (2002), who found that BAS scores were negatively related to HR acceleration during stress.

According to Heponiemi *et al.* (2003), the pronounced HR reactivity of the subjects with high BAS scores seems to be mediated by parasympathetic withdrawal. BAS sensitivity was associated with stronger vagal withdrawal during the tasks, whereas there was no association with baseline parasympathetic tone. This agrees with the finding of Ravaja (2004) that suggests that the BAS would be mediated peripherally by parasympathetic activity.

The findings by Heponiemi *et al.* (2004) also show that considering only HR reactivity, as traditionally has been done, BAS sensitive persons could be assumed to be at a higher health risk, since higher HR reactivity has been associated with neuroendocrine responses (Lovallo *et al.* 1990; Manuck *et al.* 1991) and disease risk (e.g., Krantz and Manuck 1984). When the joint effect of sympathetic and parasympathetic activity has been considered, the persons with BIS sensitivity express a higher risk.

In agreement with their findings on emotional distress, Heponiemi *et al.* (2004) found no association between BIS/BAS sensitivity and a baseline level of HR, but BAS sensitivity was associated with an elevated HR reactivity during the task-induced stress.

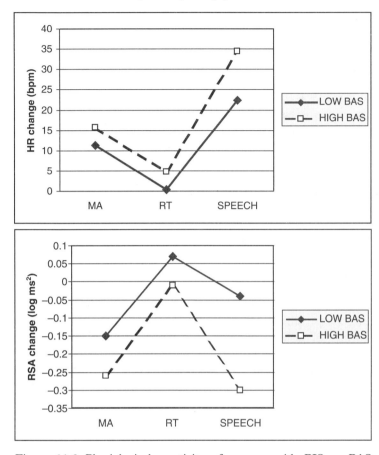

Figure 11.2 Physiological reactivity of persons with BIS or BAS sensitivity during public speech (S), mathematics (MA) and reaction time (RT)

Importance of the nature of the stressor

Diverse definitions of reinforcement are of essential importance when testing Gray's theory. Different reinforcing stimuli have been most systematically used in studies by Heponiemi *et al.* (2003, 2004). Their study addressed BIS/BAS-related stress proneness using well-known stressors with aversive and appetitive valences and widely-documented correlates with autonomic reactivity.

The findings of Heponiemi *et al.* (2003, 2004) demonstrated well the obvious importance of the nature of the stressor. Regarding emotional distress, the findings suggest that during stress, persons with BIS sensitivity, compared to those with less sensitive BIS, experience more unpleasant affects in general, and when faced with aversive stimulus especially. Then, the persons with BIS sensitivity were most likely to react with anxiety and tension. In contrast, BAS sensitivity was related to a proneness to experience more pleasant affects during stress in general, and to an increase of activated pleasant affect especially during the appetitive stressors. These findings are in line with Gray's theory and with Larsen and Diener's (1992) suggestion that an activated unpleasant affect would be associated with biologically-based sensitivity to conditioned signals of punishment, whereas activated pleasant affect would be associated with a biologically-based sensitivity to reward. Carver and White (1994) also found that BAS sensitivity predicts positive emotional reactions to cues of impending reward, whereas BIS sensitivity predicts a level of nervousness in response to impending punishment. The series of studies by Heponiemi *et al.* (2003, 2004) was however, the first in which the variance caused by different stressors was consistently tested.

Concerning physiological responses, HR seemed to be generally reactive, that is, independently of the nature of the stressor. That means that the persons with high BAS sensitivity exhibited higher HR reactivity during all tasks, while the association between BAS sensitivity and parasympathetic withdrawal (RSA reactivity) was strongest during the speech task, which has been shown to have a high appetitive valence (see Figure 11.2) . This finding is of considerable importance, since the public speech task is known to have a great deal of social relevance and ecological validity; thus, it corresponds well to the stresses of daily life. According to Heponiemi *et al.* (2003), it appears that the prospect of social rewards and success is a stronger incentive for high BAS persons than a small delayed monetary incentive or relief from noise punishment. Social interactions are intrinsically rewarding (Aitken and Trevarthen 1997) and can possibly act as an effective appetitive incentive among persons with high BAS sensitivity, thereby leading to physiological reactivity that reflects positive engagement rather than negative stress. For example, vagal withdrawal has been related to sociability in infants (Stifter and Corey 2001) and to lower levels of social problems in three-year-old children (Porges, Doussard-Roosevelt, Portales and Greenspan 1996).

BIS/BAS sensitivity and gender

The findings on BIS-BAS sensitivity or sensitivity-related reactivity have indicated only few gender differences. Women have been shown to score higher on the BIS scale (Heponiemi *et al.* 2003, 2004; Jorm *et al.* 1999) while no gender differences have been demonstrated for the BAS scale. Regarding emotional stress reactivity, Heponiemi *et al.* found (2003) that BIS sensitivity was more strongly related to unpleasant affects (i.e., anxiety, tension and disappointment) among men than among women, and was associated with unactivated unpleasant affects (dullness, tiredness, sleepiness) only among men. Thus, BIS sensitivity is slightly more typical of women, but might be of higher importance among men. The findings by Heponiemi *et al.* (2003) are the first to demonstrate gender differences in emotional BIS-BAS sensitivity. Other studies have not focused on this issue.

BIS/BAS sensitivity and performance

Heponiemi *et al.* (2003) showed that BAS sensitivity was associated with better performance during stress. For mental arithmetic and reaction time, actual performance of the participants was measured in their study as the number of correct and sufficiently fast responses. This is in line with previous findings by Gray and Braver (2002) who found that high BAS individuals were mentally more efficient. They had better performance and lower activation in the anterior cingulate cortex during a working memory task than low BAS individuals.

Future challenges

BIS sensitivity is likely to predispose a person to stress reaction in stressful situations in general, that is, regardless of the nature of the stressor and especially when faced with an aversive stressor. The higher stress-proneness of BIS persons is manifested as emotional distress and ineffective coping of the parasympathetic system. Emotional distress was characterized by negative affects in general, and anxiety, tension and depression in particular. Negative affects, especially anxiety and depression, have been found to be non-specific risk factors for poor health outcomes in general, and a prognostic factor for cardiac events and cancer in particular (Denollet 1998; Denollet, Vaes and Brutsaert 2000). Ineffective parasympathetic coping is also seen as a risk factor for coronary heart disease and hypertension (Tsuji *et al.* 1996).

BAS sensitivity, in contrast, was likely to operate as a stress buffer. Persons with high BAS sensitivity showed an appropriate stress response. Their pronounced reactivity was associated with positive emotional arousal and physiological flexibility. High BAS individuals experienced more pleasant affects during the stress in general, with an especially great increase in pleasant affect during appetitive tasks. They also expressed 'an optimal physiological stress reaction' (Porges 1992b), that is, a strong withdrawal of parasympathetic activity during stress and a quick recovery. In addition, high BAS individuals have been found to be mentally more efficient, that is, stress is not likely to decrease their level of cognitive capacity.

There are several mechanisms via which BIS sensitivity might increase stress vulnerability. First, stress-proneness might be caused by BIS-related negative emotionality, that is, it has been found that persons with high negative emotionality are not only easily distressed but also likely to cope poorly with stress (Watson, Clark and Harkness 1994). In addition, the anxiety-related tendency to approach a danger when faced with an approach-avoidance conflict may increase a behavioural stress vulnerability (e.g., Siegman and Smith 1994). Secondly, BIS sensitivity has been suggested to influence attention focus (Gray 1990). Derryberry and Reed (1994) have shown that in environmental interpretations, highly BIS sensitive persons would be biased in favour of negative cues, whereas highly BAS sensitive persons would be biased in favour of incentive signals.

Persons with BAS sensitivity, in turn, have been shown to react to incentive signals by initiating goal-directed behaviour and by focusing attention to incentive relevant cues, which may cause discounting or neglect of cues for punishment or frustration (Patterson and Newman 1993).

Thirdly, stress-proneness related to BIS sensitivity might be influenced by physiological differences between highly BIS and highly BAS persons, especially by differences in parasympathetic activity. Infants and young children with high resting parasympathetic tone show a superior ability to shift and sustain attention (Porges 1992a), are more social (Fox 1989), and react with larger HR responses to stress (Porter, Porges and Marshall 1988). In addition, the withdrawal of parasympathetic tone during stress has been associated with better performance (Porges 1972). Porges (1992b) has suggested that parasympathetic tone indexes stress and stress vulnerability, that is, chronic low parasympathetic tone accompanied by low parasympathetic reactivity indexes a person's stress vulnerability. In contrast, persons with high parasympathetic tone who have an ability to dampen parasympathetic activity in challenging situations (i.e., the capacity to react) and return to a high baseline afterwards (i.e., self-regulation) exhibit an appropriate stress response and will be less susceptible to stress.

The somatic endpoints of differences in physiological BIS–BAS reactivity need, however, to be studied more. Some studies suggest that high cardiovascular reactivity mediated through sympathetic activation (and perhaps through parasympathetic control) has more relevance to disease pathogenesis than reactivity mediated through parasympathetic withdrawal (e.g., Blascovich and Katkin 1993). For instance, endocrinological and immune functions have been shown to be more closely related to HR reactivity mediated by sympathetic reactivity than by parasympathetic reactivity (Caccioppo 1994). In addition, a high sympathetic activation has been shown to play a role in disease susceptibility (e.g., Rozanski, Blumenthal and Kaplan 1999), in increased mortality (Kleiger *et al.* 1987), and in the pathogenesis of hypertension (Singh *et al.* 1998), even though the primary role of parasympathetic system has been emphasized by some studies, as mentioned above.

Conclusion

Taken together, Gray's *Reinforcement Sensitivity Theory* offers a good model for studying psychosomatic issues and increases our understanding of the relationships between environmental stress, emotional distress and somatic disease. The findings show that dispositional sensitivity to potential reward and non-punishment is related to cardiac autonomic reactions during active coping.

Further studies are, however, needed, because previous results are still diverse, and, especially, since the health-related significance of HR reactivity may differ substantially depending on its autonomic origin. In addition, it has been emphasized (e.g., Corr 2001) that the lack of diverse definitions of reinforcement, and the widely varying psychometric measures of BIS/BAS functioning, have been the essential problems when examining Gray's theory. Thus, conflicting findings might also be caused by problems in the assessment of the concept. These future studies should examine more precisely the effects of different reinforcements and other manipulations known to activate the BAS or BIS. In addition, it would be relevant to focus on the reactions after the effects of novelty and uncertainty have waned. Future studies could also control for other personality or behavioural factors that might explain the observed relationships. Because BIS and BAS sensitivities seem to be associated with stress reactivity, it would be useful to study further how BIS and BAS sensitivities affect other stress indicators as well, for instance the role of BIS/BAS sensitivity in acute vs. long-term stress. Behavioural genetics would also offer a new challenge. Cloninger's temperament factors of novelty seeking and harm avoidance (Cloninger 1987), which are very close to the concepts of BAS and BIS sensitivity, respectively, are shown to have a genetic origin (Keltikangas-Järvinen, Elovainio, Kivimäki, Lichtermann, Ekelund and Peltonen 2003; Keltikangas-Järvinen, Puttonen, Kivimäki, Rontu and Lehtimäki 2006).

References

Aitken, K.J. and Trevarthen, C. (1997), Self/other organization in human psychological development, *Development and Psychopathology*, 9, 653–677

Arnett, P.A. and Newman, J.P. (2000), Gray's three-arousal model: an empirical investigation, *Personality and Individual Differences*, 28, 1171–1189

Baum, A., Davidson, L.M., Singer, J.E. and Street, S.W. (1987), Stress as a psychophysiological process in A. Baum and J.E. Singer (eds), *Handbook of Psychology and Health: Stress* (Hillsdale, NJ: Erlbaum), pp. 1–24

Beauchaine, T.P. (2001), Vagal tone, development, and Gray's motivational theory: toward an integrated model of autonomic nervous system functioning in psychopathology, *Development and Psychopathology*, 13, 183–214

Blascovich, J.J. and Katkin, E.S. (1993), *Cardiovascular Reactivity to Psychological Stress and Disease* (Washington: American Psychological Association)

Cacioppo, J.T. (1994), Social neuroscience: autonomic, neuroendocrine, and immune responses to stress, *Psychophysiology*, 31, 113–128

Carver, C.S. and White, T.L. (1994), Behavioral inhibition, behavioral activation, and affective responses to impending reward and punishment: the BIS/BAS scales, *Journal of Personality and Social Psychology*, 67, 319–333

Cloninger, C.R. (1987), A systematic method for clinical description and classification of personality variants, *Archives of General Psychiatry*, 44, 573–588

Corr, P.J. (2001), Testing problems in J.A. Gray's personality theory: a commentary on Matthews and Gilliland (1999), *Personality and Individual Differences*, 30, 333–352

Corr, P.J., Pickering, A.D. and Gray, J.A. (1997), Personality, punishment, and procedural learning: a test of J.A. Gray's anxiety theory, *Journal of Personality and Social Psychology*, 73, 337–344

De Pascalis, V., Fiore, A.D. and Sparita, A. (1996), Personality, event-related potential (ERP) and heart rate (HR): an investigation of Gray's theory, *Personality and Individual Differences*, 20, 733–746

Denollet, J. (1998), Personality and risk of cancer in men with coronary heart disease, *Psychological Medicine*, 28, 991–995

(2000), Type D personality: a potential risk factor refined, *Journal of Psychosomatic Research*, 49, 255–266

Denollet, J., Vaes, J. and Brutsaert, D.L. (2000), Inadequate response to treatment in coronary heart disease, *Circulation*, 102, 630–635

Derryberry, D. and Reed, M.A. (1994), Temperament and attention: orienting toward and away from positive and negative signals, *Journal of Personality and Social Psychology*, 66, 1128–1139

Dillard, J.P. and Peck, E. (2001), Persuasion and the structure of affect: dual systems and discrete emotions as complementary models, *Human Communication Research*, 27, 38–68

Dunbar, F. (1947), *Mind and Body: Psychosomatic Medicine* (New York: Randon House)

Fowles, D.C. (1980), The three arousal model: implications of Gray's two-factor learning theory for heart rate, electrodermal activity, and psychopathy, *Psychophysiology*, 17, 87–104

(1988), Psychophysiology and psychopathology: a motivational approach, *Psychophysiology*, 25, 373–391

Fox, N.A. (1989), Heart-rate variability and behavioral reactivity: individual differences in autonomic patterning and their relation to infant and child temperament in J.S. Reznick (ed.), *Perspectives on Behavioral Inhibition: the John D. and Catherine T. MacArthur Foundation Series on Mental Health and Development* (Chicago, IL: University of Chicago Press), pp. 177–195

Gable, S.L., Reis, H.T. and Elliot, A.J. (2000), Behavioral activation and inhibition in everyday life, *Journal of Personality and Social Psychology*, 78, 1135–1149

Gomez, R. and McLaren, S. (1997), The effects of reward and punishment on response disinhibition, moods, heart rate and skin conductance level during instrumental learning, *Personality and Individual Differences*, 23, 305–316

Gray, J.A. (1982), *The Neuropsychology of Anxiety: An Enquiry into the Functions of the Septo-hippocampal System* (New York: Oxford University Press)
(1990), Brain systems that mediate both emotion and cognition, *Cognition and Emotion*, 4, 269–288

Gray, J.A. and McNaughton, N. (2000), *The Neuropsychology of Anxiety: an Enquiry into the Functions of the Septo-hippocampal System* (2nd edn, Oxford: Oxford University Press)

Gray, J.R. and Braver, T.S. (2002), Personality predicts working-memory-related activation in the caudal anterior cingulate cortex, *Cognitive, Affective, and Behavioral Neuroscience*, 2, 64–75

Hagopian, L.P. and Ollendick, T.H. (1994), Behavioral inhibition and test anxiety: an empirical investigation of Gray's theory, *Personality and Individual Differences*, 16, 597–604

Heponiemi, T., Keltikangas-Järvinen, L., Kettunen, J., Puttonen, S. and Ravaja, N. (2004), BIS-BAS sensitivity and cardiac autonomic stress profiles, *Psychophysiology*, 41, 37–45

Heponiemi, T., Keltikangas-Järvinen, L., Puttonen, S. and Ravaja, N. (2003), BIS-BAS sensitivity and self-rated affects during experimentally induced stress, *Personality and Individual Differences*, 34, 943–957

Jorm, A.F., Christensen, H., Henderson, A.S., Jacomb, P.A., Korten, A.E. and Rodgers, B. (1999), Using the BIS/BAS scales to measure behavioural inhibition and behavioural activation: factor structure, validity and norms in a large community sample, *Personality and Individual Differences*, 26, 49–58

Keltikangas-Järvinen, L., Elovainio, M., Kivimäki, M., Lichtermann, D., Ekelund, J. and Peltonen, L. (2003), Association between the type 4 dopamine receptor gene polymorphism and novelty seeking, *Psychosomatic Medicine*, 65, 471–476

Keltikangas-Järvinen, L., Puttonen, S., Kivimäki, M., Rontu, R. and Lehtimäki, T. (2006), Epidermal growth factor A61G polymorphism and Cloninger's temperament dimensions, *Genes, Brain and Behavior*, 5, 11–18

Kleiger, R.E., Miller, J.P., Bigger, J.T. Jr and Moss, A.J. (1987), Decreased heart rate variability and its association with increased mortality after acute myocardial infarction, *American Journal of Cardiology*, 59, 256–262

Knyazev, G.G., Slobodskaya, H.R. and Wilson, G.D. (2002), Psychophysiological correlates of behavioural inhibition and activation, *Personality and Individual Differences*, 33, 647–660

Krantz, D.S. and Manuck, S.B. (1984), Acute psychophysiologic reactivity and risk of cardiovascular disease: a review and methodologic critique, *Psychological Bulletin*, 96, 435–464

Larsen, R.J. and Diener, E. (1992), Promises and problems with the circumplex model of emotion in M.S. Clark (ed.), *Review of Personality and Social Psychology: Emotion* (Newbury Park, CA: Sage), vol. 13, pp. 25–29

Lovallo, W.R., Pincomb, G.A., Brackett, D.J. and Wilson, M.F. (1990), Heart rate reactivity as a predictor of neuroendocrine responses to aversive and appetitive challenges, *Psychosomatic Medicine*, 52, 17–26

Manuck, S.B., Cohen, S.C., Rabin, B.S., Muldoon, M.F. and Bachen, E.A. (1991), Individual differences in cellular immune response to stress, *Psychological Science*, 2, 111–115

Matthews, G. and Gilliland, K. (1999), The personality theories of H.J. Eysenck and J.A. Gray: a comparative review, *Personality and Individual Differences*, 26, 583–626

McNaughton, N. and Corr, P. (2004), A two-dimensional neuropsychology of defense: fear/anxiety and defensive distance, *Neuroscience and Biobehavioral Review*, 28, 285–305

Patterson, C.M. and Newman, J.P. (1993), Reflectivity and learning from aversive events: toward a psychological mechanism for the syndromes of disinhibition, *Psychological Review*, 100, 716–736

Porges, S.W. (1972), Heart rate variability and deceleration as indexes of reaction time, *Journal of Experimental Psychology*, 92, 103–110

(1992a), Autonomic regulation and attention in B.A. Campbell and H. Hayne et al. (eds), *Attention and Information Processing in Infants and Adults: Perspectives from Human and Animal Research* (Hillsdale, NJ: Erlbaum), pp. 201–223

(1992b), Vagal tone: a physiologic marker of stress vulnerability, *Pediatrics*, 90, 498–504

Porges, S.W., Doussard-Roosevelt, J.A., Portales, A.L. and Greenspan, S.I. (1996), Infant regulation of the vagal 'brake' predicts child behavior problems: a psychobiological model of social behavior, *Developmental Psychobiology*, 29, 697–712

Porter, F.L., Porges, S.W. and Marshall, R.E. (1988), Newborn pain cries and vagal tone: parallel changes in response to circumcision, *Child Development*, 59, 495–505

Ravaja, N. (2004), Effects of a small talking facial image on autonomic activity: the moderating influence of dispositional BIS and BAS sensitivities and emotions, *Biological Psychology*, 65, 163–183

Rozanski, A., Blumenthal, J.A. and Kaplan, J. (1999), Impact of psychological factors on the pathogenesis of cardiovascular disease and implications for therapy, *Circulation*, 99, 2192–2217

Siegman, A.-W. and Smith, T.W. (1994), *Anger, Hostility and the Heart* (Hillsdale, NJ: Lawrence Erlbaum)

Singh, J.P., Larson, M.G., Tsuji, H., Evans, J.C., O'Donnell, C.J. and Levy, D. (1998), Reduced heart rate variability and new-onset hypertension: insights into pathogenesis of hypertension: the Framingham Heart Study, *Hypertension*, 32, 293–297

Stifter, C.A. and Corey, J.M. (2001), Vagal regulation and observed social behavior in infancy, *Social Development*, 10, 189–201

Tsuji, H., Larson, M.G., Venditti, F.J. Jr, Manders, E.S., Evans, J.C., Feldman, C.L. and Levy, D. (1996), Impact of reduced heart rate variability on risk for cardiac events: the Framingham Heart Study, *Circulation*, 94, 2850–2855

Watson, D., Clark, L.A. and Harkness, A.R. (1994), Structures of personality and their relevance to psychopathology, *Journal of Abnormal Psychology*, 103, 18–31

12 RST and clinical disorders: anxiety and depression

Richard E. Zinbarg and K. Lira Yoon

> If I have seen farther than others, it is because I stand on the shoulders of giants.
> Isaac Newton

To borrow Sir Isaac Newton's metaphor, Jeffrey Gray's shoulders must be getting very sore as there are many researchers standing on them including neuroscientists, personality psychologists and psychopathologists. This is because one of the most distinctive aspects and strengths of Gray's *Reinforcement Sensitivity Theory* (RST) is that it bridges several levels of analysis: anatomy, physiology, motivation, conditioning, personality and psychopathology. Regarding anxiety, Gray (1982; Gray and McNaughton 2000) proposed that individual differences in reactivity of the Behavioral Inhibition System (BIS) – a sub-system of the *conceptual* nervous system – not only underlies the normal personality dimension of trait anxiety/neuroticism but also underlies vulnerability to the anxiety disorders. At the anatomical level, Gray (1982) originally proposed that the septo-hippocampal system (SHS) constituted the sub-system of the central nervous system that is the seat of the BIS. Gray and McNaughton (2000) expanded the neuroanatomical seat of anxiety to include the interactions of the SHS system with the amygdala.

One can derive at least three broad sets of predictions based on RST that are directly relevant for anxiety disorders and major depressive disorder (MDD). First, predictions can be derived regarding the general structure of the various symptoms of the anxiety disorders. Relatedly, RST also provides a useful framework for understanding the relations of anxiety with panic and depression. Secondly, the psychopathology of the anxiety disorders should be characterized by features described by the major outputs of the BIS – an increase in arousal, behavioral inhibition and negative cognitive bias. Thirdly, trait anxiety/neuroticism should be a risk factor for the anxiety disorders and perhaps (non-psychotic)

MDD as well. In this chapter, we review the available evidence regarding these three sets of predictions, identify unresolved questions concerning RST and make suggestions regarding future RST research directions.

Structure of the symptoms of anxiety disorders and depression

Structure implied by RST: a hierarchical model

Our interpretation of RST is that it is one of several theoretical perspectives that imply a hierarchical model of the structure of the symptoms of anxiety disorders. RST – especially the version articulated by Gray and McNaughton (2000) – argues that the neural bases of the different anxiety disorders are not entirely overlapping. For example, it is argued that activity in the periaqueductal gray (PAG) underlies panic, SHS interactions with the amygdala underlie anxiety, and cingulate cortex (CING) and basal ganglia (BG) underlie obsessions and compulsions. The recognition of several anxiety disorders with partially distinct neural bases implies some reliable variance that should be specific to each disorder. In factor analytic terminology, this implies that the key features of the anxiety disorders should be multidimensional, with each disorder being associated with its own group (first-order) factor. On the other hand, RST also posits that there are extensive interconnections among the PAG, SHS, amygdala, CING and BG. Moreover, whether subserved by the monoaminergic inputs to all of these structures or the interconnections among them, RST hypothesizes a risk factor (threat perception) that is common to all the anxiety disorders. In factor analytic terminology, the hypothesis of a common risk factor implies that there should be a general (second-order) factor that is common to all of the anxiety disorders. Tellegen (1985) and Fowles (1988) extended RST by suggesting that this general factor is also common to unipolar (non-psychotic) depression/major depressive disorder (MDD).

Zinbarg and Barlow (1996) tested and found strong support for this hierarchical model by measuring a broad set of the key features of the anxiety disorders in a large sample of patients and a sample of no mental disorder (NMD) control participants. Several first-order factors (i.e., social anxiety, fear of fear, agoraphobia, obsessions and compulsions, and generalized dysphoric mood) provided the basis for differentiating among the anxiety disorder groups. However, the first-order factors were moderately intercorrelated, thereby giving rise to a second-order, general factor. This second-order factor differentiated each of the anxiety disorder groups and a MDD group from the NMD group. Though the evidence regarding the second-order factor is consistent with the hypothesis that there is a risk factor common to all of the anxiety disorders and MDD, there are at least two alternative explanations for these results. First, it is possible that the second-order factor was an artifact of the high levels of co-morbidity typical of treatment seeking samples. Secondly, it is possible that the second-order factor may have arisen entirely as a consequence of demoralization resulting from developing an emotional disorder rather than from a variable of etiologic significance (Frank 1973; Link and Dohrenwend 1980).

As a preliminary test of the notion that the second-order factor is not entirely a consequence of the inclusion of many individuals with co-morbid diagnoses, Zinbarg and Barlow (1996) performed some re-analyses excluding patients with co-morbid diagnoses. The average correlation among the first-order factors ($r = .33$) in the sub-sample of participants with a single diagnosis was virtually identical to that among the entire sample ($r = .34$). In addition, the four 'pure' patient groups that had at least fifteen members after excluding individuals with additional diagnoses were still significantly higher on the second-order factor than the NMD group. These results suggest that diagnostic co-morbidity cannot entirely account for the second-order factor.

Furthermore, epidemiological studies using large, representative samples have consistently found support for a factor common to all of the anxiety disorders and MDD in New Zealand (Krueger, Caspi, Moffitt and Silva 1998), the United States (e.g., Krueger 1999) and the Netherlands (Vollebergh, Iedema, Bijl, de Graff, Smit and Ormel 2001). In addition, each of these three studies produced evidence that the factor common to all of the anxiety disorders and MDD (or internalizing disorders) is at least somewhat distinct from a second broad factor that is common to the externalizing disorders. Similar results have also been reported among consumers of fifteen general health care service centers in fourteen countries, including Brazil, Chile, China, England, France, Germany, Greece, India, Italy, Japan, the Netherlands, Nigeria, Turkey and the United States (Krueger, Chentsova-Dutton, Markon, Goldberg and Ormel 2003). Thus, high levels of co-morbidity in psychiatric patients cannot entirely explain the presence of the second-order factor.

Evidence with some bearing on the notion that the second-order factor is not a result of the demoralizing effect of having an emotional disorder has come from multivariate, behavior-genetic studies conducted by Kendler and his colleagues (e.g., Hettema, Prescott, Myers *et al.* 2005; Kendler, Prescott, Myers and Neale 2003; Kendler, Walters,

Neale *et al.* 1995). Whereas the most recent reports from this group find two genetic factors within the anxiety disorders and MDD characterized by 'anxious-misery' on the one hand and 'fear' on the other (Kendler, Prescott, Myers and Neale 2003; Kendler, Walters, Neale *et al.* 1995), these two factors were moderately positively correlated which is consistent with a second-order factor common to all the anxiety disorders and MDD. Thus, these results suggest strongly that genetic factors are largely responsible for the pattern of symptom co-variance that results in the two frequently co-occurring clusters of internalizing and externalizing symptoms. Furthermore, it seems likely that the genetic factor is at least partly, if not entirely, related to the vulnerability to these disorders. Indeed, data we review later from longitudinal studies demonstrate that heritable temperamental characteristics and personality traits relevant to RST (e.g., behavioral inhibition and neuroticism) do prospectively predict the onset of new episodes of MDD and anxiety disorders.

Relation between anxiety and panic

Discussions of the relation between anxiety and a Fight-Flight-Freeze (FFF) response labeled as either fear (e.g., Barlow 1988, 1991a; Barlow, Chorpita and Turovsky 1996) or panic (e.g., Gray 1991; Gray and McNaughton 1996, 2000) have led to some debate. Some theorists view a qualitative distinction between fear/panic and anxiety to be unnecessary (e.g., Rachman 1990; Rapee 1996). Others, however, suggest that anxiety and fear/panic differ fundamentally (e.g., Barlow 1988, 1991a, 1991b; Klein 1964, 1981). The hierarchical structural model implicit in RST suggests that both of these seemingly contradictory views may be partially correct. Our interpretation of Gray's (1982) initial articulation of RST suggested that anxiety and fear/panic overlap in that anxiety involves an excitatory input to the FFF mechanism. At the same time, the two are differentiable in that anxiety also involves a simultaneous inhibitory input to the FFF mechanism whereas fear/panic arises from more purely excitatory input to this mechanism, resulting in actual triggering of the FFF response. According to this synthesis, fear/panic suggests a firing of the FFF mechanism when threat is perceived to be *present*; anxiety suggests a conflict between excitation of the FFF mechanism and inhibition of this mechanism (Zinbarg 1998; Zinbarg, Barlow, Brown and Hertz 1992). That is, anxiety may be seen as a *priming* or preparation of the FFF mechanism when threat is perceived to be more distal in time and/or space. Though the anatomical structures believed to subserve anxiety and panic have changed from Gray's (1982) initial theory to Gray and McNaughton's (2000) reformulation, nothing in the reformulation suggests to us that we should abandon our psychological interpretation of the relation between anxiety and panic.

Unfortunately, Gray and McNaughton (2000) themselves are somewhat unclear about the relation between anxiety and panic. In places, they appear to follow Graeff (1994) in adopting the view that anxiety inhibits panic. We believe this view is not so much wrong as it is overly simplistic or incomplete, as priming does involve inhibition. However, priming also involves simultaneous excitation. In other places, Gray and McNaughton do acknowledge a more nuanced view of the relation between anxiety and panic involving simultaneous excitation and inhibition of panic when anxiety is activated. Indeed, in these places, they eloquently describe how such simultaneous excitation and inhibition allows the sudden dramatic shifts involved in converting 'approach (requiring activity in the behavioral inhibition system) to avoidance (mediated by the fight-flight system) as fast as possible should conditions require this' (Gray and McNaughton 2000, p. 54, also see p. 31).

The data that exist on this issue appear to support the priming interpretation over Graeff's (1994) purely inhibitory view of the relation between anxiety and panic. Mavissakalian (1988) asked fifty-nine agoraphobic patients to keep diaries of their panic attacks and their out of home experiences for a two-week period. Panic attacks were correlated with anticipated anxiety and the actual anxiety experienced in the agoraphobic situations. Basoglu, Marks and Sengun (1992) conducted a study of panic and anxiety in thirty-nine patients who had PDA using an event-sampling technique over three twenty-four-hour periods. Of the thirty-two patients who reported at least one panic during the study, 69 per cent reported that their panics surged from an already heightened level of anxiety. Another 18 per cent reported heightened anxiety preceding some panics but not others. Only 13 per cent did not report a preceding period of elevated anxiety before any of their panics. Kenardy et al. (1992) used a computer-assisted event-sampling technique over a one-week period in a study of twenty panic patients. They found that a generally anxious mood in the hours preceding panic attacks was non-significantly higher than in control hours (not followed by panic) and that worry about panic specifically was significantly elevated in the hour preceding panic attacks relative to control hours. As noted by Bouton, Mineka and Barlow (2001), the evidence from panic provocation paradigms that baseline anxiety is the best predictor of panic in response to a variety of provocation procedures is also consistent with the hypothesis that anxiety primes panic.

Relation between anxiety and depression

There has also been debate regarding the relationship between anxiety and depression. A number of theorists have suggested that anxiety and depression are variable expressions of the same pathology, while others have hypothesized that the two differ fundamentally (see Clark and Watson 1991 for an excellent review). This debate seems to have been largely resolved by Clark and Watson's (1991) tripartite model, which acknowledged both substantial overlap between and meaningful differentiation between anxiety and depression. To account for the evidence of substantial overlap, Clark and Watson proposed that anxiety and depression share a non-specific component of generalized distress, i.e., negative affect (NA). On the other hand, to account for the evidence of meaningful differentiation, they proposed two additional factors that are more specifically related to either anxiety or depression. That is, Clark and Watson hypothesized that low positive affect (PA)/anhedonia was unique to depression and hyper-arousal was unique to anxiety.

The tripartite model prediction that hyper-arousal was specific to anxiety required reformulation in light of evidence regarding the hierarchical structure of the anxiety disorders and that autonomic hyper-arousal did not generally distinguish the anxiety disorders from MDD but rather specifically distinguished panic disorder from MDD *and* the other anxiety disorders (e.g., Zinbarg *et al.* 1994; Zinbarg and Barlow 1996; Brown, Chorpita and Barlow 1998). Mineka, Watson and Clark (1998) integrated the tripartite model with Zinbarg and Barlow's (1996) hierarchical model, but this integrative hierarchical model retained the original tripartite model hypotheses that NA is a non-specific factor common to depression and anxiety and low PA is largely specific to depression. Following Tellegen (1985) and Fowles (1988), we find it useful to relate these affective dimensions to RST constructs. PA has been linked to the RST construct of the Behavioral Activating System (BAS) whereas NA has been linked to the BIS. One of the functions attributed to the BAS is to regulate active coping responses to threat (Gray 1982; Gray and McNaughton 2000). From this point of view, what is common to anxiety and depression is the perception of threat (high NA/BIS activity). In contrast, fundamental differences between anxiety and depression may be found in BAS activity. Depression suggests loss of hope of actively coping with threat (low PA/BAS activity); anxiety implies preparation for efforts to actively cope with threat (at least moderate levels of PA/BAS activity).

RST predictions regarding the psychopathology of anxiety disorders and depression

If RST provides a valid account of the etiology of anxiety disorders, we would expect the three major outputs of the BIS – an increase in arousal, behavioral inhibition and negative cognitive bias – to be shared by most, if not all, of the anxiety disorders. The reason we hedge with respect to whether these three characteristics would be shared by all of the anxiety disorders is that Gray and McNaughton (2000) are a bit unclear with respect to whether the SHS is actually involved in all the anxiety disorders. They are clear in articulating claims that dysfunction in structures other than the SHS are primary in the case of some of the disorders classified as anxiety disorders by the *Diagnostic and Statistical Manual of Mental Disorders* (DSM-IV; APA 1994). For example, they hypothesize that amygdala and medial hypothalamus activity are central to specific phobias (PHOB). To the extent that amygdala and medial hypothalamus activity alone are involved in PHOB, then one would not predict that cognitive biases favoring the processing of threat should be associated with PHOB (as such biases are primarily attributed in RST to SHS activity). On the other hand, given that the various defense system structures are extensively interconnected, one might predict that the SHS, and hence cognitive biases, would still play a role in PHOB even if not a central one.

Arousal

Various manifestations of increased arousal are recognized as diagnostic criteria for generalized anxiety disorder (GAD) and post-traumatic stress disorder (PTSD). Unambiguous examples include muscle tension and restlessness (GAD), exaggerated startle response (PTSD) and sleep disturbance (both GAD and PTSD). Of course, the criteria for panic disorder without agoraphobia (PD) and panic disorder with agoraphobia (PDA) also include several unambiguous examples of arousal symptoms. However, in PD and PDA these symptoms are part of the criteria set for panic attacks (seen in RST as arising from activity in the PAG and its interactions with the hypothalamus and amygdala) as opposed to being specified as criteria for the anticipatory anxiety component of these diagnoses. Psychophysiological recording in laboratory studies, however, confirm that PD and PDA patients do have higher baseline levels of arousal (i.e., when not panicking) than controls (e.g., Bass, Lelliott and Marks 1989; Bystritsky, Craske, Maidenberg, Vapnik and Shapiro 1995;

Hoehn, Braune, Scheibe and Albus 1997; Larsen, Norton, Walker and Stein 2002; Middleton 1990; Roth, Margraf, Ehlers, Taylor et al. 1992). Similarly, psychophysiological and self-report measures confirm that patients who have specific phobia (PHOB), social phobia (SOC), obsessive-compulsive disorder (OCD) and agoraphobia without a history of panic disorder (AG) have higher levels of arousal than controls (e.g., Antony, Bieling, Cox, Enns and Swinson 1998; Brown, Chorpita and Barlow 1998; Boulougouris, Rabavilas and Stefanis 1977; Cook, Melamed, Cuthbert, McNeil and Lang 1988; Gerlach, Wilhelm, Gruber and Roth 2001; Hofmann, Newman, Ehlers and Roth 1995; Lelliott, Noshirvani, Marks, Monteiro et al. 1987).

Though Brown, Chorpita and Barlow (1998, p. 189) concluded that 'the disorder-specific features of GAD (i.e., worry; ...) act to decrease (suppress) autonomic arousal', they did find that their GAD latent factor had a positive zero-order correlation (r = .48) with their hyper-arousal latent factor. Moreover, their conclusion is based entirely on a negative estimate of a unique path between GAD and autonomic arousal in an analysis that used several other anxiety disorder latent factors and a NA latent factor as co-variates. This unique path can only be interpreted as the association between that *part* of GAD that is not shared with the other disorders included in their analyses and that *part* of arousal that is not shared with negative affect (Miller and Chapman 2001). Thus, when one considers *all* the features of GAD and arousal per se (rather than only that portion that is orthogonal to NA), then the only one of their results that is germane is the positive, significant zero-order correlation between these two constructs.

Consistent with the positive zero-order correlation between GAD and arousal reported by Brown, Chorpita and Barlow (1998), Zinbarg et al. (1994) found that a group with principal diagnoses of GAD reported higher scores than a NMD control group on an arousal scale (albeit not as high as the scores reported by patients with PDA). It is worth noting that a MDD group also reported higher scores than the NMD group on this same arousal scale (again, though, not as high as the scores reported by the patients with PDA). This later result is consistent with extensions of RST postulating that a hyperactive BIS is also a characteristic of MDD.

Behavioral inhibition

Avoidance is a diagnostic criterion for the vast majority of anxiety disorders with GAD and PD being the only two exceptions. More subtle and complex avoidance tendencies (often labeled as 'safety behaviors'), however, have been found to be relatively common in GAD (e.g., Craske

Rapee, Jackel and Barlow 1989; Hoyer, Becker and Roth 2001; Schut, Castonguay and Borkovec 2001; Tallis and de Silva 1992) and in PD (Radomsky, Rachman and Hammond 2002; Salkovskis, Clark and Gelder 1996). Thus, it is clear that behavioral inhibition is a feature that is ubiquitous across the anxiety disorders. In addition, there are several studies documenting so-called 'learned helplessness' passivity and active-avoidance/escape deficits in MDD patients (e.g., Kavanagh 1987; Klein and Seligman 1976; Nation and Cooney 1980) that we have interpreted as reflecting enhanced passive avoidance tendencies (Foa, Zinbarg and Olasov-Rothbaum 1992; Zinbarg *et al.* 1992; Zinbarg and Mineka 1991). Enhanced passive avoidance tendencies associated with MDD are exactly what would be predicted on the basis of the extensions of RST hypothesizing that a hyperactive BIS is also involved in MDD.

Cognitive biases associated with anxiety disorders and unipolar depression

RST predicts that a hyperactive BIS should lead to enhanced attention to threat, a tendency to disambiguate ambiguity in a threatening fashion and enhanced memory for threat. We will now review the evidence on each of these three types of cognitive bias.

Attentional biases in anxiety disorders   Two tasks, an emotional Stroop task and a dot-probe task, have been used most frequently to measure visual attentional biases toward threatening information in anxious individuals. In the emotional Stroop task, participants are presented with emotional words, which participants must attempt to ignore while performing a central task (i.e., naming the color of the ink in which the words are printed). When the 'ignored' aspect (i.e., the word's meaning) is salient enough to compete with the 'attended to' aspect (i.e., the color of the ink), there is typically a longer response latency in naming the ink color (see MacLeod 1991; Williams, Mathews and MacLeod 1996, for reviews). Individuals with anxiety disorders, relative to healthy controls, typically show longer response latencies to threat words compared to neutral words (see Mathews and MacLeod 2005; Williams, Watts, MacLeod and Mathews 1997, for reviews). For example, such findings have been reported for GAD (e.g., Mathews and MacLeod 1985), PD (e.g., Ehlers, Margraf, Davies and Roth 1988; Maidenberg, Chen, Craske, Bohn and Bystritsky 1996) and SOC (e.g., Mattia, Heimberg and Hope 1993). Furthermore, these effects have been shown even when stimuli were presented subliminally (Bradley, Mogg, Millar and White 1995; Mogg, Bradley, Williams and Mathews 1993).

For several different anxiety disorders, these Stroop effects have been shown to be specific to the domain of greatest concern to that individual (rather than to all threatening cues) (see Mineka, Rafaeli and Yovel 2003, for a review). For example, McNally *et al.* (1990) conducted a study in which fifteen PTSD patients and fifteen matched controls performed an emotional Stroop task with PTSD-related, OCD-related, positive and neutral words. In contrast to the control participants who showed no interference effect, the PTSD patients showed Stroop interference only for the PTSD words. Related studies found greater interference for physical threat words in PD (Hope, Rapee, Heimberg and Dombeck 1990), for social threat words in SOC (Hope *et al.* 1990; Lundh and Öst 1996; Maidenberg *et al.* 1996), for contamination words in OCD (Tata, Leibowitz, Prunty, Cameron and Pickering 1996), and for rape-related words in rape victims with PTSD (Foa, Feske, Murdock, Kozak and McCarthy 1991). Indeed, color-naming interference has even been found in the anxiety disorder that Gray and McNaughton (2000) suggest might not even involve anxiety – PHOB (e.g., Kindt and Brosschot 1999, for snake phobia) as well, and this effect was again found to be specific to words related to participants' concern (Watts, McKenna, Sharrock and Trezise 1986, spider-related words in spider phobics).

However, there have been some controversies regarding the Stroop task due to an inherent methodological limitation. The emotional Stroop relies exclusively on interference effects leading to alternative ways of interpreting the findings (Mogg and Bradley 1998), that is, it is not clear whether Stroop interference reflects competition at the input (attentional) stage or at the output or response selection stage (MacLeod 1991). Interference in the emotional Stroop task may even reflect emotional disruption effects (Mathews and MacLeod 2005; Mogg and Bradley 1998), that is, interference may be a result of slowed response due to a momentary increase in state anxiety (and thus behavioral inhibition) resulting from exposure to a threat word (Mogg and Bradley 1998).

The dot-probe task can assess attentional biases more directly, as attentional biases are measured through location of attention. On each trial of an emotional dot-probe task, a pair of words is presented on a computer screen. Typically, one word is a threat word and the other is neutral or positive. Each pair is presented briefly and followed by a probe that is presented in the former position of one of the words, and participants are instructed to respond to the probe as quickly as possible. Previous research has established that detection latency for such a probe is a sensitive measure of visual attention, and that individuals respond faster to a probe stimulus presented in an attended rather than unattended region of a visual display (Navon and Margalit 1983).

In the first experiment using the dot-probe paradigm in emotional disorders, MacLeod, Mathews and Tata (1986) found that patients with GAD showed faster reaction times when the probes replaced a threat word than when they replaced a neutral word indicating attention to the threat words. The controls, on the other hand, showed the opposite pattern. The results were replicated in subsequent studies with adults with PD (e.g., Asmundson, Sandler, Wilson and Walker 1992; Beck, Stanley, Averill, Baldwin and Deagle 1992; Maidenberg et al. 1996), GAD (Mathews, Mogg, Kentish and Eysenck 1995; Mogg, Mathews and Eysenck 1992), and PTSD (Bryant and Harvey 1997), and with children with anxiety disorders (Vasey, Daleiden, Williams and Brown 1995).

Similar to studies using the Stoop task, studies using the dot-probe task have provided evidence of selective attentional biases for stimuli relevant for specific concerns related to particular disorders, including SOC (Asmundson and Stein 1994; Maidenberg et al. 1996) and OCD (Tata et al. 1996). As with the Stroop results, research using the dot-probe task also demonstrated subliminal attentional biases (e.g., Hermans, Vansteenwegen and Eelen 1999; Mathews, Ridgeway and Williamson 1996; Mogg, Bradley and Williams 1995; Mogg, Millar and Bradley 2000). Thus, it has been suggested that attentional biases in anxiety is associated with automatic processes that are likely to be involved in initial orienting of attention towards threatening stimuli (e.g., Mathews and MacLeod 1994; McNally 1995; Mogg and Bradley 2005). It should also be noted that given the convergence of results across the dot-probe and Stroop paradigms, the most parsimonious explanation of the results from both paradigms is that they both demonstrate attentional bias for threat in anxiety disorders. It should also be noted that it appears that this attentional bias is not restricted to verbal stimuli, but has been observed with emotional pictures and faces as well (e.g., Bradley, Mogg, White, Groom and De Bono 1999; Mogg, Millar and Bradley 2000).

Importantly, studies examining processing efficiency using stimuli that present only one processing option have failed to demonstrate negative attentional biases in anxiety (e.g., Becker and Rinck 2004; MacLeod and Mathews 1991; Mathews and MacLeod 1987). This suggests, as MacLeod (1990) has concluded, that anxiety is 'associated with relative increases in the priorities assigned to the processing of threat-related information, under conditions that introduce competition for processing resources' (p. 24).

It is not entirely clear whether MacLeod's (1990) conclusion is consistent with Gray's (1982) original articulation of RST. The most detailed statement we can find in Gray (1982) regarding attentional bias is that the output of the BIS/SHS includes 'increased attention to the environment, and especially to novel elements in the environment' (p. 459). This quote could be interpreted to imply increased attention to threat but it could at least as easily be interpreted as implying a general increase in alertness or a selective attentional bias for novelty. In addition, the emphasis on novelty would seem to imply that an anxious individual would not show increased attention toward a threat cue if it were familiar. If so, it would appear that the original formulation of RST cannot explain the attentional bias literature as most of the threat cues used in the Stroop and dot-probe studies are probably familiar to the subjects (for a related discussion see Eysenck 1992). Clearly, however, MacLeod's (1990) conclusion is consistent with the view expressed in Gray and McNaughton's (2000, p. 277) reformulation of RST, that an overactive BIS/SHS 'will increase the immediate perception and hence subsequent storage of threatening associations under conditions of conflict'.

Attentional biases in depression Though extensions of RST proposing that an overactive BIS also characterizes depression would predict a similar pattern of attentional biases in depression as that observed in anxiety, evidence in support of attentional biases in depression is not as reliable as in anxiety disorder. Whereas some studies demonstrated the presence of attentional biases in depression using the Stroop task (e.g., Gotlib and Cane 1987; Mogg, Bradley and Williams 1995; Nunn, Mathews and Trower 1997; Segal, Gemar, Truchon and Guirguis 1995; Williams and Broadbent 1986), the dot-probe task using words (Mathews, Ridgeway and Williamson 1996; Mogg, Bradley and Williams 1995, but limited to supraliminal stimuli), and the dot-probe task using faces (Gotlib, Kasch, Traill, Joormann, Arnow and Johnson 2004; Gotlib, Krasnoperova, Yue and Joorman 2004; Koster, Raedt, Goeleven, Franck and Crombez 2005), several failed to find evidence for attentional biases in depression (e.g., Bradley, Mogg, Millar and White 1995; MacLeod, Mathews and Tata 1986; McCabe and Gotlib 1995; Mogg, Bradley and Williams 1995 (no attentional biases for subliminal stimuli); Mogg, Bradley, Williams and Mathews 1993; Mogg, Millar and Bradley 2000; Neshat-Doost, Taghavi, Moradi, Yule and Dalgleish 1997).

It has been suggested that there is little convincing evidence that depression is associated with attentional biases (MacLeod 1990; Mathews and MacLeod 1994; Williams, Mathews and MacLeod 1996; Williams et al. 1997) or that attentional biases in depression could be attributed to co-morbid anxiety (MacLeod 1990; Mineka, Rafaeli and

Yovel 2003). There are, however, several issues that need to be considered when evaluating these conclusions. First, it is important to note that these previous reviews relied on studies mostly with non-clinical populations, albeit having high levels of depressed mood (e.g., Gilboa and Gotlib 1997; Gotlib, McLachlan and Katz 1988; Hill and Dutton 1989; Hill and Knowles 1991). Second, some of the studies that did not find negative attentional biases in depression showed that depressed individuals also failed to show positive attentional biases, suggesting a lack of positive biases normally found in non-depressed individuals (e.g., Gotlib, McLachlan and Katz 1988; McCabe and Gotlib 1995).

Interestingly, studies that have demonstrated the presence of attentional biases in MDD have tended to use longer durations of stimulus exposure, typically a SOA of 1,000ms (e.g., Gotlib, Kasch et al. 2004; Gotlib, Krasnoperova et al. 2004; for null findings with a SOA of 1,000ms in children and adolescents, see Neshat-Doost, Moradi, Taghavi, Yule and Dalgleish 2000). Thus, whereas more studies are needed for a firm conclusion regarding the status of attentional biases in MDD, it seems that if MDD is associated with attentional bias, this bias appears to differ from that associated with anxiety disorders, that is, if there is attentional bias in MDD, it seems to operate in later processes, such as sustained attention for (or difficulty disengaging from) negative information, rather than in initial orienting (Bradley, Mogg and Lee 1997; Mogg and Bradley 2005).

Interpretive biases in anxiety and mood disorders   The BIS is described as being activated by conflict, typically in the form of approach-avoidance conflict, and resolves the conflict by increasing the weight placed on aversive information. As such, the stronger the BIS output the more the individual should interpret novel or ambiguous stimuli as threatening given that such stimuli should elicit conflict between positive and negative interpretations.

There is general consensus that anxious individuals favor negative interpretations of ambiguity (see Mathews and MacLeod 2005; Mineka, Rafaeli and Yovel 2003; Williams et al. 1997, for reviews), that is, individuals with panic disorder interpret descriptions of physical sensations as symptoms of catastrophic disease (e.g., Clark 1988; Richards, Austin and Alvarenga 2001), and individuals with social phobia over-estimate the likelihood of negative social events and the negative consequences of events (e.g., Foa, Franklin, Perry and Herber 1996; Lucock and Salkovskis 1988). Likewise, clinically depressed individuals endorse more negative interpretations of ambiguous situations (e.g., Miller and Norman 1986; Nunn, Mathews and Trower 1997). Though consistent with the hypothesis that anxiety and depression are associated with a negative interpretive bias, these results might reflect response bias or demand as the studies relied heavily on self-report measures (MacLeod and Cohen 1993).

To overcome these limitations, researchers developed alternative techniques, mainly based on priming paradigms, to assess interpretive bias without asking participants to emit or endorse alternative response options. Studies using a priming methodology with a non-clinical population confirmed the presence of negative interpretive biases in highly anxious, non-clinical samples (e.g., Calvo and Castillo 2001; Richards and French 1992; MacLeod and Cohen 1993; Yoon, Hong and Zinbarg 2005; Yoon and Zinbarg 2007) and dysphoric individuals (Lawson, MacLeod and Hammond 2002), or the absence of positive interpretive biases (Hirsch and Mathews 2000) in anxious individuals.

To the best of our knowledge, however, there are only two studies with patient populations that did not rely on self-report measures to assess interpretation of ambiguity. In a study comparing GADs with controls (Hazlett-Stevens and Borkovec 2004), participants performed a lexical decision task that used homographs as ambiguous primes. Each homograph was preceded by antecedent words that were either (a) associated with the threatening meaning of the prime, (b) associated with the neutral meaning of the prime, or (c) unrelated to either meaning of the. homograph. In addition, homographs were followed by threat or neutral lexical decision target words. When the meaning of homographs remained ambiguous (i.e., when preceded by unrelated antecedent words), the GAD group did not show facilitated responses to negative targets. Thus, the results failed to demonstrate interpretive biases in GAD.

Using a somewhat different design, Amir, Beard, and Przeworski (2005) investigated the effect of priming of either threat or non-threat meanings of homographs on later encounters with that homograph in SOC. The SOC group showed the same pattern of results as controls when responding to threat targets. The SOC group, however, did not benefit from prior exposure to non-threat meanings of homographs, as they were slow to respond to non-threat targets of homographs that were previously presented with non-threat targets. Thus, the results seemed to suggest that SOC might have difficulty in learning non-threat meanings of ambiguous stimuli, which is consistent with Hirsch and Mathews' (2000) findings.

Though Hazlett-Stevens and Borkovec (2004) failed to find interpretive biases in a patient population, it seems premature to conclude that clinical levels of anxiety and depression are not associated with interpretive bias. On the contrary, it seems reasonable to assume that patient populations should show this bias, as studies with non-clinical populations have successfully demonstrated the presence of interpretive biases as reviewed above. Obviously we would need further research to be more conclusive about interpretive biases in anxiety and mood disorders.

Memory biases in anxiety and mood disorders As one tenet of RST is that excessive functional output from the SHS will increase the storage of threat and subsequent retrieval of threatening associations (Gray and McNaughton 2000), a clear prediction of RST is that memory biases should be associated with anxiety and mood disorders. Research has consistently demonstrated that depressed individuals favor recall of negative material (for reviews, see Blaney 1986; Mathews and MacLeod 1994, 2005; Mineka, Rafaeli and Yovel 2003). For example, clinically depressed participants show a bias to recall experimentally presented negative words (e.g., Watkins, Mathews, Williams and Fuller 1992) or facial stimuli (Gilboa-Schechtman, Erhard-Weiss and Jeczemien 2002) when encoded in a self-referential manner. In addition, depressed individuals show elevated tendencies to report more negative (e.g., Clark and Teasdale 1982) and overgeneral autobiographical memories (e.g., Williams and Scott 1988; for a review, see Healy and Williams 1999). As such, Matt, Vazquez and Campbell (1992) concluded in their meta-analysis of studies in memory bias in depression that depressed individuals recall more negative than positive stimuli, whereas non-depressed individuals recall more positive than negative stimuli.

Implicit memory refers to 'memory for information that was acquired during a specific episode and that is expressed on tests in which subjects are not required, and are frequently unable, to deliberately or consciously recollect the previously studied information' (Schacter 1990, p. 338). Earlier studies failed to demonstrate the presence of negative implicit memory biases while successfully demonstrating the presence of explicit memory biases in depressed individuals (Denny and Hunt 1992; Hertel and Hardin 1990; Watkins, Mathews, Williamson and Fuller 1992). It has been suggested, however, that a mismatch between the encoding task and the retrieval task has contributed to these null findings (Roediger and McDermott 1992). Indeed, when stimuli were conceptually encoded and conceptual tests were used, depressed individuals show negative implicit memory biases (e.g., Bradley, Mogg and Millar 1996; Watkins, Martin and Stern 2000; Watkins, Vache, Verney, Muller and Mathews 1996; for a review, see Watkins 2002).

In contrast to reliable memory biases in MDD, there has been mixed evidence supporting the presence of memory biases in anxiety disorders (for reviews, see Coles and Heimberg 2002; Eysenck and Mogg 1992; MacLeod and Mathews 2004). On the one hand, most studies on explicit memory bias in anxiety disorders failed to find such biases including studies of patients with GAD (e.g., Mathews, Mogg, May and Eysenck 1989; Mogg, Mathews and Weinman 1987; Otto, McNally, Pollack, Chen and Rosenbaum 1994), PHOB (Watts and Dalgleish 1991) and PD (e.g., Otto *et al.* 1994). On the other hand, one study with PD patients did find enhanced recall of threatening words (McNally, Foa and Donnell 1989), and at least one study was able to demonstrate the presence of explicit memory bias in GAD (Friedman, Thayer and Borkovec 2000). In terms of implicit memory bias, the results are inconsistent. While some studies lend support for the presence of implicit memory bias, for example, in PTSD (Amir, McNally and Wiegartz 1996), social phobia (Lundh and Ost 1996) or GAD (Mathews, Mogg, May and Eysenck 1989; MacLeod and McLaughlin 1995), others found no evidence for such bias in PD (e.g., Becker, Rinck and Margraf 1994), OCD (Foa, Amir, Gershuny, Molnar and Kozak 1997) or PTSD (McNally and Amir 1996, though this study has a problem of mismatch between encoding and retrieval tasks).

To summarize the evidence on cognitive biases, it is clear that an automatic attention bias to threat is a feature associated with anxiety disorders. There is some evidence that depressed individuals show attentional biases if stimuli are presented long enough, but, unlike anxiety disorders, MDD does not seem to be associated with *automatic* attentional biases. Evidence regarding interpretive biases in anxiety disorders and MDD is a bit unclear. On the one hand, evidence from several studies is consistent with the presence of interpretive biases. On the other hand, the studies with patient populations thus far have mostly relied on self-report measures and are therefore vulnerable to response bias and demand artifacts. When it comes to memory biases, it is clear that depressed individuals exhibit memory biases, but evidence of memory biases in anxiety disorders is mixed at best.

Longitudinal studies of risk for anxiety and mood disorders

Several longitudinal studies have shown neuroticism (N) to be a predictor of later negative affect and symptoms of emotional distress (e.g., Costa and McCrae 1980; Levenson *et al.* 1988), even after entering initial symptom levels as co-variates (Gershuny and Sher 1998; Jorm *et al.* 2000). Importantly, Clark, Watson and Mineka (1994) reviewed several other longitudinal studies showing N to be a predictor of both subsequent diagnoses and chronicity of major depression, and subsequent studies found additional support for their conclusion (Hayward *et al.* 2000; Kendler *et al.* 1993; Krueger *et al.* 1996; Roberts and Kendler 1999). In addition, N is a risk factor for development of PTSD following trauma (e.g., Breslau and Davis 1992; Breslau, Davis and Adnreski 1995; Kulka *et al.* 1990; Helzer, Robin and McEvoy 1987), an especially good marker of risk for multiple diagnoses (Krueger *et al.* 1996) and a predictor of the development of panic attacks (Hayward *et al.* 2000). Similarly, Schmidt, Lerew and Jackson (1999) found trait anxiety predicted the development of panic attacks in a prospective study of Air Force Academy Cadets (though this effect appeared to be mediated by the personality trait of anxiety sensitivity). Additional longitudinal studies have shown that behaviorally inhibited children are at greater risk for the development of multiple phobias and multiple anxiety disorders in later childhood (Biederman *et al.* 1990, 1993; Hirshfeld *et al.* 1992), social phobias in adolescence (Hayward *et al.* 1998) and MDD in early adulthood (Caspi *et al.* 1996). Thus, extant data provide strong support for the hypothesis that N/trait anxiety is a marker of vulnerability for MDD and anxiety disorders, though there is a need for more research concerning vulnerability for anxiety disorders.

Unresolved questions and suggestions for future research directions

We begin our discussion of unresolved questions and suggestions for future research directions by focusing on issues most directly relevant to anxiety disorders and MDD. After raising questions specific to anxiety disorders and MDD, we will discuss one more general question that is germane to all RST researchers and theorists.

How should RST be modified to account for the complexity of the results on cognitive biases in anxiety disorders and MDD?

Gray and McNaughton (2000) appear to assume that prospective and retrospective 'risk analysis' are functionally equivalent and carried out by the same circuits. Thus, they predict that the negative bias associated with a hyperactive SHS should include increased attention to threatening stimuli, increased storage of threatening associations and increased retrieval of threatening associations. To the extent that a hyperactive SHS is involved in the anxiety disorders and MDD, the current version of RST therefore predicts that both attentional and memory biases should be characteristic of the anxiety disorders and

MDD. Certainly, it is more parsimonious to assume that attention to threat, storage of threatening associations and retrieval of threatening associations are essentially reflecting a single, relatively unified cognitive mechanism/process ('risk analysis'). The data on cognitive biases in patients, however, force us to abandon this assumption in favor of a more complex one. As reviewed above, there is strong evidence that anxiety disorders are associated with attentional bias but less support for memory bias in anxiety disorders, with the converse pattern holding for MDD. This pattern of results suggests that prospective risk analysis (attention to threat) is dissociable from retrospective risk analysis (memory for threat). In addition, any evidence that does suggest that MDD is associated with an attentional bias comes from studies using long SOAs, suggesting that an early, automatic stage of risk analysis is dissociable from a later, more strategic stage. What remains unclear, however, is how these dissociations are implemented psychologically and anatomically. Are there at least somewhat distinct sub-systems/ circuits of the BIS/SHS that subserve these different forms of risk analysis and are differentially hyperactive in anxiety disorders versus MDD? Might it be the case that when the BAS is also active it interacts with the BIS to bias risk analysis toward the prospective/automatic mode (as part of preparation for active coping with threat characteristic of anxiety) whereas BIS activity in the relative absence of BAS activity biases risk analysis toward the strategic and retrospective modes? More research is needed before questions such as these concerning different forms of risk analysis can be answered. Thus, it is clear that RST needs to be modified to account for associations between anxiety disorders and MDD with cognitive biases but at this time it is not clear what form this modification should take.

Does specific phobia essentially not involve anxiety and passive avoidance?

Gray and McNaughton (2000) appear to contradict themselves regarding these issues. On the one hand, they make statements clearly rejecting roles for anxiety and passive avoidance in specific phobia (PHOB) such as 'because they are insensitive to anxiolytic drugs, we can exclude specific phobias from our analysis and identify them with pure fear rather than anxiety' (Gray and McNaughton 2000, p. 292). Similarly, they state that 'specific phobias in general manifest as increased active avoidance of the specific phobia object while agoraphobia manifests as increased passive avoidance' (Gray and McNaughton 2000, p. 320). On the other hand, Gray and McNaughton (2000, p. 311) also claim that phobic stimuli are innate fear stimuli and that innate fear stimuli 'act on the septo-hippocampal system (probably on information relayed to it by the amygdala and as a result of anticipatory conditioning)'. Given that activity in the SHS, especially when accompanied by amygdala activation, is seen as giving rise to anxiety and passive avoidance, this later position would seem to imply that anxiety is an important component of PHOB. Our view is that whereas fear focused on a discrete, external object or situation may be the unique feature of PHOB, we see this specific feature as co-existing with the shared feature of anxiety.

One of the considerations that appears to lead Gray and McNaughton (2000) to occasionally identify PHOB with pure fear is their functional typology for defense in which they equate PHOB with the response to actual avoidable threat that, in turn, they identify with fear. Even if we agreed that PHOB could be reduced to the response to actual avoidable threat, the rabbit and fox example used by Gray and McNaughton makes clear that such situations often involve conflict as the potential prey 'must be prepared both to remain still and assess whether it has been detected ... and to flee ... Thus, both anxiety and fear will be present' (Gray and McNaughton 2000, p. 328). Moreover, whereas we agree that actual avoidable threat is relevant for fear, we distinguish between fear and PHOB and do not agree that PHOB can be reduced to the response to actual avoidable threat in the first place. For us, what distinguishes PHOB from fear is that PHOB also involves anticipatory anxiety and passive avoidance triggered by cues for threat (i.e., potential threat). For example, many people would experience at least some degree of fear if they encountered a potentially poisonous snake when out for a hike in the woods. It is not until an individual who would otherwise enjoy hiking begins to avoid going hiking in the woods that we would diagnose him/her as having a PHOB. Finally, to the extent to which RST is correct in attributing attentional bias toward threat to SHS activity, the cognitive bias literature is more consistent with the position that anxiety plays an important role in PHOB; that is, as we reviewed earlier, results from the emotional Stroop paradigm suggesting increased attention to threat have been reported in PHOB.

How should disorder be defined?

Gray and McNaughton (2000) speak of pure cases of PD or PHOB or OCD or primary *disorders* of panic, phobia, etc. without anxiety and that would not normally seek treatment. We believe such presentations most probably should not even be considered to be instances of disorder. Of course, a debate over this issue would hinge upon one's definition of disorder. Gray and McNaughton never do articulate their criterion for disorder. For us, distress and functional impairment are central characteristics of disorder. Consider an individual who experiences occasional panic attacks but does not worry about them in between attacks, is not distressed about the fact that he/she has these attacks, has not altered his/her behavior in any way to reduce the likelihood of having attacks and does not experience any functional impairment as a result of having the attacks. We would say that this person does not have PD or a disorder of any kind. If RST is to continue to be taken seriously as a leading theory of the development of anxiety disorders and MDD, RST theorists will not only need to be explicit in articulating their criteria for disorder but such criteria will need to correspond at least fairly closely to the consensual or modal view held by psychopathologists.

Should phobic stimuli be viewed as innate fear stimuli or prepared stimuli?

Gray and McNaughton (2000) are very clear in adopting the view of phobic stimuli as innate fear stimuli (as noted above) and in explicitly rejecting preparedness theory. One of us (Zinbarg and Mineka 1991; also see Mineka and Zinbarg 1995, 1996) has argued strongly in favor of the preparedness view. Mineka's (1987) experiments clearly show that when a fear-relevant conditioned stimulus (CS) is paired with modeling of fearful behavior, this does not merely cause more attention to be paid to the CS but rather causes the CS to elicit fear. If, as claimed by Gray and McNaughton, the principle that conditioning is facilitated by the similarity of events to be associated could account for Mineka's results, we would expect fear-relevant stimuli that could not have been prepared by evolution to have the same associative properties as putatively prepared fear-relevant stimuli. Some studies, however, showed that stimuli that are fear-relevant but that could not be prepared by evolution to be so (e.g., guns, broken electrical outlets) do not have the same associative properties as putatively prepared fear-relevant stimuli. For example, greater resistance to extinction has been found when the CSs were phylogenetic (i.e., prepared) fear-relevant stimuli rather than ontogenetic (i.e., not prepared) fear-relevant stimuli (Cook, Hodes and Lang 1986; Hugdahl and Karker 1981). Other studies have shown that pairing fear-relevant stimuli with non-contingent shock results in the development of a stronger illusory correlation or co-variation bias between phylogenetic fear-relevant stimuli and shock than between ontogenetic fear-relevant stimuli and shock (e.g., Amin and Lovibond

1997; Kennedy, Rapee and Mazurski 1997; Tomarken, Sutton and Mineka 1995; though see Davey and Dixon 1996, Honeybourne, Matchett and Davey 1993 and Hugdahl and Johnsen 1989).

Do nightmares in PTSD and nocturnal-panic represent freedom from inhibitory control otherwise exerted by the SHS?

Gray and McNaughton (2000) argue that nightmares in PTSD and nocturnal panic in PD are best explained as instances of release from inhibitory control otherwise exerted by the SHS. We take a different stance. First, as stated above, we believe it is more accurate to say that anxiety primes panic rather than anxiety inhibits panic. Thus, we would explain nocturnal panic as arising from hypervigilance for arousal, widely thought to be a core process in PD and is thought to be more automatic than strategic (perhaps combined with the notion that the just noticeable difference for fluctuations in arousal will decrease during sleep as baseline levels of arousal decrease). Secondly, the release from inhibition explanation of PTSD nightmares would seem to imply that flashbacks, intrusive thoughts and other of the so-called 're-experiencing' symptoms during the waking state should be much less frequent (if they should occur at all) than nightmares. On the contrary, the data bearing on the relative frequency of nightmares versus flashbacks/intrusive images/thoughts indicate that flashbacks/intrusive images/thoughts during the waking state are at least as common as nightmares among those with PTSD (e.g., Carrion, Weems, Ray and Reiss 2002; Foa, Cashman, Jaycox and Perry 1997; Franklin and Zimmerman 2001; Wohlfarth, Van den Brink, Winkel and Ter Smitten 2003). There is also evidence suggesting that dreaming is the offline reprocessing of information essential to survival (Winson 1990). Certainly, stimuli associated with a life-threatening trauma, such as is required for the diagnosis of PTSD, must constitute information that is essential for survival. According to this analysis, nightmares should be one of the expected sequelae of trauma without requiring release from inhibition (for a more detailed discussion of the notion that nightmares are part of the response to uncontrollable, unpredictable stress and how to test this possibility in animal models (see Foa, Zinbarg and Olasov-Rothbaum 1992).

What type of conflict is more central to agoraphobia: approach-avoidance or escape-avoidance?

According to Gray and McNaughton (2000, p. 322), agoraphobia is often 'an incidental consequence of the coincidence of a randomly occurring panic attack with the presence of otherwise affectively positive stimuli'. We believe that this characterization at best accounts for a small minority of cases of agoraphobia. Rather, we maintain that a conflict between escape and passive avoidance lies at the core of the vast majority of cases of agoraphobia. In the first place, many of the most prototypic situations feared by agoraphobic patients – driving, riding on public transportation, being far from home or a hospital, riding an elevator, going over a bridge, being in a crowd, etc. – do not appear to be necessarily positive. The DSM definition of agoraphobia is 'anxiety about being in places from which escape might be difficult (or embarrassing) or in which help may not be available in the event of having an unexpected or situationally predisposed panic attack or panic-like symptoms' (APA 1994, p. 396); that is, the typical worry of a patient with PDA is that he or she will feel the urge to escape and that this escape attempt will be either frustrated or perhaps even punished (in the form of embarrassment).

Do anxiolytic medications reduce attentional bias?

Given that 'hyperactivity of the septo-hippocampal system should produce a fundamentally cognitive dysfunction' (Gray and McNaughton 2000, p. 277) and that the anxiolytic medications reduce 'the acuity' of SHS processing, a relatively straightforward prediction of RST should be that anxiolytic medications should reduce cognitive bias. It might even be predicted that cognitive bias reduction should mediate the therapeutic effects of the anxiolytic medications. In fact, it could be argued that these are predictions of central theoretical significance for the current version of RST. Whereas Gray and McNaughton review a number of studies testing whether anxiolytic drugs produce a generalized amnesia and a number of studies have tested whether cognitive-behavioral therapy reduces negative cognitive bias (e.g., Lundh and Ost 2001; Mathews, Mogg, Kentish and Eysenck 1995; Mattia, Heimberg and Hope 1993; McNally and Foa 1987; Mogg, Bradley, Millar and White 1995; Westling and Ost 1995), there appears to be only four studies to date testing the effects of anxiolytic medications on negative cognitive bias (Golombok, Stavrou, Bonn, Mogg et al. 1991; Golombok, Mathews, MacLeod, Lader et al. 1990; Mattia, Heimberg and Hope 1993; Nesse and Klaas 1994). Moreover, among these four studies, the only study that found a significant effect of anxiolytic drugs on cognitive bias (Mattia, Heimberg and Hope 1993) combined patients who were treated with cognitive-behavioral therapy, phenelzine or placebo. It is therefore possible that the patients treated with cognitive-behavioral therapy may have been entirely responsible for the significant effect in that study. Thus, there is a need for more studies testing the predictions that anxiolytic medications should reduce cognitive bias and that such reductions should mediate the therapeutic effects of these medications. As it appears that the 'truly anxiolytic effect' of such medications develops over time and is not immediate even in the case of the benzodiazepines (Gray and McNaughton 2000), such studies would need to carefully assess both the immediate and more slowly developing effects of the anxiolytic medications. However, if such studies continue to fail to support these predictions, a modification of RST would seem to be called for that would specify how the anxiolytic medications are affecting the SHS/BIS if not via cognitive bias reduction.

What types of situations constitute conflicts that activate the BIS?

Though we believe that the emphasis on conflict in the reformulation of RST does nicely capture the core of the psychology of anxiety, it appears that agreement about when conflict is present and what types of conflict are sufficient for activating the BIS may be problematic. For example, Gray and McNaughton (2000) claim that awaiting the optimal moment to emit an innate flight response is reflective of pure activation of the Fight-Flight System whereas our analysis of this situation suggests that conflict is inherent in this situation. To us, it seems the point of waiting for the optimal moment to emit an innate flight response is that an innate flight response emitted at a sub-optimal moment might actually increase the likelihood of attack from a predator. Even if attack is inevitable and so the flight response does not affect the probability of attack, we would still argue that flight initiated at a sub-optimal time is more likely to be punished than flight initiated at an optimal time. Thus, if the animal does not flee, it is likely to be punished but if it flees at the wrong time it is also likely to be punished and we believe it therefore must be experiencing an avoidance-avoidance conflict.

A related issue in need of clarification is whether approach-approach conflicts activate the BIS/SHS. On the one hand, Gray and McNaughton (2000, p. 45) describe the BIS as 'a system that is active when the animal is faced with a threat which it has some reason to approach'. Similarly, pure amygdala activation is said not to involve 'the approach-avoidance conflict which underlies anxiety' (Gray and McNaughton 2000, p. 235). These statements seem to exclude the possibility that the BIS is also activated by approach-approach conflicts (or avoidance-avoidance conflicts for that matter). On the other hand, in places Gray and McNaughton (2000) do suggest that approach-approach (or avoidance-avoidance) conflicts are also possible elicitors of BIS activation. Moreover, RST places heavy emphasis on the functional equivalence of signals for punishment and signals for frustrative non-reward and any approach-approach conflict can be just as easily described as a frustration-frustration conflict. That is, approach of either goal in an approach-approach conflict involves at least the temporary omission of the reward (and thus the experience of frustration) associated with the other goal. In this way, each goal involved in an approach-approach conflict represents a threat with respect to the other goal.

If there is widespread agreement among RST researchers that avoidance-avoidance and approach-approach conflicts need to be incorporated as BIS elicitors, we would suggest that the description of the BIS offered by Gray and McNaughton and quoted above needs to be modified. Rather than focusing on situations when the individual is faced with a threat that he/she has some reason to approach, we would prefer to describe the BIS as a system that is active when the individual is faced with a threat that he/she has some reason *not to escape/actively avoid*. The differences between these two descriptions are subtle but meaningful as the latter clearly incorporates avoidance-avoidance conflicts and perhaps even the situation of awaiting the optimal moment to emit an innate flight response. Our description of the BIS encompasses the approach-approach conflict as well, that is, the reason not to escape/actively avoid the threat to goal 1 (i.e., the frustration of not obtaining goal 1 in the pursuit of goal 2) is that there is motivation to approach the threat to goal 1 (i.e., the reward associated with the achievement of goal 2). If this rhetoric strikes the reader as convoluted, we would propose then that the BIS should simply and consistently be described as a system that is active whenever the individual experiences conflicting goals. This description clearly applies equally well to approach-avoidance conflicts, avoidance-avoidance conflicts and approach-approach (frustration-frustration) conflicts without requiring any further elaboration.

Clearly, the hypothesis that avoidance-avoidance conflicts elicit BIS activity has already been subject to extensive empirical testing. Two-way active avoidance is certainly an exemplar of avoidance-avoidance conflict and analysis of the effects of anxiolytic medications and SHS lesions on two-way active avoidance has figured prominently in the derivation of the BIS in the development of RST (Gray 1982; Gray and McNaughton 2000). The notion that approach-approach conflicts are anxiogenic appears not to have been tested as extensively (if at all). However, it does seem to be testable by slightly modifying traditional two-way avoidance in the shuttle-box. We might call this paradigm 'two-way reward' and, in its simplest version, we would require the animal on each trial to jump over the hurdle in the shuttle-box to be rewarded. If it stays where it is, reward is omitted. We suspect that this simple version of the paradigm will turn out to be too easy such that even undrugged/unlesioned animals won't hesitate at all to jump back to the side associated with frustrative non-reward on the prior trial. If so, one could use more complex contingencies. Perhaps one could use a partial reinforcement schedule for the second jump (back to the starting side of the box) thereby enhancing the frustrative non-reward associated with that side of the box. Thus, the second jump would be rewarded but not as consistently as the first jump. Perhaps one could even titrate the partial reinforcement associated with the second jump, gradually reducing the reinforcement percentage to the level just below that which consistently supports making the second jump among undrugged/unlesioned animals. Imagine, for example, that a 10 per cent reinforcement schedule is associated with greater than 50 per cent of undrugged animals consistently and rapidly making the second jump but that a 5 per cent reinforcement schedule is associated with less than 50 per cent of undrugged animals making the second jump. We would then predict that the drugged (or lesioned) animal would be significantly more likely than the control animal to make the second jump when the second jump is rewarded on the 5 per cent reinforcement schedule. In contrast, if approach-approach conflicts do not tend to activate the BIS, then the drugged (or lesioned) animal should show consistently similar reductions to that shown by control animals in the likelihood of making the second jump as the reinforcement schedule is lowered.

Conclusion

The evidence on the symptom structure and psychopathology of and prospective risk factors for anxiety disorders and MDD is largely consistent with the predictions of RST. The most notable exception to this generalization is found in the literature on cognitive biases associated with anxiety disorders and MDD. Rather than finding attentional, interpretive and memory biases in all these disorders as predicted by RST, there is strong evidence for attentional and interpretive biases, with more equivocal evidence for memory biases associated with anxiety disorders. In contrast, there is strong evidence for memory biases but more equivocal evidence for automatic attentional biases associated with MDD.

Whereas the data are not entirely consistent with RST and a comprehensive comparison with other theories of anxiety disorders and MDD is beyond the scope of this chapter, it is our conviction that there are few other theories that account for as much of the data as RST does.

Moreover, there are no other theories that we know of that account for as much data as RST does in as parsimonious a fashion (basically RST relies on one central theoretical construct – that of the BIS) or spanning as many levels of analysis as does RST, including very detailed predictions of the underlying anatomical substrates. To be sure, there are many unresolved questions confronting researchers and theorists whose work is informed by RST and we anticipate that RST will need to undergo further revisions. In the final analysis, there can be no doubt that RST has been very successful in stimulating a great deal of research that has led to important insights about the nature of anxiety disorders and we fully expect RST to remain a generative theory in this regard for a long time to come.

References

American Psychiatric Association (1994), *Diagnostic and Statistical Manual of Mental Disorders* (4th edn, Washington DC: APA)

Amin, J.M. and Lovibond, P.F. (1997), Dissociations between covariation bias and expectancy bias for fear-relevant stimuli, *Cognition and Emotion*, 11, 273–389

Amir, N., Beard, C. and Przeworski, A. (2005), Resolving ambiguity: the effect of experience on interpretation of ambiguous events in generalized social phobia, *Journal of Abnormal Psychology*, 114, 402–408

Amir, N., McNally, R.J. and Wiegartz, P.S. (1996), Implicit memory bias for threat in panic disorder: application of the 'white noise' paradigm, *Behaviour Research and Therapy*, 34, 157–162

Antony, M.M., Bieling, P.J., Cox, B.J., Enns, M.W. and Swinson, R.P. (1998), Psychometric properties of the 42-item and 21-item version of the depression anxiety stress scales in clinical groups and a community sample, *Psychological Assessment*, 10, 176–181

Asmundson, G.J., Sandler, L.S., Wilson, K.G. and Walker, J.R. (1992), Selective attention toward physical threat in patients with panic disorder, *Journal of Anxiety Disorders*, 6, 295–303

Asmundson, G.J.G. and Stein, M.B. (1994), Selective processing of social threat in patients with generalized social phobia: evaluation using a dot-probe paradigm, *Journal of Anxiety Disorders*, 8, 107–117

Barlow, D.H. (1988), *Anxiety and its Disorders: the Nature and Treatment of Anxiety and Panic* (New York: Guilford Press)

 (1991a), Disorders of emotion, *Psychological Inquiry*, 2, 58–71

 (1991b), Disorders of emotions: clarification, elaboration, and future directions, *Psychological Inquiry*, 2, 97–105

Barlow, D.H., Chorpita, B.F. and Turovsky, J. (1996), Fear, panic, anxiety, and disorders of emotion in D.A. Hope (ed.), *Nebraska Symposium on Motivation: vol. 43, Perspectives on Anxiety, Panic, and Fear: Current Theory and Research in Motivation* (Lincoln, NE: University of Nebraska Press), pp. 251–328

Basoglu, M., Marks, I.M. and Sengun, S. (1992), A prospective study of panic and anxiety in agoraphobia with panic disorder, *British Journal of Psychiatry*, 160, 57–64

Bass, C., Lelliott, P. and Marks, I. (1989), Fear talk versus voluntary hyperventilation in agoraphobics and normals: a controlled study, *Psychological Medicine*, 19, 669–676

Beck, J.G., Stanley, M.A., Averill, P.M., Baldwin, L.E. and Deagle, E.A. (1992), Attention and memory for threat in panic disorder, *Behavior Research and Therapy*, 30, 619–629

Becker, E.S. and Rinck, M. (2004), Attention in fear of spiders: a signal detection approach, *Cognition and Emotion*, 18, 961–976

Becker, E.S., Rinck, M. and Margraf, J. (1994), Memory bias in panic disorder, *Journal of Abnormal Psychology*, 103, 396–399

Biederman, J., Rosenbaum, J.F., Bolduc-Murphy, E.A., Faraone, S.V., Chaloff, J., Hirshfeld, D.R. *et al.* (1993), A 3-year follow-up of children with and without behavioral inhibition, *Journal of the American Academy of Child and Adolescent Psychiatry*, 32, 814–821

Biederman, J., Rosenbaum, J.F., Hirshfeld, D.R., Faraone, S.V., Bolduc, E.A., Gersten, M. *et al.* (1990), Psychiatric correlates of behavioral inhibition in young children of parents with and without psychiatric disorders, *Archives of General Psychiatry*, 47, 21–26

Blaney, P.H. (1986), Affect and memory: a review, *Psychological Bulletin*, 99, 229–246

Boulougouris, J.C., Rabavilas, A.D. and Stefanis, C. (1977), Psychophysiological responses in obsessive-compulsive patients, *Behaviour Reseasrch and Therapy*, 15, 221–230

Bouton, M., Mineka, S. and Barlow, D.H. (2001), A modern learning theory perspective on the etiology of panic disorder, *Psychological Review*, 108, 4–32

Bradley, B.P., Mogg, K. and Lee, S.C. (1997), Attentional biases for negative information in induced and naturally occurring dysphoria, *Behaviour Research and Therapy*, 35, 911–927

Bradley, B.P., Mogg, K. and Millar, N. (1996), Implicit memory bias in clinical and non-clinical depression, *Behaviour Research and Therapy*, 34, 865–880

Bradley, B.P., Mogg, K., Millar, N. and White, J. (1995), Selective processing of negative information: effects of clinical anxiety, concurrent depression, and awareness, *Journal of Abnormal Psychology*, 104, 532–536

Bradley, B.P., Mogg, K., White, J., Groom, C. and De Bono, J. (1999), Attentional bias for emotional faces in generalized anxiety disorder, *British Journal of Clinical Psychology*, 38, 267–278

Breslau, N. and Davis, G.C. (1992), Posttraumatic stress disorder in an urban population of young adults: risk factors for chronicity, *American Journal of Psychiatry*, 149, 671–675

Breslau, N., Davis, G.C. and Adnreski, P. (1995), Risk factors for PTSD-related traumatic events: a prospective analysis, *American Journal of Psychiatry*, 152, 529–535

Brown, T.A., Chorpita, B.F. and Barlow, D.H. (1998), Structural relationships among dimensions of the DSM-IV anxiety and mood disorders and dimensions of negative affect, positive affect, and autonomic arousal, *Journal of Abnormal Psychology*, 107, 179–192

Bryant, R.A. and Harvey, A.G. (1997), Processing threatening information in posttraumatic stress disorder, *Journal of Abnormal Psychology*, 104, 537–541

Bystritsky, A., Craske, M., Maidenberg, E., Vapnik, T. and Shapiro, D. (1995), Ambulatory monitoring of panic patients during regular activity: a preliminary report, *Biological Psychiatry*, 38, 684–689

Calvo, M.G. and Castillo, M.D. (2001), Selective interpretation in anxiety: uncertainty for threatening events, *Cognition and Emotion*, 15, 299–320

Carrion, V.G., Weems, C.F., Ray, R. and Reiss, A.L. (2002), Toward an empirical definition of pediatric PTSD: the phenomenology of PTSD symptoms in youth, *Journal of the American Academy of Child and Adolescent Psychiatry*, 41, 166–173

Caspi, A., Moffitt, T.E., Thornton, A., Freedman, D. *et al.* (1996), The life history calendar: a research and clinical assessment method for collecting retrospective event-history data, *International Journal of Methods in Psychiatric Research*, 6, 101–114

Clark, D.M. (1988), A cognitive model of panic attacks in S. Rachman and J.D. Maser (eds), *Panic: Psychological Perspectives* (Hillsdale, NJ: Erlbaum), pp. 71–89

Clark, D.M. and Teasdale, J.D. (1982), Diurnal variation in clinical depression and accessibility of memories of positive and negative experiences, *Journal of Abnormal Psychology*, 91, 87–95

Clark, L.A. and Watson, D. (1991), Tripartite model of anxiety and depression: psychometric evidence and taxanomic implications, *Journal of Abnormal Psychology*, 100, 316–336

Clark, L.A., Watson, D. and Mineka, S. (1994), Temperament, personality, and the mood and anxiety disorders, *Journal of Abnormal Psychology*, 103, 103–116

Coles, M.E. and Heimberg, R.G. (2002), Memory biases in the anxiety disorders: current status, *Clinical Psychology Review*, 22, 587–627

Cook, E.W., Hodes, R.L. and Lang, P.J. (1986), Preparedness and phobia: effects of stimulus content on human visceral conditioning, *Journal of Abnormal Psychology*, 95, 195–207

Cook, E.W., Melamed, B.G., Cuthbert, B.N., McNeil, D.W. and Lang, P.J. (1988), Emotional imagery and the differential diagnosis of anxiety, *Journal of Consulting and Clinical Psychology*, 56, 734–740

Costa, P.T. and McCrae, R.R. (1980), Influence of extraversion and neuroticism on subjective well-being: happy and unhappy people, *Journal of Personality and Social Psychology*, 38, 668–678

Craske, M.G., Rapee, R.M., Jackel, L. and Barlow, D.H. (1989), Qualitative dimensions of worry in DSM-III-R generalized anxiety disorder subjects and nonanxious controls, *Behaviour Research and Therapy*, 27, 397–402

Davey, G.C.L. and Dixon, A.L. (1996), The expectancy bias model of selective associations: the relationship of judgments of CS dangerousness, CS-UCS similarity and prior fear to a priori and a posteriori covariation assessments, *Behaviour Research and Therapy*, 34, 235–252

Denny, E. and Hunt, R. (1992), Affective valence and memory in depression: dissociation of recall and fragment completion, *Journal of Abnormal Psychology*, 101, 575–582

Ehlers, A., Margraf, J., Davies, S. and Roth, W.T. (1988), Selective processing of threat cues in subjects with panic attacks, *Cognition and Emotion*, 2, 201–220

Eysenck, M.W. (1992), The nature of anxiety in A. Gale and M.W. Eysenck (eds), *Handbook of Individual Differences: Biological Perspectives* (Oxford: John Wiley and Sons), pp. 157–178

Eysenck, M.W. and Mogg, K. (1992), Clinical anxiety, trait anxiety, and memory bias in S.A. Christianson (ed.), *The Handbook of Emotion and Memory: Research and Theory* (Hillsdale, NJ: Lawrence Erlbaum Associates)

Foa, E.B., Amir, N., Gershuny, B., Molnar, C. and Kozak, M.J. (1997), Implicit and explicit memory in obsessive-compulsive disorder, *Journal of Anxiety Disorders*, 11, 119–129

Foa, E.B., Cashman, L., Jaycox, L. and Perry, K. (1997), The validation of a self-report measure of posttraumatic stress disorder: the posttraumatic diagnositc scale, *Psychological Assessment*, 9, 445–451

Foa, E.B., Feske, U., Murdock, T.B., Kozak, M.J. and McCarthy, P.R. (1991), Processing of threat-related information in rape victims, *Journal of Abnormal Psychology*, 100, 156–162

Foa, E.B., Franklin, M.E., Perry, K.J. and Herber, J.D. (1996), Cognitive biases in generalized social phobia, *Journal of Abnormal Psychology*, 105, 433–439

Foa, E.B., Zinbarg, R. and Olasov-Rothbaum, B.O. (1992), Uncontrollability and unpredictability in post-traumatic stress disorder: an animal model, *Psychological Bulletin*, 112, 218–238

Fowles, D.C. (1988), Psychophysiology and psychopathology: a motivational approach, *Psychophysiology*, 25, 373–391

Frank, J.D. (1973), *Persuasion and Healing: A Comparative Study of Psychotherapy* (Oxford: Schocken)

Franklin, C. and Zimmerman, M. (2001), Posttraumatic stress disorder and major depressive disorder: investigating the role of overlapping symptoms in diagnostic comorbidity, *Journal of Nervous and Mental Disease*, 189, 548–551

Friedman, B.H., Thayer, J.F. and Borkovec, T.D. (2000), Explicit memory bias for threat words in generalized anxiety disorder, *Behaviour Research and Therapy*, 31, 745–756

Gerlach, A.L., Wilhelm, F.H., Gruber, K. and Roth, W.T. (2001), Blushing and physiological arousability in social phobia, *Journal of Abnormal Psychology*, 110, 247–258

Gershuny, B. and Sher, K.J. (1998), The relation between personality and anxiety: findings from a 3-year prospective study, *Journal of Abnormal Psychology*, 107, 252–262

Gilboa, E. and Gotlib, I.H. (1997), Cognitive biases and affect persistence in previously dysphoric and never-dysphoric individuals, *Cognition and Emotion*, 11, 517–538

Gilboa-Schechtman, E., Erhard-Weiss, D. and Jeczemien, P. (2002), Interpersonal deficits meet cognitive biases: memory for facial expressions in depressed and anxious men and women, *Psychiatry Research*, 113, 279–293

Golombok, S., Mathews, A., MacLeod, C., Lader, M. *et al.* (1990), The effects of diazepam on cognitive processing, *Human Psychopharmacology: Clinical and Experimental*, 5, 143–147

Golombok, S., Stavrou, A., Bonn, J., Mogg, K. *et al.* (1991), The effects of diazepam on anxiety-related cognition, *Cognitive Therapy and Research*, 15, 459–467

Gotlib, I.H. and Cane, D.B. (1987), Construct accessibility and clinical depression: a longitudinal investigation, *Journal of Abnormal Psychology*, 96, 199–204

Gotlib, I.H., Kasch, K.L., Traill, S., Joormann, J., Arnow, B.A. and Johnson, S. L. (2004), Coherence and specificity of information-processing biases in depression and social phobia, *Journal of Abnormal Psychology*, 113, 386–398

Gotlib, I.H., Krasnoperova, E., Yue, D.N. and Joorman, J. (2004), Attentional biases for negative interpersonal stimuli in clinical depression, *Journal of Abnormal Psychology*, 113, 127–135

Gotlib, I.H., McLachlan, A.L. and Katz, A.N. (1988), Biases in visual attention in depressed and nondepressed individuals, *Cognition and Emotion*, 2, 185–200

Graeff, F.G. (1994), Neuroanatomy and neurotransmitter regulation of defensive behaviors and related emotions in mammals, *Brazilian Journal of Medical and Biological Research*, 27, 811–829

Gray, J.A. and McNaughton, N. (1996), The neuropsychology of anxiety: reprise in D.A. Hope (ed.), *Nebraska Symposium on Motivation*, vol. 43, *Perspectives on Anxiety, Panic, and Fear: Current Theory and Research in Motivation* (Lincoln, NE: University of Nebraska Press), pp. 61–134

(2000), *The Neuropsychology of Anxiety* (Oxford: Oxford University Press)

Gray, J.A. (1982), *The Neuropsychology of Anxiety: an Enquiry into the Functions of the Septo-hippocampal System* (NY: Clarendon Press/Oxford University Press)

(1991), Fear, panic, and anxiety: what's in a name?, *Psychological Inquiry*, 2, 77–78

Hayward, C., Killen, J.D., Kraemer, H.C. and Taylor, C.B. (1998), Linking self-reported childhood behavioral inhibition to adolescent social phobia, *Journal of the American Academy of Child and Adolescent Psychiatry*, 37, 1308–1316

(2000), Predictors of panic attacks in adolescents, *Journal of the American Academy of Child and Adolescent Psychiatry*, 39, 207–214

Hazlett-Stevens, H. and Borkovec, T.D. (2004), Interpretative cues and ambiguity in generalized anxiety disorder, *Behaviour Research and Therapy*, 42, 881–892

Healy, H. and Williams, M.G. (1999), Autobiographical memory in T. Dalgleish and M.J. Power (eds), *Handbook of Cognition and Emotion* (New York: Wiley), pp. 229–242

Helzer, J.E., Robin, L.N. and McEvoy, L. (1987), Post-traumatic stress disorder in the general population: findings of the epidemiological catchment area survey, *New England Journal of Medicine*, 317, 1630–1634

Hermans, D., Vansteenwegen, D. and Eelen, P. (1999), Eye movement registration as a continuous index of attention deployment: data from a group of spider anxious students, *Cognition and Emotion*, 13, 419–434

Hertel, P.T. and Hardin, T.S. (1990), Remembering with and without awareness in a depressed mood: evidence of deficits in initiative, *Journal of Experimental Psychology: General*, 119, 45–59

Hettema, J.M., Prescott, C.A., Myers, J.M., Neale, M.C. and Kendler, K.S. (2005), The structure of genetic and environmental risk factors for anxiety disorders in men and women, *Archives of General Psychiatry*, 62, 182–189

Hill, A.B. and Dutton, F. (1989), Depression and selective attention to self-esteem threatening words, *Personality and Individual Differences*, 10, 915–917

Hill, A.B. and Knowles, T.H. (1991), Depression and the 'emotional' Stroop effect, *Personality and Individual Differences*, 12, 481–485

Hirsch, C.R. and Mathews, A. (2000), Impaired positive inferential bias in social phobia, *Journal of Abnormal Psychology*, 109, 705–712

Hirshfeld, D.R., Rosenbaum, J.F., Biederman, J., Bolduc, E.A. et al. (1992), Stable behavioral inhibition and its association with anxiety disorder, *Journal of the American Academy of Child and Adolescent Psychiatry*, 31, 103–111

Hoehn, T., Braune, S., Scheibe, G. and Albus, M. (1997), Physiological biochemical and subjective parameters in anxiety patients with panic disorder during stress exposure as compared with healthy controls, *European Archives of Psychiatry and Clinical Neuroscience*, 247, 264–274

Hofmann, S.G., Newman, M.G., Ehlers, A. and Roth, W.T. (1995), Psychophysiological differences between subgroups of social phobia, *Journal of Abnormal Psychology*, 104, 224–231

Honeybourne, C., Matchett, G. and Davey, G.C. (1993), Expectancy models of laboratory preparedness effects: a UCS-expectancy bias in phylogenetic and ontogenetic fear-relevant stimuli, *Behavior Therapy*, 24, 253–264

Hope, D.A., Rapee, R.M., Heimberg, R.G. and Dombeck, M.J. (1990), Representations of the self in social phobia: vulnerability to social threat, *Cognitive Therapy and Research*, 14, 177–189

Hoyer, J., Becker, E.S. and Roth, W.T. (2001), Characteristics of worry in GAD patients, social phobics and controls, *Depression and Anxiety*, 13, 89–96

Hugdahl, K. and Johnsen, B.H. (1989), Preparedness and electrodermal fear-conditioning: ontogenetic vs. phylogenetic explanations, *Behaviour Research and Therapy*, 27, 269–278

Hugdahl, K. and Karker, A.C. (1981), Biological vs. experiential factors in phobic conditioning, *Behaviour Research and Therapy*, 19, 109–115

Jorm, A.F., Christensen, H., Henderson, A.S., Jacomb, P.A., Korten, A.E. and Rodgers, B. (2000), Predicting anxiety and depression from personality: is there a synergistic effect of neuroticism and extraversion?, *Journal of Abnormal Psychology*, 109, 145–149

Kavanagh, D.J. (1987), Mood, persistence, and success, *Australian Journal of Psychology*, 39, 307–318

Kenardy, J., Fried, L., Kraemer, H.C. and Taylor, C.B. (1992), Psychological precursors of panic attacks, *British Journal of Psychiatry*, 160, 668–673

Kendler, K.S., Neale, M.C., Kessler, R.C., Heath, A.C. and Eaves, L.J. (1993), A longitudinal twin study of personality and major depression in women, *Archives of General Psychiatry*, 50, 853–862

Kendler, K.S., Prescott, C.A., Myers, J. and Neale, M.C. (2003), The structure of genetic and environmental risk factors for common psychiatric and substance use disorders in men and women, *Archives of General Psychiatry*, 60, 929–937

Kendler, K.S., Walters, E.E., Neale, M.C., Kessler, R.C., Heath, A.C. and Eaves, L.J. (1995), The structure of the genetic and environmental risk factors for six major psychiatric disorders in women: phobia, generalized anxiety disorder, panic disorder, bulimia, major depression, and alcoholism, *Archives of General Psychiatry*, 52, 374–383

Kennedy, S.J., Rapee, R.M. and Mazurski, E.J. (1997), Covariation bias for phylogenetic versus ontogenetic fear-relevant stimuli, *Behaviour Research and Therapy*, 35, 415–422

Kindt, M. and Brosschot, J.F. (1999), Cognitive bias in spider-phobic children: comparison of a pictorial and a linguistic spider Stroop, *Journal of Psychopathology and Behavioral Assessment*, 21, 207–220

Klein, D.C. and Seligman, M.E. (1976), Reversal of performance deficits and perceptual deficits in learned helplessness and depression, *Journal of Abnormal Psychology*, 85, 11–26

Klein, D.F. (1964), Delineation of two drug responsive anxiety syndromes, *Psychopharmacologia*, 5, 397–408

(1981), Anxiety reconceptualized in D.F. Klein and J.Rabkin (eds), *Anxiety: New Research and Changing Concepts* (New York: Raven Press), pp. 235–263

Koster, E.H.W., De Raedt, R., Goeleven, E., Franck, E. and Crombez, G. (2005), Mood-congruent attentional bias in dysphoria: maintained attention to and impaired disengagement from negative information, *Emotion*, 5, 446–455

Krueger, R.F. (1999), The structure of common mental disorders, *Archives of General Psychiatry*, 56, 921–926

Krueger, R.F., Caspi, A., Moffitt, T.E. and Silva, P.A. (1998), The structure and stability of common mental disorders (DSM-III-R): a longitudinal-epidemiological study, *Journal of Abnormal Psychology*, 107, 216–227

Krueger, R.F., Caspi, A., Moffitt, T.E., Silva, P.A. and McGee, R. (1996), Personality traits are differentially linked to mental disorders: a multitrait-multidiagnosis study of an adolescent birth cohort, *Journal of Abnormal Psychology*, 105, 299–312

Krueger, R.F., Chentsova-Dutton, Y.E., Markon, K.E., Goldberg, D. and Ormel, J. (2003), A cross-cultural study of the structure of comorbidity among common psychopathological syndromes in the general health care setting, *Journal of Abnormal Psychology*, 112, 437–447

Kulka, R.A., Schlenger, W.E., Fairbank, J.A., Hough, R.L., Jordan, B.K., Marmar, C.R. *et al.* (1990), *Trauma and the Vietnam War Generation: Report of Findings from the National Vietnam Veterans Readjustment Study* (Philadelphia: Brunner)

Larsen, D.K., Norton, G.R., Walker, J.R. and Stein, M.B. (2002), Analysis of startle responses in patients with panic disorder and social phobia, *Cognitive Behaviour Therapy*, 31, 156–169

Lawson, C., MacLeod, C. and Hammond, G. (2002), Interpretation revealed in the blink of an eye: depressive bias in the resolution of ambiguity, *Journal of Abnormal Psychology*, 111, 321–328

Lelliott, P.T., Noshirvani, H.F., Marks, I.M., Monteiro, W.O. *et al.* (1987), Relationship of skin conductance activity to clinical features in obsessive-compulsive ritualizers, *Psychological Medicine*, 17, 905–914

Levenson, M.R., Aldwin, C.M., Bosse, R., Spiro, A. III (1988), Emotionality and mental health: longitudinal findings from the normative aging study, *Journal of Abnormal Psychology*, 97, 94–96

Link, B. and Dohrenwend, B.P. (1980), Formulation of hypotheses about the true prevalence of demoralization in the United States in B.P. Dohrenwend, B.S. Dohrenwend, M. Gould, B. Link, R. Neugebauer and R. Wunsch-Hitzig (eds), *Mental Illness in the United States* (New York: Praeger Publications), pp. 114–132

Lucock, M.P. and Salkovskis, P.M. (1988), Cognitive factors in social anxiety and its treatment, *Behaviour Research and Therapy*, 26, 297–302

Lundh, L.G. and Ost, L.G. (1996), Recognition bias for critical faces in social phobics, *Behaviour Research and Therapy*, 34, 787–794

    (2001), Attentional bias, self-consciousness and perfectionism in social phobia before and after cognitive-behaviour therapy, *Scandinavian Journal of Behaviour Therapy*, 30, 4–16

MacLeod, C. (1990), Mood disorders and cognition in M.W. Eysenck (ed.), *Cognitive Psychology: an International Review* (Oxford: John Wiley and Sons), pp. 9–56

    (1991), Half a century of research on the Stroop effect: an integrative review, *Psychological Bulletin*, 109, 163–203

MacLeod, C. and Cohen, I. (1993), Anxiety and the interpretation of ambiguity: a test comprehension study, *Journal of Abnormal Psychology*, 102, 238–247

MacLeod, C. and Mathews, A. (1991), Biased cognitive operations in anxiety: accessibility of information or assignment of processing priorities, *Behaviour Research and Therapy*, 29, 599–610

    (2004), Selective memory effects in anxiety disorders: an overview of research findings and their implications in D. Reisberg and P. Hertel (eds), *Memory and Emotion* (Oxford: Oxford University Press), pp. 155–185

MacLeod, C., Mathews, A. and Tata, P. (1986), Attentional bias in emotional disorder, *Journal of Abnormal Psychology*, 95, 15–20

MacLeod, C. and McLaughlin, K. (1995), Implicit and explicit memory bias in anxiety: a conceptual replication, *Behaviour Research and Therapy*, 33, 1–14

Maidenberg, E., Chen, E., Craske, M., Bohn, P. and Bystritsky, A. (1996), Specificity of attentional bias in panic disorder and social phobia, *Journal of Anxiety Disorders*, 10, 529–541

Mathews, A. and MacLeod, C. (1985), Selective processing of threat cues in anxiety states, *Behaviour Research and Therapy*, 23, 563–569

    (1987), An information-processing approach to anxiety, *Journal of Cognitive Psychotherapy: an International Quarterly*, 1, 105–115

(1994), Cognitive approaches to emotion and emotional disorder, *Annual Review of Psychology*, 45, 25–50

(2005), Cognitive vulnerability to emotional disorders, *Annual Review of Clinical Psychology*, 1, 167–195

Mathews, A., Mogg, K., Kentish, J. and Eysenck, M. (1995), Effect of psychological treatment on cognitive bias in generalized anxiety disorder, *Behaviour Research and Therapy*, 33, 293–303

Mathews, A., Mogg, K., May, J. and Eysenck, M. (1989), Implicit and explicit memory bias in anxiety, *Journal of Abnormal Psychology*, 98, 236–240

Mathews, A., Ridgeway, V. and Williamson, D.A. (1996), Evidence for attention to threatening stimuli in depression, *Behaviour Research and Therapy*, 34, 695–705

Matt, G., Vazquez, C. and Campbell, W.K. (1992), Mood-congruent recall of affectively toned stimuli: a meta-analytical review, *Clinical Psychology Review*, 12, 227–255

Mattia, J.I., Heimberg, R.G. and Hope, D.A. (1993), The revised Stroop color-naming task in social phobics, *Behaviour Research and Therapy*, 31, 305–313

Mavissakalian, M. (1988), The relationship between panic, phobic and anticipatory anxiety in agoraphobia, *Behaviour Research and Therapy*, 26, 235–240

McCabe, S.B. and Gotlib, I.H. (1995), Attentional processing in clinically depressed subjects: a longitudinal investigation, *Cognitive Therapy and Research*, 17, 359–377

McNally, R.J. (1995), Automaticity and the anxiety disorders, *Behaviour Research and Therapy*, 33, 747–754

McNally, R.J. and Amir, N. (1996), Perceptual implicit memory for trauma-related information in post-traumatic stress disorder, *Cognition and Emotion*, 10, 551–556

McNally, R.J. and Foa, E.B. (1987), Cognition and agoraphobia: bias in the interpretation of threat, *Cognitive Therapy and Research*, 11, 567–581

McNally, R.J., Foa, E.B. and Donnell, C.D. (1989), Memory bias for anxiety information in patients with panic disorder, *Cognition and Emotion*, 3, 27–44

McNally, R.J., Kaspi, S.P., Riemann, B.C. and Zeitlin, S.B. (1990), Selective processing of threat cues in posttraumatic stress disorder, *Journal of Abnormal Psychology*, 99, 398–402

Middleton, H.C. (1990), Cardiovascular dystonia in recovered panic patients, *Journal of Affective Disorders*, 9, 229–236

Miller, G.M. and Chapman, J.P. (2001), Misunderstanding analysis of covariance, *Journal of Abnormal Psychology*, 110, 40–48

Miller, I.V. and Norman, W.H. (1986), Persistence of depressive cognitions within a subgroup of depressed inpatients, *Cognitive Therapy and Research*, 10, 211–224

Mineka, S. (1987), A primate model of phobic fears in H.J. Eysenck and I. Martin (eds), *Theoretical Foundations of Behavior Therapy* (New York: Plenum), pp. 81–111

Mineka, S., Rafaeli, E. and Yovel, I. (2003), Cognitive biases in emotional disorders: information processing and social-cognitive perspectives in

R.J. Davidson, K.R. Scherer and H.H. Goldsmith (eds), *Handbook of Affective Science* (New York: Oxford Univeristy Press), pp. 899–1043

Mineka, S., Watson, D. and Clark, L.A. (1998), Comorbidity of anxiety and unipolar mood disorders, *Annual Review of Psychology*, 49, 377–412

Mineka, S. and Zinbarg, R. (1995), Conditioning and ethological models of social phobia in R.G. Heimberg, M.R. Leibowitz, D.A. Hope and F.R. Schneier (eds), *Social Phobia: Diagnosis, Assessment, and Treatment* (New York: Guilford Press), pp. 134–162

(1996), Conditioning and ethological models of anxiety disorders: stress-in-dynamic-context anxiety models in D.A. Hope (ed.), *Nebraska Symposium on Motivation*, vol. 43, *Perspectives on Anxiety, Panic, and Fear: Current Theory and Research in Motivation* (Lincoln, NE: University of Nebraska Press), pp. 135–210

Mogg, K. and Bradley, B.P. (1998), A cognitive-motivational analysis of anxiety, *Behaviour Research and Therapy*, 36, 809–848

(2005), Attentional bias in generalized anxiety disorder versus depressive disorder, *Cognitive Therapy and Research*, 29, 29–45

Mogg, K., Bradley, B.P., Millar, N. and White, J. (1995), A follow-up study of cognitive bias in generalized anxiety disorder, *Behaviour Research and Therapy*, 33, 927–935

Mogg, K., Bradley, B.P. and Williams, R. (1995), Attentional bias in anxiety and depression: the role of awareness, *British Journal of Clinical Psychology*, 34, 17–36

Mogg, K., Bradley, B.P., Williams, R. and Mathews, A. (1993), Subliminal processing of emotional information in anxiety and depression, *Journal of Abnormal Psychology*, 102, 304–311

Mogg, K., Mathews, A. and Eysenck, M. (1992), Attentional bias to threat in clinical anxiety states, *Cognition and Emotion*, 6, 149–159

Mogg, K., Mathews, A. and Weinman, J. (1987), Selective processing of threat cues in anxiety states: a replication, *Behaviour Research and Therapy*, 27, 317–323

Mogg, K., Millar, N. and Bradley, B.P. (2000), Biases in eye movements to threatening facial expressions in generalized anxiety disorder and depressive disorder, *Journal of Abnormal Psychology*, 109, 695–704

Nation, J.R. and Cooney, J.B. (1980), The change and maintenance effectiveness of persistence training regarding the treatment of laboratory-induced and naturally occurring depression, *Bulletin of the Psychonomic Society*, 16, 121–124

Navon, D. and Margalit, B. (1983), Allocation of attention according to informativeness in visual recognition, *Quarterly Journal of Experimental Psychology, Part A, Human Experimental Psychology*, 35, 497–512

Neshat-Doost, H.T., Moradi, A.R., Taghavi, M.R., Yule, W. and Dalgleish, T. (2000), Lack of attentional bias for emotional information in clinically depressed children and adolescents on the dot probe task, *Journal of Child Psychology and Psychiatry and Allied Disciplines*, 41, 363–368

Neshat-Doost, H.T., Taghavi, M.R., Moradi, A.R., Yule, W. and Dalgleish, T. (1997), The performance of clinically depressed children and adolescents on the modified Stroop paradigm, *Personality and Individual Differences*, 23, 753–759

Nesse, R.M. and Klaas, R. (1994), Risk perception by patients with anxiety disorders, *Journal of Nervous and Mental Disease*, 182, 465–470

Nunn, J.D., Mathews, A. and Trower, P. (1997), Selective processing of concern-related information in depression, *British Journal of Clinical Psychology*, 36, 489–503

Otto, M.W., McNally, R.J., Pollack, M.H., Chen, E. and Rosenbaum, J.F. (1994), Hemispheric laterality and memory bias for threat in anxiety disorder, *Journal of Abnormal Psychology*, 103, 828–831

Rachman, S. (1990), The determinants and treatment of simple phobia, *Advances in Behaviour Research and Therapy*, 12, 1–30

     (1991), Disorders of emotion: causes and consequences, *Psychological Inquiry*, 2, 86–87

Radomsky, A.S., Rachman, S. and Hammond, D. (2002), Panic termination and the post-panic period, *Journal of Anxiety Disorders*, 16, 97–111

Rapee, R. (1996), *Current Controversies in the Anxiety Disorders* (New York: Guilford)

Richards, A. and French, C.C. (1992), An anxiety-related bias in semantic activation when processing threat/neutral homographs, *Quarterly Journal of Experimental Psychology: Human Experimental Psychology*, 45(A), 503–525

Richards, J.C., Austin, D.A. and Alvarenga, M.E. (2001), Interpretation of ambiguous interoceptive stimuli in panic disorder and non-clinical panic, *Cognitive Research and Therapy*, 25, 235–246

Roberts, S.B. and Kendler, K.S. (1999), Neuroticism and self-esteem as indices of the vulnerability to major depression in women, *Psychological Medicine*, 29, 1101–1109

Roediger, H. and McDermott, K. (1992), Depression and implicit memory: a commentary, *Journal of Abnormal Psychology*, 101, 587–591

Roth, W.T., Margraf, J., Ehlers, A., Taylor, C.B. *et al.* (1992), Stress test reactivity in panic disorder, *Archives of General Psychiatry*, 49, 301–310

Salkovskis, P.M., Clark, D.M. and Gelder, M.G. (1996), Cognition-behaviour links in the persistence of panic, *Behaviour Research and Therapy*, 34, 453–458

Schacter, D.L. (1990), Introduction to 'Implicit Memory: Multiple Perspective', *Bulletin of the Psychonomic Society*, 28, 338–340

Schmidt, N.B., Lerew, D.R. and Jackson, R.J. (1999), Prospective evaluation of anxiety sensitivity in the pathogenesis of panic: replication and extension, *Journal of Abnormal Psychology*, 108, 532–537

Schut, A.J., Castonguay, L.G. and Borkovec, T.D. (2001), Compulsive checking behaviors in generalized anxiety disorder, *Journal of Clinical Psychology*, 57, 705–715

Segal, Z.V., Gemar, M., Truchon, C. and Guirguis, M. (1995), A priming methodology for studying self-representation in major depressive disorder, *Journal of Abnormal Psychology*, 104, 205–213

Tallis, F. and De Silva, P. (1992), Worry and obsessional symptoms: a correlational analysis, *Behaviour Research and Therapy*, 30, 103–105

Tata, P.R., Leibowitz, J.A., Prunty, M.J., Cameron, M. and Pickering, A.D. (1996), Attentional bias in obsessional compulsive disorder, *Behaviour Research and Therapy*, 34, 53–60

Tellegen, A. (1985), Structures of mood and personality and their relevance to assessing anxiety, with an emphasis on self-report in A.H. Tuma and J.D. Maser (eds), *Anxiety and the Anxiety Disorders* (Hillsdale, NJ: Lawrence Erlbaum Associates), pp. 681–706

Tomarken, A.J., Sutton, S.K. and Mineka, S. (1995), Fear-relevant illusory correlations: what types of associations promote judgmental bias?, *Journal of Abnormal Psychology*, 104, 312–326

Vasey, M.W., Daleiden, E.L., Williams, L.L. and Brown, L.M. (1995), Biased attention in childhood anxiety disorders: a preliminary study, *Journal of Abnormal Child Psychology*, 23, 267–279

Vollebergh, W.A.M., Iedema, J., Bijl, R.V., De Graff, R., Smit, F. and Ormel, J. (2001), The structure and stability of common mental disorders: the NEMESIS study, *Archives of General Psychiatry*, 58, 597–603

Watkins, P. (2002), Implicit memory bias in depression, *Cognition and Emotion*, 16, 381–402

Watkins, P.C., Martin, C.K. and Stern, L.D. (2000), Unconscious memory bias in depression: perceptual and conceptual processes, *Journal of Abnormal Psychology*, 109, 282–289

Watkins, P., Mathews, A., Williamson, D.A. and Fuller, R.D. (1992), Mood-congruent memory in depression: emotional priming or elaboration?, *Journal of Abnormal Psychology*, 101, 581–586

Watkins, P.C., Vache, K., Verney, S.P., Muller, S. and Mathews, A. (1996), Unconscious mood-congruent memory bias in depression, *Journal of Abnormal Psychology*, 105, 34–41

Watts, F. and Dalgleish, T. (1991), Memory for phobia-related words in spider phobics, *Cognition and Emotion*, 5, 313–329

Watts, F., McKenna, F.P., Sharrock, R. and Trezise, L. (1986), Colour naming of phobia-related words, *British Journal of Psychology*, 77, 97–108

Westling, B.E. and Ost, L.G. (1995), Cognitive bias in panic disorder patients and changes after cognitive-behavioral treatments, *Behaviour Research and Therapy*, 33, 585–588

Williams, J.M.G. and Broadbent, K. (1986), Distraction by emotional stimuli: use of a Stroop task with suicide attempters, *British Journal of Clinical Psychology*, 25, 101–110

Williams, J.M.G., Mathews, A. and MacLeod, C. (1996), The emotional Stroop task and psychopathology, *Psychological Bulletin*, 120, 3–24

Williams, J.M. and Scott, J. (1988), Autobiographical memory in depression, *Psychological Medicine*, 18, 689–695

Williams, J.M.G., Watts, F., MacLeod, C. and Mathews, A. (1997), *Cognitive Psychology and Emotional Disorders* (2nd edn, Chichester: John Wiley and Sons)

Winson, J. (1990), The meaning of dreams, *Scientific American*, 263, 86–96

Wohlfarth, T.D., Van den Brink, W., Winkel, F.W. and Ter Smitten, M. (2003), Screening for posttraumatic stress disorder: an evaluation of two self-report scales among crime victims, *Psychological Assessment*, 15, 101–109

Yoon, K.L., Hong, S. and Zinbarg, R.E. (2005), The effects of social anxiety on binocular rivalry between two faces, paper presented at the Association for Behavioral and Cognitive Therapies, Washington, DC.

Yoon, K.L. and Zinbarg, R.E. (2007), Threat is in the eye of the beholder: social anxiety and the interpretation of neutral facial expressions. *Behaviour Research and Therapy*, 45, 839–847

Zinbarg, R.E. (1998), Concordance and synchrony in measures of anxiety and panic reconsidered: a hierarchical model of anxiety and panic, *Behavior Therapy*, 29, 301–323

Zinbarg, R.E. and Barlow, D.H. (1996), Structure of anxiety and the anxiety disorders: a hierarchical model, *Journal of Abnormal Psychology*, 105, 181–193

Zinbarg, R.E., Barlow, D.H., Brown, T.A. and Hertz, R.M. (1992), Cognitive-behavioral approaches to the nature and treatment of anxiety disorders, *Annual Review of Psychology*, 43, 235–267

Zinbarg, R.E., Barlow, D.H., Leibowitz, M., Street, L. and Broadhead, E. (1994), The DSM-IV field trial for mixed anxiety-depression, *American Journal of Psychiatry*, 151, 1153–1162

Zinbarg, R. and Mineka, S. (1991), Animal models of psychopathology, Part II, Simple phobia, *The Behavior Therapist*, 14, 61–65

13   RST and psychopathy: associations between psychopathy and the behavioral activation and inhibition systems

John F. Wallace and Joseph P. Newman

We review the experimental evidence regarding information processing anomalies that have been observed in psychopaths, and conclude that the body of evidence is in substantially better accord with the revised *Reinforcement Sensitivity Theory* (RST), and, in particular, the current conceptualization of the BIS, than with the original version of RST. In addition, clear associations exist between psychopathy and self-report measures of the BAS and BIS constructs, and we discuss possible explanations for those associations that merit evaluation in future psychopathy research.

RST and psychopathy: associations between psychopathy and the BAS and BIS

Maladaptive behavior that is anti-social or impulsive in nature has been characterized as reflecting *disinhibition* – a decreased ability to regulate response inclinations in light of possible adverse consequences (e.g., Gorenstein and Newman 1980). Due to psychopaths' penchant for engaging in anti-social, maladaptive behavior, psychopathy is a proto-typical example of the clinical syndromes that have disinhibited behavior as a prominent feature. For instance, although psychopaths make up only 1 per cent of the general population, they constitute 15 to 25 per cent of the prison population (Hare 1996), and psychopathic offenders are two to five times more likely to re-offend than are non-psychopaths (Hemphill, Hare and Wong 1998; Quinsey, Rice and Harris 1995; Serin 1996; Walters 2003).

As described by Cleckley (1976), who has played a major role in shaping the current conceptualization of psychopathy, the core features of the syndrome include poor judgement, the failure to learn from experience (especially from punishment or negative feedback), maladaptive behavior that often occurs in the context of relatively low levels of motivation (i.e., on a whim), extreme egocentricity, lack of remorse and generally shallow or superficial emotional reactions (both positive and negative).

The original version of Gray's RST (1975, 1987; Gray and Smith 1969) has figured prominently in attempts to explain the disinhibition of psychopaths. Briefly, the original RST postulated three interacting neurological systems. The Behavioral Activation System (BAS) was hypothesized to be reactive to conditioned appetitive stimuli or reward cues (i.e., stimuli associated with appetitive outcomes), and, as the level of BAS activity increases, the initiation of goal-directed behavior becomes more likely. Conversely, the Behavioral Inhibition System (BIS) was viewed as being reactive to conditioned aversive stimuli or punishment cues (i.e., stimuli associated with aversive outcomes), as well as to stimuli that are at odds with pre-existing expectancies. The BIS promotes the inhibition of ongoing or goal-directed behavior when potential threats or discrepant stimuli are detected, and causes attention to be directed or allocated to the processing of the threatening or discrepant stimulus. The third of Gray's three systems – the Fight-Flight System (FFS) – was considered to be reactive to unconditioned or innately aversive stimuli, and mediates the behavioral and affective reactions to those stimuli (e.g., rage).

Fowles (1980) proposed an initial explanation of psychopathy in terms of RST, noting that a number of psychophysiological findings that distinguished psychopaths from non-psychopathic controls (e.g., relatively small increases in skin conductance in anticipation of aversive stimuli) were consistent with the sorts of deficits that would be expected to occur in the presence of BIS dysfunction. Consequently, Fowles (1980) proposed that the BIS of psychopaths is relatively weak or hyporeactive, and that it is this defect that causes the observable features of the syndrome.

Whereas Fowles used laboratory findings and clinical observations to draw inferences about the relationships between psychopathy and RST, self-report measures of the BAS and BIS constructs recently have been used to examine those relationships. For instance, Book and Quinsey (2004) administered a measure of BAS and BIS activation to a group of psychopaths and to members of several control groups. Those researchers found that psychopaths were both higher in BAS activation and lower in BIS activation than controls; that is, their results indicated that psychopaths not only manifest a relatively weak BIS, but a relatively strong BAS as well.

RST also was utilized by Lykken (1995) in his conceptualization of psychopathy. However, he broadened his explanatory focus to reflect the distinction between primary and secondary psychopathy (e.g., Blackburn 1979; Hare 1970). According to Cleckley (1976), primary or true psychopaths tend to experience lower levels of tension or anxiety than do most individuals. On the other hand, Cleckley viewed neurotic or secondary psychopaths as experiencing relatively high levels of negative affect (e.g., anxiety), with their anti-social behavior occurring mainly as a reaction to emotional conflicts or distress.

In accord with Cleckley's conceptualization, Lykken (1995) described primary psychopaths as manifesting fearlessness, relatively weak electrodermal responses in anticipation of punishment, and normal or below-normal levels of general emotional reactivity. However, he characterized secondary psychopaths as manifesting high levels of impulsivity and general emotional reactivity, but normal levels of fear and electrodermal activity in anticipation of punishment.

Based on his conceptualization of primary and secondary psychopathy, Lykken (1995) hypothesized that primary psychopathy is associated with a hyporeactive BIS, but normal or average levels of BAS reactivity, leading to maladaptive behavior via impaired processing of stimuli associated with potential threats or punishment. Conversely, he viewed secondary psychopathy as being associated with a hyperreactive BAS and average levels of BIS reactivity. Lykken proposed that the maladaptive behavior of the secondary psychopath reflects a stronger-than-normal response to reward cues, causing relatively inflexible BAS-mediated approach behavior. Nevertheless, he also suggested that those individuals tend to experience relatively high levels of negative affect due to the increased incidence of adverse outcomes that occur as a consequence of their inadequately-regulated approach behavior.

To assess Lykken's hypothesis that primary psychopaths manifest a weak BIS and normal BAS, whereas secondary psychopaths manifest a strong BAS and a normal BIS, two measures of the BAS and BIS constructs – the Sensitivity to Punishment and Sensitivity to Reward Questionnaire (SPSRQ) (Torrubia, Ávila, Moltó and Caseras 2001) and the BIS/BAS scales (Carver and White 1994) – were administered to a sample of 517 male inmates in the Wisconsin prison system (Newman, MacCoon, Vaughn and Sadeh 2005). Participants were identified as psychopaths or non-psychopaths using the Psychopathy Checklist-Revised (Hare 2003). Measures of trait anxiety or negative affectivity traditionally have been used to distinguish between primary and secondary psychopaths, with primary psychopathy associated with lower levels of anxiety/negative affect and secondary psychopathy associated with higher anxiety/negative affect levels (for a review, see Newman and Brinkley 1997). In this study, the Welsh Anxiety Scale (Welsh 1956) was utilized for this purpose.

As predicted, primary psychopaths had significantly lower BIS scores than did other participants, with no group differences in BAS scores, based on both measures of the BIS and BAS constructs. In addition, the BAS scores of secondary psychopaths were significantly higher than those of other participants for both of the measures. However, the prediction that secondary psychopathy would be associated with average BIS scores received only partial support: the results from one measure (the BIS/BAS scales) were not indicative of differences in BIS reactivity, but those from the other (the SPSRQ) were indicative of greater BIS reactivity in the secondary psychopathy group. Hence, although the evidence was equivocal regarding the prediction of normal BIS functioning in secondary psychopaths, the results of this study were consistent with the suggestion that secondary psychopaths' BAS is unusually strong or reactive. In addition, the hypothesis that primary psychopaths are characterized by a weak BIS and a normal BAS received strong support.

Experimental evidence

Nevertheless, in our research we have *not* embraced the idea that primary psychopathy is caused by a weak or hyporeactive BIS (e.g., Fowles 1980; Lykken 1995) as the BIS was conceptualized in the original version of RST. In particular, primary psychopaths do not manifest a general or global hyporeactivity to punishment cues. Rather, psychopaths' insensitivity to punishment cues is unambiguously situation-specific.[1]

One of the clearest illustrations of the situational specificity of psychopaths' deficit was provided by Newman and Kosson (1986). Participants in their experiment were asked to press a response button when numbers that had been designated as target stimuli were presented on a computer monitor, and not to press when numbers that had not been designated as targets were presented.

In addition, two incentive conditions were utilized. In one, participants won money for correct button press responses and lost money for incorrect responses (i.e., for pressing the response button when a non-target number was present). In the other, participants also lost money for pressing the button in the presence of a non-target number, but they

---

[1] Based on the work of Cleckley, who viewed true psychopaths as being low in trait anxiety or negative affectivity, the research of Newman and colleagues has focused on elucidating the information-processing deficits of primary psychopaths (see Schmitt, Brinkley and Newman 1999).

did *not* win money for responding correctly. Hence, the prepotent inclination or response set to press the button was less well established in the second condition than in the first, because no reward was obtained for doing so. Also note that, in both conditions, the non-target numbers clearly functioned as punishment cues (i.e., as inputs to the BIS): responding when they were present led to a loss of money.

In the first condition (in which a stronger set to press the button was established), primary psychopaths made more incorrect responses than did non-psychopaths. In other words, they manifested deficient behavioral inhibition in the presence of the punishment cues (non-target numbers). Conversely, psychopaths and non-psychopaths displayed comparable inhibition in the presence of the punishment cues in the second condition, in which the set to press the button was less well established.

We have concluded from these and similar results (e.g., Arnett, Howland, Smith and Newman 1993; Arnett, Smith and Newman 1997; Newman, Patterson, Howland and Nichols 1990; Newman, Patterson and Kosson 1987; Newman and Schmitt 1998; Schmitt, Brinkley and Newman 1999) that primary psychopaths do *not* suffer from either a general insensitivity to punishment cues or an inability to respond appropriately to stimuli associated with punishment (e.g., engage in behavioral inhibition). Rather, psychopaths manifest disinhibition (i.e., a decreased ability to regulate behavior to avoid adverse consequences) when the avoidance of an adverse outcome requires overriding a prepotent response inclination or modifying an established behavioral goal.

Furthermore, our view of psychopaths' deficit is not only more specific than the hypoactive BIS hypothesis (based on original conceptualization of the BIS), but it is also more general (Newman, Schmitt and Voss 1997). On the one hand, it is more specific in that psychopaths do *not* manifest a global insensitivity to punishment cues (i.e., their idiosyncratic responses to punishment are situation specific). On the other, it is more general in that situation-specific anomalies have been observed in the processing of stimuli that are not associated with punishment (i.e., that are affectively neutral), that is, psychopaths' information processing deficit is more pervasive than simply an idiosyncratic (albeit situation-specific) response to punishment cues.

To investigate 'whether psychopathic individuals are relatively unresponsive to contextual cues that are peripheral to their dominant response set (i.e., primary task) even though the cues are unrelated to punishment' (p. 554), Newman, Schmitt and Voss (1997) utilized a version of a task that had been developed by Gernsbacher and Faust (1991, Experiment 3). Participants were asked to determine whether two sequentially-presented stimuli were conceptually related or unrelated. On half of the trials, two words were compared, and on the other half, two pictures were compared. For instance, on each picture trial, the first of the sequentially-presented stimuli consisted of a picture and a superimposed word, and the second stimulus consisted of a picture only. Participants were instructed to ignore the superimposed word (the distractor stimulus) in the initial display, and simply decide whether the two pictures (the comparison stimuli) were conceptually related (they won money based on the speed and accuracy of their responses). However, the to-be-ignored distractor stimulus (in this case, the superimposed word) was, on some trials, related to the second of the comparison stimuli. For example, the initial display might consist of a picture of a baseball player with the word *rain* superimposed, and the second stimulus might be a picture of an umbrella.

Gernsbacher and Faust (1991) observed that, when the two comparison stimuli were conceptually unrelated (e.g., a picture of a baseball player followed by a picture of an umbrella), but the distractor stimulus (e.g., the word *rain*) was conceptually related to the second picture, the presence of the distractor interfered with participants' ability to determine that the two comparison stimuli were unrelated (i.e., response latencies were longer than when the distractor stimulus was related to the second picture than when it was not).

Likewise, in the Newman, Schmitt and Voss (1997) experiment, members of the control group were slowed in their determination that the two comparison stimuli were unrelated during trials in which the distractor stimulus was related to the second comparison stimulus. Conversely, primary psychopaths did not manifest the normal interference effect: their response latencies did not differ regardless of whether the distractor was related or unrelated to the second comparison stimulus. Thus, psychopaths apparently did not process the distractor stimuli to the same extent as did non-psychopaths, even though the distractor was not associated with punishment (see also Hiatt, Schmitt and Newman 2004; Vitale, Brinkley, Hiatt and Newman 2007; Vitale *et al.* 2005).

A related set of results (Lorenz and Newman 2002) was obtained using a lexical decision task, in which participants determined whether a briefly-presented string of letters was a word or a non-word. Typically, participants show facilitation for emotion words; that is, they are able make the lexical decision more rapidly for words having an emotional connotation or valence (e.g., sunset) than for words that are affectively neutral (e.g., bowl). In the Lorenz and Newman (2002) experiment, an equal number of positive and negative words were utilized, and, after completing the lexical decision task, participants were asked to rate the stimulus words on a scale ranging from 0 (bad) to 7 (good).

As predicted, and replicating results first reported by Williamson, Harpur and Hare (1991), primary psychopaths manifested significantly less facilitation in their identification of emotion words than did controls, and this result was evident for positive as well as negative words. Nonetheless, psychopaths were equally adept at appraising or rating the affective valence of the stimulus words when that activity was the focus of their attentional set (i.e., when they were explicitly asked to do so at the conclusion of the experiment).

As was the case for the Newman and Kosson (1986) experiment, the results obtained by Newman, Schmitt and Voss (1997) and Lorenz and Newman (2002) do not appear to be consistent with an interpretation invoking dysfunction of the BIS (based on its original conceptualization). In the Newman, Schmitt and Voss (1997) study, psychopaths were less affected than controls by the distractor stimuli, even though the distractors were not associated with punishment. Likewise, in the lexical decision experiment, psychopaths showed less facilitation for *both* positive and negative words (i.e., their deficit was not specific to the processing of words having negative affective valence).

Our preferred interpretation of the information-processing anomalies that have been observed in experimental task performance of primary psychopaths is that, for these individuals, selective attention is less likely to be re-allocated in a relatively automatic or effortless manner to the processing of information or stimuli that are extraneous to, or incongruent with, the current attentional focus (i.e., the current focus of selective attention) (e.g., MacCoon, Wallace and Newman 2004; Wallace, Schmitt, Vitale and Newman 2000). As we have observed elsewhere, 'psychopaths fail to allocate attention to non-dominant cues when their attention is allocated already to dominant cues. Whereas controls can use non-dominant cues automatically, psychopaths appear to have difficulty doing so' (MacCoon, Wallace and Newman 2004, p. 431).

It is important to note, however, that psychopaths perform as capably as do non-psychopaths when the relevant information is encompassed by their current attentional focus (i.e., when an automatic shift or re-allocation of attention is not required). Stated another way, 'psychopaths will perform normally when deliberately attending to relevant task dimensions but appear oblivious to incidental cues that rely on automatic shifts of attention' (Lorenz and Newman 2002, p. 99; see Newman and Lorenz 2003 for review).

We wish at this point to highlight the distinction between two conceptually distinct types of processes that are involved in the allocation or direction of selective attention (see Most, Scholl, Clifford and Simons 2005). The first results from the activation of cognitive control mechanisms and processes (e.g., working memory; dual-task co-ordination) associated with the frontal and prefrontal cortices. As described by Lavie, Hirst, De Fockert and Viding (2004), 'frontal cognitive control functions serve to control selective attention in accordance with task-relevant information by actively maintaining the current stimulus-processing priorities' (p. 352). Furthermore, 'goal-directed behavior requires focusing attention on goal-relevant stimuli' (p. 339), and 'frontal processes of cognitive control seem crucial for maintaining task-processing priorities between relevant and irrelevant stimuli to guide behavior in accordance with current goals' (p. 352). In other words, frontally-mediated cognitive control subserves the maintenance of the current goal orientation by allocating selective attention to the processing of stimuli that are relevant to the current behavioral goal, while decreasing interference by (i.e., the processing of) stimuli that are extraneous to, or incongruent with, that goal.

In contrast, the second type of allocation process is associated primarily with subcortical structures such as the septo-hippocampal system, and involves the relatively effortless and automatic re-allocation of selective attention from the current attentional focus to the processing of stimuli or information that may be of potential relevance, but that are extraneous to the current response set or behavioral goal. As noted by Most *et al.* (2005), 'attention must be distractible; if potentially dangerous or relevant objects appear, they should divert cognitive resources' (p. 218). They designate this process *attention capture*, and state that it involves 'instances in which stimuli draw a person's attention without that person's volition' (p. 218). 'These kinds of attentional shifts have been referred to as *reflexive, involuntary,* and *automatic*' (p. 218).

In our view, it is a deficiency involving this second type of attentional process that is the essential feature underlying the disinhibition of psychopaths (i.e., their decreased ability to regulate immediate response inclinations in the light of possible adverse consequences). That is, psychopaths' disinhibition results from difficulty utilizing information that is extraneous to their current goals or prepotent response inclinations to modify those inclinations and goals. Specifically, reduced efficacy of the subcortically-mediated reallocation of selective attention decreases the probability that information indicative of a potential problem with the current goal or response inclination will receive sufficient processing to cause the inhibition or modification of the prepotent response or the alteration of the current goal. Hence, the likelihood is increased of emitting maladaptive behavior and experiencing adverse consequences.

RST revisited

Taken together, the results that were referenced above are not consistent with the hypothesis that primary psychopathy is caused by a weak or hyporeactive BIS, at least as the BIS was described in the original RST. In particular, (a) psychopaths' idiosyncratic responses to punishment cues are situation-specific, rather than being ubiquitous (as would be expected to result from a hypoactive BIS), and (b) impairments are evident in the processing of stimuli that would not be expected to function as inputs to the original BIS (i.e., that are not punishment cues or stimuli of substantial novelty).

Nevertheless, although *experimental* evidence is not consistent with the association of primary psychopathy with BIS dysfunction, there are equally clear results based on the use of *self-report* measures that do, in fact, link primary psychopathy with the BIS (as well as secondary psychopathy with the BAS). Viewing the experimental results in light of recent revisions in RST (Gray and McNaughton 2000) may provide a way of resolving this discrepancy. In the revised RST, the BIS is associated primarily with the septo-hippocampal system (SHS) and amygdala, and becomes active when conflicts occur between concurrent goals. When the BIS is activated, ongoing or prepotent behaviors are inhibited, and information-processing activities to resolve the conflict are initiated. The prototypical conflict situation involves the activation of competing goals of approach and avoidance, but conflicts between two incompatible approach goals, or between two incompatible avoidance goals, also activate the BIS.

The reformulation of the BIS construct addresses the two objections to a weak BIS hypothesis that were described earlier. Specifically, the BIS is no longer considered to be reactive to punishment cues per se. Rather, the BIS becomes active in the presence of goal conflicts, which may or may not involve stimuli associated with punishment. Hence, the facts that psychopaths *do not* manifest a global insensitivity to punishment cues, and *do* manifest information-processing anomalies involving affectively-neutral stimuli, do not constitute objections to a model of psychopathy based on the current version of the BIS.

Indeed, Newman and colleagues (Newman *et al.*, in press) recently provided a comparison of psychopaths' deficits with the expected effects of SHS dysfunction, based largely on Gray and McNaughton's (2000) conceptualization of the functioning of the SHS. In brief, Gray and McNaughton (2000) characterized the SHS (which, as just noted, is a principal component of the BIS) as a comparator that detects conflicts among concurrently activated goals. Specifically, the hippocampus 'receives subcortical input which reflects the presence of important stimuli (potential goals). If the hippocampus does not at the same time receive a matching cortical input (i.e., the goals are novel), it determines the relative strength of the novel goal and of any prepotent goal and, if there is a significant conflict between these (i.e., neither is significantly greater than the other), then it produces an output which inhibits the prepotent goal and hence permits the orienting and exploratory programs to function properly' (Gray and McNaughton 2000, pp. 255–256).

In their review, Newman *et al.* (in press) discussed a number of features of SHS functioning that plausibly might be of relevance to the sorts of ill-conceived, maladaptive actions that are characteristic of psychopaths. For instance, a deficit in the processing of competing or conflicting goals might impair the ability to shift behavior strategies when the features of a situation suggest that the current response strategy is no longer adaptive or appropriate (e.g., when punishment is a more likely outcome than reward, or when an alternative strategy is more likely to achieve the desired end). In addition, those authors concluded that impairment of the functions attributed to the SHS might cause a number of the deficiencies in experimental task performance manifested by psychopaths. Hence, both clinical observations and experimental evidence are in substantially better accord with the revised RST and, in particular, the current conceptualization of the BIS, than with the original version.

Despite those consistencies, however, Newman *et al.* (in press) noted that psychopaths' hypothesized information-processing anomaly might have origins other than an impairment in the functioning of the SHS. For instance, psychopaths' deficient processing of stimuli that are extraneous to (or inconsistent with) the current goal might result from a dysfunction involving other neuroanatomical structures that affect the strength of the inputs that are received by the SHS, rather than from a problem in the processing of those inputs by the SHS. As one example, those authors noted that the CA3 comparator plays a crucial role in determining which stimuli will be gated in to the conflict detector: stimuli that are associated with higher levels of monoamine activity are passed on, whereas stimuli that are associated with sub-threshold levels of monoamine activity are gated out. Hence, a dysfunction that decreases the monoamine activity associated with potentially significant extraneous stimuli would be expected to have an adverse affect on the processing of those stimuli by the SHS, even in the absence of an impairment of the SHS itself.

In addition, a laterality component in the information-processing deficits of psychopaths repeatedly has been observed. In several experiments, more pronounced performance deficits have been apparent when the task involves an increased demand for processing by the left cerebral hemisphere (e.g., Howland, Kosson, Patterson and Newman 1993; Kosson 1998). For instance, Bernstein, Newman, Wallace and Luh (2000) asked the participants in their experiment to memorize, and later recall, the serial order of eight words that were presented, one at a time, on a computer monitor. Each word appeared in one of the four corners of display. After viewing the words and then attempting to recall the words in serial order, participants were asked to recall the location in which each word appeared. Psychopaths were as able as control participants to recall the serial order of the words (replicating other results demonstrating that psychopaths do *not* manifest deficient performance when the task is the focus of their attention). However, while not differing in the recall of left spatial field locations, they recalled fewer locations from the right spatial field (visual information from the right spatial field is processed primarily by the left cerebral hemisphere). Similarly, in the Lorenz and Newman (2002) experiment described above, disparities between the performance of psychopaths and control participants were evident only when right-handed responses were required (which, presumably, utilized primarily left hemisphere processing resources).

Finally, in the lexical decision experiment (Lorenz and Newman 2002), in which participants determined whether briefly-presented strings of letters were words or non-words, psychopaths were less affected by the emotional connotation of the word stimuli, that is, they evidenced less facilitation in their identification of emotion words, suggesting that they were less affected by the emotional connotations of the words than were non-psychopaths. It is not clear, however, that processing the emotional connotation of the word stimuli constituted a goal conflict with respect to the manifest task of identifying the stimuli as being words or non-words. Consequently, this result may not fit as neatly within a weak BIS or an SHS dysfunction model of psychopathy as do other results that were discussed previously (e.g., Newman and Kosson 1986; Newman, Schmitt and Voss 1997).

Therefore, although we have attempted to achieve some specificity in our description of the information-processing deficit that underlies the disinhibition of psychopaths, we do not believe that, at this time, the evidence is sufficient to support a definitive statement regarding the anatomical locus (or loci) of that deficit. This stance follows from our view that psychopaths' deficit, although similar to that which might result from SHS (or BIS) dysfunction, also could be caused by impairments of other neuroanatomical pathways and structures. Evidence suggesting a laterality component to psychopaths' information-processing deficit also requires accommodation within any neurological model of psychopathy.

Directions for future research

Although we do not, at least at present, endorse a weak BIS hypothesis of primary psychopathy, RST certainly will continue to play a major role in psychopathy research. This is because, without question, associations exist between psychopathy and self-report measures of the BAS and BIS constructs. Given the recent modifications of the BIS construct, those associations are in better accord with experimental results. In this section, we attempt to advance the theoretical development in the field by contrasting alternative hypotheses regarding the nature of the associations between psychopathy and the BAS and BIS.

One possibility is that evidence of both high BAS activation and low BIS activation within a sample of psychopaths reflects the presence of distinct sub-types among persons whose symptoms warrant a psychopathy diagnosis. That is, all psychopaths manifest disinhibition, but the disinhibition of one sub-set of psychopaths may result from the action of different psychological processes than the disinhibition of another subset. Consistent with this view, the BAS and BIS have been found to be differentially associated with the primary and secondary psychopathy sub-types. As described above, primary psychopaths score lower than controls on measures of BIS activation, whereas secondary psychopaths score higher on measures of BAS activation. This result might imply that some persons manifest psychopathic behavior due largely to the effects of a strong BAS (e.g., their attention is strongly attracted by reward cues, thus decreasing the attentional capacity that is available to process information indicative of a potential problem with a prepotent response). Others may merit the psychopathy diagnosis due largely to the effects of a weak BIS (e.g., impaired processing of information that is indicative of a conflict involving a current or prepotent goal).

A second possibility for understanding the associations of psychopathy with the BAS and BIS is derived from factor-analytic studies of the Psychopathy Checklist – Revised (PCL-R) (Hare 2003), which is the most widely used instrument for diagnosing psychopathy. The PCL-R encompasses two broad factors (e.g., Hare 2003), with psychopaths typically scoring above the mean on both (although for individual psychopaths, scores on one factor may be substantially higher than scores on the other). Based on experimental correlates of the PCL-R factors, Patrick and colleagues (e.g., Patrick 1994; Patrick, Bradley and Lang 1993) proposed that Factor 1 reflects the core features of the psychopathy (e.g., hyposensitivity to anxiety), whereas Factor 2 reflects an externalizing dimension that is common to disinhibitory conditions such as conduct disorder, anti-social personality disorder and aggression (Patrick, Curtin and Kreuger, in press).

In a recent examination of the correlations between measures of the BAS and BIS constructs and the PCL-R factors, Newman (2006) found a robust association between responses to BIS scale items and Factor 1 (controlling for the effects of Factor 2), whereas BAS scale scores were predicted by the unique variance associated with Factor 2 (controlling for the contribution of Factor 1). These results suggest that psychopathy may represent an unfortunate combination of traits that jointly predispose affected individuals to the disinhibited expression of dominant response inclinations. In particular, psychopathy might be viewed as resulting from a combination of a weak or hypoactive BIS with a strong or hyperactive BAS. Note that this view differs from that associated with the primary and secondary psychopathy sub-types, in that the factorial position implies that both a strong BAS and a weak BIS are present to some extent in most psychopaths, whereas the sub-type view implies that some psychopaths predominantly manifest a weak BIS and other psychopaths manifest a strong BAS.

A second possibility that follows from the factorial view of psychopathy is that the information-processing deficit that is fundamental to psychopathy is reflected in the variance that is common to PCL-R Factor 1 and Factor 2. We discussed previously our view that this deficit entails an impairment that adversely affects the subcortical allocation of selective attention to the processing of stimuli or information that is extraneous to the current response inclination or goal. On the other hand, the unique variance associated with Factor 1 plausibly reflects the influence of a hypoactive BIS, with the unique variance associated with Factor 2 reflecting the influence of a strong or hyperactive BAS.

This perspective implies that BIS and BAS processes do not themselves constitute the fundamental psychopathy diathesis but, instead, serve to moderate its expression. Indeed, it may be that the cognitive deficit that is fundamental to psychopathy generally is not sufficient to produce the psychopathy syndrome. Rather, the presence of either a BIS that is weaker than average or a BAS that is stronger than average (or both) may be necessary to raise the level of disinhibited behavior above the threshold that is required to merit a psychopathy diagnosis.

Specifically, the presence of either a hypoactive BIS or a hyperactive BAS is, in and of itself, conducive to impaired self-regulation and increased disinhibition (e.g., Newman and Wallace 1993). Hence, when the psychopathy diathesis is combined with either a strong BAS or a weak BIS, the presence of a dual predisposition to disinhibition creates a high probability that a person's level of disinhibited behavior will exceed the threshold that is required for producing the psychopathy syndrome. Extrapolating from this line of reasoning, it follows that the concurrent presence of both a weak BIS and a strong BAS (i.e., the individual attains PCL-R scores that are well above average on both Factor 1 and Factor 2) would create a particularly potent predisposition for expressing the psychopathy diathesis as behavioral disinhibition.

At this point, however, we do not believe that the evidence that is presently available clearly favors any one of the possible interpretations of the associations that exist between psychopathy and the BAS and BIS: proponents of any of the positions described above could cite favorable evidence. For example, the BAS and BIS constructs have been shown to be differentially associated *both* with the primary and secondary psychopathy sub-types and with PCL-R Factors 1 and 2. Consequently, we predict that attempts to elucidate the associations between psychopathy and RST will continue to play a pivotal role in psychopathy research.

Conclusion

We have proposed that the predisposition to psychopathy consists of an information-processing deficit that entails a decreased efficacy of the subcortical allocation of selective attention to stimuli or information that are extraneous to, or incongruent with, the current goal or prepotent response inclination. This deficit becomes problematic (i.e., disinhibition results) when information indicating that the current response may not be well suited to the situation or stimulus context is not adequately processed.

In addition, psychopathy is associated with self-report measures of the BAS and BIS constructs. In the context of the original RST, those relationships appeared inconsistent with experimental results, whereas experimental and self-report data are in substantially better accord when viewed in light of the revised RST. Hence, the recent revision of RST, and in particular the increased specificity of the description of the BIS, have substantially enhanced the utility of RST for understanding the cognitive, affective and behavioral characteristics associated with psychopathy. We believe that the evaluation of alternative explanations for the associations between psychopathy and the BAS and BIS constructs (such as those described above) will significantly advance psychopathy research.

References

Arnett, P.A., Howland, E.W., Smith, S.S. and Newman, J.P. (1993), Autonomic responsivity during passive avoidance in incarcerated psychopaths, *Personality and Individual Differences*, 14, 173–185

Arnett, P.A., Smith, S.S. and Newman, J.P. (1997), Approach and avoidance motivation in incarcerated psychopaths during passive avoidance, *Journal of Personality and Social Psychology*, 72, 1413–1428

Bernstein, A., Newman, J.P., Wallace, J.F. and Luh, K.E. (2000), Left-hemisphere activation and deficient response modulation in psychopaths, *Psychological Science*, 11, 414–418

Blackburn, R. (1979), Cortical and autonomic arousal in primary and secondary psychopaths, *Psychophysiology*, 16, 143–150

Book, A.S. and Quinsey, V.L. (2004), Psychopaths: cheaters or warrior-hawks?, *Personality and Individual Differences*, 36, 33–45

Carver, C.S. and White, T.L. (1994), Behavioral inhibition, behavioral activation, and affective responses to impending reward and punishment: the BIS/BAS scales, *Journal of Personality and Social Psychology*, 67, 319–333

Cleckley, H. (1976), *The Mask of Sanity* (5th edn, St Louis, MO: Mosby)

Corr, P.J. (2000), J.A. Gray's reinforcement sensitivity theory: tests of the joint subsystems hypothesis of anxiety and impulsivity, *Personality and Individual Differences*, 33, 511–532

Fowles, D.C. (1980), The three arousal model: implications of Gray's two-factor learning theory for heart rate, electrodermal activity, and psychopathy, *Psychophysiology*, 17, 87–104

Gernsbacher, M.A. and Faust, M.E. (1991), The mechanism of suppression: a component of general comprehension skill, *Journal of Experimental Psychology: Learning, Memory, and Cognition*, 17, 245–262

Gorenstein, E.E. and Newman, J.P. (1980), Disinhibitory psychopathology: a new perspective and a model for research, *Psychological Review*, 87, 301–315

Gray, J.A. (1975), *Elements of a Two-Process Theory of Learning* (London: Academic Press)

(1987), *The Psychology of Fear and Stress* (2nd edn, New York: Cambridge University Press)

Gray, J.A. and McNaughton, N. (2000), *The Neuropsychology of Anxiety: an Enquiry into the Functions of the Septo-hippocampal System* (2nd edn, New York: Oxford University Press)

Gray, J.A. and Smith, P.T. (1969), An arousal-decision model for partial reinforcement and discrimination learning in R. Gilbert and N.S. Sutherland (eds), *Animal Discrimination Learning* (New York: Academic Press), pp. 243–272

Hare, R.D. (1970), *Psychopathy: Theory and Research* (New York: Wiley)

(1996), Psychopathy: a clinical construct whose time has come, *Criminal Justice and Behavior*, 23, 25–54

(2003), *Manual for the Hare Psychopathy Checklist-Revised* (2nd edn, Toronto: Multi-Health Systems)

Hemphill, J.F., Hare, R.D. and Wong, S. (1998), Psychopathy and recidivism: a review, *Legal and Criminological Psychology*, 3, 139–170

Hiatt, K.D., Schmitt, W.A. and Newman, J.P. (2004), Stroop tasks reveal abnormal selective attention in psychopathic offenders, *Neuropsychology*, 18, 50–59

Howland, E.W., Kosson, D.S., Patterson, C.M. and Newman, J.P. (1993),
Altering a dominant response: performance of psychopaths and low
socialization college students on a cued reaction time task, *Journal of
Abnormal Psychology*, 102, 379–387

Kosson, D.S. (1998), Divided visual attention in psychopathic and
nonpsychopathic offenders, *Personality and Individual Differences*, 24, 373–391

Lavie, N., Hirst, A., De Fockert, J.W. and Viding, E. (2004), Load theory of
selective attention and cognitive control, *Journal of Experimental Psychology:
General*, 133, 339–354

Lorenz, A.R. and Newman, J.P. (2002), Deficient response modulation and
emotion processing in low-anxious Caucasian psychopathic offenders:
results from a lexical decision task, *Emotion*, 2, 91–104

Lykken, D.T. (1995), *The Antisocial Personalities* (Hillsdale, NJ: Lawrence
Erlbaum Associates)

MacCoon, D.G., Wallace, J.F. and Newman, J.P. (2004), Self-regulation:
context-appropriate balanced attention in R.F. Baumeister and K.D. Vohs
(eds), *Handbook of Self-regulation: Research, Theory, and Applications* (New
York: Guilford Press), pp. 422–444

Most, S.B., Scholl, B.J., Clifford, E.R. and Simons, D.J. (2005), What you see is
what you set: sustained inattentional blindness and the capture of
awareness, *Psychological Review*, 112, 217–242

Newman, J.P. (2006), Correlations between measures of the BAS and BIS
constructs and the PCL-R factors (unpublished raw data)

Newman, J.P. and Brinkley, C.A. (1997), Reconsidering the low-fear
explanation for primary psychopathy, *Psychological Inquiry*, 8, 236–244

Newman, J.P. and Kosson, D.S. (1986), Passive avoidance learning in
psychopathic and nonpsychopathic offenders, *Journal of Abnormal
Psychology*, 95, 257–263

Newman, J.P. and Lorenz, A.R. (2003), Response modulation and emotion
processing: implications for psychopathy and other dysregulatory psychopathology in R.J. Davidson, K. Scherer and H.H. Goldsmith (eds), *Handbook
of Affective Sciences* (New York: Oxford University Press), pp. 1043–1067

Newman, J.P., MacCoon, D.G., Buckholtz, J.W., Bertsch, J.D., Hiatt, K.D. and
Vaughn, L.J. (in press), Deficient integration of top-down and bottom-up
influences on attention in psychopaths: potential contribution of the septo-
hippocampal system in D. Barch (ed.), *Handbook of Cognitive and Affective
Neuroscience of Psychopathology* (New York: Oxford University Press)

Newman, J.P., MacCoon, D.G., Vaughn, L.J. and Sadeh, N. (2005), Validating a
distinction between primary and secondary psychopathy with measures of
Gray's BIS and BAS constructs, *Journal of Abnormal Psychology*, 114, 319–323

Newman, J.P., Patterson, C.M., Howland, E.W. and Nichols, S.L. (1990),
Passive avoidance in psychopaths: the effects of reward, *Personality and
Individual Differences*, 11, 1101–1114

Newman, J.P., Patterson, C.M. and Kosson, D.S. (1987), Response
perseveration in psychopaths, *Journal of Abnormal Psychology*, 96, 145–148

Newman, J.P. and Schmitt, W.A. (1998), Passive avoidance in psychopathic offenders: a replication and extension, *Journal of Abnormal Psychology*, 107, 527–532

Newman, J.P., Schmitt, W.A. and Voss, W. (1997), The impact of motivationally neutral cues on psychopathic individuals: assessing the generality of the response modulation hypothesis, *Journal of Abnormal Psychology*, 106, 563–575

Newman, J.P. and Wallace, J.F. (1993), Diverse pathways to deficient self-regulation: implications for disinhibitory psychopathology in children, *Clinical Psychology Review*, 13, 699–720

Patrick, C.J. (1994), Emotion and psychopathy: startling new insights, *Psychophysiology*, 31, 319–330

Patrick, C.J., Bradley, M.M. and Lang, P.J. (1993), Emotion in the criminal psychopath: startle reflex modulation, *Journal of Abnormal Psychology*, 102, 82–92

Patrick, C.J., Curtin, J.J. and Kreuger, R.F. (in press), The externalizing spectrum: structure and etiology in D. Barch (ed.), *Handbook of Cognitive and Affective Neuroscience of Psychopathology* (New York: Oxford University Press)

Quinsey, V.L., Rice, M.E. and Harris, G.T. (1995), Actuarial prediction of sexual recidivism, *Journal of Interpersonal Violence*, 10, 85–105

Schmitt, W.A., Brinkley, C.A. and Newman, J.P. (1999), The application of Damasio's somatic marker hypothesis to psychopathic individuals: risk-takers or risk-averse?, *Journal of Abnormal Psychology*, 108, 538–543

Serin, R.C. (1996), Violent recidivism in criminal psychopaths, *Law and Human Behavior*, 20, 207–217

Torrubia, R., Ávila, C., Moltó, J. and Caseras, X. (2001), The sensitivity to punishment and sensitivity to reward questionnaire (SPSRQ) as a measure of Gray's anxiety and impulsivity dimensions, *Personality and Individual Differences*, 31, 837–862

Vitale, J.E., Brinkley, C.A., Hiatt, K.D. and Newman, J.P. (2007), Abnormal selective attention in psychopathic female offenders, *Neuropsychology*, 21, 301–312

Vitale, J.E., Newman, J.P., Bates, J.E., Goodnight, J., Dodge, K.A. and Petit, G.S. (2005), Deficient behavioral inhibition and anomalous selective attention in a community sample of adolescents with psychopathic and low-anxiety traits, *Journal of Abnormal Child Psychology*, 33, 461–470

Wallace, J.F., Schmitt, W.A., Vitale, J.E. and Newman, J.P. (2000), Experimental investigations of information-processing deficiencies in psychopaths: implications for diagnosis and treatment in C.B. Gacono (ed.), *The Clinical and Forensic Assessment of Psychopathy: a Practitioner's Guide* (Mahwah, NJ: Lawrence Erlbaum Associates), pp. 87–109

Walters, G.D. (2003), Predicting institutional adjustment and recidivism with the psychopathy checklist factor scores: a meta-analysis, *Law and Human Behavior*, 27, 541–558

Welsh, G.S. (1956), Factor dimensions A and R in G.S. Welsh and W.G. Dahlstrom (eds), *Basic Readings on the MMPI in Psychology and Medicine* (Minneapolis: University of Minnesota Press), pp. 264–281

Williamson, S., Harpur, T.J. and Hare, R.D. (1991), Abnormal processing of affective words by psychopaths, *Psychophysiology*, 28, 260–273

14 Behavioural activation and inhibition in social adjustment

Gennady G. Knyazev, Glenn D. Wilson and Helena R. Slobodskaya

Gray's theory, now known as *Reinforcement Sensitivity Theory* (RST), describes three major neuropsychological systems, the Behavioural Inhibition System (BIS), the Behavioural Activation System (BAS) and the Fight-Flight System (FFS). In psychometric and experimental studies, only two of these have received confirmation. In particular, psychometric evidence does not support the existence of FFS as a unified dimension orthogonal to BIS and BAS (Wilson, Gray and Barrett 1990; Wilson, Barrett and Iwawaki 1995; Slobodskaya *et al.* 2001; Knyazev, Slobodskaya and Wilson 2004). This chapter will therefore concentrate upon the BIS and BAS dimensions. First, we comment on the position of BIS and BAS within the hierarchy of personality and temperament traits. Then we consider certain difficulties linked with research on the social implications of RST and summarize empirical evidence linking BIS and BAS with social adjustment. Finally, we offer an interpretation of this data and review scarce evidence regarding the moderating role of environmental factors and cognitive abilities on the relationship between BAS, BIS and social outcomes.

BAS, BIS and hierarchical models of personality and temperament

To a large extent, BAS and BIS could be viewed as the two highest-order dimensions of personality. Following the 'Big Five' and Eysenck's 'Giant Three', we might perhaps dub these the 'Gargantuan Two'. CFA studies of the Eysenck Personality Profiler usually find negative correlations between the Extraversion and Neuroticism factors (Eysenck, Wilson and Jackson 2000; Moosbrugger and Fischbach 2002; Knyazev, Belopolsky, Bodunov and Wilson 2004). Studies of the NEO PI-R also detect appreciable intercorrelations among the Big Five factors. Digman

(1997) proposed that these correlations give rise to two broader dimensions, which he labelled Alpha and Beta. Alpha seems to reflect the development of impulse restraint and the reduction of hostility and aggression and is similar to the opposite pole of BAS. Beta relates to self-actualization versus personal constriction and is reminiscent of inverted BIS. Research on temperament shows that a two-factor model can explain much of the variance in temperamental characteristics (Martin *et al.*, unpublished). These two factors are identified with Impulsivity and Inhibition. Thus, much research on individual differences points to the existence of two super dimensions, which are very similar to Gray's constructs of BAS and BIS.

Difficulties and pitfalls linked with research on social aspects of RST

Sensitivity to punishment and reward, which according to Gray's theory are determined by BIS and BAS activity, should play an important role in everyday social interactions. Unfortunately, there have been relatively few studies examining the various social aspects of RST and most of them are concerned with negative consequences of BIS and BAS. Gray has clearly explicated the role of BIS and BAS in anxiety disorder (Gray 1982) and anti-social behaviour (Gray 1987). Others who have applied two-factor theory to adjustment problems differ in the emphasis placed on the BAS and BIS, but all agree that attention deficit disorder with hyperactivity, and conduct disorder, stem from an overactive BAS, while an overactive BIS predisposes to emotional problems (Quay 1988; Fowles 1980). On the whole, however, the social consequences of high BAS activity are less clear than the social consequences of high BIS activity.

BIS was conceptualized by Gray (1982) as a combination of Neuroticism and Introversion, as manifested by trait anxiety. Individuals high on BIS should be shy, anxious, fearful, withdrawn and predisposed to emotional problems. The theoretical delineation of BAS is less certain. As a BAS-related trait, Gray originally proposed that Impulsivity might capture the dimension running from stable introverts to neurotic extraverts. Consequently, BAS activity should underpin positive affect and subjective energy (Matthews and Gilliland 1999). However, psychometric measures of impulsiveness show high correlations with traits such as sensation seeking and anti-social or non-conformist tendencies. In the light of this, Pickering and Gray (2001) adopted the term *impulsive anti-social sensation seeking* as a working label for the BAS-related personality dimension. Pickering and Gray (1999) cite Depue and Collins' (1999) analysis showing that impulsive sensation seeking trait measures (which incorporate positive affect) are located on the diagonal between Extraversion and Constraint, with the latter construct being anchored by EPQ-P. Consequently, they conclude that BAS reactivity should be situated somewhere between Extraversion and Psychoticism.

There are grounds, however, to doubt that BAS-related traits should incorporate positive affect. Corr (2002a) pointed out that impulsivity is related specifically to reward expectancies rather than simply to reward sensitivity. Behavioural impulsivity is characterized by intolerance of delayed reward and a high rate of temporal discounting, both of which imply negative emotions such as frustration and hostility. From such a point of view, impulsivity should relate to negative rather than positive emotions and to Psychoticism more than Extraversion. Intolerance of frustration and a predisposition to negative affect links BAS with Neuroticism, in accord with initial Gray's interpretation. Indeed, within the framework of the five-factor model, traits such as irritability, anger and immoderation, which clearly imply BAS activity, are located within the Neuroticism dimension (Costa and McCrae 1992). Thus, it could be argued that a combination of Introversion and the inhibitory aspects of Neuroticism makes up the higher pole of the BIS dimension, whereas a combination of Psychoticism with the emotional instability aspects of Neuroticism constitutes the extreme pole of the BAS dimension. It has recently been proposed, however, that impulsivity may not be a good anchor for BAS-related personality trait and Extraversion may offer the best correspondence with functional outcomes of the BAS (Depue and Collins 1999; Smillie, Pickering and Jackson, 2006). Whether this is indeed the case is a matter for future investigations.

A definition of BAS as *impulsive anti-social sensation seeking* shifts this dimension distinctly in the direction of psychopathology. This ties in with the fact that in the DSM-IV (American Psychiatric Association 1994) impulsivity is associated with various disorders such as impulse-control disorders, anti-social personality disorder, mania and dementia.

BIS and social adjustment

Research on childhood behavioural inhibition and disinhibition, operationalized in terms of laboratory behavioural measures and physiological indicators, has provided ample evidence linking inhibition in toddlerhood and early childhood with later social anxiety disorder and disinhibition with disruptive behaviour. (For a review of these studies see Hirshfeld-Becker *et al.* 2003.) Table 14.1 summarizes empirical evidence linking BAS and BIS with social adjustment, with an emphasis

Table 14.1 *Summary of evidence linking behavioural inhibition (BIS) and activation (BAS) with social adjustment*

Study	Sample	BAS and BIS measures	Results
Windle 1994	Male US military veterans (N = 4462)	MMPI indices of BIS and BAS	**BIS** – low social support, generalized anxiety and major depressive disorders **BAS** – aggression, substance abuse, anti-social personality disorder
Farrington 1995	South London males age 8 through 32 (N = 411)	Test of psychomotor impulsivity	Childhood **Impulsivity** predicted later delinquency
Fonseca and Yule 1996	(1) 44 male delinquents, 20 controls (age 11–15) (2) 27 conduct disorders, 26 controls (age 7–11)	A card task aimed at measuring sensitivity to reward	**Sensitivity to reward** – anti-social behaviour
Tranah, Harnett and Yule 1998	20 conduct disorders, 20 controls	I_6 Impulsiveness scale	**Impulsiveness** – conduct disorder
Slobodskaya et al. 2001	Adolescents 14–16 years (N = 251)	GWPQ	**BIS** – Emotional disorder (+), Delinquent behaviour (−) **BAS** – Conduct disorder, Hyperactivity
Moeller et al. 2001	Cocaine-dependents (N = 98)	Barratt Impulsivity Scale	**Impulsivity** – higher average cocaine use and withdrawal symptoms
Muris et al. 2001, 2003	Adolescents 12–18 years (N = 968)	Classified on BIS symptoms	**BIS** – anxiety disorder, depression
Franken 2002	Alcoholics, controls (N = 58)	BIS/BAS scales	**BAS** predicted alcohol craving
Knyazev et al. 2002	Adolescents 12–16 years (N = 457)	GWPQ	**BIS** – Emotional disorder, somatic complaints **BAS** – Conduct disorder, Hyperactivity

Table 14.1 (*cont.*)

Study	Sample	BAS and BIS measures	Results
Neal, Edelmann and Glachan 2002	Anxiety and depression self-help organizations Adults (N = 234)	Retrospective Self-report of inhibition	**Anxiety** – increased sensitivity to environmental stimuli **Inhibition** – social phobia, depression
Corruble *et al.* 2003	Depressed in-patients (N = 127)	Impulsivity Rating Scale; Barratt Impulsivity Scale; Impulse Control Scale	**Impulsivity** – recent suicide attempts in severe depression
Jackson and Francis 2004	Undergraduate students (N = 400)	EPP Anxiety and Impulsivity scales	**Anxiety** – anxious attitude to church **Impulsivity** – rewarding attitude to church
Colder and O'Connor 2004	Children, 9–12 years (N = 63)	SPSRQ; reaction time	**Sensitivity to punishment** – internalizing **Impulsivity/fun seeking** – externalizing
Knyazev and Wilson 2004	Adolescents 11–17 years (N = 768)	GWPQ-S	**BIS** – Emotional symptoms **BAS** (+) BIS (−) – Conduct problems, Hyperactivity
Kopecky, Sawyer and Behnke 2004	Undergraduate students, 19.27 years (N = 136)	SPSRQ	**Sensitivity to punishment** – state anxiety during public speaking
Aluja 2004	Women 19–45 years (N = 325)	SPSRQ	**Sensitivity to punishment** – sexual anxiety **Sensitivity to reward** – higher sexual excitability and satisfaction levels
Kane *et al.* 2004	22 bulimic women, 23 co-morbid bulimia-alcohol abuse, 21 controls 18–34 years	Eysenck's Impulsiveness Scale; BIS/BAS scales; CARROT	**Impulsivity** – eating disorder, alcohol problems

Table 14.1 (*cont.*)

Study	Sample	BAS and BIS measures	Results
Knyazev *et al.* 2004b	Adolescents, 16.11 years (N = 4501)	GWPQ-S	**BAS** – substance use, vulnerability to deviant peers' influence
Knyazev 2004	Adolescents, 16.11 years (N = 4501)	GWPQ-S	Influence of **BAS** on substance use was mediated by social attitudes
Perkins and Corr 2005	68 managers, 42 years	Worrying scale: Occupational Personality Questionnaire	**Worrying** – better performance in more cognitively able individuals
Lauriola *et al.* 2005	Adults, 46.99 years (N = 240)	BIS/BAS scales; Barratt Impulsiveness Scale	**Fun seeking** – health risk-taking
Meyer, Oliver and Roth 2005	Undergraduates, 20.07 years (N = 202)	BIS/BAS scales	**BIS** – distress **BAS** – active, directive responses to threat
Slobodskaya, Safronova and Windle, in press	Adolescents, 14.4 years (N = 255)	GWPQ	**BIS** – emotional problems **BAS** – conduct problems

on more recent findings. This evidence converges in showing that high BIS activity impairs social adjustment primarily via heightened anxiety levels and concomitant symptoms of depression. The predisposition to such a behavioural style, when it appears in early childhood, tends to persist throughout the entire lifespan.

In a recent (unpublished) study by H.R. Slobodskaya and M.V. Safronova, using a sample of 1,013 adolescents aged ten to eighteen years, the BIS scale of a short version of the GWPQ (GWPQ-S) (Wilson, Barrett and Gray 1989; Slobodskaya *et al.* 2003) was negatively associated with perceived physical health and positively associated with sport activity, suggesting that high-BIS adolescents are inclined to worry about their health and try to improve it. They had lower self-esteem and a lower estimate of their personal safety and social support. On the positive side, they tended to have higher grade point averages (GPA), smoked less and reported less drug use.

These findings show that high BIS activity is not without certain advantages. Caution, which is linked with BIS, may reduce the likelihood of exposure to risky situations. Another possibility is that, on exposure to a risky situation, the person with a highly active BIS withdraws more readily. Knyazev, Slobodskaya, Kharchenko and Wilson (2004) found that, in relation to substance use, both such tendencies did apply for females. Males, however, were different; here BIS actually seemed to work in the opposite direction, being associated with higher levels of drug use. Gender-role expectations might account for this sex difference. Avoidance of femininity by males has a strong affective component (Archer 1984), implying a role for BIS. Since higher activity and a degree of delinquency could be regarded as more 'appropriate' gender-role behaviour for males, a fear of seeming effeminate may push high BIS males toward hyperactive and delinquent behaviour. It should be emphasized, however, that the effect size of this gender-specific departure was small and, overall, BIS is inclined to reduce the likelihood of dangerous acting-out behaviours.

Within the framework of the joint subsystems hypothesis (Corr 2002b), these effects could be partly explained by the inhibitory influence of BIS on BAS-specific behaviour. However, there could be an additional reason for the beneficial effects of BIS. There is evidence that human anxiety differs from that manifested in lower mammals. One recent study has demonstrated that although the amygdala has an important role in mediating initial responses to fearful stimuli, anxiety in primates is focused more in cortical regions (Kalin et al. 2001). This neuropsychological evidence concurs with existing psychological data linking human anxiety with cognitive processes such as rehearsal and rumination. Thus, human anxiety appears to be more cognitive than emotional and this links it with other cognitive abilities that are generally beneficial for social adjustment.

BAS and social adjustment

Evidence summarized in Table 14.1 confirms a substantial link between BAS and delinquent, anti-social behaviour. The link between BAS and addictive behaviour is particularly important because it was predicted by most theorists in the field (e.g., Cloninger 1987). Empirical evidence shows that BAS predicts alcohol craving (Franken 2002), binge eating (Kane et al. 2004) and involvement in drugs (Knyazev, Slobodskaya, Kharchenko and Wilson 2004). BAS, as indexed by the GWPQ-S, is a better predictor of substance use than EPQ Psychoticism (Knyazev, Slobodskaya, Kharchenko and Wilson 2004). It is possible, however, that impulsivity, rather than sensitivity to reward, may account for the observed association between substance use and BAS measures (Dawe and Loxton 2004).

BAS influences a variety of variables measuring social attitudes and relationships with the social environment which act as risk and protective factors in relation to substance use. Thus, high BAS predisposes to conflict with adults, affiliation with deviant peers, tolerant attitudes toward law-breaking, low educational aspiration and poor relationships with parents (Knyazev 2004). In the latter study, the first three variables partly mediated relationships between BAS and substance use but after controlling for their influence, BAS was still significantly associated with the outcome.

Some data indicate that high BAS provides a degree of protection against emotional disturbances, such as anxiety symptoms (Slobodskaya *et al.* 2001; Knyazev *et al.* 2002), and promotes body development in males (Mussap 2006). It should be noted, however, that high BAS is associated with lower subjective wellbeing (Knyazev 2004) and increases the probability of suicide attempts in depression (Corruble *et al.* 2003).

Why the balance between BAS and BIS is important for social adjustment

Summing up, empirical studies show that in modern society, both an overactive BAS and overactive BIS predispose to adjustment problems. From an evolutionary point of view, BAS and BIS are manifestations of two basic motivations common to most animal species. BIS reflects a need for safety, whereas BAS mediates approach to important objects. Clearly, optimal survival and reproduction will be afforded by some balance in the activity of the BIS and BAS. The exact pitching of this balance depends on the degree of danger and the availability of important objects in the real world for a particular animal within its particular (ever-changing) environment. In dangerous and poor environments, highly active BIS and BAS would benefit for survival. But for human beings living in a civilized society, the likelihood of lethal attack by predators or death by starvation is relatively low; most threats and attractions are of a social nature. To function effectively in this environment, an individual must rely more upon cognitive abilities and social networks. The importance of social inclusion at the human level is indicated by the fact that social phobia and stage fright are more widespread than fear of snakes and spiders. Excessive activity either within the BIS or the BAS may result in inappropriate behaviour and social maladjustment. An overly active BIS results in social withdrawal and emotional turmoil; an overly active BAS results in risky, anti-social behaviour.

Within the framework of the so-called 'person-centred' approach, empirical studies have found evidence that three personality types, labelled *Resilients, Overcontrollers* and *Undercontrollers*, can be replicated across methods, languages and ages (Robins *et al.* 1996). Resilients are found to be high on all the Big Five characteristics, intelligent, socially and academically competent and well-adjusted. Overcontrollers are characterized as low on extraversion and emotional stability and vulnerable to internalizing problems. Undercontrollers are low on agreeableness and conscientiousness, impulsive, with academic problems, and at greater risk for co-morbid internalizing and externalizing problems. Thus, basically, Resilients represent a 'good' part of the population while Overcontrollers and Undercontrollers are problematic in one way or another. Recently, it has been shown that Overcontrol represents high behavioural inhibition, Undercontrol high behavioural activation, and Resilience low scores on both dimensions (Knyazev and Slobodskaya 2006).

It is interesting that a group with both high BAS and high BIS is lacking in this empirical classification. According to Gray's theory, BAS and BIS are reciprocally connected. Besides, following Corr's joint subsystems hypothesis, each of these systems operates to inhibit behaviour governed by the other. That means that a person with one system that is highly active should tend to show less behaviour that is peculiar to the other system. Therefore, a balance between the two systems may be readily achieved only at low levels of activity in both systems, which is the case for Resilients. Persons with both systems highly active should be rare within the population. It might be supposed that such persons would be least favoured in terms of social adjustment because they combine higher levels of both internalizing and externalizing problems, and there is some evidence to this effect (Windle 1994; Knyazev and Wilson 2004). However, more detailed analysis reveals that, owing to the mutually inhibitory effects of the two systems, problem behaviour in such persons is less marked than it is in persons who combine one overactive dimension with a deficient other (Knyazev and Wilson 2004).

Moderating role of the environment and cognitive abilities

Social outcomes of BIS and BAS activity are moderated by environmental factors. Thus, the impact of Psychoticism, BAS and Extraversion on substance use is softened by a better relationship with one's parents and exacerbated by affiliation with deviant peers (Knyazev, Slobodskaya, Kharchenko and Wilson 2004; Knyazev 2004). It could be speculated that environmental influences also modulate BAS and BIS activity. Younger people tend to be higher on Neuroticism and Extraversion, and lower on Agreeableness and Conscientiousness (Costa and McCrae 1989) implying that activity of both BAS and BIS decreases with age. The extent of this modulation during childhood and adolescence might depend both on peculiarities of the environment and individual susceptibility to environmental influences. There is considerable research on interactions between child temperament and the family environment in predicting later social outcomes but within the RST framework such research is scarce. Since such modulation represents a kind of learning, its effectiveness should depend on the child's cognitive abilities. For example, Nakao et al. (2000) showed that children with high intellect had stronger influences on their personality from their family environment than those with low intellect.

Existing evidence suggests that the impact of unfavourable temperamental predispositions on social adjustment is indeed moderated by cognitive abilities. Asendorpf and Van Aken (1994) showed that higher intelligence relates to better adjustment in inhibited children. A recent study by Perkins and Corr (2005) showed that, in more cognitively able managers, worrying (which is an attribute of BIS) was positively correlated with performance but as ability declined this relationship disappeared. In a study by Finn and Hall (2004), the relationship between disinhibition and alcohol problems was moderated by intelligence and short-term memory capacity. High disinhibition and high ability participants had fewer alcohol problems than did high disinhibition and low ability participants.

To reveal how cognitive abilities influence the relationship between BAS and social interactions with peers, we used data from our previous study (Knyazev et al. 2002). In 227 adolescents (108 boys) aged thirteen to sixteen years, cognitive abilities were measured by a Russian test of verbal IQ, BAS was evaluated by its proxy EPQ Psychoticism and relations with peers were rated by teachers on a seven-point scale of 'How well he/she communicates with peers'. The association of P with the outcome was significantly negative in the group with below-median IQ scores but was not significant in the group with IQ scores above the median (Figure 14.1).

These, albeit scarce, data confirm that high cognitive abilities ameliorate unfavourable influences of high BAS and BIS activity on social adjustment. Extension of this research, particularly using longitudinal designs in the developmental perspective, is needed for understanding

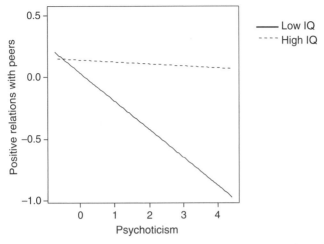

Figure 14.1 A graphical plot of the relation between psychoticism and teacher ratings of relations with peers as moderated by verbal IQ

how BAS and BIS activity is tempered in the process of interaction with the environment and the exact role of cognitive abilities in this process. Another unexplored but intriguing issue is the relationship of BAS and BIS with emotional intelligence and their interactions in prediction of social outcomes.

Conclusion

Empirical evidence shows that high BIS and BAS are both detrimental to social adjustment. High BIS predisposes to anxiety and depression whereas high BAS predisposes to delinquency and risky health behaviours. A balance between the two systems, with low levels of activity in both, appears to be optimal for social adjustment. In the case of high levels of activity in both, some protection may be afforded by their mutually inhibitory action, although BIS probably offers more beneficial moderating effects than BAS. Some evidence suggests that environmental factors and cognitive abilities moderate the influence of BAS and BIS on social adjustment. Certain difficulties experienced within the field of social behaviour are shared with other areas of RST research. The most serious problem is flux and controversy in the conceptualization of BAS. RST needs to account for other areas of personality research beyond Eysenck's theory. A growing body of evidence indicates that two super dimensions at the highest level of hierarchy explain the co-variance among personality and temperament traits and by implication these dimensions are similar to BAS and BIS. If RST fails to encompass this evidence, another theory will have to do it.*

References

Aluja, A. (2004), Sensitivity to punishment, sensitivity to reward and sexuality in females, *Personality and Individual Differences*, 36, 5–10

American Psychiatric Association (1994), *Diagnostic and Statistical Manual of Mental Disorders* (4th edn, Washington, DC: APA)

Archer, J. (1984), Gender roles as developmental pathways, *British Journal of Social Psychology*, 23, 245–256

Asendorpf, J.B. and van Aken M.A.G. (1994), Traits and relationship status: stranger versus peer group inhibition and test intelligence versus peer group competence as early predictors of later self-esteem, *Child Development*, 65, 1786–1798

Carver, C.S. and White, T.L. (1994), Behavioural inhibition, behavioural activation and affective responses to impending reward and punishment: the BIS/BAS scales, *Journal of Personality and Social Psychology*, 67, 319–333

Cloninger, C.R. (1987), A systematic method for clinical description and classification of personality variants: a proposal, *Archives of General Psychiatry*, 44, 573–588

Colder, C.R. and O'Connor, R.M. (2004), Gray's reinforcement sensitivity model and child psychopathology: laboratory and questionnaire assessment of the BAS and BIS, *Journal of Abnormal Child Psychology*, 32, 435–451

Corr, P.J. (2002a), J.A. Gray's reinforcement sensitivity theory and frustrative nonreward: a theoretical note on expectancies in reactions to rewarding stimuli, *Personality and Individual Differences*, 32, 1247–1253

    (2002b), J.A. Gray's reinforcement sensitivity theory: tests of the joint subsystems hypothesis of anxiety and impulsivity, *Personality and Individual Differences*, 33, 511–532

Corruble, E., Benyamina, A., Baylec, F., Falissardd, B. and Hardy, P. (2003), Understanding impulsivity in severe depression? A psychometrical contribution, *Progress in Neuro-Psychopharmacology and Biological Psychiatry*, 27, 829–833

Costa, P.T. and McCrae, R.R. (1989), *The NEO-PI/NEO-FFI Manual Supplement* (Odessa, FL: Psychological Assessment Resources)

    (1992), *Revised NEO Personality Inventory (NEO-PI-R) and NEO Five-Factor Inventory (NEO-FFI) Professional Manual* (Odessa, FL: Psychological Assessment Resources)

Dawe, S. and Loxton, N.J. (2004), The role of impulsivity in the development of substance use and eating disorders, *Neuroscience and Biobehavioral Reviews*, 28, 343–351

* The first author was supported by a grant from the Russian Foundation for Basic Research # 05-06-80033-a and the third author gratefully acknowledges the support by the Russian Foundation for Basic Research (# 04-06-80028), the Russian Humanitarian Foundation (# 04-06-00-477) and the Regional Public Foundation of Russian Medicine Support.

Depue, R.A. and Collins, P.F. (1999), Neurobiology of the structure of personality: dopamine, facilitation of incentive motivation, and extraversion, *Behavioural and Brain Sciences*, 22, 491–569

Digman, J.M. (1997), Higher-order factors of the big five, *Journal of Personality and Social Psychology*, 73, 1246–1256

Eysenck, H.J., Wilson, G.D. and Jackson, C.J. (2000), *Eysenck Personality Profiler (Short V6)* (Worthing: Psi-Press)

Farrington, D.P. (1995), The development of offending and antisocial behaviour from childhood: key findings from the Cambridge Study in Delinquent Development, *Journal of Child Psychology and Psychiatry*, 36, 929–964

Finn, P.R. and Hall, J. (2004), Cognitive ability and risk for alcoholism: short-term memory capacity and intelligence moderate personality risk for alcohol problems, *Journal of Abnormal Psychology*, 113, 569–581

Fonseca, A.C. and Yule, W. (1996), Personality and antisocial behaviour in children and adolescents: an enquiry into Eysenck's and Gray's theories, *Journal of Abnormal Child Psychology*, 23, 767–781

Fowles, D.C. (1980), The three arousal model: implications of Gray's two-factor learning theory for heart rate, electrodermal activity, and psychopathy, *Psychophysiology*, 17, 87–104

Franken, I.H.A. (2002), Behavioral approach system (BAS) sensitivity predicts alcohol craving, *Personality and Individual Differences*, 32, 349–355

Gray, J.A. (1982), *The Neuropsychology of Anxiety: an Inquiry into the Functions of the Septo-hippocampal System* (Oxford: Oxford University Press)

(1987), *The Psychology of Fear and Stress* (2nd edn, Oxford: Oxford University Press)

Hirshfeld-Becker, D.R., Biederman, J., Calltharp, S., Rosenbaum, E.D., Faraone, S.V. and Rosenbaum, J.F. (2003), Behavioral inhibition and disinhibition as hypothesized precursors to psychopathology: implications for pediatric bipolar disorder, *Biological Psychiatry*, 53, 985–999

Jackson, C.J. and Francis, L.J. (2004), Are interactions in Gray's reinforcement sensitivity theory proximal or distal in the prediction of religiosity: a test of the joint subsystem hypothesis, *Personality and Individual Differences*, 36, 1197–1209

Kalin, N.H., Shelton, S.E., Davidson, R.J. and Kelley, A.E. (2001), The primate amygdala mediates acute fear but not the behavioral and physiological components of anxious temperament, *Journal of Neuroscience*, 21, 2067–2074

Kane, T.A., Loxton, N.J., Staiger, P.K. and Dawe, S. (2004), Does the tendency to act impulsively underlie binge eating and alcohol use problems? An empirical investigation, *Personality and Individual Differences*, 36, 83–94

Knyazev, G.G. (2004), Behavioural activation as predictor of substance use: mediating and moderating role of attitudes and social relationships, *Drug and Alcohol Dependence*, 75, 309–321

Knyazev, G.G., Belopolsky, V.I., Bodunov, M.V. and Wilson, G.D. (2004), The factor structure of the Eysenck personality profiler in Russia, *Personality and Individual Differences*, 37, 1681–1692

Knyazev, G.G. and Slobodskaya, H.R. (2006), Personality types and behavioural activation and inhibition in adolescents, *Personality and Individual Differences*, 41, 1385–1395

Knyazev, G.G., Slobodskaya, H.R., Kharchenko, I.I. and Wilson, G.D. (2004), Personality and substance use in Russian youths: the predictive and moderating role of behavioural activation and gender, *Personality and Individual Differences*, 37, 827–843

Knyazev, G.G., Slobodskaya, H.R., Safronova, M.V. and Kinsht, I.A. (2002), School adjustment and health in Russian adolescents, *Psychology, Health and Medicine*, 7, 2, 143–155

Knyazev, G.G., Slobodskaya, H.R. and Wilson, G.D. (2004), Comparison of construct validity of the Gray-Wilson personality questionnaire and the BIS/BAS scales, *Personality and Individual Differences*, 37, 1565–1582

Knyazev, G.G. and Wilson, G.D. (2004), The role of personality in the co-occurrence of emotional and conduct problems in adolescents: a confirmation of Corr's 'joint subsystems' hypothesis, *Personality and Individual Differences*, 37, 43–63

Kopecky, C.C., Sawyer, C.R. and Behnke, R.R. (2004), Sensitivity to punishment and explanatory style as predictors of public speaking state anxiety, *Communication Education*, 53, 281–285

Lauriola, M., Russo, P.M., Lucidi, F., Violani, C. and Levin, I.P. (2005), The role of personality in positively and negatively framed risky health decisions, *Personality and Individual Differences*, 38, 45–59

Martin, R.P., Halverson, C., Havill, V. and Lu, Y., Temperamental associations with personality in children: the role of impulsivity and inhibition (unpublished manuscript)

Matthews, G. and Gilliland, K. (1999), The personality theories of H.J. Eysenck and J.A. Gray: a comparative review, *Personality and Individual Differences*, 26, 583–626

Meyer, B., Oliver, L. and Roth, D. (2005), Please don't leave me! BIS/BAS, attachment styles, and responses to a relationship threat, *Personality and Individual Differences*, 38, 151–162

Moeller, F.G., Dougherty, D.M., Barratt, E.S., Schmitz, J.M., Swann, A.C. and Grabowski, J. (2001), The impact of impulsivity on cocaine use and retention in treatment, *Journal of Substance Abuse Treatment*, 21, 193–198

Moosbrugger, H. and Fischbach, A. (2002), Evaluating the dimensionality of the Eysenck Personality Profiler-German version (EPP-D): a contribution to the Super Three vs. Big Five discussion, *Personality and Individual Differences*, 33, 191–211

Muris, P., Meesters, C. and Spinder, M. (2003), Relationships between child- and parent-reported behavioural inhibition and symptoms of anxiety and depression in normal adolescents, *Personality and Individual Differences*, 34, 759–771

Muris, P., Merckelbach, H., Schmidt, H., Gadet, B. and Bogie, N. (2001), Anxiety and depression as correlates of self-reported behavioural inhibition in normal adolescents, *Behaviour Research and Therapy*, 39, 1051–1061

Mussap, A.J. (2006), Reinforcement sensitivity theory (RST) and body change behaviour in males, *Personality and Individual Differences*, 40, 841–852

Nakao, K., Takaishi, J., Tatsuta, K., Katayama, H., Iwase, M., Yorifuji, K. and Takeda, M. (2000), The influences of family environment on personality traits, *Psychiatry and Clinical Neuroscience*, 54, 91–95

Neal, J.A., Edelmann, R.J. and Glachan, M. (2002), Behavioural inhibition and symptoms of anxiety and depression: is there a specific relationship with social phobia?, *British Journal of Clinical Psychology*, 41, 361–374

Perkins, A.M. and Corr, P.J. (2005), Can worriers be winners? The association between worrying and job performance, *Personality and Individual Differences*, 38, 25–31

Pickering, A.D. and Gray, J.A. (1999), The neuroscience of personality in L. Pervin and O. John (eds), *Handbook of Personality* (2nd edn, New York: Guilford Press), pp. 277–299

(2001), Dopamine, appetitive reinforcement, and the neuropsychology of human learning: an individual differences approach in A. Eliasz and A. Angleitner (eds), *Advances in Individual Differences Research* (Lengerich: PABST Science Publishers), pp. 117–149

Quay, H.C. (1988), The behavioural reward and inhibition system in childhood behavior disorders in L.M. Bloomingdale (ed.), *Attention Deficit Disorder* (New York: Pergamon), vol. 3, pp. 176–186

Robins, R.W., John, O.P., Caspi, A., Moffitt, T.E. and Stouthammer-Loeber, M. (1996), Resilient, overcontrolled and undercontrolled boys: three replicable personality types, *Journal of Personality and Social Psychology*, 70, 157–171

Slobodskaya, H.R., Knyazev, G.G., Safronova, M.V. and Wilson, G.D. (2003), Development of a short form of the Gray-Wilson personality questionnaire: its use in measuring personality and adjustment among Russian adolescents, *Personality and Individual Differences*, 35, 1049–1059

Slobodskaya, H.R., Safronova, M.V., Knyazev, G.G. and Wilson, G.D. (2001), Reactions of Russian adolescents to reward and punishment: a cross-cultural study of the Gray-Wilson personality questionnaire, *Personality and Individual Differences*, 30, 1211–1224

Slobodskaya, H.R., Safronova, M.V. and Windle, M. (2005), Personality, temperament and adolescent adjustment in modern Russia, *Personality and Individual Differences*, 39, 167–178

Smillie, L.D., Pickering, A.D. and Jackson, C.J. (2006), The new reinforcement sensitivity theory: implications for personality measurement, *Personality and Social Psychology Review*, 10, 320–375

Tranah, T., Harnett, P. and Yule, W. (1998), Conduct disorder and personality, *Personality and Individual Differences*, 24, 741–745

Wilson, G.D., Barrett, P.T. and Gray, J.A. (1989), Human reactions to reward and punishment: a questionnaire examination of Gray's personality theory, *British Journal of Psychology*, 80, 509–515

Wilson, G.D., Barrett, P.T. and Iwawaki, S. (1995), Japanese reactions to reward and punishment: a cross-cultural personality study, *Personality and Individual Differences*, 19, 198–112

Wilson, G.D., Gray, J.A. and Barrett, P.T. (1990), A factor analysis of the Gray-Wilson personality questionnaire, *Personality and Individual Differences*, 10, 1037–1045

Windle, M. (1994), Temperamental inhibition and activation: hormonal and psychosocial correlates and associated psychiatric disorders, *Personality and Individual Differences*, 17, 61–70

15 Reinforcement sensitivity in the workplace: BIS/BAS in business

Adrian Furnham and Chris Jackson

Personality theorists usually get ever more adventurous as they set out empirically to test their ever more sophisticated theories. Most naturally begin in the laboratory, sometimes even the animal house, testing fundamental (biological and behavioural) tenets of the theory, which develops and changes as it is tested. However, demands both for ecological validity and applicability mean they soon find themselves testing theoretical assumptions on 'real people in real settings'. These settings are most frequently the clinic, the classroom and the office/factory.

Any inspection of work of the trait theorists like Eysenck, Cattell and latterly Costa and McCrae shows how they usually first became interested in the *clinical* applications of their work, then the *educational* applications and finally the *occupational* and organizational applications. Perhaps because Eysenck was at the Institute of Psychiatry (though neither a trained nor practising clinician) he took a great deal of interest in clinical issues with all three dimensions (i.e., Extraversion, Neuroticism and Psychoticism) having obvious clinical implications. Being both a trained clinician and a student of Eysenck, it is no surprise that Jeffrey Gray too, chose to test many of his ideas first on rats and then on patients.

Raymond Cattell, of the three, seemed more interested in the educational sphere, both because of his educational training but also because of his work on intelligence. Similarly Hans Eysenck was always interested in learning theory and intelligence and always took an active interest in how both personality *and* intelligence predicted educational behaviours and outcomes. Indeed, following Burt, the *British Journal of Educational Psychology* from the 1950s to the 1970s published many papers by Eysenck and Cattell on personality trait processes in educational settings (Cattell 1967; Eysenck and Cookson 1969).

However, the world of work seemed of less interest as a place to test the theories. In a review of Eysenck's personality theory and organizational psychology, Furnham (1997) pointed out that even an amazingly productive renaissance man such as Hans Eysenck had done comparatively little work testing his theory in organizational settings. This was less true of Cattell, who published various papers on the personality profile of people in different organizations, as well as many works on motivation of all sorts. Even Costa and McCrae have let others test their theories in work settings rather than do it themselves (Judge, Heller and Mount 2002).

Early work based on either the Eysenckian orthogonal, three-factor model or the Cattellian oblique, sixteen-factor model found that there are fairly consistent patterns across jobs. Eysenck (1967) noted that whereas introversion-extraversion varied accordingly to the particular job (i.e., sales: high; research-and-development: low), neuroticism was consistent in that all successful people tend to be stable. Extraverts do badly at monotonous, detailed, routine tasks and best in people-oriented, varied tasks. Introverts are less prone to distraction. Further, there is significant evidence that Eysenck's three factors predict negative job outcomes like accidents and absenteeism. Unstable extraverts make mistakes; unstable introverts are prone to psychological and physical illnesses (Furnham 1999, 2005).

The work inspired by Cattell's theory has also shown small but consistent, significant and logical correlations between personality factors and such things as absenteeism, entrepreneurship, performance and turnover (Furnham 1994). However, in their manual Cattell, Eber and Tatsuoka (1970) have elaborate equations showing how his sixteen factors need to be specifically weighted and combined to predict such things as the performance of retail and wholesale sales staff. Many results show that the neuroticism factors (C = Emotional Stability, Q4 Tension; O = Apprehensive) are negatively related to job performance.

It may be of some surprise to many to learn that while Jeffrey Gray was at the Institute of Psychiatry following Hans Eysenck, he started and directed a very successful Organisational Consultancy (Psychology at Work Ltd). Despite this, his incredible CV shows very, very little evidence of him taking any interest in the world of work, save perhaps a small number of papers with the editor of this volume (Corr and Gray 1995a, 1995b, 1995c, 1996). However, there is now an active and ongoing research effort, inspired by Gray's theory, to test it in the workplace. This chapter will both review this work and offer some ideas that follow from it. It should be acknowledged that many ideas are based on Gray's early formulation of his theory. Certain features have changed (see McNaughton and Corr 2004; McNaughton and Corr, chapter 2).

Two approaches

There seems to be a very important difference in the research effort of two groups bent on the same purpose. First, there are personality theorists who wander into the 'real world' in an attempt to test their theories. Secondly, there are organizational psychologists who notice dramatic, stable and important individual differences at work and search out the personality literature in an attempt to find a theory and a measure to explain them.

The basic tenet of 'classic personality theory' approach is to measure personality as the independent variable and to see how it relates to some work-related behaviour (like accidents, motivation, pay, satisfaction, productivity). The approach has been piecemeal and there is very little evidence of a concerted, systematic and programmatic research effort, which is perhaps not that unusual. The selection of work-related variables is somewhat opportunistic, because researchers are usually unable to get measures of the precise behaviour they are interested in. Essentially, studies such as these are nearly always seen by personality researchers simply as supporting evidence for their ideas. The office or factory simply replace the laboratory and provide ecologically valid evidence.

On the other hand, researchers in organizational psychology are usually interested in examining personality correlates of specific work behaviours which might help them select, appraise, promote or train individuals. This research tradition has a number of limitations. First, the choice of personality theories and tests has been arbitrary and uni-formed. Personality tests have been favoured mainly because they have been commercially exploited rather than because they are reliable and valid. Secondly, statistical analyses have been simple and naïve. As a rule, simple correlations have been computed rather than partial cor-relations, or even more preferably multivariate statistics to prevent type II errors (finding more significant differences than actualiy occur). Given that both independent and dependent variables are multifactorial, it is essential that sufficiently robust and sensitive multivariate statistics are used to analyse results. Thirdly, studies in this area are frequently exploratory and atheoretical rather than based on a sound theory or programmatic research endeavour. As a result, interesting results are rarely followed up and the theoretical implications rarely exploited. Fourthly, researchers often ignore possible organizational and societal factors that either directly or indirectly affect the dependent variable; that is, work-related behaviours are rarely solely under the control of the individual and may be moderated by powerful organizational factors which need to be taken into account.

BIS/BAS theory has neither infiltrated trait psychology in a big way nor organizational psychology, though this pattern may be changing (Campbell *et al.* 2003). This may mean that neither approach is fully informing the other and the concept has fallen through the cracks from a business perspective.

Measuring the construct

One reason why Gray's theories may have failed to attract much attention is not that they did not appear self-evidently very relevant to the world of work, but rather that they seemed difficult to measure. For most organizational psychologists personality is always an independent variable and some aspect of work behaviour (i.e., productivity, accidents) the dependent variable. What they favour is a simple, robust and valid measure of the personality construct in question. However, it was well over a decade before researchers developed measures of the BIS/BAS concepts. Torrubia and Tobena (1984) devised a 'susceptibility to punishment' scale which showed predictable and satisfactory correlations with Eysenck's measure. Wilson, Barrett and Gray (1989) were less successful, however. They devised a five-dimension measure – approach, active avoidance, passive avoidance, extinction and fight-flight – which, although they showed satisfactory internal consistency, did not correlate with the Eysenckian dimensions as hypothesized (Jackson 2002a, 2003). Later, Carver and White (1994) developed these BIS/BAS scales which have attracted a reasonable amount of interest and research (Johnson, Turner and Iwala 2003) and Jackson developed the JAMS (Jackson's Appetitive Motivation Scale; Jackson and Smillie 2004; Smillie and Jackson 2005) and a more general measure of functional and dysfunctional learning known as the Learning Styles Profiler (LSP) (Jackson 2005).

Whilst the various measures have been used in subsequent papers on the SPSRQ (Torrubia *et al.* 2001), it is not until comparatively recently that good psychometric housekeeping, on all available scales, has taken place. Thus, Caseras, Ávila and Torrubia (2003) compared eight anxiety and impulsivity questionnaires. Indeed, they noted that 'Contrary to most personality models, Gray's model has no standard way to assess the personality dimensions that arise from the theory' (p. 999). Similarly O'Connor, Colder and Hawke (2004) looked at the dimensional structure of SPSRQ but concluded that 'further improvements in this self-report measure should be considered on future research' (p. 985).

Thus, over thirty years on we still do not have a proven psychometrically robust and valid measure of the concept. This never seemed to concern Gray himself, but it may, rightly or wrongly, be a major explanation for ignorance of the theory and research in organizational psychology. New measures such as the JAMS and LSP have some potential to correct this problem.

Applications to organizational psychology

Over fifteen years ago Furnham (1992) recognized the potential application of Gray's theory to work settings. The practical application of Gray's theory to occupational settings is appealingly obvious, particularly with respect to motivation. It may seem apparent that it would be a waste of time to try to motivate an extravert (high on BAS) with threats of dire punishment (such as sacking, no pay rise), and it would prove equally unsuccessful to attempt to entice an introvert (high on BIS) with promise of pay and benefits. However, it should be noted that the theory clearly stipulates that, because introverts have some BAS activity and extraverts some BIS activity, everyone is sensitive to *both* reward and punishment but to varying degrees. The stronger the reward or the punishment, the less differentiating its effect. To exact the highest level of performance from individuals, motivators must encourage the BAS extravert with potential rewards and prompt the BIS introvert with judicious use of punitive threats. Further, they need to get the optimal reward-punishment right for their particular employees. Thus, BAS extraverted organizations, like those involved in selling, could best motivate and satisfy their staff by providing regular, but varied, rewards. Equally, a primarily BIS introverted organization, as in many bureaucracies, can best shape or motivate staff by the suggestion of imposed sanctions.

The degree of neuroticism heightens an individual's sensitivity to reward or punishment. The introvert, sensitive to punishment, who displays high neuroticism becomes, and indeed is, more sensitive to both reward and punishment, with the greatest increase being toward punishment; that is, the neurotic introvert becomes more concerned with reward but is even more anxious about punishment than the low neurotic introvert. As neuroticism increases, the extravert (sensitive to reward) becomes more sensitive to both reward and punishment, with high increases in reward sensitivity. Although extraverts and introverts increase in sensitivity to reward and punishment as neuroticism increases, each has the highest increase of sensitivity to that trait commonly attributed to extraversion or introversion.

Thus, an extraverted neurotic, being highly sensitive to reward, is less socializable in terms of legal and organizational norms and more likely to become maladaptive or difficult. Given moderate levels of extraversion, high (neurotic) individuals are usually more responsive to control techniques than low (stable) individuals. Whether reward or punishment is the controlling factor, the oversocialized individual will respond readily and may tend to become overcontrolled, while undersocialized individuals may show little or no response to control measures. Consequently, the low neuroticism (stable) individual may necessitate the use of rigid control and severe disciplinary measures (Wakefield 1979).

According to Gray's *Reinforcement Sensitivity Theory* (RST), once the BAS has been activated it should produce motor activity, overall motivation and feelings of desire, elation and hope: optimistic, reward-sensitive, motivated behaviour. On the other hand, BIS arouses anxiety (avoidance) and inhibition (the latter theory suggests avoidance tendencies are inhibited). Whilst a cursory glance over the literature suggests that high BAS but low BIS levels may be beneficial for work, this is clearly an oversimplification. Thus, studies have shown, as predicted, that whilst BIS is clearly a vulnerability factor of anxiety and depression, so BAS may be related to drug and alcohol abuse. Thus, the impulsive BAS individual may be particularly prone to accidents, mishaps and mistakes while the anxiety-sensitive BIS related to absenteeism, perfectionism and difficult task avoidance. However, there are adaptive levels of both BIS and BAS where they can be beneficial. Indeed, Perkins and Corr (2005) argued anxiety at work can be good in situations that require caution, self-discipline and anticipation of threat. They found that (only) for cognitively able individuals, worrying was positively correlated with performance but as ability declined, the relationship disappeared.

Clearly, different jobs call for different abilities and temperaments. Optimistic, fun-seeking, reward-sensitive drive associated with high BAS levels is clearly an asset in jobs associated with the service sector, sales and entertainment, even the military. Equally, it is possible to see situations where moderate BIS scores may be useful in research or safety-related occupations.

Personality in the prediction of work performance

There is now increasing consensus that psychometrically assessed personality traits are useful in predicting both job performance (Barrick, Stewart and Piotrowski 2002; De Fruyt and Salgado 2003; Hough and Furnham 2003; Tett, Jackson, Rothstein and Reddon 1994) and other organizational criteria, such as job satisfaction and absenteeism (Ones, Viswesvaran and Schmidt 2003). Within the Psychoticism-Extraversion-Neuroticism framework of personality (PEN) (Eysenck 1967), meta-analyses provide evidence that extraversion can predict job performance (e.g., De Fruyt and Salgado 2003), and there is some evidence that psychoticism may interact with intelligence to predict creative achievement (Eysenck 1994). However, neuroticism is often associated with poor work outcomes (Judge and Ilies 2002) and undesirable work outcomes, including burnout and emotional exhaustion (Wright and Cropanzano 1998; Wright and Staw 1999). Gray's RST theory tends to shift neuroticism away from pathology, as BIS is seen to be adaptive.

Outside of Eysenck's personality framework, the Big Five model of personality has gained pre-eminence in applied work, particularly in America. Conscientiousness (low psychoticism) is generally predictive of success across a range of work-related criteria and specific occupations (Barrick and Mount 1991), in team performance (Neuman and Wright 1999) and in leadership (Judge, Bono, Ilies and Gerhardt 2002). For example, using meta-analysis, Judge *et al.* (2002) report that conscientiousness correlates on average .28 with leadership and is generally the best personality predictor. Together with high mental ability, it seems that conscientious people are often seen as ideal employees. Mount and Barrick (1998, p. 856) state:

there are now two dispositional predictors in our field whose validity generalizes: general mental ability and conscientiousness. Thus no matter what job you are selecting for, if you want employees who will turn out to be good performers, you should hire those who work smart and work harder.

Reviewers of the literature now agree that there are three stable individual difference factors that consistently account for between one-quarter and one-third of the variance with respect to a wide variety of work-related behaviours and over a wide variety of job types: they are intelligence, stability (i.e., low neuroticism) and conscientiousness.

Various meta-analyses seem to suggest that three individual difference factors are consistently predictive of job outcomes across a variety of jobs. They are intelligence, neuroticism and conscientiousness. Intelligence is more important in complex jobs which require analysis and new learning. Stability is important because it is seriously implicated in stress reactions at work, which are associated with absenteeism, poor productivity and low job satisfaction. Equally, conscientiousness is related to achievement-orientation, diligence, dutifulness and adhering to the work ethic. It is, however, doubtful whether these factors work in isolation; that is, there is, very probably, an interaction effect. Thus, there may be an adaptive value of worrying about task-related things. Whilst studies and meta-analyses consistently highlight the same factors as predictive of work success there remains less evidence on the nature of the process that explains how the relationship works.

What are the implications of this basic work-related finding for RST?

Some researchers suggest conscientiousness as the opposite of impulsivity based on the following reasoning. Conscientiousness is about being organized, reliable, thorough, dependable and efficient. Those who score low on conscientiousness and its sub-scales are described as being hasty, impulsive, careless, impatient, immature and distractible. From this perspective, it follows that low impulsiveness (or high conscientiousness) will generally predict higher performance in the workplace.

From a theoretical perspective, such ideas are potentially in conflict with RST. If *high* conscientiousness is in part *low* impulsivity, and both of these are similar to *low* BAS, and they all predict high work performance, then the conclusion is that people *low in reward sensitivity* are likely to be the high work performers. This seems wrong, since many studies in organizational psychology argue that motivation of workers by rewards is fundamental to business success (Eisenberger *et al.* 1991; Furnham 2005). In short, the organizational literature such as it is strongly suggests that reward-oriented people (i.e., high BAS) will tend to be better performers in the workplace.

What however is missing is a careful mapping of BIS and BAS onto the Big Five at both the domain (superfactor) and facet (primary factor) level. Gray mapped his BIS/BAS onto the Eysenck PEN system and not the Big Five model. Further, there are multiple measures of both the BIS/BAS concepts and the Big Five. Within the Big Five as measured by the NEO-PI-R, impulsiveness (NS) is a facet of neuroticism, as is anxiety (NI). Overall, the neuroticism total score is negatively correlated with all the facets of conscientiousness (Costa and McCrae 1992). However, within the Eysenckian PEN system, with the move from the EPI to the EPQ, the impulsivity items moved from neuroticism to psychoticism (Rocklin and Revelle 1981). For Gray (1981) BAS was a mixture of high N (Neuroticism), E (Extraversion) and P (Psychotism). The question is: what maps onto low Neuroticism, high Conscientiousness (and probably high Openness as a proxy for intelligence)?

If the problems for BAS (assuming a negative correlation between BAS and conscientiousness) in the prediction of workplace performance were not enough, then these are compounded by BIS. According to RST, BIS equates to anxiety which is a major primary scale of neuroticism. In general, neuroticism is associated with poor work performance in some reviews (Judge and Ilies 2002) and has also be linked to undesirable work outcomes, including burnout and emotional exhaustion (Wright and Cropanzano 1998; Wright and Staw 1999). It should be pointed out that

BIS is not a pure measure of neuroticism. Neuroticism tends to be viewed negatively within the work environment. Evidence from meta-analyses is more equivocal on the prediction of work performance from neuroticism, with the suggestion that the relationship is consistent but small (Furnham 2005). Neuroticism is more affected with poor morale than low productivity. In contrast, Smillie, Yeo, Furnham and Jackson (2006) provide evidence of a positive relationship between neuroticism and performance. They use a longitudinal design to show that neurotics are good performers on busy days, but poor performers when they are less busy. The issue is inevitably the level at which N is optimal.

RST argues that high BIS scorers are sensitive to punishment. In theory, (threat of) punishment is provided by managers and organizations to encourage staff to be more productive and therefore high BIS should be related to high performance in the workplace. At best, such a relationship seems to be rarely reported in the literature. Indeed, it is not certain whether it has been tested, partly because it remains inappropriate to extrapolate from measures of neuroticism to BIS because they are different but related concepts.

If RST is to be useful in the prediction of workplace behaviour, we must explain the findings that run counter to RST theory, although there remains little data in the area. Why may low BAS (measured as low impulsivity) be associated with high performance when we should expect high BAS to be associated with high performance? Why is high BIS so rarely related to high performance in the workplace? One explanation is that it is rarely directly measured so we have little data.

We attempt to answer these questions as follows:

(1) BAS and impulsivity are not the same thing and therefore it does not follow that impulsivity and BAS are highly positively correlated.
(2) High BIS scorers might be motivated to avoid punishment and management might motivate staff by providing punishment, but it is a mistake to assume that avoidance of punishment provided by management leads to high performance; that is, BIS may lead to good performance when the avoidance of certain costly behaviours has been suppressed by punishment.

Future of RST in the prediction of workplace behaviour

Whereas personality research is to do with the study of the causes of individual differences in affect, cognition, behaviour and experiences,

RST is much more limited in that it represents more essential types of learning and reflects our instincts to engage in reward or punishment avoidant behaviour. If RST is to be useful in the prediction of work performance then we need to integrate RST with the social-cognitive basis of behaviour. This kind of integration provides a broader model which might have the potential to explain the complex goal-oriented behaviour which we can observe in the workplace.

The social-cognitive perspective conceptualizes personality as the outcome of idiographic, contextually sensitive cognitive processes. Good examples of this perspective are provided by Bandura (1999) who advocates self-efficacy and VandeWalle (1997) who proposes goal orientation as situationally specific cognitive predictors of behaviour. Until recently, the RST viewpoint has not taken account of the socio-cognitive viewpoint.

We attempt to achieve theoretical integration between RST and the socio-cultural perspective first by focusing on Cloninger's split of personality into temperament and character (e.g., Cloninger, Svrakic and Przybeck 1993) in which temperament refers to stable and instinctive causes of behaviour and character refers to socio-cognitive causes of behaviour. Secondly, we believe the increasingly predominant approach and avoidance motivation model of personality provides the best conceptual lens to bring all these different research threads together. Approach and avoidance has been advocated by many researchers since James, but most recently by Gable, Reis and Elliot (2003) and Jackson (2005; in press). Approach and avoidance motivation differ as a function of valence, such that approach motivation occurs when behaviour is instigated by the possibility of reward and positive outcomes, whereas avoidance motivation occurs by a desire to avoid punishment and negative outcomes (Elliot 1999).

Figure 15.1 provides a simple introduction to our proposed biosocial model of personality in which socio-cognitive character variables are seen as cognitive expressions of temperaments or instincts. Temperament is a distal predictor of personality mediated by more proximal social-cognitive components. Thus, a mouth-watering slice of pizza may evoke an immediate instinctive, biologically-based desire to approach (a temperament-based approach motivation), yet a dieter might modify these instincts by means of socio-cognitive goals (such as a goal to 'look good') such that the pizza is not in fact eaten.

Approach and avoidance in temperament

There are several biological models of personality such as the one proposed by Zuckerman, but RST (Gray 1982, 1987; Gray and

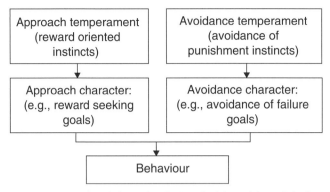

Figure 15.1 A simple introduction to the biosocial model of personality in which sociocognitive character variables are seen as cognitive expressions of temperaments or instincts

McNaughton 2000) is well developed, formulated around principles of approach and avoidance and recognized as a likely cause of personality (e.g., Gray 1982; Matthews and Gilliland 1999) with resultant psychometric implications (Jackson 2002a, 2002b, 2003, 2005; Jackson and Smillie 2004). According to the model, the Behavioural Activation System (BAS) activates approach behaviour when reward cues are detected and the Behavioural Inhibition System (BIS) activates avoidance behaviour when aversive and fear-provoking stimuli are detected (e.g., snakes, blood). It should be pointed out that whereas this was true of the original Gray (1982) model, it is not strictly true in the revised Gray and McNaughton (2000) model. In the revision, BIS is more associated with goal conflict than simple avoidance behaviour. Gray's model seeks to explain the whole of personality from a physiological perspective and leaves no room for alternative more cognitive-based explanations (Matthews and Gilliland 1999). We believe more can be achieved if we limit the broadness of RST by restricting its activity to just the temperament component of personality. Alternative and similar concepts for temperament include biological, non-conscious procedurally learnt, non-controlled or instinctive (see Cloninger, Svrakic and Przybeck 1993; Elliot and Thrash 2002) as shown in Figure 15.1.

Cloninger and colleagues (e.g., Cloninger, Svrakic and Przybeck 1993) developed a broad biosocial model in which processes similar to RST are located in the subcortical part of the brain, yet we know BIS has frontal lobe connections. They argue that cortical or conscious processes of the brain relate to character. Alternative concepts for character include conscious, social, learnt, controlled, agentic doing, self-regulated, self-aware, voluntary or cognitive. According to Cloninger's model, perceptual memory processes relating to temperament operate independently of conceptual processes related to character and research supports the disassociation of these processes in the central nervous system (Roediger, Rajaram and Srinivas 1990).

Cloninger's model attempts integration of biology and social-cognitive constructs. It brings into personality psychology well established principles that procedural learning (data-driven habit and skill learning) is different to propositional learning (concept-driven learning) and based on different parts of the brain. Nevertheless, the model has serious limitations: (1) the model has a very clinical orientation; (2) Cloninger's choice of character variables seems to have little a priori theoretical basis and instead is based on observation and factor analysis (Cloninger et al. 1993); (3) Cloninger's model is in fact completely trait-oriented and fails to utilize well-known socio-cognitive models; (4) Cloninger fails to capitalize on approach and avoidance as a unifying theme; (5) temperament and character are not seen as joint systems; (6) character should mainly be explainable as shared environment effects as opposed to additive genetic effects, yet Gillespie, Cloninger, Heath and Martin (2003) find additive genetic components with no shared environment effects. Other researchers have also developed conscious components of personality. For example, Newman and Wallace's (1993) term 'response modulation' describes sensory sampling of the world and 'self-regulation' as the modification of BAS and BIS outputs.

Proximal and distal pathways and redefinition of character

Approach and avoidance temperament may be considered distal predictors of behaviour, and character or conscious scales as proximal mediators of the distal scales. Proximal character components are therefore cognitive expressions of distal temperament. Our use of structural equation modelling (SEM) terms is deliberate since SEM provides both a theoretical perspective as well as an applied investigative methodology, in which the prediction of actual behaviour is expressly built into the personality model. This aim extends and develops initial exploratory work by Elliot and Thrash (2002), Humphreys and Revelle (1984) and Jackson and Francis (2004) who advocate models of approach and avoidance pathways with instinctive and situational components. Further support is derived from research into the functional and dysfunctional basis of learning (Jackson 2005). Revelle's recent work conceptualizes personality as the organization of affect, behaviour, cognition and goals using a classification system similar to that developed in this project (Ortony, Norman and Revelle 2005).

Moreover, since we disagree with Cloninger's definition of character, we draw upon a general socio-cultural model of behaviour prediction recently described in the applied literature. Chen, Gully, Whiteman and Kilcullen (2000) propose and validate a socio-cognitive applied model which suggests that academic performance can be predicted from goals (Locke and Latham 1990), general self-efficacy, specific self-efficacy for a particular situation (Bandura 1999), goal orientation (learning and performance, as described by VandeWalle 1997), state anxiety and ability. Their model was not tested outside of the limited educational domain and we seek to generalize the model to the workplace.

The basis for the proposed biosocial model of personality is mainly derived from Bandura 1999; Chen *et al.* 2000; Cloninger, Svrakic and Przybeck 1993; Elliot and Thrash 2002; Humphreys and Revelle 1984; and Ortony, Norman and Revelle 2005. Figure 15.2 describes the

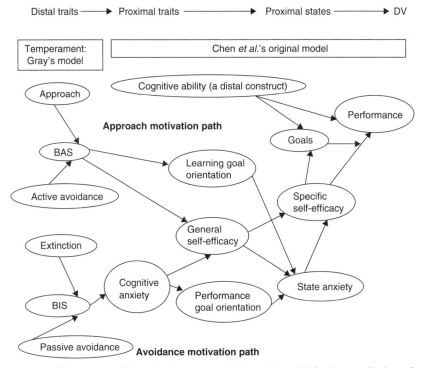

Figure 15.2 Hypothesized general biosocial model in the prediction of performance

proposed generic biosocial model and includes precursors of BAS and BIS (Wilson, Gray and Barrett 1990; Jackson 2002a, 2003). For simplicity, our model excludes Gray and McNaughton's (2002) Fight-Flight-Freeze System. We recognize, however, that this model may be less relevant to the old 1982 model than the recently revised model by Gray and McNaughton (2000).

In short, our integrated model that will be useful in the prediction of work performance achieves the following novel outcomes:

(1) A marriage between RST as championed by Gray and the social-cognitive theory such that social cognitions are seen as proximal mediators of distal biological constructs.

(2) Relegation of RST to temperament to allow the social-cognitive perspective room to flourish.

(3) Relegation of social-cognitive theory to character to allow RST room to flourish.

(4) The opportunity to integrate social and cognitive models along the lines suggested by Chen *et al.* (2000), such as self-efficacy, learning and performance orientation, as well as other models such as social learning, locus of control and attributional style, etc. This will have the effect of unifying the biological and social-cognitive approaches to trait personality within a single theory of wide-ranging application.

(5) The opportunity to test for redundancy in various overlapping social-cognitive models. Chen *et al.*'s (2000) model may be over-complex since more recent research suggests commonality between many of the negative emotion scales (Judge, Erez, Bono and Thoreson 2002) and overlap in scales representing each pathway (Gable, Reis and Elliot 2003). Jackson's pilot work (see below) also suggests usefulness of a simple model.

(6) The opportunity to view social-cognitions as constructs providing direction to instinctive energy of RST behaviour as proposed by Revelle's laboratory (Humphreys and Revelle 1984; Revelle 1993, 1995).

(7) The opportunity to determine if interactions between activation and avoidance pathways are found at either the distal RST or the proximal social-cognitive perspective (Jackson and Francis 2004; Ortony, Norman and Revelle 2005).

(8) The opportunity to explore some of the properties of temperament and character within a single model that may allow us to understand how to conduct better interventions when improvements in behaviour are needed.

Biosocial model and performance at work

The best known applied model of personality is the five-factor model (the 'Big Five') which is thought to predict job performance as a result of the stable and consistent behaviours that personality traits are thought to represent. However, such models can be criticized as tautological and failing to address primary motivations. Meta-analysis on the predictiveness of work performance by the Big Five suggests that its validity is relatively low (Hurtz and Donovan 2000), although much better if theory-driven (Hogan and Holland 2004). Our proposed biosocial model hopefully predicts work performance in a non-circular, theoretical and valid way that identifies ways of improving behaviour. It is worth noting that even small positive changes in validity can dramatically improve selection success. Jackson (2001) provided solitary evidence that BAS positively predicts sales performance and Smillie, Yeo, Furnham and Jackson (2006) showed that a scale highly related to BIS can predict sales performance when within person changes across time are taken into account. We therefore identify a gap in the literature relating biosocial constructs to work performance.

Figure 15.3 shows separate results of two self-report cross-sectional surveys using blue collar workers (N = 70) and part-time employed

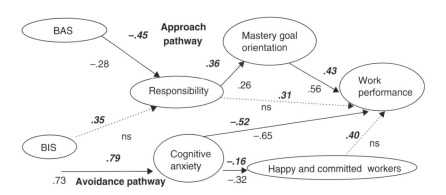

Standardized beta weights in italics and bold above the arrows represent blue collar workers (N =70; AGFI = .92, GFI = .96, CFI = .94; RMSEA = .09); standardized beta weights below the line represent students reporting on part-time work activities (N = 282, AGFI =.90, GFI = .95, CFI = .93; RMSEA = .07). Disturbances and error variances omitted for clarity. All paths significant unless labelled ns.

Figure 15.3 Two pilot studies providing evidence in favour of the biosocial approach

students $(N = 282)$. BAS (temperament) is mediated by responsibility and goal mastery (character) in prediction of work performance. BIS (temperament) is mediated by cognitive anxiety (character) in prediction of work performance and worker happiness. Note replicability across models and identifiable approach and avoidance pathways. In both studies, multiple regression showed no Big Five scale of personality was a significant predictor of work performance. Results emphasize (a) superiority of biosocial approach over traditional models, (b) project feasibility and (c) how cognitive interventions (e.g., training) should focus on character.

Significance of the proposed integration of RST with the sociocognitive model

The Big Five model of personality has become the dominant framework for understanding trait personality. Whilst many consider the Big Five to provide an adequate taxonomy of personality, it also has many problems (e.g., Block 1995) and ultimately personality traits are known to show useful but relatively low validity. Some argue that models such as the Big Five simply reflect the underlying actions of BIS and BAS (Jackson 2002a; Smits and Boeck 2006). In contrast, socio-cognitive models offer more situational and contextually sensitive explanation (e.g., Matthews, Schwean, Campbell, Saklofske and Mohamed 2000). Whilst social and cognitive theorists claim their models are predictive of behaviour, they fail to account for stability and heredity of personality.

Our proposed integration of RST with the socio-cognitive perspective provides a significant and innovative opportunity to integrate trait and socio-cognitive approaches to personality by developing a general, theoretical and testable model of wide applicability and appeal to personality researchers and practitioners. This project rests on logical extensions from, and integration of, the work of many earlier researchers (e.g., Chen et al. 2000; Cloninger, Svrakic and Przybeck 1993; Elliot and Thrash 2002; Gray and McNaughton 2000; Humphreys and Revelle 1984; Revelle 1993, 1995). Our proposed model offers a possible opportunity to unify an area of psychology that has long suffered from the deleterious effects of schism, yet from the safety of knowing that recent research and replicated pilot studies fully support our approach. We hope our biosocial model will lead to improved validity compared to existing personality models, and provide insight into how interventions might be possible (e.g., deficiencies in character could be expected to be more amenable to cognitive interventions). Thus, the biosocial model has the promise of revolutionizing the study of personality and its applications. Additionally, our application to the workplace addresses the significant problems of selection, motivation and training of staff.

Jackson (2005, in press) has developed this line of thinking away from RST and more towards a general model of learning in personality. This model is based on the learning characteristics of the biologically-based scale of sensation seeking. Jackson argues and demonstrates that cognitive control of sensation seeking leads to functional learning and positive behavioural outcomes whereas lack of cognitive control of sensation seeking leads to dysfunctional learning and negative behavioural outcomes. The model is applied to organizational, educational and clinical areas.

Conclusion

Gray's BIS/BAS theory is not only interesting and important, it is also fecund in the sense that it suggests many applied implications. In this chapter we have noted one serious omission in the application of the theory, notably behaviour at work. It is not difficult to see how the theory may be applied but up to now two factors may have prevented this. The first factor is the development and perhaps even commercialization of a simple but valid measure of the construct. The second factor is whether the organization is able and willing to provide performance data which may be matched up with employees' BIS/BAS scores. However, our work and tentative theory development in this area suggests that Gray's theory is particularly useful for understanding and then predicting behaviour in the workplace.

We must acknowledge that Gray's theory developed and changed in his lifetime: compare Gray (1982) with Gray and McNaughton (2000). McNaughton and Corr (2004) have helpfully pointed to five fundamental and critical changes between the latter and former theory. They are: first, a distinction between fear and anxiety with the former moving an animal (and presumably a human) *away* from danger but the latter *toward* danger. Secondly, there are clear categorical and neuroanatomical distinctions between panic, phobia, anxiety and obsession. Thirdly, anxiety is generated by concurrent and equivalent activation of the fear and approach system. Next, BIS is being distributed among a number of neural structures; finally, the functions of the septo-hippocampal system are distributed across functions of anxiety and memory. It is clearly the first difference which affects our tentative theory the most and could indeed lead to opposite predictions (see Jackson, submitted).

At this stage, however, our ideas are still forming (see Jackson 2005; in press). We have come up with at least a useful heuristic. What, however, we are certain of is that RST theory has not up to now been, but can and indeed should be, applied to behaviour at work. Managers talk of 'carrot and stick' organizations meaning those that attempt to shape behaviour by a judicious mix of punishments and rewards. Organizational psychology textbooks are full of advice on how to motivate individuals. Though it is difficult to translate the fundamentally important pharmacological and neuroanatomical work of Gray and his colleagues to the world of work, it is a goal worth pursuing. It may indeed enrich and enliven both areas of research.

References

Bandura, A. (1999), Social cognitive theory of personality in A. Pervin and O.P. John, *Handbook of Personality: Theory and Research* (2nd edn, New York: Guilford Press), pp. 102–138

Barrick, M. and Mount, M. (1991), The 'Big 5' personality dimensions and job performance, *Personnel Psychology*, 44, 1–25

Barrick, M., Stewart, G. and Piotrowski, M. (2002), Personality and job performance, *Journal of Applied Psychology*, 87, 43–51

Block, J. (1995), A contrarian view of the five-factor approach to personality description, *Psychological Bulletin*, 117, 187–215

Campbell, L., Simpson, J., Stewart, M. and Manning, J. (2003), Putting personality in social context: extraversion, emergent leadership and the availability of rewards, *Personality and Social Psychology Bulletin*, 29, 1547–1559

Carver, C.S. and White T. (1994), Behavioral inhibition, behavioural activation, and affective responses to impending reward and punishment: the BIS/BAS scales, *Journal of Personality and Social Psychology*, 67, 319–333

Caseras, X., Ávila, C. and Torrubia, R. (2003), The measurement of individual differences in behavioural inhibition and behavioural activiation systems, *Personality and Individual Differences*, 34, 999–103

Cattell, R. (1967), The theory of fluid and crystallised intelligence, *British Journal of Educational Psychology*, 37, 209–224

Cattell, R., Eber, H. and Tatsuoka, M. (1970), *Handbook of the 16 PF Questionnaire* (Champaign: IPAT)

Chen, G., Gully, S.M., Whiteman, J.A. and Kilcullen, R.N. (2000), Examination of relationships among trait-like individual differences, state-like individual differences and learning performance, *Journal of Applied Psychology*, 85, 835–847

Cloninger, C.R., Svrakic, D.M. and Przybeck, T.R. (1993), A psychobiological model of temperament and character, *Archives of General Psychiatry*, 50, 975–990

Corr, P.J. and Gray, J.A. (1995a), Explaining success and failure in insurance selling, *Selection and Development Review*, 11, 1–2

(1995b), Attributional style, socialisation and cognitive ability as predictors of sales success: a predictive validity study, *Personality and Individual Differences*, 18, 241–252

(1995c), Relationship between attributional style and Lie scores in an occupational sample motivated to fake good, *Personality and Individual Differences*, 18, 433–435

(1996), Attributional style as a personality factor in insurance sales performance in the UK, *Journal of Occupational and Organizational Psychology*, 69, 83–87

De Fruyt, F. and Salgado, J. (2003), Applied personality psychology: lessons learnt from the IWO field, *European Journal of Personality*, 17, 123–131

Elliot, A.J. (1999), Approach and avoidance motivation and achievement goals, *Educational Psychologist*, 34, 169–189

Elliot, A.J. and Church, M. (1977), A hierarchical model of approach and avoidance achievement motivation, *Journal of Personality and Social Psychology*, 72, 218–232

Elliot, A.J. and Thrash, T.M. (2002), Approach-avoidance motivation in personality: approach and avoidance temperaments and goals, *Journal of Personality and Social Psychology*, 82, 804–818

Eysenck, H. (1967), *The Biological Basis of Personality* (Springfield, IL: Thomas)

(1994), *Genius* (Cambridge: Cambridge University Press)

Eysenck, H.J. and Cookson, D. (1969), Personality in primary school children: ability and achievement, *British Journal of Educational Psychology*, 39, 109–130

Flanagan, J.C. (1954), The critical incident technique, *Psychological Bulletin*, 51, 327–359

Furnham, A. (1992), *Personality at Work* (London: Routledge)

(1994), *Personality at Work* (London: Routledge)

(1997), Eysenck's personality theory and organisational behaviour in H. Nyborg (ed.), *The Scientific Study of Human Nature* (Oxford: Pergamon), pp. 462–490

(2005), *The Psychology of Behaviour at Work* (Hove: Psychologist Press)

Furnham, A. and Heaven, P. (1999), *Personality and Social Behaviour* (London: Arnold)

Gable, S.L., Reis, H.T. and Elliot, A.J. (2003), Evidence of bivariate systems: an empirical test of appetition and aversion across domains, *Journal of Research in Personality*, 37, 349–372

Gillespie, N., Cloninger, C.R., Heath, A.C. and Martin, N.G. (2003), The genetic and environmental relationship between Cloninger's dimensions of temperament and character, *Personality and Individual Differences*, 35, 1931–1946

Gray, J.A. (1982), *The Neuropsychology of Anxiety: an Enquiry into the Function of the Septo-hippocampal System* (New York: Oxford University Press)

(1987), The neuropsychology of emotion and personality in S.M. Stahl, S.D. Iverson and E.C. Goodman (eds), *Cognitive Neurochemistry* (Oxford: Oxford University Press)

Gray, J.A. and McMaughton, N. (2000), *The Neuropsychology of Anxiety* (Oxford: Oxford University Press)

Hogan, J. and Holland, B. (2004), Using theory to evaluate personality and job performance relations: a socioanalytic perspective, *Journal of Applied Psychology*, 88, 100–112

Hough, L. and Furnham, A. (2003), Use of personality variables in work settings in W. Borman, D. Ilgen and R. Klimoski (eds), *Handbook of Psychology* (New York: John Wiley), vol. 12, pp. 131–169

Humphreys, M.S. and Revelle, W. (1984), Personality, motivation and performance: a theory of the relationship between individual differences and information processing, *Psychological Review*, 91, 153–184

Hurtz, G. and Donovan, J. (2000), Personality and job performance: the big five revisited, *Journal of Applied Psychology*, 85, 869–879

Jackson, C.J. (2001), Comparison between Eysenck and Gray's models of personality in the prediction of motivational work criteria, *Personality and Individual Differences*, 31, 129–144

(2002a), Mapping Gray's model of personality onto the Eysenck Personality Profiler (EPP), *Personality and Individual Differences*, 32, 495–507

(2002b), *Learning Styles and its Measurement: an Applied Neuropsychological Model of Learning for Business and Education* (Australia: Cymeon)

(2003), Gray's RST: a psychometric critique, *Personality and Individual Differences*, 34, 533–544

(2005), *An Applied Neuropsychological Model of Functional and Dysfunctional Learning: Applications for Business, Education, Training and Clinical Psychology* (Australia: Cymeon)

(in press), Measurement issues concerning a personality model spanning temperament, character and experience in G. Boyle, G. Matthews and D. Saklofske (eds), *Handbook of Personality and Testing* (Sage Publishers)

(submitted), How ear performance interacts with neuroticism to predict disinhibitory approach

Jackson, C.J. and Francis, L.J. (2004), Are interactions in Gray's Reinforcement Sensitivity Theory proximal or distal in the prediction of religiosity: a test of the joint subsystems hypothesis, *Personality and Individual Differences*, 36, 1197–1209

Jackson, C.J. and Smillie, L.D. (2004), Appetitive motivation predicts the majority of personality and an ability measure: a comparison of BAS measures and a re-evaluation of the importance of RST, *Personality and Individual Differences*, 36, 1627–1636

Johnson, S., Turner, R. and Iwala, N. (2003), BIS/BAS levels and psychiatric disorder: an epidemiological study, *Journal of Psychopathology and Behavioural Assessments*, 25, 25–36

Judge, T. and Ilies, R. (2002), Relationship of personality to performance motivation, *Journal of Applied Psychology*, 87, 797–807

Judge, T., Heller, D. and Mount, M. (2002), Five-factor model of personality and job satisfaction: a meta-analysis, *Journal of Applied Psychology*, 87, 530–541

Judge, T.A., Erez, A., Bono, J.E. and Thoresen, C.J. (2002), Are measures of self-esteem, neuroticism, locus of control and generalized self-efficacy indicators of a common core construct, *Journal of Personality and Social Psychology*, 83, 693–710

Locke, E.A. and Latham, G.P. (1990), *A Theory of Goal Setting and Task Performance* (Englewood Cliffs, NJ: Prentice Hall)

Matthews, G. and Gilliland, K. (1999), The personality theories of H.J. Eysenck and J.A. Gray: a comparative review, *Personality and Individual Differences*, 26, 583–626

Matthews, G., Schwean, V.L., Campbell, S.E., Saklofske, D.H., Mohamed, A. (2000), Personality, self-regulation and adaptation: a cognitive-social framework in M. Boekarts, P.R. Pintrich and M. Zeidner (eds), *Handbook of Self-regulation* (New York: Academic Press), pp. 171–207

McNaughton, N. and Corr, P. (2004), A two-dimensional neuropsychology of defense: fear/anxiety and defensive distance, *Neuroscience and Biobehavioural Reviews*, 28, 285–305

Mount, M., Barrick, M. and Stewart, G. (1998), Five factor model of personality and performance in jobs involving interpersonal interactions, *Human Performance*, 11, 145–165

Neuman, G. and Wright, J. (1999), Team effectiveness: beyond skills and cognitive ability, *Journal of Applied Psychology*, 84, 376–387

Newman, J.P. and Wallace, J.F. (1993), Diverse pathways to deficient self-regulation: implications for disinhibitory psychopathology in children, *Clinical Psychology Review*, 13, 690–720

O'Connor, R., Colder, C. and Hawke, L. (2004), Confirmatory factor analysis of the sensitivity to punishment and sensitivity to reward questionnaire, *Personality and Individual Differences*, 37, 985–1002

Ones, D., Viswesvaran, C. and Schmidt, F. (2003), Personality and absenteeism, *European Journal of Personality*, 17, 19–35

Ortony, A., Norman, D.A. and Revelle, W. (2005), Effective functioning: a three level model of affect, motivation, cognition, and behavior in J.M. Fellous and M.A. Arbib (eds), *Who Needs Emotions? The Brain Meets the Machine* (New York: Oxford University Press), pp. 173–202

Perkins, A. and Corr, P. (2005), Can worriers be winners? The association between worrying and job performance, *Personality and Individual Differences*, 38, 25–32

Revelle, W. (1993), Individual differences in personality and motivation: non-cognitive determinants of cognitive performance in A. Baddelely and L. Weiskrantz, *Attention: Selection, Awareness and Control: a Tribute to Donald Broadbent* (Oxford, Oxford University Press), pp. 346–373

(1995), Personality processes, *Annual Review of Psychology*, 46, 295–328

(1997), Extraversion and impulsivity: the lost dimension? in H. Nyborg (ed.), *The Scientific Study of Human Nature: Tribute to Hans J. Eysenck at Eighty* (Denmark: Pergamon), pp. 189–212

Revelle, W., Humphreys, M.S., Simon, L. and Gilliland, K. (1980), The interactive effect of personality, time of day, and caffeine: a test of the arousal model, *Journal of Experimental Psychology: General*, 109, 1–31

Rocklin, T. and Revelle, W. (1981), The measurement of extraversion, *British Journal of Social Psychology*, 20, 279–283

Roediger, H.L., Rajaram, S. and Srinivas, K. (1990), Specifying criteria for postulating memory systems, *Annals of the New York Academy of Sciences*, 608, 572–589

Seligman, M.E. and Schulman, P. (1986), Explanatory style as a predictor of productivity and quitting among life insurance sales agents, *Journal of Personality and Social Psychology*, 50, 832–838

Smillie, L.D. and Jackson, C.J. (2005), The appetitive motivation scale and other BAS measures in the prediction of approach and active-avoidance, *Personality and Individual Differences*, 38, 981–994

Smillie, L.D., Jackson, C.J. and Dalgliesh, L.I. (submitted) Reward-responsiveness, fun and drive: the BIS/BAS scales as an example of the non-equivalence of trait impulsivity and reactivity of the behavioural activation system

Smillie, L., Yeo, G., Furnham, A. and Jackson, C.J. (2006), The moderating effect of neuroticism on daily recorded work performance criteria, *Journal of Applied Psychology*, 91, 139–155

Smits, D.J.M. and Boeck, P.D. (2006), From BIS/BAS to the Big Five, *European Journal of Personality*, 20, 255–270

Spielberger, C.D. (1983), *Manual for the State-Trait Anxiety Inventory* (Palo Alto, CA: Consulting Psychologists Press)

Tett, R., Jackson, D., Rothstein, M. and Reddon, J. (1994), Meta analysis of personality-job performance relations, *Personnel Psychology*, 47, 157–172

Torrubia, A., Ávila, C., Moltó, J. and Caseras, X. (2001), The sensitivity to punishment and sensitivity to reward questionnaire (SPSRQ) as a measure of Gray's anxiety and impulsivity dimensions, *Personality and Individual Differences*, 31, 837–862

Torrubia, A. and Tobena, A. (1984), A scale for the assessment of susceptibility to punishment as a measure of anxiety: preliminary results, *Personality and Individual Differences*, 5, 371–375

VandeWalle, D. (1997), Development and validation of a work domain goal orientation instrument, *Educational and Psychological Measurement*, 57, 995–1015

Wakefield, J. (1979), *Using Personality to Individualise Instruction* (San Franciso: Edits)

Wilson, G.D., Barrett, P.T. and Gray, J.A. (1989), Human reactions to reward and punishment: a questionnaire examination of Gray's personality theory, *British Journal of Psychology*, 80, 509–515

Wilson, G.D., Gray, J.A. and Barrett, P.T. (1990), A factor analysis of the Gray-Wilson personality questionnaire, *Personality and Individual Differences*, 11, 1037–1045

Wright, T.A. and Cropanzano, R. (1998), Emotional exhaustion as a predictor of job performance and voluntary turnover, *Journal of Applied Psychology*, 83, 486–493

Wright, T.A. and Staw, B.M. (1999), Affect and favorable work outcomes: Two longitudinal tests of the happy-productive worker thesis, *Journal of Organisational Behaviour*, 20, 1–33

16 Formal and computational models of Reinforcement Sensitivity Theory

Alan D. Pickering

Jeffrey Gray (Gray 1970, 1981, 1987) developed a 'bottom-up' approach to personality which began with the identification of large-scale brain-behavioural systems in animals (based on lesion and psychopharmacological evidence). The systems which he emphasized were: a reward system (later termed the Behavioural Activation System or BAS); a punishment system; an arousal system; and a Fight-Flight System. His view of personality was that inter-individual differences in the functioning of each discrete system should give rise, in human beings, to a major dimension (or trait) of personality. The theory also talked particularly about the sensitivity (i.e., reactivity) of each system to its characteristic inputs (i.e., the inputs which activated that system rather than any of the others). Inter-individual differences in the sensitivities of the systems were taken to be the causal basis of human personality traits. As the names 'reward system' and 'punishment system' implied, the characteristic inputs of the systems were reinforcing stimuli. To capture these aspects of the theory, I suggested the name *Reinforcement Sensitivity Theory* (RST) for the personality theory which he developed.[1]

Basic tenets of the original RST

In the original version of the theory (which I shall call 'old RST' in this chapter), the personality trait corresponding to variations in functioning of the BAS was suggested to be impulsivity. The punishment system (so-called because it was thought that this system responded to

---

[1] Up until the mid-1990s, the theory was usually called 'Gray's theory of personality'. Jeffrey Gray felt it was too pompous to use this term for the theory in articles on which he was a co-author, and so urged me to come up with a name for the theory. I considered reinforcement reactivity theory and motivational input sensitivity theory (MIST), which would have done equally well, but settled on RST. The name RST really took root after I used it liberally in our 1997 article (Pickering, Corr, Powell, Kumari, Thornton and Gray 1997).

conditioned stimuli signalling impending punishment) was referred to as the Behavioural Inhibition System (BIS): the personality trait corresponding to variations in functioning of the BIS was suggested to be anxiety. This theory, and the data arising from tests of the theory, has been reviewed at length elsewhere (Matthews and Gilliland 1999; Pickering, Díaz and Gray 1995; Pickering *et al.* 1997). The theory also spawned several closely related biological theories of personality by other distinguished researchers (e.g., Cloninger 1986; Depue and Collins 1999).

From the late 1990s onwards, a variety of revisions to the basic theory began to emerge: there was a (re-)emphasis on the interactions between reward and punishment systems (Pickering 1997; Corr 2001); the trait which most closely corresponded to variations in BAS functioning was reconsidered (Depue and Collins 1999; Pickering and Gray 1999, 2001); and a start was made at formalizing the theory more precisely (Pickering 1997; Pickering and Gray 2001). However, the most important revisions to the theory were required in response to the book by Gray and McNaughton (2000). This book detailed some fairly radical revisions to the nature of the fundamental brain-behavioural systems upon which RST rests. This chapter will use the term 'new RST' to describe the personality theory reflecting the changes proposed by Gray and McNaughton (2000).

A number of recent papers have clarified the nature of new RST, and the differences compared with old RST, in very explicit terms (Corr 2002, 2004; McNaughton and Corr 2004) and so only a brief resumé will be given here. Little empirical work on new RST has emerged and so one purpose of this book is to encourage other researchers to consider new RST. The current chapter tries to provide guidance in this connection by exploring the relationship between the two versions of RST in formal terms.

Key differences between old and new RST

The main change underpinning the changes between old and new RST concern the BIS. In old RST this system was considered to respond, inter alia, to conditioned stimuli signalling impending punishment. In new RST the BIS is considered to respond to response conflict (i.e., situations in which, for example, both reward and punishment systems are strongly activated). This notion will be elaborated later in the present chapter. New RST proposes that trait anxiety corresponds to variation in BIS functioning, exactly as in old RST. However, it is inappropriate, in new RST, to refer to the BIS as a punishment system. In new RST, responding to punishing inputs (both conditioned and

Table 16.1 *Key elements of two-system ('old') RST and three-system ('new') RST (Imp = impulsivity; Ext = extraversion; N= neuroticism)*

OLD RST
Behavioural Activation System = BAS
Behavioural Inhibition System = BIS

SYSTEM	RESPONDS TO	OUTPUTS	TRAIT
BAS	Conditioned Reward	Approach + Arousal	Imp (Ext)
BIS	Conditioned Punishment	Inhibition + Arousal	Anxiety (N)

NEW RST
Fight-Flight-Freeze System = FFFS

SYSTEM	RESPONDS TO	OUTPUTS	TRAIT
BAS	Reward	Approach + Arousal	Imp (Ext)
FFFS	Punishment	Fight-Flight-Freezing	???
BIS	Goal conflict	inhibition + Arousal	Anxiety (N)

unconditioned) is controlled by the flight-fight system. This is now termed the Fight-Flight-Freeze System (FFFS) in recognition that animals may freeze in the presence of (distant or weak) fear-provoking stimuli; they fight or flee only when the danger is much more proximal or intense. Fear (the emotional state related to FFFS activation) and anxiety (the emotional state related to BIS activation) are distinguished in new RST, but there is as yet no clear proposal for the trait corresponding to variation in FFS functioning.

The key differences between old and new RST are summarized in Table 16.1.

RST has always been a complex theory, although it masquerades as a simple one (Pickering, Díaz and Gray 1995; Pickering *et al.* 1997). New RST is obviously more complex than old RST, in that it has an extra system and an increased number of possible system interactions. When one attempts to describe a complex theory in words the results are often cumbersome and/or ambiguous. That is why most areas of science use formal models to express their theories more precisely. The goal of this chapter, as already noted, is to explore some formal modelling approaches that one might use with RST. A formal modelling approach was first used, in connection with old RST, by Gray and Smith (1969), although their model did not address personality. They modelled reward and punishment systems, and their interactions, in order to explain characteristic effects in animal discrimination learning. Their model did, however, include parameters corresponding to the sensitivities of the reward and punishment systems. We have previously adapted the Gray and Smith approach to study personality-related predictions under old RST (Pickering 1997). The present chapter is the first step towards repeating and extending this exercise for 'new' RST. It is hoped that this may lead to a clearer set of predictions that can be investigated empirically.

System inputs, sensitivities and outputs

RST is described in terms of three key concepts: system inputs, system outputs and system sensitivities. The starting point for our modelling is to try to express these notions using formal symbols. Sensitivity connotes the reactivity of the system to its inputs. If we have a given amount of input, I, then a more sensitive (reactive) system will be stimulated to a greater extent by that input than a less sensitive (reactive) system. It is therefore natural to capture the amount of incoming stimulation, received by a system, in terms of the input multiplied by the system sensitivity. If sensitivity is denoted by w, then the total stimulation of the system by input I will be $I \star w$. We will also define a quantity called the activation, A (or activity), of the system. In the simplest case this will be equal to the total stimulation received: $A = I \star w$. The output from the system will be related to its activation. There are an infinite number of possible forms of the relationship between a system's activation and its output. More formally one would say that the output, O, is a function of the level of system activation, and this can be written: $O = f(A)$.

Some functions are perhaps more likely than others in biological systems. The simplest (or linear) function is when each fixed amount of activation produces a fixed amount of output:

$$O = k_0 + k_1 * I * w \tag{1}$$

where k_0 and k_1 are the familiar intercept and slope parameters of the linear function.

Such a linear relationship may hold (approximately) over a part of a system's range; however, most biological systems cannot increase their output for ever. At high levels of stimulation the increase in output may start to level off (saturate) with increased stimulation. There may also be a threshold of stimulation, below which there is no output. These features would contribute to generating a non-linear output function.

So far we have a very simple system, which receives an excitatory input. This input then creates a level of activation of the system (proportional to the input multiplied by the system sensitivity), and then generates an output according to some linear or non-linear function of the system activation. We need complicate this representation of our system only a little further in order to have the building blocks for a basic model of RST. Let us now suppose we have two systems, system R and system P, and we will denote features of the system by adding subscripts to the letters we have used so far. For example, I_R and w_R denote the input to, and sensitivity of, system R, while O_P denotes the output from system P.

A two-system decision model

The choice of subscripts above was not arbitrary. The subscript R will be used to denote a system that responds to rewarding stimuli, whereas system P will be used to denote a system that responds primarily to punishing stimuli. In 'old' RST, system R was the BAS while system P was the BIS (as long as the punishment stimuli were conditioned, secondary reinforcers). In 'new' RST, the revision means that system P is now the FFFS, rather than the BIS, and the type of punisher (conditioned or unconditioned) is irrelevant.

We can write a simple decision rule that decides the probability that a particular system gains control over behaviour, as a function of the output from the two systems above. This is precisely what Gray and Smith (1969) attempted in their original formal model of reward and punishment systems. Specifically, Gray and Smith proposed that the probability of observing approach behaviour, that is, the probability that the reward system would gain control of behaviour (P_R), was increased by reward system output and decreased by punishment system output. In other words, the outputs of the two systems acted in antagonistic fashion (with respect to each other) on a decision mechanism. The decision mechanism determined which of the two systems would gain control over behaviour. In formal terms, Gray and Smith modelled this as a function of the difference between the system outputs; specifically:

$$P_R = \Phi([O_R - O_P])/\sigma \tag{2}$$

where $\Phi(z)$ is the cumulative distribution function for the standard normal distribution and σ is the standard deviation of the quantity $(O_R - O_P)$. This function is that which is used to generate normal probability tables: $F(-2)$ is approximately 0.025, $F(0)=0.5$, and $F(2)$ is approximately 0.975. This generates the familiar 5% two-tailed rejection region for the normal distribution for z-scores lying outside the range $-2 \leq z \leq 2$. The general shape of this function is shown in Figure 16.1.

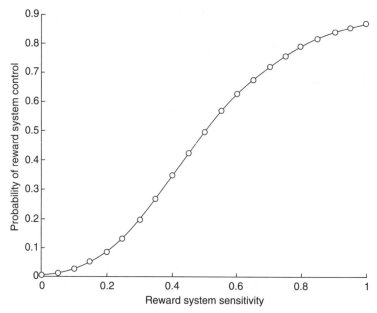

Figure 16.1 A simulation of the probability of reward system control over behavior as a function of reward system sensitivity

The two-system RST model is now ready to be written down. We use the simplest output function for the systems (i.e., equation (1) with $k_0 = 0$ and $k_1 = 1$) and thus can rewrite equation (2) as follows:

$$P_R = \Phi([I_R * w_R - I_p * w_p])/\sigma \tag{3}$$

where $I_R * w_R$ and $I_P * w_P$ are the mean values of the quantities over many occurrences, and the quantity $(I_R * w_R - I_P * w_P)$ is assumed to have a standard deviation equal to σ. This equation describes P_R for an individual with system sensitivities w_R and w_P, across a set of situations for which there is a normal distribution of input strengths affecting each system (mean input strengths are I_R and I_P for reward and punishment systems respectively).[2] Note also, for the two-system model, that $P_P = (1 - P_R)$.

---

[2] To estimate the parameter σ from equation (3) we employ the fact that the expected standard deviation of the difference of variables drawn from two independent normal distributions is the square root (sqrt) of the sum of the variances of the two normal distributions. Thus, if the standard deviation of the distributions of I_R and I_P is s in both cases, then the standard deviation of the distribution of $I_R * w_R$ will be $w_R * s$. Similarly we can write $w_p * s$ for the standard deviation of $I_P * w_P$. Thus, σ, the standard deviation of $(I_R * w_R - I_P * w_P)$, will be s * sqrt($w_R^2 + w_p^2$).

To see what predictions this simple model will make, we begin by arbitrarily constraining the possible range of values of the parameters. We will let the system sensitivities (w_R, w_P) vary from 0 (no sensitivity) to 1 (maximum sensitivity). The same ranges will be used for the strength of the inputs to the systems (I_R, I_P). Let us suppose the punishment system of a particular individual has a mid-range sensitivity ($w_p = 0.5$), and further suppose the reward and punishment system are simultaneously receiving mid-strength inputs, which are sampled from two independent normal distributions (mean I_R = mean I_P = 0.5; s.d. of I_R distribution = s.d. of I_P distribution = 0.2). Let us next calculate what happens to the probability of the response system gaining control (e.g., the probability of approach behaviour) as we vary the sensitivity of the reward system (w_R) of the individual from 0 to 1. The result is shown in Figure 16.1.

First one should note that the model is entirely symmetrical and, with w_R fixed at 0.5, an identical graph could have been plotted with punishment system sensitivity varying across the x-axis and probability of punishment system control (e.g., the probability of avoidance behaviour) on the y-axis. Notice also that when the reward system sensitivity equals the punishment system sensitivity ($w_R = w_P = 0.5$) the probability of the reward system gaining control over behaviour is equal to the probability of the punishment system gaining control over behaviour (= 0.5).

The punishment system sensitivity (w_P) was 0.5 and the mean strength of input to each system was equal ($I_R = I_P = 0.5$; s.d. of I_R and $I_P = 0.2$). The graph shows the result for the basic two-system model (and illustrates the general shape of the cumulative distribution function for a normal distribution). The next thing to consider is how this model might be reflected in the responses of a sample of individuals, when filling out personality trait questionnaires. RST supposes that the causal bases of major personality dimensions derive from the sensitivities of the systems (e.g., w_R and w_P above). It seems unreasonable, to me at least, to assume that an individual would be able to introspect directly about their own particular values of w_R and w_P when completing a questionnaire. These sensitivity values must, I assume, be directly related to the functional capacity of neural assemblies and systems in the particular brain regions housing the systems concerned. However, the sensitivities are 'latent' properties of the system. By this I mean that they can reveal their settings, for a particular person, only when the individual's systems are activated by incoming stimuli. This view means that personality trait questionnaire responses, like other aspects of behaviour, must be driven by the 'functional outcomes' of system activation, which will only indirectly reflect the values of system sensitivities such as w_R and w_P.

This is a major argument of this chapter and represents a departure from my previous thinking when formally modelling RST (see Pickering 1997). The theoretical predictions of the models are critically affected by this position.

In the case of personality questionnaire responses, these must also reflect an individual's ability to introspect about the 'functional outcomes' of the activated and interacting systems, or at least the typical value of such outcomes, remembered and estimated over a range of situations. The process of introspection and recollection, and its conversion to questionnaire responses, will doubtless be a noisy one, but we assume that this subjective assessment will at least correlate with objective reality.

What functional outcomes might an individual try to remember and estimate when completing a personality questionnaire? In this chapter we will suggest a number of different possibilities, and indicate that different questionnaires, or sub-groups of questionnaire items, may depend upon the subjective estimates of different functional outcomes.[3] One possibility is that some questionnaire responses would reflect an individual's estimate, across a range of situations, of the probability that the reward system (or punishment system) would gain control over behaviour. An individual seems likely to be able to estimate how often they tend to approach sources of pleasure (a direct manifestation of P_R) or how often they tend to avoid doing something if it is likely to bring them into contact with a source of pain (a direct manifestation of P_P). In the terms of our model, this suggests that some personality trait questionnaire responses would be partly based upon an estimate of one's personal value of P_R (or P_P) across various situations differing in I_R and I_P. One would expect that such estimates might underlie a considerable part of the variance in responses on special-purpose reward-sensitivity scales (e.g., Carver and White's 1994 BAS scale, or the signals of reward scale developed in Spain: Torrubia *et al.* 2001) and punishment-sensitivity scales (Carver and White's BIS scale; the signals of punishment (SP) scale from Spain: Torrubia and Tobeña 1984; Torrubia *et al.* 2001). For example, in Carver and White's BAS scale (particularly the drive sub-scale) there are items which seem to ask directly about the probability of

---

[3] The possibility that a personality scale might contain sub-sets of items, each depending on subjective assessments of different types of functional outcomes, requires some further thought. If such a scale were derived by factor analytic methods, it is possible that the scale score will reflect an underlying latent variable which influences all sub-sets of items. In this way the scale score might reflect a latent brain system property (such as system sensitivity), without an individual being able to introspect on such properties directly.

approach behaviour in response to reward ('If I see a chance to get something I want, I move on it right away' and 'When I go after something I use a "no holds barred" approach'). Similarly, in the SP scale, there are items concerned with avoidance behaviour under the threat of punishment ('Do you generally avoid high places or cliffs that are not well protected?').

There is a possible source of confusion here in that punishment-related scales may be referred to as BIS scales, as they were developed under old RST, when the BIS was thought to be the system which responded to punishments. Such scales are now perhaps better referred to as punishment sensitivity scales, as they may not directly relate to the functioning of the BIS; under new RST, the causal basis of punishment sensitivity scales is ascribed to variations in the functioning of the FFFS.

In addition to special-purpose scales, RST has argued that trait measures of extraversion or impulsive anti-social sensation seeking reflect the functioning of the reward system (see Pickering and Gray 1999, 2001; Pickering 2004b), and so these scales might correlate with individuals' estimates of the probability of reward system control over behaviour. Trait anxiety was considered to be the trait corresponding to functioning of the BIS under old RST, and remains so under the new revision (see McNaughton and Corr 2004). However, anxiety measures do correlate strongly with special purpose punishment system trait measures (e.g., see Díaz and Pickering 1993). Thus, trait anxiety scale responses might be expected to correlate with individuals' estimates concerning the probability of punishment system control over behaviour. This is despite the fact that, under new RST, the BIS (thought to be responsible for trait anxiety) does not have any specific link with punishment per se. However, the emotional state of fear (linked by Gray and McNaughton to the punishment-based FFFS) seems very likely to be a frequent occurrence in individuals who are highly trait anxious.

The simple model outlined above leads to one striking prediction for the trait measures that are influenced directly by (or correlate with) individuals' estimates of their personal values of P_R or P_P. If one trait measure (a reward trait) is affected by estimated personal P_R, and another (a punishment trait) is affected by estimated personal P_P, then the correlation between these two measures will be negative. This follows because, in the model, P_R and P_P are perfectly inversely correlated: one's behaviour (in the relevant situations) is either controlled by a reward system or by the punishment system and so $P_R = 1 - P_P$. However, as noted earlier, the conversion of these objective parameter values for an individual into a subjective estimate of the parameter, which then influences personality scale ratings, is likely to be a very noisy process.

A considerable part of this 'conversion noise', which contributes to variance in punishment trait responses, is likely to be independent of the conversion noise contributing variance to the reward trait measure. In addition to noise in the conversion process, there will be other sources of variance in each of the trait measures that are not related to one another, or to reward and punishment system effects. Finally, specific reward trait questionnaires are likely to draw upon an individual's estimate of R_R in rewarding situations (i.e., where I_R is generally large and I_P is generally small). By contrast, specific punishment trait questionnaires are likely to draw upon an individual's estimate of R_P in punishing situations (i.e., where I_P is generally large and I_R is generally small). This feature will attenuate the negative correlation between the estimates of P_R and P_P. Thus, for all these reasons, the negative correlation between the trait measures would be expected to be much weaker than -1.

There are several important aspects to this predicted negative correlation between reward and punishment traits. First, this correlation will occur even when there is independence between w_R and w_P. RST supposes that an individual's values for w_R and w_P, acquired through a mixture of genetic and environmental processes, are unrelated to one another. This independence in a key property of the brain systems does not lead to the prediction that the traits, arising from w_R and w_P, will be independent of one another. In fact, the systems, of which w_R and w_P are key properties, are functionally interdependent rather than independent. If individuals completed personality questionnaires by being able to introspect directly into their personal values of w_R and w_P, then the affected personality trait measures would be unrelated (as long as w_R and w_P each selectively affected different trait measures). However, this chapter contends that the ability to make that kind of introspection is extremely unlikely, and so a negative correlation is predicted.

Note in the foregoing paragraphs that we talk about reward traits and punishment traits: this terminology is adopted because the responses to items on the reward trait sale are assumed to be a reflection of a functional outcome of the reward system specifically (P_R) while the items on the punishment trait scale are assumed to be a reflection of a functional outcome of the punishment system specifically (P_P).

In the past (e.g., Pickering 1997) authors have acknowledged the functional interdependence between the systems of RST, and have often ascribed it to the reciprocal inhibition between the reward and punishment systems. This reciprocal inhibition has appeared in diagrams of the systems' interactions since the paper by Gray and Smith (1969). However, in the basic model, described by Gray and Smith and reiterated above, there is no reciprocal inhibition (although it can easily be added, see below). The key aspect of the interdependence between the two systems is their antagonistic effects on the decision mechanism that determines which system gains control of behaviour. This antagonism is explicitly represented in equations (2) and (3) above by the fact that the outputs of the reward and punishment systems (O_R and O_P) act in opposing directions on P_R, and also by the fact that $P_P = 1 - P_R$.

The predicted negative relationship between a reward trait and a punishment trait has important implications for a psychometrician who might attempt to develop new specific and direct measures of such traits. Although such measures are predicted to be negatively related, in the past, it was argued that such trait measures should be uncorrelated. Thus, part of the validation of reward and punishment trait measures derived, in the past, from showing they were independent of one another (e.g., Carver and White 1994, p. 323).

Is there any evidence for the predicted negative relationship between putative reward and punishment traits? We (Pickering, Dawkins, Lessiter, Tharp, Jones, Halari, Powell and Powell in preparation) were able to take a preliminary look using a reasonably large corpus of questionnaire responses collected from over 200 healthy participants (Lessiter 1999). As noted in our chapter on the BAS elsewhere in this volume, the participants completed eight putative reward trait measures. The putative reward traits were found to form two orthogonal factors (if one excluded extraversion). Extraversion had robust positive correlations with both factors ($r > 0.4$, $p < 0.001$ in each case). The participants also completed three trait measures that may be punishment traits (EPQ-Neuroticism: Eysenck and Eysenck 1975; Cloninger' Harm Avoidance: Cloninger 1989; and the BIS scale: Carver and White 1994). These putative punishment traits were all robustly positively intercorrelated ($r > 0.6$, $p < 0.0001$ in every case).

As predicted, extraversion scores were correlated negatively with each putative punishment trait measure (BIS: $r = -0.21$, $p = 0.002$; Harm Avoidance: $r = -0.45$, $p < 0.001$; Neuroticism: $r = -0.23$, $p < 0.001$). The first factor, formed from four of the other seven reward traits, correlated negatively with BIS ($r = -0.14$, $p < 0.05$) and Harm Avoidance ($r = -0.23$, $p = 0.001$) but had a near-zero correlation with Neuroticism ($r = 0.01$). The second reward trait factor (based on the remaining three reward traits) had a small but significant negative correlation with Neuroticism (-0.13, $p < 0.05$), a non-significant negative correlation with Harm Avoidance (-0.09, $p > 0.1$), but a very small positive correlation with the BIS scale ($r = 0.03$). Of the twenty-four individual correlations between the eight putative reward traits and the three putative punishment traits, eleven were significantly negative (at $p < 0.05$, uncorrected for multiple comparisons), and four others were non-significantly negative. However, of the nine positive correlations, six were significant (at $p < 0.05$ uncorrected); and the significant ones were drawn from three of the reward scales (BAS, Cloninger's Reward Dependence, and Mason, Claridge and Jackson's 1995 Impulsive Nonconformity). Note that BAS and Impulsive Nonconformity loaded on one of the reward trait factors while Reward Dependence loaded on the other. In addition, the positive correlations between the BAS scale and punishment trait measures derived primarily from the reward responsiveness sub-scale, a point we shall return to later.

These findings suggest that many putative reward traits do indeed have inverse correlations with putative punishment traits. However, the findings are necessarily weak because the mapping of traits onto systems in RST is unclear. For example, in the original formulations of RST by Gray, extraversion was suggested to be influenced by the reward system and to be inversely (and less strongly) influenced by the punishment system. Thus, if this claim is correct, then one would expect extraversion to correlate negatively with (other) traits that are positively related to punishment system functioning. However, if extraversion is primarily a marker of the reward system functioning, as others have argued (e.g., Depue and Collins 1999), then the observations above are consistent with the formal model presented in this chapter. The finding that some putative reward traits are positively correlated with putative punishment traits is completely unexpected in terms of the model presented so far. It is particularly surprising as one of the measures concerned (the BAS) was specifically designed to capture variations in reward system functioning, while inspection of the items of the other measures (Impulsive Nonconformity and Reward Dependence), gives one little reason to anticipate positive correlations with putative punishment (anxiety, neuroticism) measures. It is clear that putative reward trait measures (judged by past claims, or face validity of the items) can be quite divergent and, as suggested above, may be influenced by different functional outcomes of reward system functioning.

In principle, then, using a formal model can also help one to correct past statements about RST which may be erroneous (e.g., 'the traits influenced by reward system functioning and by punishment system functioning should be independent of one another'). Another such statement is potentially challenged by the formal model above. RST claims that variations in the sensitivity of the systems to their characteristic inputs are the causal basis of major personality dimensions (hence the word sensitivity in the name Reinforcement Sensitivity Theory). RST has also suggested that some traits are related to the functioning of one system specifically (thus we talked above about 'reward' and 'punishment' traits). These two tenets of the theory lead naturally to statements claiming, for example, that 'the reward system trait arises specifically from inter-individual variations in the sensitivity of the reward system to its inputs' (analogous statements can be made about the punishment system traits). In terms of the formal model above, such a statement would correspond to saying that a specific trait measure would be derived exclusively from variations in the parameter w_R (or w_P). The model presented above directly challenges such statements. We assumed that some trait measures might reflect variations in individuals' estimates of their own personal value of P_R (or P_P) across a range of situations. The model makes it clear, from equation (3), that P_R (and P_P) is a function of both w_R *and* w_P. So reward trait variation is predicted to be influenced by both reward and punishment system sensitivities, in direct contradiction of the type of statement in quotation marks above. It should be clear that the model also predicts that punishment trait variation is influenced by both reward and punishment system sensitivities. Thus, the naming of the traits as 'reward' or 'punishment' does not derive from their dependence upon the sensitivity of one system specifically; rather it derives from their dependence on a functional outcome of one system (which in turn depends on the sensitivities of both systems).

It is important at this point to consider briefly the relationship between the points just made and the version of RST which has become known as the joint subsystems theory (Corr 2001, 2002, 2004). The central idea of Corr's proposal is that responses controlled by the reward system would often be expected to be affected by both reward and punishment traits, as would responses controlled by the punishment system. This central idea has obvious resonances with the points made in this chapter. However, Corr was assuming that reward traits are a direct reflection of reward system sensitivity (w_R) and punishment traits are a direct reflection of punishment system sensitivity (w_P; see Corr 2002, p. 516, n. 1). I have made a similar assumption previously (Pickering 1997); for the reasons given above I now believe this assumption to be highly implausible.

Extending the two-system model

The simple two-system model above can be extended in a variety of ways. This is the subject of ongoing work and there is not space to explore all the possibilities in great depth here. Obvious extensions are to add non-linearity in the functions determining system outputs and to add reciprocal inhibitory connections between the reward and punishment systems.

These changes are unlikely to alter the fundamental behaviour of the model described above and (for technical reasons) they are more easily explored as part of a dynamically interacting network model in the style of Pickering (1997) (see below).

A more important modification to the model is to consider other possible functional outcomes of system activation and interaction, which might be reflected in an individual's responses to personality question-naires. The most obvious would be to suggest that subjects are able to introspect about their typical (or average) levels of system output, across a range of situations. System outputs might be the neural basis of emotional states and/or related feelings and thereby could influence responses to certain questionnaire items (while other kinds of items, as in the examples given earlier in this chapter, might be influenced by the probability that a particular system would gain control; i.e., by P_R or P_P). Extraversion measures might be an example of a reward trait measure that could reflect subjective estimates of mean levels of reward system output. Many typical extraversion items are concerned with the enjoyment of activities or with experiencing positive emotions; under RST such emotions are ascribed to reward system functioning. In similar fashion, trait measures containing items concerning the experi-ence of negative emotions might reflect mean levels of punishment system output.

If the mean output from the reward system influenced trait measure A (but not B), and if the mean output from the punishment system influenced trait B (but not A), we would, of course, still refer to A as the reward trait and B as the punishment trait. However, for the simple model presented above, these two traits would be uncorrelated with one another. This follows because w_R and w_P are assumed to be independent of one another in the model, as are I_R and I_P. Thus, the outputs (which are functions of $I_R^*w_R$ and $I_P^*w_P$) would be independent of one another. This prediction is obviously in marked contrast to the prediction for traits influenced by personal estimates of P_R or P_P. Predicted ortho-gonality between reward and punishment traits also contrasts with Jane Lessiter's data, summarized above, in which putative reward and pun-ishment traits were found most often to be negatively correlated, but sometimes were significantly positively correlated. However, if the reward and punishment systems mutually antagonize one another, as is widely argued, then reward and punishment traits of this kind (i.e., based on mean system output levels, rather than those based on P_R or P_P) are likely to be negatively correlated with one another.

To test the prediction made in the previous paragraph we employed a two-system dynamically interacting neural network model developed by

Pickering (2004a) as an extension of the earlier work by Pickering (1997). The model is described in more detail in Smillie, Pickering and Jackson (2006). In this model, which involved mutually inhibitory interactions between a reward and punishment system,[4] reward and punishment trait responses for each simulated subject were determined by the outputs of the two systems averaged over a wide range of 200 input contexts. Each input context was a pair of values for I_R and I_P, with each drawn randomly from independent normal distributions with a mean of 0.5 and a standard deviation of 0.2. One hundred subjects were simulated: each subject had an individual combination of values for w_R and w_P. Each sensitivity lay between 0 and 1 and was drawn from a normal distribution with a mean of 0.5 and a standard deviation of 0.2 (the distributions for w_R and w_P were independent). The mean reward system output for a simulated individual (over the 200 experiences) was taken to reflect their reward trait score, and punishment trait scores were based on mean punishment system outputs. The correlation between these indices was negative ($r = -0.84$), as predicted, even though the model had only a moderate degree of mutual inhibition between the systems. This correlation value obviously did not include any noise in the processes of making the personal estimates of mean reward and punishment system outputs and converting those estimates into questionnaire responses. As argued above, such noise would inevitably drive the real value of such correlations further towards zero.

Another obvious modification is to add further systems to the model. Gray and Smith's original model was an extension of the model presented in this chapter, in that they included a third system. Their model also had a non-specific arousal system that was positively activated by outputs from both the reward and the punishment systems. The output from the arousal system was then used to energize whichever behaviour (i.e., the output of the system in overall control) was selected by the decision mechanism. The energization of the reward system response by the arousal system output, denoted here as E_R, was assumed to be a simple linear function of both reward and punishment system outputs:

$$E_R = \alpha * O_R + \beta * O_P \qquad (4)$$

---

[4] In this model the output from each system inhibits the activation of the other system. There is no explicit decision mechanism, but this competitive interaction between the two systems is such that, even when there is only a moderate difference in the initial activations of the two systems, the system that is initially the more active system will end up producing a larger output, while the other system will produce a relatively small output.

where α and β are positive constants. An analogous equation could be constructed for the energization of the punishment system response, E_P, with different values for the constants. Gray and Smith also suggested that the speed of some approach behaviours (such as an animal's alley running speed, which their model was simulating) would be a function of P_R multiplied by E_R. It is plausible that the mean intensity of a reward system controlled behaviour would often be a function of P_R multiplied by E_R. This mean intensity index ($E_R{}^{\star}P_R$) would therefore be positively influenced by w_R and negatively influenced by w_P, because P_R is influenced by the sensitivities in this way (see equation (3) above). At the same time, the mean intensity index would also be positively influenced by both w_R and w_P, because E_R is influenced by the sensitivities in this way (see equation (4) above, and note that system outputs are positively related to system sensitivities).

It seems likely that some personality questionnaires might be influenced by an individual's estimates of the average intensity of their behaviours controlled by the reward system. This is a third possible functional outcome on which reward trait item responses might be based, in addition to the earlier suggestions that they might be influenced by personal estimates of either P_R or the mean output of the reward system across situations. For example, several items of the BAS scale (especially the reward responsiveness sub-scale) may reflect estimates of the average intensity of reward-controlled behaviours ('When I get something I want, I feel excited and energised'; 'When I see an opportunity for something I like, I get excited right away'; 'It would excite me to win a contest'; 'When good things happen to me it would excite me strongly').

Another possibility (the fourth functional outcome that might be reflected in reward trait responses) is that reward trait items (such as the BAS reward responsiveness items noted above) may be influenced by the mean level of output from the arousal system, averaged over memories of rewarding contexts (i.e., these items may be based upon estimates of a personal value for E_R, rather than estimates of $E_R{}^{\star}P_R$). A similar argument may be made for some punishment scales, with items potentially relating to the estimated level of the arousal system activation or output, averaged over punishing contexts (e.g., BIS scale: 'If I think something unpleasant is going to happen to me, I usually get pretty "worked up"'). Such items may thus be based on an estimate of a personal mean value for E_P. Reward and punishment scales that may be directly influenced by estimates of arousal system output (i.e., by E_R or E_P) are thus more likely to be positively correlated. This is because both arousal system outputs, in either rewarding or punishing contexts, reflect the sum of outputs from the reward and punishment systems.

The sum of the outputs from the two systems in rewarding contexts is likely to be positively correlated, across individuals, with the sum of the outputs from the two systems in punishing contexts.

In keeping with this, the positive correlations between the BAS and punishment trait scales noted above (Pickering *et al.*, in preparation) derived largely from the reward responsiveness sub-scale; as just noted, this sub-scale has items that are easily seen as reflecting estimates of mean arousal system output. Carver and White (1994) also reported that, of the three BAS sub-scales, only the reward responsiveness sub-scale was positively correlated (r = 0.28) with the BIS scale.

The kind of analysis that has just been presented is obviously highly speculative and post hoc. However, having a formal model offers a route for a more careful development of RST-related personality scales. Researchers might try to develop sets of items that relate to specific functional outcomes (e.g., mean arousal system output under reward or probability of punishment system control over behaviour). By doing this, they could use formal models to make predictions about the nature of the interrelationships between the new scales. It may even be possible to test between alternative versions of the formal model with such scales. Without this serious and positivist approach to theories such as RST it seems unlikely to me that much further progress and clarification will be achieved.

In the next section, we consider the addition of a different third system: the BIS. Specifically, we will add a BIS which performs the role ascribed to it in the revised account offered by Gray and McNaughton: that of resolving goal conflict.

A three-system decision model for 'new' RST

As we have already seen, the model shows that the individual will be in a state of conflict when the activation of the reward system ($I_R{}^\star w_R$) is approximately equal to the activation of the punishment system ($I_P{}^\star w_P$): the individual will be undecided as to whether to engage in reward system behaviours (such as approach) or punishment system behaviours (such as freezing or flight). Indeed, when the two activations are exactly equal the probability of either system gaining control over behaviour is 0.5 (see Figure 16.1). McNaughton and Corr (2004) use the terms 'avoidance' and 'approach' to describe behaviours controlled by punishment and reward system outputs respectively, and 'fear' or 'frustration' to describe the motivational state of punishment system activation. They state that, under the new version of RST, derived from Gray and McNaughton (2000), the BIS is activated by the type of conflict described above, that is, when 'approach and avoidance tendencies are not only each present but relatively closely matched in intensity of activation' (p. 298).

The BIS is activated under the circumstances just described because the BIS's role in 'new RST' is to resolve conflicts; it is proposed that conflict resolution is achieved by the BIS biasing the decision mechanism to favour punishment system (FFFS) control. For example, McNaughton and Corr (2004) state that 'the normal resolution of conflict by the BIS involves an increase in the effects of fear or frustration that favours avoidance over approach' (p. 298). Figure 6 from their paper shows the biasing operation of the BIS explicitly.

It is simple to operationalize this conflict resolution within the formal model presented in this chapter. Equation (3) is rewritten:

$$P_R = \Phi([I_R * w_R - I_p * w_p - I_C * w_C]/\sigma) \tag{5}$$

where I_C is the input to the conflict resolution system (i.e., to the BIS) and w_C is a parameter reflecting the individual's sensitivity to conflict (i.e., BIS sensitivity). Note that the minus sign before $I_C{}^*w_C$ means that the term acts in the same direction as $I_p{}^*w_P$ by reducing P_R (and increasing P_P), thereby giving the appropriate bias.

We need an expression for I_C in terms of the reward and punishment system outputs. First we should consider the relative size of the two conflicting system outputs. We need I_C (the input to the BIS) to be largest, as Corr and McNaughton stated (see above), when the reward and punishment systems are each generating approximately equal outputs. Next, if the relative sizes of the conflicting system outputs were held constant, one would expect more input to a conflict resolution system as the size of the conflicting system outputs increased. In other words, if reward system and punishment system outputs were equal, but both were small, then this should generate less input to the conflict resolution device (the BIS) than when both outputs were equal and large.

To render the above properties of I_C in mathematical form we can make use of the expressions for quantities Q_1 and Q_2 below,[5] in which the output from each system is equal to its activation ($I *w$):

$$Q_1 = (I_R * w_R)^N/((I_P * w_P)^N + (I_R * w_R)^N)$$
$$Q_2 = \sqrt{((I_R * w_R) * (I_P * w_P))} \tag{6}$$

---

[5] The precise form of the mathematics given in equations (6) and (7) is not important; the equations are just one simple way of representing the conflict resolution of the BIS by an explicit formula with the appropriate properties (as shown in Figure 16.2).

where N is a positive value (4 in the simulations below) and sqrt(x) denotes the square root of x. Q_1 is influenced by the relative size of the two system outputs and $Q_1 = 0.5$ when conflict is at a maximum, that is, when the activation of the reward system ($I_R{}^\star w_R$) equals the activation of the punishment system ($I_P{}^\star w_P$). Q_1 will equal 0 or 1 when conflict is at a minimum. One minimum conflict state ($Q_1 = 1$) is when the reward system output is maximal (output $= 1$) and the punishment system is not generating any output (output $= 0$). The other minimum conflict state ($Q_1 = 0$) occurs when the output of the punishment system is 1 and that of the reward system is 0. Conflict should also be related to the size of the system outputs and this is reflected by the quantity Q_2, which increases as the strength of either system output increases. Thus, we can write an expression for I_C which involves both Q_1 and Q_2. A simple expression which will generate the appropriate relationship between I_C and Q_1 and Q_2, and which constrains I_C to lie between 0 and 1, is as follows:

$$I_C = Q_2 * (1 - 2 * ABS(0.5 - Q_1)) \quad (7)$$

where ABS(x) means the absolute value of x (i.e., ignoring the sign of x).

The computation of I_C from reward and punishment system outputs using equations (6) and (7) is illustrated in Figure 16.2. The graph shows that the mathematical formulation behaves according to the theoretical action of the BIS. The maximum input to the BIS conflict resolution system occurs when the activations of the reward and punishment systems are equal (i.e., when the sensitivities are both equal to 0.5, given equal inputs to each system). Input to the BIS (and hence its activation level) does not simply increase with increasing reward and punishment system activation; rather, with the activation of one system fixed, BIS input rises and then falls with increasing activation of the other system. This non-monotonicity of the BIS input, inherent in the new formulation of RST, will create a much greater complexity in the relationships between system activation and the sensitivities of the reward and punishment systems (in old RST, the relationships were all monotonic). We will explore this below in a final simulation. Moreover, Figure 16.2 also shows that the strength of the conflict resolution input increases as the activation of the two systems increases (the four curves depicted are, from bottom to top, generated by increasing strength inputs to the reward and punishment systems).

Figure 16.2 shows that the strength of BIS activation experienced, under the new three-system version of RST, is going to be influenced by the sensitivities of all three systems (i.e., sensitivities of the reward and

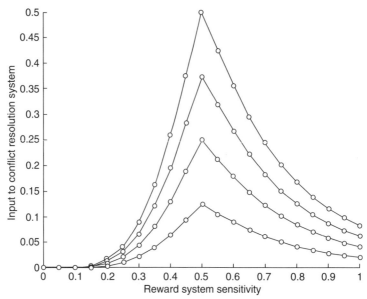

Figure 16.2 A simulation of the value of the input to the conflict resolution system (I_C) changing as a function of reward system sensitivity (see equations (7) and (8)). The punishment system sensitivity (W_P) was 0.5. The parameter N in equation 7 was set to 4 (this parameter just controls how sharply peaked the curves are, with lower values of N being associated with less sharply peaked curves). The inputs to each system were equal ($I_R = I_P$). The four curves were, from bottom to top, generated with increasing levels of system inputs ($I_R = I_P = 0.25$; $I_R = I_P = 0.50$; $I_R = I_P = 0.75$; $I_R = I_P = 1.0$)

punishment systems, plus the sensitivity of the BIS itself, which would be multiplied by the BIS input shown in Figure 16.2 to give the BIS activation). In line with the key point made earlier about 'reward' and 'punishment' traits, a BIS (or conflict resolution) trait is so named because it relates to variations in a functional outcome of the BIS such as an individual's estimate of their mean BIS activation (or output) levels across a range of situations. A BIS trait does not depend selectively upon the sensitivity of the BIS alone.

The next simulation in this chapter will be to repeat the simulation which generated Figure 16.1 but to look additionally at the effect of adding the conflict-resolution system (BIS), using the formulation just presented. Figure 16.1 was generated using equation (3) (old RST) and so the figure for the new RST model could, in principle, be generated by equation (5) (the new RST extension of equation (3)). Unfortunately, the standard deviation, σ, of the quantity $(I_R {}^\star w_R - I_P {}^\star w_P - I_C {}^\star w_C)$ in equation (5), is awkward to derive analytically from the standard deviation, s, of the quantities I_R and I_P. This awkwardness stems from the nature of the formulae for calculating I_C from I_R and I_P (see equations (6) and (7)). Thus, it is easier to use a numerical simulation.

To do this used the same parameter settings as were used in simulating Figure 16.1. We assumed a series of individuals with a mid-range punishment system sensitivity ($w_p = 0.5$) and began by assuming no conflict resolution system (achieved by setting $w_C = 0$). We varied the sensitivity of their reward systems from minimum (0) to maximum (1). We estimated the probability of the reward system gaining control from a sample of 500 events per plotted point in the figure. The events in the sample varied in terms of the values of the reward inputs (I_R) and punishment inputs (I_P). The values of I_R and I_P were drawn from independent normal distributions with means equal to 0.5 and standard deviations equal to 0.2 (exactly as for Figure 16.1). For each sampled event, the reward system gained control whenever the quantity $(I_R {}^\star w_R - I_P {}^\star w_P - I_C {}^\star w_C)$ was greater than zero. The probability of this occurring could then be estimated across the 500 events of each sample. This simulation generated the line joining the circles in Figure 16.3, which is a direct replication of Figure 16.1 (as there is no BIS). Note that the function is not completely smooth but is otherwise virtually identical to the plot in Figure 16.1. The difference in smoothness is because Figure 16.1 plots the theoretical probability of reward system control at each point under the assumed normal distributions, whereas Figure 16.3 numerically estimates the probability from a finite sample of 500 events (and is therefore subject to sampling error at each plotted point).

Next the simulation was repeated for a series of subjects with mid-range conflict resolution system sensitivity ($w_C = 2.0$; for convenience BIS sensitivity was scaled between 0 and 4, unlike the other sensitivities which ranged between 0 and 1). The calculation of the input to the conflict resolution system (I_C), for each sampled event, used equations (6) and (7). The resulting plot is shown in Figure 16.3 with crosses. Finally, a similar plot (triangles) was shown for individuals with maximum conflict resolution system sensitivity ($w_C = 4.0$).

We can see the influence of the conflict resolution system in Figure 16.3. Note that the probability of reward system control is reduced for individuals with mid-range conflict resolution system sensitivity. It is further reduced for individuals with maximally sensitive conflict resolution systems. However, the points at which these reductions are largest occur in the mid-range of reward system sensitivities (0.4–0.8) in the figure. This happens because the figure is for individuals with mid-range punishment

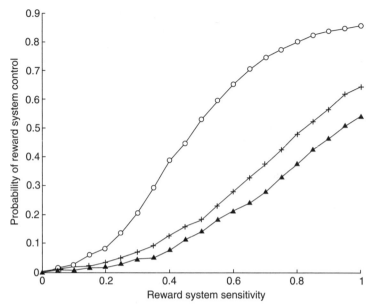

Figure 16.3 A simulation of the probability of reward system control over behavior as a function of reward system sensitivity, adopting the three-system formulation of new RST. The punishment system sensitivity (W_P) was 0.5 and the inputs to the reward and punishment systems $(I_R$ and $I_P)$ were sampled from independent normal distributions with mean $= 0.5$ and s.d. $= 0.2$. The plot with circles is for individuals without a conflict resolution system $(W_C = 0)$; the plot with crosses is for individuals with a mid-range sensitive conflict resolution system $(W_C = 2.0)$; the plot with triangles is for individuals with a maximally sensitive conflict resolution system $(W_C = 4.0)$

system sensitivities $(w_P = 0.5)$ and the conflict resolution system is activated whenever the reward and punishment system are activated to an approximately equal extent. When the reward system sensitivity is low (0–0.3) this is much lower than the punishment system sensitivity (0.5) and so there is little conflict resolution system activation. Similarly, relatively little conflict resolution system activation occurs when the reward system is very sensitive (0.9–1.0), as this is much higher than the punishment system sensitivity. However, there is more conflict resolution system activation in this case than for the low reward sensitivity portion of the graph, because the overall levels of reward and punishment activation are higher (and conflict resolution is directly related to the product of reward and punishment system activations; see term Q_2 in equations (6) and (7)).

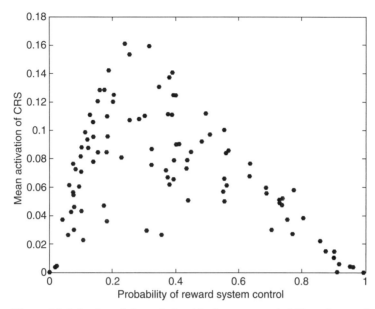

Figure 16.4 A plot of the relationship between probability of reward system control over behaviour and the mean activation level of the conflict resolution system (CRS). Simulation details are given in the text

A final simulation, using the above model, was employed to look at the relationship between mean conflict resolution system (i.e., BIS) activation levels (given by $I_C *w_C$) and the probability of reward system control (each taken over 500 events per simulated individual). The simulation used for Figure 16.3 was rerun, except that the sensitivities of the three systems (w_R, w_P and w_C) were each drawn at random, for each of 100 simulated individuals, from three independent normal distributions. The mean of each distribution was 0.5 and standard deviation of each was 0.2 (sensitivity values which fell by chance outside the range 0.01–1.0 were clipped to these limits). Although the overall relationship was negative (r =−0.37 in the particular simulation shown in Figure 16.4) the scatter plot revealed that the regression was non-linear (see Figure 16.4).[6] This is expected: individuals who have a very high probability of reward system control (approaching 1, across all 500 events) are likely to have high w_R

[6] The relationship between mean level of conflict resolution system activation and probability of punishment system control is the mirror-image non-linear plot to that shown in Figure 16.4 (with r = 0.37), as the probabilities of reward and punishment system control sum to 1.

and low w_P, and so will not generate much activation of the conflict resolution system. Likewise, individuals with a very low probability of reward system control (approaching 0) are likely to have low w_R and high w_P, and consequent low conflict resolution system activation. Individuals with more equal values of w_R and w_P are more likely to elicit moderate probabilities of reward system control and also the highest levels of conflict resolution system activation. Note also that the mean probability of reward system control (=0.38) is below 0.5, reflecting the operation of the conflict resolution system biasing behavioural control to the punishment system overall. Indeed, one can simulate the probability of reward system control with and without conflict resolution system intervention: one finds that the mean probability of reward system control, without conflict resolution system, is 0.55. Each individual's reduction in reward system control was linearly and strongly related to the mean level of conflict resolution system activation (r = 0.7).

Imagine one had a personality questionnaire measuring anxiety (i.e., the conflict resolution system trait) based on individuals' estimated mean levels of activation (or output) of their conflict resolution systems. The above simulation suggests that such a trait score would relate in a complex non-linear fashion (akin to what was depicted in Figure 16.4) to a reward system trait questionnaire (if this were based on estimated probabilities of reward system control). The relationship between the conflict resolution system trait scores and punishment system trait questionnaire (if this were based on estimated probabilities of punishment system control) would be expected to be a mirror-image complex non-linear relationship to that shown in Figure 16.4. However, given the likely degree of conversion noise (discussed at various points earlier) in individuals' estimation of such parameters and their conversion to personality questionnaire responses, such relationships might be difficult to detect in real data.

A three-system dynamically interacting neural network model

As noted earlier in this chapter, it is important to consider other possible bases for questionnaire responses. To this end, this chapter concludes by reporting simulations based on a three-system dynamically interacting neural network (DINN) model. This model is similar to the two-system DINN model used earlier in this chapter, but with an added conflict resolution system. The model was previously employed by Pickering (2004a), and is described in more detail in Smillie, Pickering and Jackson (2006). The architecture of the model is outlined in

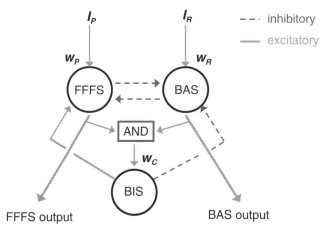

Figure 16.5 A dynamically interacting neural network (DINN) model of new RST involving three systems. FFFS = Fight-Flight-Freeze (punishment) System. BIS = Behavioural Inhibition (conflict resolution) System. BAS = Behavioural Activation (reward) System. I_R and I_P are system inputs; W_R, W_P, and W_C are system sensitivities

Figure 16.5. This type of model, as we saw earlier, allows one to look at mean levels of system activation (or output). The three-system DINN model is equivalent to the three-system decision model used in the preceding section of this chapter.

In the three-system DINN model, the punishment and reward systems mutually inhibit one another (to a moderate extent) and their outputs jointly activate the conflict resolution system (BIS) such that the maximum BIS activation occurs when the reward and punishment system outputs are of equal magnitude. The output of the conflict resolution system activates the punishment system and inhibits the reward system, thereby biasing behavioural control in favour of the punishment system.

The simulations with this model were similar to those reported by Pickering (2004a) but with minor alterations so that the parameters were as similar as possible to those employed in the three-system decision model reported earlier in this chapter. The parameters and simulation details used were the same as those for the two-system DINN model described earlier in this chapter; and, as for the other two systems, the conflict resolution system sensitivities (w_C) were drawn at random from an independent normal distribution (mean = 0.5; s.d. = 0.20).

The simulation revealed a large negative correlation between mean reward system output and mean punishment system output (r = −0.87); this was barely changed from that obtained with the two-system DINN model (r = −0.84). In addition, the relationship, across simulated individuals, between their mean reward system output and mean conflict resolution system output was quite similar to the non-linear relationship revealed by the three-system decision model (as shown in Figure 16.4). The relationship between the mean punishment system and mean conflict resolution system output was a mirror image of that between the reward and conflict resolution systems.

These three-system simulations, either using a decision model or a DINN model, reveal that the negative relationship between reward and punishment system traits are unchanged relative to the older two-system version of RST (assuming that the trait scores are based either on estimated probabilities of system control or on mean system output levels). They also reveal that the conflict resolution system trait (based on mean system outputs) will be likely to have complex, hard-to-detect relationships with traits based on functional outcomes of the reward and punishment systems.

Conclusion

This chapter has shown that having simple formal models of a theory like RST can be very beneficial for clarifying the possible ambiguities that may occur with a complex scientific theory if it is expressed only in words. Application of the simple model, which has been available in its basic form since 1969, reveals a number of striking predictions which RST should make. These predictions are, in some cases, entirely at odds with the predictions made by, or properties of, RST when that theory has been expressed verbally.

RST supposes that certain personality traits (e.g., impulsivity or extraversion) are primarily influenced by the functioning (output) of a single, specific brain system (e.g., the system which responds to rewarding stimuli; the BAS). Other personality traits (e.g., neuroticism or anxiety) are presumed to be influenced by the output of other systems (e.g., the system which responds to punishing stimuli, the FFFS in 'new' RST or the BIS in 'old' RST). RST further supposes that each system's functioning is dependent upon the functioning of the other systems with which it interacts. The formal models emphasize this aspect of RST. Traditional, verbally-expressed versions of RST argue that the personality traits involved will be uncorrelated with one another because the sensitivities of the underlying brain systems (to their specific inputs) are independent of one another across individuals. It is argued in this chapter that this view is likely to be wrong, as individuals' personality questionnaire responses are unlikely to be determined by latent properties of the brain systems (such as their sensitivities), which are not available to introspection. Instead, it is proposed that questionnaire responses, like other forms of behaviour, are much more likely to be determined by functional outcomes of system interactions which are open to introspection and subjective estimation. Several examples of such functional outcomes were considered, including the probability that a particular system gains control over behaviour or the mean activation/output level of a system (both being estimated by individuals over a range of situations).

Armed with this proposal regarding the nature of questionnaire responses, the formal model demonstrates that there should be a negative correlation between the reward system trait and the punishment system trait. The negative relationship is predicted because the outputs of each system have opposing effects upon the decision mechanism that determines which system gains control over behaviour (in the decision version of the model) or mutually inhibit the other system (in the dynamically interacting neural network version of the model). Some evidence regarding the intercorrelations between putative reward system and putative punishment system traits was presented; this was largely consistent with this prediction.

Initial model simulations were also run for the revised 'three-system' version of RST, which includes a system (the BIS) which acts to resolve conflicts such as those that might occur when both the reward system and punishment system are activated to a comparable extent. These simulations revealed that a negative correlation between reward and punishment system traits is still predicted in the new RST. These simulations also revealed that any personality trait, related to functional outcomes of the BIS (such as estimated mean output levels), may have complex non-linear relationships with reward and punishment system traits.

The chapter also clarifies what is meant by referring to a personality measure as a reward (or punishment) system trait. This does not imply that such a trait will be influenced selectively by reward (or punishment) system sensitivity. Indeed, the models used here show that such traits will also be influenced by the sensitivities of the other systems in the model. Instead, a reward trait is so called because it relates specifically and selectively to a functional outcome of the reward system.

The rendering of the models in this chapter have a number of weaknesses and oversimplifications, of course. In particular, the samples of events used to estimate system functional outcomes are equivalent for all simulated individuals. In the real world, an individual with a sensitive reward system would tend to approach a greater number of appetitive stimuli, when compared with an individual with a less sensitive reward system. Thus, these two types of individuals are likely to base their estimates of system functioning on differing samples of events. Simplification is an essential part of model-building, however, and it is hoped that the current models can cast some light on the present, sometimes densely swirling, fog of debate surrounding RST.

References

Carver, C.S. and White, T.L. (1994), Behavioral inhibition, behavioral activation, and affective responses to impending reward and punishment: the BIS/BAS, scales, *Journal of Personality and Social Psychology*, 67, 319–333

Cloninger, C.R. (1986), A unified biosocial theory of personality and its role in the development of anxiety states, *Psychiatric Developments*, 3, 167–226

Cloninger, C.R. (1989), *The Tridimensional Personality Questionnaire* (St Louis, MO: Department of Psychiatry and Genetics, Washington University School of Medicine)

Corr, P.J. (2001), Testing problems in J.A. Gray's personality theory: a commentary on Matthews and Gilliland (1999), *Personality and Individual Differences*, 30, 333–352

(2002), J.A.Gray's reinforcement sensitivity theory: tests of the joint subsystems hypothesis of anxiety and impulsivity, *Personality and Individual Differences*, 33, 511–532

(2004), Reinforcement sensitivity theory and personality, *Neuroscience and Biobehavioral Reviews*, 28, 317–332

Depue, R.A. and Collins, P.F. (1999). Neurobiology of the structure of personality: Dopamine, facilitation of incentive motivation, and extraversion, *Behavioral and Brain Sciences*, 22, 491–517

Díaz, A. and Pickering, A.D. (1993), The relationship between Gray's and Eysenck's personality spaces, *Personality and Individual Differences*, 15, 297–305

Eysenck, H.J. and Eysenck, S.B.G. (1975), *Manual of the Eysenck Personality Questionnaire (Junior and Adult)* (London: Hodder and Stoughton)

Gray, J.A. (1970), The psychophysiological basis of introversion-extraversion, *Behaviour Research and Therapy*, 8, 249–266

(1981), A critique of Eysenck's theory of personality in H.J. Eysenck (ed.), *A Model for Personality* (Berlin: Springer), pp. 246–276

(1987), *The Psychology of Fear and Stress* (Cambridge: Cambridge University Press)

Gray, J.A. and McNaughton, N. (2000), *The Neuropsychology of Anxiety: an Enquiry into the Functions of the Septo-hippocampal System* (2nd edn, Oxford: Oxford University Press)

Gray, J.A. and Smith, P.T. (1969), An arousal-decision model for partial reinforcement and discrimination learning in R. Gilbert and N.S. Sutherland (eds), *Animal Discrimination Learning* (London: Academic Press), pp. 243–272

Lessiter, J. (1999), *A Dopaminergic Model of Reward Motivation: a Test of Implications for Personality and Schizophrenia* (unpublished doctoral thesis, University of London)

McNaughton, N. and Corr, P. (2004), A two-dimensional neuropsychology of defense: fear/anxiety and defensive distance, *Neuroscience and Biobehavioral Reviews*, 28, 285–305

Mason, O., Claridge, G. and Jackson, M. (1995), New scales for the assessment of schizotypy, *Personality and Individual Differences*, 18, 7–13

Matthews, G. and Gilliland, K. (1999), The personality theories of H.J. Eysenck and J.A. Gray: a comparative review, *Personality and Individual Differences*, 26, 583–626

Pickering, A.D. (1997), The conceptual nervous system and personality: from Pavlov to neural networks, *European Psychologist*, 2, 139–163

(2004a), A formal model of 'new' reinforcement sensitivity theory, paper presented at the twelfth European Conference on Personality, Groningen, The Netherlands, 18–22 July 2004

(2004b), The neuropsychology of impulsive antisocial sensation seeking: from dopamine to hippocampal function? in R.M. Stelmack (ed.), *On the Psychobiology of Personality: Essays in Honor of Marvin Zuckerman* (Oxford: Elsevier), pp. 455–478

Pickering, A.D., Corr, P.J., Powell, J.H., Kumari, V., Thornton, J.C. and Gray, J.A. (1997), Individual differences in reactions to reinforcing stimuli are neither black nor white: to what extent are they Gray? in H. Nyborg (ed.), *The Scientific Study of Human Nature: Tribute to Hans J. Eysenck at 80* (London: Elsevier Sciences), pp. 36–67

Pickering, A.D., Díaz, A. and Gray, J.A. (1995), Personality and reinforcement: an exploration using a maze-learning task, *Personality and Individual Differences*, 18, 541–558

Pickering, A.D. and Gray, J.A. (1999), The neuroscience of personality in L. Pervin and O. John (eds.), *Handbook of Personality* (2nd edn, New York: Guilford Press), pp. 277–299

(2001), Dopamine, appetitive reinforcement, and the neuropsychology of human learning: an individual differences approach in A. Eliasz and A. Angleitner (eds.), *Advances in Individual Differences Research* (Lengerich: PABST Science Publishers), pp. 113–149

Pickering, A.D., Dawkins, L., Lessiter, J., Tharp, I., Jones, L., Halari, R., Powell, J.F., and Powell, J.H. (in preparation), Investigating the Behavioural Activation System

Smillie, L.D., Pickering, A.D. and Jackson, C.J. (2006), The new reinforcement sensitivity theory: implications for personality measurement, *Personality and Social Psychology Review*, 10, 320–335

Torrubia, R., Ávila, C., Moltó, J. and Caserás, X. (2001), The sensitivity to punishment and sensitivity to reward questionnaire (SPSRQ) as a measure of Gray's anxiety and impulsivity dimensions, *Personality and Individual Differences*, 15, 837–862

Torrubia, R. and Tobeña, A. (1984), A scale for the assessment of 'susceptibility to punishment' as a measure of anxiety: preliminary results, *Personality and Individual Differences*, 5, 371–375

17 Reinforcement Sensitivity Theory: a critique from cognitive science

Gerald Matthews

Reinforcement Sensitivity Theory (RST) draws on forty years of research conducted by Jeffrey Gray, and now incorporates significant modifications introduced by Philip Corr, Alan Pickering, Neil McNaughton and others (see Corr 2004; McNaughton and Corr 2004). RST is now a highly visible feature of the panorama of models of human personality. The purpose of this chapter is to provide a critique of the theory, from a cognitive science standpoint. RST is an ambitious, multifaceted account of the biological bases of personality, comprising several 'theories within a theory'. Table 17.1 discriminates the logically distinct facets of RST, whose validity may be separately evaluated, as follows.

First, there is an epistemological facet. RST is based on animal models of emotion and motivation (McNaughton and Gray 2000); one may question whether such models are valid for understanding human personality. Secondly, there is a neurophysiological facet. RST sets out a 'conceptual nervous system' or a specification of discrete brain systems that influence personality. Figure 17.1 illustrates the three fundamental systems specified by the latest, modified version of RST (Corr 2004). The Fight-Flight-Freeze System (FFFS) mediates reactions to all aversive stimuli, including both conditioned and unconditioned stimuli. It relates to fear, but not anxiety. The behavioral activation system (BAS) mediates reactions to conditioned and unconditioned appetitive stimuli. In the current theory, the behavioral inhibition system (BIS) is activated by goal conflict, typically when the organism faces an approach-avoidance conflict associated with concurrent activation of the FFFS and BAS. Its activation corresponds to anxiety and worry, but not fear. The issue is then whether the functional organization of personality, motivation and emotion is indeed based on these three systems.

Thirdly, there is a neurobehavioral facet describing how activation of the key brain structures controls behavior. The FFFS and BAS control avoidance and approach behavior, respectively. The BIS inhibits prepotent conflicting behaviors, focuses attention on threat, and initiates

Table 17.1 *Multiple facets of RST*

Facet	Key issue	Key evidence
Epistemological	Can we use animal models to explain human behavior?	A basic conceptual issue that is not directly tested by evidence
Neuropsychological	Does RST correctly describe and differentiate the key brain systems for personality?	Neuroanatomical and neurophysiological evidence on the functional organization of motivation and emotion
Neurobehavioral	Do the brain systems influence behavior as specified by RST?	Studies of neural mediation of emotion and motivation effects on behavior
Neuro-trait	Do IDs in brain systems map onto personality traits as specified by RST?	Psychophysiological and psychometric studies linking trait measures to neural systems
Psychological	Does RST provide an adequate explanation for observed relationships between personality, emotion and behavior?	Experimental psychological studies linking behavioral and subjective indices to standard traits
Adaptive	Does RST explain the adaptive significance of personality traits?	Studies of the role of strategies for adaptation in generating associations between traits and significant real-life outcomes

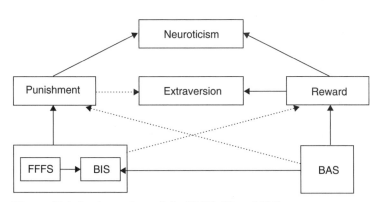

Figure 17.1 A schematic model of RST (Corr 2004)

scanning of memory to assess risk and resolve goal conflict. In addition, McNaughton and Corr (2004) discuss how behavioral outputs may vary according to the notion of defensive distance. Perhaps, RST has correctly specified the neuroanatomically defined systems, but mis-specified how variation in system activation relates to overt behavior. A particular challenge in this respect is the cognitive-psychological view that much of behavior is controlled by symbolic information-processing, rather than being directly contingent upon activation level of neural systems (Matthews 2000; Pylyshyn 1999).

Fourthly, there is what might be called a 'neuro-trait' facet: the correspondences between parameters of neural systems and phenotypic trait constructs. Modified RST assumes that sensitivity to input of the BAS corresponds to impulsivity (which, in turn, correlates highly with Extraversion or E), and the BIS corresponds to trait anxiety (highly correlated with Neuroticism or N). The FFFS is also related to trait anxiety, as the BIS and the FFFS jointly influence individual differences in punishment sensitivity (Corr 2004, p. 319). Corr (2004) also defines N independently, as the sum of punishment and reward sensitivities, whereas E reflects the difference in sensitivities; reward minus punishment. The theory might fail if the traits defined neurologically (stable, differential sensitivities of systems) did not, in fact, correspond to the psychometrically defined personality traits.

The fifth facet refers to the theory's explanations for the psychological rather than the neurophysiological correlates of traits. The key finding is that the relevant traits interact with motivational factors to influence outcomes including learning, performance and subjective mood (Corr 2004). The original theory predicted that reward signals would enhance learning in high impulsives (and extraverts), whereas punishment signals would enhance conditioning in persons high in Anx (and N), a pattern of interactions referred to as the *separable subsystems hypothesis* (SSH). The modified theory (Corr 2002, 2004) introduces the *joint subsystems hypothesis* (JSH). In certain specified conditions, the BAS may antagonize responses to aversive stimuli, and the punishment system may antagonize response to appetitive stimuli, so that, paradoxically, anxiety may interact with reward, and impulsivity with punishment. Weaknesses of this element of the theory would be shown by failures to find predicted effects of personality and motivational factors on psychological outcomes.

The sixth, adaptive facet is not explicitly part of RST, but merits some consideration nonetheless. The issue is how the behavioral expressions of the personality traits influence adaptation, in both the evolutionary sense, and in the broader sense of coping familiar from emotion and stress theory (e.g., Lazarus 1991). How does variability in the sensitivity of brain systems translate into different 'strategies for living', that is, handling the challenges of life such as forming intimate relationships, working and raising children? Much of the interest in personality traits relates to their correlation with real-life criteria such as stress symptoms, work behaviors and interpersonal strife. RST would be incomplete if adaptive choices were not, in fact, related to the brain systems.

I will examine where fault lines may be exposed in these different facets of the theory in three sections. First, I will briefly question the epistemology of RST, and explore the adequacy of its conceptual nervous system as a basis for understanding the neural architecture, motivational control of behavior and stabilities in personality. In the next two sections, I will explore the psychological implications of the theory in somewhat greater depth, reviewing, in turn, data on subjective emotion and data on performance variability and its adaptive significance. The chapter aims not to provide a full literature review, but to identify the key issues on whose resolution the fate of RST depends. I will conclude with a summary of the potential weaknesses of the theory.

Termites in the foundations: the validity of the conceptual model

Are animal models appropriate?

RST is based on a strong identification between animal and human models for motivation. The Gray and McNaughton (2000) animal model of anxiety, the axial pillar on which RST rests, receives impressive support from rat studies of the effects of brain lesions and anxiolytic drugs on learning and behavior. It is assumed that the neurophysiological and neurobehavioral conclusions from these studies can be generalized to humans with rather little modification.

There is no consensus among psychologists on the validity of this rather large assumption: see LeDoux (1998) and Lazarus (1991) for contrary perspectives.

The key issue is the role of symbolic information-processing in human behavior. From the cognitive science standpoint (e.g., Pylyshyn 1999) processing requires computations performed on discrete symbolic representations, so that, just as in a digital computer, we can distinguish the mental software from the (neural) hardware that supports it. Studies of personality that have adopted cognitive-psychological methods have shown how individual differences in behavior may be highly contingent upon information-processing demands that do not map onto neurological constructs in any simple way (Matthews 2000). By contrast, McNaughton and Corr (2004, p. 297), in the context of describing multiple mechanisms for detection of threat, state that '[t]he slow and sophisticated processes would normally be referred to as cognitive processes but

486   The Reinforcement Sensitivity Theory of Personality

their operation is no different in principle, although more complex in practice, than more "reflexive" responses'. Within cognitive science, symbolic, 'cognitive' processes are very much different in principle from neural processes that use no symbolic representation. Cognitive science models, in addition to 'hardware' and 'software' levels, also differentiate a third type of explanation, referred to as the 'knowledge' (Newell 1982) or 'semantic' level (Pylyshyn 1999). Behavior may be explained by reference to the meanings that the person attributes to stimuli, in relation to personal goals. Thus, traits relate to biases in appraisals of events, choice of coping strategies and other aspects of self-regulation (Matthews, Schwean *et al.* 2000). This type of understanding also corresponds to work on human motivation that suggests that basic needs are complemented by self-directed motivations towards competence, autonomy and social connection (Deci and Ryan 2000).

The point is not that knowledge-level constructs are unrelated to neural functioning, but that the neural concomitants of self-regulative processes may not support good explanatory models for the psychological phenomena. Thus, there are good reasons for doubting whether animal models provide the conceptual equipment needed to explain the multifarious ways in which personality and emotion are expressed.

Neurophysiology and the control of behavior

The neurophysiological model on which RST is based (Gray and McNaughton 2000; McNaughton and Corr 2004) is a sophisticated account of the neural structures involved in fear and anxiety. The neural substrate for the BAS has received less attention. However, other physiological models of emotion present a somewhat different picture of brain function. Basic emotions theories (e.g., Ekman 1999) posit from five to ten fundamental emotions, with (in biologically-based accounts) each emotion corresponding to a distinctive neural substrate (Panksepp 1998). By contrast with RST, anger is supported by a separate system to other basic negative affects such as sadness and disgust. Conversely, basic emotions theories typically do not differentiate anxiety and fear, and some variants of basic emotions theory propose specifically social basic emotions such as separation distress. RST seems to attribute effects of personality on social behavior to BIS, BAS and/or FFFS, whereas it may be necessary to explore the role of specifically social brain systems. A case in point might be sources of the association between neuroticism and insecure attachment styles (Hagekull and Bohlin 2003).

A different set of challenges to RST is posed by another leading neuropsychological model of emotion (Rolls 1999). Like RST, it specifies discrete and fundamental reward and punishment. However, Rolls (1999, Figure 1) represents fear and apprehension (anxiety) as simply representing different intensities of emotion driven by presentation of a negative reinforcer. As in basic emotions theories, anxiety and fear are not sharply distinguished. In addition, Rolls (1999) takes a rather different neurobehavioral tack in linking motivational systems to behavior. Specifically, his model differentiates two routes to action. The first is based on implicit stimulus-reinforcement learning that accommodates reinforcement history, current motivational state and other factors influencing the reward value of the outcome. Its control over action is supported by projections from emotion centers (amygdala and orbitofrontal cortex) to the basal ganglia. By contrast with RST, which links the basal ganglia (specifically, the ventral striatum and ventral pallium) to the BAS, Rolls (1999) sees the implicit route as operating equally for gaining rewards or avoiding punishment, on the basis of a cost-benefit computation.

The second, explicit route to action is explicitly language based, supported by cortical language, motor and planning areas. Rolls describes it as affording multistep syntactic planning that allows implementation and regulation of long-term plans for action, that may override the implicit system. Importantly, it may be unique, or at least uniquely developed, in humans by comparison with other primates, whose linguistic capabilities remain moot. Thus, the rodent data on which RST is based neglect the language-based system and its role in translating human emotions into action. This neglect may be rather a large omission from the neurobehavioral component of the theory. Indeed, cognitive neuroscience studies suggest that anxiety may be linked to the functioning of specific cortical systems that implement motivational control over attention (Derryberry and Reed 1997).

The issue of control merits emphasis. Figure 17.2 sketches some of the different causal models prevalent in emotion research. The figure is intended to illustrate different conceptualizations of emotional control of behavior, *not* any full model. The traditional neuropsychological view corresponds in its essentials to Panksepp's (1998) biological model and Eysenck's (1981) skepticism about the value of cognitive psychology. Emotion is a concomitant of multiple brain systems that must be understood neurologically; 'cognition' as understood by cognitive psychologists is at best epiphenomenal froth. A more sophisticated perspective is provided by animal models such as LeDoux's (1998) that admit of a separate cortical system for higher-order cognition that plays a role in emotion. However, the role is of a satellite nature, in modulating the operation of lower level systems. LeDoux (1998) sees control of emotional response as residing primarily in the amygdala: 'the

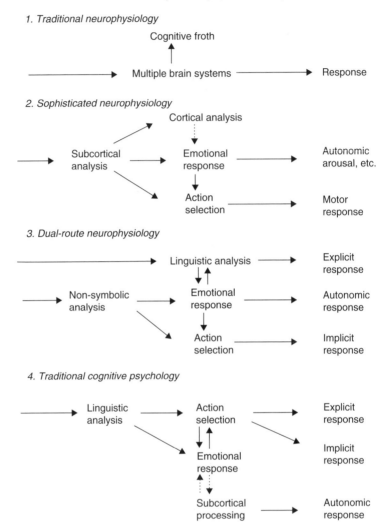

Figure 17.2 Four outline conceptualizations of how cognition and emotion may control behavior

amygdala has a greater influence on the cortex than the cortex has on the amygdala, allowing emotional arousal to dominate and control thinking' (p. 303). My reading of RST is that it adopts a similar stance, in affording the greater part of behavioral control to subcortical systems. Of course, such a position might be correct for rats but not humans.

The 'dual-route' conceptual model shown in Figure 17.2 corresponds to Rolls (1999), which, via the explicit linguistic system, allows an autonomous cortical control over behavior. Here, there are two independent but interacting control systems, with emotion providing an interface between them. Emotional responses provide the explicit system with limited information on the functioning of the implicit system, and a conduit for exerting control over that system. The dynamics of shifts of control between the two systems are open to debate; Rolls (1999), somewhat like LeDoux (1998), takes the reasonable position that the implicit system is most useful when fast action to an immediate threat or opportunity is needed. However, at least in some circumstances, it allows for entirely language-based control over behavior, so that it is autonomic arousal rather than cognition that is epiphenomenal.

Finally, Figure 17.2 shows a traditional cognitive model (e.g., Lazarus 1999), in which cognitive appraisal is the primary and necessary causal influence on emotion, with physiological changes exerting a more indirect effect, mediated by cognitions. I have highlighted here a feature of current cognitive theory that should be better known by neuropsychologists, namely, that implicit, unconscious actions may be either cortically or sub-cortically controlled. In an important critique of biological theories of emotion, Clore and Ortony (2000) point to fast, associative, meaning-based processing as being a key mode of cognitive control. Lack of conscious awareness does not imply subcortical and/or non-symbolic processing, and symbolic cognition is not obliged to be slow and deliberative.

The problem for RST is that the empirical evidence showing inter-action between traits and motivational factors is open to the alternative explanation that behavioral effects may reflect symbolic cognitive mechanisms, rather than the subcortical processes described by RST. Worse, individual differences in subcortical processes and their con-comitant psychophysiological activity may reflect variation in cortical control. Taking the issue without prejudice, validating RST requires some criteria for identifying the level of control. At present, responses such as the startle reflex (Corr 2002) can most plausibly be attributed to subcortical control, whereas data from information-processing tasks such as semantic priming (Matthews and Harley 1993) are best explained in terms of cognitive biases. However, there remains a vast middle-ground of ambiguous data, for example, on motivational effects on discrimination learning (e.g., Zinbarg and Revelle 1989) for which the level of control remains ambiguous.

Traits as neurological constructs

Traditionally, trait psychology has been a 'top-down' enterprise that begins with a molar phenotype for a quality of personality for which neurological bases are sought (Zuckerman 1991). Within the top-down model, the mappings between phenotypic traits and brain systems may be complex, so that there is no *isomorphism* between traits and brain systems (Matthews 2004; Zuckerman 1991). RST suggests a contrasting 'bottom-up' approach, such that phenotypic traits are indeed directly isomorphic with brain systems, as in the classical theories of Eysenck and Gray. In fact, RST softens this position somewhat, to the extent that both the BIS and FFFS may relate to anxiety. In addition, certain structures such as anterior cingulate and amygdala may participate in more than one of the three basic systems (see McNaughton and Corr 2004). There may also be diffuse modulation of the systems by serotonergic and noradrenergic systems.

The difficulties here are both conceptual and psychometric. The conceptual difficulty is whether individual differences in neurophysiological functioning are in fact expressed directly in self-report data. RST is paradoxical in that it seeks to assess an implicit parameter of individual functioning through questionnaire assessment. Seemingly, some objective measurement (behavioral or physiological) would be more true to the tenets of the theory, especially given the well-known difficulties of assessing motivation by self-report. I will not review the psychophysiological data here (see Corr 2004; Matthews and Gilliland 1999), but it is fair to say that support for RST from such data is mixed, at best. One difficulty is that trait anxious individuals typically do not show the elevated autonomic nervous system activity that would be expected if anxiety relates to reactivity of a punishment system. To cite one recent example, Heponiemi *et al.* (2004) found that the Carver-White BIS scale failed to predict either baseline cardiac activity or reactivity to a stressful task (although the BAS scale related to parasympathetic withdrawal). Another general difficulty concerns arousal. Gray (1991) distinguished a separate noradrenergic arousal system that was activated by both BAS and BIS, but appeared to exert some independent influence on response energization. McNaughton and Corr (2004, Figure 5) cite arousal as an output of the BIS, but Corr (2004) does not refer to arousal as an explanatory device. It remains unclear whether outputs of the BIS and arousal systems should be or could be differentiated in psychophysiological studies.

The psychometric argument relates primarily to the use of factor analysis to isolate fundamental traits. A longstanding difficulty for Gray's theory has been that factor analytic studies consistently identify E and N as fundamental axes, not impulsivity and anxiety. The rejoinder (e.g., Corr 2004), is that factor analysis is a fallible technique that is trumped by theoretical arguments. Of course, researchers should not place all their eggs in the factor-analytic basket, but concerns remain, which are highlighted by attempts to develop questionnaire measures of the BIS and BAS.

There are various BIS and BAS scales, generally based on Gray's earlier RST. For the most part, these scales are acceptably reliable and factor appropriately in isolation. In other respects, problems arise. First, factor structures fail to correspond to theoretical expectation. Wilson, Barrett and Gray (1989) developed the Gray–Wilson Personality Questionnaire (GWPQ) on theoretical grounds, so as to define the three motivational systems (as understood at that time), in terms of constructs from the six relevant animal learning paradigms. However, the factor solution did not conform to prediction; for example, Fight and Flight scales failed to converge on the expected common factor.

Secondly, it is difficult to separate BIS and BAS scales from general negative and positive affectivity, and, indeed, N and E. I will give two examples here. Heubeck, Wilkinson and Cologen (1998) factored the Carver and White (1994) BIS/BAS scale with scales for E and N (from the EPQ), and positive and negative affectivity. A confirmatory factor analysis supported a two-factor solution, grouping together (1) BIS, N and negative affectivity, and (2) BAS, E and positive affectivity. Knyazev, Slobodskaya and Wilson (2004) performed a similar exercise in a Russian sample, using measures of N, E and P, trait anxiety, impulsivity, along with the Carver-White scales and a short version of the GWPQ. A factor analysis gave a three-factor solution, corresponding to N, P and E. Both BIS scales and trait anxiety had high loadings on the N factor. The BAS scales divided into those loading on the P factor (e.g., fun seeking, approach) and those loading on the E factor (e.g., drive, reward). Impulsivity related to P, not E. There seems to be a disconnect here between the emotional and behavioral attributes of the BAS. The study also failed to show any distinct FFFS factor; scales related to anxiety, fear and avoidance gravitated towards a general N or negative affectivity factor.

Thus, the RST skeptic may reasonably assert that (1) much of the variance in BIS and BAS scales simply relates to N and E, and (2) the prediction that BIS and FFFS correspond to separate traits is rather spectacularly disconfirmed by the evidence available (Knyazev, Slobodskaya and Wilson 2004). Of course, RST predicts overlap with N and E, so the nature of whatever variance may be unique to BIS and BAS scales is important. Lack of focus on divergent validity makes this a difficult issue to address. However, the attachment of several BAS scales to P rather than E in the Knyazev, Slobodskaya and Wilson (2004) study might imply that it is reward rather than punishment behavior that requires fractionation (cf., Morrone-Strupinsky and Depue 2004). Difficulties are compounded by the uncertain psychometric status of impulsivity, which has become the Flying Dutchman of personality structure, flitting between Extraversion, Neuroticism and Psychoticism according to preference. Whiteside and Lynam (2001) distinguished four orthogonal impulsivity dimensions that related to different 'Big Five' traits; RST will need to engage with such complexities before the psychometric problems can be resolved.

Bad feelings: personality and negative emotion

Mediators of personality effects on mood

The simplest model of basic emotions or moods posits two dimensions of energetic arousal and tense arousal (Thayer 1989), or positive affect and negative affect (PA and NA: Watson 2000). These dimensions may correspond to brain reward and punishment systems respectively. Empirical studies have typically focused on generic negative affect. Corr (2004, p. 323) refers thus to Larsen and Ketelaar's (1991) study of personality and mood induction: 'NA was highest in E − /N + (high Anx) individuals; but inconsistent with theory was the finding that PA was highest in E + /N − (low Anx) individuals, not E + /N + (high Imp) individuals'. The study is noteworthy because of its demonstration that personality factors *interact* with induced mood broadly as predicted by RST. In fact, the problematic negative association between PA and N noted by Corr (2004) was not robust. Larsen and Ketelaar (1991, p. 136) found that 'neurotic subjects did not show differential positive-affect responsivity to the mood-induction manipulations, relative to the stable subjects', that is, there was no significant interaction between N and PA (or main effect of N). A replication study (Rusting and Larsen 1997) obtained similar results.

Thus far, the results fit classic RST[1] quite well: E moderated the PA response, but N did not, whereas N but not E moderated the NA response. Indeed, in many studies, the equation between E and PA and N and NA works quite well, as long as we are content to interpret Eysenck's axes in terms of Gray's theory (Matthews, Jones and

---

[1] One problematic feature of the results – on which the authors do not comment – is that the significant interaction between N and the mood induction was not driven by differential sensitivity of N+ persons to the negative mood induction. N+ and N− individuals showed a similar increase in negative mood relative to the neutral condition. The interaction reflects a lack of effect of N on NA in the *positive* induction condition; put differently, the positive induction appeared to calm N+s but not N−s, relative to the neutral condition.

Chamberlain 1990). The issue of which version of RST works better remains open to the extent that a few correlational and mood induction studies have shown the E – low NA and N – low PA associations predicted by modified RST (see Matthews, Deary and Whiteman 2003).

A more fundamental difficulty for RST is whether effects of traits on mood response are, in fact, directly mediated by variation in sensitivity of brain reward and punishment systems. An important, but disregarded, feature of the Larsen and Ketelaar (1991) study is that it used no overtly appetitive or aversive stimuli at all! In fact, participants *imagined* negative events (e.g., being expelled from school in an embarrassing manner) or positive events (enjoying the beach in Hawaii). The procedure leaves open a cognitive interpretation for the findings, perhaps related to Clore and Ortony's (2000) fast associative retrieval process. Personality may influence availability of events in long-term memory: perhaps, high N persons are more likely to have experienced being embarrassed at school, or to have gone to Hawaii and argued with their partner. Alternatively, personality may influence the ease with which memories may be accessed. Trait effects on induced mood are found also with studies using overt stimuli such as film-clips (e.g., Morrone-Strupinsky and Depue 2004), but, again, reaction to the stimulus may be filtered through the individual's cognitive appraisals and memory retrieval.

In fact, we have a typical case of the ambiguity over control mechanisms often found in human studies. Presumably, a proponent of RST could interpret the imagery mood induction in terms of model type 2 in Figure 17.2. Extraverts and introverts access the same cognitive representation of a positive event but the BAS activates more strongly in response to that representation in extraverts: control resides at the subcortical level. However, in terms of models type 3 and 4, we could equally claim that it is the properties of the cognitive representation that are sensitive to personality, and individual differences in emotion are cognitively controlled.[2]

Recent work by the author supports a cognitive interpretation of personality effects on mood. Mood change, with respect to baseline, in studies of stressful task performance appears to be substantially related to the person's appraisals and coping strategies, as specified by Lazarus (1991, 1999) and others. Broadly, challenge appraisal and task-focused

---

[2] I am avoiding the long-running controversy in cognitive psychology over whether mental images are coded propositionally (in language-like form) or whether they are supported by a separate representational code. In this context, it is reasonable to suppose that imagining a specified event involves at least a partial linguistic representation.

coping relate to positive mood response; threat appraisals and emotion-focused coping relate to negative mood response (Matthews and Zeidner 2004). These cognitive processes may mediate personality effects, given that E typically relates to challenge and task-focus, and N to threat and emotion-focus. Matthews *et al.* (2006) found that more neurotic individuals showed elevated emotional distress following performance of demanding laboratory tasks, but the effect was fully mediated by emotion-focused coping.

Fractionating negative affect

Modified RST (Corr 2004) makes a sharp distinction between fear and anxiety as separate emotions supported by different neurological systems, but fear and anxiety do not emerge as separate state dimensions in studies of mood. Typically, 'fearful' as a mood descriptor relates to Thayer's tense arousal dimension, which corresponds to the affective component of state anxiety (Matthews, Jones and Chamberlain 1990; Thayer 1989). It is possible that BIS and FFFS activations are experienced as similar subjective states, even though they are neurophysiologically distinct, implying inconsistency in relations between state anxiety, personality and behavior. If so, RST needs to supply some independent measure of whether the person is experiencing fear or anxiety.

Although the fear/anxiety distinction is problematic, recent psychometric studies show the limitations of the simple PA/NA model. Matthews, Campbell *et al.* (2002) showed that state dimensions related to mood, motivation and subjective cognition cohered around three fundamental higher-order factors. *Task engagement* integrated energy, task motivation and concentration. *Distress* was defined by tension, negative hedonic tone and lack of perceived control and confidence. *Worry* was a purely cognitive factor, related to self-focused attention, low self-esteem and high cognitive interference. N related most reliably to high distress and high worry. There is an intriguing parallel to RST in this model of subjective states in that it shows two quite distinct forms of aversive mental state, in the forms of distress and worry. Somewhat like fear, distress appears to be sensitive to immediate external demands such as task workload (although it is also substantially correlated with appraisal and coping factors). Furthermore, angry mood loads on distress, perhaps indicating a 'fight' component to the state factor. Somewhat like anxiety in modified RST, worry is not directly driven by task demands, but signals a need to reflect on the personal significance of events. Indeed, Corr (2004, p. 324) states that BIS activation is experienced subjectively as worry and rumination. The distress-FFFS and worry-BIS linkages should not be pushed too far; for example, the human data provide no indication that distress is a necessary precursor to worry. However, it is intriguing that human aversive states may be divided into two largely independent factors in this way – and that N relates to both dimensions.

Role of metacognition

A final twist to the analysis of mood states is that cognitive effects may be moderated by *metacognition*, that is, the person's beliefs about their own cognitive and emotional states. The concept is best known from clinical studies suggesting that metacognitive styles may play a causal role in the aetiology and maintenance of anxiety disorders (Wells 2000; Wells and Matthews 2005). For example, 'meta-worry' (worry about worry) and beliefs that worry is a useful problem-solving activity are implicated in Generalized Anxiety Disorder. Another metacognitive construct, anxiety sensitivity, referring to appraisals of bodily arousal, predicts various anxiety pathologies over and above trait anxiety (Schmidt, Lerew and Jackson 1999). RST seeks to map different anxiety disorders onto different neurological systems; panic, phobia and obsessive-compulsive disorder are linked by McNaughton and Corr (2004) to different levels of the defensive avoidance hierarchy, increasing in cytoarchitectonic and behavioral complexity. However, even the most 'primitive' of these disorders – panic, linked to undirected escape – turns out to have pivotal cognitive and metacognitive components. Clark's (1996) model of panic implicates faulty cognitions of bodily symptoms as playing a key role in panic attacks, e.g., misinterpreting cardiac acceleration as an impending heart attack. Styles of metacognition are also substantially correlated with trait anxiety and other traits related to negative affectivity, in non-clinical samples (Wells 2000).

Matthews, Hillyard and Campbell (1999) showed that about 40 per cent of the variance in dispositional test anxiety could be explained by Wells' (2000) metacognitive trait scales, even though the metacognitive items make no reference to being evaluated. Metacognitive traits also predicted the level of state worry experienced during an actual examination. Metacognition may also be important for the behavioral consequences of anxiety. Studies of sports anxiety (see Zeidner and Matthews 2005 for a brief review) show that athletes differ in their metacognitions of the anxiety commonly experienced during competition. Some find anxiety motivating and beneficial, whereas others appraise it as a sign of loss of focus.

In sum, human anxiety states are better understood as concomitants of cognitively-mediated representations of threat, rather than as the raw output of brain systems for anxiety (Averill 1980). Subcortical systems may play an important role in dynamic interaction with those cortical sites supporting symbolic representation, but the central roles of cognitive appraisals and metacognitions in human anxiety are incompatible with a simple neurological account of anxiety. Indeed, as Lazarus (1991) rather mischievously suggested, we may need to understand the psychology of anxiety in order to make sense of its physiological concomitants and expressions.

A cloudy crystal ball: RST and the prediction of performance

RST predicts how personality traits will interact with motivational factors in influencing psychological outcomes (see Matthews and Gilliland 1999 for reviews of data). I concur with Corr's (2004, p. 323) appraisal, that, at this early stage of research on the modified version of RST 'it is yet to be seen whether the revised theory is better able to generate consistent and interpretable data' than the old model. In fact, the general conclusions to be drawn are uncontentious. Reward and punishment manipulations quite often moderate the effects of traits such as E and N on learning and performance. Sometimes the effects observed are compatible with either standard or modified RST, but sometimes they are not. Furthermore, the precise personality effect found varies from study to study, even when task paradigms are highly similar. Rather than review this complex literature, this section will focus on identifying the broad types of finding that may prove problematic for RST.

Conditioning and learning

The most popular behavioral approach to testing RST has been to use simple conditioning and learning tasks, including classical conditioning, operant conditioning and passive avoidance paradigms (e.g., Corr, Pickering and Gray 1995). Such tasks seem especially appropriate because of the animal learning basis for RST. A brief dip into the conditioning literature will illustrate the problems that arise (see Matthews and Gilliland 1999 for a full critique). The simplest prediction, from 'classic RST', assuming separable subsystems, is that reward will enhance learning in high impulsives; punishment will enhance learning in anxious persons. Classic RST also separates learning with conditioned and unconditioned stimuli, but this distinction no longer appears to be a systematic moderator factor (McNaughton and Corr 2004). Some studies do indeed support the simple prediction, especially those studies using traditional conditioning paradigms such as associative conditioning of the eye-blink response (Spence 1964) and verbal operant conditioning (Gupta 1990). Corr, Pickering and Gray (1997) also found that high anxiety related to superior procedural learning under punishment.

Other studies show various departures from expectation. For example, Zinbarg and Revelle (1989) showed that, across four studies, anxiety and impulsivity interacted in their effects on a discrimination learning task. With 'go cues' (reward signals), high anxiety facilitated learning among low impulsives, but with 'no-go cues' (punishment signals), anxiety facilitated learning among high impulsives. The results conflict with the simple prediction that Imp+ subjects should learn faster with go cues, and Anx+ subjects should learn faster with no-go cues. Different patterns of interaction between anxiety and impulsivity have been observed in other studies (e.g., Corr 2002). Other studies support the JSH, in showing 'complementary-trait effects'; that is, the 'wrong' personality trait influences learning. As examples, Corr, Pickering and Gray (1995, Experiment 3), in a discrimination learning study, found that high trait anxiety related to lower speed of response to approach cues, and Corr, Pickering and Gray (1995, Experiment 2) found that E was negatively correlated with associative learning with an aversive UCS (but not appetitive or neutral UCSs).

Compounding these difficulties is the wide range of personality scales used, including Eysenckian measures, miscellaneous impulsivity scales, BIS-BAS scales, and other scales that seem potentially relevant, such as the Cloninger scales. There is an obvious risk of Type I error when multiple scales are employed and analyzed. It remains unclear whether some of these measures are more predictive than others. As Corr (2004, p. 324) states, 'there is a diversity and complexity of findings in RST research, which at times are highly confusing and suggestive of a failure of RST to provide a coherent account of the causal dynamics of personality'.

Corr (2004) cites studies that seem to support both SSH and JSH in different experimental conditions; the new RST may perhaps afford excessive 'wiggle-room' for explaining unexpected findings. The solution, of course, is to specify ante hoc the conditions which promote or prevent interaction between systems. Corr (2004) lists the moderator factors which, it is hoped, will bring consistency to the empirical findings. He states (p. 329), 'that there is some support for the JSH but the precise pattern of effects seem highly dependent: (a) on the type of task employed; (b) the specific scales used to measure PUN and REW traits (of which there are many); (c) the operational definition of reward and

498   The Reinforcement Sensitivity Theory of Personality

punishment; and (d) the expectancies of reward and punishment either preexisting or induced during early stages of the experimental procedure'. The statement is reasonable, but it is fair to add also that at this early stage of research on modified RST, the empirical database that would specify precisely (a), (b), (c) and (d) is lacking.

The conservative position is that more data are needed to evaluate the success of the new theory, but there are some warning signs in the existing data. What empirical findings would disconfirm modified RST? First, there are some personality-learning associations that are prohibited by both the SSH and JSH. Specifically, anxiety should not relate to indices of decreased BIS[3] or increased BAS activity, whereas impulsivity should not relate to indices of increased BIS or decreased BAS activity. However, some findings are at least suggestive of these prohibited relationships. For example, in a study of sexual response, Barr and McConaghy (1974) found that anxiety enhanced appetitive electrodermal conditioning. Levey and Martin (1981) report on an eye-blink conditioning study conducted by Eysenck and Levey that found that, with a strong, presumably aversive, air-puff UCS, impulsivity was positively associated with learning. With a weak UCS, low impulsives learned faster. It is hard to see how high impulsives could show faster conditioning to a strong aversive stimulus, likely to activate the BIS. Some features of the Zinbarg and Revelle (1989) study also seem problematic. Why should anxiety facilitate learning of go (reward) cues among low impulsive subjects? Presumably learning of this type is mediated by the BAS, which should be either unaffected (SSH) or inhibited (JSH) by anxiety. Likewise, how can RST explain the detrimental effect of high anxiety on learning of no-go cues among low impulsive subjects? Anxiety should facilitate, not impair, performance on learning of this kind.

A second type of disconfirmation would follow if the factors that moderate whether the SSH or JSH is supported (Corr 2004, p. 325) failed to operate as predicted. It is premature to arrive at any final judgment, but existing studies illustrate potential problems. Corr (2002) showed complementary trait effects in two paradigms, one based on the startle response (Study 1), and one using a signal detection task (Study 2). One factor said by Corr (2004, p. 325) to promote interaction between reward and punishment systems is the use of weak appetitive/ aversive stimuli. Study 2 manipulated reinforcement via verbal feedback which can reasonably be described as 'weak'. However, Study 1 used,

---

[3] I will, in line with most empirical reports, refer to the BIS in this section, although modified RST leaves open the possibility that it is an integrated punishment system (BIS and FFSS; see Figure 17.1) that mediates personality effects.

among other materials, unpleasant slides (e.g., mutilated bodies). Can we be confident that such images are weak rather than strong? An influential psychophysiological study of sensation seeking (Smith *et al.* 1989) used sexual and violent words (e.g., 'slaughter') as high intensity stimuli and, presumably, images are stronger than words. The problem – familiar from studies of personality and arousal (Matthews and Gilliland 1999) – is that there is neither consensus nor adequate methodology for deciding on stimulus strength, allowing room for post hoc rationalization. Had the Corr (2004) study showed support for the SSH in Study 1 and JSH in Study 2, the (not implausible) argument might have been that images of dead bodies are a stronger aversive stimulus than the negative feedback signal (the word 'INCORRECT').

Another of Corr's (2004) moderator factors is that mixed appetitive and aversive stimuli should tend to give results supporting the JSH. Corr (2004, Study 1) used mixed stimuli, whereas in Study 2, reinforcement was manipulated between subjects, and so was non-mixed. The designs would then seemingly promote the JSH (Study 1) and SSH (Study 2), although, in fact, both studies suggested interaction between BIS and BAS. Again, the difficulty is predicting rather than postdicting findings. Given the variation in stimulus materials and design in the Corr (2002) studies, one could find a rationale for supporting either the JSH or SSH in each of the two studies. Future research on RST needs urgently to develop a stronger set of principles for prediction.

Attention and performance

Gray (1991) deserves credit for predicting that anxiety should relate to a bias in attention towards threatening stimuli, a prediction confirmed in various cognitive-psychological studies (e.g., Fox *et al.* 2001). However, Matthews and Gilliland (1999) referred to two basic problems in using RST as a basis for predicting performance on attentional tasks. First, it is rather unclear what increased 'sensitivity' to motivational signals means in the context of attention, i.e., whether it refers to greater distractibility, or to some enhancement of processing. Secondly, it neglects an important general principle of research on stress and emotion (Hockey 1984), that stressor effects on performance are rarely uniform across tasks, varying critically with information-processing demands. For example, the threat bias linked to anxiety appears to be more reliable for selective attention than for focused attention on a single stimulus source (Fox *et al.* 2001). Matthews and Gilliland (1999) discussed various instances of dependence of anxiety effects on information-processing parameters for which RST has no means to offer an explanation.

Modified RST takes one step forward and one step backward. On the positive side, RST now offers a more detailed account of attentional outputs, discriminating environmental scanning, external scanning (risk assessment) and internal scanning (memory) (McNaughton and Corr 2004, p. 298). The link with risk assessment is intriguing in that the human experimental literature suggests that anxiety does not necessarily relate to heightened sensitivity to threat in general, but to difficulties in disengagement from threat once detected (Fox *et al.* 2001). Perhaps the anxious person may be engaged in risk assessment prior to disengagement, although risk assessment in humans is highly dependent upon linguistically-mediated cognitive operations such as use of heuristics (Johnson and Tversky 1984). On the negative side, anxiety effects on behavior might now be mediated not just by the BIS (and suppression of the BAS), but also by the FFFS, whose range of outputs include active avoidance, escape and freezing. It is not very clear how these outputs would be expressed on information-processing tasks – McNaughton and Corr (2004, p. 293) relate the Stroop test for selective attention to active avoidance – but the general point is that the effects of anxiety on behavior are overdetermined. Taking together all the various outputs of the BIS and FFFS, we have six or more possible explanations for any given experimental finding, which may provide rather too much latitude.

Elsewhere, I have argued that the attempt to explain all the multifarious effects of anxiety and neuroticism on performance by a single brain system – even a system with multiple outputs – is doomed to failure (Matthews 2000; Matthews, Derryberry and Siegle 2000; Matthews, Deary and Whiteman 2003). Performance effects relate to multiple levels of processing – neural, symbolic and semantic – and to multiple mechanisms within each level. Most pertinently in the present context, anxiety relates to higher-level, strategically-controlled functions such as making predictive inferences (Calvo and Castillo 2001). Several studies by Derryberry (see Derryberry and Reed 1997; Matthews *et al.* 2000) show that anxiety relates to several functionally distinct cortical attentional systems, including components of a 'posterior' system controlling spatial attention, and an 'anterior' system that controls several executive functions. Similarly, Wells and Matthews (1994) relate anxiety to strategies for regulating threat, such as voluntary search for danger stimuli.

A cognitive-adaptive perspective

RST describes the adaptive functions of the brain systems in general terms, but has little to say about the adaptive significance of individual differences. The assumption appears to be that variation in the sensitivities of systems reflects random variation that exerts a 'bottom-up' control over higher-level systems, including behavior. A contrary 'top-down' view (Matthews 2004; Matthews and Zeidner 2004) is that phenotypic traits are higher-order, emergent qualities that should be studied in their own right. The cognitive-adaptive theory of personality (Matthews 1997, 2004) proposes that traits are multiply distributed, across and within the cognitive science levels of explanation; that is, traits are expressed not only in individual differences in neural functioning, but also, independently, in variation in information-processing parameters, and in high-level goals and self-knowledge. In addition, at each explanatory level, traits relate to biases in multiple systems. What gives unity to a trait is not an isomorphic brain system, but a common adaptation. Each trait represents a generic strategy for managing some class of life demands or opportunities; a strategy that is supported by multiple biases.

Thus, neuroticism may be seen as a preference for avoidance and anticipation of threat, as opposed to direct confrontation (Matthews 2004). The neurotic adaptation is supported not just by high sensitivity of brain systems for punishment (should this prove to be true), but also by biases in the symbolic processing of threat stimuli, and by negative self-concept and preferences for emotion-focused coping. In fact, given that neuroticism appears to relate more to social than to physical threats, the higher-level expressions of the trait may typically control behavior. Because of the ambiguity and complexity of social threats (see Matthews 2004 for an adaptive analysis), simple S-R mappings or conditioned responses are unlikely to be sufficient for successful adaptation. Similarly, Matthews (1997; Matthews and Zeidner 2004) relates extraversion to choices of adaptation towards cognitively-challenging social settings that offer both potential gains (e.g., social networking) and costs (e.g., social failure). As with neuroticism, analysis of the various physiological, cognitive and affective correlates of extraversion suggests that they help, in different ways, to support an adaptation towards social challenge.

The contrast with RST is that cognitive-adaptive theory sees traits as emerging from a multitude of typically small biases in physiological and psychological functioning, in line with the small magnitude of correlations often found in validity studies (Matthews and Zeidner 2004). The trait is more readily seen in molar behavior, as the person tackles some challenge of life, than at the neurological level. Temperamental variability in sensitivity to reward and punishment may well feed forward into personality, as one of several discrete influences. However, most of the behavioral expressions of traits are not directly mediated by variance in the activation of reward and punishment systems. Although more research is needed, existing studies typically show that psychophysiological indices are generally ineffective as mediators of associations between personality and performance (Matthews 1997).

Conclusion

More research is needed before any final verdict on RST may be brought in, but the challenges to the theory may be summarized as follows:

1. *Relevance of animal models.* RST assumes that animal models of emotion and motivation provide an appropriate basis for explaining human personality data. The issue is in part an issue of core assumptions (or negative heuristic) but, from the cognitive science standpoint, it is open to question. Specifically, symbolic information-processing and high-level knowledge-based cognition may not map onto neurological constructs in any tractable manner (Pylyshyn 1999). Thus, biological theories may not be capable of providing an adequate account of the cognitive processes that appear to mediate many of the effects of personality traits on emotion and behavior. Rolls' (1999) differentiation of an explicit, language-based system for behavioral control from a more primitive implicit system lends weight to this criticism. Indeed, control of emotion and behavior is the key issue. Cognitive theory and the more sophisticated psychobiological theories provide viable alternatives to neural reductionism in which individual differences in behavior call for cognitive as well as (or instead of) neurological explanations. Corr (2004) does refer to expectancy as a possible moderator factor, but this potentially cognitive aspect of RST requires elaboration.

2. *Scope of the theory.* RST claims to provide a general explanation for the full range of personality phenomena. This position may be excessively ambitious. A different perspective (Matthews and Zeidner 2004) is that personality traits may be distributed across multiple mechanisms, to be understood at different levels of abstraction from the neural substrate. RST may be valid for some phenomena, especially those close to neurology, but irrelevant to higher-level expressions of traits. If RST is just one piece of some more elaborate jigsaw, then progress requires some statement about the range of phenomena that RST is apt for explaining.

3. *Mis-specifications of the theory.* Several of the basic assumptions of RST appear to conflict with other influential theories or data. The most striking of these is the differentiation of fear and anxiety as separate systems, which conflicts with basic emotions theory (e.g., Ekman 1999),

and does not lend itself to operationalization in human studies. At the same time, I have discussed recent evidence that grouping all negative emotions together as 'negative affect' may be overly simplistic (Matthews, Campbell *et al.* 2002). RST may also be incorrect in its assumptions about personality structure, given the failure of theoretically-derived constructs to cohere around factors as the theory predicts (e.g, Knyazev, Slobodskaya and Wilson 2004), although it is legitimate to question whether factor analysis is a suitable tool for identifying biologically-based systems (Corr 2004).

4. *Methodological issues.* As with Eysenck's arousal theory of personality (see Matthews and Gilliland 1999), RST has generated a range of empirical findings, some of which are consistent with prediction and some of which are not. Like arousal theory, RST risks falling into the trap of relying on post hoc rationalizations of data. Indeed, arousal itself has appeared as a moderator factor in empirical data (Corr 2002), for reasons that are not apparent from theory. A related issue (Eysenck and Eysenck 1985) is that motivational manipulations may be confounded by arousal: testing RST badly needs independent measures of the level of activity of brain motivational and arousal systems. Corr (2004) makes a brave attempt at a theoretically-motivated account of the factors that determine whether SSH or JSH predictions are supported, but it remains to be seen whether these moderator factors can be rigorously specified ante hoc. RST still appears to lack experimental paradigms that provide robust, repeatable interactive effects of personality and motivational manipulations on performance and/or psychophysiological outcomes.

5. *Functional significance of traits.* It is difficult to reconcile the bottom-up nature of RST with evidence that traits relate to active self-regulation and the person's strategic control of real-life demands and social encounters (Matthews, Schwean *et al.* 2000). Cognitive-adaptive theory (Matthews and Zeidner 2004) claims that individual differences in adaptation are pivotal to understanding personality traits, which cannot be understood solely in terms of feed-forward from underlying brain systems.

References

Averill, J.R. (1980), A constructivist view of emotion in R. Plutchik and H. Kellerman (eds), *Emotion: Theory, Research and Experience*, vol. 1, *Theories of Emotion* (San Diego: Academic Press), pp. 305–339

Barr, R.F. and McConaghy, N. (1974), Anxiety in relation to conditioning, *Behaviour Therapy and Research*, 5, 193–202

Calvo, M.G. and Castillo, M.D. (2001), Bias in predictive inferences during reading, *Discourse Processes*, 32, 43–71

Clark, D.M. (1996), Panic disorder: from theory to therapy in P.M. Salkovskis (ed.), *Frontiers of Cognitive Therapy* (New York: Guilford Press), pp. 318–344

Clore, G.L. and Ortony, A. (2000), Cognition in emotion: sometimes, always, or never? in R.D. Lane and L. Nadel (eds), *Cognitive Neuroscience of Emotion* (New York: Oxford University Press), pp. 24–61

Corr, P.J. (2002), J.A. Gray's reinforcement sensitivity theory: tests of the joint subsystem hypothesis of anxiety and impulsivity, *Personality and Individual Differences*, 33, 511–532

— (2004), Reinforcement sensitivity theory and personality, *Neuroscience and Biobehavioral Reviews*, 28, 317–332

Corr, P.J., Pickering, A.D. and Gray, J.A. (1995), Personality and reinforcement in associative and instrumental learning, *Personality and Individual Differences*, 19, 47–72

— (1997), Personality, punishment, and procedural learning: a test of J.A. Gray's anxiety theory, *Journal of Personality and Social Psychology*, 73, 337–344

Deci, E.L. and Ryan, R.M. (2000), The 'what' and 'why' of goal pursuits: human needs and the self-determination of behavior, *Psychological Inquiry*, 11, 227–268

Derryberry, D. and Reed, M.A. (1997), Motivational and attentional components of personality in G. Matthews (ed.), *Cognitive Science Perspectives on Personality and Emotion* (Amsterdam: Elsevier), pp. 443–473

Ekman, P. (1999), Basic emotions in T. Dalgleish and M.J. Power (eds), *Handbook of Cognition and Emotion* (New York: Wiley), pp. 45–60

Eysenck, H.J. (1981), General features of the model in H.J. Eysenck (ed.), *A Model for Personality* (New York: Springer-Verlag), pp. 1–37

Eysenck, H.J. and Eysenck, M.W. (1985), *Personality and Individual Differences* (New York: Plenum)

Fox, E., Russo, R., Bowles, R. and Dutton, K. (2001), Do threatening stimuli draw or hold visual attention in subclinical anxiety?, *Journal of Experimental Psychology: General*, 130, 681–700

Gray, J.A. (1991), Neural systems, emotion and personality in J. Madden IV (ed.), *Neurobiology of Learning, Emotion and Affect* (New York: Raven Press), pp. 273–306

Gray, J.A. and McNaughton, N. (2000), *The Neuropsychology of Anxiety: an Enquiry into the Functions of the Septo-hippocampal System* (2nd edn, Oxford: Oxford University Press)

Gupta, S. (1990), Impulsivity/sociability and reinforcement in verbal operant conditioning: a replication, *Personality and Individual Differences*, 11, 585–590

Hagekull, B. and Bohlin, G. (2003), Early temperament and attachment as predictors of the five factor model of personality, *Attachment and Human Development*, 5, 2–18

Heponiemi, T., Keltikangas-Järvinen, L., Kettunen, J., Puttonen, S. and Ravaja, N. (2004), BIS-BAS sensitivity and cardiac autonomic stress profiles, *Psychophysiology*, 41, 37–45

Heubeck, B.G., Wilkinson, R.B. and Cologon, J. (1998), A second look at Carver and White's (1994) BIS/BAS scales, *Personality and Individual Differences*, 25, 785–800

Hockey, G.R.J. (1984), Varieties of attentional state: the effects of the environment in R. Parasuraman and D.R. Davies (eds), *Varieties of Attention* (New York: Academic), pp. 156–189

Johnson, E.J. and Tversky, A. (1984), Representations of perceptions of risks, *Journal of Experimental Psychology: General*, 113, pp. 20–31

Knyazev, G.G., Slobodskaya, H.R. and Wilson, G.D. (2004), Comparison of the construct validity of the Gray-Wilson Personality Questionnaire and the BIS/BAS scales, *Personality and Individual Differences*, 37, 1565–1582

Larsen, R.J. and Ketelaar, T. (1991), Personality and susceptibility to positive and negative emotional states, *Journal of Personality and Social Psychology*, 55, 132–140

Lazarus, R.S. (1991), *Emotion and Adaptation* (Oxford: Oxford University Press) (1999), *Stress and Emotion: a New Synthesis* (New York: Springer)

LeDoux, J.E. (1998), *The Emotional Brain: the Mysterious Underpinnings of Emotional Life* (London: Phoenix)

Levey, A.B. and Martin, I. (1981), Personality and conditioning in H.J. Eysenck (ed.), *A Model for Personality* (Berlin: Springer), pp. 123–168

Matthews, G. (1997), Extraversion, emotion and performance: a cognitive-adaptive model in G. Matthews (ed.), *Cognitive Science Perspectives on Personality and Emotion* (Amsterdam: Elsevier), pp. 339–442

(2000), A cognitive science critique of biological theories of personality traits, *History and Philosophy of Psychology*, 2, 1–17

(2004), Neuroticism from the top down: psychophysiology and negative emotionality in R. Stelmack (ed.), *On the Psychobiology of Personality: Essays in Honor of Marvin Zuckerman* (Amsterdam: Elsevier Science), pp. 249–266

Matthews, G., Campbell, S.E., Falconer, S., Joyner, L., Huggins, J., Gilliland, K., Grier, R. and Warm, J.S. (2002), Fundamental dimensions of subjective state in performance settings: task engagement, distress and worry, *Emotion*, 2, 315–340

Matthews, G., Deary, I.J. and Whiteman, M.C. (2003), *Personality Traits* (2nd edn, Cambridge: Cambridge University Press)

Matthews, G., Derryberry, D. and Siegle, G.J. (2000), Personality and emotion: cognitive science perspectives in S.E. Hampson (ed.), *Advances in Personality Psychology* (London: Routledge), vol. 1, pp. 199–237

Matthews, G., Emo, A.K., Funke, G., Zeidner, M., Roberts, R.D., Costa, P.T. Jr and Schulze, R. (2006), Emotional intelligence, personality, and task-induced stress, *Journal of Experimental Psychology: Applied*, 12, 96–107

Matthews, G. and Gilliland, K. (1999), The personality theories of H.J. Eysenck and J.A. Gray: a comparative review, *Personality and Individual Differences*, 26, 583–626

Matthews, G. and Harley, T.A. (1993), Effects of extraversion and self-report arousal on semantic priming: a connectionist approach, *Journal of Personality and Social Psychology*, 65, 735–756

Matthews, G., Hillyard, E.J. and Campbell, S.E. (1999), Metacognition and maladaptive coping as components of test anxiety, *Clinical Psychology and Psychotherapy*, 6, 111–125

Matthews, G., Jones, D.M. and Chamberlain, A.G. (1990), Refining the measurement of mood: the UWIST mood adjective checklist, *British Journal of Psychology*, 81, 17–42

Matthews, G., Schwean, V.L., Campbell, S.E., Saklofske, D.H. and Mohamed A.A.R. (2000), Personality, self-regulation and adaptation: a cognitive-social framework in M. Boekarts, P.R. Pintrich and M. Zeidner (eds), *Handbook of Self-regulation* (New York: Academic), pp. 171–207

Matthews, G. and Zeidner, M. (2004), Traits, states and the trilogy of mind: an adaptive perspective on intellectual functioning in D. Dai and R.J. Sternberg (eds), *Motivation, Emotion, and Cognition: Integrative Perspectives on Intellectual Functioning and Development* (Mahwah, NJ: Lawrence Erlbaum), pp. 143–174

McNaughton, N. and Corr, P.J. (2004), A two-dimensional neuropsychology of defense: fear/anxiety and defensive distance, *Neuroscience and Biobehavioral Reviews*, 28, 285–305

McNaughton, N. and Gray, A. (2000), Anxiolytic action on the behavioural inhibition system implies multiple types of arousal contribute to anxiety, *Journal of Affective Disorders*, 61, 161–176

Morrone-Strupinsky, J.V. and Depue, R.A. (2004), Differential relation of two distinct, film-induced positive emotional states to affiliative and agentic extraversion, *Personality and Individual Differences*, 36, 1109–1126

Newell, A. (1982), The knowledge level, *Artificial Intelligence*, 18, 87–127

Panksepp, J. (1998), *Affective Neuroscience: the Foundations of Human and Animal Emotions* (New York: Oxford University Press)

Pylyshyn, Z.W. (1999), What's in your mind? in E. Lepore and Z.W. Pylyshyn (eds), *What is Cognitive Science?* (Malden, MA: Blackwell), pp. 1–25

Rolls, E.T. (1999), *The Brain and Emotion* (New York: Oxford University Press)

Rusting, C.L. and Larsen, R.J. (1997), Extraversion, neuroticism, and susceptibility to positive and negative affect: a test of two theoretical models, *Personality and Individual Differences*, 22, 607–612

Schmidt, N.B., Lerew, D.R. and Jackson, R.J. (1999), Prospective evaluation of anxiety sensitivity in the pathogenesis of panic: replication and extension, *Journal of Abnormal Psychology*, 108, 532–537

Smith, B.D., Davidson, R.A., Smith, D.L., Goldstein, H. and Perlstein, W. (1989), Sensation seeking and arousal: effects of strong stimulation on electrodermal activation and memory task performance, *Personality and Individual Differences*, 10, 671–679

Spence, K.W. (1964), Anxiety (drive) level and performance in eyelid conditioning, *Psychological Bulletin*, 61, 129–139

Thayer, R.E. (1989), *The Biopsychology of Mood and Arousal* (Oxford: Oxford University Press)

Watson, D. (2000), *Mood and Temperament* (New York: Guilford Press)

Wells, A. (2000), *Emotional Disorders and Metacognition: Innovative Cognitive Therapy* (Chichester: Wiley)

Wells, A. and Matthews, G. (1994), *Attention and Emotion: a Clinical Perspective* (Hove: Erlbaum)

(2005), Cognitive vulnerability to anxiety disorders: an integration in L.B. Alloy and J.H. Riskind (eds), *Cognitive Vulnerability to Emotional Disorders* (Hillsdale, NJ: Lawrence Erlbaum), pp. 303–325

Whiteside, S.P. and Lynam, D. (2001), The Five Factor Model and Impulsivity: using a Structural Model of Personality to Understand Impulsivity, *Personality and Individual Differences*, 30, 669–689

Wilson, G.D., Barrett, P.T. and Gray, J.A. (1989), Human reactions to reward and punishment: a questionnaire examination of Gray's personality theory, *British Journal of Psychology*, 80, 509–515

Zeidner, M. and Matthews, G. (2005), Evaluation anxiety in A.J. Elliot and C.S. Dweck (eds), *Handbook of Competence and Motivation* (New York: Guilford Press), pp. 141–163

Zinbarg, R. and Revelle, W. (1989), Personality and conditioning: a test of four models, *Personality and Social Psychology*, 57, 301–314

Zuckerman, M. (1991), *Psychobiology of Personality* (Cambridge: Cambridge University Press)

18 The contribution of Reinforcement
Sensitivity Theory to personality theory

William Revelle

The breadth of Jeffrey Gray's contributions to psychology is barely touched in the various chapters of this book. This is not a criticism of the authors, but of the task that the editor set them. For to honor Jeffrey Gray in a single volume is an impossible task. As all of the contributers have said so well, Jeffrey was a remarkable man. Warm and caring to his friends and colleagues, linguistically skilled, familiar with theater and music in multiple languages, Jeffrey developed a biological model of personality that has become so well established that it has persisted even after he drastically changed it. To those who study personality psychology, the preceding chapters of this book are essential requirements that allow us to take advantage of the careful research and broad scholarship that went into Jeffrey Gray's work.

Personality theory is concerned with describing and explaining the observed complexity of individual differences in the patterning of affect, behavior, cognition and desires over time and space. At the descriptive level, there is moderately strong consensus that three to six broad domains can be used to organize how people describe themselves and others. People differ in the power they exert over others, in the affection they show others, in the quality of their work, in their tendency to react emotionally, in the openness of their interests to intellectual inquiry and in their basic intellectual ability. In his discussions of adult personality, particularly in the workplace, Hogan and his colleagues have distinguished between personality as we see ourselves (our identity) and personality as others see us (our reputation). He categorizes the tasks that we face as those of getting along and getting ahead and suggests that much of human behavior is in interaction with other humans as we are faced with agentic and communal roles (Hogan, Hogan and Roberts 1996; Hogan and Kaiser 2005; Hogan and Roberts 2004).

Although there is agreement that most if not all of the dimensions of personality at the descriptive level have moderate additive heritabilities

(McGue and Bouchard 1998), this says nothing about the mechanism. For those who worry about mechanism (i.e., the readers of this book), the path from genes to behavior must go through proteins, biological networks, structures and systems, which in turn are tuned by the individual's history of environmental experience. (Individual differences in the capacity to learn language or to be religious are heritable, but what language one uses or what religion one espouses is a function of environmental experience.)

The proposed biological mechanisms should be consistent with our knowledge of evolutionary theory. A fundamental assumption of evolution is preservation of function across species. Hearts, lungs, the circulatory system and the central nervous system did not evolve independently in different species but rather were selectively modified to meet particular evolutionary challenges. It might be comforting to think that human affect, behavior and cognition are unique, but the uniqueness is one of degree, not of kind.

Jeffrey Gray took advantage of this assumption of evolutionary preservation and studied the rat, particularly the rat's response to anti-anxiety drugs, to study human personality. Earlier versions of 'the Gray model' have become so well established in the field that they can be thought of as the 'standard model' for the biological basis of personality. Variations of the dimensional analysis of the Behavioral Inhibition System and the Behavioral Approach System have been integrated into most causal theories of personality. Whether it is the BIS and BAS of Gray (1970), of Fowles (1980, 1984), or of Depue and Collins (1999), the two systems approach has been the foundation of biologically driven theories.

But the original Gray model was wrong. It failed the basic criterion of science in that it did not predict what it should have predicted and did not match our growing understanding of biological mechanisms. The best evidence for the model's failure was, of course, in the later work of Jeffrey Gray and his colleagues (Corr 2004; Gray and McNaughton 2000; Pickering and Gray 2001). This was the real strength of Jeffrey's contributions: he was able to develop a testable theory that could be rejected based upon data. Not only did he develop such a theory, he was the one who was able to put together the evidence of its failure. But not content with merely testing (and rejecting) his prior work, Jeffrey continued to develop a much more complex model that is both biologically more accurate and simultaneously harder to test. For the newer theory attempts to model the complexity of three interacting brain systems, each with multiple sub-systems.

Although many of us have referred to 'Gray's theory of personality', as Pickering (chapter 16) points out, Jeffrey himself thought this was pompous and preferred to use the term – suggested by Pickering – *Reinforcement Sensitivity Theory* (RST). I think this label is unfortunate, for although this book discusses Reinforcement Sensitivity Theory, Jeffrey's major contribution to personality theory should probably better be known as Three Systems Theory (3ST). The biologically and behaviorally based distinctions between the Behavioral Inhibition System, the Behavioral Approach System and the Fight-Flight-Freeze System has had a greater impact upon personality theory than the fundamental analysis of how these systems respond to appetitive and aversive cues in the process of learning. Just as the original distinction between analyzing behavior in terms of action tendencies (BAS) and inhibition of action (BIS) made contact with non-biological models of action (e.g., Atkinson and Birch 1970) that focused on general action and 'negaction' tendencies, so can we hope that the Three Systems Theory will lead to broader conceptualizations of the complexity of human behavior.

RST is a projective test. Everyone brings their own theoretical biases and fits them into RST. RST is a fundamental approach to the problem of the biological basis of personality. RST recognizes the importance of analyzing ongoing behavior in the face of potentially aversive and rewarding cues in a goal directed motivational context that depends upon past histories of rewards and punishments. In contrast to many personality researchers who limit themselves to single behaviors associated with single dimensions of personality, the contributors to this volume have focused on the complex interplay of three systems and two types of cues as they lead to learning and performance.

Much of this book focuses on differential responses of the three systems to cues for punishment and reward (with a particular emphasis upon the BIS and BAS), but ignores that much of behavior is not directly motivated by environmental reinforcers. Most of animal and human learning is not directly reinforced but is rather learning how to parse the continuous flow of input from the sensory system into meaning. Infants exposed to the buzzing confusion of the stream of sounds and light that adults associate with words, sentences and objects need to learn to parse the stream into words that then lead to associations with objects and action (Hespos and Spelke 2004). For adults, much of our learning is implicit and semantic and not directly associated with reinforcement (Reber, Gitelman, Parrish and Mesulam 2003). For the rat, as we have known for years, exploring mazes will lead to knowing the structure of mazes, even without direct rewards. It is only when reinforcements are made explicit that the learning results in motivated action (Blodgett 1929; Tolman 1948; Tolman and Honzik 1930).

Although it is possible to learn without reinforcement, that there are different brain systems to (learn how to) approach, to avoid and to inhibit is fundamental to current personality theory. The discussions in the preceding chapters have focused on learning to approach given appetitive cues and learning to avoid given aversive cues, and the use of an inhibitory system to resolve conflict in the case when the cues themselves are conflicting. However, a broader interpretation of these three systems (Furnham and Jackson, chapter 15) is that we can distinguish between general tendencies for action and inaction, approach, avoidance and inhibition (Atkinson and Birch 1970; Elliot and Thrash 2002; Humphreys and Revelle 1984; Kuhl and Blankenship 1979; Revelle 1993; Revelle and Michaels 1976).

The authors of the preceding chapters uniformly have recognized the complex patterns of predictions that a thoughtful analysis of RST produces. The scope of the chapters is inspiring, for they range from discussions of evolutionary reasons for three systems (Ávila and Torrubia, chapter 7), to discussions of the molecular genetics and neurophysiology of each system (Reuter, chapter 10) to techniques in measurement (Pickering and Smillie, chapter 4; Torrubia, Ávila and Caseras, chapter 6), and the implications for psychopathology (Knyazev, Wilson and Slobodskaya, chapter 14; Wallace and Newman , chapter 13; Zinbarg and Yoon, chapter 12), health (Keltikangas-Järvinen, chapter 11) and performance in the workplace (Furnham and Jackson, chapter 15).

RST1 and RST2: does it make a difference?

The basic contribution of the original theory, RST1, was not that specific neural structures related to specific behaviors, but that it was possible to integrate aspects of the central nervous system (CNS) into a conceptual nervous system (cns) composed of approach and inhibition systems. RST1 gave plausible (and different) neural underpinnings to the descriptive and causal theory of Hans Eysenck (1967). RST1 and its variants became the standard model of biologically oriented personality theories. Indeed, even as the axes of RST1 slowly rotated towards Extraversion and Neuroticism, the explanation of Eysenck's E/N dimensions became more 'Gray like' (e.g., Corr, chapter 1; Gomez and Cooper, chapter 9; Matthews and Gilliland 1999).

Most tests of the human personality aspects of the theory were not at the biological level but rather at the conceptual systems level. This is a point of irritation for Pickering (chapter 16) who thinks that the human level results were not directly applicable to the theory. Tests of reward or punishment sensitivity could involve conditioning (e.g., Zinbarg and

Mohlman 1998; Zinbarg and Revelle 1989) and classification tasks (Rogers and Revelle 1998) as they related to self-report inventories. These studies did not attempt to relate these behaviors to parts of the septal-hippocampal loop, but were expressed at the conceptual level of rewards, punishments and positive and negative affect.

RST2 was a major revision of RST1 at both the physiological level and at the conceptual level, with much of the emphasis of aversive cue sensitivity switching towards the FFFS, but the changes in predictions were not as immediately obvious. Indeed, most references to Gray's theory of personality are still references to RST1 and are oblivious to RST2. One of the goals of this book is to bring the newer model to the broader research community. In addition to this text, the recent articles by Corr (2004) and Smillie, Pickering and Jackson (2006) do much to enlighten personality researchers not directly connected to the 'RST mafia'.

Basic theory

The distinctions between RST1 and RST2 are laid out in the early chapters by Corr (chapter 1), McNaugton and Corr (chapter 2) and are formally modeled by Pickering (chapter 16). These reviews are very helpful in highlighting the changes that RST underwent both in the biological bases of the three systems as well as the behavioral implications of the new model.

In a masterful review, Corr (chapter 1) directly addresses the question of why use RST2 when RST1 is so well understood. Does the human theorist really need to care about the subtleties of brain function (McNaugton and Corr, chapter 2)? Yes and No. No in terms of distinctions between the relative importance of the medial hypothalmus versus the amygdala. But yes in terms of the revised importance of the Fight-Flight-Freeze System and the modified role of the Behavioral Inhibition System. RST2 has dropped the conditioned/unconditioned aversive stimuli distinction and now emphasizes that the FFFS is involved in reactions to all aversive stimuli, the BAS in reactions to all appetitive stimuli, and the BIS in resolving goal conflicts in general (that is, not just approach-avoidance, but also avoidance-avoidance and approach-approach; see also Zinbarg and Yoon, chapter 12).

In agreement with some of the human clinical literature, RST2 now distinguishes between fear and anxiety. It adds an emphasis upon both defensive distance and defensive direction. An analysis of the defensive distance for eliciting fight, freezing or flight will be an important addition to human models. In the rat, defensive distance may be directly measured, but in the human the concept is more in the cognitive representation of threat. Evaluating biases in cognitive estimates of the strength and distance of aversive cues will be a useful framework for testing the application of the model as it relates to trait and state measures of anxiety.

As a powerful demonstration of the utility of the original model, RST1, Ávila and Torrubia's review (chapter 7) integrates RST1's biological approach with modern studies of the effect of anxiety and extraversion on conditioning. They review Newman's interpretation of Gray (Newman and Wallace, chapter 13; see also Patterson and Newman 1993) and point out that it is the differences in the learning of aversive associations in conditions that can lead to reward and punishments that are essential to understanding disinhibition. They also examine Corr's separable versus joint subsystems distinction (SSH and JSH) and outline the conditions when SSH is true (strong appetitive/ aversive stimuli, extreme scores, no mix of aversive and appetitive stimuli, no need for rapid attentional shifts). They make the interesting point that approach tendencies are continuously reviewed and can be extinguished whereas inhibitory tendencies are prone to be maintained through successful advoidance. As is seen also in many of the other chapters, Ávila and Torrubia discuss how human research is different from animals and emphasize the role of expectations and the motivational context.

Too many theories in personality are verbal descriptions of complex patterns of affect, cognition and behavior. RST tends to fall into this trap and has many different interpretations. This is a particular problem in the way many of us address the implications of RST. Some of these theoretical descriptions include structural models of relationships (e.g., Furnham and Jackson, chapter 15; Humphreys and Revelle 1984) that are admittedly unclear in the specific pattern of predictions.

Pickering (chapter 16) addresses this problem and begins to formalize the model in terms of a static model of the pattern of predicted relationships. He recognizes the need to convert these static models into dynamic simulations and reports some progress in this endeavor (see also Smillie, Pickering and Jackson 2006). He further points out that, although logically the variables of interest are the sensitivity weights associating cues for reward and punishment with activation of the BAS and FFFS, these weights are probably not open to self-awareness, but that the affective, behavioral and cognitive reactions produced by BAS and FFFS are open to self-report. This highlights a major complication in terms of testing the theoretical predictions with respect to self-report personality variables, for the fundamental variables are not open to awareness.

Although RST is a theory of three systems, the emphasis has traditionally been upon the BIS and more recently the FFFS. The biological underpinnings of anxiety from the RST perspective are well reviewed by Gray and McNaughton (2000) but those of the BAS are underplayed. This lack of emphasis on the BAS is compensated for by Pickering and Smillie (chapter 4) who do an excellent job at reviewing the physiological structures proposed to underlie the BAS.

In addition to the biological correlates, they ask whether the BAS is perhaps oversold. In 1995 I suggested that the BAS has been associated with most of the approach traits (extraversion, impulsivity, novelty seeking and positive affectivity) as well as states of positive affect (Revelle 1995). Pickering and Smillie (chapter 4) ask whether this promiscuity of associations is due to the importance of the BAS, or due to theoretical difficulties in defining the concept.

The original association of BAS with impulsivity was unfortunate, and Pickering and Smillie review the biopsychological and behavioral data suggesting that dopaminergic functioning and the reward system are more aligned with extraversion than with impulsivity. Unfortunately, although extraversion can be better measured than impulsivity (e.g., Revelle 1997), purified measures of extraversion leave something to be desired. Even correcting for attenuation does not lead to perfectly correlated measures (Goldberg et al. 2006). This is a problem not for RST but for the broader study of personality. This problem of measurement can partly be resolved by focusing on discriminant validity, particularly focusing on what a putative measure does not measure, rather than the convergent validities of our psychological constructs.

Biological correlates

Reuter (chapter 10) provides a very thoughtful analysis of current work in molecular genetics and the current work trying to associate candidate genes with candidate brain structures. This work is hindered by the problems of measurement of RST constructs at the personality item/scale level. The proposed measurement of endophenotypes of RST identified by fMRI and PET requires better identification of those endophenotypes than is currently possible. RST is a link between genetics, the proteins for which genes code, the structures and transmitters associated with those proteins, and higher-level approach and inhibition and fighting/fleeing behaviors that we see at the level of the whole organism. The multiplicity of genes associated with the dopaminergic system that is presumably the underpinning of the BAS makes it quite clear that the data force us to reject the one gene-one disease (OGOD) model, or its generalization to the one gene-one system hypothesis (OGOSH).

De Pascalis (chapter 8) thoroughly reviews the problems of correlating psychophysiological measures with putative measures derived from RST. The patterns of correlations are generally supportive of BIS/BAS distinctions, but are less consistent with respect to specific localizations of function. The early work by Sutton and Davidson (1997) suggesting a lateralization of functioning for the BIS versus the BAS has been called into question by the effects of anger and approach on frontal activation (Harmon-Jones, Sigelman, Bohlig and Harmon-Jones 2003). De Pascalis' conclusion matches that of many of the other authors in this volume, that there is a great deal of promise but a great deal that needs to be known before we can definitively assess RST1 or RST2.

Keltikangas-Järvinen (chapter 11) reviews the physiological and health risks associated with a reactive negative system (equated with the BIS) and a reactive positive system (equated with the BAS.) The emphasis upon BIS vs. BAS leads to thinking of affect as one bipolar dimension and similarly tends to focus on BIS-BAS as a bipolar dimension. Perhaps this is a misinterpretation, for the evidence for the multidimensionality of affect is compelling (Matthews *et al.* 2002; Rafaeli and Revelle 2006). Keltikangas-Järvinen recognizes the problem of measurement with BIS-BAS but does not focus so much on the complexity of a theory where the two systems interact with each other. Furthermore, by focusing on health correlates of BIS and BAS, the possibility of curvilinear, non-monotonc, associations is ignored; that is, it is important to consider the functional significance of both systems. It is likely that there are benefits and costs associated with each system and the optimal level is at some middle point (see below for a further discussion of the challenge on optimality for theory testing).

Are animal models appropriate for human personality?

The RST was derived from work primarily based upon rats. (Jeffrey used to confess that he was a 'rat psychologist who would surface every seven years to see what had happened in human personality'. Concluding that not much had happened, he would return to the rat lab.) A recurring theme throughout the book is that Gray's theory is rat-based and humans are more complicated. Is a biologically-driven theory, derived from rats, applicable to humans? Many of the chapters address this issue, and most suggest that the answer is yes. Much of behavior is reflexive or routine and does not involve complex cognition (Ortony, Norman and Revelle 2005). That the behavior reflects prior experience and situational context is given, but that a rat-based model is adequate for developing theories for complex human feelings, thoughts and actions may be challenged.

Matthews (chapter 17) rises to this challenge and suggests that a cognitive science approach of computation is the most useful level of analysis. But this fails to address the important contributions of behavior genetics and physiology. Even taking a cognitive science approach, we should distinguish between the information being processed and the computational limitations of the processor. Individual differences in the activation of the three systems lead to different information being stored in associative memories and different bias settings in the coding of environments based upon these prior memories, as well as different resource limitations. Nonetheless, Matthews' request for a formal computational model is appropriate and a connectionist architecture along the lines sketched out by Pickering (chapter 16) is a beginning.

McNaughton and Corr (chapter 3) respond to Matthews' critique in a forthright defense of the use of animal models to study human personality. To add to this debate is not necessary, but irresistible. It should be noted that almost sixty years ago Tolman (1948) discussed animal models of cognition in a computational form that would appeal to the most cognitive of psychologists. To Matthews, the contribution of cognitive science is the requirement for computational models, but to others, the great breakthrough from strict behaviorism to cognitive psychology was the introduction of latent constructs and intervening variables. The conceptual nervous system approach of Hebb, particularly as utilized by Gray, follows this approach by creating high-level summaries (BAS/BIS/FFFS) and idealizations of low level 'wetware'.

Can biological theories address cognitive problems?

That one's biology affects one's cognitions is the primary focus of those who study energetic components of mood and emotion. Changes in arousal and affect, by changing resource availability and resource allocation, affect the relative strengths and foci of competing cognitive processes (Humphreys and Revelle 1984; Revelle 1993). But this is a two-way street, for changing cognitions will change arousal and affect. That the internal, cognitive representations of external contingencies of reinforcement need to be considered has been clear for decades. Weiner and Schneider (1971) showed that the interaction of test anxiety with task difficulty effects, so clearly demonstrated by Spence, Farber and McFann (1956), was due to subjects interpreting their performance as success or failure (and thus rewarding or punishing). When success/failure was made explicit by the experimenter, the anxiety by feedback interaction drove the results; that is, the experimental participants' cognitive interpretations of the situation overcame any potential physiological differences in anxiety-related drive.

A recurring theme in cognitive models of personality and performance is that there are multiple levels of control. Low-level, reactive responses to stimuli can be controlled by routines that have become automaticized and require little to no cognitive resources. Although much of human behavior probably occurs at this routine level, higher-level reflective processes can (and do) override them to facilitate the approach of long-term goals and to resolve conflict (Ortony, Norman and Revelle 2005). Similar hierarchical models of control have been proposed by Broadbent (1971), Mulder (1986) and Revelle (1993).

But such levels of control are not unique to cognitively-oriented models. RST2 specifically incorporates levels of control into the neurophysiology of anxiety with prefrontal cortically-based linguistic control systems overriding and interacting with subcortical and archicortical control of anxiety (Gray and McNaughton 2000). (See also MacLean 1990 for an earlier neurologically-based hierarchical model of control and Corr, chapter 1, for the place of cognitive control in RST2.)

RST and psychopathology

A fundamental hypothesis to the dimensional approach to psychopathology is that psychopathology represents extreme scores on normal personality traits. Separately, a basic statistical concept is that small differences in the means or variances of two groups on an underlying dimension can lead to large differences in the relative frequencies in which these two groups are seen at extreme scores of this dimension. The combination of the continuity hypothesis with the extremity effect allows for powerful tests of theory by using psychopathological groups, for small mean differences in the groups can be detected in the relative frequency of rare events. The phenomenon of disinhibition and psychopathy is an excellent example of this approach. Psychopathy is characterized as extreme disinhibition. Although the incidence of 'psychopaths' is less than 1 per cent in the population, they represent up to 25 per cent of the population of prisons. Using prisoners is thus a powerful technique for studying subtle correlates of disinhibition with personality traits associated with the RST.

Wallace and Newman (chapter 13) consider the proposed distinction between primary and secondary psychopaths in terms of the old and the new RST and find that the pattern of relationships is much more compatible with the revised model. Traditionally, primary psychopaths are characterized as having low BIS activity while secondary psychopaths have a superactive BAS. Factor analyses of the Psychopathy Checklist leads to a two-(correlated) factor solution with factor 1 reflecting BIS- and factor 2 BAS+. Wallace and Newman suggest that BIS/BAS moderate the expression of the general trait.

Knyazev, Wilson and Slobodskaya (chapter 14) take an evolutionary perspective to suggest that both an overactive BIS or BAS can lead to maladjustment and suggest that some balance in the activation level of the two systems is optimal. Based upon an analysis of Corr's joint subsystems hypothesis they suggest that low levels of both might lead to more favorable adjustment. In emphasizing the role that cognitive ability plays as a control process, they report that ability moderates the negative effects of high BAS, with low ability students showing larger BAS effects. In their treatment of the BIS/BAS system as a 'gargantuan two' they describe what is functionally Wundt's organization of Galen's four temperaments in terms of BIS/BAS balance. Although not described in so many words, their conclusion is that the phlegmatic (low BIS and low BAS) is most socially adjusted and that extreme scores and in particular a lack of BIS/BAS balance hinders resiliency and stability.

Zinbarg and Yoon (chapter 12) provide a very compelling review of how RST (both old and new) fits into the clinical literature on depression and different sub-types of anxiety. They take full advantage of the experimental psychopathology literature and relate it to the structural differences discussed in Gray and McNaughton. Zinbarg and Yoon show how a hierarchical model of anxiety can be conceptualized in terms of RST. More importantly, Zinbarg and Yoon propose, based upon the experimental and correlational clinical data, theoretical challenges to RST that need to be addressed.

RST in the broader context

A potential weakness of RST is that it has failed to be seen as relevant to the broader psychological community. Furnham and Jackson (chapter 15) provide a brief review of the lack of contact between RST and work-related concepts. As they point out, this partly reflects the general lack of connection between mainstream personality researchers and organizational theorists, but also reflects the lack of an emphasis upon measurement of the RST constructs. Although personality trait approaches are making inroads into industrial/organizational psychology, this is either through poorly defined (but popular) measures such as the Myers-Briggs type inventory (see Pittenger 2005 for a strong critique of this practice) or much better defined but still non-RST-related inventories such as the NEO-PI-R (Costa and McCrae 1992) or Hogan Personality Inventory (Hogan and Hogan 1995). What is missing is a theory-based set of predictions of what leads to effective performance in the work place.

Furnham and Jackson (chapter 15) follow earlier proposals (e.g., Humphreys and Revelle 1984) and view RST constructs as biological/ temperamental distal causes that combine with those motivational and situational demand variables that have been referred to as 'characterological' and that lead to behavior. Their model abstracts the common thread of RST and recent work on human motivation (e.g., Elliot and Church 1997; Elliot and Thrash 2002) with a focus on approach and inhibition of behavior. It would be useful also to generalize the model to examine how goals such as promotion of gains versus prevention of losses (Higgins *et al.* 2003) relate to the more distal components of the RST. Their broad approach, which integrates the biological structures of RST with cognitive representations of goals as well as past histories of experience, emphasizes the strength of RST as an integrative theory.

Issues for the future

How to measure the basic components?

A requirement for any theory is that it should specify how to be tested. To test RST requires adequate measurement of the fundamental constructs. But, as has been suggested in multiple chapters, there has been remarkably little concern as to how to measure individual differences in BIS, BAS or FFFS. This is partly because each of these constructs is specified at the biological/conceptual nervous system level and results in a complex patterning of affect, behavior and cognition in the context of an individual's desires (or goals). Many of the predictions of the model are of the type that, for example, people who have an active BAS and a weak BIS and a weak FFFS when faced with a cue for reward and also a cue for punishment will do X. But this does not lead to an easy self-report or observational item. Torrubia, Ávila and Caseras (chapter 6) address the measurement problem and attempt to directly develop self-report scales to assess the RST. Part of the difficulty in measurement results from what Wittmann (1988) describes as 'Brunswickian Symmetry'. Broad constructs predict at broad levels of analysis and are not nearly as effective at narrow levels. Similarly, narrow trait measures are not particularly useful for predictions of broad criteria.

The failure to line up reinforcement sensitivity scales directly with the axes of the Eysenck PEN or the Big Five/Five Factor models does not invalidate RST, but rather suggests that the fundamental axes of RST are not well understood in their identification at the trait level. This might be a result of measuring traits using self-report inventories. As Pickering proposes, people are probably not aware of their sensitivities to cues for positive and negative reinforcement, but rather are aware of the patterning of behaviors associated with those cues. In addition, it is likely that the observed surface traits reflect complex combinations of the underlying parameters of the RST. A similar problem occurred with the original formulation of BIS/BAS theory with respect to the surface traits of extraversion and neuroticism. Extraversion was seen as the difference between BAS and BIS, while neuroticism was seen as their sum.

In an attempt to relate biological constructs to surface traits, Gray mapped the BAS and BIS onto impulsivity and anxiety. Given the importance of the Eysenck (1967) two space of E and N, and the original model of anxiety as reflecting the BIS, this was a rational choice at the time as Gray was attempting to integrate BIS/BAS within the Eysenckian framework while simultaneously explaining anxiety. The identification of the BAS with impulsivity was an unfortunate choice, partly because of the multidimensional structure of impulsivity. Just as the meaning of extraversion has changed over the years, so has the meaning and measurement of impulsivity. Impulsivity is probably a mix of sensitivity to reward and a lack of inhibitory control.

Just as the measurement of sensitivity to aversive events and tendencies towards behavioral inhibition can be shown to have a hierarchical structure (Zinbarg and Yoon, chapter 12), so part of the confusion on the measurement of BAS (Pickering and Smillie, chapter 4) probably reflects a hierarchical structure of approach-like traits. Hierarchical factor models are typical in the measurement of intelligence, where lower-level ability factors are found to be correlated and a higher-order factor (g) can be extracted (Carroll 1993) and loadings on g and orthogonal lower-order factors can be found using the Schmid Leiman transformaton (Jensen and Weng 1994; Schmid and Leiman 1957). Unfortunately, with the exception of Zinbarg and his colleagues (Zinbarg et al. 2005, 2006) such hierarchical models are not common in the non-cognitive domains of personality. The BAS-like traits are a probable candidate for showing a general factor running through all of the measures with specific sub-domains represented in each test.

At the broadest level, a general factor common to the entire approach domain can be taken as representing BAS_g, but each particular test is only partially saturated with BAS_g, and has specific components. A classic example of this are the BAS scales from Carver and White's BIS/BAS scales (Carver and White 1994). The BAS scale breaks down into three correlated sub-factors, the common component of which could be seen as BAS_g. This point is reminiscent of the debate between Eysenck (1967) and Guilford (1975) as to whether there is a common factor to sociability and impulsivity (i.e., extraversion), with Eysenck arguing for a common higher-order factor, and Guilford criticizing extraversion as shotgun marriage of two unrelated traits.

Optimal level of activation of all three systems, separately and combined

Activation of any one system is going to have costs and benefits. But all three systems are working in unison and the problem becomes one of finding the optimal value for all three systems in a changing world. Are the costs of one system the benefits of the others? Consider this analysis for the Behavioral Approach/Activation System. Low levels of BAS, and low responsiveness to cues for reward, will lead to sluggish behavior and a low frequency of reward. Increasing the BAS will lead to an increasing frequency of reward. But activation bears an energetic cost and risk from predation or other threats. Even more activation leads to more energy expenditure (and greater risk). If the benefits saturate and the costs grow, there will be an optimal level of BAS activity. An unfettered BAS is manic, not adaptive. More moderate levels of BAS will avoid both sluggishness and mania.

Similarly, low activation of the FFFS will make one a convenient target for predators and lead to inadequate avoidance (by either fighting or fleeing). But too high a setting will lead to constant avoidance and an inability to ever engage in a task. In that the BIS resolves conflicts between BIS and FFFS through inhibition of both, once again, a moderate level leads to more systematic and sensitive control.

The challenge of optimality is that it implies that correlations with effective functioning will be curvilinear rather than monotonic. The 'Goldilocks principle' of not too little, not too much, likely applies to the three systems, separately as well as in combination.

An important question from an evolutionary point of view is how is diversity maintained. If the functioning of a system uniformly increases survival and offers reproductive advantage, genetic variation in the function of that system will be reduced over time. If, however, there are disadvantages for very high or very low functioning of a system, for example, of the BIS or of the BAS, then selection can lead to a balanced polymorphism. Although most researchers examine the characteristics of high BIS and high BAS, Ávila makes the interesting suggestion that those with a less active BIS are able to learn a broader repertoire of approach tasks and have a lower resistance to extinction than those with a more active BIS, and that an active BAS leads to more difficulty extinguishing a dominant response for reward than a less active BAS.

RST1 and its variants became the standard model for the biologically oriented and RST2 should as well. However, RST1 and RST2 propose different mechanisms. At the basic structural level, these are very different. At the affective, behavioral and cognitive levels they are also different, but in more subtle ways. Teasing out the implications of the RST2 (3ST) will be a research agenda for years to come.

Unresolved problems

Is the BIS a universal conflict resolver? Corr (chapter 1) and Zinbarg and Yoon (chapter 12) raise the questions about approach-approach and avoidance-avoidance conflicts. Impulsive behavior is not just not inhibiting actions that lead to aversive outcomes, it is also being distracted from doing one positive action by some other cues for some other positive action. (Writing a chapter in honor of Jeffrey Gray is a positive behavior, but impulsively checking just one more reference on the Web is another positive act that needs to be inhibited.)

What is rewarding and what is aversive? There are some prepared stimuli that are threatening (for primates, snakes and spiders seem to be prepared, guns and electric outlets are not) and rewarding (infant faces, be they humans or dogs elicit positive affect), while there are many stimuli that come to be seen as threatening or rewarding after many trials. A sailboard is not automatically a cue for either reward or a threat of danger, but is a cue for reward for the experienced windsurfer, a cue for danger from a novice who has fallen into cold water while trying to stand up on a board, and a flat plank of fiberglass to someone who has never seen the water. But where do these expectations come from? That some people find windsurfing or sailing small boats in high winds to be rewarding while others find it aversive presumably reflects years of experience on the water, with or without traumatic events.

What is the role of cognition? There is a clear role of cognition as a high-level control process in the manifestations of BIS/BAS/FFFS inter-actions. Cognitive control processes presumably are used to inhibit behavior without involving BIS activation, but these control processes can be hindered by fatigue or distraction. People learn to inhibit exhibiting stereotypic thinking but this takes cognitive and energetic resources. When evening people are asked about minority groups in the morning, they are more likely to stereotype than they are later in the day (Bodenhausen 1990). (That this is not just a direct time of day effect is shown when morning people stereotype more later in the day.)

Testability: how could we know we were wrong?

Matthews (chapter 17) raises the important question that a theory needs to be open to the possibility of disproof. That RST1 has morphed into RST2 is a sign of the testability (and rejection) of the original model. Unfortunately, the formal models of Pickering and his colleagues (chapter 16 and Smillie, Pickering and Jackson 2006) suggest that RST2 makes more complicated predictions than RST1 and that these predictions might be harder to reject, for the very complexity of the model allows it to make many, seemingly contradictory, predictions. However, we can hope that as the formal modelers are forced to specify particular ranges of parameter values, testable prediction will result.

The application of 3ST to complex behaviors in complex organizations (Furnham and Jackson, chapter 15) suggests the possibility of integration with other motivational models (e.g., achievement motivation theory as developed by Atkinson and his colleagues has seen a resurgence of interest with models of Elliot and his colleagues and is very compatible with 3ST).

RST1 and RST2 are conceptual frameworks thought to organize human and rat brain structure data. But RST1 and RST2 have been applied by some at a level that is untouched by biological theorizing. The BAS/FFFS/BIS theory at this higher level uses the terms of the biological systems but does not stand or fall on changes in our understanding of biology. This is both a strength and a weakness of the theory. Gray and his closest collaborators thought of RST2 as a biological model that could be tested at the biological level. As formulated at a generalized level, in terms of making predictions about job performance and psychopathology, the real contribution was a focus on separating a BAS from a FFFS and BIS.

Conclusion

This book is a small tribute to the contribution of Jeffrey Gray. Wrapped up as he was in his broad ranging studies of how the brain works, he perhaps did not realize the enormous contribution he had made to the study of personality. His careful and analytical approach, combined with an openness to the ideas of others, were an inspiration to far more people than just those who collaborated in this book. The impact of his work upon the field of personality in particular and psychology in general will continue to influence the research agenda in personality theory for the coming decades.

References

Atkinson, J.W. and Birch, D. (1970), *The Dynamics of Action* (New York: Wiley)

Blodgett, H.C. (1929), The effect of the introduction of reward upon the maze performance of rats, *Univ. Cal. Pub. Psychol*, 4, 113–134

Bodenhausen, G.V. (1990), Stereotypes as judgmental heuristics: evidence of circadian variations in discrimination, *Psychological Science*, 1, 319–322

Broadbent, D.E. (1971), *Decision and Stress* (London: Academic Press)

Carroll, J.B. (1993), *Human Cognitive Abilities: a Survey of Factor-Analytical Studies* (New York: Cambridge University Press)

Carver, C.S. and White, T.L. (1994), Behavioral inhibition, behavioral activation, and affective responses to impending reward and punishment: the BIS/BAS scales, *Journal of Personality and Social Psychology*, 67, 319–333

Corr, P.J. (2002), J.A. Gray's reinforcement sensitivity theory: tests of the joint subsystem hypothesis of anxiety and impulsivity, *Personality and Individual Differences*, 33, 511–532

(2004), Reinforcement sensitivity theory and personality, *Neuroscience and Biobehavioral Reviews*, 28, 317–332

Costa, P.T. Jr and McCrae R.R. (1992), *Revised NEO Personality Inventory (NEO PI-R) and the NEO Five-Factor Inventory (NEO-FFI) Professional Manual* (Odessa, FL: Psychological Assessment Resources)

Depue, R.A. and Collins, P.F. (1999), Neurobiology of the structure of personality: dopamine, facilitation of incentive motivation, and extraversion, *Behavioral and Brain Sciences*, 22, 491–569

Elliot, A.J. and Church, M.A. (1997), A hierarchical model of approach and avoidance achievement motivation, *Journal of Personality and Social Psychology*, 72, 218–232

Elliot, A.J. and Thrash, T.M. (2002), Approach-avoidance motivation in personality: approach-avoidance temperaments and goals. *Journal of Personality and Social Psychology*, 82, 804–818.

Elliott, E.S. and Dweck, C.S. (1988), Goals: an approach to motivation and achievement, *Journal of Personality and Social Psychology*, 54, 5–12

Eysenck, H.J. (1967), *The Biological Basis of Personality* (Springfield: Thomas)

Fowles, D.C. (1980), The three arousal model: implications of Gray's two factor learning theory for heart rate, electrodermal activity and psychopathy, *Psychophysiology*, 17, 87–104

(1984), Arousal: implications of behavioral theories of motivation in M.G.H. Coles, J.R. Jennings and J.P. Stern (eds), *Psychophysiological Perspectives: Festschrift for Beatrice and John Lacey* (New York: Van Nostrand), pp. 143–156

Goldberg, L.R., Johnson, J.A., Eber, H.W., Hogan, R., Ashton, M.C., Cloninger, C.R. and Gough, H.C. (2006), The international personality item pool and the future of public-domain personality measures, *Journal of Research in Personality*, 40, 84–96

Gray, J.A. (1970), The psychophysiological basis of introversion–extraversion, *Behaviour Research and Therapy*, 8, 249–266

——— (1982), *The Neuropsychology of Anxiety: an Enquiry into the Functions of the Septo-hippocampal System* (Oxford: Oxford University Press)

Gray, J.A. and McNaughton, N. (2000), *The Neuropsychology of Anxiety: an Enquiry into the Functions of the Septo-hippocampal System* (Oxford: Oxford University Press)

Guilford, J.P. (1975), Factors and factors of personality, *Psychological Bulletin*, 82, 802–814

Harmon-Jones, E., Sigelman, J.D., Bohlig, A. and Harmon-Jones, C. (2003), Anger, coping, and frontal cortical activity: the effect of coping potential on anger-induced left frontal activity, *Cognition and Emotion*, 17, 1–24

Hespos, S.J. and Spelke, E.S. (2004), Conceptual precursors to spatial language, *Nature*, 430, 453–456

Higgins, E.T., Idson, L.C., Freitas, A.L., Spiegel, S. and Molden, D.C. (2003), Transfer of value from fit, *Journal of Personality and Social Psychology*, 84, 1140–1153

Hogan, R. and Hogan, J. (1995), *The Hogan Personality Inventory Manual* (2nd edn, Tulsa, OK: Hogan Assessment Systems)

Hogan, R., Hogan, J. and Roberts, B.W. (1996), Personality measurement and employment decisions: questions and answers, *American Psychologist*, 51, 469–477

Hogan, R. and Kaiser, R.B. (2005), What we know about leadership, *Review of General Psychology*, 9, 169–180

Hogan, R. and Roberts, B.W. (2004), A socioanalytic model of maturity, *Journal of Career Assessment*, 12, 207–217

Humphreys, M.S. and Revelle, W. (1984), Personality, motivation, and performance: a theory of the relationship between individual differences and information processing, *Psychological Review*, 91, 153–184

Jensen, A.R. and Weng, L.-J. (1994), What is good g?, *Intelligence*, 18, 231–258

Kuhl, J. and Blankenship, V. (1979), The dynamic theory of achievement motivation: from episodic to dynamic thinking, *Psychological Review*, 85, 239–248

MacLean, P.D. (1973), *A Triune Concept of Brain and Behavior* (Toronto: University of Toronto Press)

——— (1990), *The Triune Brain in Evolution: Role in Paleocerebral Functions* (New York: Plenum)

Matthews, G., Campbell, S.E., Falconer, S., Joyner, L.A., Huggins, J., Gilliland, K., Grier, R. and Warm, J.S. (2002), Fundamental dimensions of subjective state in performance settings: task engagement, distress, and worry, *Emotion*, 4, 315–340

Matthews, G. and Gilliland, K. (1999), The personality theories of H.J. Eysenck and J.A. Gray: a comparative review, *Personality and Individual Differences*, 26, 583–626

McGue, M. and Bouchard, T.J. Jr (1998), Genetic and environmental influences on human behavioral differences, *Annual Review of Neuroscience*, 21, 1–24

Mulder, G. (1986), The concept and measurement of mental effort in G.R. J. Hockey, A.W.K. Gaillard and M.G.H. Coles (eds), *Energetics and Human Information Processing* (Dordrecht: Martinus Nijhoff), pp. 175–198

Ortony, A., Norman, D.A. and Revelle, W. (2005), Effective functioning: a three level model of affect, motivation, cognition, and behavior in J.M. Fellous and M.A. Arbib (eds), *Who Needs Emotions? The Brain Meets the Machine* (New York: Oxford University Press), pp. 173–202

Patterson, C.M. and Newman, J.P. (1993), Reflectivity and learning from aversive events: toward a psychological mechanism for syndromes of disinhibition, *Psychological Review*, 100, 716–736

Pickering, A.D. and Gray, J.A. (2001), Dopamine, appetitive reinforcement, and the neuropsychology of human learning: an individual differences approach in A. Eliasz and A. Angleitner (eds), *Advances in Individual Differences Research* (Lengerich: PABST Science Publishers), pp. 113–149

Pittenger, D.J. (2005), Cautionary comments regarding the Myers-Briggs type indicator, *Consulting Psychology Journal: Practice and Research*, 57, 210–221

Rafaeli, E. and Revelle, W. (2006), A premature consensus: are happiness and sadness truly opposite affects?, *Motivation and Emotion*, 30, 1–12

Reber, P.J., Gitelman, D.R., Parrish, T.B. and Mesulam, M.-M. (2003), Dissociating explicit and implicit category knowledge with fMRI?, *Journal of Cognitive Neuroscience*, 15, 574–685

Revelle, W. (1993), Individual differences in personality and motivation: 'non-cognitive' determinants of cognitive performance in A. Baddeley and L. Weiskrantz (eds), *Attention: Selection, Awareness and Control: a Tribute to Donald Broadbent* (Oxford: Oxford University Press), pp. 346–373

(1995), Personality processes, *Annual Review of Psychology*, 46, 295–328

(1997), Extraversion and impulsivity: the lost dimension in H. Nyborg (ed.), *The Scientific Study of Human Nature: Tribute to Hans J. Eysenck at Eighty* (Elsevier Science Press), pp. 189–212

Revelle, W. and Michaels, E.J. (1976), The theory of achievement motivation revisited: the implications of inertial tendencies, *Psychological Review*, 83, 394–404

Rogers, G.M. and Revelle, W. (1998), Personality, mood, and the evaluation of affective and neutral word pairs, *Journal of Personality and Social Psychology*, 74, 1592–1605

Schmid, J. and Leiman, J.M. (1957), The development of hierarchical factor solutions, *Psychometrika*, 22, 53–61

Smillie, L.D. and Jackson, C.J. (2006), Functional impulsivity and reinforcement sensitivity theory, *Journal of Personality*, 74, 47–83

Smillie, L.D., Pickering, A.D. and Jackson, C.J. (2006), The new reinforcement sensitivity theory: implications for personality measurement, *Personality and Social Psychology Review*, 10, 320–335

Spence, K.W., Farber, I.E. and McFann, H.H. (1956), The relation of anxiety (drive) level to performance in competitional and non-competitive paired-associates learning, *Journal of Experimental Psychology*, 52, 296–305

Sutton, S.K. and Davidson, R.J. (1997), Prefrontal brain asymmetry: a biological substrate of the behavioral approach and inhibition systems, *Psychological Science*, 8, 204–210

Tolman, E.C. (1948), Cognitive maps in rats and men, *Psychological Review*, 55, 189–208

Tolman, E.C. and Honzik, C.H. (1930), Introduction and removal of reward and maze performance in rats, *Uni. Cal. Pub. Psychol*, 4, 257–275

Weiner, B. and Schneider, K. (1971), Drive versus cognitive theory: a reply to Boor and Harmon, *Journal of Personality and Social Psychology*, 18, 258–262

Wittmann, W.W. (1988), Multivariate reliability theory: principles of symmetry and successful validation strategies in R.B. Cattell and J.R. Nesselroade (eds), *Handbook of Multivariate Experimental Psychology* (New York: Plenum), pp. 505–560

Zinbarg, R.E. and Mohlman, J. (1998), Individual differences in the acquisition of affectively valenced associations, *Journal of Personality and Social Psychology*, 74, 1024–1040

Zinbarg, R. and Revelle, W. (1989), Personality and conditioning: a test of four models, *Journal of Personality and Social Psychology*, 57, 301–314

Zinbarg, R.E., Revelle, W., Yovel, I. and Li, W. (2005), Cronbach's alpha, Revelle's beta, McDonald's omega: their relations with each and two alternative conceptualizations of reliability, *Psychometrika*, 70, 123–133

Zinbarg, R., Yovel, I., Revelle, W. and McDonald, R. (2006), Estimating generalizability to a universe of indicators that all have one attribute in common: a comparison of estimators for omega, *Applied Psychological Measurement*, 30, 121–144

General Index

activated pleasant (AP) affect 292, 293, 301, 306
activated unpleasant (AUP) affect 292, 293, 301, 305, 306
agoraphobia 69, 367, 380
amygdala 63–64, 80, 112, 180
anger 27, 265
animal cognition and human personality 95–115
  biology *and* cognition 111–114
  biology or cognition: fallacies 97–111
  cognitions are emotionally neutral 104
  cognitions are hardware-free 106–108
  cognitions are unconstrained 105–106
  cognitive anthropocentrism 99–101
  cortex as seat of cognition 110–111
  emotion 95–96, 113–114
  language as cognition 101–104
  primary anthropocentrism 98–99
  radical behaviourism 96, 108–109
  silent cognitions 97, 109–110
animals
  between-species differences 29–30
  as models 485–492, 502, 515–516
  see also animal cognition and human personality; defence: 'state' level analysis
anthropocentrism 98–99, 99–101
anxiety 5–8, 518
  clinical effects of drugs 74–76
  conflict 49–50
  defensive direction 47–48
  and monoamine systems 163–164
  scales 191, 215–218
  separation anxiety 72
  social anxiety 72
  trait anxiety 52, 177, 376
  see also anxiety disorders; anxiolytic drugs; neural systems of fear and anxiety
anxiety disorders 360–385, 361–363
  arousal 366–367

attentional biases 368–371, 499–500
behavioural inhibition 367
defining disorder 378
and depression 360, 361, 362–363, 365, 518
interpretive biases 372–374
longitudinal studies of risk 375–376
memory biases 374–375
and panic 74, 81, 180, 363–364, 376, 380
and phobia 377–378, 379
structure 361–363
see also agoraphobia
anxiolytic drugs 9, 16, 52, 58, 74–76, 81, 381
AP *see* activated pleasant (AP) affect
Appetitive Motivation Scale 142, 196, 197
arousal/arousability 4, 5, 7, 8, 162, 366–367, 490
Ascending Reticular Activating System (ARAS) 3, 5
attention 404–405, 499–500
  see also attentional bias
attention deficit disorder with hyperactivity 416
attentional bias
  anxiety disorders 368–371, 499–500
  anxiolytic medications 381
  depression 371–372
AUP *see* activated unpleasant (AUP) affect
autonomic activity and BIS/BAS 274–281
  cardiovascular activity 275–281
  electrodermal activity (EDA) 274, 276–281

Barratt Impulsiveness Scale 132–133
BAS *see* Behavioural Approach System
basal ganglia 361
behaviour 5, 122–135, 486–489
Behavioural Activation System *see* Behavioural Approach System (BAS)

Index of names